Barker
Burton
Zieve

Handbook of
AMBULATORY
MEDICINE

Handbook of
AMBULATORY
MEDICINE

Philip D. Zieve, M.D.

Professor of Medicine
The Johns Hopkins University School of Medicine
Chairman, Department of Medicine
Johns Hopkins Bayview Medical Center
Baltimore, Maryland

Adapted from

Principles of AMBULATORY MEDICINE
Fourth Edition

edited by

L. Randol Barker, John R. Burton, and Philip D. Zieve

Williams & Wilkins

BALTIMORE • PHILADELPHIA • HONG KONG
LONDON • MUNICH • SYDNEY • TOKYO

A WAVERLY COMPANY

Editor: David C. Retford
Managing Editor: Kathleen Courtney Millet
Production Coordinator: Kimberly S. Nawrozki
Copy Editor: Bill Cady
Designer: Wilma E. Rosenberger
Illustration Planner: Ray Lowman

Copyright © 1995
Williams & Wilkins
351 West Camden Street
Baltimore, Maryland 21201-2436 USA

Accurate indications, adverse reactions, and dosage schedules for drugs are provided in this book, but it is possible that they may change. The reader is urged to review the package information data of the manufacturers of the medications mentioned.

Printed in the United States of America

Library of Congress Cataloging-in-Publication Data

Handbook of ambulatory medicine / [edited by] Philip D. Zieve.
     p.   cm.
   "Adapted from Principles of ambulatory medicine, fourth edition, edited by L. Randol Barker, John R. Burton, and Philip D. Zieve."
   Includes index.
   ISBN 0-683-09374-6
   1. Family medicine — Handbooks, manuals, etc.   2. Ambulatory medical care — Handbooks, manuals, etc.   I. Zieve, Philip D., 1932–   .   II. Principles of ambulatory medicine.
   [DNLM: 1. Ambulatory Care — handbooks.   WB 39 C6413 1995]
RC55.C54   1995
616 — dc20
DNLM/DLC
for Library of Congress   94-47181
                                              CIP

                      95 96 97 98 99
    1 2 3 4 5 6 7 8 9 10

PREFACE

Abridgments of large texts are very much in vogue now, in part because of the cost of large books and in part because of the haste to acquire essential information as efficiently and expeditiously as possible. This book is the essence of the 4th edition of *Principles of Ambulatory Medicine,* edited by L. Randol Barker, John R. Burton, and myself.

The objective of this book is to provide the most important information of the larger text and to serve as a springboard to the larger text when more detailed descriptions are required.

Philip D. Zieve, M.D.

ACKNOWLEDGMENTS

The following contributed a chapter or chapters to *Principles of Ambulatory Care*, fourth edition, from which this book is adapted.

Unless otherwise indicated, hospital appointments are at Johns Hopkins Bayview Medical Center, Baltimore, Maryland, and faculty appointments are at The Johns Hopkins University School of Medicine.

Frank C. Arnett, Jr., M.D.
Professor of Internal Medicine
The University of Texas
Health Science Center
Houston, Texas

L. Randol Barker, M.D., Sc.M.
Co-Chief, Division of General
 Internal Medicine
Associate Professor of Medicine

Linda F. Barr, M.D.
Assistant Professor of Medicine
Division of Pulmonary and Critical
 Care Medicine
The Johns Hopkins Hospital

John G. Bartlett, M.D.
Chief, Division of Infectious
 Diseases
The Johns Hopkins Hospital
Stanhope Bayne-Jones Professor of
 Medicine

Eric B. Bass, M.D., M.P.H.
Staff Physician, General Internal
 Medicine
The Johns Hopkins Hospital
Assistant Professor of Medicine

William E. Beatie, M.D.
Instructor in Orthopaedic Surgery

**Jeffrey S. Bender, M.D.,
F.A.C.S.**
Associate Professor of Surgery
Director, Trauma and Surgical
 Critical Care

Richard G. Bennett, M.D.
Associate Professor of Medicine

Marc R. Blackman, Ph.D.
Chief, Division of Endocrinology
Associate Professor of Medicine

David G. Borenstein, M.D.
Professor of Medicine
Medical Director, The Spine Center
Department of Medicine
The George Washington University
 Medical Center
Washington, D.C.

Gary R. Briefel, M.D.
Director of Hemodialysis
Associate Professor of Medicine

E. James Britt, M.D.
Clinical Director, Pulmonary
 Division
University of Maryland Hospital
Associate Professor of Medicine
University of Maryland School of
 Medicine
Baltimore, Maryland

John R. Burton, M.D.
Clinical Director, Division of
 Geriatric Medicine and
 Gerontology
Professor of Medicine

**M. Janette Busby-Whitehead,
M.D.**
Associate Professor of Internal
 Medicine
Program on Aging
University of North Carolina
 School of Medicine
Chapel Hill, North Carolina

Ronald P. Byank, M.D.
Chairman, Department of
 Orthopaedic Surgery
Associate Professor of Orthopaedic
 Surgery

Nisha Chibber Chandra, M.D.
Associate Professor of Medicine

Lawrence J. Cheskin, M.D.
Assistant Professor of Medicine
Assistant Professor of International
   Health (Human Nutrition)
The Johns Hopkins School of
   Hygiene and Public Health

Andrea M. Corse, M.D.
Instructor in Neurology
Neuromuscular Division

**Vanessa E. Cullins, M.D.,
M.P.H.**
Assistant Professor of Obstetrics
   and Gynecology

Susan J. Denman, M.D.
Vice President for Medical Affairs
Philadelphia Geriatric Center
Professor of Medicine
Temple University
Philadelphia, Pennsylvania

J. Raymond DePaulo, Jr., M.D.
Professor of Psychiatry
Director, The Affective Disorders
   Clinic
The Johns Hopkins Hospital

Burton C. D'Lugoff, M.D.
Associate Professor of Medicine
Associate Professor of Psychiatry

**Christopher J. Early, M.B.,
B.C.H.**
Assistant Professor of Neurology

David M. Ennis, M.D.
Chief Fellow in Infectious Disease
University of Alabama at
   Birmingham
Birmingham, Alabama

Lori Fantry, M.D.
Assistant Professor of Medicine

Michael I. Fingerhood, M.D.
Staff Physician, Center for
   Chemical Dependence and
   General Internal Medicine
Assistant Professor of Medicine

Robert S. Fisher, M.D., Ph.D.
Chief, Epilepsy Center
Barrow Neurological Institute
Phoenix, Arizona

Louis F. Fries, M.D.
Associate Professor of International
   Health
The Johns Hopkins School of
   Hygiene and Public Health

Preston M. Gazaway, M.D.
Assistant Professor of Gynecology
   and Obstetrics

Sheldon H. Gottlieb, M.D.
Clinical Chief, Division of
   Cardiology
Associate Professor of Medicine

Robert I. Gregerman, M.D.
Professor of Medicine
University of Texas at San Antonio
San Antonio, Texas

Richard J. Gross, M.D., Sc.M.
Assistant Professor of Medicine and
   Public Health

Neal A. Halsey, M.D.
Professor and Division Director
International Health-Division of
   Disease Control
Joint Appointment
Department of Pediatrics

S. Mitchell Harman, M.D.
Staff Physician, Endocrinology
Gerontology Research Center,
   National Institute on Aging
Associate Professor of Medicine

David B. Hellmann, M.D.
Associate Professor of Medicine
Acting Director, Department of
   Medicine
The Johns Hopkins Hospital

Edward W. Hook III, M.D.
Professor of Medicine
Department of Medicine/Infectious
   Diseases
University of Alabama at
   Birmingham
Medical Director
STD Control Program
Jefferson County Department of
   Health
Birmingham, Alabama

Janet Horn, M.D.
Assistant Professor of Medicine
Division of Infectious Disease

George R. Huggins, M.D.
Chairman, Department of
  Obstetrics and Gynecology
Associate Professor of Obstetrics
  and Gynecology

Constance J. Johnson, M.D.
Director of Outpatient Neurology
Assistant Professor of Neurology

Calvin E. Jones, M.D.
Associate Professor of Surgery
Chief, Division of Vascular Surgery

**Peter W. Kaplan, M.B., B.S.,
M.R.C.P.**
Chief of Neurology
Associate Professor of Neurology

**Philip O. Katz, M.D., F.A.C.P.,
F.A.C.G.**
Associate Professor of Medicine
Deputy, Chairman of Medicine

David E. Kern, M.D., M.P.H.
Co-Director, Division of General
  Internal Medicine
Associate Professor of Medicine

Frederick T. Koster, M.D.
Associate Professor of Medicine
University of New Mexico School of
  Medicine
Albuquerque, New Mexico

Edward S. Kraus, M.D.
Staff Physician
Department of Nephrology
Associate Professor of Medicine

Ralph W. Kuncl, M.D., Ph.D.
Associate Professor of Neurology
Department of Neurology

Bruce S. Lebowitz, D.P.M.
Director, Podiatry Clinic
Department of Orthopaedic
  Surgery

Frederick A. Lenz, M.D., Ph.D.
Associate Professor of
  Neurosurgery

Richard F. Lewis, M.D.
Instructor in Neurology
The Johns Hopkins Hospital

Mark C. Liu, M.D.
Associate Professor of Medicine

Douglas MacLeod, D.M.D.
Formerly Chief, Department of
  Dentistry

Esteban Mezey, M.D.
Professor of Medicine
Division of Gastroenterology

Patrick A. Murphy, M.D.
Professor of Medicine
Chief, Division of Infectious
  Diseases

David N. Neubauer, M.D.
Assistant Professor of Medicine
Department of Psychiatry
Director, Acute Psychiatric Unit
Faculty, The Johns Hopkins Sleep
  Disorders Center

John K. Niparko, M.D.
Associate Professor
Department of Otolaryngology–
  Head and Neck Surgery

Nathaniel F. Pierce, M.D.
Professor of Medicine

Michael J. Purtell, M.D.
Assistant Professor of Medicine
Division of Hematology-Oncology

Peter V. Rabins, M.D., M.P.H.
Professor of Psychiatry and
  Behavioral Sciences

Stephen G. Reich, M.D.
Staff Physician, Neurology
The Johns Hopkins Hospital
Assistant Professor of Neurology

Robert P. Roca, M.D., M.P.H.
Director, Geriatrics Services
Sheppard and Enoch Pratt Hospital
Towson, Maryland
Associate Professor of Psychiatry

Kevin A. Rossiter, M.D.
Assistant Professor of Medicine
Division of Renal Medicine

David A. Sack, M.D.
Associate Professor of International
  Health

Andrew P. Schachat, M.D.
Professor of Ophthalmology
Director, Ocular Oncology Service

Chester W. Schmidt, Jr., M.D.
Chairman, Psychiatry
Professor of Psychiatry

Marvin M. Schuster, M.D.
Director, Division of Digestive
    Diseases
Professor of Medicine
Joint Appointment in Psychiatry

Stephen D. Sears, M.D., M.P.H.
Vice President for Medical Affairs
Kennebec Valley Medical Center
Augusta, Maine

Edward P. Shapiro, M.D.
Director, Cardiac Non-Invasive
    Service
Associate Professor of Medicine

Gardner W. Smith, M.D.
Chairman, Section of Surgical
    Sciences
Professor of Surgery

Philip L. Smith, M.D.
Co-Director, Baltimore Regional
    Sleep Disorders Center
Professor of Medicine
Instructor of Anesthesiology

David A. Spector, M.D.
Associate Professor of Medicine
Director, Division of Renal
    Medicine

Robert J. Spence, M.D.
Associate Professor of Surgery
Chief of Plastic Surgery
Assistant Professor of Plastic
    Surgery

Ray E. Stutzman, M.D.
Director of Outpatient Urology
The Johns Hopkins Hospital
Associate Professor of Urology

**John T. Sullivan, M.B., Ch.B.,
F.R.A.C.P.**
Medical Director, Center for
    Chemical Dependence
Associate Professor of Medicine

Peter B. Terry, M.D.
Staff Physician, Pulmonary
    Medicine
Professor of Medicine

**Alexander S. Townes, M.D.,
F.A.C.P.**
Chief of Staff
Veterans Administration Medical
    Center
Professor of Medicine
Vanderbilt University School of
    Medicine
Nashville, Tennessee

Martin D. Valentine, M.D.
Professor of Medicine
The Johns Hopkins Asthma and
    Allergy Center

Larry Waterbury, M.D.
Chief, Division of Hematology-
    Oncology
Associate Professor of Medicine and
    Oncology

S. Elizabeth Whitmore, M.D.
Assistant Professor of Dermatology

Fredrick M. Wigley, M.D.
Associate Professor
Director, Division of Rheumatology

Robert A. Wise, M.D.
Associate Professor of Medicine
Associate Director, Division of
    Pulmonary Medicine

Michael E. Zenilman, M.D.
Assistant Professor of Surgery
Albert Einstein College of Medicine
New York, N.Y.

Philip D. Zieve, M.D.
Chairman, Department of Medicine
Physician-in-Chief
Professor of Medicine

CONTENTS

Section VIII   Musculoskeletal Problems

Section IX   Metabolic and Endocrinological Problems

Section X   Neurological Problems

Section I
Psychiatric and Behavioral Problems

DEFINITIONS

A. Abnormal illness behavior — the inappropriate magnitude and duration of symptoms and of disability in response to a diagnosed disease

B. Somatization — the linkage of unexplained or amplified physical symptoms to psychological factors or conflicts

REACTIVE EMOTIONAL STATES (DEMORALIZATION)

A. Adjustment disorders (Table 1.1)
   1. Somatic symptoms (e.g., fatigue, chest pain, dyspnea) that result from difficulty in adjusting to environmental demands (e.g., marital discord, job stress)
   2. Important strategies
      a) Elicit the relevant history (ask open-ended questions; e.g., "how are things at home?")
      b) Rule out major depression (see Chapter 3)
      c) Temper the workup; e.g., avoid excessive use of laboratory tests
   3. Management
      a) Many patients get better after one office visit that includes empathetic listening, partial physical examination, and reassurance
      b) Follow up by phone or brief visit in 1 week
      c) Prescribing of drugs for anxiety or insomnia may not relieve symptoms but can be considered in selected cases
      d) If there is no response to these maneuvers, re-evaluate and look for other syndromes [e.g., panic disorder (Chapter 2), major depression (Chapter 3), alcoholism (Chapter 7), a somatoform disorder (see below)]

B. Psychological factors affecting medical condition
   1. Criteria: Table 1.2
   2. Common conditions: Table 1.3
   3. Management: same as for Adjustment disorders (see above)

Table 1.1. Diagnostic Criteria for Adjustment Disorder

A. The development of emotional or behavioral symptoms in response to an identifiable stressor(s) occurring within 3 months of the onset of the stressor(s).

B. These symptoms or behaviors are clinically significant as evidenced by either of the following:
   (1) Marked distress that is in excess of what would be expected from exposure to the stressor
   (2) Significant impairment in social or occupational (academic) functioning

C. The stress-related disturbance does not meet the criteria for any specific Axis 1 disorder and is not merely an exacerbation of a preexisting Axis I or Axis II disorder.

D. Does not represent Bereavement.

E. The symptoms do not persist for more than 6 months after the termination of the stressor (or its consequences).
   Acute: if the symptoms have persisted for less than 6 months
   Chronic: if the symptoms have persisted for 6 months or longer

Table 1.2.   Diagnostic Criteria for Psychological Factors Affecting Physical Condition

A. The presence of a general medical condition (coded on Axis III).
B. Psychological factors adversely affect the general medical condition in one of the following ways:
  (1) The factors have influenced the course of the general medical condition as shown by a close temporal association between the psychological factors and the development or exacerbation of, or delayed recovery from, the general medical condition.
  (2) The factors interfere with the treatment of the general medical condition.
  (3) The factors constitute additional health risks for the individual.
  (4) The factors elicit stress-related physiological responses that precipitate or exacerbate symptoms of a general medical condition (e.g., chest pain or arrhythmia in a patient with coronary artery disease).

Adapted from American Psychiatric Association: *Diagnostic and Statistical Manual of Mental Disorders*, 4th ed. Washington, DC, American Psychiatric Association, 1994.

Table 1.3.   Common Conditions in Which Psychophysiological Symptoms Are Important

Physiological System	Symptomatic Condition	For Further Information, See Chapter
Cardiovascular	Migraine headache	61
	Vasovagal syndrome (fainting)	63
	Hypertension (usually asymptomatic)	45
	Supraventricular tachycardia	42
	Angina	41
Gastrointestinal	Irritable bowel syndrome	26
	The following symptoms may occur singly or together: anorexia, nausea, vomiting, abdominal cramps, diarrhea, constipation, aerophagia, acid-peptic symptoms	22, 23, 25
Genitourinary	Menstrual disturbance	60
	Difficulties in micturition: frequency (in both sexes), retention (females), hesitancy (in males)	6
	Sexual disorders	
	Dyspareunia	
	Anorgasmia	
	Inhibited sexual excitement	
	Delayed ejaculation; premature ejaculation	
Musculoskeletal	Pain secondary to increased muscle tension: occipital or bitemporal headaches, backaches, myalgia in various muscle groups	48, 61
	Fatigue	
	Tremor	64
	Rheumatoid arthritis	53
Respiratory	Hyperventilation syndrome	2
	Bronchospasm	39
	Dyspnea	38
Skin	Hyperhidrosis	82
	Pruritus	82

SOMATOFORM DISORDERS

A. Somatization disorder
  1. Criteria: Table 1.4
  2. Presence of 3 of following 7 symptoms highly sensitive and specific for diagnosis: shortness of breath without exertion, dysmenorrhea, burning sensations in sexual organs, difficulty swallowing, amnesia, vomiting, pain in extremities
  3. Rare in men
  4. Management
      a) Review all medical records to determine range of complaints and adequacy of evaluations
      b) Avoid hospitalization, consultations, and invasive laboratory tests
      c) Be aware of promoters of symptoms (e.g., major depression, sick family members, increased attention from relatives or friends, lack of emotional support in childhood)
      d) Do not expect complete resolution of symptoms
      e) Schedule regular brief visits
      f) Do not ascribe symptoms entirely to psychological causes but focus on life problems rather than on symptoms
B. Undifferentiated somatoform disorder
  1. Criteria: Table 1.5
  2. Evaluation and management: same as for Somatization disorder
C. Conversion disorder
  1. Criteria: Table 1.6
  2. More often in women; generally begins in adolescence or early adulthood
  3. Management

Table 1.4.   Diagnostic Criteria for Somatization Disorder

A. History of many physical complaints beginning before the age of 30, occurring over a period of several years, and resulting in treatment being sought or significant impairment in social or occupational functioning.

B. Each of the following criteria must have been met at some time during the course of the disorder. To count a symptom as significant, it must not be fully explained by a known general medical condition, or the resulting complaints or impairment are in excess of what would be expected from the history, physical examination, or laboratory findings.

  (1) Four pain symptoms: a history of pain related to at least four different sites or functions (such as head, abdomen, back, joints, extremities, chest, rectum, during sexual intercourse, during menstruation, or during urination)

  (2) Two gastrointestinal symptoms: a history of at least two gastrointestinal symptoms other than pain (such as nausea, diarrhea, bloating, vomiting other than during pregnancy, or intolerance of several different foods)

  (3) One sexual symptom: a history of at least one sexual or reproductive symptom other than pain (such as sexual indifference, erectile or ejaculatory dysfunction, irregular menses, excessive menstrual bleeding, vomiting throughout pregnancy)

  (4) One pseudoneurological symptom: a history of at least one symptom or deficit suggesting a neurological disorder not limited to pain (conversion symptoms such as blindness, double vision, deafness, loss of touch or pain sensation, hallucinations, aphonia, impaired coordination or balance, paralysis or localized weakness, difficulty swallowing, difficulty breathing, urinary retention, seizures; dissociative symptoms such as amnesia or loss of consciousness other than fainting)

Adapted from American Psychiatric Association: *Diagnostic and Statistical Manual of Mental Disorders*, 4th ed. Washington, DC, American Psychiatric Association, 1994.

Table 1.5.   Diagnostic Criteria for Undifferentiated Somatoform Disorder

A. One or more physical complaints (e.g., fatigue, loss of appetite, gastrointestinal or urinary complaints).
B. Either (1) or (2):
  (1) After appropriate investigation, the symptoms cannot be explained by a known general medical condition or pathophysiological mechanism (e.g., the effects of injury, medication, drugs, or alcohol).
  (2) When there is a related general medical condition, the physical complaints or resulting social or occupational impairment[s] are grossly in excess of what would be expected from the physical findings.
C. The symptoms cause clinically significant distress or impairment in social, occupational, or other important areas of functioning.
D. The duration of the disturbance is at least 6 months.
E. [The disturbance] is not better accounted for by another disorder (e.g., another Somatoform Disorder, Sexual Dysfunction, Mood Disorder, Anxiety Disorder, Sleep Disorder, or Psychotic Disorder).
F. The symptom is not intentionally produced or feigned.

Adapted from American Psychiatric Association: *Diagnostic and Statistical Manual of Mental Disorders*, 4th ed. Washington, DC, American Psychiatric Association, 1994.

Table 1.6.   Diagnostic Criteria for Conversion Disorder

A. One or more symptoms or deficits affecting voluntary motor or sensory function suggesting a neurological or general medical condition.
B. Psychological factors are judged to be associated with the symptom or deficit because the initiation or exacerbation of the symptom or deficit is preceded by conflicts or other stressors.
C. The symptom or deficit is not intentionally produced or feigned (as in Factitious Disorder or Malingering).
D. The symptom or deficit cannot, after appropriate investigation, be fully explained by a neurological or general medical condition and is not a culturally sanctioned behavior or experience.
E. The symptom or deficit causes clinically significant distress or impairment in social, occupational, or other important areas of functioning or warrants medical evaluation.
F. The symptom or deficit is not limited to pain or sexual dysfunction, does not occur exclusively during the course of Somatization Disorder, and is not better accounted for by another mental disorder.

Adapted from American Psychiatric Association: *Diagnostic and Statistical Manual of Mental Disorders*, 4th ed. Washington, DC, American Psychiatric Association, 1994.

      a) Be certain an adequate medical evaluation has been done
      b) Be aware of promoters of symptoms (see Somatization disorder)
      c) Do not be overly blunt about psychological origins of symptoms
      d) Be optimistic about recovery
D. Hypochondriasis
    1. Criteria: Table 1.7
    2. Sexes affected equally; onset generally in the third decade but may occur later
    3. Anxiety, depression, drug dependency, and iatrogenic disease are common complications
    4. Management: same as for Somatization disorder
E. Pain disorder
    1. Criteria: Table 1.8

Table 1.7. Diagnostic Criteria for Hypochondriasis

A. Preoccupation with fears of having, or the idea that one has, a serious disease based on the person's misinterpretation of bodily symptoms.
B. The preoccupation persists despite appropriate medical evaluation and reassurance.
C. The belief in A is not of delusional intensity (as in Delusional Disorder, Somatic Type) and is not restricted to a circumscribed concern about appearance (as in Body Dysmorphic Disorder).
D. The preoccupation causes clinically significant distress or impairment in social, occupational, or other important areas of functioning.
E. The duration of the disturbance is at least 6 months.
F. The preoccupation does not occur exclusively during the course of Generalized Anxiety Disorder, Obsessive-Compulsive Disorder, Panic Disorder, a major depressive episode, Separation Anxiety, or another Somatoform Disorder.

Specify if: with poor Insight: if, for most of the time during the current episode, the person does not recognize that the concern about having a serious illness is excessive or unreasonable

Reprinted with permission from American Psychiatric Association: *Diagnostic and Statistical Manual of Mental Disorders*, 4th ed. Washington, DC, American Psychiatric Association, 1994.

Table 1.8. Diagnostic Criteria for Pain Disorder

A. Pain in one or more anatomical sites is the predominant focus of the clinical presentation and is of sufficient severity to warrant clinical attention.
B. The pain causes clinically significant distress or impairment in social, occupational, or other important areas of functioning.
C. Psychological factors are judged to have an important role in the onset, severity, exacerbation, or maintenance of the pain.
D. The pain is not better accounted for by a Mood, Anxiety, or Psychotic Disorder and does not meet criteria for Dyspareunia.

Adapted from American Psychiatric Association: *Diagnostic and Statistical Manual of Mental Disorders*, 4th ed. Washington, DC, American Psychiatric Association, 1994.

   2. Onset usually in fourth or fifth decade
   3. Management
      a) Similar to that for Somatization disorder
      b) Avoid benzodiazepines and narcotic analgesics
   F. Body dysmorphic disorder
      1. Criteria: Table 1.9
      2. Onset typically between adolescence and age 30
      3. Management
         a) Generally similar to that for Somatization disorder
         b) Avoid surgery

DISORDERS WITH VOLUNTARY SYMPTOM PRODUCTION
   A. Factitious disorder with physical symptoms
      1. Criteria: Table 1.10
      2. Onset usually in early adulthood
      3. Management
         a) Try to avoid unnecessary hospitalization
         b) Schedule early psychiatric consultation
   B. Malingering
      1. Deliberate simulation of physical or psychological symptoms to achieve a *specific* benefit

Table 1.9.   Diagnostic Criteria for Body Dysmorphic Disorder

A. Preoccupation with an imagined defect in appearance. If a slight physical anomaly is present, the person's concern is markedly excessive.
B. The preoccupation causes clinically significant distress or impairment in social, occupational, or other important areas of functioning.
C. The preoccupation is not better accounted for by another mental disorder (e.g., dissatisfaction with body shape and size in Anorexia Nervosa).

Reprinted with permission from American Psychiatric Association: *Diagnostic and Statistical Manual of Mental Disorders*, 4th ed. Washington, DC, American Psychiatric Association, 1994.

Table 1.10.   Diagnostic Criteria for Factitious Disorder With Physical Symptoms

A. Intentional production or feigning of physical or psychological signs or symptoms.
B. The motivation for the behavior is to assume the sick role.
C. External incentives for the behavior (such as economic gain, avoiding legal responsibility, or improving physical well-being, as in Malingering) are absent.

Adapted from American Psychiatric Association: *Diagnostic and Statistical Manual of Mental Disorders*, 4th ed. Washington, DC, American Psychiatric Association, 1994.

2. Suspect whenever symptoms are excessive and are accompanied by obvious social or familial benefit
3. Differs from factitious disorder (above), wherein sole goal is to become a patient, or from conversion disorder, wherein symptoms are not intentional
4. Management
   a) Tactfully make patient aware that malingering is suspected
   b) Remove gratifications
   c) Consider psychiatric consultation

DRUG-RELATED ANXIETY: TABLE 2.1

ANXIETY DISORDERS

A. Adjustment disorders with anxiety
1. Criteria: Table 2.2
2. Management
   a) Advise patient to avoid use of caffeine and other stimulants
   b) Short-term counseling
   c) Relaxation training (see below)
   d) Consider a 1–2-month course of a benzodiazepine (see below)
B. Generalized anxiety disorders
1. Criteria: Table 2.3
2. Usually begins in teens or twenties and fluctuates thereafter with stresses of life
3. Management (see General Approach to Treatment, below)
   a) Take a medical history, and do a focused physical examination
   b) Counsel patient to avoid caffeine, other stimulants, and alcohol
   c) Inquire about life stresses, and help patient to address them
   d) Encourage use of relaxation techniques (see below)
   e) If there is sleep disturbance or hyperactivity, consider a 1–2-month course of benzodiazepines (see below)
   f) If there is excessive worry, consider use of buspirone or a tricyclic antidepressant (see below) for 6–12 months
C. Phobias
1. Criteria
   a) As a group, enduring fears of harmless objects or situations, leading patients to avoid contact with them

Table 2.1. Drugs and Other Substances That May Exacerbate (or Produce) Anxiety

Toxic symptoms
  Anticholinergic drugs
  Drugs of abuse[a]
    Marijuana and other drugs that alter perception
    Stimulant drugs of abuse
    Inhalants
    Phencyclidine
    Hallucinogens
Sympathomimetic drugs
  Decongestants (found in most over-the-counter cold remedies)
  β_2 Bronchodilators
  Weight reduction agents
Thyroid hormone
Xanthine-containing drugs, foods, and beverages
  Bronchodilators with theophylline
  Many over-the-counter cold and arthritis remedies
  Caffeine (use and discontinuation)
Withdrawal symptoms
  Sedative-hypnotics
  Alcohol
  Tobacco

[a] See Chapter 8.

Table 2.2. Diagnostic Criteria for Adjustment Disorder

A. The development of emotional or behavioral symptoms in response to an identifiable stressor(s) occurring within 3 months of the onset of the stressor(s).
B. These symptoms or behaviors are clinically significant as evidenced by either of the following:
   (1) Marked distress that is in excess of what would be expected from exposure to the stressor
   (2) Significant impairment in social or occupational (academic) functioning
C. The stress-related disturbance does not meet the criteria for any specific Axis I disorder and is not merely an exacerbation of a preexisting Axis I or Axis II disorder.
D. [The disturbance] does not represent Bereavement.
E. The symptoms do not persist for more than 6 months after the termination of the stressor (or its consequences).
   Acute: if the symptoms have persisted for less than 6 months
   Chronic: if the symptoms have persisted for 6 months or longer

Reprinted with permission from American Psychiatric Association: *Diagnostic and Statistical Manual of Mental Disorders*, 4th ed. Washington, DC, American Psychiatric Association, 1994.

Table 2.3. Diagnostic Criteria for Generalized Anxiety Disorder

A. Excessive anxiety and worry (apprehensive expectation), occurring more days than not for at least 6 months, about a number of events or activities (such as work or school performance).
B. The person finds it difficult to control the worry.
C. The anxiety and worry are associated with at least three of the following six symptoms (with at least some symptoms present for more days than not for the past 6 months):
   (1) Restlessness or feeling keyed up or on edge
   (2) Being easily fatigued
   (3) Difficulty concentrating or mind going blank
   (4) Irritability
   (5) Muscle tension
   (6) Sleep disturbance (difficulty falling or staying asleep, or restless unsatisfying sleep)
D. The focus of the anxiety and worry is not confined to features of an Axis I disorder, e.g., the anxiety or worry is not about having a panic attack (as in Panic Disorder), being embarrassed in public (as in Social Phobia), being contaminated (as in Obsessive-Compulsive Disorder), being away from home or close relatives (as in Separation Anxiety Disorder), gaining weight (as in Anorexia Nervosa), or having a serious illness (as in Hypochondriasis), and is not part of Posttraumatic Stress Disorder.
E. The anxiety, worry, or physical symptoms cause clinically significant distress or impairment in social, occupational, or other important areas of functioning.
F. [The disturbance is] not due to the direct effects of a substance (e.g., drugs of abuse, medication) or a general medical condition (e.g., hyperthyroidism), and does not occur exclusively during a Mood Disorder, Psychotic Disorder, or a Pervasive Developmental Disorder.

Reprinted with permission from American Psychiatric Association: *Diagnostic and Statistical Manual of Mental Disorders*, 4th ed. Washington, DC, American Psychiatric Association, 1994.

    b) Specific phobia: Table 2.4
    c) Social phobia: Table 2.5
  2. Epidemiology
    a) Among the commonest psychiatric problems
    b) Specific phobias are twice as common in women; if they begin in childhood, usually resolve; if they begin in adulthood, don't resolve without treatment
    c) Social phobias are equally common in men and women; decline with age

Table 2.4.   Diagnostic Criteria for Specific Phobia

A. Marked and persistent fear that is excessive or unreasonable, cued by the presence or anticipation of a specific object or situation (e.g., flying, height, animals, receiving an injection, seeing blood).

B. Exposure to the phobic stimulus almost invariably provokes an immediate anxiety response, which may take the form of a situationally bound or situationally predisposed panic attack. Note: in children, the anxiety may be expressed by crying, tantrums, freezing, or clinging.

C. The person recognizes that the fear is excessive or unreasonable.

D. The phobic situation(s) is avoided or else endured with intense anxiety or distress.

E. The avoidance, anxious anticipation, or distress in the feared situations interferes significantly with the person's normal routine, occupational (academic) functioning, or . . . social activities or relationships with others, or there is marked distress about having the phobia.

F. In individuals under 18 years, the duration is at least 6 months.

G. The anxiety, panic attacks, or phobic avoidance associated with the specific object or situation . . . [is] not better accounted for by another mental disorder, such as Obsessive-Compulsive Disorder (e.g., fear of contamination), Posttraumatic Stress Disorder (e.g., avoidance of stimuli associated with a severe stressor), Separation Anxiety Disorder (e.g., avoidance of school), Social Phobia (e.g., avoidance of social situations because of fear of embarrassment), Panic Disorder with Agoraphobia, or Agoraphobia Without History of Panic Disorder.

Adapted from American Psychiatric Association: *Diagnostic and Statistical Manual of Mental Disorders*, 4th ed. Washington, DC, American Psychiatric Association, 1994.

3. Management (see General Approach to Treatment, below)
   a) Desensitization: generally increased exposure to the anxiety-provoking stimulus while, at the same time, utilizing a relaxation technique (see below)
   b) Participant modeling — sharing the anxiety-provoking stimulus with the patient
   c) Social skills training, especially assertiveness training, by use of modeling and role playing
D. Panic disorder
   1. Criteria: Table 2.6
   2. Epidemiology
      a) Strong genetic component
      b) Onset usually in second or third decade, often during a time of stress
      c) Frequently associated with major depression, generalized anxiety disorder (see above), agoraphobia (Table 2.6), or obsessive-compulsive disorder
      d) Increased cardiovascular mortality
   3. Management (see General Approach to Treatment, below)
      a) Take a medical history, and perform a focused physical examination
      b) Counsel patient to avoid caffeine, stimulant drugs, alcohol, and marijuana
      c) Inquire about life stresses, and help patient to address them
      d) Drugs for prophylaxis
         1) Alprazolam 0.25 mg 3 times/day (other benzodiazepines may not prevent attacks); or
         2) Tricyclic antidepressants, usually imipramine (see Chapter 3); or

Table 2.5.   Diagnostic Criteria for Social Phobia

A. A marked and persistent fear of one or more social or performance situations in which the person is exposed to unfamiliar people or to possible scrutiny by others. The individual fears that he or she will act in a way (or show anxiety symptoms) that will be humiliating or embarrassing. Note: in children, there must be evidence of capacity for social relationships with familiar people, and the anxiety must occur in peer settings, not just in interactions with adults.

B. Exposure to the feared social situation almost invariably provokes anxiety, which may take the form of a situationally bound or situationally predisposed panic attack. Note: In children, the anxiety may be expressed by crying, tantrums, freezing, or withdrawal from the social situation.

C. The person recognizes that the fear is excessive or unreasonable. Note: in children, this feature may be absent.

D. The feared social or performance situations are avoided or else endured with intense anxiety or distress.

E. The avoidance, anxious anticipation, or distress in the feared social or performance situation(s) interferes significantly with the person's normal routine, occupational (academic) functioning, or . . . social activities or relationships with others, or there is marked distress about having the phobia.

F. In individuals under 18 years, the duration is at least 6 months.

G. The fear or avoidance is not due to the direct effects of a substance (e.g., drugs of abuse, medication) or a general medical condition, and is not better accounted for by Panic Disorder With or Without Agoraphobia, Separation Anxiety Disorder, Body Dysmorphic Disorder, a Pervasive Developmental Disorder, or Schizoid Personality Disorder.

H. If a general medical condition or other mental disorder is present, the fear in A is unrelated to it; e.g., the fear is not of stuttering, trembling (in Parkinson's disease), or exhibiting abnormal eating behavior (in Anorexia Nervosa or Bulimia Nervosa).

Adapted from American Psychiatric Association: *Diagnostic and Statistical Manual of Mental Disorders*, 4th ed. Washington, DC, American Psychiatric Association, 1994.

          3) Monoamine oxidase (MAO) inhibitors, usually phenelzine (see Chapter 3)

     e) Behavioral modification as for Phobias (see above)

E. Obsessive-compulsive disorder
1. Criteria: Table 2.7
2. Epidemiology
   a) Onset usually in adolescence or early adulthood
   b) Frequently associated with major depression (Chapter 3), simple phobia (see above), and panic disorder (see above)
   c) Evidence for genetic component
3. Management (see General Approach to Treatment, below)
   a) In the medical history and physical examination, look for medical conditions, medications, or dietary products (e.g., caffeine) that may exacerbate anxiety
   b) Clomipramine (Anafranil) 25 mg/day to start, up to 250 mg/day; improvement may take 6–8 weeks; or
   c) Fluoxetine (Prozac) 20 mg/day to start, up to 40–60 mg/day (2 doses early in the day)
   d) Behavioral modification

F. Posttraumatic stress disorder
1. Criteria: Table 2.8
2. Epidemiology
   a) Twice as likely as the general population to have another psychiatric disorder (especially obsessive-compulsive disorder,

Table 2.6.   Diagnostic Criteria for Panic Disorder Without and With Agoraphobia

Without Agoraphobia

A. Both (1) and (2):
   (1) Recurrent unexpected panic attacks
   (2) At least one of the attacks has been followed by a month (or more) of (a) persistent concern about having additional attacks; (b) worry about the implications of the attack or its consequences (e.g., losing control, having a heart attack, "going crazy"); or (c) a significant change in behavior related to the attacks
B. Absence of Agoraphobia (defined below).
C. The panic attacks are not due to the direct effects of a substance (e.g., drugs of abuse, medication) or a general medical condition (e.g., hyperthyroidism).
D. The anxiety is not better accounted for by another mental disorder, such as Obsessive-Compulsive Disorder (e.g., fear of contamination), Posttraumatic Stress Disorder (e.g., in response to stimuli associated with a severe stressor), Separation Anxiety Disorder, or Social Phobia (e.g., fear of embarrassment in social situations).

With Agoraphobia

A. Both (1) and (2):
   (1) Recurrent unexpected panic attacks
   (2) At least one of the attacks has been followed by a month or more of (a) persistent concern about having additional attacks; (b) worry about the implications of the attack or its consequences (e.g., losing control, having a heart attack, "going crazy"); or (c) a significant change in behavior related to the attacks
B. The presence of agoraphobia, i.e., anxiety about being in places or situations from which escape might be difficult (or embarrassing) or in which help may not be available in the event of having an unexpected or situationally predisposed panic attack. Agoraphobic fears typically involve characteristic clusters of situations that include being outside the home alone; being in a crowd or standing in a line; being on a bridge; and traveling in a bus, train, or car.
   Note: Consider the diagnosis of Specific Phobia, if limited to one or only a few specific situations, or Social Phobia, if the avoidance is limited to social situations.
C. Agoraphobic situations are avoided (e.g., travel is restricted) or else endured with marked distress or with anxiety about having a panic attack, or [they] require the presence of a companion.
D. The panic attacks are not due to the direct effects of a substance (e.g., drugs of abuse, medication) or a general medical condition (e.g., hyperthyroidism).
E. The anxiety or phobic avoidance is not better accounted for by another mental disorder, such as Specific Phobia (e.g., avoidance limited to a single situation like elevators), Separation Anxiety Disorder (e.g., avoidance of school), Obsessive-Compulsive Disorder (e.g., fear of contamination), Posttraumatic Stress Disorder (e.g., avoidance of stimuli associated with a severe stressor), or Social Phobia (e.g., avoidance limited to social situations because of fear of embarrassment).

Adapted from American Psychiatric Association: *Diagnostic and Statistical Manual of Mental Disorders*, 4th ed. Washington, DC, American Psychiatric Association, 1994.

       dysthymia (Chapter 3), substance abuse, bipolar affective disorder (Chapter 3), and antisocial personality)
   b) Benzodiazepines are effective but may be relatively contraindicated in people at risk for chemical dependency
   c) Desensitization (see above) usually required
   d) Psychotherapy may be needed

GENERAL APPROACH TO TREATMENT

A. Nonpharmacological
   1. Explanation of the disorder — to relieve feelings of isolation and to give hope for improvement

Table 2.7.   Diagnostic Criteria for Obsessive Compulsive Disorder

A. Either obsessions or compulsions:

Obsessions as defined by (1), (2), (3), and (4):
   (1) Recurrent and persistent thoughts, impulses, or images that are experienced, at some time during the disturbance, as intrusive and inappropriate and cause marked anxiety or distress
   (2) The thoughts, impulses, or images are not simply excessive worries about real-life problems
   (3) The person attempts to ignore or suppress such thoughts or impulses or to neutralize them with some other thought or action
   (4) The person recognizes that the obsessional thoughts, impulses, or images are a product of his or her own mind (not imposed from without as in thought insertion)

Compulsions as defined by (1) and (2):
   (1) Repetitive behaviors (e.g., handwashing, ordering, checking) or mental acts (e.g., praying, counting, repeating words silently) that the person feels driven to perform in response to an obsession or according to rules that must be applied rigidly
   (2) The behaviors or mental acts are aimed at preventing or reducing distress or preventing some dreaded event or situation; however, these behaviors or mental acts either are not connected in a realistic way with what they are designed to neutralize or prevent or are clearly excessive

B. At some point during the course of the disorder, the person has recognized that the obsessions or compulsions are excessive or unreasonable. Note: this does not apply to children.

C. The obsession or compulsions cause marked distress; are time-consuming (take more than an hour a day); or significantly interfere with the person's normal routine, occupational functioning, or usual social activities or relationships with others.

D. If another Axis I disorder is present, the content of the obsessions or compulsions is not restricted to it (e.g., preoccupation with food in the presence of an Eating Disorder; hair pulling in the presence of Trichotillomania; concern with appearance in the presence of Body Dysmorphic Disorder; preoccupation with drugs in the presence of a Substance Use Disorder; preoccupation with having a serious illness in the presence of Hypochondriasis; or guilty ruminations in the presence of Major Depressive Disorder).

E. [The disorder is] not due to the direct effects of a substance (e.g., drugs of abuse, medication) or a general medical condition.

Adapted from American Psychiatric Association: *Diagnostic and Statistical Manual of Mental Disorders*, 4th ed. Washington, DC, American Psychiatric Association, 1994.

  2. Self-regulation techniques
     a) Progressive muscle relaxation and diaphragmatic breathing (Table 2.9)
     b) Biofeedback — electromyographic information via electrodes placed on a muscle or muscle group — allows patient to reduce tension (requires referral to a psychology laboratory)
     c) Self-hypnosis (therapists usually available in larger communities)
     d) Meditation techniques (e.g., Zen, yoga)
B. Pharmacological
  1. Benzodiazepines
     a) Information about available preparations (Table 2.10)
     b) Tolerance to anxiolytic effects less common than to hypnotic effects
     c) Physical dependence does develop, and withdrawal signs and symptoms (e.g., irritability, disturbed sleep, anorexia) should be anticipated

Table 2.8.   Diagnostic Criteria for Posttraumatic Stress Disorder

A. The person has been exposed to a traumatic event in which both of the following have been present:
  (1) The person has experienced, witnessed, or been confronted with an event or events that involve actual or threatened death or serious injury or a threat to the physical integrity of oneself or others
  (2) The person's response involved intense fear, helplessness, or horror. Note: in children, it may be expressed instead by disorganized or agitated behavior
B. The traumatic event is persistently reexperienced in at least one of the following ways:
  (1) Recurrent and intrusive distressing recollections of the event, including images, thoughts, or perceptions.
  (2) Recurrent distressing dreams of the event. Note: in children, there may be frightening dreams without recognized content
  (3) Acting or feeling as if the traumatic event were recurring (includes a sense of reliving the experience, illusions, hallucinations, and dissociative flashback episodes, including those that occur upon awakening or when intoxicated); note: in young children, trauma-specific reenactment may occur
  (4) Intense psychological distress at exposure to internal or external cues that symbolize or resemble an aspect of the traumatic event
  (5) Physiological reactivity upon exposure to internal or external cues that symbolize or resemble an aspect of the traumatic event
C. Persistent avoidance of stimuli associated with the trauma and numbing of general responsiveness (not present before the trauma), as indicated by at least three of the following:
  (1) Efforts to avoid thoughts, feelings, or conversations associated with the trauma
  (2) Efforts to avoid activities, places, or people that arouse recollections of the trauma
  (3) Inability to recall an important aspect of the trauma
  (4) Markedly diminished interest in participation in significant activities
  (5) Feeling of detachment or estrangement from others
  (6) Restricted range of affect (e.g., unable to have loving feelings)
  (7) Sense of a foreshortened future (e.g., does not expect to have a career, marriage, children, or a normal life span)
D. Persistent symptoms of increased arousal (not present before the trauma), as indicated by at least two of the following:
  (1) Difficulty falling or staying asleep
  (2) Irritability or outbursts of anger
  (3) Difficulty concentrating
  (4) Hypervigilance
  (5) Exaggerated startle response
E. Duration of the disturbance (symptoms in B, C, and D) is more than 1 month.
F. The disturbance causes clinically significant distress or impairment in social, occupational, or other important areas of functioning.
  Acute: if duration of symptoms is less than 3 months
  Chronic: if duration of symptoms is 3 months or more
  With Delayed Onset: onset of symptoms at least 6 months after the stressor

Adapted from American Psychiatric Association: *Diagnostic and Statistical Manual of Mental Disorders*, 4th ed. Washington, DC, American Psychiatric Association, 1994.

  1) Dosage of drug and duration of treatment should be minimized
  2) Withdrawal symptoms should be explained to patient
  3) Patients should be seen weekly
  4) Tapering of the drug should take 4–6 weeks
  5) Switching to a longer acting preparation before tapering may minimize symptoms of withdrawal
 d) Abuse of drugs among patients with anxiety is not common unless there is a history of abuse of other substances

Table 2.9. Essential Steps in Progressive Muscle Relaxation (A), Rapid Muscle Relaxation Techniques (B), and Diaphragmatic Breathing (C)

	Exercise
Muscle(s):	A. Progressive Muscle Relaxation[a]
Forehead/scalp	Raise the eyebrows high; hold; feel strain; relax.
Forehead	Scowl or frown; bunch eyebrows with nose upward; relax.
Eyes	Squeeze eyes shut; hold; feel strain in temples; relax.
Mouth	Smile broadly until mouth quivers slightly; relax; press lips tightly inward; hold; relax.
Jaw	Grit teeth gently but firmly; hold; relax; part lips slightly.
Neck/arm/shoulder	Press head back against right hand; relax; repeat exercise with left hand.
Neck/arm/shoulder	Press head forward against right hand placed on forehead; relax; repeat with left hand.
Back/legs/abdomen	Sitting, grip chair sides firmly; raise legs slightly; lift buttocks 1 inch from chair; point toes forward, then backward; relax.
Hands/arm	Make fist; clench tightly; relax.

B. Rapid Relaxation[b]

Step 1: Sit or lie down. The quieter the place, the better.
Step 2: Take a deep breath through your mouth, hold it for 10 seconds, and exhale slowly.
Step 3: Mentally repeat the word "relax" 4 times in a calm manner.
Step 4: Gradually space out repeating "relax" until each repetition takes about 7 seconds.
Step 5: Keep practicing until you achieve the level of relaxation you desire.

C. Diaphragmatic Breathing

While sitting or lying down with a pillow at the small of your back:
1. Breathe in slowly and deeply by pushing your stomach out.
2. Say the word "relax" silently to yourself prior to exhaling.
3. Exhale slowly, letting your stomach come in.
4. Repeat entire procedure 10 times consecutively, with emphasis on slow, deep breaths.

Practice should take place 5 times/day, 10 consecutive diaphragmatic breaths each sitting. Time for mastery is after 1–2 weeks of daily practice.

[a] Subject instructed to practice this seated comfortably or reclining.
[b] For immediate relaxation in everyday stressful situation.

2. Antidepressants (see Chapter 3)
3. Buspirone (BuSpar)
   a) Comparable effectiveness to benzodiazepines (especially for cognitive, interpersonal aspects of anxiety)
   b) Nonsedating; no amplification of effects of alcohol
   c) No tolerance or dependence yet observed
   d) Available in 5- and 20-mg tablets; starting dose of 5 mg 3 times/day may be increased to 10 mg 3 times/day
   e) Two weeks until maximum effect
   f) Side effects: nervousness, headache, light-headedness, nausea

Table 2.10.   Usual Dose and Pharmacokinetics of Anxiolytic Benzodiazepines

Drug (Trade Name), Year Introduced	Onset of Effect After Oral Dose[a]	Available Strengths (mg)	Oral Daily Dose Range Divided 2 or 3 Times/Day (mg)	Active Metabolites Present	Elimination Half-Life[b] (hr)
Alprazolam (Xanax) 1981	Intermediate	0.25, 0.5, 1 (scored tablets)	0.75–6	No	8–16
Chlordiazepoxide[c] (Librium; Libritabs) 1960	Intermediate	5, 10, 25 (capsules) 5, 10, 25 (tablets)	15–100	Yes	5–30
Clonazepam[d] (Klonopin) 1990	Intermediate	0.5, 1, 2 (tablets)	1.5–20	Yes	18–50
Clorazepate dipotassium[c] (Tranxene; Tranxene-SD) 1972	Rapid	3.75, 7.5, 15 (capsules) 11.25, 22.5 (tablets)	15–60	Yes	36–200
			22.5 (single doses are intended for patients stabilized on 3.75 or 7.5 mg 3 times/day)	Yes	36–200
Diazepam[c] (Valium) 1961	Rapid	2, 5, 10 (tablets)	4–40	Yes	20–50
Diazepam (Valrelease) 1982	Slow	15 (capsules)	15–30 (single dose is equivalent to 5 mg of Valium 3 times/day)	Yes	20–50
Halazepam (Paxipam) 1981	Slow to intermediate	20, 40 (tablets)	80–160	Yes	50–100
Lorazepam[c] (Ativan) 1977	Intermediate	0.5, 1, 2 (tablets)	1–6	No	10–20
Oxazepam[c] (Serax) 1963	Slow to intermediate	10, 15, 30 (capsules) 15 (tablets)	30–120 30–120	No	5–10
Prazepam (Centrax) 1977	Slow	5, 10 (capsules)	20–60	Yes	36–200

[a] Drugs with more rapid onset of action are those more rapidly absorbed.
[b] Elimination half-life of lipophilic activity.
[c] Generic available.
[d] Clonazepam is not Food and Drug Administration approved for treatment of anxiety. Approved as an anticonvulsant.

4. β-Adrenergic blockers (see Chapter 46)
   a) May be most effective drugs in reducing autonomic symptoms of anxiety (e.g., palpitations)
   b) Do not prevent panic attacks
5. Antihistamines
   a) Alternatives to benzodiazepines, especially in people with obstructive lung disease
   b) Very sedating
   c) Hydroxyzine (Vistaril, Atarax) 10–25 mg 3 times/day, a common choice

3/ AFFECTIVE DISORDERS

DYSTHYMIC DISORDER (DEPRESSIVE NEUROSIS)
A. Criteria: Table 3.1
B. Epidemiology
1. Far more common in women
2. Onset usually between ages 18 and 30
3. Often precipitated by stress
4. Episodes of major depression (see below) common
C. Management
1. Detection of disorder and expression of interest often therapeutic
2. Weekly visits for 3–6 weeks to provide support and advice are important
3. Antidepressant drugs (see below) often useful if symptoms persist
4. Benzodiazepines, if prescribed, should not be used for more than 1–2 weeks
D. Prognosis
1. Commonly chronic, often with waxing and waning
2. Chronic medical disorders, severe social maladjustments predict poor outcome

MAJOR AFFECTIVE DISORDERS
A. Major depression
1. Criteria: Table 3.2
2. Epidemiology
a) Two to three times more common in women
b) Occurs at any age
3. Management
a) Available drugs (Table 3.3)
1) Tricyclic antidepressants (TCAs)

Table 3.1. American Psychiatric Association Diagnostic Criteria for Dysthymic Disorder

A. Depressed mood for most of the day, for more days than not, as indicated either by subjective account or [by] observation made by others, for at least 2 years.
B. Presence, while depressed, of two (or more) of the following:
(1) Poor appetite or overeating
(2) Insomnia or hypersomnia
(3) Low energy or fatigue
(4) Low self-esteem
(5) Poor concentration or difficulty making decisions
(6) Feelings of hopelessness
C. During the 2-year period of the disturbance, the person has never been without the symptoms in A and B for more than 2 months at a time.
D. No major depressive episode during the first 2 years of the disturbance, i.e., not better accounted for by chronic Major Depressive Disorder or Major Depressive Disorder in partial remission.
E. [There] has never been [been] . . . a manic episode or an unequivocal hypomanic episode.
F. [The disturbance] does not occur exclusively during the course of a chronic psychotic disorder, such as Schizophrenia or Delusional Disorder.
G. [The symptoms are] not due to the direct effects of a substance (e.g., drugs of abuse, medication) or a general medical condition (e.g., hypothyroidism).

Adapted from American Psychiatric Association: *Diagnostic and Statistical Manual of Mental Disorders*, 4th ed. Washington, DC, American Psychiatric Association, 1994.

Table 3.2.   American Psychiatric Association Diagnostic Criteria for Major Depressive Episode

A. At least five of the following symptoms have been present during the same 2-week period and represent a change from previous functioning; at least one of the symptoms is either (1) depressed mood or (2) loss of interest or pleasure:
   (1) Depressed mood most of the day, nearly every day, as indicated by either subjective report (e.g., feels sad or empty) or observation made by others (e.g., appears tearful)
   (2) Marked diminished interest or pleasure in all, or almost all, activities most of the day, nearly every day (as indicated either by subjective account or observation made by others)
   (3) Significant weight loss or weight gain when not dieting (e.g., more than 5% of body weight in a month), or decrease or increase in appetite nearly every day
   (4) Insomnia or hypersomnia nearly every day
   (5) Psychomotor agitation or retardation nearly every day (observable by others, not merely subjective feelings of restlessness or being slowed down)
   (6) Fatigue or loss of energy nearly every day
   (7) Feelings of worthlessness or excessive or inappropriate guilt (which may be delusional) nearly every day (not merely self-reproach or guilt about being sick)
   (8) Diminished ability to think or concentrate, or indecisiveness, nearly every day (either by subjective account or as observed by others)
   (9) Recurrent thoughts of death (not just fear of dying), recurrent suicidal ideation without a specific plan, or a suicide attempt or a specific plan for committing suicide
B. The symptoms cause clinically significant distress of impairment in social, occupational, or other important areas of functioning.
C. [The symptoms are] not due to the direct effects of a substance (e.g., drugs of abuse, medication) or a general medical condition (e.g., hypothyroidism).
D. [The symptoms have not occurred] within 2 months of the loss of a loved one (except if associated with marked functional impairment, morbid preoccupation with worthlessness, suicidal ideation, psychotic symptoms, or psychomotor retardation).

Adapted from American Psychiatric Association: *Diagnostic and Statistical Manual of Mental Disorders*, 4th ed. Washington, DC, American Psychiatric Association, 1994.

   (a) Secondary amine TCAs (Table 3.3) recommended for prescription by nonpsychiatrists
   (b) Give a total dose at bedtime
   (c) Do not change a dosage or a preparation before the patient has had an adequate trial (2 weeks)
   (d) If there is no improvement within 6–8 weeks, change regimen (measure drug level first)
   (e) Starting doses should be reduced by 50% in older patients
   (f) Be aware of drug interactions (Table 3.4)
2) Selective serotonin-reuptake inhibitors — no more effective than TCAs but fewer side effects
3) Monoamine oxidase inhibitors
   (a) Not first-line agents because of risk of hypertensive crisis (Table 3.4)
4) Bupropion (Wellbutrin) — fewer side effects than TCAs; full effect not seen for 4 weeks
5) Benzodiazepines, e.g., alprazolam (Xanax), effective in relieving associated anxiety, should not be used for more than a month
   b) Duration of treatment
      1) Two-month trial at a therapeutic dosage to establish efficacy

Table 3.3.   Selected Characteristics of Antidepressant Drugs

A. Tricyclic Antidepressants (TCAs)

Generic Name	Proprietary Name	Strengths of Oral Preparations (mg)	Usual Effective Total Daily Doses (Range) (mg)	Therapeutic Plasma Level (ng/ml)	Average Elimination Half-Life (Range) (hr)	Side Effects Antihistamine (Sedation)	Side Effects Antiadrenergic (Orthostatic Hypotension)	Side Effects Anticholinergic[a]	Side Effects Weight Gain
Secondary amines									
Desipramine[c]	Norpramin	10, 25, 50	200 (50–100)	125–300[b]	18 (12–50)	1+	2+	1+	1+
Nortriptyline[c]	Aventyl, Pamelor	10, 25, 50, 75, 100	100 (50–150)	50–150	26 (18–88)	1+	1+	1+	1+
Protriptyline	Vivactil	5, 10	40 (15–60)	70–170	76 (54–124)	1+	2+	1+	0
Tertiary amines									
Amitriptyline[c]	Elavil, Endep	10, 25, 50, 75, 100	150 (50–300)	>120[b]	24 (16–46)	3+	3+	3+	4+
Doxepin[c]	Sinequan, Adapin	10, 25, 50, 100	150 (50–300)	>90[b]	17 (10–47)	3+	1+	1+	3+
Imipramine[c]	Tofranil, SK-Pramine, Presamine	10, 25, 50, 100	150 (50–300)	150–250[b]	22 (12–34)	2+	3+	1+	3+
Clomipramine	Anafranil	50, 100	250 (50–300)	100–250	32 (19–37)	1+	3+	3+	2+

B. Selective Serotonin Reuptake Inhibitors

Generic Name	Proprietary Name	Strengths of Oral Preparations (mg)	Usual Effective Total Daily Doses (Range) (mg)	Average Elimination Half-Life (Range) (hr)	Side Effects Insomnia	Side Effects Anxiety	Side Effects Sedation or Lethargy
Fluoxetine	Prozac	10, 20	20 (10–80)	168 (72–360)	1+	1+	1+
Sertraline	Zoloft	50, 100	100 (25–200)	24 (10–30)	1+	1+	1+

Generic Name	Proprietary Name	Strengths of Oral Preparations (mg)	Usual Effective Total Daily Doses (Range)[d] (mg)	Average Elimination Half-Life (Range) (hr)	Side Effects	
					Risk of Hypertensive Crisis	Hypotension
Paroxetine	Paxil	20, 30	20 (20-50)	24 (3-65)	1+	1+
Trazodone	Desyrel[c]	50, 150, 300	300 (150-400)	8 (4-14)	0	3+

C. Monoamine Oxidase Inhibitors (MAOIs)

Generic Name	Proprietary Name	Strengths of Oral Preparations (mg)	Usual Effective Total Daily Doses (Range)[d] (mg)	Average Elimination Half-Life (Range) (hr)	Side Effects	
					Risk of Hypertensive Crisis	Hypotension
Tranylcypromine	Parnate	10	30 (20-60)	2 (1.5-3)	2+	2+
Phenelzine	Nardil	15	45 (30-90)	2 (1.5-4)	1+	2+
Isocarboxazid	Marplan	10	30 (20-60)	?	1+	2+

D. Other Drugs for Depression

Generic Name	Proprietary Name	Strengths of Oral Preparations (mg)	Usual Effective Total Daily Doses (Range) (mg)	Average Elimination Half-Life (Range) (hr)	Major Advantages	Major Disadvantages
Bupropion	Wellbutrin	75, 100	300-450[e]	14 (8-24)	Few anticholinergic effects; no orthostasis or other cardiac effects. No weight gain.	May be more likely than TCA to induce seizures. Can increase anxiety and insomnia in early phase of treatment. Three times a day schedule.
Alprazolam	Xanax	0.25, 0.5, 1	0.75-4[e]	16 (9-26)	A benzodiazepine without anticholinergic or other tricyclic side effects.	Not established as fully effective in depressions. Some addictive potential. Fairly sedating. Three times a day schedule.
Venlafaxine	Effexor	25, 37.5, 50, 75, 100	75-225	5 (3-7)[f], 11 (9-13)[g]	Fewer side effects than TCAs	Occasionally causes sustained hypertension

[a] Dry mouth, blurred vision, decreased intestinal motility, decreased bladder tone, tachycardia.
[b] Upper limit not established.
[c] Available in generic preparation.
[d] Twice-daily schedule.
[e] Three times a day schedule.
[f] Unaltered drug.
[g] Active metabolite.

Table 3.4.   Drugs That May Interact With Tricyclic Antidepressants (TCAs)

Drug	Interaction
Anticholinergic antispasmodics	Enhanced anticholinergic side effects
Antihypertensive drugs	Enhanced orthostatic hypotension (exception: clonidine and guanethidine; TCA may interfere with antihypertensive effectiveness)
Antiparkinsonian drugs (L-dopa and anticholinergic drugs)	Enhanced anticholinergic side effects (also decreased L-dopa effect)
Cimetidine	Increased imipramine effect
Dilantin	May block TCA effectiveness
Fluoxetine (Prozac)	Increases TCA plasma levels 2-fold or more
Methylphenidate (Ritalin)	May increase TCA plasma levels
Monoamine oxidase inhibitors (MAOIs)	Levels of both TCAs and MAOIs may be increased; enhanced risk of hypertensive crisis
Sedating drugs (alcohol, antihistamines, anxiolytics, hypnotics, neuroleptics)	Enhanced sedation
Sympathomimetics (decongestants, weight reduction agents, stimulants)	TCA may potentiate blood pressure-raising effects of these drugs

Table 3.5.   Cognitive Distortions in Depression

All-or-nothing thinking: Thinking occurs in black and white terms with no recognition of a middle ground. Things are wonderful or awful. One's actions reflect either perfection or total failure.

Overgeneralization: Words like "always" and "never" may portray a single negative event as a never-ending pattern of defeat.

Selective abstraction: A single negative detail is focused on and ruminated about until it colors everything.

Disqualifying the positive: Positive experiences are often discounted as not relevant, not real, or not deserved.

Arbitrary inferences: It is assumed that things are or will be negative, regardless of the facts.

Magnification and/or minimization: One's own failures and others' successes are magnified; one's own successes and others' failures are minimized.

Emotional reasoning: Bad feelings are taken as the litmus test of reality.

Should statements: Repetitive "I should/should not" or "I must/must not" statements often contribute to depression, resentment, guilt, and hopelessness.

Labeling and mislabeling: Mistakes or shortcomings become sweeping self-condemnations.

Personalization: Depressed individuals often assume they are the cause of some unfortunate or unpleasant event for which, in actuality, they are not responsible.

Adapted from Burns DD: *Feeling Good: The New Mood Therapy.* New York, New American Library, 1980.

  2) If a regimen is effective, it should be maintained for 6 months
  3) Tapering should be done by reducing dosage 25% per week to avoid withdrawal symptoms (nausea, dizziness, headache, increased perspiration and salivation), unless toxic side effects (Table 3.3) have occurred
 c) Office psychotherapy
  1) See patient at least every other week for 6–8 weeks
  2) At each visit emphasize that major depression is a treatable disease
  3) The patient should avoid major life decisions while depressed

      4) Frank discussion of suicidal feelings should be part of each visit
      5) The patient should be asked about drug side effects at each visit, and heart rate and rhythm and sitting and standing blood pressure should be recorded
      6) Cognitive distortions (Table 3.5) should be gently corrected
   d) Criteria for referral to a psychiatrist
      1) No improvement despite 8 weeks of treatment with an adequate dose of an antidepressant
      2) Inability or refusal to take an antidepressant
      3) Overtly suicidal patient
      4) Patient with delusions, hallucinations, or depressive stupor

B. Mania
  1. Criteria: Table 3.6
  2. Epidemiology
   a) Equally common in men and women
   b) First episode usually before age 30
   c) Much less common than major depression
  3. Management
   a) Always refer to a psychiatrist
   b) Lithium carbonate the most useful drug
      1) Dosage determined by the treating psychiatrist
      2) Levels should be checked at least 6 times/year
      3) Side effects common, especially physiological tremor, thyroid dysfunction (goiter and/or hypothyroidism), and partial nephrogenic diabetes insipidus (Chapter 58)
      4) Drug interactions: Table 3.7
   c) If mania is severe, lithium and a neuroleptic (Chapter 4) will

Table 3.6.   American Psychiatric Association Diagnostic Criteria for a Manic Episode

A. A distinct period of abnormally and persistently elevated, expansive, or irritable mood, lasting at least 1 week (or any duration if hospitalization is necessary)
B. During the period of mood disturbance, at least three of the following symptoms have persisted (four if the mood is only irritable) and have been present to a significant degree:
(1) Inflated self-esteem or grandiosity
(2) Decreased need for sleep (e.g., feels rested after only 3 hours of sleep)
(3) More talkative than usual or pressure to keep talking
(4) Flight of ideas or subjective experience that thoughts are racing
(5) Distractibility (i.e., attention too easily drawn to unimportant or irrelevant external stimuli)
(6) Increase in goal-directed activity (either social, at work or school, or sexually) or psychomotor agitation
(7) Excessive involvement in pleasurable activities that have a high potential for painful consequences (e.g., the person engages in unrestrained buying sprees, sexual indiscretions, or foolish business investments)
C. The mood disturbance is sufficiently severe to cause marked impairment in occupational functioning or in usual social activities or relationships with others or to necessitate hospitalization to prevent harm to self or others
D. [The symptoms are] not due to the direct effects of a substance (e.g., drugs of abuse, medication) or a general medical condition (e.g., hyperthyroidism).

Adapted from American Psychiatric Association: *Diagnostic and Statistical Manual of Mental Disorders*, 4th ed. Washington, DC, American Psychiatric Association, 1994.

Table 3.7.   Important Drug Interactions With Lithium

Drugs that may enhance lithium toxicity
 Angiotensin-converting enzyme inhibitors[a]
 Amiloride[b]
 Calcium channel blockers[a]
 Ethacrynic acid[b]
 Furosemide[b]
 Indomethacin (and probably other nonsteroidal anti-inflammatory drugs)[b]
 Methyldopa[a]
 Phenytoin[a]
 Carbamazepine[a]
 Spectinamycin[b]
 Sprionolactone[b]
 Tetracycline[b]
 Thiazide diuretics[b]
 Triamterene[b]
Drugs that may diminish lithium effect
 Acetazolamide[c]
 Theophyline[c]
Drugs that may aggravate lithium tremor
 Neuroleptics[a]
 Tricyclic antidepressants[a]

[a] Mechanism not established.
[b] Decreased renal excretion.
[c] Increased renal excretion.

be prescribed by the treating psychiatrist, usually in the hospital
4. Prognosis
 a) With treatment, most patients recover within months, but 20% with major depression have not fully recovered in 2 years
 b) Relapses common and become more frequent with advancing age

SUICIDE PREVENTION
A. Risks for successful suicide
 1. Severe depression
 2. Older age
 3. Male sex
 4. Alcoholism
 5. Living alone
 6. Previous suicide attempt
 7. Refusal to accept referral for psychiatric treatment
B. Strategies to prevent suicide
 1. Recognition, treatment, and prevention of major depressive episodes
 2. Direct inquiry of depressed patients about suicidal ideas and plans
 3. Use of small prescriptions of potentially lethal drugs
 4. Family supervision of medications
 5. Hospitalization if risk is high

4/ SCHIZOPHRENIA

EPIDEMIOLOGY AND NATURAL HISTORY
A. Epidemiology
   1. Equal frequency in males and females
   2. Onset usually in young adulthood
   3. More common in lower socioeconomic groups
   4. Relatives of schizophrenics are at higher risk of developing schizophrenia
B. Natural history
   1. Prodromal phase
      a) Gradual withdrawal from social relationships
      b) Indifference to appearance, suspicious attitudes, ignoring of social graces
      c) Gradual deterioration of scholastic and vocational abilities
      d) Dysphoria (anxiety or depression) common
   2. Acute psychotic episodes
      a) Delusions
      b) Hallucinations
      c) Blunted, flattened, or inappropriate affect
      d) Preoccupation with fantasies
      e) Inability to carry out goal-oriented behavior
      f) Stereotyped, bizarre, sometimes rigid posturing
      g) If treated (see below), respond in several weeks to 2 months; then revert to prodromal state, regressing further after each psychotic episode

DIAGNOSIS
A. Criteria: Table 4.1
B. Differential diagnosis
   1. Organic mental disorders (Chapter 5) characterized by delirium, disorientation, and impaired intellectual function
   2. Simple psychotic symptoms (e.g., delusions or auditory hallucinations) may be seen in the demented elderly
   3. Use of illicit drugs (Chapter 8)
   4. Use of prescription drugs occasionally (Table 4.2); no prodrome
   5. Major affective disorders (Chapter 3): disturbance in mood precedes psychotic symptoms; the opposite of the situation in schizophrenics

TREATMENT
A. Neuroleptic agents (Table 4.3)
   1. Control of combativeness, hyperactivity, and agitation usually within 24–48 hours
   2. Subsidence of delusions, hallucinations, negativism, and withdrawal within 1–2 weeks, often continued improvement over 4–8 weeks
   3. Starting dose the equivalent of 300–400 mg of chlorpromazine a day in divided doses
   4. Haloperidol 2–5 mg, a good choice for intramuscular injections
   5. Early side effects
      a) Sedation with drugs that are less potent per unit weight (Table 4.3)

Table 4.1.   Diagnostic Criteria for Schizophrenia

A. Characteristic Symptoms: At least two of the following, each present for a significant portion of time during a 1-month period (or less if successfully treated):
   (1) Delusions
   (2) Hallucinations
   (3) Disorganized speech (e.g., frequent derailment or incoherence)
   (4) Grossly disorganized or catatonic behavior
   (5) Negative symptoms, i.e., affective flattening, alogia, or avolition
   (Note: Only one A symptom is required if delusions are bizarre or hallucinations consist of a voice keeping up a running commentary on the person's behavior or thoughts or two or more voices conversing with each other.)
B. Social/Occupational Dysfunction: For a significant portion of the time since the onset of the disturbance, one or more major areas of functioning, such as work, interpersonal relations, or self-care, is markedly below the level achieved prior to the onset (or when the onset is in childhood or adolescence, failure to achieve expected level of interpersonal, academic, or occupational achievement).
C. Duration: Continuous signs of the disturbance persist for at least 6 months. This 6-month period must include at least 1 month of symptoms that meet criterion A (i.e., active phase symptoms), and may include periods of prodromal or residual symptoms. During these prodromal or residual periods, the signs of the disturbance may be manifested by only negative symptoms or two or more symptoms listed in criterion A present in an attenuated form (e.g., odd beliefs, unusual perceptual experiences).
D. Schizoaffective and Mood Disorder Exclusion: Schizoaffective Disorder and Mood Disorder with Psychotic Features have been ruled out because either: (1) no major depressive or manic episodes have occurred concurrently with the active phase symptoms; or (2) if mood episodes have occurred during active phase symptoms, their total duration has been brief relative to the duration of the active and residual periods.
E. Substance/General Medical Condition Exclusion: The disturbance is not due to the direct effects of a substance (e.g., drugs of abuse, medication) or a general medical condition.

Adapted from American Psychiatric Association: *Diagnostic and Statistical Manual of Mental Disorders*, 4th ed. Washington, DC, American Psychiatric Association, 1994.

  b) Anticholinergic effects (dry mouth, stuffy nose, blurred vision, urinary retention in the elderly) with phenothiazines
  c) Parkinson's syndrome (tremor, rigidity, etc.) — greatest risk with drugs that are more potent per unit weight (Table 4.3)
    1) Attempt to reduce dose, or change to another drug
    2) Use an antiparkinsonian agent (Chapter 65)
    3) Tends to abate within 1–2 months
  d) Acute dystonias (sudden onset of contractions of neck, spine, extraocular muscles, tongue)
    1) Most commonly with haloperidol and piperazine class of phenothiazines (Table 4.3)
    2) Remit with Benadryl, 25–50 mg i.m., or Cogentin, 2 mg i.v.; then give an antiparkinsonian drug for 1 month
  e) Akathisia (pacing, fidgeting)
    1) Response to treatment not predictable
    2) Treat as for Parkinson's syndrome (above)
  f) Orthostatic hypotension — usually limited to aliphatic and piperidine classes of phenothiazines (Table 4.3) and to chlorprothixene
  g) Cholestatic jaundice — reversible
  h) Neuroleptic malignant syndrome (rapid onset rigidity and high fever) — hospitalize

Table 4.2.   Prescription Drugs That Have Been Reported Occasionally to Cause Hallucinations or Other Manifestations of Psychosis

Angiotensin-converting enzyme inhibitors	Fluoxetine (Prozac)
Acyclovir (Zovirax)	Ganciclovir (Cytovene)
Albuterol (Proventil; Ventolin)	Histamine H_2-receptor antagonists
Amiodarone (Cordarone)	Isoniazid (INH, others)
Amantadine (Symmetrel)	Levodopa (Sinemet)
Amphetamine-like drugs	Methyldopa (Aldomet)
Anabolic steroids	Methylphenidate (Ritalin)
Anticonvulsants	Metronidazole (Flagyl)
Antidepressants, tricyclic	Nalidixic acid (NegGram)
Antihistamines	Narcotics
Atropine and anticholinergics	Pentazocine (Talwin)
Baclofen (Lioresal)	Pseudoephedrine
Benzodiazepines	Nonsteroidal anti-inflammatory drugs
β-Adrenergic blockers	Pergolide (Permax)
Bromocriptine (Parlodel)	Phenelzine (Nardil)
Bupropion (Wellbutrin)	Phenylephrine (Neo-Synephrine)
Caffeine	Prazosin (Minipress)
Chloroquine (Aralen)	Procainamide (Pronestyl)
Ciprofloxacin (Cipro)	Procaine Penicillin G
Clonidine (Catapres)	Quinacrine (Atabrine)
Cocaine	Quinidine
Corticosteroids (prednisone, cortisone, ACTH, other)	Salicylates
Cyclobenzaprine (Flexeril)	Selegiline (Eldepryl)
Cyclosporine (Sandimmune)	Sulfonamides
Deet (Off)	Tamoxifen (Nolvadex)
Digitalis glycosides	Thyroid hormones
Disopyramide (Norpace)	Trazodone (Desyrel)
Disulfiram (Antabuse)	Verapamil
Ethchlorvynol (Placidyl)	Zidovudine (Retrovir)

Adapted from: Drugs that cause psychiatric symptoms. *Med Lett* 35:65, 1993 (includes references to reports).

    i) Older schizophrenics more prone to side effects, doses should be lower (by equivalent of 100–200 mg chlorpromazine)
6. Long-term drug treatment
   a) All patients should be treated for at least 2 years after an acute episode; most, indefinitely
   b) Moderate dose (e.g., equivalent of 100–200 mg of chlorpromazine a day) usually adequate
   c) If patient cannot maintain medication schedule, consider a long-acting intramuscular agent (Prolixin 1–2 ml once a week)
   d) If neuroleptics are ineffective or have intolerable side effects, consider Clozaril, a tricyclic dibenzodiazepine, starting at 25 mg once or twice a day, increasing 25 mg every other day to 100 mg, then increasing 50 mg every other day to 300–450 mg by 2 weeks
   e) Late side effects of drugs
     1) Parkinsonism — try another drug (long-term use of antiparkinsonian agents to be avoided)
     2) Tardive dyskinesia (involuntary choreiform movements or tics, sometimes with dystonia) (see above) — poor prognosis for remission, but if symptoms occur, neuroleptics should be tapered and discontinued if possible

Table 4.3.   Available Strengths and Equivalent Doses of Commonly Used Neuroleptic Antipsychotic Agents

Generic Name	Trade Name	Available Strengths of Oral Preparations (mg)	Approximate Equivalent Dose (mg)
Phenothiazines			
Aliphatic			
Chlorpromazine[a]	Thorazine	10, 25, 50, 100, 200	100
Triflupromazine	Vesprin	10, 25	30
Piperidines			
Mesoridazine	Serentil	10, 25, 100	50
Piperacetazine	Quide	10, 15	12
Thioridazine[a]	Mellaril	10, 15, 25, 50, 100, 150, 200	95
Piperazines			
Fluphenazine[a,b]	Prolixin, Permitil	1, 2.5, 5, 10	2
Perphenazine[a]	Trilafon	2, 4, 8, 16	10
Trifluoperazine[a]	Stelazine	1, 2, 5, 10	5
Thiozanthenes			
Aliphatic			
Chlorprothixene	Taractan	10, 25, 50, 100	65
Piperazine			
Thiothixene[a]	Navane	1, 2, 5, 10, 25	5
Dibenzazepine			
Loxapine	Loxitane, Daxolin	10, 25, 50	15
Butyrophenone			
Haloperidol[a,c]	Haldol	0.5, 1, 2, 5, 10	2
Indolone			
Molindone	Moban	5, 10, 25	10

[a] Generic available.
[b] Long-acting fluphenazine decanoate or enanthate, for injection, comes in a concentration of 25 mg/ml; also available for injection as fluphenazine hydrochloride, a short-acting preparation.
[c] Haloperidol for injection comes in a concentration of 2 mg/ml.

B. Overall management
   1. Regular office visits to review status, medications, side effects, etc. (frequency a function of stability of patients)
   2. Family education and support important
   3. Maximum use of social services

5/ MENTAL ILLNESS IN THE ELDERLY

DEPRESSION
A. Depressive symptoms
   1. Symptoms of depression more common in the elderly; major depression (Chapter 3) less common
   2. Adjustment disorder with depressed mood (Chapter 3) quite common
   3. Dysthymic disorder (Chapter 3) — suspect if there are depressive symptoms for more than 2 years, interspersed with regular fluctuations in mood
B. Depression disorder (Chapter 3)
   1. Hypochondriasis, agitation, suspiciousness, even frank paranoia may accompany depression
   2. Requires treatment (Chapter 3)
      a) Tricyclic antidepressants with pronounced anticholinergic activity (amitriptyline and doxepin should be avoided)
      b) Tricyclics with highest potential of causing orthostatic hypotension (amitriptyline and imipramine) should be avoided
      c) Nortriptyline and desipramine are the tricyclics of choice, starting at 10–25 mg at bedtime
      d) Limited reported experience with fluoxetine (Prozac) in the elderly
      e) Electroconvulsive therapy (ECT) sometimes safer than drugs
      f) Low-dose neuroleptics (see Chapter 4) sometimes necessary to control paranoid delusions
C. Depression-induced cognitive impairment
   1. Mood disorder and cognitive function can improve with antidepressant treatment
   2. Up to 50% do eventually develop a progressive dementia
   3. When to consider
      a) Cognitive impairment of less than 3–6 months duration
      b) A history of depression
      c) When dementia is associated with hypochondriacal or bizarre delusions
      d) When patients dwell on their cognitive impairment (uncommon in Alzheimer's disease)
      e) If demented patients report early morning awakening, lack of energy, or feelings of guilt
   4. If uncertain of diagnosis, a trial of an antidepressant (Chapter 3) for 4 weeks is warranted
D. Depression coexisting with brain disease
   1. Stroke, Alzheimer's disease, and Parkinson's disease are common disorders of the elderly commonly complicated by depression
   2. Important to treat both physical and mental disorders, focusing first on the disorder causing the more severe impairment

DEMENTIA
A. Definition: a global decline in cognitive function from a previous level, without altered consciousness
B. Causes: Table 5.1

Table 5.1.   Major Causes and Approximate Frequency Distribution of Progressive Dementias in the Elderly[a]

1. Senile dementia, Alzheimer type	50%
2. Vascular (multi-infarct)	20%
3. Parkinson's, other neurological conditions	10%
4. Combination of 1 and 2	5%
5. Frontal dementias, Lewy body dementias	5%
6. Other causes (hypothyroid, B_{12} deficiency, chronic alcoholism, syphilis, cause unknown)	5%
7. Uncommon or mixed with above	10%

[a]In younger patients the commonest causes include AIDS dementia and dementia related to complications of drug abuse or trauma.

C. Evaluation
   1. Search for reversible causes
      a) Medication toxicity (especially benzodiazepines); depression and thyroid disease are the most common
      b) Do history, physical examination, mental status examination, and screening tests (CBC, serum electrolytes, serum creatinine, liver function tests, serum calcium and phosphorus, T_4, TSH, serum vitamin B_{12}, STS)
      c) Computed tomography (CT) scan for dementia of less than 2 years
   2. Determine whether the dementia is cortical or subcortical
      a) Subcortical
         1) Most reversible dementia
         2) Common causes: Parkinson's disease, multiple sclerosis, Huntington's disease, normal pressure hydrocephalus, dementia syndrome of depression, most multi-infarct dementias
         3) Characterized by memory loss, apathy, slowness, movement disorder but intact language (e.g., patient can name objects, repeat a phrase, follow 3-step commands), normal visuospatial function (e.g., can copy a diagram)
      b) Cortical
         1) Characterized by memory loss, aphasic language (e.g., substituting a letter in a word or saying an incorrect word), apraxia, agnosia
         2) Alzheimer's disease the most common diagnosis (see below)
   3. Specific disease
      a) Alzheimer's disease
         1) Other causes have been excluded
         2) Slowly progressive
         3) Cognitive disorder has cortical features (as above)
      b) Multi-infarct dementia
         1) Stepwise course
         2) Evidence of vascular disease and hypertension
         3) Abnormal neurological examination common
      c) Frontal dementias
         1) Slowly progressive, with pronounced changes in behaviors and personality
         2) Frontal atrophy on CT scan

D. Management
  1. Assessment
    a) Elicit specific problems in behavior and deal with them (e.g., tell the patient he can no longer drive a car or cook or smoke, unobserved)
    b) Make legal and financial plans early
  2. Good general medical care
    a) Minimize use of drugs that may affect cognitive function (e.g., benzodiazepines, cimetidine, β-blockers, clonidine, methyldopa, anticholinergics)
    b) Be alert to medical conditions that may further affect cognitive function
  3. Management of noncognitive behavioral changes
    a) Avoid insomnia by discouraging daytime napping
    b) Eliminate tasks that the patient no longer can do and finds frustrating (see above)
    c) Neuroleptic medications should be used sparingly to control, for example, hallucinations, delusions, aggression, e.g., thiothixene (Navane) 1 mg at bedtime, increased if necessary to 2 mg twice a day
    d) Aggressive behavior that does not respond to neuroleptics may respond to carbamazepine (Tegretol), 100 mg/day, increased if necessary to 200 mg twice a day
    e) Depression (see above)
    f) Catastrophic reactions — decompensated behavior when patient is confronted with a situation in which he is forced to face his impairment; best to avoid such provocations if at all possible
  4. Family support
    a) Allow the family to ventilate
    b) Encourage use of support groups
  5. Longitudinal care — plan early for the possible eventual need for nursing home placement
  6. Decisions about limiting therapy: use living will, other advance directives if patients are still competent to sign them; arrange for durable power of attorney when necessary
  7. Drugs for dementia
    a) No effective drug available
    b) Tacrine (Cognex) has been approved for use but is expensive, requires monitoring for hepatic function, and has no noticeable effect on cognition

DELIRIUM

A. Definition: clouding of consciousness and inattentiveness with secondary changes in behavior, cognition, or perception
B. Causes: Table 5.2
C. Diagnosis
  1. Changes in consciousness and attentiveness distinguish delirium from dementia
  2. Abrupt onset (hours to days) also a difference between delirium and dementia
  3. Cognitive impairment and rapid fluctuation in symptoms distinguish delirium from schizophrenia and other psychoses

Table 5.2.   Etiological Classification of Delirium

IN A MEDICAL OR SURGICAL ILLNESS (NO FOCAL OR LATERALIZING NEUROLOGICAL SIGNS; CEREBROSPINAL FLUID USUALLY CLEAR)

  Metabolic disorders: hepatic stupor, uremia, hypoxia, hypercapnia, hypoglycemia, porphyria, hyponatremia

  Congestive heart failure

  Pneumonia, septicemia, typhoid fever, other febrile illnesses (especially in elderly)

  Hyperthyroidism and hypothyroidism

  Postoperative and posttraumatic states

IN NEUROLOGICAL DISEASE THAT CAUSES FOCAL OR LATERALIZING SIGNS OR CHANGES IN THE CEREBROSPINAL FLUID

  Cerebrovascular disease

  Subarachnoid hemorrhage

  Hypertensive encephalopathy

  Cerebral contusion

  Subdural hematoma

  Tumor

  Abscess

  Meningitis

  Encephalitis

  Status epilepticus (by EEG)

  Postconvulsive delirium

ABSTINENCE STATES AND EXOGENOUS INTOXICATIONS (SIGNS OF OTHER MEDICAL, SURGICAL, AND NEUROLOGICAL ILLNESSES ABSENT OR COINCIDENTAL)

  Withdrawal of alcohol (delirium tremens), barbiturates, and nonbarbiturate sedative drugs, following chronic intoxication

  Drug intoxication due to benzodiazepines, opiates, neuroleptics, antidepressants, antihistamines, H_2 blockers, centrally acting antihypertensives, anticholinergics, digitalis, illicit drugs (see Chapter 8), etc.

BECLOUDED DEMENTIA

  Any dementing or other brain disease in combination with infective fevers, drug reactions, heart failure, or other medical or surgical disease

Adapted from Adams RD: Delirium and other acute confusional states. In: Isselbacher KJ, et al (eds): *Harrison's Principles of Internal Medicine*, 9th ed. New York, McGraw-Hill, 1980.

  4. Electroencephalogram (EEG) shows generalized slowing in contrast to depression or schizophrenia, and slowing is more marked in delirium than in dementia

D. Management

  1. Treat the underlying disease

  2. Reorient and reassure patient; avoid darkened rooms, even at night; avoid overstimulation

  3. If agitation, hallucinations, or delirium persist, consider a neuroleptic in low dose

6/ COMMON SEXUAL DISORDERS

ORGANIC ETIOLOGIES: TABLES 6.1–6.4

GENERAL APPROACH: TABLE 6.5

PSYCHOGENIC SEXUAL DESIRE DISORDERS

A. Diagnostic classification
  1. Hypoactive sexual desire disorder (loss of libido)
    a) Not associated with a medical or psychiatric disorder (e.g., major depressive disorder)
    b) Causes marked distress
  2. Sexual aversion disorder
    a) Extreme aversion to genital contact
    b) Not associated with a medical or psychiatric disorder
    c) Causes marked stress to patient
B. Causes: in addition to excluding organic etiologies (see above) and a psychiatric disorder such as major depression, alcohol or other substance abuse should be considered; also marital strife can interfere with sexual desire and performance
C. Treatment
  1. Treat underlying medical or psychiatric condition
  2. Stop all drugs that may interfere with sexual desire (Table 6.4)
  3. Loss of desire due to intercurrent stress can be helped by supportive counseling
  4. Aversion disorders usually require referral to a psychiatrist

SEXUAL AROUSAL DISORDERS

A. Diagnostic classification
  1. Female arousal disorders
    a) Persistent or recurrent inability to achieve or maintain an adequate lubrication-swelling response of sexual excitement before completion of sexual activity
    b) Not associated with a major medical or psychiatric disorder (e.g., major depressive disorder) or with alcohol or substance abuse
    c) Causes marked distress
  2. Male erectile disorder (impotence)
    a) Persistent or recurrent inability to attain or maintain an adequate erection before completion of sexual activity
    b) Same as 1. b) above
    c) Same as 1. c) above
B. Causes
  1. See Tables 6.1–6.4
  2. If desire is intact, hypogonadism not likely
  3. In younger men, drugs are the commonest cause of impotence; in older men, vascular (often associated with diabetes mellitus) or neurological disease
  4. In women, vaginitis or atrophic vaginal changes may contribute
  5. Psychogenic
    a) Any psychological problems may contribute, including

Table 6.1.   Medical Conditions That May Affect Sexual Response in Both Sexes

Organic Factor	Sexual Disorders
Alcoholic neuropathy	Hypoactive arousal, hypoactive orgasm
Angina pectoris or recent myocardial infarction	Hypoactive desire
Any chronic systemic disease	Hypoactive desire, hypoactive arousal
Chronic pain	Hypoactive desire
Degenerative arthritis and disc disease of lumbosacral spine	Hypoactive desire, hypoactive arousal
Diabetes mellitus	Hypoactive arousal, retrograde ejaculation (men)
	Hypoactive orgasm (women)
Endocrine disorders (thyroid deficiency states, Addison's disease, Cushing's disease, hypopituitarism, hyperprolactinemia)	Hypoactive desire, variable effect on arousal
Multiple sclerosis	Hypoactive desire, hypoactive arousal, hypoactive orgasm
Cord lesions	
Low lesion	Hypoactive reflex arousal (psychogenic arousal, and reflex ejaculation may be preserved)
High lesion	Hypoactive psychogenic arousal (reflex arousal, and ejaculation may be preserved)
Radical pelvic surgery	Hypoactive arousal, hypoactive orgasm
Temporal lobe lesions	Hypoactive or increased desire
Vascular disease	
Large vessel (Leriche's syndrome)	Hypoactive arousal
Small vessel (pelvic vascular insufficiency)	Hypoactive arousal

preoccupation with sexual performance and stressful life situations

   b) If uncertain about organic versus psychogenic cause in men, refer to a sleep laboratory for nocturnal penile tumescence study
C. Treatment
   1. Treat underlying medical or psychiatric condition
   2. Prosthetic devices that cause erection
      a) Semirigid Silastic rods placed in the penis create a permanent modest erection
      b) Hydraulic device, when implanted, allows voluntary stiffening of the penis
   3. Intracavernosal injection of vasodilating substances (papaverine, phenoxybenzamine, or phentolamine) or prostaglandin E
      a) Patients inject themselves, using a 28-gauge needle
      b) Erection begins in 8–10 minutes, lasts 2–4 hours
      c) More effective for neurogenic impotence than for impotence due to vascular disease
      d) Best done after instruction by a urologist

Table 6.2. Medical Conditions That May Affect Sexual Response in Men Only

Organic Factor	Sexual Disorders
Dyspareunia (genital pain during intercourse)	Hypoactive desire, hypoactive arousal, and hypoactive orgasm are disorders that may occur with any of the organic factors listed at the left
Disturbed penile anatomy (chordee, Peyrone's disease, traumatic fracture, traumatic amputation)	
Penile skin infections	
Prostatic infections	
Testicular disease (orchitis, epididymitis, tumor, trauma)	
Urethral infections (gonorrhea, nonspecific urethral infections)	
Hypogonadal androgen-deficient states (Klinefelter's syndrome, testicular agenesis, Kallman's syndrome, testicular tumors, orchitis, hyperprolactinemia, castration)	Hypoactive desire, hypoactive arousal, hypoactive orgasm
Mechanical problems (inguinal hernia, hydrocele)	Hypoactive arousal
Surgical procedures	
Abdominoperineal bowel resection	Hypoactive arousal
Lumbar sympathectomy	Hypoactive orgasm
Radical perineal prostatectomy	Hypoactive arousal

4. Yohimbine, 1 tablet p.o. 3 times/day, occasionally effective for psychogenic impotence
5. No drugs are known that stimulate female arousal
6. Psychogenic arousal disorders, if of recent onset, may respond to counseling; otherwise, referral to a sex therapist may be warranted

ORGASM DISORDERS

A. Diagnostic classification
1. Female orgasmic disorder (inhibited orgasm)
   a) Persistent delay or absence of orgasm following a normal sexual arousal stage
   b) Not associated with a major medical or psychiatric disorder or with alcohol or substance abuse
   c) Causes marked distress
2. Male orgasmic disorder (inhibited orgasm) [see 1. a), b), and c) above]
3. Premature ejaculation
   a) Persistent or recurrent ejaculation with minimal sexual stimulation before, on, or shortly after penetration and before desired
   b) Causes marked distress
B. Causes
1. See Tables 6.1–6.4
2. Organic conditions that inhibit orgasm are mostly neurological
3. Autonomic diabetic neuropathy, the commonest cause of inhibited orgasm in women
4. Premature ejaculation, the most common male orgasmic disorder

Table 6.3.   Medical Conditions That May Affect Sexual Response in Women Only

Organic Factor	Sexual Disorders

Complications of surgery
  Ovarian approximation to vagina
  Posthysterectomy scarring
  Shortened vagina
Dyspareunia (painful intercourse)
  Agenesis of the vagina
  Clitoral phymosis
  Imperforate hymen, rigid hymen, tender
    hymenal tags
  Infections of external genitalia: herpes
    genitalis, labial cysts, furuncles,
    Bartholin cyst infections
  Infections of the vagina: herpes genitalis,
    Candida albicans, Trichomonas
  Injuries due to birth trauma: episiotomy
    scars, tears, uterine prolapse
  Irritations of the vagina: chemical dermatitis
    (douches), atrophic vaginitis,
    intercourse with insufficient lubrication
Miscellaneous pelvic problems
  Cystitis, urethritis, urethral prolapse
  Endometriosis, ectopic pregnancy, pelvic
    inflammatory disease, ovarian cysts
    and tumors, pelvic tumors
  Intrauterine device complications
	Hypoactive desire, hypoactive arousal, hypoactive orgasm, and vaginismus are disorders that may occur with any of the organic factors listed at the left.

    5. Psychologically caused inhibited orgasm, a common problem in women, not in men (in whom it is associated with severe personality disturbances)

C. Treatment

  1. Men

    a) Treat underlying medical or psychiatric disorder

    b) For premature ejaculation, squeeze penis around coronal ridge for 10 seconds to inhibit ejaculation; repeat as necessary

  2. Women

    a) If problem of recent onset, treat underlying medical or psychiatric condition

    b) If of long duration, prognosis poor; consider psychiatric referral

SEXUAL PAIN DISORDERS

A. Diagnostic classification

  1. Dyspareunia

    a) Recurrent or persistent genital pain before, during or after intercourse

    b) Not caused exclusively by vaginismus or lack of lubrication and is not better accounted for by a psychiatric (e.g., somatization disorder) or medical condition or by medication, alcohol, or illicit drugs

    c) Causes marked distress

Table 6.4. Common Drugs and Substances That May Affect Sexual Response[a]

Drugs	Sexual Disorders Reported
Alcohol and sedatives (high dose)	Hypoactive desire, hypoactive arousal, delayed orgasm
Amiodarone	Hypoactive desire
Androgens	Increased desire (women)
	Hypoactive or increased desire, and/or hypoactive arousal
Anticonvulsants	
Carbamazepine	Hypoactive arousal
Phenytoin	Hypoactive desire, hypoactive arousal
Antidepressants	
Fluoxetine	Hypoactive desire, hypoactive orgasm
Tricyclics	Hypoactive or increased desire and/or hypoactive arousal
Antihypertensives	
Centrally acting (β-blockers, clonidine, guanabenz, methyldopa, reserpine)	Hypoactive desire, hypoactive arousal, (?) hypoactive orgasm
α-Blockers, hydralazine	Hypoactive arousal
Peripherally acting (guanethidine, guanadrel)	Retrograde ejaculation, hypoactive desire
Antipsychotics	Hypoactive or increased desire, hypoactive arousal, retrograde ejaculation (Merllaril)
Digoxin	Hypoactive desire, hypoactive arousal
Disopyramide	Hypoactive arousal
Disulfiram	Hypoactive arousal, delayed ejaculation
Diuretics	Hypoactive arousal
Estrogens, progesterone	
Men	Hypoactive desire, hypoactive arousal, hypoactive orgasm
Women	Hypoactive desire
H_2 blockers (cimetidine, famotidine, ranitidine)	Hypoactive desire, hypoactive arousal
L-Dopa	Increased desire (elderly men)
Lithium	Hypoactive desire, hypoactive arousal
Marijuana (high dose)	Hypoactive arousal (low dose may produce increased desire in men)
Metoclopramide	Hypoactive desire, hypoactive arousal
Narcotics	Hypoactive desire, hypoactive arousal, hypoactive orgasm
Stimulants (high dose) (cocaine, amphetamines)	Hypoactive desire, hypoactive arousal, hypoactive orgasm (low dose may produce increased desire)
Verapamil	Hypoactive arousal

[a] See also: Drugs that cause sexual dysfunction: an update. *Med Lett* 34:73, 1992 (contains exhaustive table, with references for each drug listed), and Buffum J: Prescription drugs and sexual function. *Psychiatr Med* 10 (2): 181, 1992.

  2. Vaginismus
    a) Recurrent or persistent involuntary spasm of the musculature of the outer third of the vagina that interferes with intercourse
    b) As in 1. b) above
    c) As in 1. c) above
B. Causes
  1. See Tables 6.2 and 6.3

Table 6.5.   Suggested Questions Regarding Sexual Practices and Problems

Suggested Opening (Legitimizing Statement)

"Something that I ask each of my patients about is sexual activity. Is that alright with you?"
Suggested Initial Question(s)

(Open-ended question) "Can you tell me about your present sexual activity (practices)? . . . "

OR

(Closed, somewhat leading question) "Have you noticed any problem in your ability to have
and enjoy sexual relations?"

OR

(Closed, but facilitative question) "Do you have any problems or questions related to your
current sexual activities? . . . "
Screening Questions for Sexual Dysfunction (ask for clarification of any positive response)

(Both sexes) "Have you noticed any loss of interest in having sex?"

(Men) "Any problems having an erection?"

(Women) "Any problems with lubrication and/or swelling of the vagina when you are sexually
aroused?"

(Both sexes) "Any problems having an orgasm?"

(Both sexes) "Any pain during intercourse?"
Screening Questions Regarding Sexual Orientation

(Both sexes) "Have you ever had sex with men, women, or both?"

OR

(Men) "Do you ever have sex with another man?"

(Women) "Do you ever have sex with another woman?"
Screening Question for Risk of or History of Sexually Transmitted Disease[a]

(Both sexes) "In the past few years about how many partners have you had for sexual
relations?"

(Both sexes) "Have you ever had any kind of infection that you got from having sex? . . . "
Open Question to Obtain Additional Information

"Is there any other information or any other questions about your sexual activities that you
would like to discuss with me? . . . "

[a] See list of safe and unsafe sexual practices (Table 20.1) and instructions for use of a condom (Table 20.2).

    a) Commonest causes are infections or atrophic vaginitis in
women, urethral or prostatic infection in men

  2. Vaginismus almost always psychogenic

C. Treatment

  1. Treat underlying medical or psychiatric condition

  2. Vaginismus treated by desensitization (progressive gentle increase
in stimulation, first of the body, then of the genitalia)

7/ ALCOHOLISM AND ASSOCIATED PROBLEMS

DEFINITION, MANIFESTATIONS, AND SCREENING
A. Definition of alcoholism
   1. Broad definition: recurring trouble associated with drinking alcohol
      a) Trouble may include the need for increased amounts of alcohol to achieve the desired effect (tolerance) and symptoms of withdrawal
      b) May be characterized by inability to control use of alcohol, drinking alone, avoiding situations where alcohol is not present, gulping drinks, continuing to drink alcohol despite problems caused by drinking
   2. National Council on Alcoholism and Drug Dependency: a primary, chronic disease with genetic, psychosocial, and environmental influences, characterized by impaired control over drinking, preoccupation with alcohol despite adverse consequences, and distorted thinking, especially denial
B. Manifestations
   1. Medical, legal, psychosocial (Table 7.1)
   2. Expected effects according to blood alcohol level for person without tolerance to alcohol (Table 7.2)
C. Screening
   1. If manifestations are not diagnostic (see above), look for evidence of inability to control use of alcohol — even intermittently — and for denial (manifested by rationalizations, humor, hostility, reticence)
   2. CAGE questions (Fig. 7.1) — 70–90% sensitive, 80–95% specific

TREATMENT AND PROGNOSIS
A. General principles of treatment
   1. Goal: achievement of abstinence or progressively longer periods of abstinence from alcohol (and other drugs), with improved life functioning for patients and their families
   2. Break down denial and motivate: comfort, show empathy, offer hope (Fig. 7.2)
   3. Use of formal intervention: a meeting with the alcoholic and a group of people important to him or her, defining the problem, the proposed solution, and the consequences (e.g., divorce, loss of job) if the solution is not accepted
   4. Employee assistance programs
   5. Avoid a psychoanalytic approach
B. Detoxification
   1. Major withdrawal manifestations
      a) Tremulousness within 8–12 hours
      b) Seizures within 8–24 hours
      c) Hallucinations within several days
      d) Delirium tremens in 48 hours (commonly) to 14 days (uncommonly)

Table 7.1.   Medical, Psychiatric, Legal, and Other Findings Suggestive (0 to *) to Highly Suggestive (to ***) or Diagnostic (****) of Alcoholism**

Presenting Complaint and History			
****	Drinking problem, recurring	*	Unexplained syncope
***	Blackouts with drinking	*	Depression
***	Spouse/other complains of patient's drinking	*	Suicide attempt
		*	Sexual dysfunction
***	Driving-while-intoxicated (DWI) record	*	Legal problem
***	Prison record	*	Noncompliance in treatment
***	Change in alcohol/drug tolerance	*	School learning problem
**	Frequent requests for mood-changing drugs	*	Hypertension
			Headache
**	Gastrointestinal bleeding, especially upper		Palpitations
			Abdominal pain
**	Traumatic injuries, fracture		Amenorrhea
**	Parent, grandparent, or relative alcoholic		Weight loss
**	Friends alcoholic or other chemical dependence		Vague complaints
			Insomnia
**	Family or other violence		Anxiety
**	Child abuse or neglect		Marital discord
**	First seizure in an adult		Financial problem
**	Job performance problem		

Alcohol or Other Drug Use History			
****	Alcohol use recurring, interfering with health, job or social functioning	***	Patient states that he has consciously stopped drinking completely for any length of time
***	Patient says, "I can stop drinking anytime," or the equivalent; or patient gets evasive or angry or talks glibly during taking of drinking history	**	Other drug misuse or dependence
		*	Cigarette smoker

Physical Examination			
***	Odor of beverage alcohol on breath	**	Unexplained bruises, abrasions, or cuts
***	Parotid gland enlargement, bilateral	*	Borderline tachycardia
***	Spider nevi or angioma	*	Thin extremities in proportion to trunk
***	Tremulousness, hallucinosis	*	Splenomegaly
**	Cigarette stains on fingers	*	Hypertension
**	Breath mint odor		Diaphoresis
**	Many scars or tattoos		Alopecia
**	Hepatomegaly		Abdominal tenderness
**	Gynecomastia		Cerebellar signs (e.g., nystagmus)
**	Small testicles		

Table 7.1.   Continued

Laboratory Abnormalities			
****	Blood alcohol level > 300 mg/100 ml	**	Anemia, macrocytic or megaloblastic,
***	Blood alcohol level > 100 mg/100 ml		microcytic, or mixed
	without impairment	*	Hyperuricemia
***	High serum ammonia	*	Creatine kinase elevation
***	γ-Glutamyl transpeptidase elevation	*	Hypophosphatemia or hypomagnesemia
**	Blood alcohol level positive, any amount		Electrolyte imbalance (hyponatremia,
**	High amylase (nonspecific for pancreas)		hypokalemia)
**	Abnormal liver function tests (especially		Low white blood cell or platelet count
	AST > ALT)		Hyperlipoproteinemia, type 4 or 5

Diagnosis			
****	Hepatitis, alcoholic	**	Attempted suicide
***	Pancreatitis, acute or chronic	**	Gastritis
***	Cirrhosis	**	Refractory hypertension
***	Portal hypertension	**	Cerebellar degeneration
***	Wernicke-Korsakoff syndrome	**	Peripheral neuropathy
***	Frequent trauma	**	Aspiration pneumonia
***	Cold injury	*	Gout
***	Nose and throat cancer	*	Cardiomyopathy
**	Other chemical dependence	*	Tuberculosis
**	Drownings	*	Anxiety
**	Burns, especially third degree	*	Depression
**	Leaves hospital against medical advice	*	Marital discord or family problem

Table 7.2.   Expected Effects According to Blood Alcohol Level for a Person Without Tolerance to Alcohol

Blood Alcohol Level (mg/dl)	Expected Effect	Approximate Location of Physiological Disturbance
25–50	Relaxation, sedation	
50–100	Coordination impaired; euphoric; loud conversation; apparent reduction of social inhibitions	Cerebral cortex
100–200	Ataxia; depressed fine motor ability, decreased mentation, attention span, and memory; poor judgment; labile mood; beginning of slurred speech	Limbic system and cerebellum
200–300	Marked ataxia and slurred speech, nausea and vomiting, tremor, irritable	Reticular activating system
300–400	Stage 1 anesthesia (unconsciousness) memory lapse	Reticular activating system
>400	Respiratory failure, coma, death	Medulla oblongata

1. Integrate alcohol use inquiry into interview so that it follows inquiry about less sensitive habits.
   Example: "We have talked about your usual diet and your smoking. Can you tell me how you use alcoholic beverages" (or "How about alcoholic beverages . . . ?)"
   If the patient says that he/she has never used alcohol and shows no sign of discomfort, inquire about problem use in others (e.g., "Anyone in your family or other close persons who have a drinking problem?"). This helps to identify a risk factor for alcoholism and to identify patients who may suffer because of the alcoholism of another person.

2. **General Questions:** For patients who report present or past use of alcohol, screen for evidence of alcoholism, with a general question such as the following:
   "Has (Did) your use of alcohol caused (cause) any kinds of problems for you?" or "Have you ever been concerned about your drinking?"

3. **CAGE Questions:**[a] If the patient has not disclosed a problem with drinking, use these four focused questions and probe for clarification of positive or ambivalent responses.
   I'd like to ask you a few more questions about alcohol that I ask all of my patients . . . "
   C "Have you ever felt you ought to CUT DOWN on your drinking (use of _____)?"
   A "Have people ANNOYED you by criticizing your drinking (use of _____)?"
   G "Have you ever felt bad or GUILTY about your drinking (use of _____)?"
   E "Have you ever had a drink first thing in the morning (EYE OPENER) to steady your nerves or get rid of a hangover? (For other substances: "Have you found that you have to take some _____ most days/some days to feel okay?")

[a] Modifications of questions for substances other than alcohol are shown in parentheses.

Figure 7.1. Recommended approach to the use of interviewing to screen all patients for alcoholism and for problems with alcohol in the family.

2. Minor withdrawal manifestations
   a) More common
   b) Anorexia, nausea, vomiting
   c) Tachycardia, systolic hypertension, diaphoresis
   d) Weakness, varying disorientation, difficulty concentrating
3. Criteria for inpatient detoxification: Table 7.3
4. Developing a score to select treatment (Table 7.4)
   a) Score <10, drugs not indicated
   b) Score 10–20, clinical judgment determines if drugs indicated
   c) Score 10, drugs indicated
5. Drugs — benzodiazepines the drugs of choice
   a) Important to recognize withdrawal early, treat early, monitor frequently

STATING THE DIAGNOSIS

1. Tell the patient the diagnosis (e.g., "I think that you have the disease alcoholism . . . and I am very concerned about you").
2. Acknowledge the patient's reaction (e.g., "I can see that this is making you pretty uncomfortable . . . ").

EXPLAINING THE DISEASE MODEL

3. Ask the patient to tell you his/her idea of what alcoholism is. (Patient usually describes stereotype model of a skid-row alcoholic . . . "and that's not me!" . . .)
4. Clarify the patient's model by stating four basic facts:
   a) Alcoholism is a disease ("a disease like other medical diseases . . . e.g., diabetes").
   b) Like other diseases, alcoholism has an early stage way before what you described.
   c) Like other diseases, alcoholism is not the patient's fault.
   d) Alcoholism can be treated and the chances of recovery are excellent.

MAKING THE MODEL SPECIFIC

5. Ask the patient if he/she knows why you think he/she has alcoholism.
6. Tell the patient the evidence that he/she has alcoholism. (Always restate concern for the patient; if appropriate, stress features of early alcoholism.)

TELLING ABOUT TREATMENT

7. Ask the patient what he/she knows about the treatment of alcoholism.
8. Tell the patient the basic facts about treatment:
   a) Abstinence
   b) Requires the help of other people

GETTING THE PATIENT (AND FAMILY) TO ACCEPT TREATMENT

9. Offer the patient treatment options that you know of (always include a local program that offers detoxification and Alcoholics Anonymous).
10. Get the patient to select a treatment plan and to make contact promptly (e.g., call available detoxification program, call local AA office and let patient speak with AA representative).
11. With the patient's permission, contact his/her spouse or other significant person(s) (tell the diagnosis and plan, and initiate plans for family treatment).

FOLLOWING THROUGH

12. Schedule follow-up, appointment in 1 or 2 weeks (consider 1 or 2 days if patient has not agreed to make a treatment decision).

Figure 7.2. Recommended approach for one-on-one confrontation of the patient in whom alcoholism has been diagnosed.

Table 7.3.   Indications for Referring a Withdrawing Alcoholic for Inpatient Detoxification

1. Evidence of hallucinations, severe tachycardia, severe tremor, fever, extreme agitation, or a past history of severe withdrawal symptoms
2. History of seizure disorder
3. Presence of ataxia, nystagmus, confusion, or ophthalmoplegia, which may be indicative of Wernicke's encephalopathy
4. Severe nausea and vomiting that would prevent the ingestion of medication
5. Evidence of acute or chronic liver disease that may alter the metabolism of drugs used in the treatment of withdrawal
6. Presence of cardiovascular disease, such as severe hypertension, ischemic heart disease, or arrhythmia, for which the sympathetic surge of catecholamines during withdrawal poses particular risk
7. Pregnant women
8. Presence of associated medical or surgical condition requiring treatment
9. Lack of medical or social support system to allow outpatient detoxification

Table 7.4.   Addiction Research Foundation Clinical Institute Withdrawal Assessment for Alcohol (CIWA-A)[a]

Patient _____	Date | __ | __ | __ | y m d	Time _____ : _____ (24 hour clock, midnight = 00:00)

Pulse or heart rate, taken for one minute: _____   **Blood pressure:** ___ / ___

NAUSEA AND VOMITING — As "Do you feel sick to your stomach? Have you vomited?" Observation.

0 no nausea and no vomiting
1 mild nausea with no vomiting
2
3
4 intermittent nausea with dry heaves
5
6
7 constant nausea, frequent dry heaves, and vomiting

TACTILE DISTURBANCES — Ask "Have you any itching, pins and needles sensations, any burning, any numbness, or do you feel bugs crawling on or under your skin?" Observation.

0 none
1 very mild itching, pins and needles, burning, or numbness
2 mild itching, pins and needles, burning, or numbness
3 moderate itching, pins and needles, burning, or numbness
4 moderately severe hallucinations
5 severe hallucinations
6 extremely severe hallucinations
7 continuous hallucinations

TREMOR — Arms extended and fingers spread apart. Observation.

0 no tremor
1 not visible but can be felt fingertip to fingertip
2
3
4 moderate, with patient's arms extended
5
6
7 severe, even with arms not extended

AUDITORY DISTURBANCES — Ask "Are you more aware of sounds around you? Are they harsh? Do they frighten you? Are you hearing anything that is disturbing you? Are you hearing things you know are not there?" Observation.

0 not present
1 very mild harshness or ability to frighten
2 mild harshness or ability to frighten
3 moderate harshness or ability to frighten
4 moderately severe hallucinations
5 severe hallucinations
6 extremely severe hallucinations
7 continuous hallucinations

Table 7.4.   Continued

PAROXYSMAL SWEATS — Observation.
0 no sweat visible
1 barely perceptible sweating, palms moist
2
3
4 beads of sweat obvious on forehead
5
6
7 drenching sweats

VISUAL DISTURBANCES — Ask "Does the light appear to be too bright? Is its color different? Does it hurt your eyes? Are you seeing anything that is disturbing to you? Are you seeing things you know are not there?" Observation.
0 not present
1 very mild sensitivity
2 mild sensitivity
3 moderate sensitivity
4 moderately severe hallucinations
5 severe hallucinations
6 extremely severe hallucinations
7 continuous hallucinations

ANXIETY — Ask "Do you feel nervous?" Observation.
0 no anxiety, at ease
1 mildly anxious
2
3
4 moderately anxious, or guarded, so anxiety is inferred
5
6
7 equivalent to acute panic states as seen in severe delirium or acute schizophrenic reactions

HEADACHE, FULLNESS IN HEAD — Ask "Does your head feel different? Does it feel like there is a band around your head?" Do not rate for dizziness or lightheadedness. Otherwise, rate severity.
0 not present
1 very mild
2 mild
3 moderate
4 moderately severe
5 severe
6 very severe
7 extremely severe

AGITATION — Observation.
0 normal activity
1 somewhat more than normal activity
2
3
4 moderately fidgety and restless
5
6
7 paces back and forth during most of the interview or constantly thrashes about

ORIENTATION AND CLOUDING OF SENSORIUM — Ask "What day is this? Where are you? Who am I?"
0 oriented and can do serial additions
1 cannot do serial additions or is uncertain about date
2 disoriented for date by no more than 2 calendar days
3 disoriented for date by more than 2 calendar days
4 disoriented for place and/or person

Total CIWA-A Score _____
Rater's Initials _____
Maximum Possible Score 67

[a] This scale is not copyrighted and may be used freely.

    b) Oral route (Table 7.5) preferred; use low dose first; switch to high dose if no effect in a few hours
  6. Detoxification without drugs
    a) For ambulatory patients without another serious illness
    b) Environmental modification: Table 7.6
    c) A reliable person should be able to observe the patient for at least 2 days

Table 7.5.   Characteristics of Benzodiazepines Used Orally in the Treatment of Alcohol Withdrawal

Drug	Onset of Action	Rate of Metabolism	Liver Metabolized	Low Dose (mg)[a']	High Dose (mg)[b']
Chlordiazepoxide	Intermediate	Long	Yes	25	100
Diazepam	Fast	Long	Yes	2–5	10–20
Lorazepam	Intermediate	Intermediate	No	0.5	2
Oxazepam	Slow	Short	No	10–15	30

[a'] Every 6 hours.
[b'] Every 2–4 hours.

Table 7.6.   Environmental Modification in Treating Alcohol and Other Sedative Withdrawal

Sense	Therapeutic	Countertherapeutic
Visual	Lights on, not bright	Lights off
	Familiar people, pictures, clock, clothes	Marked shadows
Sound	Soft music	Loud or abrupt noises
	Soft conversation	
	Reassurance and reality	
	Orientation by staff	
Touch	Reassuring touch by staff (e.g., taking pulse, hand on shoulder)	Bed clothes
		High bed
	Comfortable chair	Restraints
	Low bed	IVs and tubes
	Regular clothes	
General	Respect	Hostility, even if subtle
	Positivity, optimism	Negativity or pessimism

Modified from Baum R, Iber FL: Initial treatment of the alcoholic patient. In: Gitlow SE, Peyser HS (eds): *Alcoholism: A Practical Treatment Guide*. New York, Grune & Stratton, 1980, pp 73–87.

C. Specific aspects of treatment
    1. Group therapy
       a) The best approach to recovery
       b) Alcoholics Anonymous (AA) the most effective group
    2. Psychotherapy
       a) Not effective until patient is abstinent
       b) Supportive therapy useful for reinforcing group treatment
    3. Treatment of the family
       a) Important to educate and support closest family members, learn about drinking patterns in the home
       b) Refer close family to Al-Anon
    4. Disulfiram (Antabuse)
       a) For selected patients in active recovery (e.g., AA)
       b) Patients taking disulfiram and alcohol experience noxious side effects (e.g., flushing, headaches, anxiety, malaise, sweating) for one-half hour to several hours
       c) Contraindicated if there is coexistent hypertension, diabetes mellitus, coronary heart disease, hypothyroidism, pregnancy, or alcoholic liver disease
       d) A practical plan for use (Table 7.7)
    5. Avoid prescription of sedatives except for detoxification (see above)

Table 7.7.   Suggested Approach to Supervised Use of Disulfiram

1. Satisfy the following indications: the patient is willing to take medication several times a week under supervision, the patient can recall making the decision to take the first drink of a relapse, and the patient is actively involved in an organized outpatient treatment program.
2. Rule out contraindications, and ask yourself the following question: "Can this patient survive a disulfiram-alcohol reaction?"
3. Ensure sober state prior to the initiation of treatment.
4. Be sure patient and spouse know how to avoid hidden alcohol in foods, over- the-counter medications, toiletries, etc.
5. Have the patient read, discuss, and sign a consent form prior to initiating treatment.
6. Begin with a dose of 1 tablet (250 mg) daily.
7. *Keep the medication bottle in the office*, and have the patient come in 3 times a week to be dispensed two (or three) doses by the office staff. After 1 month, decrease the visits to twice a week, and increase the number of pills dispensed accordingly. After another month, make the visits weekly, and continue these for the duration of disulfiram treatment. See the patient at least monthly, and repeat laboratory testing every 3 months.
8. If the patient misses more than one or two appointments in a row, have the office staff contact the people on the consent form, and stop administering the medication.

6. Regular follow-up necessary for several years; neither the patient nor the therapist should be unduly discouraged by relapses
D. Prognosis
 1. Factors associated with a good prognosis
  a) Clinician commitment and patient motivation
  b) A crisis (e.g., threat of job loss) used to motivate
  c) Appropriate treatment for at least 2 years
  d) A continued threatened loss if treatment is stopped
  e) Intact family, job, health, cognitive function
  f) Prompt recognition and intervention when relapse occurs
 2. Factors associated with a poor prognosis
  a) No perceived threat of loss
  b) Inappropriate treatment (e.g., disulfiram alone, use of sedatives, limited treatment)
  c) Continued self-destructive tendencies
  d) Cognitive impairment or psychosis
  e) Acceptance of a derelict status

8/ ILLICIT USE AND ABUSE OF DRUGS AND SUBSTANCES

SELECTED DRUGS OF ABUSE

A. Sedative-hypnotics and benzodiazepines
   1. Usual effects
      a) Depression of cortical function, relaxation of inhibitions
      b) In abusers, elevation of mood, reduction in anxiety
   2. Acute adverse effects
      a) Overdose may lead to slurred speech, impaired judgment, unsteady gait
      b) Greater overdose may lead to stupor, coma, respiratory depression, vasomotor collapse, death
      c) Benzodiazepines, if taken alone, almost never cause death
   3. Chronic adverse effects
      a) No organ toxicity
      b) Confusion, irritability, slurred speech, ataxia, anterograde amnesia (most frequently with triazolam, midazolam, diazepam)
   4. Treatment
      a) Nonbenzodiazepine overdose is an emergency, requires treatment in an emergency room
      b) Withdrawal requires tapering (see Chapter 2) — see Table 8.1 for symptoms and time course
B. Heroin and other opioids
   1. Usual effects
      a) Brief euphoria, then several hours of a pleasant, dreamy state (especially after intravenous injection)
      b) Possibly itching, talkativeness, increased activity, conjunctival suffusion
      c) Miosis and respiratory depression
   2. Acute adverse effects
      a) Depressed consciousness and depressed respiration
      b) Pulmonary edema
      c) Seizures (propoxyphene and meperidine)
   3. Chronic adverse effects
      a) Effects of dirty needles (e.g., endocarditis, HIV infection, hepatitis)
      b) Heroin nephropathy (more common in African Americans)
      c) MPTP, a meperidine analog, has sometimes caused severe parkinsonism
      d) Withdrawal characterized by anxiety, nausea, yawning, diarrhea, sweating, rhinorrhea, dilated pupils, piloerection; ultimately, vomiting and muscle spasms
   4. Treatment
      a) Overdose must be treated in an emergency room (cardiorespiratory support plus naloxone, an opioid antagonist)
      b) Detoxification: methadone, buprenorphine, clonidine — all should be done by licensed drug treatment programs

Table 8.1. Characteristics of Dependence on Drugs of Abuse

Drug	Physiological Effect	Withdrawal Symptoms + Signs (1–7 Days After Last Dose)
Opioids	Pupillary constriction Analgesia Constipation Respiratory depression	Pupillary dilation Myalgia Diarrhea Stimulation of respiratory centers ("yawning") Rhinorrhea Gooseflesh Nausea and vomiting Restlessness Insomnia Nausea
Alcohol, barbiturates, benzodiazepines	Induction of sleep (hypnosis) Sedation Alcohol usually decreases but may increase seizure activity (other sedatives decrease seizure activity)	Minor symptoms Onset 24–72 hr after last dose Duration 72–96 hr after last dose Tremulousness Anxiety Irritability Autonomic hyperactivity (sweats, tachycardia, hypertension) Delirium Seizures Death (alcohol and barbiturates) Major symptoms Onset 72 hr to 1 week after last dose Duration up to 2 weeks after last dose
Cocaine	Pupillary dilation Tachycardia Hypertension	Bradycardia Hyperphagia Fatigue Hypersomnolence

C. Inhalants: solvent abuse
  1. Usual effects
     a) Immediate and of short duration
     b) Similar to alcohol intoxication
  2. Acute adverse effects
     a) Headache and nausea — similar but milder to the hangover produced by alcohol
     b) Sometimes, tactile hallucinations, spatial distortions
     c) Sudden deaths from arrhythmias or suffocation (from covering the head with the bag containing the solvent)
  3. Chronic adverse effects
     a) Concern, without definitive evidence, of organ damage (central nervous system, liver, kidneys, bone marrow)
     b) Cerebellar damage (partly reversible) and peripheral neuropathy after long-term use
  4. Treatment
     a) Because effects of acute abuse are transient, abusers rarely present for treatment
     b) Intense counseling, rehabilitation (see below)
D. Cocaine and other commonly abused stimulants
  1. Usual effects
     a) Euphoria, tachycardia, hypertension, dilated pupils
     b) Parkinsonian signs and symptoms, aphonia, dysphonia
  2. Acute adverse effects
     a) Hyperpyrexia, arrhythmias, hypertension
     b) Risk of myocardial infarction, stroke, seizures, shock, death
  3. Chronic adverse effects
     a) Hyperactivity, jitteriness, irritability when using drug; depression, lethargy when not using drug
     b) Sleep disturbance, weight loss
     c) Heavy users may exhibit rapid, repetitious, ritualistic body movements
     d) Occasional reversible delusional disorder
  4. Treatment
     a) Suicide risks or patients who cannot maintain abstinence long enough to begin outpatient treatment should be hospitalized
     b) Rehabilitation (see below)
     c) No drugs are useful
E. Marijuana/hashish
  1. Usual effects
     a) Elation, tachycardia, red eyes, later relaxation
     b) With larger doses, distorted perception
     c) Impaired short-term memory, impaired logical thinking
     d) High doses can produce hallucinations
  2. Acute adverse effects
     a) Rare
     b) Acute anxiety, paranoia
     c) Delirium, dysphoria (disorientation, catatonia, panic, heavy sedation)
  3. Chronic adverse effects
     a) Loss of energy, impaired memory, apathy
     b) Impaired pulmonary function
     c) Risk of teratogenicity

4. Treatment
   a) Acute anxiety best treated in mental health center or
      emergency room
   b) Delusional or delirious patients should be treated in an
      emergency room
F. Phencyclidine (PCP)
   1. Usual effects
      a) Exhilaration, euphoria, inebriation, tranquilization, perceptual
         disturbances
      b) Disorientation, hallucinations, anxiety, paranoia,
         hyperexcitability, irritability
   2. Acute adverse effects
      a) Acts of violence
      b) Delirium
      c) Psychosis (risk of schizophrenic psychosis within 2 years —
         even if abstinent)
      d) Ataxia, nystagmus, slurred speech, ptosis
      e) High doses can result in coma, respiratory depression, seizures,
         death
   3. Chronic adverse effects
      a) Persistent changes in personal habits
      b) Impaired memory or speech, impaired sleep, mood changes,
         paranoid thinking, unusual excitability or lethargy
   4. Treatment: in an emergency room
G. Lysergic acid diethylamide (LSD)
   1. Usual effects
      a) Depersonalization, altered time perception, labile mood,
         perceptual distortions, feelings of increased insight
      b) Slight increase in blood pressure and heart rate, fever,
         incoordination, dilated pupils, salivation and lacrimation,
         hyperreflexia, and occasional vomiting
   2. Acute adverse effects
      a) Acute panic reaction
      b) Hallucinations
   3. Chronic adverse effects
      a) Flashbacks: recurrence of the initial LSD experience, even
         though the drug has not been taken recently
      b) No withdrawal syndrome
   4. Treatment
      a) Referral to an emergency room or to a drug treatment
         program
      b) Agitated patients should be given diazepam 20 mg p.o. or i.m.
         before referral
H. Atropenic drugs
   1. In high doses, produce hallucinations, delirium, excitement,
      insomnia, amnesia
   2. Toxic overdose is a medical emergency, dictating immediate
      referral to an emergency facility
I. Arecoline (betel/areca nuts)
   1. Mostly used in Southeast Asia and India
   2. In low doses produces arousal
   3. Chronically causes grinding down of the teeth, red teeth, cancer
      of the oral cavity

   4. Poisoning requires treatment in an emergency facility
J. Anabolic androgenic steroids
   1. Usual effects
      a) No clear-cut reproducible effects
      b) No clear-cut effect on strength
   2. Chronic adverse effects
      a) Decrease in sperm count, decrease in size of testes;
         masculinization in men, acne
      b) Decreased glucose tolerance, unfavorable lipid profile
      c) Drug-induced hepatitis
      d) Increase in aggressiveness

PHARMACOLOGICAL APPROACHES TO TREATMENT OF DRUG ABUSE

A. Detoxification
   1. Outpatient (see also Chapter 7)
      a) For most patients
      b) Patients should be seen daily, given only the medication to be
         taken between visits
   2. Inpatient
      a) If the patient is unable to stop using illicit substances
      b) If the patient has medical problems that would be exacerbated
         by detoxification
      c) If there is a history of major withdrawal symptoms (e.g.,
         seizures)
      d) If there is a risk of suicide or of harm to others
      e) If there is multiple drug dependence
B. Methadone maintenance
   1. Cost-effective way to control opioid addiction
   2. Patients take methadone at least 3 times/week
   3. Methadone maintenance often indefinite
C Naltrexone
   1. An opioid antagonist that highly motivated patients can take 3
      times/week to block the effects of opioids
   2. Patients must be detoxified before taking naltrexone; otherwise
      there will be an acute withdrawal reaction

REHABILITATION

A. Principal types of programs
   1. Residential treatment programs
      a) Therapeutic communities
         1) Six months or more of treatment
         2) Aggressively confrontational group therapy
         3) Often effective if patients remain for duration (high dropout
            rate early)
      b) Intermediate-term residential programs
         1) Typically 4 weeks
         2) Traditional, less aggressive group therapy with a strong
            educational focus
         3) Not clearly more effective than outpatient programs
   2. Intensive outpatient treatment programs
      a) Sessions in evening 4–6 times/week for 4–6 weeks or longer
      b) Education and group counseling
   3. Self-help groups

      a) Narcotics Anonymous similar to Alcoholics Anonymous
      b) Provide a sequence of steps that the addict must take to
         recover from addiction
      c) Not an alternative to treatment
B. Common obstacles to recovery
   1. Difficulty in accepting total abstinence
   2. Difficulty in severing ties with drug users
   3. Difficulty in overcoming the anxiety of forming new relationships
   4. Difficulty in overcoming boredom

Section II
Allergy and Infectious
Diseases

9/ ALLERGY AND RELATED CONDITIONS

ALLERGIC RHINITIS AND SIMILAR NASAL CONDITIONS

A. Epidemiology and natural history
1. Onset usually between ages 10 and 20
2. During next 10 years, one-third get better; one-half get worse
3. Severity tends to decrease after age 40
B. Diagnosis of noninfectious rhinitis
1. Infectious rhinitis is typically purulent
2. Causes
    a) Typical seasonal allergy
    b) Year-round allergy
    c) Miscellaneous: Table 9.1
3. History
    a) Obstruction of nasal airflow, dry mouth, nasal discharge (usually clear), itching of the nose and soft palate, sneezing
    b) Cough; discharge, itching, puffiness of eyes
    c) Careful history will often identify specific cause of symptoms in patients with seasonal allergy (Table 9.2)
    d) In patients with year-round allergy, differentiation from nonallergic rhinitis may be difficult (see below)
    e) Symptoms of vasomotor rhinitis seem to be due to an inappropriate reactivity of the nasal membranes to a variety of nonallergic stimuli (e.g., cold, pleasant scents, combustion odors, stress)
4. Physical examination
    a) Swollen pale or blue nasal turbinates and nasal membranes
    b) Look for polyps: resemble peeled green grapes
5. Laboratory: in patients with allergic rhinitis, Giemsa stain of nasal

Table 9.1. Miscellaneous Nonallergic Causes of Noninfectious Rhinitis

RHINITIS MEDICAMENTOSA
  Sympatholytic antihypertensive medication
    α-Blockers
    β-Blockers
    Guanethidine
    Methyldopa
    Reserpine
  Aspirin sensitivity (other NSAID also)
  Topical decongestant abuse (rebound rhinitis)
ENDOCRINE CAUSES
  Hypothyroidism
  Pregnancy
  Oral contraceptives
ANATOMICAL CAUSES
  Nasal polyp
  Deviated nasal septum
  Nasal tumor
VASOMOTOR RHINITIS

NSAID, nonsteroidal anti-inflammatory drug.

discharge typically shows many eosinophils (40% or more of cells), and often there is a blood eosinophilia

C. Management of allergic rhinitis (Table 9.3)
  1. Avoidance and environmental control
     a) Remove as many irritants as possible (e.g., smoke)
     b) If symptoms are worse at home, consider animal dander allergy, contaminated humidifiers, or dust mites
     c) Change air filters frequently if forced air heat is used at home
     d) Minimize dust exposure (e.g., use of washable rugs and curtains, plastic-covered mattresses and pillows)
  2. Drug therapy

Table 9.2. Seasonal Occurrence of Pollens in Selected Regions

Pacific Northwest	North Central	Northeast
Trees: Apr–May	Trees: Mar–May	Trees: Apr–May
Grasses: Apr–Oct	Grasses: May–Aug	Grasses: May–July
Weeds: June–Sept	Ragweed: Aug–Sept	Ragweed: Mid-Aug–Sept
North California	Other weeds: June–Sept	Other weeds: May–Sept
Trees: Feb–May	**Midwest**	**Mid-Atlantic**
Grasses: Apr–Sept	Trees: Mar–May	Trees: Mar–May
Sagebrush: July–Oct	Grasses: May–July	Grasses: May–June
Other weeds: Mar–Oct	Ragweed: Aug–Oct	Ragweed: Mid-Aug–Sept
South California	Other weeds: July–Oct	Other weeds: May–Sept
Trees: Feb–June	**South Central**	**Southeast**
Grasses: Apr–Oct	Mountain cedar: Dec–Feb	Trees: Feb–May
Sagebrush: July–Oct	Other trees: Feb–Apr	Grasses: May–Oct
Other weeds: June–Oct	Grasses: Feb–Aug	Ragweed: Aug–Oct
	Ragweed: Aug–Oct	Other weeds: May–Oct
	Other weeds: June–Oct	

Table 9.3. Management of Allergic Rhinitis

AVOIDANCE AND ENVIRONMENTAL CONTROL
  Control dust
  Isolate furred animals
  Obtain machine-washable polyester pillows
  Seal mattress in zippered cover
  Close windows, use air conditioning
  Adjust humidity to 30–40% in winter
  Filter air
    Electrostatic
    High-efficiency particulate air filter
PHARMACOLOGICAL TREATMENT [a]
  Antihistamine alone (for discharge, sneezing, itchy eyes)
  Decongestant alone (for obstruction)
  Antihistamine-decongestant combination
  Topical disodium cromoglycate (cromolyn)
  Topical corticosteroid
  Systemic corticosteroid
IMMUNOTHERAPY
  Rational choice of allergens
    History
    Skin testing
  Adequate dosage essential

[a] See details in Tables 9.4–9.6.

Table 9.4.   Representative Antihistamines Useful in Treatment of Allergic Rhinitis

Class and Generic Name	Trade Name	Duration of Action (hr)	Sedation	Recommended Adult Dose (mg)	Available Preparations (mg)
ETHANOLAMINES					
Diphenhydramine [a,b]	Benadryl	4–6	Marked	25–50 q.i.d.	Capsule (25, 50), elixir (12.5/5 ml)
Carbinoxamine [c]	Clistin	3–4	Moderate	4 q.i.d.	Tablet, elixir
Clemastine	Tavist	8–12	Mild	2.68 b.i.d.	Tablet (2.68)
	Tavist-1 [b]	8–12	Mild	1.34 b.i.d.	Tablet (1.34)
Doxylamine	Decapryn	4–6	Moderate	12.5–25 q.i.d.	Tablet, syrup
ETHYLENEDIAMINES					
Tripelennamine [a,c]	Pyribenzamine	4–6	Moderate	50 q.i.d.	Tablet (25, 50), elixir (37.5/5 ml)
ALKYLAMINES					
Chlorpheniramine [a–c]	Chlor-Trimeton	4–6	Mild	4 q.i.d.	Tablet (4), syrup (2/5 ml)
Dexchlorpheniramine [c]	Polaramine	4–6	Mild	2 q.i.d.	Tablet (2), syrup (2/5 ml)
Brompheniramine [a–c]	Dimetane	4–6	Mild	4 q.i.d.	Tablet (4), elixir (2/5 ml)
Triprolidine [a,b]	Actidil	8–12	Mild	2.5 b.i.d.	Tablet (2.5), syrup (1.25/5 ml)
PHENOTHIAZINES					
Promethazine [a]	Phenergan	4–6	Moderate	12.5–25 q.i.d.	Tablet (12.5, 25, 50), syrup (2.5/5 ml)
Trimeprazine [a,c]	Temaril	4–6	Moderate	2.5–7.5 q.i.d.	Capsule (2.5), syrup (2.5/5 ml)
PIPERIDINES					
Azatadine	Optimine	8–12	Moderate	1–2 b.i.d.	Tablet
Cyproheptadine [d]	Periactin	4–6	Marked	4 q.i.d.	Tablet (4), syrup (2/5 ml)
BUTYROPHENONE					
Terfenadine	Seldane	8–12	Little or none	60 b.i.d.	Tablet (60)
MISCELLANEOUS					
Loratadine	Claritin	12–24	Little or none	10 daily	Tablet (10)
Astemizole	Hismanal	Up to several weeks	Little or none	10 daily on empty stomach	Tablet (10)
PIPERAZINE					
Hydroxyzine [a,d]	Atarax, Vistaril	6–12	Moderate	10–25 b.i.d., t.i.d.	Capsule (10, 25, 50, 100), suspension (10/5 ml)

[a] Generic available.
[b] Over-the-counter drug.
[c] Sustained-release preparation available.
[d] More useful in urticaria and pruritus.

a) Goal is reduction of symptoms, with minimal side effects (complete elimination of symptoms usually not possible)
b) Antihistamines (Table 9.4)
   1) Avoid sustained release preparations until the right drug is found
   2) Choose one drug from a class; if that does not work, choose a drug of another class
   3) More effective if given in anticipation of symptoms
c) Sympathomimetic decongestants (Table 9.5)
   1) Particularly effective in patients with marked obstructive symptoms
   2) Neurostimulatory — may counteract antihistamine-induced sedation
   3) To avoid rhinitis medicamentosa, utilize only when relief of symptoms is crucial (e.g., bedtime)
   4) Check blood pressure 1–3 hours after first administering (occasionally, hypertension is induced)
d) Topical corticosteroids (Table 9.6) — for patients whose symptoms cannot be controlled by antihistamines or decongestants
e) Systemic corticosteroids — occasionally necessary (e.g., 3–4 days of prednisone, 20 mg/day) to relieve severe obstruction so that topical steroids can then be administered
f) Aerosolized cromolyn (every 4 hours by metered dose to each nostril) to prevent symptoms: high cost but no risk of sedation
3. Management of eye symptoms
a) If no response to antihistamines, use topical α-adrenergic agents (e.g., Vasocon, Prefrin), 2 drops 3–4 times/day
b) If symptoms continue and are severe, steroid eye drops (e.g., HMS Liquifilm) can be used but not persistently without periodic slitlamp examination because of herpetic keratitis; wearers of contact lenses should not use steroid drugs without an ophthalmologist's approval
1. Referral to an allergist
a) If measures outlined above are not adequate to confirm diagnosis and to evaluate for immunotherapy:
b) Immunological tests
   1) To establish role of suspected allergens
   2) Scratch or intracutaneous tests using solutions of allergens
   3) RAST (*R*adio*A*llergo*S*orbent *T*est):
      (a) More expensive, less sensitive, no more specific than skin tests
      (b) Should be used when skin cannot be tested (e.g., generalized dermatitis)
c) Immunotherapy
   1) Frequent subcutaneous injections of selected allergen extract in progressively higher doses until a maintenance dose is reached; then given once or twice a month for 2–3 years
   2) Reduces symptoms in 95% of patients with seasonal ragweed or pollen allergy
   3) Local and systemic allergic reactions may occur; latter may

Table 9.5.   Representative Antihistamine-Decongestant Combinations Useful in Treatment of Allergic Rhinitis

Trade Name	Contents	mg/unit	Form Available	Usual Adult Dose
Deconamine SR	Chlorpheniramine	8	TDC[a]	1 q 12 hr
	Pseudoephedrine	120		
Ornade	Chlorpheniramine	12	TDC ("spansule")	1 q 12 hr
	Phenylpropanolamine	75		
Naldecon	Chlorpheniramine	5	Timed-release tablet	1 q 8–12 hr
	Phenyltoloxamine	15		
	Phenylephrine	10		
	Phenylpropanolamine	40		
Nolamine	Chlorpheniramine	4	Timed-release tablet	1 q 8–12 hr
	Phenindamine	24		
	Phenylpropanolamine	50		
Fedahist	Chlorpheniramine	8	"Timecaps"	1 q 12 hr
	Pseudoephedrine	120		
	Chlorpheniramine	10	"Gyrocaps"	1 q 12 hr
	Pseudoephedrine	65		
Dimetapp	Brompheniramine	12	Extentab	1 q 12 hr
	Phenylpropanolamine	75		
Bromfed	Brompheniramine	12	TDC	1 q 12 hr
	Pseudoephedrine	120		
Bromfed-PD	Brompheniramine	6	TDC	1 q 12 hr
	Pseudoephedrine	60		
Atrohist Plus	Chlorpheniramine	8	Timed-release tablet	1 q 12 hr
	Pseudoephedrine	60		
	Phenylpropanolamine	50		
	Hyoscyamine	0.19		
	Atropine SO_4	0.04		
	Scopolamine HBr	0.01		

Product	Components	Amount	Form	Dosage
Actified	Triprolidine Pseudoephedrine	2.5 60	Tablet or capsule	1 t.i.d.
Trinalin	Azatadine Pseudoephedrine	1 120	Timed-release tablet	1 q 12 hr
Seldane-D	Terfenadine Pseudoephedrine	60 120	Timed-release tablet	1 q 12 hr
Drixoral	Pseudoephedrine d-Brompheniramine	120 6	Timed-release tablet	1 q 12 hr
Extendryl	Pseudoephedrine Chlorpheniramine Phenylephrine Methscopolamine	120 8 20 2.5	TDC TDC	1 q 12 hr
Extendryl "Jr"	(Half the strength of Extendryl)			1 q 12 hr
Extendryl "Chewable"	Chlorpheniramine Phenylephrine Methscopolamine	2 10 1.25	Chewable tablet	1 q 4–6 hr
Rondec-T	Carbinoxamine Pseudoephedrine	4 60	Tablet	1 t.i.d.
Rondec-TR	Carbinoxamine Pseudoephedrine	8 120	Timed-release tablet	1 b.i.d.
Tavist-D	Clemastine Phenylpropanolamine	1 75	Tablet	1 b.i.d.

^aTimed disintegration capsule.

Table 9.6.   Forms and Dosage of Topical Steroids for Allergic Rhinitis

Trade Name	Drug	Form	Dispenser	Dosage
Beconase AQ	Beclomethasone	Aqueous solution	Manual pump, metered dose	Two sprays in each nostril b.i.d.
Beconase Inhalation Aerosol	Beclomethasone	Micronized powder	Freon-propelled	Two puffs in each nostil b.i.d.
Vancenase AQ	Beclomethasone	Aqueous solution	Manual pump, metered dose	Two sprays in each nostril b.i.d.
Vancenase PocketHaler	Beclomethasone	Micronized powder	Freon-propelled	Two puffs in each nostril b.i.d.
Nasalide	Flunisolide	Aqueous solution	Manual pump, metered dose	Two sprays in each nostril b.i.d.
Nasacort	Triamcinolone	Micronized powder	Freon-propelled	Two puffs in each nostril q.d.
Decadron Turbinaire	Dexamethasone	Micronized powder	Freon-propelled	Two puffs in each nostril b.i.d.-t.i.d.

require parenteral epinephrine (patient should be observed
for 30 minutes after allergen is injected)
D. Management of rhinitis due to topical decongestant abuse
    1. Discontinue decongestant
    2. Prescribe aerosolized corticosteroid (see above) for 1–2 weeks
    3. In very severe cases, systemic corticosteroids may have to be used
       for several days first
E. Management of intranasal polyps
    1. Topical corticosteroids or polypectomy
    2. Refer to an otolaryngologist to confirm diagnosis, plan treatment
F. Management of vasomotor rhinitis
    1. Avoid environmental irritants (see above)
    2. Oral decongestants (see above and Chapter 79)
    3. For more severe symptoms, intranasal corticosteroids (see above)
       may be of help

GENERALIZED ALLERGIC AND ALLERGIC-LIKE REACTIONS
A. Urticaria/angioedema
    1. Definitions
        a) Urticaria (hives): raised erythematous areas of edema involving
           the superficial dermis
        b) Angioedema — edema extending into the deep dermis
    2. Characteristics
        a) They occur anywhere on the body, but angioedema typically
           occurs on the face and distal extremities
        b) Usually itch
        c) Do not remain in the same area of skin longer than 24 hours
           (if they last longer than 72 hours, consider vasculitis)
        d) Chronic urticaria continues to appear for 6 weeks or longer
        e) Onset of acute urticaria within minutes to hours after exposure
    3. Etiology: Table 9.7
    4. Management
        a) Intense itching responds to subcutaneous epinephrine (0.2–0.3
           ml of a 1:1000 aqueous solution)
        b) Antihistamines (see Table 9.4 and above)
            1) Hydroxyzine particularly effective for itching (if no
               response, cyproheptadine may be tried)
            2) An H_2 antagonist (cimetidine or ranitidine) may enhance
               effectiveness of conventional (H_1) antihistamines
            3) Cold urticaria responds best to cyproheptadine
            4) Pressure urticaria usually does not respond to
               antihistamines, may require systemic corticosteroids
            5) Solar urticaria requires hydroxyzine and sunscreens
        c) Acute generalized urticaria signifies a risk of a life-threatening
           reaction (see below) on re-exposure
B. Anaphylaxis/anaphylactoid reactions
    1. Characteristics
        a) Initially, diffuse erythema, followed by generalized urticaria
        b) Progressive respiratory obstruction may ensue
        c) Vomiting, abdominal cramps, diarrhea may occur
        d) Vascular collapse can occur, with or without other symptoms
    2. Etiology: Table 9.8
    3. Management: Table 9.9

Table 9.7.   Etiology of Urticaria/Angioedema

ACUTE (EPISODE LASTING 6 WEEKS OR LESS)
  Allergy (IgE-mediated)
    Foods, drugs, insect stings
  Infection
    Virus (mononucleosis, hepatitis)
    Bacterial (β-hemolytic streptococcus)
  Idiosyncrasy
    NSAID
    Iodinated contrast material
  Physical agents
    Dermatographism
    Heat
      Generalized ("cholinergic")
      Localized
    Cold
    Solar
    Pressure
  Idiopathic
CHRONIC OR RECURRING
  Hereditary angioneurotic edema
  Hepatitis
  Parasitic infestation
  Neoplasm (especially Hodgkin's lymphoma)
  Collagen-vascular disease
    Systemic lupus erythematosus
    Polyarteritis
  Idiopathic

IgE, immunoglobulin E; *NSAID,* nonsteroidal anti-inflammatory drug.

C. Penicillin allergy
  1. History of
    a) Almost half show no allergy when challenged
    b) Prudent to prescribe another antibiotic (not a cephalosporin) if one is needed
    c) Refer to allergist for skin testing (Pre-pen, the major determinant, and penicillin G as a substitute for the minor determinant)
  2. Penicillin reactions (Table 9.10)
    a) Late reaction (rash) best treated with reassurance and an antihistamine
    b) Accelerated and immediate reactions treated as above for urticaria and anaphylaxis
    c) Ampicillin rash
      1) Commonly nonallergic nonpruritic maculopapular
      2) In 9% of all patients and in 50% of patients with mononucleosis given ampicillin
      3) Rechallenge with ampicillin not a risk
D. Hymenoptera venom allergy
  1. Skin testing, by an allergist, important to establish which venom is causative (e.g., bee, wasp, hornet, yellow jacket)
  2. Avoidance of recurrent exposure is critical, especially wearing shoes out of doors

Table 9.8. Causes of Anaphylaxis or Anaphylactoid Reactions[a]

Route of Administration[b]	Agent
Injection	Heterologous antisera
	Snake venom, rabies, diphtheria, antilymphocyte serum, antitumor antibody, clostridia
	Heterologous culture media for vaccines
	Flu, measles
	Antibiotics
	β-Lactam: penicillin, semisynthetic penicillins, cephalosporins
	Others: tetracyclines, aminoglycosides, chloramphenicol, amphotericin B, vancomycin, polymyxin, bacitracin
	Other drugs
	Protamine
	Venoms
	Hymenoptera
	Others: deer fly (*Chrysops discalis*), kissing bug (*Reduviidae*), snake, other insects, Gila monster
	Blood products
	Red blood cells
	Plasma factors: IgA, α-globulin, clotting factors
	Hormones
	Insulins, ACTH, methylprednisolone,[c] progesterone[c]
	Enzymes
	Chymotrypsin, chymopapain, trypsin, penicillinase, L-asparaginase, streptokinase
	Allergen extracts
	Diagnostic
	Therapeutic
	Miscellaneous
	Dextran, dialyzer hypersensitivity
	Generalized anesthesia induction
	Thiobarbiturates, myorelaxants
Ingestants	Foods
	Nuts, berries, beans, legumes, seafood, many others
	Drugs
	Others
	Bee pollen tablets
Inhalant	Penicillin, cromolyn
	Polymerized corn starch powder
Topical	Skin: antibiotics, certain physical stimuli, *p*-phenylenediamine, latex rubber
	Intravaginal: sperm and seminal products
	Ophthalmic: fluorescein dye
Physical stimuli	Exercise, cholinergic, cold
Unknown	Idiopathic anaphylaxis, systemic mastocytosis
Miscellaneous	Echinococcus cyst

From Shatz GS: Anaphylaxis. In: Korenblat PE, Wedner HJ (eds): *Allergy Theory and Practice*, 2nd ed. Philadelphia, WB Saunders, 1992.

IgA, immunoglobulin A; *ACTH*, adrenocorticotropic hormone.

[a] Incomplete list.

[b] Certain antigens may have more than one route of administration.

[c] Immunological mechanism possible but not proved.

Table 9.9.   Treatment of Anaphylaxis or Anaphylactoid Reaction

1. When applicable, place tourniquet above site of injection or sting to obstruct venous return or stop the administration of the causative agent. Remove tourniquet temporarily every 10–15 minutes.
2. Place patient in recumbent position and elevate lower extremities.
3. Administer aqueous epinephrine 1:1000, 0.3–0.5 ml s.c. or i.m. (or, if necessary, 0.1 in 10 ml of saline solution given i.v. over several minutes) and repeat as necessary.
4. When applicable, inject aqueous epinephrine 1:1000, 0.1–0.3 ml at the site of the injection.
5. Establish and maintain airway, first with oral airway. If necessary, use endotracheal tube.
6. Give oxygen as needed.
7. Monitor vital signs frequently.
8. If patient is not responding, give diphenhydramine hydrochloride (Benadryl), 50 mg i.v. over 3 minutes (maximum, 200 mg/kg in 24 hours).
9. If blood pressure cannot be obtained, give normal saline intravenously and maintain blood pressure with norepinephrine bitartrate (Levophed), 1 or 2 ampules (32 μg/min) in 500 ml of 5% glucose in water. Titrate to maintain blood pressure.
10. If severe asthma without shock, give aminophylline 500 mg i.v. over 10–20 minutes.
11. While corticosteroids will not be of help for the acute anaphylaxis, they may prevent protracted anaphylaxis.

Modified from: *Asthma and the Other Allergic Diseases*, NIAID Task Force Report. NIH publ. no. 79–387, May 1979.

3. An emergency self-treatment kit containing a syringe preloaded with epinephrine should be prescribed (e.g., Ana-Kit) as well as kept in the physician's office
4. Immunotherapy by an allergist should be offered (risk of reaction on re-sting reduced from 50% to 5%) if a systemic reaction occurred after the first sting

E. Food allergy
   1. Less common in adults than in young children
   2. In adults usually manifests as urticaria/angioedema or anaphylaxis in minutes to hours after ingestion of food
   3. Common causes: Table 9.11
   4. Can be detected by skin testing, but specificity is only 50–60%
   5. Definite test is double-blind food challenge unless the reaction was anaphylactic (too dangerous)

F. Reactions to iodinated contrast materials
   1. Risk: urticaria/angioedema (see above)
   2. Anaphylactoid: cough, dyspnea, wheezing, syncope with or without urticaria/angioedema
   3. Vasomotor: exaggerated flushing, nausea, paresthesias, mild transient hypotension
   4. Treat as above for generalized allergic reactions

G. Reactions to aspirin and other nonsteroidal anti-inflammatory drugs (NSAIDs)
   1. Urticaria/angioedema, anaphylactoid reaction, or asthma
   2. Usually a history of allergy
   3. Symptoms may occur immediately or some hours later
   4. Management as above for generalized allergic reactions
   5. After a reaction, avoid all preparations containing aspirin or NSAIDs (Table 9.12)

Table 9.10. Estimated Incidence of Allergic Reactions to Penicillin

Type of Reaction	Manifestations	Time of Occurrence After First Dose of Penicillin	Percentage of Treated Patients Showing Reaction
Late reactions	Skin rash	≥72 hr	1.4
Accelerated reactions	Urticaria	1–72 hr	0.3
Immediate reactions	Generalized urticaria	2–30 min	0.3
	Anaphylaxis	2–30 min	0.04
	Anaphylactic deaths [a]		0.001

Modified from: *Asthma and the Other Allergic Diseases*, NIAID Task Force Report. NIH publ. no. 79–387, May 1979. Results are based upon 70–80 million therapeutic courses of penicillin or semisynthetic penicillin or cephalosporin given per annum in the United States.
[a] From 400–800 deaths/year in the United States.

Table 9.11. Foods That Most Often Cause Allergic Reactions

MOST COMMON
  Seafood
  Eggs
  Nuts
  Seeds
OTHERS
  Milk
  Chocolate
  Grains (barley, rice, wheat)
  Fruits (citrus, melons, bananas, strawberries)
  Vegetables (tomatoes, celery, spinach, corn, potatoes, soybeans)

Table 9.12. Aspirin Preparations and Aspirin-Containing Products

Alka-Seltzer[a]	Excedrin[a]
Anacin[a]	4-Way Cold Tablets[a]
Anahist	Fiorinal
Arthritis Pain Formula[a]	Goody's Headache Powders[a]
Ascodeen-30	Measurin
Ascriptin[a]	Midol[a]
Aspergum[a]	Momentum Muscular Backache Formula[a]
Bayer Aspirin[a]	Pabirin
Bufferin[a]	Panalgesic[a]
Cama Inlay-Tabs[a]	Percodan
Cirin	Persistin
Congespirin[a]	Phenaphen
Cope	Quiet World Analgesic/Sleeping Aid[a]
Coricidin[a]	Rhinex
Darvon Compound	St. Joseph Cold Tablets for Children[a]
Dristan[a]	Sine-Off Tablets, Aspirin Formula[a]
Duradyne DHC Tablets	Stanback[a]
Durasesic Tablets	Stero-Darvon
Easprin	Supac
Ecotrin[a]	Synalgos
Empirin[a]	Triaminicin[a]
Emprazil	Vanquish[a]
Equagesic	Viro-Med[a]

[a] Over-the-counter medications.

10/ UNDIFFERENTIATED ACUTE FEBRILE ILLNESS

CAUSES

A. Infections
  1. Most common cause
     a) Abrupt onset of fever especially suggestive
     b) Usually self-limited (likely viral)
  2. Prognostic signs and symptoms sometimes develop after a day or more
     a) Most common infections: viral (e.g., mononucleosis, hepatitis, varicella, rubeola, rubella, recent HIV infection), Lyme disease, localized bacterial infection
B. Drugs (Table 10.1)
  1. Fever may occur abruptly or may be delayed for several weeks
  2. Fever may be low grade or high grade
  3. Chills uncommon
  4. Sometimes with allergic skin manifestations (see Chapter 9)
  5. Sometimes progresses to serum sickness (rash, lymphadenopathy, arthritis, nephritis, edema)
  6. Procainamide and hydralazine sometimes cause a lupus-like syndrome (fever, arthralgias, elevated antinuclear antibody titers)
  7. Defervescence in 1–2 days when drug is stopped but may not occur for weeks if half-life of drug is long
  8. Rechallenge ill-advised unless drug is critical to care
C. Other causes
  1. Vascular occlusive events or vasculitis
  2. Acute hemolysis
  3. Recent immunization
D. Chronic fever: common causes

Table 10.1. Drugs That Frequently Cause Fever due to Hypersensitivity

Allopurinol	Nifedipine
Amphotericin B	Nitrofurantoin
Antihistamines	p-Aminosalicylic acid
Atropine	Penicillamine
Barbiturates	Penicillins
Bleomycin	Phenolphthalein [b]
Captopril	Phenytoin
Cephalosporins	Procainamide
Clofibrate	Propylthiouracil
Ethambutol	Pyrazinamide
Heparin	Quinidine
Hydralazine	Salicylates [c]
Ibuprofen	Streptomycin
Iodides [a]	Sulindac
Isoniazid	Sulfonamides
Methyldopa	

[a] Including intravenous contrast media.
[b] Found in many nonprescription laxatives.
[c] When toxic levels occur.

Table 10.2.   Acute Undifferentiated Febrile Illness: Summary of Sequential Evaluation Process

Evaluation Process	Comment
INITIAL EVALUATION	
1. History, physical examination; if negative and not seriously ill, observation for 7–10 days; frequent phone contact	Spontaneous defervescence common, benign illness common
2. More thorough evaluation of "special risk" patients, including laboratory studies	Increased risk that fever is caused by serious illness, usually infection
3. If seriously ill, more extensive laboratory studies; may need hospitalization and treatment	
REPEAT EVALUATIONS (AT WEEKLY INTERVALS)	
1. Carefully repeated history and physical examination, expanded laboratory evaluation	Thorough re-evaluation often detects cause of fever
2. Discontinue recent drugs, document fever	
AFTER 3 WEEKS	
1. Begin evaluation for true fever of unknown origin, often requires hospitalization	Spontaneous defervescence uncommon, fever usually due to serious illness with substantial risk of mortality

1. Chronic infections (e.g., tuberculosis, endocarditis, osteomyelitis, cytomegalovirus infection, occult abscesses, HIV infection)
2. Collagen-vascular or rheumatic disease (especially systemic lupus, temporal arteritis, rheumatic fever, rheumatoid arthritis)
3. Neoplasms (especially lymphoma, leukemia, renal cell carcinoma, hepatoma, pancreatic cancer, lung cancer)
4. Miscellaneous (e.g., hyperthyroidism, inflammatory bowel disease, sarcoidosis, recurrent pulmonary emboli)

DIAGNOSIS

A. Objectives
   1. Early diagnosis in relatively few instances of serious illness that require specific treatment
   2. Avoidance of unnecessary diagnostic studies and of "blind therapy" for the majority of patients, who have benign, self-limited disease
B. Evaluation scheme: Table 10.2

11/ BACTERIAL INFECTIONS OF THE SKIN

SUPERFICIAL INFECTIONS CAUSED PREDOMINANTLY BY *STREPTOCOCCUS PYOGENES*

A. Impetigo
   1. Mostly in preschool children
   2. Begins as a pruritic, focal, superficial eruption of small vesicles
   3. Usually no history of preceding trauma
   4. After a few days, vesicles become pustules that break, become crusted, with an erythematous base
   5. Regional lymphadenopathy common but no systemic symptoms
B. Ecthyma
   1. Discrete ulcerating lesions (3–10 mm in diameter) with an adherent necrotic crust, surrounding erythema
   2. Most commonly on anterior tibial surface at sites of minor trauma or insect bites
   3. Spreads distally if untreated; there may be regional adenopathy
   4. No systemic symptoms
C. Erysipelas
   1. Rapidly spreading area of marked erythema with warmth, local pain, elevated sharp margin between involved and uninvolved skin, firm edema
   2. Regional tender adenopathy common
   3. Chills and fever common
D. Management
   1. Cultures usually not of help in cases of impetigo, ecthyma, or mild erysipelas
   2. Blood cultures indicated in cases of erysipelas that is extensive or associated with systemic toxicity
   3. Systemic antibiotic therapy required (Tables 11.1 and 11.2)
E. Complications
   1. Acute glomerulonephritis
      a) Not prevented by antibiotic therapy
      b) Average latency of 2 weeks
      c) If nephritogenic strains of streptococcus are known to be in the community, follow-up urinalysis in 2 weeks is appropriate
   2. Metastatic infection possible if erysipelas is neglected or severe

PUSTULAR INFECTIONS CAUSED BY *STAPHYLOCOCCUS AUREUS*

A. Folliculitis
   1. Inflammation of individual hair follicles, often with superficial pustules
   2. Little pain or surrounding erythema
   3. Especially common in bearded part of face
B. Furunculosis
   1. Deeper infection of follicles or cutaneous glands
   2. Most common on hairy parts of skin
   3. Begins with pruritus, tenderness, erythema followed by swelling, marked pain

Table 11.1. Antibiotic Selection for Skin Infections due to *S. pyogenes* or *S. aureus*

Infection	Antibiotic[a]	Route
STREPTOCOCCAL		
Impetigo	Penicillin V	Oral
	Benzathine penicillin	Intramuscular
	Erythromycin	Oral
Ecthyma	As for impetigo	
Erysipelas	Penicillin V	Oral
Mild	Erythromycin	Oral
Severe	Penicillin G	Intravenous
STAPHYLOCOCCAL		
Folliculitis	None	
Furunculosis, boils	Dicloxacillin	Oral
	Erythromycin	Oral
Bullous impetigo	As for furunculosis	
Carbuncle	Dicloxacillin	Oral
	Nafcilin	Intravenous
	Vancomycin	Intravenous
Cellulitus	As for carbuncle	

[a] A single antibiotic is given. Choices are in order of preference and include an alternate choice for patients allergic to penicillin. See the text for duration of therapy and adjunctive treatment. Dosage recommendations are in Table 11.2.

Table 11.2. Antibiotic Dosage and Schedule for Skin Infections due to *S. pyogenes* and *S. aureus* in Adults[a]

Antibiotic	Dosage
AMBULATORY TREATMENT	
Mild Infection	
Benzathine penicillin	1,200,000 units i.m. once
Penicillin V	500 mg p.o. 3 times/day
Erythromycin	250–500 mg p.o. 3 times/day
Dicloxacillin	250 mg p.o. 3 times/day
PARENTERAL TREATMENT	
Severe Infection	
Penicillin G	600,000–2,000,000 units i.v. every 6 hours
Nafcillin	1.0–1.5 g i.v. every 4 hours
Vancomycin	0.25–0.5 g i.v. every 6 hours

[a] Choice of antibiotics for specific infections is described in the text and summarized in Table 11.1. The duration of therapy is described in the text.

  4. Eventually, lesion becomes elevated, more painful; usually drains spontaneously
  5. May be recurrent, especially in diabetics or in nasal carriers of *S. aureus*
C. Hydradenitis suppurativa: chronic furunculosis of sweat glands of axilla, perineum, or groin
D. Carbuncles
  1. Coalescent mass of deeply infected follicles or sebaceous glands with multiple sinus tracts
  2. Usually occur on the back of the neck or upper back
  3. Once formed, usually worsen and enlarge
  4. Systemic toxicity common

    5. Increased frequency in diabetics
E. Management
    1. Cultures usually unnecessary
    2. Folliculitis requires only twice daily cleaning with a mild soap,
       avoidance of cosmetics or abrasive soaps
    3. Furuncles should be managed initially by application of moist heat
       (compresses or baths) 30 minutes 4 times/day
        a) Larger or very painful lesions or lesions that do not drain
           spontaneously should be drained when they are localized and
           fluctuant
        b) Antibiotics usually not required unless there are multiple
           furuncles, carbuncles, or associated diabetes mellitus (in which
           case see Tables 11.1 and 11.2)
    4. Carbuncles may require drainage; if there is systemic toxicity,
       hospitalization is warranted
    5. Recurrent furunculosis
        a) Culture nares to determine carrier state; if identified, apply
           bacitracin ointment to anterior nares 3 or 4 times/day for 2
           weeks
        b) Have patient bathe and shampoo 3 times/day with a
           hexachlorophene soap and change bed linen and bath towels
           daily
        c) Evaluate for diabetes mellitus
    6. Hydradenitis suppurativa difficult to manage, best referred to a
       dermatologist
F. Complications: be alert to metastatic infection

CELLULITIS AND OTHER WOUND INFECTIONS
A. Indices of severity
    1. Findings that require hospitalization and/or surgical intervention:
       Table 11.3
    2. Organisms that may cause life-threatening infection: Table 11.4
B. Cellulitis due to *S. pyogenes* and *S. aureus*
    1. A spreading infection of skin and subcutaneous tissues; involved
       area enlarges steadily and is painful, tender, intensely
       erythematous
    2. Chills and fever common
    3. Management
        a) Any wound drainage should be cultured
        b) See Tables 11.1 and 11.2
        c) Gentle, moist heat
        d) During recovery period, involved area should be rested
C. Secondarily infected ulcers (see Chapter 71)
    1. Best controlled by careful cleaning, debridement
    2. Systemic antibiotics only if local measures fail and after culture of
       ulcer
    3. Local antibiotics may be of help (e.g., polymyxin-bacitracin-
       neomycin ointment 3 times/day)
D. Cutaneous diphtheria
    1. Risk of myocarditis or neuropathy in 3%
    2. Outbreaks reported mainly in Native Americans or urban
       indigents

Table 11.3. Wound Infections: Findings That Necessitate Hospitalization and/or Surgical Intervention

Finding	Comment
Extensive cellulitis or erysipelas with systemic toxicity	Needs parenteral antibiotics, close observation
Diminished arterial pulse in cool, swollen, pale, infected extremity	Possible fasciitis, a surgical emergency
Cellulitus with cutaneous necrosis and/or subcutaneous gas	Needs parenteral antibiotics and possible surgical drainage/debridement
Closed space infection of the hand	Needs surgical drainage

Table 11.4. Causes of Life-Threatening Bacterial Cellulitis

Cause	Important Features
Gram-negative enteric bacilli, especially *Escherichia coli*	Occur in fecally contaminated wounds; gas may be present; surgical drainage required for gas or pus
Mixed anaerobic and enteric aerobic bacteria	Occur in fecally contaminated wounds; gas may be present; symptoms may progress rapidly and may include exquisite pain; surgical drainage required
Bacillus anthracis	Causes anthrax when minor wound is inoculated by spore-contaminated animal products (animal hides and hair, especially from goats); local chancre-like lesion devlops, followed by systemic toxicity
Erysipelothrix rhusiopathiae	Erysipelas-like lesion with central clearing; due to wound contamination with fish or meat products; treated with penicillin V or tetracycline
Pasteurella multocida	Erysipelas-like lesion that follows a dog or cat scratch or bite; treated with penicillin V or tetracycline
Marine vibrios	Necrotizing cellulitis after minor wound is contaminated by seawater or contact with shellfish
Aeromonas hydrophilia	Wound contaminated by freshwater swimming

3. Suspect when wounds develop a gray-yellow or gray-brown covering membrane and surrounding erythema
4. Organisms seen on methylene blue stains of smears from the wound, confirmed by culture
5. Presumptive cases should be treated with equine diphtheria antitoxin (20,000–40,000 units i.m. or i.v. after testing for hypersensitivity to horse serum) and either erythromycin (1.5 g/day) or procaine penicillin (1.2 million units/day i.m.) for 7–10 days

E. Bites
1. Prophylaxis for tetanus (Chapter 18) for all bite wounds
2. Human
   a) Untreated, a severe necrotizing cellulitis results

    b) Minor wounds should be washed, treated with dicloxacillin (250 mg 3 times/day) and ampicillin (500 mg 3 times/day) or, if penicillin allergy, clindamycin (150–300 mg 3 times/day) for 7–10 days

    c) Severe wounds require debridement

   3. Dog and other domestic animals

    a) Minor wounds should simply be cleaned

    b) Puncture wounds should be irrigated by injection of sterile saline through a 20-gauge needle

    c) Extensive or deep wounds require debridement plus antibiotics as for human bites

    d) Rabies precautions for all bites (including bites by domestic pets) — see Chapter 18

   4. Wild animals — treat as for domestic animal bites except that risk of rabies is greater

 F. Puncture wounds

   1. Tetanus prophylaxis (Chapter 18)

   2. Low-risk wounds (no soil or fecal contamination, healthy tissue) can be washed and observed

   3. If infection develops, culture drainage if any, treat with dicloxacillin (250 mg 3 times/day) or erythromycin (250–300 mg 3 times/day)

   4. For contaminated wounds or wounds in a diabetic or in an ischemic extremity, treat with ciprofloxacin 750 mg every 12 hours or another quinolone; surgical drainage may be required

 G. Felon

   1. An infection of the pulp of the distal phalanx of a finger

   2. Abscess formation, tissue necrosis are common

   3. If not adequately treated, severe damage may ensue

   4. Surgical drainage required, with antibiotic therapy dictated by Gram stain and culture

 H. Paronychia

   1. Infection immediately adjacent to a nail

   2. Occurs most frequently in nail biters, in people whose hands are frequently in water, and in diabetics or in toe because of an ingrown toenail

   3. Hands should be kept as dry as possible and an anticandidal cream (e.g., nystatin cream) or a broad-spectrum antibiotic cream (e.g., clotrimazole or miconazole cream) 2 times/day for several weeks should be applied

   4. If no response to these measures, drainage may be of help (sliding an 18-gauge needle, bevel down, along the nail into the infected area)

   5. For management of ingrown toenails, see Chapter 85

12/ ACUTE GASTROENTERITIS AND ASSOCIATED CONDITIONS

EPIDEMIOLOGY
A. Sources and modes of transmission of etiological agents (Tables 12.1 and 12.2)
   1. A vast majority of episodes of illness follow ingestion of normally safe foods that have been made unsafe by faulty preparation or preservation
   2. A small minority of episodes of illness follow ingestion of foods that are always unsafe, i.e., because of seafood toxins, mushroom toxins, heavy metals
   3. Symptoms of viral gastroenteritis overlap with those of bacterial gastroenteritis (Table 12.3)
B. Populations at risk
   1. Individuals of all ages
   2. A single episode may not confer protective immunity
   3. Older adults are at increased risk of dying from gastrointestinal illnesses
   4. Travelers to developing countries have a high risk of diarrheal illness

PATHOGENESIS
A. Invasive versus enterotoxigenic syndromes: Table 12.4
B. Enteroadherent *Escherichia coli* infection, neither invasive nor enterotoxigenic, primarily in children

EVALUATION
A. History
   1. Food eaten within past 48 hours
   2. Similar illness in others
   3. Probable incubation period (see Tables 12.1 and 12.2)
   4. History of taking antimicrobials within past 2 weeks (supporting the diagnosis of *Clostridium difficile* toxin-associated diarrhea)
   5. History of neurological symptoms (suggestive of, for example, botulism)
   6. History of risk factors for HIV infection
B. Physical examination
   1. Fever suggests an invasive process
   2. Poor skin turgor and postural hypotension suggest significant loss of salt and water
C. Laboratory studies
   1. Obtain if there is a suggestion of a common source outbreak (stool and food cultures, stool toxin assays)
   2. Obtain if there is diarrhea for more than 24 hours, fever, blood in the stool, significant volume depletion
      a) Stool culture for *Salmonella, Shigella, Helicobacter, Yersinia*
      b) Stool examination for fecal leukocytes (a count of >10 leukocytes/high-power field suggests an invasive pathogen; mix

Table 12.1. Characteristics of Acute Illness due to Ingestion of Infectious Agents

Agent	Pathogenesis	Usual Clinical Features	Epidemiological Features					Diagnosis	Specific Therapy
			Frequency in USA	Usual Pattern	Source (Reservoir)	Transmission to Humans	Incubation Period		
Bacteria									
Bacillus cereus	Enterotoxin produced in food or in intestine	Vomiting if preformed toxin in food, diarrhea	Not common	CSO	Soil	Foodborne	2–16 hr	Culture suspected food	None
Helicobacter jejuni	Invasion of large and small intestine	Fever, abdominal pain, diarrhea	Relatively common	S, CSO	Animal feces	Foodborne or waterborne [a]	24–48 hr	Culture stool, blood	Erythromycin (see text)
Clostridium botulinum	Neurotoxin produced in food	Vomiting, diarrhea, symmetric motor paralysis, cranial nerves, respiratory paralysis, death	Uncommon	CSO	Animal feces, soil	Foodborne (canned, low pH, anaerobic)	12–36 hr	Culture food, identify toxin in food, blood, stool	Polyvalent antitoxin
Clostridium difficile	Cytotoxin and enterotoxin produced in large intestine secondary to overgrowth	Fever, abdominal pain, diarrhea (often bloody) in a patient currently or recently on antibiotics	Common in hospitalized or recently hospitalized patients	S	Ubiquitous, especially in healthcare environments (spores)	Probably not necessary but may occur in hospitals [a]	1–10 days after beginning antibiotics (rarely up to 6 weeks after antibiotics stopped)	Identify toxin in stool	Metronidazole or vancomycin (see text)
Clostridium perfringens	Enterotoxin released during sporulation in large intestine	Diarrhea, occasionally vomiting	Relatively common	CSO	Human feces, animal feces, soil	Foodborne (meats)	12–24 hr	Culture suspected food	None
Escherichia coli									
Enterotoxigenic	Enterotoxin produced in small intestine	Voluminous watery diarrhea without fever (traveler's diarrhea)	Relatively common (travelers)	CSO, S	Human feces	Foodborne	24–48 hr	Culture stool, identify enterotoxin production by bacteria	None
Invasive	Invasion of large intestinal mucosa	Fever, diarrhea (often bloody)	Rare	CSO, S	Human feces	Foodborne (cheeses)	24–48 hr	Culture stool	Same as Shigella (see text)

Organism	Mechanism	Clinical features	Frequency		Reservoir	Transmission	Incubation	Diagnosis	Antibiotics to which organism is sensitive
Adherent	Adheres tightly to small bowel mucosa	Acute diarrhea, which may be prolonged	Unknown, probably uncommon	S	Human feces	Probably foodborne	24–48 hr	Culture stool, small bowel	None
Hemorrhagic (e.g., E. coli)	Verotoxin produced in large bowel	Hemorrhagic colitis, which may be followed by hemolytic uremic syndrome	Relatively common	CSO	Animal feces	Foodborne	24–48 hr	Culture stool	None
Salmonella (many species)	Invasion of small and large intestine	Fever and diarrhea	Relatively common	CSO	Animal feces; eggs	Foodborne (many foods, see text) person-to-person[a]	12–48 hr	Culture stool	Ampicillin or chloramphenicol, in selected cases only (see text)
Salmonella typhi	Invasion of small intestine mucosa, systemic dissemination	Protracted illness: fever, malaise, headache, constipation more often than diarrhea, splenomegaly, occasionally intestinal perforation	Uncommon	S	Human feces	Person-to-person, foodborne[a]	4 days–3 weeks	Culture blood, stool, antibacterial antibodies	Chloramphenicol
Shigella spp.	Invasion of large intestine	Fever, diarrhea (often bloody)	Relatively common	S	Human feces	Person-to-person[a]	12–48 hr	Culture stool	Trimethoprim-sulfamethoxazole (see text)
Staphylococcus aureus	Enterotoxin produced in food	Vomiting dominates, diarrhea	Very common	CSO	Human skin, nares, mouth	Foodborne (many foods, see text)	2–8 hr	Culture food, and food handlers	None
Streptococcus group A	Invasion of upper respiratory tract	Streptococcal pharyngitis (see Chapter 14)	Uncommon (by this mode of transmission)	CSO	Human pharynx, skin lesions	Foodborne	1–3 days	Culture throat, food, skin lesions of food handlers	Penicillin (see Chapter 14)
Vibrio cholerae	Enterotoxin produced in small intestine	Voluminous watery diarrhea without fever	Rare	CSO, S	Human feces	Waterborne and foodborne	12 hr–5 days	Culture stool, antibacterial and antitoxin antibody	Tetracycline
Vibrio parahaemolyticus	Probably both invasion	Diarrhea, abdominal	Uncommon	CSO, S	Seawater	Foodborne (various	15–24 hr	Culture stool	None

Table 12.1. Continued

Agent	Pathogenesis	Usual Clinical Features	Epidemiological Features						Specific Therapy
			Frequency in USA	Usual Pattern	Source (Reservoir)	Transmission to Humans	Incubation Period	Diagnosis	
	and enterotoxin production; exact mechanism unknown	cramps				types of seafood from estuary and seawater			
Vibrio vulnificus	Mechanism unknown	Fever, abdominal pain, diarrhea; septicemia "metastatic" cutaneous lesions	Uncommon	S	Seawater	Foodborne (various types of seafood from estuary and seawater)	24 hr–2 days	Culture stool	Antibiotics for Gram-negative sepsis; tetracycline
Yersinia enterocolitica	Invasion of small and large intestine	Fever, abdominal pain, which may suggest appendicitis, diarrhea	Uncommon	CSO, S	Animal feces	Foodborne, person-to-person	Probably 3–7 days	Culture stool	Doxycycline or trimethoprim-sulfamethoxazole
Viruses									
Parvovirus-like agents (Norwalk agent)	Invasion of small intestine	Vomiting and diarrhea	May be relatively common	CSO	Human feces	Foodborne and waterborne, person-to-person (secondary cases)	1–3 days	Rise in antiviral antibody (not generally available)	None
Rotavirus	Invasion of small intestine	Severe gastroenteritis in young children, mild in adults	Relatively common	S	Human feces	Person-to-person (secondary cases)	1–3 days	Virus antigen in stool; Rise in antiviral antibody	None
Protozoa and Helminths									
Entamoeba histolytica	Invasion of large intestine	Diarrhea, often chronic and bloody	Uncommon (travelers)	CSO, S	Human feces	Foodborne and waterborne, person-to-person	Few days to months	Examine stool for trophozoites	Metronidazole or quinacrine (see text)
Giardia lamblia	Colonization and occasional invasion of small intestine	Diarrhea, flatulence with foul-smelling stools	Uncommon (travelers)	CSO, S	Human feces	Waterborne, person-to-person	1–4 weeks	Examine stool for trophozoites	Metronidazole (see text)

Organism	Pathogenesis	Clinical	Frequency	CSO, S	Reservoir	Transmission	Incubation	Diagnosis	Treatment
Trichinella spiralis	(a) Encysted trichinae mature, mate, reproduce in small intestine (b) Larvae penetrate intestine, migrate to muscles where they cause inflammation and become encysted	Diarrhea, puffy eyes, muscle aching, fever, occasionally severe heart failure; eosinophilia typical	Uncommon	CSO, S	Animal muscle (swine, many wild animals)	Foodborne	2-28 days	Skin tests, antibody, muscle biopsy	Thiabendazole occasionally steroids (see text)
Cryptosporidia	Colonization	Diarrhea, acute in children and healthy adults, chronic in HIV-infected patients	Common in patients with AIDS	S	Human and animal feces	?Probably animal to person	?2-7 days	Examine stool for trophozoites	None known

CSO, common source outbreak; S, sporadic.

a Anal-oral transmission may occur in homosexual men.

Table 12.2.   Characteristics of Acute Illness due to Ingestion of Chemical Agents

Agent	Pathogenesis	Clinical Features	Epidemiological Features					Diagnosis	Specific Therapy
			Frequency in USA	Pattern	Source	Transmission to Humans	Incubation Period		
Seafood									
Ciguatoxin	Toxin with character of cholinesterase inhibitor	Vomiting and diarrhea, paresthesia (warmth, extremities), metallic taste, blurred vision, sharp pains in extremities, respiratory paralysis	Uncommon (Florida)	CSO, S	Food chain of bottom-dwelling fish caught in Florida, Hawaii (red snapper, barracuda)	Foodborne	1–6 hr	Clinical and epidemiological features	None (sensory symptoms may last days to months)
Domoic acid	Neuroexcitatory amino acid produced by phytoplankton and concentrated by mussels	Vomiting, cramps, headache, neurologic symptoms, seizures, coma, death	Unknown (Canada)	CSO, S		Foodborne	Minutes to 48 hr	Clinical and epidemiological features	Supportive care
Scombroid, fish poisoning	Histamine intoxication	Histamine reaction (flushing, headache, dizziness, burning of mouth and throat; urticaria, pruritis, and bronchospasm)	Uncommon (frozen and fresh fish can be affected)	CSO, S	Bacteria acting on fish flesh (tuna, mackerel, bonito, skipjack, mahi mahi)	Foodborne	Minutes to 1 hr	Clinical and epidemiological features	None (lasts few hours to few days)
Paralytic shellfish toxin	Neurotoxin causing motor paralysis	Paresthesia (warmth, extremities), floating sensation, dysphonia,	Uncommon	CSO, S	Toxic dinoflagellates concentrated in filter feeding bivalves (mussels,	Foodborne	<30 minutes	Clinical and epidemiological features	None (lasts few hours to few days)

		dysphagia, weakness, and respiratory paralysis			clams, oysters, scallops				
Mushrooms									
Muscarine	Muscarinic cholinergic response	Colicky abdominal pain, nausea, vomiting, diarrhea, salivation, miosis, blurred vision, bradycardia, hypotension	Uncommon	CSO, S	Amanita muscaria	Foodborne	Few minutes to few hours	Clinical and epidemiological features	Atropine 0.1–0.5 mg s.c. or i.v.
Phalloidine (and other toxins)	Diverse cytotoxin effects, multisystemic	Stage 1: nausea, abdominal pain, vomiting, bloody diarrhea, marked weakness, hypotension (shock) Stage 2: clinical improvement (day 2 or 3) Stage 3: severe hepatic failure, delirium, frequent fatal outcome		CSO, S	Amanita phalloides and other Amanita species	Foodborne	6–15 hr	Clinical and epidemiological features	None
Miscellaneous									
Heavy metals (antimony, cadmium, copper, iron, tin, zinc)	Upper gastrointestinal irritation	Metallic taste to food, nausea, vomiting, or diarrhea	Uncommon	CSO, S	Containers made of alloy that includes a heavy metal	Foodborne (food prepared in, stored in, or eaten from a container from which heavy metal leached)	5 minutes–8 hr	Clinical and epidemiological features	None

Table 12.2.   Continued

Agent	Pathogenesis	Clinical Features	Frequency in USA	Pattern	Source	Transmission to Humans	Incubation Period	Diagnosis	Specific Therapy
					Epidemiological Features				
Monosodium glutamate (MSG)	Idiopathic reaction	Burning sensation in chest, neck, abdomen, extremities	Relatively common	S	Foods prepared with large amounts of MSG	Foodborne (Chinese restaurant foods)	3 minutes–2 hr	Clinical and epidemiological features	None

Data from Gosselin RE, Hodge HC, Smith RP, Gleason MN: *Clinical Toxicology of Commercial Products*, 5th ed. Baltimore, Williams & Wilkins, 1984; and Hughes JM, Merson MH: Current concepts: fish and shellfish poisoning. *N Engl J Med* 295:1117, 1976. CSO, common source outbreak; S, sporadic.

Table 12.3.   Comparison of Symptoms of Viral Bacterial Gastroenteritis in Adults

	Percentage With Symptom				
	Viral Gastroenteritis		Bacterial Gastroenteritis		
Symptom	Rotavirus[a]	Norwalk Agent[b]	Salmonella[b]	Shigella[b]	S. aureus
Nausea	2	85	50	45	62
Vomiting	9	84	23	39	86
Abdominal cramps	26	62	78	60	86
Diarrhea	33	44	73	100	67
Fever	5	32	49	72	10
Headache	NR[c]	37	33	6	8

[a] From Wenman WM, Hinde D, Felthman S, Gurwith M: Rotavirus infection in adults. Results of a prospective family study. N Engl J Med 301:303, 1979.
[b] From Adler JL, Zicki R: Winter vomiting disease. J Infect Dis 119:668, 1969.
[c] NR, not reported.

Table 12.4.   Characteristics Distinguishing Invasive and Enterotoxigenic Diarrhea

Feature	Invasive Diarrhea	Enterotoxigenic Diarrhea
History	Fever, abdominal pain, tenesmus, may have blood in stool	Watery diarrhea with little or no fever or other systemic symptoms
Physical examination	Fever, abdominal tenderness; proctoscopy may be indicated	May be signs of salt and water depletion
Laboratory studies	Stool culture (may be diagnostic)	Stool culture usually negative unless special culture techniques available
	Fecal leukocytes in large numbers[a]	
	White blood cell count may be elevated	No or few fecal leukocytes
		White count usually normal but may be elevated
Therapy	Oral fluids and electrolytes (usually only small quantities needed)	Oral fluids and electrolytes
		Bismuth subsalicylate, other symptomatic medications as needed[c]
Course	Antimicrobials often indicated[b] Improvements in 1–2 days, particularly if appropriate antimicrobials used	Antimicrobials not indicated Duration of 1–2 days usually; may last up to 5 days

[a] Use a drop of methylene blue stain with liquid stool.
[b] See text for recommendations for specific bacterial pathogens.
[c] See text for details.

       stool with methylene blue, place under a coverslip, examine in 2–3 minutes)
- c) White blood cell count (elevated or shifted to younger forms suggests invasive infection)
- d) Special studies (e.g., looking for *Giardia, Entamoeba, Cryptosporidium, C. difficile* toxin) as indicated

D. Management
  1. Symptomatic treatment

   a) Most acute diarrheal disease in the United States can be treated
      symptomatically only (exceptions: giardiasis, amebiasis, *C.
      difficile* colitis, severe shigellosis and salmonellosis)
   b) Fluids
      1) If stool volume is relatively small, young, healthy patients
         should drink lots of fluid, avoid spicy food; otherwise, eat
         what they like; foods with complex carbohydrates (e.g., rice,
         cereals, toast) may facilitate fluid resorption
      2) If stool volume is relatively large or if patients feel weak,
         have signs of volume depletion, or are elderly, replacement
         should consist of fluids that contain electrolytes and glucose
         (available commercially as, for example, Pedialyte, or as salt-
         sugar packets to be dissolved in water, as, for example,
         Orlyte)
         (a) Solutions can be made at home also: 1 teaspoon salt
             and 4 teaspoons sugar in a liter of water
         (b) Drink 1–2 liters in first 1–2 hours, then 1 –2 liters/day
             until symptoms resolve
         (c) Soft drinks and Gatorade not satisfactory
      3) Severe diarrhea or vomiting that exceeds ability to replace
         fluids warrants hospitalization
   c) Other measures
      1) Diphenoxylate with atropine (Lomotil) or loperamide
         (Imodium or generic) if frequent diarrhea would be
         embarrassing
         (a) Potentially harmful if invasive bacteria are causing
             diarrhea
         (b) Avoid in frail elderly
      2) Kaopectate not useful
      3) Bismuth subsalicylate (Pepto-Bismol) useful (2 tablets or 30
         ml every ½ to 1 hour, as needed, up to 8 doses/24 hours)
      4) Protracted vomiting will usually respond to Compazine 25-
         mg rectal suppository 2 or 3 times/day
2. Specific treatment
   a) Shigellosis: trimethoprim-sulfamethoxazole (1 double-strength
      tablet every 12 hours for 3 days); quinolones are an alternative
   b) Salmonellosis
      1) No treatment for gastroenteritis (prolongs carrier state)
      2) If systemic symptoms (e.g., high fever), ampicillin or
         chloramphenicol 500 mg 4 times/day for 1 week
   c) Helicobacter
      1) No clear-cut clinical effect of treatment
      2) Erythromycin 500 mg 4 times/day for 5 days usually
         prescribed
   d) Antibiotic-associated diarrhea
      1) Stop antibiotic (switch to another if necessary)
      2) If *C. difficile*-induced
         (a) Bismuth subsalicylate (see above) often is of help
         (b) Metronidazole (Flagyl) 250 mg 4 times/day for 5 days
         (c) If relapsing or severe illness, vancomycin 250–500 mg
             4 times/day for 7–14 days
   e) *E. coli* infection

        1) Hemorrhagic colitis caused by some *E. coli* does not
           respond to antibiotics
        2) Traveler's diarrhea does respond to antibiotics (see Chapter
           19)
     f) Giardiasis: quinacrine hydrochloride, 100 mg 3 times/day for 5
       days, or metronidazole, 750 mg 3 times/day for 5 days
     g) Amebiasis: metronidazole, 750 mg 3 times/day for 10 days,
       followed by diiodohydroxyquin (Diodoquin), 650 mg 3 times/
       day for 3 weeks

E. Course
  1. Dehydrated patient will feel immediately better when replete
  2. Patients with invasive infection, when treated, note decrease in
     symptoms in 24–36 hours
  3. If symptoms persist for more than 3 or 4 days, patient and stool
     should be re-examined

13/ GENITOURINARY INFECTIONS

GENERAL EVALUATION

A. Urine examination
  1. Collection
    a) Midstream collection voided into a sterile container
    b) Catheterization of bladder only for women who are very obese or have other disabilities making midstream collection impossible
  2. Urinalysis
    a) Refrigerate urine if it cannot be processed within 10–15 minutes
    b) Bacteria seen through an oil immersion lens in an uncentrifuged specimen has a 90% correlation with a subsequent culture growing >1 million bacteria/ml of urine
    c) White blood cells (WBC) of >7/mm^3 seen through a low-power lens in women or any number of WBC in men indicates an abnormality (not necessarily an infection)
    d) Centrifuged urine: white cell casts indicate pyelonephritis; >10 WBC/high-power field abnormal
    e) Urine dipstick: if nitrite test and leukocyte oxidase test are both positive, infection present 90% of time
  3. Culture
    a) Always indicated in patients with systemic symptoms, patients recently discharged form a hospital, pregnant women, men
    b) Not needed in otherwise-healthy young women
    c) Specimen should be refrigerated during transport to laboratory
    d) Symptomatic infection usually associated with 10^5 or more bacteria/ml of urine, but some symptomatic patients have counts as low as 10^2 or 10^3/ml (see Urethral syndrome below)
    e) Species
      1) Even small numbers of Gram-negative organisms suspicious
      2) Multiple species suggest contamination unless, for example, patient has been chronically catheterized
      3) Large numbers of skin flora (e.g., *Staphylococcus epidermidis* or diphtheroids) can be ignored
      4) Fungi usually inconsequential
B. Localizing the site of infection
  1. Usually not necessary
  2. Relapse after standard treatment (see below) suggests, for example, upper tract infection, prostatitis, or persistent colonization of the introitus
  3. Antibody-coated bacteria test unreliable, should not be done
  4. Urethral and/or ureteral catheterization cumbersome and almost never warranted
C. Indications for sonography: Table 13.1
D. The patient with irritative symptoms
  1. Typically frequency and urgency of urination, dysuria, occasionally hematuria

Table 13.1. Indications for Evaluation of Patients With Urinary Tract Infections With Ultrasonography

Acute pyelonephritis in male patients
Acute pyelonephritis in women with persistent high fevers or leukocytosis after 2 or 3 days of antimicrobial treatment
Renal colic (see Chapter 32)
Palpable bladder or renal mass
Urea-splitting organism — usually *Proteus* spp.
Frequently recurrent urinary tract infections in women (more than 3 or 4/year)
Failure to eradicate infection with appropriate therapy

Table 13.2. Antimicrobial Agents for Uncomplicated Urinary Tract Infections (3-Day Therapy)

Agent	Dose
FIRST CHOICE (effective and inexpensive)	
Trimethoprim-sulfamethoxazole (Bactrim, Septra, generic)	1 DS q 12 hr
SECOND CHOICE (effective)	
Nitrofurantoin (Furadantin)	50 or 100 mg q 12 hr
A Quinolone	
Ciprofloxacin (Cipro)	250 or 500 mg q 12 hr
Norfloxacin (Noroxin)	100 mg q 12 hr
Ofloxacin (Floxin)	200 mg q 12 hr
Tetracycline	500 mg q 12 hr
Doxycycline	100 mg q 12 hr
THIRD CHOICE (less effective but can be used during pregnancy)	
β-Lactams (amoxicillin, cephalexin, etc.)	250–500 mg q 8 hr

  2. Chills and fever almost always indicate pyelonephritis (see below)
  3. Vaginal infections and sexually transmitted infections may mimic urinary tract infections (see Chapter 77)

MANAGEMENT OF SYMPTOMATIC URINARY TRACT INFECTIONS IN WOMEN

A. Treatment of first, occasional, or uncomplicated infection (Table 13.2)
  1. Generally total relief of symptoms within 24 hours
  2. In very symptomatic patients, could add Pyridium 200 mg 3 times/ day for a day or two
  3. If patient remains symptomatic, no follow-up necessary
  4. Education: Table 13.3
B. Management of recurrent infection
  1. Recurrent infections are usually reinfections rather than relapses
  2. Each recurrence should be treated as a first infection (see above)
  3. If there are 3 or more recurrences in a year, sonography of urinary tract is indicated
    a) If structural problems detected, refer to a urologist or gynecologist
    b) If no structural problems detected, consider prophylactic antimicrobials
  4. Prophylactic antimicrobials
    a) Nitrofurantoin, 50 mg, or trimethoprim-sulfamethoxazole, 40/ 200 mg, or cephalexin, 250 mg, all at bedtime

Table 13.3.   Points to Consider in Educating Women Who Have Had an Uncomplicated Infection

Infections are often recurrent. However, the following measures may decrease the recurrence rate:

1. Avoid a full bladder. This is an especially important reminder during travel.
2. High fluid intake (1 liter in 2–3 hours) may eradicate an infection that has just become symptomatic.
3. Irritation to the urethra, as occurs with sexual intercourse, is associated with the movement of bacteria into the bladder.
4. Voiding after intercourse, therefore, helps to prevent recurrent infection.
5. Diaphragm use is associated with development of urinary tract infection.

Infections in the absence of structural urological disorder are rarely, if ever, associated with the development of chronic renal failure.
Prompt recognition and treatment will help to control symptoms.
Even if recurrent infections are frequent, there is much that can be done to control symptoms.

   b) If recurrent infection noted only after sexual intercourse, a single dose of an antimicrobial should be given after intercourse
   c) Continue for 6 months; if, after cessation, infections recur, resume for a longer period (such as a year)

ASYMPTOMATIC BACTERIURIA
A. Associated with pregnancy
   1. Risk of symptomatic infection and, perhaps, of premature birth
   2. Should be treated (Table 13.2 and above)
B. Unassociated with pregnancy
   1. More common in women and in both sexes with advancing age
   2. Screening and treatment not warranted

SYNDROMES IN WOMEN THAT MIMIC URINARY TRACT INFECTIONS
A. Urethral syndrome (dysuria-pyuria syndrome)
   1. Characterized by frequency and urgency of urination, dysuria, >10^5 bacteria/ml of urine
   2. Most patients have pyuria (see above)
   3. Many patients have bacterial infection and respond to appropriate antimicrobials (see above)
   4. Venereal infections
      a) Especially chlamydia, gonorrhea, and herpes simplex (see Chapter 77)
      b) Pelvic examination mandatory
      c) Treatment (see Chapter 77)
   5. Unidentified etiology
      a) First reassure, prescribe sitz baths and Pyridium 200 mg 3 times/day for 5–10 days
      b) If symptoms persist, refer to a urologist for cystoscopy
      c) Educational points: Table 13.3
   6. Interstitial cystitis
      a) Affects middle-aged women
      b) Suprapubic discomfort, especially when bladder is full
      c) Urinalysis often normal, but hematuria may be present

   d) Difficult to diagnose (refer to a urologist, if suspected, for
      cystoscopy and, often, a biopsy)
   e) No effective therapy
7. Vaginitis and cervicitis (see Chapter 77)

INFECTIONS UNIQUE TO MEN

A. Bacterial cystitis
   1. Presentation the same as in women (see above)
   2. Urine culture mandatory
   3. Examination of prostate, sonography, urological consultation
      appropriate
   4. Treat for at least 7–10 days (Table 13.2)
   5. Schedule follow-up in 4–6 weeks (relapse common)
B. Prostatitis
   1. Acute bacterial prostatitis
      a) Abrupt onset fever, chills, low back pain, perineal pain
         (sometimes worse with defecation), frequency and urgency of
         urination, dysuria, sometimes hematuria
      b) Prostate swollen and boggy
      c) Urine and prostate sometimes contain WBC; culture often
         grows the pathogen (usually *Escherichia coli*)
      d) If systemic symptoms severe, hospitalize
      e) Otherwise, treat with a quinolone (Table 13.2); second choice,
         trimethoprim-sulfamethoxazole (β-lactams are ineffective)
      f) Bed rest and sitz baths 2–3 times/day may relieve pain
      g) Acute urinary retention, an occasional complication, requires
         urgent urological consultation as well as hospitalization
      h) Prostate may feel irregular for several months
      i) Recurrence more common in elderly
   2. Chronic bacterial prostatitis
      a) Presents with mild frequency, urgency, dysuria, occasionally a
         urethral discharge, sometimes painful ejaculation with
         hematospermia; no fever
      b) Prostate feels irregular, may be mildly tender
      c) Usually, *E. coli* is causative (less often, other Gram-negative
         organisms)
      d) Most patients have been intermittently symptomatic, controlled
         with short courses of antimicrobials
      e) If organism is sensitive, ciprofloxacin 250 mg twice a day for 2
         weeks is effective in 60%
      f) If infection cannot be cured, ½ tablet of regular strength
         trimethoprim-sulfamethoxazole taken at bedtime indefinitely
         usually controls symptoms
      g) Urology consultation is important
   3. Nonbacterial prostatitis (prostatosis)
      a) Signs and symptoms of chronic prostatitis (including pyuria)
         but no demonstrable infection
      b) Most patients cannot be cured, but treatment with
         ciprofloxacin, as above, may control symptoms
      c) An antispasmodic (e.g., oxybutynin 5 mg 2–3 times/day) may
         help
      d) Urology consultation warranted if no response to treatment
   4. Prostatodynia

      a) Symptoms of prostatic inflammation but negative physical examination, no WBC in urine or in prostatic secretions, negative urine culture

      b) Refer to a urologist to confirm diagnosis, rule out another process (e.g., bladder cancer or interstitial cystitis), suggest treatment (e.g., phenoxybenzamine, an α-sympathetic blocker, and a muscle relaxant)

C. Epididymitis
1. Often presents as inflammation of entire hemiscrotum
2. Chills, fever, frequency and urgency of urination, dysuria common
3. Pyuria usual
4. Causes
      a) Most cases due to *Chlamydia trachomatis*
      b) Gonorrhea in less than 5%
      c) Gram-negative infection from urinary tract, usually in men over 50
      d) Mumps, if immunity postvaccination has waned
5. Confirm impression by urine culture
6. Differential diagnosis
      a) Torsion of the testicle: in young boys (epididymitis occurs after puberty); elevation of testis intensifies pain (relieves pain of epididymitis); no pyuria
      b) Acute orchitis: urethral discharge or pyuria suggests epididymitis
      c) Tumor of the testicle with hemorrhage: tumor usually hard, nontender
      d) Hydrocele: painless, transilluminates
7. Treatment (Table 13.2)
      a) Doxycycline or ofloxacin for 14 days for chlamydia infection
      b) Ceftriaxone 250 mg i.m. once, plus doxycycline (for possible coinfection with chlamydia) for gonorrhea
      c) Bed rest, scrotal support, and sitz baths may minimize symptoms
8. Course and follow-up
      a) Induration and edema in region of epididymis may persist for 6–8 weeks
      b) Older patient should be evaluated for bladder outlet obstruction after acute symptoms are controlled (see Chapter 34)

D. Urethritis
1. Nongonococcal
      a) More common than gonococcal
      b) Most common cause is chlamydia infection
      c) Symptoms: discharge from the urethra, dysuria, itching of distal penis; no fever; 25% asymptomatic
      d) Culture not recommended (expensive), but it is useful to swab urethra (Calgiswab, type 1)
      e) Calgiswab smear shows *50 in nongonococcal urethritis; >50 in gonococcal urethritis*
      f) Treat with doxycycline 100 mg twice a day
      g) Sexual partners should be treated; patient should use a condom until symptoms abate
      h) If symptoms continue, culture warranted to exclude chronic

bacterial prostatitis (see above), and patient should be referred to a urologist to exclude urethral stricture or other intraurethral lesions

2. Gonococcal
   a) Symptoms as above
   b) Urethral smear shows many WBC, as above, and Gram stain shows extracellular or intracellular Gram-negative diplococci
   c) Treatment: Table 13.4
   d) Sexual partners should be treated; patient should use a condom until symptoms abate

PERSISTENT URINARY TRACT INFECTION IN MEN AND WOMEN

A. Recognition
   1. Treatment with an appropriate antimicrobial should result in abatement of symptoms and sterile urine within 72 hours
   2. If symptoms persist, culture urine
   3. If culture positive, consider further investigation
B. Causes
   1. Patient has not taken antimicrobial or has taken it but subsequently vomited
   2. Organism is totally resistant (unusual)
   3. Renal function is so poor (e.g., serum creatinine > 3 mg/dl) that antimicrobial has not reached urine
   4. Antimicrobial does not work at current urine pH
   5. There is a major structural anomaly of the urinary tract
   6. Organism is a fungus

RECURRENT INFECTION DUE TO RELAPSE IN MEN AND WOMEN

A. Characteristics
   1. Recurrent infection with the same organism implies persistence of bacteria in tissue within the urinary tract
   2. Urine sterile during or within 6 months of treatment of acute infection
   3. An underlying structural problem often present
   4. Much less common in women than reinfection (relapse characterized by reappearance of same serotype, e.g., of E. coli; reinfection, of a different serotype)
B. Management
   1. Sterilization not possible if a structural abnormality exists
   2. If bladder is atonic, intermittent straight catheterization by patient or a family member may prevent recurrent infection
   3. If other abnormalities exist, suppressive therapy may decrease

---

Table 13.4.   Management of Urethritis in Men

Treatment for gonococcal urethritis and nongonococcal urethritis simultaneously:

Ceftriaxone (Rocephin) 250 mg i.m. as single dose

plus

Doxycycline 100 mg twice a day for 7 days

or

Ofloxacin 400 mg q 12 hr for 5 days

Report to local health department. They will follow up and treat sexual partners.

symptomatic episodes of infection: sulfisoxazole (Gantrisin) 500
mg twice a day or trimethoprim-sulfamethoxazole, 1 tablet twice a
day for 6 weeks, repeated several times as necessary

ACUTE PYELONEPHRITIS IN MEN AND WOMEN

A. Definition: a bacterial infection of the kidney, most often from
   ascending infection
B. Diagnosis
   1. Symptoms
      a) Often flank pain, fever, abdominal pain, frequency and urgency
         of urination, dysuria
      b) There may be none of these symptoms or only symptoms of
         bladder irritation
   2. In men, a structural abnormality is likely; in women, much less
      likely
C. Management
   1. Men should be hospitalized for parenteral antibiotics, sonography,
      perhaps urological consultation
   2. Women can be treated at home if not severely ill, have no
      complicating illnesses, and are reliable; if no response in 24–48
      hours, they should be hospitalized
      a) Antimicrobial therapy: Table 13.2
      b) Forcing fluids may be detrimental but replace excess losses due
         to fever or vomiting
   3. If acute attack subsides, reculture urine in 3–4 weeks; if the same
      organism is still in the urine, consider 6 weeks therapy with an
      antibiotic

14/ RESPIRATORY TRACT INFECTIONS

UPPER RESPIRATORY TRACT INFECTIONS
A. Common cold
  1. Incidence
     a) Adults average 2–4 colds/year
     b) School children often introduce infection into the home
  2. Transmission mostly by direct physical contact with virus-contaminated surfaces (e.g., hands) rather than by aerosol
  3. Characteristics
     a) Incubation period of 48–72 hours
     b) Begins with mild malaise, rhinorrhea, sneezing, scratchy throat, variable loss of taste and smell
     c) Symptoms reach maximum severity on second to fourth day
     d) Fever absent usually but, if present, rarely exceeds 1°F
     e) Cough, hoarseness may begin later — worse in smokers
     f) Symptoms usually last 1 week but in 25% up to 2 weeks
  4. Treatment
     a) Aspirin for fever and myalgias
     b) Bed rest unnecessary
     c) Topical decongestants (Table 14.1) for nasal congestion — prescribe for no more than 5 days (to avoid rebound rhinitis)
     d) Oral decongestants (Sudafed, 30 mg over the counter or 60 mg by prescription) are of some help
     e) Combinations of oral decongestants and antihistamines (Table 14.1) are also often of help
     f) Expectorants and antimicrobials are useless
  5. Prevention
     a) Vitamin C provides no established benefit
     b) Development of a successful vaccine seems unlikely (too many viral serotypes)
B. Flu syndrome
  1. Epidemiology
     a) Major pandemics of varying severity periodically (last occurred in 1978)
     b) Annual epidemics in United States each winter
     c) Virus (usually influenza virus) spread by aerosol
  2. Characteristics
     a) Abrupt onset of fever, chills, headache, myalgias, malaise, lasting for 3–7 days
     b) As other symptoms wane, respiratory symptoms develop: cough, nasal discharge, hoarseness, sore throat, lasting for another week or so
     c) Physical findings: toxic-appearing patient, flushed, hot; watery red eyes; tender cervical nodes; occasionally, localized rales
     d) Laboratory: mild granulocytopenia
  3. Treatment
     a) Amantadine reduces fever and shortens duration of illnesses caused by influenza if given within a day or two of onset

Table 14.1. Over-the-Counter Cold Medications[a]

	Generic Name	Trade Name	Effectiveness	Side Effects
Antihistamines	Chlorpheniramine	75 products listed in PDR	Reduces sneezing, nasal mucus, symptom score	Drowsiness
	Diphenhydramine HCl	Benadryl	No difference from placebo	Drowsiness
	Terfenadine	Seldane	Reduces nasal, headache, eye symptoms in 1 of 2 studies	Tachyarrhythmia in combination with erythromycin
	Triprolidine	Actifed	No difference from placebo	No
	Astemizole	Hismanol	Seasonal allergic rhinitis	Weight gain
Decongestants	Pseudoephedrine/phenylephrine spray	89 products listed in PDR	Reduces congestion, sneezing	Tachycardia, palpitations, elevated diastolic blood pressure, fatigue, dizziness, bladder outlet obstruction
Expectorants	Oxymetazoline spray	Dristan, Afrin	Improved symptom score	Rebound nasal congestion
	Guaifenesin	64 products listed in PDR	Marginal reduction sputum quantity, not in cough frequency	No
Anticholinergics	Ipratropium spray	Atrovent aerosol	Reduces nasal discharge and sneezing	Dry throat
	Atropine methonitrate spray		Reduces nasal discharge	Dry throat
Combinations	Decongestant/antihistamine	Many[b]	Reduces congestion, postnasal drip, rhinorrhea	Dry mouth, insomnia, nervousness

[a] See package insert for dose and schedule information.
[b] See Chapter 9, Table 9.5.

1) Dosage: 200 mg, then 100 mg twice a day for 5 days (once a day in frail elderly and in patients with renal failure)
2) Side effects — insomnia, nervousness, dizziness, difficulty concentrating — are uncommon, abate when drug is stopped
3) Indications
    (a) Unvaccinated persons with chronic disease
    (b) Patients with influenzal pneumonia
    (c) Persons whose activities are vital to the community, e.g., hospital personnel

4. Complications
  a) Airway hyperreactivity
    1) Manifested by wheezing, coughing, or both
    2) May last for weeks, occasionally for months
    3) Treat with a bronchodilator (Chapter 40) and, if necessary, 15–30 mg codeine at bedtime
  b) Pneumonia
    1) A special risk in the elderly
    2) Primary influenzal pneumonia — rare
      (a) Typical symptoms of influenza rapidly progress to cyanosis, delirium, respiratory distress syndrome
      (b) Immediate intensive care in a hospital is indicated
    3) Secondary bacterial pneumonia and bronchitis
      (a) Initial illness followed by improvement for several days, then fever again and purulent or bloody sputum
      (b) Predominant pathogen is *Streptococcus pneumoniae*, but *Haemophilus influenzae* and *Staphylococcus aureus* are also common (see section on pneumonia, below)
  c) Nonpulmonary complications — rare
5. Prevention — see Chapter 18

C. Pharyngitis
  1. General considerations
    a) Many patients not cultured; and if cultured, usual office procedure detects only streptococci
    b) No dominant organism
    c) If there is a presumptive diagnosis of bacterial pharyngitis (see below), erythromycin, 500 mg twice a day for 10 days, is drug of choice
  2. Group A streptococcal pharyngitis
    a) Abrupt-onset sore throat, malaise, fever, headache
    b) The combination of fever, tender nodes at angle of jaw, creamy white tonsillar exudate occurs in less than 10% of cases
    c) Cough, rhinorrhea not usually present
    d) Scarlet fever (diffuse red blush, initially truncal, blanches with pressure; ultimately desquamates) rare but specific
    e) Throat culture mandatory if diagnosis is suspected (Gram stain, streptococcus antigen tests are not sensitive enough)
    f) Treatment strategy based on presence or absence of tonsillar exudate, temperature higher than 100°F, tender anterior cervical adenopathy
      1) If all three signs present, treat (see below) before knowing the result of the culture

        2) If only one sign present, await result of culture before treating

        3) If no signs present, neither culture nor treat (unless history of rheumatic fever, in which case culture)

    g) Treatment strategy independent of clinical signs; treat before knowing results of culture:

        1) Patients with a history of rheumatic fever who are not taking prophylactic antibiotics

        2) Young patients with a strong family history of rheumatic fever

        3) All new cases of pharyngitis in an epidemic of streptococcal pharyngitis in a semiclosed population (e.g., military personnel)

    h) Treat symptomatic family contacts of patients with streptococcal pharyngitis if culture is positive (asymptomatic family contacts need not be cultured)

    i) Preferred treatment

        1) Parenteral benzathine penicillin 1.2 million units once

        2) If injection cannot be given, oral penicillin V 250 mg 3 times/day for 10 days

        3) If penicillin allergy, give erythromycin 250 mg every 6 hours for 10 days

3. Gonococcal pharyngitis

    a) Suspect if sore throat associated with urethritis or vaginitis

    b) Gram stain not useful

    c) Use calcium alginate swab, plate immediately on Thayer-Martin medium, send to regional or state laboratory

    d) Treat with ceftriaxone, 250 mg i.m. once (preferred), or erythromycin, 500 mg 4 times/day for 7 days

    e) Follow-up culture 7 days after completion of treatment

    f) Cotreatment for chlamydia (doxycycline 100 mg twice a day for 7 days) indicated

4. Diphtheria

    a) Suspect when there is a grayish membrane in the nose or on the tonsils, uvula, or pharynx

    b) Hospitalize for diagnosis and treatment

5. Other bacteria: other organisms often grown, do not warrant treatment

6. Vincent's angina

    a) Anaerobic infection characterized by fever, tender adenopathy, large grayish-brown pseudomembrane in pharynx, foul odor

    b) Hospitalize for treatment

D. Rheumatic fever

  1. Nonsuppurative inflammatory lesions of the heart, joints, and central nervous system after a group A streptococcal pharyngitis

  2. Latent period between infection and attack is 1–5 weeks (mean, 19 days)

  3. Diagnosis (Jones criteria)

    a) Two major criteria (carditis, polyarthritis, chorea, subcutaneous nodules, erythema marginatum)

    b) One major criterion, two minor criteria (fever, arthralgia, heart block, elevated acute-phase reactants such as granulocyte count, erythrocyte sedimentation rate, or C-reactive protein)

    c) Evidence of recent streptococcal infection: positive throat culture or rising titers of antistreptococcal antibodies (e.g., antistreptolysin-O titer, anti-DNAse B, antihyaluronidase)

4. Treatment: bed rest, analgesics, salicylates, and, depending on severity, corticosteroids

5. Prophylaxis against recurrence

    a) For young patients, patients at high risk of recurrent streptococcal infection (parents of young children, school teachers, medical and military personnel, people living in crowded conditions), people who have had acute rheumatic fever within 5 years

    b) Regimens

      1) Benzathine penicillin 1.2 million units i.m. every 4 weeks (preferred)

      2) Penicillin V 125–250 mg twice a day

      3) Sulfadiazine 1 g/day (for patients with penicillin allergy)

    c) May be discontinued if no history of carditis at age 18 or 5 years after last attack, whichever is longer

E. Chronic or relapsing sore throat

  1. Causes: Table 14.2

  2. Chronic tonsillitis

    a) Recurrent sore throats; very large tonsils; chronically enlarged, periodically tender lymph nodes

    b) Treat with clindamycin, 300 mg every 8 hours, or amoxicillin-clavulanate (Augmentin), 500 mg every 8 hours, for 7 days (to eliminate β-lactamase-producing organisms that inactivate penicillin)

F. Acute sinusitis

  1. Diagnosis

    a) In autumn, winter, spring, usually follows a viral upper respiratory infection; in summer, often associated with swimming, diving, or allergic rhinitis

    b) Pain (over infected sinus) initially dull, then throbbing, exacerbated by coughing, percussion over sinus

    c) May present without pain, usually as a cold that has persisted

Table 14.2. Causes of Chronic or Relapsing Sore Throat

Primary Site of Pain	Condition	See for Details
Pharynx	Chronic tonsillitis	
	Smoking (especially marijuana)	Chapter 8
	Postnasal drip	Chapter 39
	Infectious mononucleosis	Chapter 38
	Chronic fatigue syndrome	Chapter 38
	Agranulocytosis	
	Acute leukemia	
	Pemphigus	
Not the pharynx	Septic thyroiditis	Chapter 57
	Subacute thyroiditis	
	Angina (radiating to neck)	Chapter 42
	Psychogenic	Chapter 1

    for more than 2 weeks, accompanied by cough, purulent nasal discharge, headache

    d) Examination (pharynx, nose, ears, teeth, transillumination of sinuses) often unrevealing

    e) Most sensitive test: radiological examination including four views to visualize all paranasal sinuses — not necessary if diagnosis is obvious

  2. Treatment

    a) Culture unnecessary

    b) Ampicillin or amoxicillin, 250–500 mg, 4 times/day for 10 days (trimethoprim-sulfamethoxazole, 2 tablets 2 times/day for 10 days if patient allergic to penicillin)

    c) Augmentin if response is slow or if there is relapse

    d) Symptomatic therapy

      1) Neo-Synephrine spray, 0.25–0.5%, initial squirt followed by a second squirt in 5–10 minutes every 4 hours for 2–4 days, then an oral decongestant (see above, common cold)

      2) Pain relief may necessitate use of codeine

    e) If no response (or if symptoms intensify) in several days, refer to an otolaryngologist for further diagnosis and treatment

G. Chronic sinusitis

  1. Diagnosis

    a) Persistent purulent nasal discharge and postnasal drip despite adequate treatment of acute sinusitis

    b) Pain and tenderness minimal to absent

    c) X-rays may show clouding of cavities, thickening of the mucosal lining or bony sclerosis

  2. Treatment

    a) Penicillin V or ampicillin as above for 1 month (preferred)

    b) Alternatives: Augmentin, 250–500 mg, or clindamycin, 300–450 mg, every 8 hours

    c) Refer to an otolaryngologist for drainage if symptoms do not resolve

H. Pharyngeal abscess

  1. Most commonly peritonsillar and retropharyngeal

    a) Peritonsillar

      1) Characterized by severe odynophagia, muffled voice, trismus, fever, malaise

      2) Swelling of superior pole of anterior tonsillar pillar

      3) Tonsil may or may not be enlarged but displaced medially

    b) Retropharyngeal

      1) Same symptoms as peritonsillar abscess except trismus not common and breathing may be compromised

      2) Swelling seen in posterior oropharynx

  2. Management: incision and drainage by an otolaryngologist or an oral surgeon followed by antibiotics and warm saline gargles

I. Epiglottitis

  1. Abrupt onset of sore throat, dysphagia, progressive respiratory distress

  2. Stridor common, fever usual

  3. Oropharynx relatively uninvolved (may be red)

  4. Soft tissue x-rays may show edema of epiglottis, narrowing of the aperture

5. Diagnosis confirmed by indirect laryngoscopy, revealing epiglottal edema; procedure only done if emergency intubation can be done if necessary
6. Hospitalization mandatory

LOWER RESPIRATORY TRACT INFECTIONS

A. Acute bronchitis
  1. Characteristics
    a) Cough, productive in one-half of cases, persisting for more than a week or two after an upper respiratory infection
    b) Culture not of help
    c) A diagnosis of exclusion after pneumonia and noninfectious cause of cough (Chapter 39) have been ruled out
  2. Management
    a) Cough suppression (Chapter 39)
    b) If cough (with no or clear sputum) persists for several days and is accompanied by fever and malaise, treatment with erythromycin 500 mg 4 times/day for 14 days is reasonable; if symptoms do not abate in 5–7 days, azithromycin or clarithromycin 500 mg twice a day may be effective
    c) If cough (with colored sputum) persists and is accompanied by fever and malaise, ampicillin, amoxicillin, trimethoprim-sulfamethoxazole, and doxycycline are relatively inexpensive and are effective; if symptoms do not abate in 5–7 days, treat as above (2. b))
    d) Persistent hacking cough after 2 weeks of antibiotics may respond to bronchodilators or inhaled corticosteroids (Chapter 40)
B. Acute exacerbations of chronic bronchitis
  1. Characteristics
    a) Change in color, consistency and amount of sputum
    b) Possibly increased cough, dyspnea, fatigue
    c) Usually no fever or chills
    d) Gram stain and culture of sputum not of help
  2. Management
    a) Routine therapy of chronic bronchitis (Chapter 40)
    b) Avoid cough suppressants and sedatives
    c) Smoking cessation critical
    d) Reliable patients should be given a 7–10-day prescription of tetracycline (250 mg 4 times/day) or ampicillin (250–500 mg 4 times/day) to be taken at first sign of chest cold
C. Pneumonia
  1. Syndromes (Table 14.3)
    a) Bacterial pneumonias typically present with abrupt-onset shaking chills, fever, pleuritic chest pain, cough productive of purulent or rusty sputum
    b) Nonbacterial pneumonias characterized by prodrome of headache, myalgia followed by fever, malaise, nonproductive hacking cough, substernal chest pain
  2. Evaluation
    a) Physical examination usually does not distinguish bacterial from nonbacterial pneumonia (signs of consolidation suggest bacterial infection)

Table 14.3. Clues to the Presumptive Diagnosis and Treatment of Acute Pneumonia [a]

Organisms	Seasonal Incidence	Incubation Period (Days)	Epidemiological Setting	Clinical Clues	Antibiotics [b]
COMMON BACTERIA					
S. pneumoniae	All year		Elderly; smokers; cardiopulmonary disease, alcoholism	None [c]	Erythromycin (mild cases only), penicillin (when diagnosis known), cephalosporins, trimethoprim-sulfamethoxazole (not tetracycline, quinolones)
H. influenzae	All year		Same	None [c]	Amoxicillin, amoxicillin-clavulanate, trimethoprim-sulfamethoxazole, quinolones (erythromycin often not effective)
Moraxella catarrhalis	All year		Chronic obstructive pulmonary disease	None	Erythromycin (not amoxicillin), trimethoprim-sulfamethoxazole, quinolones
Legionella pneumophila	All year Summer outbreaks	2–10	Construction sites; air-cooling apparatus	Diarrhea [c] Fever > 40°C	Erythromycin (not β-lactams), quinolones
Chlamydia pneumoniae (TWAR)	All year	Not known	Young adults, person-to-person	Diarrhea [c] Pharyngitis Laryngitis	Erythromycin (not β-lactams)
Anaerobes	All year	1–5	Aspiration	Consolidation in dependent lobe	Amoxicillin-clavulanate, clindamycin, penicillin VK
Gram-negative aerobes	All year	1–5	Aspiration, alcoholism, elderly, recent hospitalization with antibiotics, institutionalization	Delirium; sepsis	Clindamycin (usually needs i.v. antibiotics)
UNCOMMON BACTERIA (<1% incidence)					
Psittacosis	All year	6–15	Exposure to birds, especially parrots, turkeys, pigeons, (20% have no bird exposure)		Erythromycin, doxycycline

	Season	Incubation (days)	Epidemiology	Symptoms	Treatment
Q fever	All year	14–28	Contact with sheep, goats, cattle, especially at parturition		Doxycycline, quinolones
Tularemia (pulmonary)	All year	2–4	Handling infected rodents, rabbits		Doxycycline
Plague (pneumonia)	Spring to fall	2–4	Handling infected rodents, humans, cats	Delirium, sepsis, bubo	Gentamicin, doxycycline
OTHER PATHOGENS					
Mycoplasma pneumoniae	Summer to fall	14–28	Multiple members of household ill, often at 3–4-week intervals	Pharyngitis, laryngitis, bullous myringitis, dry hacking cough persisting > 1 week	Erythromycin, tetracycline, doxycycline, quinolones
Respiratory syncytial virus	Spring	2–8	Contact with bronchiolitis in children, nosocomial spread		
Influenza A & B	Winter, spring	1–3	Accompany school absenteeism	Severe headache, myalgias	Amantadine, rimantadine (influenza A only)
Parainfluenza 1, 2, 3	All year	3–8	Croup in household	Conjunctivitis	
Adenovirus	Winter	4–5	Closed populations	Conjunctivitis	
Hantavirus	Spring to fall	Unknown	Close contact with deer mice in southwest states	Severe myalgias, pulmonary edema, low albumin	Ribavirin
Pneumocystis carinii	All year	Unknown	HIV risk group		Trimethoprim-sulfamethoxazole

[a] Tuberculosis and some fungal pneumonias may be indistinguishable from acute pneumonia (symptoms for <7 days).
[b] See practical information regarding strengths, dose, and side effects in Table 14.4.
[c] No differences in prodromal symptoms and respiratory tract symptoms among these four pathogens.

       b) White blood cell count of >15,000 suggests bacterial pneumonia

       c) Chest x-ray does not distinguish bacterial from nonbacterial pneumonia (and may be normal)

       d) Gram stain of sputum useful in demonstrating, e.g., pneumococci, staphylococci, *Haemophilus*

       e) Sputum cultures usually not of help

       f) If no response to treatment after 3–5 days and patient has been ill less than 14 days, obtain and store an acute-phase serum sample and, after 3 weeks of illness, obtain a convalescent sample and send to state or regional health laboratory (see Table 14.3)

   3. Management

     a) Hospitalization

       1) Over age 60, significant underlying disease

       2) White blood cell count < 5000, O^2 saturation < 90%

       3) Suspicion of aspiration

       4) Extrapulmonary complications (e.g., pleural effusion, metastatic infection)

       5) Hospitalization within the last 4 weeks or residence in a nursing home

       6) Sputum smear showing a predominance of Gram-negative bacteria

       7) Inability to be cared for at home

       8) Failure to respond to therapy

       9) Toxic, dyspneic, cyanotic, fatigued patients; hemoptysis; difficulty clearing secretions

     b) Antimicrobial therapy: Tables 14.3 and 14.4

     c) Follow-up

       1) Phone contact in 24 hours

       2) Follow-up office visit in 3–4 days (most patients will feel better)

       3) Another chest x-ray if no improvement in 5–7 days or if there is a relapse

       4) All patients over 40 and all smokers or ex-smokers should have a chest x-ray in 4–6 weeks to exclude lung cancer

   4. Pneumonia in a patient with HIV infection (see Chapter 20)

D. Pleurodynia

   1. Symptoms: abrupt-onset severe paroxysmal pain of thorax or abdomen, worse with cough or breathing, fever, headache, anorexia

   2. Physical examination normal except chest splinting to avoid pain

   3. Chest x-ray normal

   4. Recovery in 3–4 weeks

Table 14.4. Oral Antimicrobial Drugs Used in Ambulatory Treatment of Respiratory Infections

Drug[a] (Trade Name)	Available Strengths (mg)	Usual Adult Dose and Schedule	Common Side Effects	Drug and Food Interactions and Instructions
Penicillin V	250, 500	250–500 mg 3 or 4 times daily	Diarrhea, nausea, vomiting, vaginitis, skin rash	Rash with infectious mononucleosis or concomitant allopurinol, false-positive Clinitest (use Clinistix or Tes-tape)
Ampicillin	250, 500	250–500 mg 3 or 4 times daily		
Amoxicillin	250, 500	250–500 mg 3 or 4 times daily		
Amoxicillin-clavulanate (Augmentin)[b]	250, 500	250–500 mg every 8 hours		
Erythromycin	250, 500	250–500 mg 3 or 4 times daily	Nausea, vomiting, abdominal pain, diarrhea (less with azithromycin and clarithromycin)	False elevation of aminotransferase, raises serum theophylline and terfenadine levels, potentiates warfarin and glucocorticoids, increases risk of lovastatin-induced rhabdomyolysis
Azithromycin (Zithromax)[b]	250	500 mg loading dose 250 mg daily 1 hr before eating, for 4 days		
Clarithromycin (Biaxin)[b]	250, 500	500 mg twice daily		
Tetracycline	250, 500	250–500 mg 3 or 4 times daily	Skin photosensitivity, nausea, vomiting, heartburn, diarrhea, mucosal candidiasis	Food, milk, antacids, iron interfere with absorption
Doxycycline	100	100 mg twice daily		
Trimethoprim (T) plus Sulfamethoxazole (S)	80 T/400 S (single strength) 160 T/800 S (double strength)	2 single-strength or 1 double-strength twice daily	Skin rash, gastrointestinal upset, elevates serum creatinine	Prolongs half-life of warfarin, phenytoin, and oral hypoglycemics

Table 14.4. Continued

Drug[a] (Trade Name)	Available Strengths (mg)	Usual Adult Dose and Schedule	Common Side Effects	Drug and Food Interactions and Instructions
Clindamycin	150, 300	150–450 mg 4 times daily	*Clostridium difficile*-induced diarrhea	To avoid possible esophageal irritation, take with a full glass of water
Cefuroxime axetil (Ceftin)[b]	125, 250, 500	250–500 mg twice daily	Nausea, vomiting, diarrhea	Absorption enhanced with food, false-positive Clinitest
Cefaclor (Ceclor)[b]	250	250–500 mg every 8 hours		
Ciprofloxacin (Cipro)[b]	250, 500, 750	500 mg twice daily	Nausea, diarrhea, vomiting, restlessness	Prolongs half-life of theophylline; antacids interfere with absorption; central nervous system side effects increased with caffeine
Ofloxacin (Floxin)[b]	400	400 mg twice daily		

[a]No trade name is listed for those available in generic preparations.
[b]Courses of these cost more than $50.

15/ TUBERCULOSIS IN THE AMBULATORY PATIENT

TUBERCULOSIS: DEFINITIONS, DIAGNOSIS, AND TREATMENT

A. Definitions
1. Primary
   a) In an immunocompetent adult, manifest by conversion to a positive tuberculin skin test; patients are not infectious
   b) In an immunosuppressed patient (e.g., a patient with HIV infection), severe progressive disease may develop
2. Reactivation
   a) In a patient who was infected and never treated or was inadequately treated and, when old or immunosuppressed, develops clinically active disease
   b) Patients are infectious
B. Diagnosis
1. History
   a) Symptoms almost always of weeks to months duration
   b) Common nonspecific symptoms: weight loss, fever (particularly late evening), night sweats, anorexia, malaise
   c) Common pulmonary symptoms: cough with productive sputum, hemoptysis, pleuritic chest pain
   d) Important to know, if possible, whether patient has had tuberculosis (Tbc), whether tuberculin skin test has been done and, if so, whether it was positive, whether previous chest films are available, whether any close associate has had Tbc, whether the patient has been in a developing country
2. Physical examination
   a) May be negative
   b) Helpful findings if positive: rales localized to the upper posterior chest, bronchovesicular breathing and whispered pectoriloquy (signs of cavitation), evidence of pleural effusion, supraclavicular and infraclavicular retraction, lymphadenopathy, evidence of weight loss, fever
3. Tuberculin skin tests
   a) Five units of intermediate-strength purified protein derivative (PPD) applied intradermally on the volar forearm
   b) Read at 48 hours
   c) A positive test is 10 mm or more of induration (ignore erythema); in HIV-infected people, even 2 mm of induration may be considered positive
   d) Control tests with ubiquitous antigens on other arm (e.g., *Candida* or mumps)
   e) Useful to detect recently infected, otherwise-healthy young people, to evaluate close associates of people with active disease
   f) Not useful to evaluate patients with nonspecific symptoms because prevalence of positive reaction may be high in patients without active disease and because patients with active disease may be anergic
   g) If test is positive, it should not be repeated (to avoid a severe reaction)

      h) Cross-reactions with related mycobacteria (not *Mycobacterium tuberculosis*) occur

      i) Booster phenomenon

         1) A positive test on repeat injection 1 week after a negative test in a patient who had a remote infection

         2) Useful in elderly (common) and in hospital employees, who are tested frequently

   4. Laboratory evaluation

      a) Chest x-ray

         1) Posteroanterior (PA) and lateral views

         2) Apical lordotic view if suspicion of disease is high and PA and lateral views are normal

         3) Negative very rarely in patients with pulmonary Tbc

         4) Typical but nonspecific findings: apical scarring, hilar adenopathy with peripheral infiltrate, upper lobe cavitation

      b) Cultures and smears

         1) Obtain sputum 3 times

         2) Positive smear highly suggestive of active disease (possibility of atypical organism)

         3) Positive culture diagnostic

         4) Stimulation of sputum by inhalation of aerosolized hypertonic saline sometimes necessary

         5) If organism cultured, important to establish drug sensitivity

   5. Miscellaneous tests

      a) Complete blood count: hematocrit value may be normal or low

      b) White blood cell count and differential count usually normal; monocytosis sometimes seen

      c) Urinalysis should be done routinely; sterile pyuria suggests renal Tbc, so urine cultures should be obtained

      d) Liver function tests if disseminated disease is suspected

   6. Tbc in HIV-infected patients

      a) An AIDS indicator condition (Chapter 20) in an HIV-infected patient

      b) If Tbc precedes the advent of another AIDS indicator condition, the presentation of Tbc is usually typical (see above); tuberculin skin test is usually positive

      c) If Tbc follows the advent of another AIDS indicator condition, presentation is often atypical (e.g., involvement of the lower lobes of the lung, more extrapulmonary disease), and tuberculin skin test is negative half the time

C. Treatment

   1. Treat on the basis of a presumptive diagnosis (cultures take 4 weeks)

   2. Chemotherapy (Tables 15.1 and 15.2)

      a) Second-line drugs

         1) For people with resistant disease, with previously treated disease, who have had adverse reactions to the standard drugs

         2) Refer to an expert in treatment of Tbc

      b) Ethambutol should not be given to patients with renal impairment

      c) Extrapulmonary disease treated identically to pulmonary disease (some recommend 9 months treatment)

Table 15.1. Regimen Options for the Initial Treatment of Tuberculosis Among Children and Adults

	Tuberculosis Without HIV Infection			Tuberculosis With HIV Infection
Option 1	Option 2	Option 3		
Administer daily INH, RIF, and PZA for 8 weeks, followed by 16 weeks of INH and RIF daily or 2–3 times/week.[a] In areas where the INH resistance rate is not documented to be <4%, EMB or SM should be added to the initial regimen until susceptibility to INH and RIF is demonstrated. Continue treatment for at least 6 months and 3 months beyond culture conversion. Consult a Tbc medical expert if the patient is symptomatic or smear or culture positive after 3 months.	Administer daily INH, RIF, PZA, and SM or EMB for 2 weeks, followed by 2 times/week[a] administration of the same drugs for 6 weeks (by DOT), and subsequently, with 2 times/week administration of INH and RIF for 16 weeks (by DOT). Consult a Tbc medical expert if the patient is symptomatic or smear or culture positive after 3 months.	Treat by DOT 3 times/week with INH, RIF, PZA, and EMB or SM for 6 months.[b] Consult a Tbc medical expert if the patient is symptomatic or smear or culture positive after 3 months.		Options 1, 2, or 3 can be used, but treatment regimens should continue for a total of 9 months and at least 6 months beyond culture conversion.

From Centers for Disease Control and Prevention: Initial therapy for tuberculosis in the era of multidrug resistance: recommendations of the Advisory Council for the Elimination of Tuberculosis. *MMWR* 42(No. RR-7): May 21, 1993.

DOT, directly observed treatment; *EMB*, ethambutol; *INH*, isoniazid; *PZA*, pyrazinamide; *RIF*, rifampin; *SM*, streptomycin.

[a] All regimens administered 2 times/week or 3 times/week should be monitored by DOT for the duration of therapy.

[b] The strongest evidence from clinical trials is the effectiveness of all four drugs administered for the full 6 months. There is weaker evidence that SM can be discontinued after 4 months if the isolate is susceptible to all drugs. The evidence for stopping PZA before the end of 6 months is equivocal for the 3 times/week regimen, and there is no evidence on the effectiveness of this regimen with EMB for less than the full 6 months.

Table 15.2. Drugs for the Treatment of Mycobacterial Disease in Adults

Commonly Used Agents	Available Strengths of Oral Tablets or Capsules (mg)	Dosage			Most Common Side Effects	Tests for Side Effects	Drug Interactions[a]
		Total Once Daily Dose	Twice Weekly Dosage	Three Times Weekly Dosage			
Isoniazid[b]	100, 300	5–10 mg/kg up to 300 mg p.o. or i.m.	15 mg/kg p.o. or i.m.	15 mg/kg up to 900 mg p.o. or i.m.	Peripheral neuritis, hepatitis, hypersensitivity	Aminotransferases (not as a routine)	Carbamazepine: increased toxicity, both drugs Disulfiram: psychosis, ataxia Phenytoin: toxicity increased
Rifampin	600	10 mg/kg up to 600 mg p.o.	10 mg/kg up to 600 mg p.o.	10 mg/kg p.o.	Hepatitis, febrile reaction, purpura (rare)	Aminotransferases (not as a routine)	May reduce the effect of the following drugs due to increased hepatic metabolism: oral contraceptives, quinidine, corticosteroids, anticoagulants, disopyramide, diazepam, barbiturates, methadone, digitoxin, digoxin, oral hypoglycemics; p-aminosalicylic acid may interfere with absorption of rifampin
Streptomycin		15–20 mg/kg up to 1 g i.m.	25–30 mg/kg up to 1 g i.m.	25–30 mg/kg up to 1 g i.m.	Eighth nerve damage, nephrotoxicity	Vestibular function, audiograms; blood urea nitrogen and creatinine	Neuromuscular blocking agents — may be potentiated to cause prolonged paralysis
Pyrazinamide	500	15–30 mg/kg up to 2 g p.o.	50–70 mg/kg p.o.	50–70 mg/kg up to 3 g p.o.	Hyperuricemia, hepatotoxicity	Uric acid, aminotransferases	
Ethambutol	100, 400	15–25 mg/kg p.o.	50 mg/kg p.o.	25–30 mg/kg up to 2.5 g p.o.	Optic neuritis (reversible with discontinuation of drug; very rare at 15 mg/kg), skin rash	Red-green color discrimination and visual acuity;[c] difficult to test in a child under 3 years	

Adapted from American Thoracic Society: Treatment of tuberculosis and tuberculosis infection in adults and children. *Am Rev Respir Dis* 134: 355, 1986; and *MMWR* 42:2, 1993.

[a] Reference should be made to current literature, particularly on rifampin, because it induces hepatic microenzymes and therefore interacts with many drugs.

[b] With pyridoxine 25 mg daily for poorly nourished or pregnant patients, to prevent peripheral neuropathy.

[c] Initial examination should be done at start of treatment.

    d) If isoniazid is given, pyridoxine 25 mg/day should be taken to prevent neuropathy if patient is eating poorly, is pregnant, or has another disease associated with neuropathy (e.g., diabetes mellitus)

D. Course in treated patients
1. Follow-up schedule
    a) See patient at least monthly to ensure compliance, monitor for drug side effects
    b) Sputum culture monthly for the first 3 months and at 5 or 6 months (latter should be negative)
    c) Chest x-ray at 3 months and between 6 and 12 months to exclude progression of disease and in documenting status when Tbc is cured
    d) If treated for 9 months, further follow-up not necessary; if treated for 6 months, see every few months for another year to detect relapse
2. Usual response
    a) If organisms are sensitive and drugs are tolerated, prognosis is excellent
    b) Some symptomatic improvement within 1 week; afebrile within 10 days; at baseline state of health in 1–2 months
    c) Noninfectious after a few days to a few weeks
3. Respiratory isolation
    a) At home, cover mouth and nose when coughing or sneezing; wear a surgical mask in a public place
    b) Should have negative sputum before being in shelters for homeless or in places where HIV-infected people might be exposed
4. Possible complications
    a) Drug resistance
        1) Never add one drug to a failing regimen
        2) Refer to the local health department before changing the regimen
        3) Keep the patient in respiratory isolation until cured
        4) Treatment may require up to 6 drugs, may take 18–36 months
    b) Drug toxicity (Table 15.2)

PREVENTION OF TUBERCULOSIS

A. Case detection among known contacts
1. Tuberculin testing of all household and intimate contacts and retesting of nonreactors in 2–3 months, usually done at local health department
2. Reactors have chest x-rays; if no evidence of active disease, they are treated with isoniazid for 1 year (see below)
B. Role of tuberculin testing (see above) in prevention
1. Test status should be evaluated sometime in young adulthood, repeated periodically in high-risk populations (urban, chronically ill, history of residence in an underdeveloped country); physicians and hospital personnel at risk should be tested yearly
C. Isoniazid prophylaxis
1. Dose: 300 mg/day for 6–12 months (latter period for immunosuppressed persons)

2. For the following groups:
   a) Close contacts of active cases, especially young children and HIV-infected people, regardless of PPD status
   b) Persons with recent skin test conversion (see above)
   c) Persons with positive skin tests and a chest x-ray suggestive of old Tbc
   d) Persons with a history of active Tbc who were never treated
   e) Persons with positive skin test who are to be given corticosteroids or immunosuppressive therapy, who have silicosis, who have had a gastrectomy, or who have a disease altering cellular immunity (e.g., HIV infection)
   f) Persons under 35 years with a positive skin test
3. Monitoring guidelines
   a) Monthly inquiry about symptoms (e.g., anorexia, nausea, fatigue) or signs of liver toxicity (e.g., dark urine, icterus, fever) or of neurological toxicity (e.g., persistent paresthesias)
   b) Provide no more than 1 month's supply of isoniazid
   c) Routine monitoring of hepatic function not necessary, but liver function tests must be done if there are signs and symptoms of toxicity
   d) Measurement of aminotransferase activity monthly in high-risk groups: persons over 35 years, daily "drinkers," persons taking other potentially hepatotoxic drugs, patients with a history of liver disease; discontinue isoniazid if levels are 3 or more times normal

16/ SELECTED SPIROCHETAL INFECTIONS: SYPHILIS AND LYME DISEASE

SYPHILIS
A. Stages of the disease: Table 16.1
   1. Differential diagnosis of a genital sore: Table 16.2 (refer to a sexually transmitted disease (STD) clinic if syphilis suspected)
   2. Sensitivity and specificity of serological tests at different stages (Table 16.3)
     a) Nontreponemal tests detect reagin, a nonspecific antibody to cardiolipin; VDRL and RPR are used most often
     b) Treponemal tests (fluorescent treponemal antibody-absorption test [FTA-ABS] and microhemagglutination test for *Treponema pallidum* [MHA-TP]) detect specific antibodies to *T. pallidum*
     c) Biological false positive test: reactive nontreponemal test, nonreactive treponemal test
       1) Less than 6 months: pneumonia, hepatitis, pregnancy, mononucleosis, measles, often smallpox vaccination
       2) More than 6 months: diseases of disordered immunity (e.g., systemic lupus erythematosus, rheumatoid arthritis), chronic liver disease, intravenous drug addicts, elderly
     d) Cerebrospinal fluid (CSF)-VDRL is the test of choice in workup for neurosyphilis, but its sensitivity varies (low in asymptomatic patients or with tabes dorsalis)
     e) Screening serology: use nontreponemal test
     f) Pattern after treatment: Figure 16.1
B. Treatment
   1. Regimens
     a) For primary, secondary, early latent syphilis, and for contacts of infected patients, 2–4 million units benzathine penicillin G i.m. (some advocate a repeat dose in 1 week)
       1) For penicillin-allergic patients, tetracycline, 500 mg 4 times/ day for 2 weeks, or doxycycline, 100 mg 2 times/day for 2 weeks
       2) For tetracycline or doxycycline-intolerant, penicillin-allergic patients, ceftriaxone 250 mg/day i.m. for 10 days
     b) For late latent, cardiovascular syphilis or for patients with gummas, 2.4 million units benzathine penicillin G i.m. weekly for 3 weeks
       1) Exclude neurosyphilis first
       2) For penicillin-allergic patients, tetracycline, 500 mg 4 times/ day for 4 weeks, or doxycycline, 100 mg 2 times/day for 4 weeks
     c) For confirmed neurosyphilis (see above), 12–24 million units of aqueous crystalline penicillin G i.v. daily (2–4 million units every 4 hours) for 10–14 days

Table 16.1. Outline of the Clinical Stages of Syphilis

Stage	Characteristic Findings	Usual Onset After Exposure	Duration of Stage in Untreated Patients	Dark Field
Primary	Chancre — may be absent or not visible (e.g., in vagina or mouth)	10–90 days (average 21 days)	2–6 weeks	+ (chancre, lymph nodes)
Secondary	Rash, condyloma latum, lymphadenopathy	6 weeks to 6 months	2–6 weeks; recurrences in 25% over 4-year period	+ (especially moist lesions)
Latent				
Early	None	< 1 year after infection	May be lifelong, since only one-third of untreated patients develop tertiary syphilis	–
Late	None	> 1 year after infection		
Late (tertiary)				
Benign	Gumma	2–10 years	Indolent	–
Cardiovascular	Aorta aneurysm	10–30 years	Progressive; may be fatal	Aorta may be +
	Aortic insufficiency			
	Coronary artery disease especially of the ostia			
Neurosyphilis				
Asymptomatic	None	2–35 years	Progressive; may be fatal	
Acute syphilitic meningitis	Headache, cranial nerve lesions, papilledema	6 weeks to 2 years	Not applicable	
Meningovascular	Signs of infection depend on area involved	2–10 years		Brain may be +
Paresis	Minor personality changes to frank psychosis	15–35 years		
Tabes dorsalis	Signs of posterior column degeneration	5–30 years		

Table 16.2. Differential Diagnosis of a Genital Sore

Primary syphilis (chancre)
  Incubation period 10–90 days (average, 21 days)
  Usually painless (in absence of secondary infection)
  Not vesicular
  Usually single indurated ulcer, but multiple leasions are seen in 30% of cases
  Spirochete on dark-field examination
  Nontender inguinal adenopathy
Herpes simplex
  Incubation period 24–48 hours
  Usually painful
  Vesicular
  Usually multiple ulcers
  Multinucleated giant cells on Giemsa stain plus virus on culture
  Tender inguinal adenopathy
Chancroid
  Multiple soft superficial erosions
  Nontender adenopathy; *Haemophilus ducreyi* on Gram stain of dried smear (small Gram-
    negative bacillus)
Granuloma inguinale
  Soft, occasionally raised, granulating lesions in inguinal area: Donovan bodies on smear
    (histiocytes with intracytoplasmic encapsulated Gram-negative bacilli)
Other considerations
  Trauma, carcinoma, scabies, lichen planus, psoriasis, fixed drug eruption (especially
    phenolphthalein), fungus infection, folliculitis

---

1) If compliance is ensured, procaine penicillin G, 2.4 million units i.m. once a day, plus probenecid, 500 mg 4 times/day, is a reasonable outpatient alternative
2) If patient is penicillin-allergic, infectious disease consultation is indicated to suggest an alternative regimen

2. Effectiveness
   a) Primary and secondary syphilis
      1) Judged by disappearance of signs and symptoms, 4-fold fall in VDRL titer within 1 year
      2) Of penicillin-treated patients, 5% and, of tetracycline-treated patients, 20% have persistent or recurrent infection
   b) Latent syphilis: treatment appears to be 100% effective
   c) Cardiovascular syphilis: treatment probably arrests the disease but does not reverse its effects (e.g., aortic aneurysm)
   d) Neurosyphilis
      1) Treatment often reverses signs and symptoms of acute meningovascular syphilis and stabilizes tabes dorsalis but may have no effect in patients with general paresis
      2) In addition to signs of disease, CSF cell count is an index of response (repeat every 6 months until clear if initial tap shows pleocytosis; if no improvement in 6 months or if not clear by 2 years, re-treat)

3. Jarisch-Herxheimer reaction
   a) Usually a mild fever within 6–8 hours of first injection of penicillin
   b) Resolves within a few hours, does not occur after subsequent injections

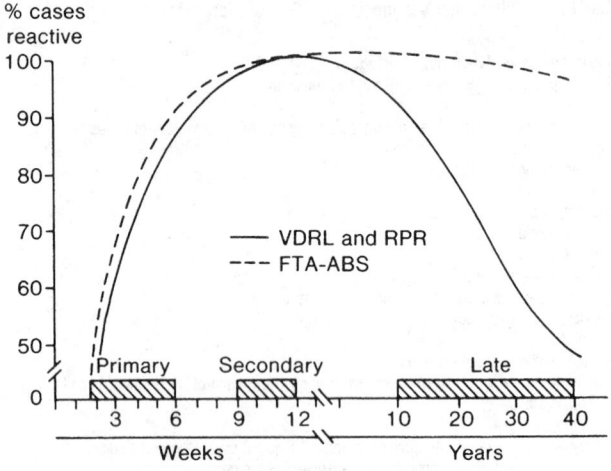

Figure 16.1.   Serology of untreated syphilis. (Adapted from Wallace AL, Norins LC: Syphilis serology today. *Prog Clin Pathol* 2:198, 1969.)

      c) Occurs in 50% of patients with primary syphilis, 75–90% with secondary syphilis, 30% with late disease

      d) Rarely, may be characterized by high fever, chills, headaches, myalgias, arthralgias, sore throat, transient hypotension; corticosteroids often administered, but efficacy uncertain

    4. Follow-up

      a) Nontreponemal titer the most useful index of effectiveness

      b) If initial titer is 1:4 or greater, test should be repeated every 3 months for a year to see if a 4-fold fall has occurred (if not, re-treat as above)

      c) If nontreponemal titer remains high at 1 year, CSF examination warranted

      d) If initial titer low (e.g., in late latent syphilis), no way to assess adequacy of treatment

      e) All identified sexual contacts must be evaluated for syphilis (and treated as above) before serological test results are known if patient has primary, secondary, or early latent syphilis

C. HIV infection and syphilis

    1. Strong association warrants testing for HIV infection in all patients suspected to have syphilis

    2. HIV-infected patients with syphilis should be treated as above, but nontreponemal tests should be repeated monthly for 6 months to look for treatment failure (see Follow-up, above)

LYME DISEASE

A. Epidemiology

    1. Most common tick-borne illness in the United States

Table 16.3. Sensitivity and Specificity of Serological Tests for Syphilis [a] at Different Stages

| | Percentage of Sensitivity (Sens.) and Specificity (Spec.) | | | | | | | |
| Stage of Syphilis | VDRL | | RPR | | FTA-ABS | | MHA-TP | |
	Sens.	Spec.	Sens.	Spec.	Sens.	Spec.	Sens.	Spec.
Primary	80 (59–87)	98 (80–99)	86 (81–100)	98 (80–99)	98 (93–100)	98 (84–99)	82 (64–90)	99 (98–100)
Secondary	100 (99–100)	98	100 (99–100)	98	100 (99–100)	98	100	99
Latent	96 (73–100)	98	99	98	100 (96–100)	98	100 (96–100)	99
Tertiary (late)	71	98	73	98	96	98	94	99

[a] The consensus figures for the sensitivity and specificity are for tests done in the CDC Reference Laboratory on samples derived from a well-run STD clinic. The figures in parentheses demonstrate the variability in published reports. Responsible factors include (a) study of populations with different prevalences of syphilis and other confounding illnesses, (b) variable performance by the laboratory, and (c) different clinical criteria for the diagnosis of syphilis (see the text).

  2. Caused by spirochete *Borrelia burgdorferi,* carried in most cases
     by ticks that have attached to deer and/or mice at some point in
     their life cycle
  3. Most common in the northeastern United States but has been
     reported in 45 states
B. Stages
  1. Primary Lyme disease
     a) Incubation period 3–32 days
     b) Most common sign: an expanding lesion at site of bite, starting
        as a red macule or papule, spreading with a clearing center
        (erythema chronicum migrans), warm, not pruritic or painful
     c) Flu-like symptoms common
     d) Regional or generalized adenopathy often present
     e) Resolves, even if untreated, in 3–4 weeks
  2. Secondary Lyme disease
     a) Within 1–6 months of bite
     b) Dermatological manifestations
        1) Multiple annular lesions
        2) Usually accompanied by severe lethargy, myalgias,
           generalized adenopathy, splenomegaly
     c) Cardiac manifestations in 4–10%
        1) Arrhythmias, heart block, cardiomyopathy, heart failure
        2) Atrioventricular block, the most common abnormality,
           usually resolves, even without treatment, within 6 weeks
     d) Neurological manifestations in 20%
        1) Meningitis — headache, stiff neck, nausea, vomiting,
           malaise, fatigue — lasting for weeks to months
           (a) One-half have depressed consciousness, cognitive or
               behavioral abnormalities, sometimes with seizures,
               ataxia, paresis
           (b) CSF shows mononuclear cells (usually < 500);
               moderately elevated protein, normal glucose
               concentrations
           (c) Abnormal electroencephalogram
           (d) Computed tomography scan usually normal but may
               show focal areas of increased attenuation with contrast
               enhancement
        2) Cranial and peripheral neuropathies the most characteristic
           abnormality
           (a) Most commonly, facial nerve palsies
           (b) Asymmetrical radicular pain common, with decreased
               sensation, weakness, lost reflexes
     e) Rheumatological manifestations in 60%; self-limited episodes
        of asymmetric arthritis, especially in the knees
  3. Tertiary Lyme disease
     a) Weeks to years after the primary infection
     b) Rheumatological manifestations
        1) Most commonly in knees
        2) Lasts weeks to months, sometimes, a chronic arthritis
           develops
     c) Dermatological manifestations: acrodermatitis chronica
        atrophicans
        1) Mostly in elderly, 6–8 months after initial infection

  2) A red or violaceous, sometimes nodular discoloration in swollen skin of acral areas
  3) Lesions may be painful or pruritic
  4) May become atrophic or sclerotic
 d) Neurological manifestations
  1) Encephalopathy, polyneuropathy, leukoencephalopathy
  2) May begin years after primary infection

C. Diagnosis
 1. History of tick bite and compatible clinical findings are important
 2. Available tests: ELISA or immunofluorescent assays, Western blot techniques — not standardized, poorly reproducible

D. Treatment
 1. Primary Lyme disease
  a) Nonpregnant women and other adults: doxycycline, 100 mg 2 times/day for 10–21 days, or amoxicillin, 250 mg 3 times/day for 10–12 days, depending on response
  b) Amoxicillin preferred for pregnant or lactating women
  c) In patients intolerant of or allergic to tetracycline or penicillin, erythromycin 250 mg 4 times/day may be used but is less effective (cefuroxime axetil or azithromycin may also work)
  d) Treatment shortens course, reduces incidence, and attenuates manifestations of later disease
 2. Secondary and tertiary Lyme disease
  a) Patients with acrodermatitis, minor cardiac, or neurological manifestations should be treated as are patients with primary disease (patients with Bell's palsy should be treated for a month)
  b) Patients with more severe cardiac or neurological disease or with arthritis should be treated with penicillin, 20 million units/day i.v., or ceftriaxone, 2 g 2 times/day i.v., for 14 days
   1) Corticosteroids may be of help if carditis does not respond to antimicrobials
   2) Patients with arthritis may respond also to doxycycline, 100 mg twice a day, or amoxicillin, 500 mg 3 times/day, for a month

E. Prevention
 1. Remove ticks within 48 hours of attachment
 2. Wearing of light-colored, long trousers treated with an insect repellent when at risk of tick exposure
 3. Antimicrobial prophylaxis not recommended after a tick bite

17/ AMBULATORY CARE FOR SELECTED INFECTIONS, INCLUDING OSTEOMYELITIS, LUNG ABSCESS, AND ENDOCARDITIS

OSTEOMYELITIS

A. Clinical presentation: Table 17.1
B. Laboratory evaluation
  1. Radiology
    a) Plain films not abnormal until 30–50% of bone resorbed (10–14 days)
    b) Earliest x-ray changes are lytic lesions; other findings include soft tissue swelling, periosteal reaction, cortical irregularity, demineralization, and sequestrum formation
    c) If diagnosis suspected and x-ray normal, technetium bone scan or indium-111 leukocyte scan can be of help: good sensitivity (70–90%), poor specificity (50–75%)
  2. Needle aspiration (by an orthopedist) and culture
    a) Imperative for diagnosis and treatment
    b) If subperiosteal pus is obtained, surgical drainage is mandatory
    c) If no pus is obtained, a needle is inserted into bone to obtain a specimen
    d) Cultures often contaminated, so organisms recovered in small concentrations or that grow only in broth may not be the cause of the infection
    e) Gram stain an important adjunct to culture
C. Treatment
  1. Strict immobilization not necessary
  2. Antimicrobial treatment
    a) Acute osteomyelitis
      1) 3–6-week course
      2) Staphylococcal infection
        (a) Preferred: penicillinase-resistant penicillin (e.g., nafcillin) 1.5–2.0 gm every 6 hours
        (b) Alternative: parenteral cefazolin (1.0–1.5 gm every 8 hours), vancomycin (500 mg every 6 hours), or clindamycin (600 mg every 8 hours)
        (c) Intravenous antimicrobials for 1 or 2 weeks or until the patient is afebrile, followed by oral clindamycin (300 mg every 6 hours) or oral dicloxacillin or cephalexin (500 mg every 6 hours), may be effective, but is not a well-established regimen yet in adults
      3) Choice of antimicrobial for Gram-negative infection should be based on in vitro sensitivity

Table 17.1. Types of Osteomyelitis

	Hematogenous	Secondary to Contiguous Infection	Complications of Vascular Insufficiency
Approximate proportion of all cases	20%	50%	30%
Commonest age group(s)	1–16 years	Any age	>50 years
	>50 years		
Bones involved	Long bones (children)	Hip, femur, tibia, digits	Feet
	Vertebrae (adults)		
Predisposing causes	Trauma	Surgery	Diabetes mellitus
	Bacteremia	Soft tissue infection	Vascular insufficiency
Usual bacteria	Staphylococcus aureus	Often polymicrobial: Gram-negative bacilli,	Usually polymicrobial: Gram-negative bacilli,
	Gram-negative bacilli	S. aureus	anaerobes, streptococci, S. aureus
Presentation			
Initial episode	Fever, local pain swelling, tenderness,	Fever, local pain swelling, tenderness,	Ulceration drainage ± pain
	limited movement	limited movement	
	Sinus drainage ± pain	Sinus drainage ± pain	
Recurrent episode	Sinus drainage ± pain	Sinus drainage ± pain	Drainage ± pain

      b) Chronic osteomyelitis
         1) Surgical excision of dead tissue and adequate debridement are important
         2) Antimicrobial therapy is based on bacteriological diagnosis, but no firm guidelines exist for establishing dosage schedule; general agreement that prolonged treatment (e.g., 6 months or more) is warranted

D. Late complications
  1. Major one is recurrent infection, heralded by fever, draining sinuses, local pain, change in x-ray or bone scan
  2. Amyloidosis now rare
  3. Epidermoid carcinoma in a draining sinus in 0.2–1.5% of cases after many years

LUNG ABSCESS

A. Clinical presentation
  1. Primary lung abscesses (80% of cases) occur primarily in people prone to aspiration (e.g., alcoholics) but may be seen in otherwise-healthy people
  2. Secondary lung abscesses (20% of cases) are complications of another disease (e.g., lung cancer or a disease of altered immunity)
  3. Primary pathogens are anaerobes, but some aerobic bacteria (e.g., *Staphylococcus aureus, Klebsiella pneumoniae*) may cause abscesses

B. Laboratory evaluation
  1. Chest x-ray, complete blood count, blood cultures, Gram stain, Ziehl-Neelsen stain (for tuberculosis) of sputum
  2. Ideal specimen for identification of anaerobes is a transtracheal aspirate but not necessary in typical patients (e.g., with a condition that predisposes to aspiration or with putrid sputum)
  3. Bronchoscopy not useful for obtaining of a specimen to culture

C. Treatment
  1. Anaerobic: Table 17.2
  2. Aerobic: dependent on culture and sensitivity
  3. Inadequate response
    a) If there is no continued improvement at home and patient is taking penicillin, switch to clindamycin or add metronidazole (Flagyl) 500 mg 4 times/day
    b) Failure to show progressive improvement may suggest need for bronchoscopy (to exclude obstruction)
    c) Surgery for totally refractory abscesses, life-threatening hemorrhage, or obstruction

ENDOCARDITIS

A. Management in hospital indicated for diagnostic evaluation, initial intravenous administration of antibiotics
B. Management out of hospital
  1. Antimicrobial treatment
    a) Selected on basis of in vitro sensitivity tests with an emphasis on bacteriocidal activity
    b) Typically, 4–6 weeks of intravenous therapy, but with a home care agency, most of treatment course can be at home

Table 17.2.   Antimicrobial Regimens for Primary Lung Abscess

Intravenous[a]	Oral[a]	Comments
Aqueous penicillin G 5–10 million units/day	Penicillin G or V 500–750 mg 4 times/day *or* Amoxicillin 500 mg 4 times/day *or* Amoxicillin-clavulanate 250–500 mg every 8 hours[b]	Regarded as standard *Advantages:* inexpensive and well tolerated *Disadvantages:* about 20% fail to respond, and additional patients have delayed response *Advantage:* coverage for organisms that produce β-lactamase *Disadvantage:* expensive
Clindamycin 600 mg every 6–8 hours	Clindamycin 300 mg 4 times/day	*Advantage:* optimal response rates *Disadvantages:* expensive; side effects include 10–20% with diarrhea and occasional patients with pseudomembranous colitis

[a] Intravenous treatment until patient is afebrile and clinically improved; oral treatment is given either to complete an arbitrary total course of 3–6 weeks of treatment or until chest x-rays show clearance or a small, stable residual lesion.

[b] Both strengths listed are for amoxicillin; both contain 125 mg of clavulanate.

      c) Two-week courses have been advocated by some for *Streptococcus viridans* and *Streptococcus bovis* infection

      d) Prosthetic valve endocarditis requires at least 6 weeks of treatment with intravenous drugs selected on basis of in vitro sensitivity

  2. Follow-up

      a) Complications: heart failure, relapse, mycotic aneurysms, recurrence with new organisms

      b) Blood cultures warranted 2–3 days after antibiotics discontinued: relapse requires second course of treatment and/or surgery, depending on condition of valve, sensitivity of organism

      c) Valve replacement, if necessary, usually because of refractory heart failure, should be deferred, if possible, until 6 weeks after antibiotics have been discontinued

      d) Mycotic aneurysms (in 15% of cases) most commonly appear several months or more after treatment

         1) Intracranial arteries most often involved; chest and abdominal arteries next most often

         2) Demonstrated by computed tomography scanning if intracranial, by arteriography otherwise

         3) Surgery almost always indicated

      e) Antibiotic prophylaxis indicated with endoscopy, surgery, dental procedures (see Chapter 53)

18/ IMMUNIZATION TO PREVENT INFECTIOUS DISEASE

PATIENT ASSESSMENT
A. History
   1. Previous immunizations, especially for deciding whether to give tetanus toxoid/antitoxin, to consider diphtheria in the diagnosis of acute pharyngitis, and for deciding what immunizations are needed for persons traveling outside the United States
   2. Prior allergic reactions or other untoward reactions to vaccines or their components — contents of vaccine should be determined from package insert
   3. Immunosuppressed persons should not receive live virus vaccines, nor if virus is shed (e.g., polio) should vaccine be given if an immunosuppressed person is a close contact of the patient
   4. In general, live virus vaccines should not be given to pregnant women (and pregnancy should be prevented for 3 months after the vaccine is given)
   5. Many live virus vaccines should not be given within 2 weeks of administration of immune globulin (yellow fever and oral polio are exceptions)
   6. Vaccines should not be given to acutely febrile patients
B. Physical and laboratory evaluation — usually unnecessary

IMMUNIZATION PROCEDURES
A. General considerations
   1. Simultaneous vaccine administration
      a) Inactivated vaccines can be given simultaneously at the same site
      b) An inactivated and a live attenuated virus vaccine can be given simultaneously at separate sites
      c) Some live virus vaccines can be given together (e.g., measles, mumps, rubella)
   2. Possible side effects should be explained; patient should be observed for 15 minutes after injection
   3. A written record of vaccinations should be kept by the patient
B. Current recommendations (Table 18.1)
   1. Hepatitis A
      a) Pooled human immune globulin
         1) 80–90% effective in acutely exposed persons in preventing hepatitis
         2) Should be given to family members of intimate contacts of persons with hepatitis A (0.02 ml/kg) and to travelers to developing countries (see Chapter 19 for dosage schedules)
      b) Vaccines will be available in the United States within the next few years
   2. Hepatitis B (see Chapter 28 and Table 18.1)
      a) Hepatitis B immune globulin (HBIG)
         1) 75% effective if given at time of exposure

Table 18.1. Characteristics and Administration of Commonly Used Vaccines and Immune Globulin Preparations

Vaccine or Immune Globulin	Type of Preparation	Population to Be Immunized[a]	Usual Age and Immunization Schedule[b]	Common Adverse Reactions[c]
Diphtheria toxoid	Toxoid	All	Childhood; series of 3 primary injections (day 0, 1 mo, 6–12 mo) with boosters every 10 yr[d]	Local pain and swelling
Tetanus toxoid	Toxoid	All	Childhood; series of 3 i.m. injections (day 0, 1 mo, 6–12 mo) with boosters every 10 yr[d]	Local pain and swelling
Tetanus immune globulin (TIG)	High-titered human immune globulin	Unimmunized person with wound	Single i.m. injection (250 units)	Not significant
Whole cell pertussis vaccine	Killed bacteria	All children	Series of 5 injections (2, 4, 6 mo) with boosters to age 6	Fever pain and local swelling, occasionally severe neurological reactions
Acellular pertussis vaccine	Fractionated killed bacteria and toxoid	All	15–18 mo and 4–6 yr	Reduced relative to whole cell vaccine
Measles vaccine	Live attenuated virus[e]	All children	≥15 mo and 4–6 yr or 11–13 yr	Fever, rash
Rubella vaccine	Live attenuated virus[e]	All children and unimmunized women	Child ≥ 15 mo and 4–6 yr or 11–13 yr, women through childbearing age with measles vaccine as MMR	Arthralgias, fever
Mumps vaccine	Live attenuated virus[e]	All children and young adults without history of mumps	Child ≥ 15 mo and 4–6 yr or 11–13 yr with measles vaccine as MMR	Not significant
Polio vaccine Oral (OPV) Parenteral (IPV)	Live attenuated virus Killed virus	All All	Ages 2, 4 mo, 15–18 mo, and 4–6 yr Children or adults (preferred for adults); primary series of 3 doses	Rare paralytic disease Not significant
Haemophilus influenzae type B	Conjugated purified polysaccharide	All children, high-risk adults (asplenic)	Children, some adults; series of 3 injections beginning at 2 mo	Not significant
Hepatitis B vaccine	Recombinant proteins from yeast	All (eventually)	Childhood, selected adults; 3 injections (0 time, 1 mo, 6 mo in adults; birth, 1–2 mo, 6–12 mo in children)	Not significant
Hepatitis B immune globulin	High-titered human γ-globulin	Persons exposed to hepatitis B	0.06 ml/kg at time of exposure and again 1 mo later	Not significant

Influenza vaccine	Killed virus (whole virus and "split virus" preparations); preparations of virus change yearly	Persons at high risk, elderly or chronically ill	Child or adult; Adults: single injection (whole virus) repeated yearly; Children under 12: split virus preparation, 2 doses	Fever, local tenderness
Immune globulin (IG)	Pooled human γ-globulin	Persons exposed to hepatitis A and B or measles	Usually adults; Hepatitis A: 0.02 ml/kg, once; Hepatitis B: 0.06 ml/kg, twice; Measles: 0.25 ml/kg, once	Pain
Meningococcal vaccine	Purified polysaccharide (serogroups A, C, Y, W135)	Only during epidemic disease; persons at high risk	All ages; young adult military; Single injection	Erythema at injection site
Rabies vaccine	Killed virus	Persons bitten by possibly rabid animal or at high risk of exposure	All ages — postexposure and pre-exposure; Postexposure: 5 doses of vaccine i.m. (days 0, 3, 7, 14, 30); Pre-exposure: 3 doses of rabies vaccine, intradermal or i.m. (days 0, 7, 21, or 28)	Pain, rare neurological reactions, urticaria
Rabies immune globulin (HRIG)	High-titered human γ-globulin	Unimmunized persons with suspicious animal bite	Any age; single injection, up to ½ infiltrated into wound	Not significant
Pneumococcal vaccine	Polyvalent purified polysaccharide (23 serotypes)	Persons with asplenia, or chronic illness, elderly	Age (over 2 yr); single injection, booster after ≥ 5 years (for high-risk only) (see text)	Erythema at injection site
Bacillus Calmette-Guérin vaccine (BCG)	Live attenuated bacteria	Newborns in developing countries and persons with excessively high risk of developing tuberculosis	Infants and children; single injection, intradermal	Prolonged granuloma or ulcer at injection site, lymphadenitis

a Populations cited represent general ambulatory patients. Certain subjects (HIV-infected, other immunocompromised persons) may benefit from specifically tailored immunization programs (see Chapter 20).

b All injections are intramuscular unless otherwise specified. Schedules given are for adults unless the vaccine is used solely in pediatric age group.

c Reactions listed are most common and/or serious. This listing is not exhaustive. Allergic hypersensitivity is possible with almost any vaccine but is rare.

d Boosters of diphtheria and tetanus are particularly important for those traveling to underdeveloped countries. Diphtheria and tetanus vaccines should be given in combined [tetanus and diphtheria toxoid (TD)] preparation. (See also Table 18.6.)

e Given as the combination mumps, measles, and rubella vaccine (MMR). (See additional details about measles vaccine in Tables 18.5 and 18.6.)

        2) Enhanced protection if given at same time as hepatitis B vaccine

        3) If exposed persons have antibody to hepatitis B core antigen (HB_cAg) or hepatitis B surface antigen (HB_sAg), prophylaxis unnecessary

    b) Recombinant hepatitis B vaccine

        1) Should be given in an arm for maximal effect

        2) Booster doses not currently recommended

        3) Recommendations for prophylaxis after perinatal or sexual exposure (Table 18.2) or percutaneous, ocular, or mucous membrane exposure (Table 18.3)

        4) Recommendations for hepatitis B vaccine for other persons at increased risk

          (a) Health care personnel exposed to blood or blood products

          (b) Homosexually active men

          (c) Family members or sexual partners of chronic HB_sAg carriers

          (d) Prostitutes

          (e) Persons who regularly receive blood or blood products

          (f) Patients in hemodialysis units

          (g) Inmates and staff of institutions for the mentally retarded

          (h) Users of injected illicit drugs

          (i) Selected international travelers (see Chapter 19)

3. Hepatitis C — no effective preparations available

4. Tetanus

    a) Majority of cases in elderly, usually unimmunized

    b) Usually follows (by 4–21 days) penetrating wounds, including animal bites

    c) Immunization schedules: see Tables 18.1 and 18.4

5. Diphtheria

    a) See Table 18.1

    b) For asymptomatic immunized contacts of patients with diphtheria, 600,000 units benzathine penicillin i.m. or 250 mg erythromycin 4 times/day for 7 days *plus* primary vaccination and daily surveillance for evidence of diphtheria

6. Mumps

    a) See Table 18.1

    b) Unvaccinated adults born before 1957 can be ensured to be immune

Table 18.2.　Recommendations for Hepatitis B Prophylaxis After Perinatal or Sexual Exposure

Exposure	HBIG		Vaccine	
	Dose	Recommended Timing	Dose	Recommended Timing
Perinatal	0.5 ml i.m.	Within 12 hours of birth	0.5 ml i.m.	Within 12 hours of birth [a]
Sexual	0.06 ml/kg i.m.	Single dose within 14 days of last sexual contact	1.0 ml i.m.	First dose at time of HBIG treatment [a]

From: *MMWR* 39(Suppl 2): 1990.
[a] The first dose can be given the same time as the HBIG dose but at a separate site; subsequent doses should be given as recommended for specific vaccine.

Table 18.3.   Recommendations for Hepatitis B (HB) Prophylaxis After Percutaneous or Permucosal Exposure

| Exposed Person | HB$_s$Ag Positive | Treatment When Source Is Found to Be | |
		HB$_s$Ag Negative	Source Not Tested or Unknown
Unvaccinated	HBIG × 1 [a] and initiate HB vaccine [b]	Initiate HB vaccine [b]	Initiate HB vaccine [b]
Previously vaccinated	Test exposed for anti-HBs	No treatment	No treatment
Known responder	1. If adequate, [c] no treatment		
	2. If inadequate, HB vaccine booster dose		
Known nonresponder	HBIG × 2 or	No treatment	If known high-risk source, may treat as if source were HB$_s$Ag positive
	HBIG × 1 plus 1 dose HB vaccine		
Response unknown	Test exposed for anti-HB$_s$	No treatment	Test exposed for anti-HB$_s$
	1. If inadequate, [c] HBIG × 1 plus HB vaccine		1. If inadequate, [c] HB vaccine booster dose
	2. If adequate, no treatment		2. If adequate, no treatment

From: *MMWR* 39 (Suppl 2): 1990.
[a] HBIG dose, 0.06 ml/kg i.m.
[b] Adult dose, 1.0 ml i.m.
[c] Adequate anti-HB$_s$ is ≥10 sample ratio units (SRU) by radioimmunoassay or positive by electroimmunoassay.

Table 18.4. Summary Guide to Tetanus Prophylaxis in Routine Wound Management (United States)

History of Absorbed Tetanus Toxoid Doses	Clean, Minor Wounds		All Other Wounds [a]	
	TD [b]	TIG [c]	TD [b]	TIG [c]
Uncertain or <3	Yes	No	Yes	Yes
≥3 [d]	No [e]	No	No [f]	No

From Centers for Disease Control: Update on adult immunization: recommendations of the Immunization Practices Advisory Committee (ACIP). *MMWR* 40(RR-12): 1991.

[a] Such as, but not limited to, wounds contaminated with dirt, feces, and saliva; puncture wounds; avulsions; and wounds resulting from missiles, crushing, burns, and frostbite.

[b] Td, tetanus and diphtheria toxoids, adsorbed (for adult use). For children <7 years old, DTP (DT, if pertussis vaccine is contraindicated) is preferred to tetanus toxoid alone. For persons ≥7 years old, Td is preferred to tetanus toxoid alone.

[c] TIG, tetanus immune globulin.

[d] If only three doses of fluid toxoid have been received, a fourth dose of toxoid, preferably an adsorbed toxoid, should be given.

[e] Yes, >10 years since last dose.

[f] Yes, >5 years since last dose. (More frequent boosters are not needed and can accentuate side effects.)

Table 18.5. Current Recommendations for Measles Vaccination (United States)

	Criteria for Adequate Protection
Routine childhood schedule	
Most areas	Two doses, [a, b] first dose at ≥15 months, second dose at 4–6 years (entry to kindergarten or first grade) [c]
High-risk areas [d]	Two doses, [a,b] first dose at 12 months, second dose at 4–6 years (entry to kindergarten or first grade) [c]
Colleges and other educational institutions post-high school	Documentation of receipt of two doses of measles vaccine after the first birthday [b] or other evidence of measles immunity [e]
Medical personnel beginning employment	Documentation of receipt of two doses of measles vaccine after the first birthday [b] or other evidence of measles immunity [e]

From: *MMWR* 38(Suppl 9): 1989.

[a] Both doses should preferably be given as combined measles, mumps, rubella vaccine (MMR).

[b] No less than 1 month apart. If no documentation of any dose of vaccine, first dose of vaccine should be given at the time of school entry or employment, and second dose, no less than 1 month later.

[c] Some areas may elect to administer the second dose at an older age or to multiple age groups.

[d] A county with more than five cases among preschool-aged children during each of at least 5 years, a county with a recent outbreak among unvaccinated preschool-aged children, or a county with a large inner-city urban population. These recommendations may be applied to an entire county or to identified risk areas within a county.

[e] Prior physician-diagnosed measles disease, laboratory evidence of measles immunity, or birth before 1957.

7. Measles
   a) For current recommendations for vaccination, see Table 18.5
   b) For recommendations for control of measles outbreak, see Table 18.6
   c) Immunocompromised persons should receive 0.5 ml/kg of immune globulin
8. Rubella
   a) See Table 18.1
   b) Newly vaccinated women should not become pregnant for 3 months

Table 18.6. Recommendations for Measles Outbreak Control[a]

Outbreaks in preschool-aged children	Lower age for vaccination to as low as 6 months of age in outbreak area if cases are occurring in children <1 year of age[b]
Outbreaks in institutions: daycare centers, K–12th grades, colleges, and other institutions	Revaccination of all students and their siblings and of school personnel born in or after 1957 who do not have documentation of immunity to measles[c]
Outbreaks in medical facilities	Revaccination of all medical workers born in or after 1957 who have direct patient contact and who do not have proof of immunity to measles[c]
	Susceptible personnel who have been exposed should be relieved from direct patient contact from the 5th to 21st day after exposure (regardless of whether they received measles vaccine or IG) or — if they become ill — for 7 days after they develop rash

From: *MMWR* 38(Suppl 9): 1989.

[a] Mass revaccination of entire populations is not necessary. Revaccination should be limited to populations at risk, such as students attending institutions where cases occur.

[b] Children initially vaccinated before the first birthday should be revaccinated at 15 months of age. A second dose should be administered at the time of school entry or according to local policy.

[c] Documentation of physician-diagnosed measles disease, serological evidence of immunity to measles, or documentation of receipt of two doses of measles vaccine on or after the first birthday.

9. Influenza
    a) See Table 18.1 and Chapter 14
    b) Amantadine prophylaxis in influenza A epidemics (see also Chapter 14)
        1) For unvaccinated persons at high risk because of underlying disease
        2) For adults in critical occupations who have not been immunized with the current vaccine
        3) For persons in semiclosed institutional environments, especially nursing homes
        4) Give 200 mg/day during outbreak; give 100 mg/day to persons over 70; give 50 mg/day to frail elderly
        5) Amantadine can be given for 2 weeks after vaccination, then stopped as antibodies develop
10. Pneumococcal disease
    a) See Table 18.1; vaccination for high-risk patients (asplenia, sickle cell anemia, cardiopulmonary disease, diabetes mellitus, nephrotic syndrome, cirrhosis)
    b) Efficacy 44–81% against 23 serotypes of pneumococcus in vaccine (responsible for 90% of cases)
    c) Booster doses should be given only to persons at very high risk and then no more often than every 5 years
11. Tuberculosis — no indication for vaccination (BCG) in adults in United States
12. Rabies
    a) For postexposure prophylaxis, see Table 18.1
    b) For pre-exposure prophylaxis where risk of exposure is high, see Table 18.1 (does not eliminate need for postexposure prophylaxis with vaccine; hyperimmune globulin need not be given)

19/ MEDICAL ADVICE FOR THE INTERNATIONAL TRAVELER

IMMUNIZATIONS
A. Yellow fever
  1. Endemic zones: Figures 19.1 and 19.2
  2. Vaccine
    a) See Table 19.1
    b) Available only in yellow fever vaccine centers (call local health department)
    c) Contraindicated in immunosuppressed persons
    d) Mild side effects (headache, myalgia, fever) 5–10 days after administration
B. Cholera
  1. Infection rare in prudent travelers

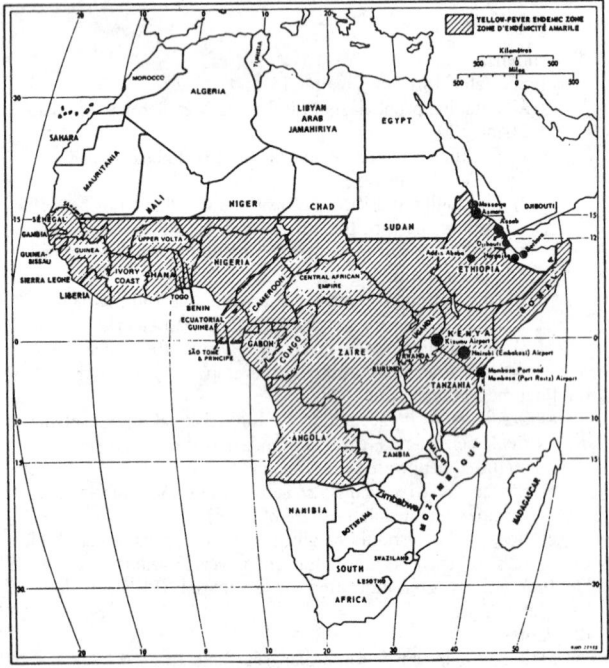

Figure 19.1. Yellow fever endemic zone in Africa. (From: *Health Information International Travel.* Supplement to *MMWR* 32: August, 1983. Washington DC, US Department of Health and Human Services, HHS publication no (CDC) 83–8280, 1983.)

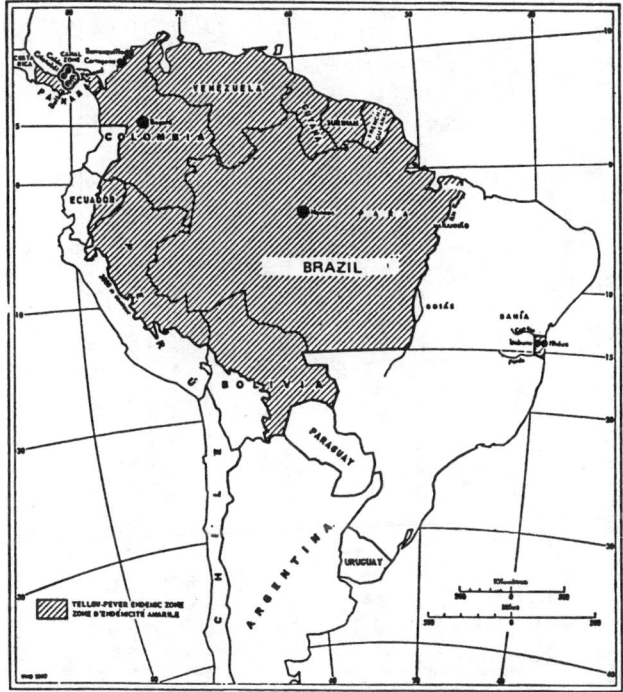

Figure 19.2. Yellow fever endemic zone in the Americas. (From: *Health Information International Travel.* Supplement to *MMWR* 32: August, 1983. Washington DC, US Department of Health and Human Services, HHS publication no (CDC) 83–8280, 1983.)

   2. Vaccine ineffective
   3. May be required for entry into some countries (if so, see Table 19.1)
C. Typhoid fever
   1. Travelers in developing countries who leave usual routes, eat local food are at risk
   2. Two vaccines, both effective (Table 19.1)
D. Polio
   1. If traveling to a developing country outside the Americas and vaccination was more than 10 years ago, booster dose of vaccine indicated (Table 19.1)
   2. Oral polio vaccine (OPV) should not be given to immunocompromised persons or to pregnant women
E. Tetanus and diphtheria
   1. Tetanus immunization (Table 19.1) should be maintained in all travelers

Table 19.1.   Vaccines and Immune Globulin for International Travel (See Details in Text and in Product Instructions)

Vaccine/Immune Globulin	Patient	Route	Dose	Booster	Comments
Yellow fever	>9 mo	s.c.	0.5 ml	0.5 ml q 10 yr	May be required
Cholera	6 mo–4 yr	s.c. or i.m.	0.2 ml	0.2 ml q 6 mo	May be required
	5–10 yr		0.3 ml	0.3 ml q 6 mo	Limited efficacy
	>10 yr		0.5 ml	0.5 ml q 6 mo	
Typhoid parenteral	<10 yr	s.c.	0.25 ml	0.25 ml q 3 yr	Local reactions common
	>10 yr		0.50 ml	0.5 ml q 3 yr	
Typhoid oral (TY21)	>1 yr	p.o.	1 dose q.o.d. × 4	Repeat series q 5 yr	Keep refrigerated, avoid antibiotics
Poliomyelitis					
OPV	All ages	p.o.	3 doses	1 dose pretravel	IPV is preferable for adults
IPV	All ages	s.c.	3 doses	1 dose q 10 yr	
Japanese encephalitis	<3 yr	s.c.	0.5 ml	1 dose at 1 and 4 yr	Just licensed by the FDA
	>3 yr		1 ml		
Immune globulin					
Short term (<3 mo)	<23 kg	i.m.	0.5 ml		Immune globulin is used for prophylaxis of hepatitis A; consider screening for anti-HAV in frequent travelers
	23–45 kg		1.0 ml		
	>45 kg		2.0 ml		
Long term (>3 mo)	<23 kg	i.m.	1.0 ml	1.0 ml q 6 mo	
	23–45 kg		2.5 ml	2.5 ml q 6 mo	
	>45 kg		5.0 ml	5.0 ml q 6 mo	
Tetanus-diphtheria	>7 yr	i.m.	3 doses	1 dose q 10 yr	Always use combined vaccine
Meningitis A, C, Y, W135	>2 yr	i.m.	0.5 ml	Unclear	For specific areas of travel
Rabies	All ages	i.m.	1.0 ml	1 dose q 2 yr	Still requires postexposure treatment
	All ages	i.d.	0.1 ml (3 doses)	1 dose q 2 yr	
Hepatitis B	All ages	i.m.	1.0 ml (3 doses)	Unclear	Protection lasts 5–7 yr

OPV, oral polio vaccine; IPV, inactivated (parenteral) polio vaccine; FDA, Food and Drug Administration; HAV, hepatitis A virus; i.d., intradermal.

    2. Diphtheria immunization (Table 19.1) should be maintained in all travelers to developing countries

F. Hepatitis A
    1. A risk for travelers to developing countries, especially outside usual tourist routes
    2. Immune globulin should be given (Table 19.1); no contraindications to use

G. Hepatitis B
    1. Health care workers and travelers who plan to stay longer than 6 months or who will have sexual contacts in a developing country are at risk
    2. Vaccination (Table 19.1) appropriate for travelers at risk

H. Rabies
    1. Pre-exposure prophylaxis (Table 19.1) for long-term travelers to endemic areas [booster dose (1 ml) every 2 years]
    2. If vaccinated traveler is exposed to rabies, postexposure immunization (Table 19.1) should still be given

I. Tuberculosis
    1. Tuberculosis status should be known prior to travel to an endemic area
    2. Bacillus Calmette-Guérin vaccine not recommended

J. Measles, mumps, rubella, influenza
    1. Persons not immunized against measles, mumps, or rubella should be vaccinated before travel outside the United States

K. Japanese encephalitis
    1. In epidemics in Asia; endemic in tropical areas of Southeast Asia
    2. Vaccination (Table 19.1) indicated for long-term or rural travelers — effective and safe
    3. Side effects of vaccine in 10–20% (fever, headache, myalgias, malaise)

L. Miscellaneous
    1. Typhus vaccine no longer available, little risk for travelers
    2. Plague vaccination not recommended unless direct contact with wild rodents in plague enzootic areas
    3. Meningococcal meningitis
      a) Vaccination for travelers to sub-Saharan Africa, Saudi Arabia, Nepal (mountain travelers), Tanzania, and Burundi
      b) See Table 19.1

M. Timing of vaccinations
    1. Multiple vaccines can be given at same visit except oral polio and oral typhoid vaccines (separate by 2 weeks)
    2. Complete vaccinations by 1 week before departure
    3. When vaccines are given together, administer with separate syringes at different sites
    4. Immune globulin can be given concurrently with killed virus vaccines and with live virus yellow fever and polio vaccines; other live virus vaccines should be given 14 days before or 3 months after administration of immune globulin

MALARIA PROPHYLAXIS

A. Epidemiology
    1. Transmitted usually by *Anopheles* mosquitoes but can be acquired

from blood transfusion or by contaminated needles and syringes used by abusers of illicit drugs

2. Risk varies depending on country and season [Centers for Disease Control (CDC) maintains an information line: 404–639–1610]

B. Avoidance of mosquito exposure
   1. Travelers should sleep in screened rooms and under mosquito nets
   2. Travelers, between dusk to dawn, should cover exposed body with clothing or insect repellent (deet); outside nighttime activity should be avoided
   3. Chemoprophylaxis
      a) For all travelers to endemic areas
      b) Begin 1–2 weeks before entering and 4 weeks after leaving malarious area
      c) For prophylaxis where chloroquine-resistant *Plasmodium falciparum* (CRPF) malaria is not a risk, prescribe chloroquine or hydroxychloroquine (Table 19.2)
         1) Side effects (itching, nausea, disorientation) are mild
         2) Better tolerated if taken with meals
      d) For CRPF prophylaxis, mefloquine (Table 19.2) should be prescribed
         1) Mefloquine resistance reported in eastern Thailand, rural Cambodia — see below
         2) Side effects (dizziness, nausea) are mild and transient
         3) Should be avoided by persons taking drugs that interfere with cardiac conduction
         4) Should be avoided by persons with a seizure disorder or psychosis
      e) For CRPF prophylaxis when mefloquine cannot be taken or where there is mefloquine resistance (see above)
         1) Doxycycline (Table 19.2) — be aware of occasional sun sensitivity and gastrointestinal intolerance
         2) Proguanil (Table 19.2) — not available in United States; may be more useful in East Africa (not Southeast Asia) if taken with chloroquine
      f) Travelers taking chloroquine alone or chloroquine plus Proguanil in areas of CRPF should take along a supply of Fansidar (Table 19.2) to be taken if they develop a febrile illness
      g) For travelers to areas where *Plasmodium vivax* or *ovale* is a risk and who stay an extended period or who get bitten by mosquitoes, Primaquine should be given during last 2 weeks of chloroquine prophylaxis

FOOD AND WATER

A. Precautions
   1. Avoidance of uncooked food, unpasteurized milk (including cheeses)
   2. Avoidance of stored cooked food if refrigeration is poor
   3. Avoidance of unpeeled fruit
   4. Avoidance of unpurified water (including ice and hot tap water); acceptable:
      a) Boiled water, including coffee or tea
      b) Carbonated beverages
      c) Beer or wine

Table 19.2. Drugs Used in the Prophylaxis of Malaria

Drugs	Adult Dose	Pediatric Dose
Chloroquine phosphate (Aralen)	500 mg salt p.o. once/week	5 mg/kg base (8.3 mg/kg salt) p.o. once/week, up to a maximal dose of 300 mg base
Hydroxychloroquine sulfate (Plaquenil)	400 mg salt p.o. once/week	5 mg/kg base (6.5 mg/kg salt) p.o. once/week, up to maximal adult dose of 310 mg base
Mefloquine	228 mg base (250 mg salt) p.o. once/week	15–19 kg: ¼ tablet/week 20–30 kg: ½ tablet/week 31–45 kg: ¾ tablet/week >45 kg: 1 tablet/week
Doxycycline	100 mg p.o. once/day	>8 years of age: 2 mg/kg of body weight p.o./day, up to adult dose of 100 mg/day
Proguanil (not available in United States)	200 mg p.o. once/day in combination with weekly chloroquine	<2 yr: 500 mg/day 2–6 yr: 100 mg/day 7–10 yr: 150 mg/day >10 yr: 200 mg/day
Primaquine	15 mg base (26.3 mg salt) p.o. once/day for 14 days	0.3 mg/kg base (0.5 mg/kg salt) p.o. once/day for 14 days
For presumptive therapy: pyrimethamine-sulfadoxine (Fansidar)	3 tablets (75 mg pyrimethamine and 1500 mg sulfadoxine as a single dose)	5–10 kg: ½ tablet 11–20 kg: 1 tablet 21–30 kg: 1.5 tablets 31–45 kg: 2 tablets >45 kg: 3 tablets

B. Diarrhea
  1. Prophylaxis
     a) Routine use of antimicrobials not recommended
     b) Indications
        1) Travelers with pre-existing conditions (e.g., cardiovascular disease) that would put them at risk were they dehydrated
        2) Travelers who would be at high risk for <3 weeks
     c) Drugs — taken during travel and for 2 days after leaving a developing country
        1) Doxycycline, 100 mg/day with meals (possible photosensitivity and gastrointestinal intolerance)
        2) Trimethoprim-sulfamethoxazole, 1 double-strength tablet/day
        3) Ciprofloxacin, 500 mg/day, or norfloxacin, 400 mg a day — preferred agents in most cases
  2. Treatment
     a) Rehydration — sufficient, in itself, for mild illness
        1) Mild — soups and juices
        2) Severe
           (a) Oral rehydration solution (ORS) (available in pharmacies in most countries) taken to approximate fluid losses
           (b) If ORS not available, mix ½ teaspoon salt, ½ teaspoon baking soda, 4 tablespoons sugar (use 1 teaspoon salt if no baking soda) in 1 liter boiled water
     b) Antimicrobial treatment — for a moderately severe or severe illness
        1) Start soon after diarrhea begins; continue for 3 days
        2) Ciprofloxacin (500 mg twice a day), norfloxacin (400 mg twice a day), doxycycline (100 mg twice a day), or trimethoprim-sulfamethoxazole (1 double-strength tablet twice a day)
        3) If shigellosis suspected (blood in stool, fever, severe abdominal cramps), quinolone preferred
     c) Antimotility drugs (Lomotil or Imodium preferred)
        1) For temporary relief, e.g., before a long bus ride
        2) Not recommended routinely (may prolong dysentery)
     d) Bismuth subsalicylate (Pepto-Bismol) may be of help (30 ml or 2 tablets every ½–1 hour up to 8 doses/day)
     e) Kaopectate useless
  3. Consultation with a physician
     a) Repeated vomiting or failure to improve within 2–3 days
     b) Blood in stool
     c) Fever higher than 101°F, especially if accompanied by shaking chills

SCHISTOSOMIASIS
A. Epidemiology
  1. Relatively common in developing world
  2. Contracted by wading or swimming in freshwater
  3. Symptoms typically delayed for 6 months to several years (transient fever, cough, malaise may occur in 4–5 weeks)
B. Diagnosis

1. Freshwater exposure in an endemic area warrants serological testing and a complete blood count (eosinophilia may occur early)
2. If serology positive, urinalysis and stool examination for ova are indicated

C. Treatment: proven or strongly suspected cases should be treated with praziquantel (600 mg tablets, 20 mg/kg 3 times separated by 4–6 hours, all in 1 day)

MISCELLANEOUS HEALTH CONCERNS

A. Jet lag
   1. Recovery takes several days to weeks
   2. Avoid overeating, alcohol ingestion during air travel
   3. Schedule a day of rest after passing six or more time zones
B. Injectable medications and blood transfusions: avoid in developing countries; leave if possible before accepting
C. High altitude
   1. Symptoms may occur on rapid ascent to 8000 feet or higher: mild — dizziness, nausea, headache, fatigue — or severe — difficulty concentrating, extreme dyspnea, severe headache
   2. Symptoms usually resolve in day or two; if not, descent may be necessary; oxygen will relieve acute symptoms
   3. Avoid overexertion, tobacco, alcohol
   4. Diamox (125–250 mg 3 times/day) reduces acclimatization time if started 1 day before ascent, continued for 2–3 days after ascent

20/ AMBULATORY CARE FOR THE HIV-INFECTED PATIENT

GENERAL CONSIDERATIONS

A. Epidemiology
   1. Major risk groups: homosexual and bisexual men, intravenous drug users, prostitutes, hemophiliacs (who received plasma concentrates before they were further purified)
   2. Heterosexual transmission becoming more common
   3. AIDS (acquired immune deficiency syndrome) follows infection by up to 10 years
B. Transmission
   1. HIV in highest concentrations in blood and semen, in lower concentrations in cervical and vaginal secretions, saliva, tears, breast milk
   2. Sexual transmission
      a) Risk greater if multiple partners, receptive anal intercourse, a sexually transmitted disease (especially a disease that causes genital ulcers, e.g., syphilis)
      b) Prevention: see Tables 20.1 and 20.2
   3. Transfusion of blood and blood products — risks now very small (1:153,000 per unit transfused)
   4. Needles
      a) Sharing of needles by drug addicts
      b) Use of improperly cleaned needles or syringes in developing countries

Table 20.1. Safe Sex Guidelines

Safe Sex Practices
- Massage
- Hugging
- Mutual masturbation
- Social kissing (dry)
- Body-to-body rubbing
- Voyeurism, exhibitionism, fantasy

Possibly Safe Sex Practices
- French kissing (wet)
- Anal intercourse with condom[a]
- Vaginal intercourse with condom[a]
- Limiting the number of partners with whom one has sex

Unsafe Sex Practices
- Semen, vaginal fluid, menstrual blood, or urine in mouth or in contact with the skin where there is an open cut or sore
- Anal intercourse without condom[a]
- Vaginal intercourse without condom[a]
- Rimming (oral-anal contact)
- Fisting (possible percutaneous inoculation with blood from trauma caused by inserting fist into anus)
- Having sex when either partner has an open genital sore

[a] See instructions for condom users in Table 20.2.

Table 20.2.   Instructions for Condom Users

- Use a condom every time you have intercourse.
- Always put the condom on the penis before intercourse begins.
- Put the condom on when the penis is erect.
- Do not pull the condom tightly against the tip of the penis. Leave a small empty space — about 1 or 2 cm — at the end of the condom to hold semen. Some condoms have a nipple tip that will hold semen.
- Unroll the condom all the way to the bottom of the penis.
- If the condom breaks during intercourse, withdraw the penis immediately and put on a new condom.
- After ejaculation, withdraw the penis while it is still erect. Hold onto the rim of the condom as you withdraw so that the condom does not slip off.
- Use a new condom each time you have intercourse. Throw used condoms away.
- If a lubricant is desired, use water-based lubricants such as contraceptive jelly. Lubricants made with petroleum jelly may damage condoms. Do not use saliva because it may contain virus.
- Store condoms in a cool, dry place if possible.
- Condoms that are sticky or brittle or otherwise damaged should not be used.

[a] Adapted from: *Popul Rep XIV* (3): 1986.

    5. Perinatal transmission: 7–39% risk that HIV-infected mothers will infect their infants

    6. Casual contact no risk (e.g., household contacts), but hepatitis precautions should be used (see Chapter 28)

C. Natural history (Fig. 20.1)

    1. Initial infection usually manifests itself as a mild flu-like illness

    2. Antibodies to HIV usually demonstrable within 6–24 weeks after infection (may take 6 months)

    3. Percentage of CD4 cells best indicator of prognosis (see Table 20.3 for equivalencies of absolute counts and percentages)

    4. Skin test reactivity to ubiquitous antigens also a prognostic indicator (anergy correlates with progression of disease)

D. Classification of HIV infection: Tables 20.4 and 20.5

SEROLOGICAL DIAGNOSIS AND ASSOCIATED COUNSELING

A. Serological tests

    1. Enzyme-linked immunosorbent assay (ELISA)

       a) Initial test to detect HIV infection

       b) Sensitivity and specificity 99%

       c) False positive tests (negative Western blot (WB) — see below) generally in members of low-risk groups who have had multiple pregnancies, multiple transfusions or who have immunological abnormalities other than due to HIV infection

       d) False negative tests early in disease (see above)

    2. Western blot

       a) Confirmatory test if ELISA is positive twice

       b) Indeterminate test may reflect early disease or absence of HIV infection — should be repeated every 8–12 weeks for 6 months (if still indeterminate at 6 months, can be considered negative)

B. Indications for testing

    1. Mandatory: military; many prison populations, Job Corps; donors of blood, semen, or organs

    2. Voluntary

       a) All persons with a sexually transmitted disease

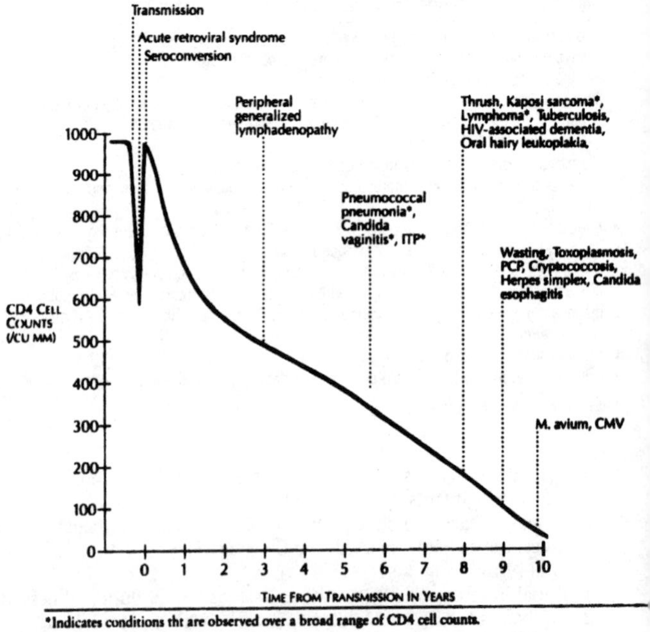

Figure 20.1. Natural history of HIV infection based on CD4 cell counts. Decline in CD4 cell count is based on sequential tests in 318 seroconverters in the MAC study (*J Infect Dis* 165:352, 1992). Approximate time of complications relative to CD4 cell count is based on experience of MACS with 888 AIDS-defining diagnoses (A. Muñoz, personal communication) and multiple published reports. (From Bartlett JG: *The Johns Hopkins Hospital Guide to Medical Care of Patients With HIV Infection*, 4th ed. Baltimore, Williams & Wilkins, 1994.)

  b) Current or former intravenous drug users
  c) Hemophiliacs
  d) Persons who received blood or blood products between 1978 and 1985
  e) Prostitutes
  f) Persons from developing countries that have high rates of HIV infection
  g) Sexual partners of persons at high risk of HIV infection
  h) Persons with signs or symptoms suggestive of HIV infection
  i) Persons who consider themselves at risk of HIV infection or who request testing
  j) Health care workers who perform invasive procedures
C. Pretest and posttest counseling: Table 20.6

Table 20.3.   Equivalence for Absolute Numbers of CD4 Cells and CD4 Percentages

CD4 Cells (per mm³)	CD4 Cell Percentage of Total Lymphocytes
>500	>29
200–500	14–29
<200	<14

Adapted from Centers for Disease Control and Prevention: 1993 Revised Classification System for HIV Infection and Expanded Surveillance Case Definition for AIDS Among Adolescents and Adults. *MMWR* 41(RR-17): 1992.

Table 20.4.   1993 Revised HIV Classification System

CD4+ T-Cell Categories	Clinical Categories		
	(A) Asymptomatic Acute (Primary) HIV or PGL	(B) Symptomatic, Not (A) or (C) Conditions	(C) AIDS Indicator Conditions [a]
(1) ≥500/mm³	A1	B1	C1
(2) 200–499/mm³	A2	B2	C2
(3) <200/mm³ (AIDS indicator T-cell count [a])	A3	B3	C3

PGL, persistent generalized lymphadenopathy.

[a] Row 3 and Column C illustrate the expanded AIDS surveillance case definition. Persons with AIDS indicator conditions (Category C, see Table 20.5) as well as those with CD4+ T-lymphocyte counts < 200/mm³ (Categories A3 or B3) became reportable as AIDS cases in the United States and Territories effective January 1, 1993.

EARLY EVALUATION AND MANAGEMENT OF THE HIV-INFECTED PATIENT

A. History
1. One-half of all HIV-positive patients have had a flu-like illness early in course (see Fig. 20.1), lasting 1–2 weeks, or an aseptic meningitis
2. Less commonly, early transient polyneuropathy, brachial neuritis, or esophageal ulceration with odynophagia
3. HIV-oriented review of symptoms: Table 20.7
4. Sexual history
5. History of tuberculosis (Tbc) or of a positive purified protein derivative (PPD) test
6. History of immunosuppressive therapy
7. Immunization history
8. History of illicit use of drugs
B. Physical examination — special emphasis on oral cavity, skin, lymph nodes, female reproductive system (see below)
C. Laboratory evaluation
1. Complete blood count, hepatitis B surface antigen, syphilis serology, CD4 count
2. PPD, unless history of positive test; if PPD negative, skin tests with ubiquitous antigens
3. Chest x-ray if patient anergic or has a positive PPD or has a history of or symptoms of respiratory disease
D. Follow-up care
1. Health maintenance schedule: Table 20.8
2. Immunizations

Table 20.5.   AIDS Indicator Conditions in HIV-Infected Persons

Candidiasis
  Bronchi
  Trachea
  Esophagus
  Lungs
Cervical cancer, invasive [a]
Coccidiodomycosis, disseminated or extrapulmonary
Cryptococcosis, extrapulmonary
Cryptosporidiosis, extrapulmonary
Cytomegalovirus disease (other than liver, spleen, or nodes)
Encephalopathy, HIV-related (dementia)
Herpes simplex
  Chronic ulcer(s) of >1 month's duration
  Bronchitis
  Pneumonitis
  Esophagitis
Histoplasmosis, disseminated or extrapulmonary
Isosporiasis, intestinal of >1 month's duration
Kaposi's sarcoma
Lymphoma
  Burkitt's
  Immunoblastic
  Primary of the brain
Mycobacterium
  M. avium complex, disseminated or extrapulmonary
  M. kansasii, disseminated or extrapulmonary
  M. tuberculosis, pulmonary [a] or extrapulmonary
  Other species, disseminated or extrapulmonary
Pneumocystis carinii pneumonia
Pneumonia, two or more episodes within a year [a]
Progressive multifocal leukoencephalopathy
Salmonella septicemia, recurrent
Toxoplasmosis, brain
Wasting syndrome due to HIV (>10% weight loss and either chronic weakness and fever or
  chronic diarrhea ≥ 30 days)

Adapted from Centers for Disease Control and Prevention: 1993 Revised Classification System for HIV Infection and Expanded Surveillance Case Definition for AIDS Among Adolescents and Adults. *MMWR* 41(RR-17): 1992.
[a] Added in the 1993 Revised Classification System.

    a) Table 20.8
    b) Hepatitis B vaccine in B surface antigen- and antibody-negative
       patients at continued risk for hepatitis B
    c) In general, live attenuated vaccines (Chapter 18) should not be
       given

SYMPTOMATIC HIV-INFECTED PATIENT

A. Constitutional manifestations and lymphadenopathy
   1. Fatigue, the commonest symptom
   2. Fever, night sweats, weight loss
     a) May be presenting symptoms of an opportunistic infection
     b) Warrant a complete blood count, liver function tests, blood
       cultures, urine and sputum cultures if appropriate
     c) If initial evaluation is unrevealing, consider blood, bone
       marrow, stool cultures for *Mycobacterium avium intracellulare*
       (MAI) and computed tomography or gallium scans to look for
       occult infection

Table 20.6.   HIV Pretest and Posttest Counseling: Points for Discussion

Pretest counseling
1. Meaning of positive test
   - Positive test means HIV infection
   - Positive test does NOT mean AIDS[a]
   - Positive test means individual is an HIV carrier
2. Confidentiality of test results and medical information
3. Availability of anonymous and confidential counseling and testing sites
4. Potential adverse psychosocial consequences if information becomes known, e.g., possible adverse effects on employment, housing, insurance status
5. Sources of additional AIDS/HIV-related information[b]
6. Means for reducing risk of HIV transmission or exposure (depends on patient's current or likely high-risk behaviors)
   - "Safe Sex" practices (see Tables 20.1 and 20.2)
   - Sterilization of intravenous drug equipment
   - Treatment for drug addiction
   - Discontinuation of sharing intravenous needles

Posttest counseling
1. Interpretation of HIV antibody test results
2. Information about long-term chances of developing symptoms
3. Planning for medical follow-up
4. Referral to psychosocial support services
5. Reinforcement of recommendations for prevention of HIV transmission/exposure
6. Discussion of notification of sexual partner(s) or needle-sharing partner(s)
7. Reproductive issues in women

[a] Most people with a positive test will develop AIDS. Length of time from infection to development of AIDS is variable but averages 10 years.
[b] A single source for information is The National AIDS Information Clearing House, P.O. Box 6003, Rockville, MD 20850 (1-800-458-5231).

    3. Lymphadenopathy
       a) Common during first 6 months after diagnosis
       b) Not predictive of course
       c) Consider other diseases (e.g., another sexually transmitted disease in patients with inguinal adenopathy; lymphoma)
B. Clinical manifestations by organ system (see also Table 20.5)
    1. Features of common opportunistic infections in HIV-infected patients: Table 20.9
    2. Antimicrobial agents used in treatment and prophylaxis of opportunistic infections: Table 20.10
    3. Neurological syndromes: Table 20.11
C. Antiretroviral treatment
    1. Zidovudine (AZT)
       a) For asymptomatic patients (see Table 20.8 for recommendations), benefits probably a small percentage of patients
       b) For patients with AIDS, benefits about 20% of patients, usually for several months only
       c) Preparations and dosage schedule: 100-mg capsules or 50 mg/ml elixir; usual dose, 500–600 mg/day (100 mg every 4 hours or 200 mg every 8 hours while awake) indefinitely
       d) Toxicity mostly hematological
         1) Monitor complete blood count in 2 weeks, then every month for 3 months, then every 3 months

Table 20.7. HIV-Oriented Review of Symptoms

General: Weight loss, fever, night sweats
Skin: New rashes, pigmented lesions, itching
Lymphoid system: Asymmetrical or rapidly growing lymph nodes
HEENT: Changes in vision, unusual headaches, congestion or runny nose, oral lesions
Respiratory: Cough, shortness of breath, decrease in exercise tolerance
Gastrointestinal: Pain or difficulty in swallowing, nausea or vomiting, diarrhea, painful defecation
Neuropsychiatric: Difficulty thinking, depression, change in personality, numbness or tingling, muscle weakness, loss of sensation

Table 20.8. HIV Health Maintenance and Monitoring Schedule Based on Most Recent CD4 Count

	CD4 Cell Count (per mm³)			
	>600	500–600	200–499	<200
History and physical	Every 12 mo	Every 12 mo	Every 6 mo	Every 6 mo
CD4 cell count	Every 6 mo	Every 3–4 mo	Every 3–6 mo[a]	
Syphilis serology	Every 12 mo	Every 12 mo	Every 12 mo	Every 12 mo
Hepatitis B serology	Once	Once	Once	Once
Tuberculosis screening[b]	Every 12 mo	Every 12 mo	Every 12 mo	Every 12 mo
Pap smear	Every 12 mo	Every 12 mo	Every 12 mo	Every 12 mo
Pneumococcal vaccine	Once	Once	Once	Once
Influenza vaccine[c]	Yearly Oct–Dec	Yearly Oct–Dec	Yearly Oct–Dec	Yearly Oct–Dec
Tetanus vaccine	Every 10 yr	Every 10 yr	Every 10 yr	Every 10 yr
Antiretroviral therapy	No	No	Yes	Yes
P. carinii pneumonia prophylaxis	No	No	No	Yes

[a] Repeat at 3-month intervals when approaching 200.
[b] When anergic 2 years in a row or if positive, do not need to repeat.
[c] May not be cost effective especially at low CD4 cell count when response to the vaccine is often suboptimal.

    2) Dose adjustments: Table 20.12
  2. Dideoxyinosine (ddI)
    a) For patients with CD4 counts < 200/mm³, symptomatic patients with CD4 counts < 300/mm³, patients who have failed treatment with AZT or who have developed toxic reactions to AZT
    b) Available as a buffered powder (45, 67, 100, 250, and 375 mg) for solution in water or as a chewable tablet (25, 50, 100, 150 mg); dose based on weight (Table 20.13)
    c) Adverse reactions most often peripheral neuropathy (usually reversible), diarrhea, pancreatitis (dose related)
  3. Dideoxycytidine (ddC)
    a) For patients with CD4 counts below 300/mm³ or for patients who have failed treatment with AZT
    b) Available in tablets (0.375 and 0.75 mg); starting dose is 0.75 mg every 8 hours plus AZT 200 mg every 8 hours
    c) Major toxic effect is peripheral neuropathy, pancreatitis much less often than with ddI

Table 20.9. Principal Features of Common Opportunistic Infections in HIV-Infected Patients

Organ System/Organism	Mode of Transmission/ Isolation Procedures	Major Clinical Features	Definitive Diagnosis: Method/Source	Antimicrobial Agents[a]
RESPIRATORY SYSTEM				
Pneumocystis carinii[b,c]	Not human-to-human Patient with PCP not contagious to others No respiratory isolation	Dry cough, mild SOB, subacute presentation, may have no findings on PE	Cytological stain: bronchial lavage or lung tissue	1. TMP/SMX *or* 2. Pentamidine *or* 3. Dapsone-TMP *or* 4. Atovaquone
Mycobacterium tuberculosis[b,d]	Aerosolized droplets Human-to-human Respiratory isolation	Productive cough, SOB, fever usually with findings on PE	Smear or culture: bronchial lavage	Isoniazid, rifampin, ethambutol, and pyrazinamide
NEUROLOGICAL SYSTEM				
Cryptococcus neoformans[b,c] (meningitis)	Not human-to-human Patient not contagious No isolation	Headache, fever, change in mental status: often no findings on PE	Positive India ink or cryptococcal antigen or culture: CSF	1. Amphotericin B (flucytosine is added only in severe cases) *or* 2. Fluconazole
Toxoplasma gondii[a,c] (cerebritis or abscess)	Not human-to-human Patient not contagious No isolation	Headache, seizures, focal neurological deficit, ± fever	1. Head CT with contrast 2. Toxoplasma serology not of help 3. Definitive Dx: brain biopsy 4. Dx often made by response to empiric Rx	1. Pyramethamine and sulfadiazine and folinic acid *or* 2. Clindamycin as alternative to sulfa
Herpes simplex or varicella-zoster (encephalitis)	Human-to-human Wound and skin precautions if peripheral lesions present	Headache, seizures, change in mental status, ± fever	1. Head CT — cerebritis or WNL 2. LP — pleocytosis 3. EEG — focal temporal slowing 4. Brain biopsy — culture: definitive 5. Empiric Rx often tried	Acyclovir
Progressive multifocal	? mode of transmission	Change in mental status	1. Head CT with contrast or MRI:	None

Table 20.9. Continued

Organ System/Organism	Mode of Transmission/Isolation Procedures	Major Clinical Features	Definitive Diagnosis: Method/Source	Antimicrobial Agents [a]
leukoencephalopathy [b] (papovavirus)	No isolation		distinctive pattern 2. Brain biopsy — definitive	
ORAL CAVITY AND GASTROINTESTINAL SYSTEM				
Thrush (Candida albicans) [c]	Not human-to-human No isolation	Typical white plaques in mouth	Potassium hydroxide microscopy or culture: scraping of plaque	1. Nystatin or 2. Clotrimazole or 3. Ketaconazole or 4. Fluconazole
Candida esophagitis [b,c]	Same as above	Dysphagia/odynophagia ± thrush	Biopsy of esophagus for pathology	1. Ketaconazole or 2. Amphotericin B or 3. Fluconazole
Herpes simplex esophagitis [b,c]	Human-to-human transmission Contact of mucous membrane/open skin wound with lesion Wound and skin precautions if peripheral lesions present	Dysphagia/odynophagia ± oral mucocutaneous HSV infections	1. Biopsy of esophagus for pathology, culture 2. May be assumed with definite oral herpes and esophageal symptoms	Acyclovir
Cytomegalovirus [b,c] esophagitis/ileocolitis	Human-to-human Sexual, intravenous, vertical, breast milk, ? other No isolation (? pregnant caretakers)	Esophagitis: same as above Ileocolitis: cramping abdominal pain ± fever ± diarrhea	Biopsy of site for pathology culture	1. Ganciclovir 2. Foscarnet
Salmonella sp. [c]	Fecal-oral transmission Enteric precautions	Diarrhea, fever, systemic toxicity	Stool culture	1. Amoxicillin or 2. TMP/SMX or 3. Quinolones

	Isolation	Presentation	Diagnosis	Treatment
Cryptosporidium[b]	No human-to-human, No isolation	Chronic, profuse diarrhea	1. Stool O & P exam, 2. Biopsy	?
Isospora belli	No human-to-human, No isolation	Chronic, profuse diarrhea	1. Stool O & P exam, 2. Biopsy	TMP/SMX
OTHER ORGAN SYSTEMS				
Skin				
Mucocutaneous herpes simplex virus[c,e]	Human-to-human, Contact of mucous membrane or open skin with active lesion, Skin and wound precautions until lesion crusted	Classic vesicular lesion and distribution	Smear (Tzanck prep) or culture	Acyclovir
Varicella-zoster (shingles)	Same as HSV	Same as HSV in dermatomal distribution	Same as above: only culture differentiates from HSV	Acyclovir
Eye				
Cytomegalovirus[b,c] (retinitis)	Same as for cytomegalovirus under GI above	Asymptomatic or loss of vision	1. Opthalmologist-diagnosed classical retinal lesion, 2. Positive CMV urine or blood cultures	1. Ganciclovir, 2. Foscarnet
DISSEMINATED INFECTIONS				
M. avium intracellulare[b,c]	No human-to-human, No isolation	"Wasting" syndrome, diarrhea/abdominal pain, fever of unknown origin	1. Blood cultures, 2. Stool cultures, 3. Tissue biopsy (bone marrow, liver, colon)	Requires multiple agents. Suggested: Rifampin or rifabutin; Ethambutol + Ciprofloxacin or ofloxacin; Clofazimine or clarithromycin; Amikacin
Histoplasmosis[b,e]	No human-to-human, No isolation	Nonspecific: FUO, weight loss, Pulmonary Sx	1. Bone marrow biopsy and culture, 2. Blood culture	1. Amphotericin B (ketoconazole, fluconazole — maintenance), 2. Itraconazole

Table 20.9.   Continued

Organ System/Organism	Mode of Transmission/ Isolation Procedures	Major Clinical Features	Definitive Diagnosis: Method/Source	Antimicrobial Agents[a]
			3. Biopsy of lymph node, liver, lungs	
Coccidioidomycosis [b,e]	No human-to-human No isolation	Same as above plus CNS: meningoencephalitis Cutaneous: nodules, ulcers	1. Sputum/tissue pathology 2. Cultures: bone marrow, blood, lymph node, liver, urine 3. ± Serology	1. Amphotericin B 2. Fluconazole 3. Itraconazole

PCP, P. carinii pneumonia; SOB, shortness of breath; PE, physical examination; TMP/SMX, trimethoprim-sulfamethoxazole; CSF, cerebrospinal fluid; CT, computed tomography; Dx, diagnosis; Rx, treatment; WNL, within normal limits; LP, lymphocyte predominant; EEG, electroencephalogram; MRI, magnetic resonance imaging; HSV, herpes simplex virus; O & P, ova and parasite; GI, gastrointestinal; CMV, cytomegalovirus; FUO, fever of unknown origin; Sx, sign(s); CNS, central nervous system.
[a] For details regarding treatment, see Table 20.10.
[b] AIDS-defining illness (see Table 20.5).
[c] Requires maintenance or prophylaxis after initial treatment.
[d] See Chapter 15 for details.
[e] Maintenance should be considered.

Table 20.10. Practical Information About Antimicrobial Agents Used for the Treatment of Opportunistic Infections Listed in Table 20.9

Antimicrobial Agent	Organism(s) and Syndromes	Dosage/ Schedule/Route	Duration/ Maintenance	Common Adverse Effects	Drug Interactions	Dosage Change With Renal/Hepatic Failure	Available Strengths, Preparations
ANTIFUNGAL							
Nystatin	• *Candida:* Thrush	Suspension 100,000 units t.i.d. p.o. *or* Troches (lozenge) 200,000 units 5 times/d p.o.	1–2 wk ± maintenance or p.r.n.	1. Transient N & V 2. Unpleasant taste	None	None	100,000 units/5 ml of suspension 200,000 units/troche
Clotrimazole	Same as nystatin	Troches 10 mg 5 times/d p.o.	1–2 wk ± maintenance or p.r.n.	1. GI side effects 2. ↑ LFTs — reversible	None	None	10 mg/troche
Fluconazole	• *Candida* sp.: Esophagitis • *C. neoformans:* Meningitis	200 mg/d p.o. 100 mg/d p.o. 400 mg/d p.o. 200 mg/d p.o.	First day ≥4 wk First day 10–12 wk, then maintenance of 200 mg/d	1. GI side effects 2. Headache 3. ↑ LFTs	1. Warfarin: potentiated 2. Phenytoin: increased levels 3. Hypoglycemics: increased levels	↓ with renal failure	Tablets: 50, 100, 200 mg
Ketoconazole	• *Candida:* 1. Thrush 2. Esophagitis • Histoplasmosis • Coccidioidomycosis	200 mg/d p.o. 200–400 mg/d p.o. 200–400 mg/d p.o. 200–400 mg/d p.o.	2 wk or until Sx resolve + Maintenance Rx Maintenance only Maintenance only	1. N & V 2. Mild ↑ LFTs 3. Severe hepatitis (1/15,000) 4. Adrenal insufficiency	1. H₂ blockers, antacids; prevent absorption of ketoconazole 2. Warfarin: anticoagulant effect enhanced 3. Hypoglycemics: severe ↓ glucose 4. Rifampin: causes ↓ levels of ketoconazole	Renal — none Precaution with hepatic failure	200-mg capsule

Table 20.10. Continued

Antimicrobial Agent	Organism(s) and Syndromes	Dosage/Schedule/Route	Duration/Maintenance	Common Adverse Effects	Drug Interactions	Dosage Change With Renal/Hepatic Failure	Available Strengths, Preparations
Amphotericin B[a]	• Candida: Esophagitis / Other organs	0.6–1.0 mg/kg/d i.v.	1. Up to 500 mg total / 2. 1.5–2.0 g total	1. ↓ renal function 2. Anemia, thrombocytopenia (leukopenia — rare) 3. Reactions associated with infusion: fever, chills, headache 4. Thrombophlebitis 5. Anaphylaxis, hepatotoxicity — rare	5. Phenytoin: may alter concentration of either / May cause additive nephrotoxicity with aminoglycosides	When creatinine > 3.5, ↓ daily dose by ½ or use same dose q.o.d.	
	• C. neoformans: Meningitis	0.5–1.0 mg/kg/d i.v.	To total of 1.0 g, then maintenance of at least 100 mg/wk				
	• Histoplasmosis: Disseminated	0.5–1.0 mg/kg/d i.v.	Total = 2.0–2.5 g				
	• Coccidioidomycosis: Disseminated	0.5–1.0 mg/kg/d i.v.	Total = 2.0–2.5 g				
5-Flucytosine (usage limited due to bone marrow suppression)	• C. neoformans: Meningitis (synergistic with amphotericin)	50–150 mg/kg/d in 4 divided doses p.o. (i.v. available on request) can reduce amphotericin dose)	Only to be used with amphotericin × 6 wk	1. N & V, diarrhea 2. Bone marrow suppression 3. Hepatotoxicity	Should avoid when using other marrow suppressive drugs	1. ↓ in renal failure 2. Caution in hepatic failure	Capsules: 250, 500 mg
ANTIPROTOZOAN Trimethoprim (TMP)-sulfamethoxazole (SMX)	• P. carinii pneumonia	5 mg/kg TMP component i.v. q 6 hr or equivalent (2 DS tabs q.i.d.) p.o. 1 DS daily or 1 SS daily or 1 DS 3×/wk	21 days / Maintenance	1. N & V 2. Rash; drug fever 3. Hematological: bone marrow 4. Reversible renal impairment	1. ? potentiation of warfarin, phenytoin 2. Avoid when using other drugs	1. Renal — "use cautiously"	DS tablets: 160 mg TMP component, 800 mg SMX component

Drug	Indication	Dose	Duration	Adverse reactions			Formulation
Dapsone-TMP	• P. carinii pneumonia	100 mg dapsone p.o. 320 mg TMP b.i.d. p.o.	Maintenance	Same as TMP-SMX	Same as TMP-SMX	Same as TMP-SMX	100-mg tablet (dapsone)
Pyrimethamine-sulfadoxine	• P. carinii pneumonia	25 mg pyrimethamine/ 500 mg sulfa/wk *or* 50 mg pyrimethamine/ 1000 mg sulfa q 2 wk	Maintenance	Same as TMP-SMX	Same as TMP-SMX	Same as TMP-SMX	Tablets: pyrimethamine: 25 mg sulfadoxine: 500 mg
Pentamidine	• P. carinii pneumonia	4 mg/kg i.v. daily slowly (i.m. causes sterile abscesses)	21 days	1. Rapid infusion: tachycardia, orthostatic hypotension 2. Renal insufficiency 3. Hypo/hyperglycemia 4. Bone marrow ↓	None	No guidelines available	300 mg (for i.v. use)
		300 mg aerosolized q mo	Maintenance	Bronchospasm	None		
Clindamycin + primaquine	• P. carinii pneumonia	600 mg i.v. q 6 hr or 300–450 mg p.o. q 6 hr	21 days				
Atovaquone	• P. carinii pneumonia	750 mg p.o. t.i.d.	21 days	Rash, nausea, diarrhea			250-mg tablet
Pyrimethamine	• T. gondii cerebritis/ abscess (used in conjunction with sulfadiazine or clindamycin)	100–200-mg loading dose → 75–100 mg/d P.O. (must supplement with folinic acid → 10–50 mg/d)	≥ 6 weeks	1. Hematological: ↓ bone marrow (↓ WBC, ↓ platelets, megaloblastic anemia)	Avoid other bone marrow toxic drugs	No guidelines available	25-mg tablet
		25–50 mg/d p.o.	Maintenance				
Sulfadiazine	• T. gondii (with pyrimethamine,	6–8 g/d in 4 divided doses p.o.	≥ 6 weeks	Same as TMP-SMX	Same as TMP-SMX	Same as TMP-SMX	500-mg tablet

Table 20.10. Continued

Antimicrobial Agent	Organism(s) and Syndromes	Dosage/ Schedule/Route	Duration/ Maintenance	Common Adverse Effects	Drug Interactions	Dosage Change With Renal/Hepatic Failure	Available Strengths, Preparations
	folinic acid	2–4 g/d in 4 divided doses	Maintenance				
Clindamycin	• T. gondii (alternative to sulfadiazine)	900–1200 mg q 6–8 hr i.v.	≥ 6 weeks	1. N & V, diarrhea 2. Pseudo-membranous colitis	1. Enhanced action of curare-like drugs 2. Worsened colitis	1. None 2. Avoid with hepatic dysfunction	Capsules: 75, 150, 300 mg
		300–450 mg q 6–8 hr p.o.	Maintenance	3. Mild elevation of aminotransferases 4. Hypersensitivity			
ANTIVIRAL Acyclovir	• Herpes simplex infections						
	1. Esophagitis	5 mg/kg i.v. q 8 hr or 10 mg/kg i.v. q 8 hr	7–10 days or until lesions crusted or gone	1. N & V, light-headedness 2. Renal insufficiency with rapid infusion	1. Possible additive nephrotoxicity with aminoglycosides	↓ with renal failure	200-mg capsule
	2. Encephalitis	Mucocut: 200–400 mg b.i.d.–t.i.d. p.o.	Maintenance	3. Neurotoxicity 4. Hematological effects unusual			
	• Varicella-zoster infections 1. Shingles	10 mg/kg i.v. q 8 hr or 600–800 mg 5 × /d p.o.	7–10 days or until lesions crusted				
Ganciclovir	2. Encephalitis • Cytomegalovirus infections 1. Retinitis 2. Colitis 3. Other disseminated	10 mg/kg i.v. q 8 hr 5 mg/kg i.v. q 12 hr induction, then 5 mg/kg i.v. daily	2–3 weeks Maintenance (dose not clearly established)	1. Neutropenia, thrombocytopenia 2. Neurotoxicity — confusion 3. GI– N & V		↓ with renal failure	

Table 20.10. Continued

Antimicrobial Agent	Organism(s) and Syndromes	Dosage/ Schedule/Route	Duration/ Maintenance	Common Adverse Effects	Drug Interactions	Dosage Change With Renal/Hepatic Failure	Available Strengths, Preparations
Foscarnet	• Cytomegalovirus infection	60 mg/kg i.v., q 8 hr 90 mg/kg i.v. daily	14–21 d Maintenance	Renal failure 1. Genital ulcerations 2. Hypocalcemia, hypophosphatemia, hypokalemia, hypomagnesemia	1. Renal toxicity with other nephrotoxic drugs 2. ↑ Risk of hypocalcemia with pentamidine	↓ or D/C with renal failure	

N & V, nausea and vomiting; *GI,* gastrointestinal; *LFT,* liver function test; *Sx,* symptom(s); *DS,* double strength; *SS,* single strength; *WBC,* white blood cell count.
[a]Dosage based on cumulative, not daily, dose.

Table 20.11.   Neurological Syndromes in HIV-Infected Patients

Diffuse Brain Disease
  Encephalitis (toxoplasmosis, herpes simplex, cytomegalovirus, acute HIV)
  AIDS dementia complex

Meningitis
  Aseptic (acute HIV infection)
  Cryptococcal
  Tuberculous
  Lymphomatous

Focal Brain Disease
  Toxoplasmosis
  Primary central nervous system
  Progressive multifocal leukoencephalopathy (papovavirus)
  Tuberculoma
  Cryptococcoma
  Herpes simplex/varicella-zoster virus encephalitis

Peripheral Neuropathies/Radiculopathies/Myelopathies
  Neuropathies/radiculopathies
  Mononeuritides (brachial plexopathy)
  Guillain-Barré syndrome
  Sensorimotor polyneuropathy
  Cytomegalovirus polyradiculopathy
  Varicella-zoster (may involve multiple dermatomes)

Myelopathies
  Transverse myelitis (varicella-zoster virus, cytomegalovirus, lymphoma)
  HIV vacuolar myelopathy

Table 20.12.   Recommendations for Management of AZT Bone Marrow Toxicity

Toxicity	Options
Hgb ≥ 7.5 g/dl	Discontinue AZT and 1. Await bone marrow recovery or transfuse and reinitiate AZT at 300 mg/day *or* 2. Administer erythropoietin at 50 units/kg s.c. 3 times/week *or* 3. Change to ddl
Absolute neutrophil count ≤ 750/mm^3	Discontinue AZT and 1. Await bone marrow recovery and initiate AZT at 300 mg/day *or* 2. Administer G-CSF or GM-CSF[a] at dosages of 1–10 mg/kg/day *or* 3. Change to ddl

Hgb, hemoglobin; *G-CSF*, granulocyte colony-stimulating factor; *GM-CSF*, granulocyte-macrophage colony-stimulating factor.
[a] GM-CSF should *only* be used if antiretroviral therapy is used.

Table 20.13.   Recommendations for Starting Dose of ddI

Weight (kg)	Tablets [a] (mg. b.i.d.)	Powder
>60	200	250
<60	125	167

[a] See text for available strengths.

21/ DISORDERS OF THE ESOPHAGUS

DYSPHAGIA

A. History
1. Difficulty in swallowing solids suggests anatomical obstruction
2. Difficulty in swallowing solids and liquids suggests a motility disturbance
3. Difficulty in initiating a swallow, regurgitation of liquid through the nose, or aspiration with swallowing suggests oropharyngeal disease
4. Retrosternal fullness after swallowing or feeling that food is sticking on the way down suggests esophageal disease

B. Diagnostic procedures
1. Barium swallow
    a) The first study to do and the easiest for the patient
    b) The radiologist must be told the suspected diagnosis
    c) A negative study does not exclude either anatomical or motor disorders of the esophagus, and
    d) A positive study seldom permits a specific diagnosis, so
    e) Barium swallow is almost always followed by endoscopy or manometry
2. Endoscopy, the most direct procedure to diagnose an inflammatory or neoplastic disease
3. Manometry, best procedure for evaluation of esophageal motor function

C. Causes
1. Cancer of the esophagus
    a) Suspect especially in patients over 40
    b) Predisposing factors: smoking, alcohol, lye strictures, achalasia, Plummer-Vinson syndrome (see below), chronic reflux
    c) Most tumors are squamous cell (middle to distal third of esophagus); adenocarcinoma occurs in distal esophagus after chronic reflux
    d) Associated with dysphagia for solid food for several months, then dysphagia for solids and liquids
    e) Both barium swallow and endoscopy are required
    f) Computed tomography scan indicated after the diagnosis is confirmed, to evaluate presence of extraesophageal extension and of hepatic metastases
    g) Treatment
        1) Surgery or radiation — neither very successful
        2) Maintaining an open esophagus the major aim if the tumor is not resectable
2. Achalasia
    a) Characterized by the complete absence of esophageal peristalsis and by failure of lower esophageal sphincter (LES) relaxation
    b) Patients complain of progressive dysphagia for solids and liquids and, often, of regurgitation of ingested material
    c) Patients may complain of nocturnal cough and may even develop aspiration pneumonia

d) Chest x-ray often suggests the diagnosis: absent gastric air bubble and an air-fluid level behind the heart; mediastinum may appear widened
e) Barium swallow shows smooth tapered narrowing of the distal esophagus, retention of barium and secretions in the dilated proximal esophagus, absent peristalsis
f) Manometry confirms absent peristalsis, reveals failure of LES to relax after a swallow, and elevated LES pressure
g) Treatment: pneumatic dilation (preferred if possible) or surgery
h) Increased risk of squamous cell cancer of the esophagus even after successful treatment

3. Diffuse esophageal spasm
a) Characterized by nonperistaltic simultaneous esophageal contractions
b) Patients complain of intermittent dysphagia for liquids and solids and of substernal pain (see below)
c) Barium swallow often nonspecific, so that motility studies are necessary to make diagnosis
d) Treatment: Table 21.1

4. Scleroderma of the esophagus
a) Involved in 80% of people with the disease
b) Main symptoms are dysphagia and heartburn
c) Low LES pressure causes reflux, and impaired peristalsis results in retention of acid in esophagus; esophageal stricture common
d) Treatment is symptomatic (Table 21.2)

5. Esophageal webs and rings
a) Webs are usually proximal, sometimes associated with iron deficiency (Plummer-Vinson syndrome)
b) Rings are distal, usually asymptomatic, but may cause intermittent dysphagia for solid food and, if food impacts, regurgitation
c) Diagnosis
   1) Best made by barium swallow with a barium-coated marshmallow
   2) Endoscopy sometimes useful
d) Treatment
   1) Chew food well
   2) Treat iron deficiency if present
   3) Bougienage frequently disrupts a lower ring

6. Globus hystericus
a) No true dysphagia, but a "lump" in the throat
b) Cause unknown
c) Treatment supportive, but reflux should be ruled out or, if present, treated (Table 21.2)

ESOPHAGEAL CHEST PAIN

A. Causes
1. Nutcracker esophagus — characterized by high-amplitude contractions — common cause
2. Diffuse esophageal spasm (see above) — uncommon cause
3. Nonspecific motility disorders — common cause

Table 21.1.   Therapy for Spastic Esophageal Motility Disorders Associated With Chest Pain

Treatment Modality	Dose	Mode of Administration	Major Complications
Reassurance			
Nitrates [a]			
Nitroglycerin	0.4 mg s.l.	Usually before meals and p.r.n.	Headache
Isosorbide [a]	10–30 mg p.o.	30 min before meals	
Anticholinergics			
Dicyclomine (Bentyl)	10–20 mg p.o.	4 times/day	Dry mouth, blurred vision
Sedatives/antidepressants			
Diazepam (Valium)	2–5 mg p.o.	4 times/day	Drowsiness
Trazodone (Desyrel)	50–100 mg p.o.	4 times/day	Drowsiness, impotence
Doxepin (Sinequan) [a]	50 mg p.o.	At bedtime	Drowsiness
Calcium channel blockers [a]			
Nifedipine (Procardia)	10–30 mg	4 times/day	Dizziness, nausea, dyspepsia
Diltiazem (Cardizem)	90 mg	4 times/day	Headache, edema, nausea
Smooth muscle relaxants [a]			
Hydralazine [a]	20–50 mg p.o.	3 times/day	Headache, lupus-like syndrome
Static dilatation	50 French		None
Pneumatic dilatation [b]		Repeat as needed	Perforation (3–5%)
Esophagomyotomy [c]			Thoracotomy required; gastroesophageal reflux (20%)

[a] Orthostatic hypotension is a common complication of this class of drugs.
[b] May be indicated if dysphagia is a prominent symptom.
[c] Rarely indicated (intractability).

Table 21.2. Treatment of Gastroesophageal Reflux

Intervention	Specific Change	Mechanism of Improvement
PHASE 1		
Elevate head of bed (6-8-inch blocks)		Decreases acid contact time
Avoid drugs that decrease LES pressure	Theophylline, nitrates, calcium channel blockers, benzodiazepines	Avoids decrease of lower sphincter pressure
Avoid irritants	Citrus, coffee	
Stop smoking		Avoids direct mucosal damage
Avoid eating before sleep	3 hours	Removes inhibition of H_2 blockers, increases lower sphincter pressure
Antacid	As needed	Avoids gastric distention
Alginic acid (Gaviscon)	As needed	Decreases gastric acid
		Barrier protectant
PHASE II		
H_2 antagonists[a]		
Cimetidine (Tagamet)	400 mg 2 times/day (nonerosive symptomatic disease)	Decreases acid secretion
	800 mg 2 times/day (erosive esophagitis)	
Ranitidine (Zantac)	150 mg 2 times/day (nonerosive symptomatic disease)	
	300 mg 2 times/day (erosive esophagitis)	
Famotidine (Pepcid)	20 mg 2 times/day (nonerosive symptomatic disease)	
	40 mg 2 times/day (erosive esophagitis)	
Nizatidine (Axid)	150 mg 2 times/day (all forms of reflux disease)	
Cisapride[b]	10 mg 4 times/day	Both cisapride and metoclopramide increase lower esophageal sphincter pressure, increase esophageal clearance, and accelerate gastric emptying
Metoclopramide (Reglan)	5-10 mg 4 times/day	
Bethanechol (Urecholine)	25 mg 4 times/day	Increases lower sphincter pressure, accelerates esophageal clearance
Sucralfate (Carafate)	1 g 4 times/day	Mucosal protection (not FDA approved for treatment of reflux)
Proton pump inhibition		
Omeprazole (Prilosec)	20 mg/day (A.M.)	Decreases acid secretion
PHASE III		
Surgery	Nissen fundoplication	Creates intra-abdominal esophagus and increased lower sphincter pressure
	Belsey Mark IV repair	
	Hill procedure	

FDA, Food and Drug Administration.
[a]Nocturnal H_2 antagonists are insufficient antireflux therapy.
[b]Not yet approved by the FDA.

B. Diagnosis
  1. Important to distinguish from cardiac ischemia
  2. If diagnosis is not clear, therapeutic trial of antireflux therapy (Table 21.2) for 3–4 weeks is appropriate
  3. If therapeutic trial unsuccessful, consider referral for esophageal pH monitoring to see if pain correlates with reflux
  4. If pH monitoring unrevealing, consider manometry with provocative testing (edrophonium)
C. Treatment
  1. Reassure patient that pain is not due to heart disease
  2. Motility disorders may respond to nitrates, to calcium channel blockers, or to hydralazine (Table 21.1)
  3. Tricyclic antidepressants may be effective, especially if there are other signs of depression

GASTROINTESTINAL REFLUX
A. Cause unknown
B. History
  1. Typical symptom is heartburn, aggravated by meals and by lying down
  2. Some have pain consistent with angina
  3. Some have hoarseness, cough, or wheezing
C. Diagnosis
  1. Therapeutic trial of antireflux therapy indicated (see below) if symptoms are mild
  2. Barium swallow with double contrast is the simplest, least expensive procedure
    a) Reflux *plus* mucosal irregularities, stricture, or ulcer necessary to make diagnosis
    b) Relatively low sensitivity — best used to rule out complications
  3. Endoscopy
    a) Best study for diagnosis and evaluation of reflux esophagitis or of other complications of reflux (e.g., stricture or Barrett's esophagus)
    b) If esophagitis present, diagnosis of reflux essentially established
    c) If there is a stricture, it should be biopsied to rule out carcinoma
    d) If there is Barrett's esophagus, it should be biopsied to confirm diagnosis and to rule out dysplasia or in situ carcinoma
    e) More sensitive than barium swallow but still relatively insensitive
  4. Intraesophageal acid perfusion; reproduction of symptoms with relief by saline highly suggestive of diagnosis
  5. If diagnosis still in doubt, consider ambulatory pH monitoring, the most sensitive and specific test available
C. Treatment: Table 21.2
D. Complications: hemorrhage, ulcers, stricture, Barrett's epithelium

HIATUS HERNIA
A. Herniation of a part of the stomach through the diaphragm through the normal esophageal hiatus
B. Very common defect, especially in elderly
C. No correlation with reflux esophagitis
D. No treatment necessary

22/ ABDOMINAL PAIN

TYPES

A. Visceral
1. From spasm or stretch of a hollow viscus, from distention of the capsule of a solid organ, or from inflammation or ischemia of a visceral structure
2. Usually felt directly over affected structure (small bowel an exception except for terminal ileum)

B. Parietal
1. Well-localized, often with rebound tenderness
2. If widespread, indicates generalized peritonitis; if inflammation is severe, may be associated with a rigid abdomen

C. Referred
1. Gallbladder pain may radiate to the intrascapular area
2. Esophageal pain may mimic the referred pain of myocardial ischemia
3. Severe visceral pain may be referred to the back

D. Caused by metabolic disease
1. Direct effect, e.g., acute intermittent porphyria, lead poisoning, familial Mediterranean fever
2. Indirect effect, e.g., peptic ulcer or pancreatitis secondary to hypercalcemia

E. Neurogenic
1. A burning sensation along the course of the affected nerve
2. Spinal root disease (e.g., herpes zoster) or peripheral neuropathy (e.g., diabetic mellitus) may be the cause

F. Psychogenic, as part of a somatoform disorder or a stress-related syndrome (e.g., irritable bowel syndrome or peptic disease)

CLUES TO DIAGNOSIS

A. Rapidity and onset of pain: Table 22.1
B. Nature and location of pain: Table 22.2

PHYSICAL EXAMINATION

A. General appearance: cold and clammy if patient is in shock; warm and moist if patient is septic
B. Position of patient: truncal flexure suggests pancreatitis; pacing and writhing suggest colic; immobile position suggests peritonitis
C. Inspection: e.g., flank or periumbilical discoloration from hemorrhagic pancreatitis, protruding hernia
D. Auscultation: e.g., hyperperistaltic or hypoperistaltic bowel sounds, high tinkling of bowel obstruction, bruits; attempt to elicit a succussion splash if there is suspicion of gastric outlet obstruction
E. Percussion to detect rebound tenderness, masses, tympany (over an area of dilated bowel), or absence of liver dullness in a patient with free air in the abdomen
F. Palpation to detect local or generalized tenderness
G. Rectal examination to detect localized tender area or masses
H. Genital and pelvic examination

Table 22.1.   Causes of Acute Abdominal Pain According to Rapidity of Onset

Intestinal Causes	Extraintestinal Causes
Abrupt onset (instantaneous)	
Perforated ulcer	Ruptured or dissecting aneurysm
Ruptured abscess or hematoma	Ruptured ectopic pregnancy
Intestinal infarct	Pneumothorax
Ruptured esophagus	Myocardial infarct
	Pulmonary infarct
Rapid onset (minutes)	
Perforated viscus	Ureteral colic
Strangulated viscus	Renal colic
Volvulus	Ectopic pregnancy
Pancreatitis	Splenic infarct
Biliary colic	
Mesenteric infarct	
Diverticulitis	
Penetrating peptic ulcer	
High intestinal obstruction	
Appendicitis (gradual onset more common)	
Gradual onset (hours)	
Appendicitis	Cystitis
Strangulated hernia	Pyelitis
Low small intestinal obstruction	Salpingitis
Cholecystitis	Prostatitis
Pancreatitis	Threatened abortion
Gastritis	Urinary retention
Peptic ulcer	Pneumonitis
Colonic diverticulitis	
Meckel's diverticulitis	
Crohn's disease	
Ulcerative colitis	
Mesenteric lymphadenitis	
Abscess	
Intestinal infarct	
Mesenteric cyst	

Adapted from Ridge JA, Way LW: Abdominal pain. In: Sleisenger MH, Fordtran JS (eds): *Gastrointestinal Disease*, 5th ed. Philadelphia, WB Saunders, 1993, p 156.

LABORATORY TESTS
A. Complete blood count, urinalysis, test for occult blood in stool

RADIOLOGY
A. Plain and upright films of the abdomen to look for displacement of the intestine by masses, distribution of air consistent with obstruction, ileus, volvulus, or perforation
B. Contrast studies — often replaced now by endoscopy
   1. Upper gastrointestinal (GI) series if there is suspicion of upper GI obstruction
   2. Barium enema (preceded always by digital and proctoscopic examination) if there is suspicion of lower intestinal obstruction
C. Ultrasonography (Table 22.3) if there is a suspicion of gallstones, pancreatic pseudocysts, or aortic aneurysm or there is a palpable abdominal mass

Table 22.2.   Nature and Location of Gastrointestinal Pain

Organ Involved	Nature of Pain	Location of Pain
Esophagus	Burning, constricting	Upper lesions: high substernal Lower lesions: low sternal or referred upward Severe: back
Stomach	Gnawing discomfort, sensation of hunger	Epigastric Left upper quadrant
Duodenum	Gnawing discomfort, sensation of hunger	Epigastric
Small intestine	Aching, cramping, bloating, sharp	Diffuse Periumbilical Terminal ileum: right lower quadrant
Colon	Aching, cramping, bloating, sharp	Lower abdomen Sigmoid: left lower quadrant Rectum: midline and sacrum
Pancreas	Excruciating, constant	Upper abdomen radiating to back
Gallbladder	Severe, later dull ache	Right upper quadrant Radiates to right scapula or interscapular area
Liver	Ache, occasionally sharp	Right lower rib cage Right upper quadrant if liver is enlarged

D. TcHIDA or PipHIDA radioisotopic study if there is a suspicion of common or cystic bile duct obstruction

E. Computed tomography (CT) (Table 22.3) to evaluate masses

F. Magnetic resonance imaging (MRI) (Table 22.3) used selectively to define masses (especially in liver, kidneys, or adrenals)

ENDOSCOPY

A. Upper gastrointestinal endoscopy
   1. Procedure of choice to diagnose upper GI disease
   2. Should be performed promptly if pain is associated with bleeding

B. Proctoscopy
   1. In any patient with abdominal pain and rectal bleeding
   2. In any patient with suspected inflammatory bowel disease
   3. To evaluate rectal disease (hemorrhoids, fissures)

C. Colonoscopy
   1. In patients with abdominal pain and rectal bleeding
   2. In patients with suspected diffuse inflammatory bowel disease
   3. In patients with known polypoid lesions of the colon — for biopsy or resection

TREATMENT

A. Dependent on cause

B. Avoid analgesia unless pain is severe

C. If pain is persistent and analgesia is needed, avoid opiates

Table 22.3. Ultrasound, Computed Tomographic (CT) Scanning, and Magnetic Resonance Imaging (MRI): Comparison of the Technique and the Patient Experience

Characteristic	Ultrasound	CT	MRI
Basis of tissue attenuation	Tissue elasticity, acoustic impedance	Electron density; linear attenuation coefficient	Nuclear resonance
Radiation dose or toxic effect	None known at diagnostic energy levels	8–10 rad (skin exposure)	None known
Morphological detail	Good	Excellent	Excellent
Contrast medium useful	No	Iodinated intravascular and oral agents; diatrizoate meglumine Gastrografin)	No (in abdomen)
Time for examination	½–1 hour	½–1 hour	1 hour
Operator skill	Substantial	Minimal	Minimal
Ease of interpretation	Complex — many artifacts	Straightforward	Moderately straightforward
Preparation	Nothing by mouth after midnight (for pelvis, 3 glasses of water 1 hour before study and do not void)	Evacuate barium from recent GI studies (or wait 1 week)	None
Cooperation	Lie still, supine, be able to hold breath	Lie still, supine, be able to hold breath	Lie still, supine, breathe quietly

Adapted from Ferrucci JT Jr: Body ultrasonography (first of two parts). *N Engl J Med* 300: 538, 1979.

23/ PEPTIC ULCER DISEASE

RISK FACTORS: TABLE 23.1

DIAGNOSIS

A. History
1. Most common symptom is a vague epigastric discomfort or a feeling of intense hunger; if there is actual pain, it is burning or aching
2. Discomfort of duodenal ulcer typically 1–3 hours after a meal or may awaken patient in early A.M.; relieved by food, antacids, or vomiting
3. Discomfort of gastric ulcer not predictably relieved by eating (may be made worse)
4. Some patients experience nausea and vomiting
5. Weight loss in 50% of patients with gastric ulcer; patients with duodenal ulcer often gain weight

B. Physical examination
1. Localized epigastric tenderness is common
2. Succussion splash 4 or more hours after eating suggests gastric outlet obstruction
3. Always test stool for occult blood

C. Upper gastrointestinal (GI) series
1. Duodenal ulcer: sensitivity 40–80%; ulcers of <0.5 cm often missed
2. Gastric ulcer: sensitivity 65–80%; malignancy missed in approximately 10%
3. Double contrast and air contrast increase sensitivity

D. Endoscopy
1. Sensitivity 90% for duodenal and gastric ulcer
2. Indications
   a) Refractory pain of long standing
   b) Symptoms but negative GI series
   c) Suspected outlet obstruction
   d) GI bleeding

Table 23.1.   Risk Factors for Peptic Ulcer Disease

Male sex
First-degree relative with duodenal ulcer
Genetic marker
   Elevated levels of pepsinogen I
   Presence of HLA-B5 antigen
   Decreased red blood cell acetylcholinesterase
Stress
Cigarette smoking
Zollinger-Ellison syndrome
Chronic renal failure — for duodenal ulcer disease only
Chronic obstructive pulmonary disease — for duodenal ulcer disease only
Alcoholic cirrhosis — for duodenal ulcer disease only
Drugs: aspirin, nonsteroidal anti-inflammatory drugs
Helicobacter pylori gastritis

      e) Equivocal GI series
      f) Gastric ulcers that are not clearly benign on GI series or are >2.5 cm
      g) Apparently benign gastric ulcers at some point in therapy (e.g., after 8 weeks)

E. Gastric analysis — of limited usefulness
F. Serum gastrin level — to screen for Zollinger-Ellison syndrome (see below)
G. Identification of *Helicobacter pylori*
    1. An important cofactor in the etiology of duodenal and gastric ulcer disease
    2. Should be looked for in any patient with refractory or recurrent duodenal or gastric ulcer
    3. Can be identified by culture, on biopsy, or by indirect tests that measure urease

TREATMENT

A. Nonpharmacological
    1. Dietary modification does not affect the cause of peptic ulcer disease
    2. Stopping smoking is the most important nonpharmacological intervention
B. Pharmacological — duodenal ulcer
    1. Expect relief in 7–10 days, healing (85–90%) in 4–6 weeks
    2. H_2 receptor antagonists (Table 23.2)
    3. Antacids: rarely used as sole agents, no advantage over H^2 receptor antagonists
    4. Omeprazole (Table 23.2): especially valuable for refractory ulcers and for reflux esophagitis
    5. Anticholinergic agents: limited usefulness because of side effects
    6. Prostaglandins (misoprostol): unacceptable side effects
    7. Sucralfate (Table 23.2)
    8. Eradication of *H. pylori* (Table 23.3) accelerates healing, reduces recurrence rate; recommended for refractory or recurrent ulcers
    9. General recommendations
      a) Choice of initial therapy should be based on cost, personal preference, side effects, drug interaction
      b) If ulcer does not heal in 6–8 weeks, prescribe omeprazole or attempt to eradicate *H. pylori* if present
    10. Maintenance (Table 23.2)
      a) Reserve for patients at higher risk of recurrence: e.g., patients over 60; men; patients with chronic obstructive lung disease, ischemic heart disease, or renal failure; patients with a history of a bleeding or perforated ulcer; patients who smoke; patients whose ulcers have recurred 2 or more times 1 year after diagnosis
      b) People without high risk have a 20% 1-year recurrence rate; do not need maintenance therapy
      c) Maintenance therapy, when given, usually for a year
C. Pharmacological — gastric ulcer
    1. Basically, same drugs as used for duodenal ulcer
    2. Eradication of *H. pylori* reduces recurrence rate

Table 23.2. Drugs Approved for Treatment of Peptic Ulcer Disease

Drug	Available Strengths	Initial Dose [a,b]	Maintenance Dose	Principal Side Effects
Cimetidine (Tagamet) [c]	200 mg 300 mg 400 mg 800 mg	300 mg 4 times/day 400 mg twice/day 800 mg at bedtime	400 mg at bedtime	Gynecomastia, confusion, impotence, blood dyscrasia, drug interaction (see text)
Ranitidine (Zantac)	150 mg 300 mg	150 mg twice/day 300 mg at bedtime	150 mg at bedtime	Gynecomastia, impotence, hepatitis (rare)
Famotidine (Pepcid) [c]	20 mg 40 mg	20 mg twice/day 40 mg at bedtime	20 mg at bedtime	Headache, decreased libido, depression, mild increase in aminotransferase
Nizatidine (Axid)	150 mg 300 mg	150 mg twice/day [d] 300 mg at bedtime	150 mg at bedtime	Sweating, urticaria (<1%), somnolence, elevated liver enzymes
Sucralfate (Carafate) [c]	1 g	1 g 4 times/day [d] 2 g twice/day	1 g twice/day 2 g at bedtime	Constipation
Omeprazole (Prilosec)	20 mg	20 mg once/day (A.M.)	Not approved	Nausea, headache

[a] Duodenal ulcer, 4–6 weeks.
[b] Gastric ulcer, 8–12 weeks (document healing).
[c] Available in liquid suspension.
[d] Not approved for gastric ulcer by the Food and Drug Administration (FDA).

Table 23.3.   Treatment of *H. pylori* Infection

Regimen	Dose	Duration of Therapy	Success Rate
Bismuth [a,b]	2 tabs 4 times/day	2 weeks	81%
Metronidazole [c]	250 mg 3 times/day	2 weeks	
Tetracycline	500 mg 3 times/day	2 weeks	
Bismuth [a]	15 ml 4 times/day	2 weeks	83%
Metronidazole [c]	500 mg 3 times/day	2 weeks	
Tetracycline	500 mg 4 times/day	2 weeks	
Metronidazole [a,c]	500 mg 3 times/day	12 days	89%
Amoxicillin	750 mg 3 times/day	12 days	
Omeprazole	20 mg 2 times/day	2 weeks	83%
Amoxicillin	500 mg 4 times/day	2 weeks	

[a] Patients were also treated with ranitidine 150 mg twice a day or 300 mg h.s. if duodenal ulcer was present.
[b] For example, Pepto-Bismol.
[c] Clarithromycin 500 mg twice a day may be substituted for metronidazole.

3. Treat for 8 weeks; document healing by endoscopy
4. Stop nonsteroidal anti-inflammatory drugs
5. Strongly discourage smoking

D. Surgery
   1. Indications: perforation, uncontrolled hemorrhage, gastric outlet obstruction, intractable symptoms
   2. Before surgery, rule out Zollinger-Ellison syndrome

ZOLLINGER-ELLISON SYNDROME

A. Caused by a gastrin-secreting tumor, usually multiple, commonly in the head of the pancreas; two-thirds are malignant although slow growing
B. Consider diagnosis in patients with refractory or frequently recurrent ulcers, with postbulbar or jejunal ulcers (although most are in the bulb), with anastomotic ulcers after surgery, with chronic diarrhea
C. Diagnosis based on elevated serum gastrin level; provocative tests (secretin test, calcium infusion test) needed if results are equivocal
D. Treatment
   1. Omeprazole the drug of choice
   2. Gastrectomy the operation of choice if medical treatment fails

NONULCER DYSPEPSIA

A. Persistent epigastric discomfort sometimes with nausea, vomiting, or bloating and no evidence of ulcer disease
B. Associated diseases
   1. Irritable bowel syndrome
   2. Cholelithiasis
   3. Gastroesophageal reflux
   4. Chronic pancreatic disease
C. Essential dyspepsia
   1. If no other evidence of disease, treat with an antiulcer regimen (Table 23.2) for 3–4 weeks
   2. If no response to drugs, endoscopy indicated (consider earlier in patients over 60, especially if symptoms are severe and of recent onset)
   3. If endoscopy negative, some advocate eradication of *H. pylori* (see above) if present

GASTRITIS

A. Acute erosive or hemorrhagic gastritis
  1. Seen in severely ill patients, patients taking nonsteroidal anti-inflammatory drugs, after heavy alcohol ingestion
  2. Symptoms: nausea, vomiting, sometimes bleeding
B. Nonerosive or chronic antral gastritis
  1. Common histological diagnosis in the elderly
  2. Caused by *H. pylori* infection
  3. Not clear whether associated with symptoms
  4. Treatment same as for essential dyspepsia (see above)

24/ GASTROINTESTINAL BLEEDING

COMMON CAUSES: TABLE 24.1

DETECTION OF BLOOD IN STOOL

A. Most commonly used test is modified guaiac slide test (Hemoccult); in screening programs, 1–8% have positive tests of whom 8–15% have colon cancer and 9–36% have polyps
B. Sensitivity low but improved by testing of multiple specimens
C. Laxatives increase number of true and false positive tests
D. False negative results are more likely in patients taking high doses of vitamin C
E. Positive tests, without clinical significance, may result from hemoglobin- or peroxidase-rich foods (e.g., rare red meat or uncooked broccoli, turnips, or cauliflower) or from iron salts
F. Obtain 2 different samples from 3 different stools over a 3-day period every year in patients over 40

EVALUATION OF PATIENTS WHO HAVE GASTROINTESTINAL BLEEDING

A. Lower gastrointestinal (GI) tract
  1. Hematochezia
    a) In patients under 40, first test is flexible proctosigmoidoscopy; if inconclusive, air contrast barium enema should be done
    b) In patients over age 40, first test is colonoscopy, even if there is rectal disease (e.g., hemorrhoids or even rectal cancer)
  2. Occult blood in stool: colonoscopy should be done

Table 24.1. Common Causes of Gastrointestinal Bleeding

Occult bleeding
  Gastritis, especially due to nonsteroidal anti-inflammatory agents or to ethanol
  Peptic ulcer disease
  Colonic polyps
  Colonic cancer
  Gastric cancer
  Esophagitis
Melena
  Peptic ulcer disease
  Hemorrhagic gastritis
  Gastric carcinoma
Hematochezia
  Diverticulosis
  Angiodysplasia
  Rectal outlet disorders (hemorrhoids, cryptitis, fissures)
  Inflammatory bowel disease
  Colonic polyps
  Colonic cancer
Hematemesis
  Peptic ulcer disease
  Esophageal varices
  Mallory-Weiss tear
  Hemorrhagic gastritis
  Gastric cancer

B. Upper GI tract
   1. Upper GI series is sometimes done first if there are upper GI symptoms and the bleeding is slow, chronic, or occult
   2. If an inflammatory process is suspected (esophagitis or gastritis) or if bleeding is acute, upper endoscopy should be done

SELECTED LESIONS THAT BLEED

A. Colonic polyps
   1. Should be suspected in any patient over 40 who has GI bleeding or a change in bowel habits (but may not cause symptoms)
   2. Bleeding may be occult or may occur as intermittent hematochezia
   3. Risk of polyps becoming malignant is related to their histological type and their size (Table 24.2)
      a) Hyperplastic polyps, the most common, probably have no malignant potential
      b) Villous and tubular adenomas
         1) Colonoscopic polypectomy indicated if there is no cancer or if cancer is confined to the mucosa of the polyp
         2) If cancer has invaded the stalk, surgery is indicated
   4. Once a polyp is detected, stool should be tested for blood yearly, and colonoscopy should be performed after 1 year and then, if negative, every 3–5 years; multiple polyposis syndromes (familial polyposis, Gardner's syndrome, Turcot syndrome) are rare inherited conditions that have high malignant potential
B. Colorectal cancer
   1. Epidemiology
      a) Third leading cause of death from cancer in the United States
      b) Incidence increases with age: two-thirds occur in people over 65
      c) High-fat, low-fiber diet appears to increase risk
      d) Sixty percent can be seen by flexible sigmoidoscopy
      e) The three main predisposing conditions are colonic polyps, familial polyposis, and ulcerative colitis; require increased surveillance
   2. Screening tests
      a) Test yearly 2 specimens from 3 consecutive stools for occult blood [by Hemoccult (see above)]
      b) Yearly rectal examination in patients over 40
      c) Flexible sigmoidoscopy in 2 consecutive years, then, if no lesions are seen, every 5–10 years if patients are asymptomatic and their stools have no occult blood
   3. Diagnosis

Table 24.2. Polyps: Relationship of Size, Histological Type, and Risk of Carcinoma

Histological Type	% That Are Cancerous		
	Under 1 cm	1–2 cm	Over 2 cm
Tubular adenoma	1.0	10.2	34.7
Intermediate type	3.9	7.4	45.8
Villous adenoma	9.5	10.3	52.9

a) Less than 10% are asymptomatic; this group has the best chance of cure
b) Major presenting symptoms are abdominal pain and change in bowel habits and hematochezia
c) Physical examination depends on size and activity of tumor: right-sided lesions or lesions in the rectal cul-de-sac may be palpable; patients with metastatic disease may have palpable hard livers, ascites, etc.
d) Barium enema may identify the tumor — accuracy excellent except at opposite ends of the colon (proctoscopy essential for that reason)
e) Endoscopy ordinarily the definitive diagnostic test and is important in evaluating the rest of the colon in a patient with an identifiable lesion
f) Carcinoembryonic antigen (CEA)
   1) Not specific for colon cancer
   2) Found in blood of many patients with colon cancer
   3) Helpful in postoperative management of patients if CEA was elevated at time of diagnosis

4. Treatment
   a) Preoperative evaluation
      1) Liver function tests, computed tomography (CT) of the liver, CEA
      2) Multiple metastases a contraindication to surgery (not so a single hepatic metastasis)
      3) Apparent hepatic metastases should be confirmed by needle biopsy
      4) If an ostomy is anticipated, preoperative discussion with an enterostomy therapist is of help
5. Prognosis: Table 24.3
6. Follow-up care
   a) If there is an ostomy, close follow-up by the surgeon and an enterostomy therapist is important
   b) Physical examination, liver function tests, CEA levels every 2–6 months for 3–5 years; if CEA rises or liver function tests become abnormal, a CT scan of the abdomen is appropriate, although the outcome is unaffected by early detection
   c) Colonoscopy within 6–12 months postoperatively; if negative, repeated in 1 year and then every 3 years if no recurrent cancer or polyps are detected

Table 24.3.   Colon Carcinoma

Classification [a]	Staging and 5-Year Survival	
	Microscopic Findings	Percentage of 5-Year Survival
A	Disease limited to mucosa	95
B	Tumor extends to serosa	60–70
C	Tumor extends to serosa and nodes involved	<40
D	Distant metastases	<5

[a] Modification of the Dukes classification.

    d) Yearly testing for fecal occult blood; if positive, colonoscopy should be done

C. Arteriovenous malformation of the colon

  1. Common source of GI bleeding, especially in the elderly, in patients with chronic renal failure, and in patients with aortic stenosis

  2. Appears most commonly in the cecum and ascending colon

  3. Often causes hematochezia, but occult blood loss may also occur

  4. Diagnosis best made by selective arteriography or by colonoscopy, although the presence of a lesion does not guarantee that it is the source of bleeding

  5. Lesions that have been observed to bleed should be excised (colonoscopic removal or cauterization may be possible)

25/ CONSTIPATION AND DIARRHEA

CONSTIPATION

A. Definition
1. Often defined as the infrequent, difficult passage of stool
2. Frequency of bowel movements varies widely in normal people
3. Constipation best defined as a reduction in normal frequency of bowel movements
4. Almost always, constipation is due to a delay in colonic transit due to one of a variety of causes (Table 25.1)

B. Evaluation
1. History
   a) Be certain that there is not a misconception about the normal frequency of bowel movements
   b) Look for a history suggestive of a systemic illness (Table 25.1)
   c) Look for symptoms suggestive of a local process (abdominal pain or rectal bleeding)
   d) Take a careful drug and dietary history (Table 25.1)
   e) In adults under 50, consider irritable bowel syndrome,

Table 25.1. Various Causes of Constipation

IDIOPATHIC (POSSIBLE MECHANISMS)
   Dietary factors — low residue
   Motility disturbances — colonic inertia or spasm (irritable bowel syndrome)
   Sedentary living
STRUCTURAL ABNORMALITIES
   Anorectal disorders — fissures, thrombosed hemorrhoids
   Strictures
   Tumors
ENDOCRINE/METABOLIC
   Hypercalcemia
   Hypokalemia
   Hypothyroidism
   Pregnancy
NEUROGENIC
   Cerebrovascular events
   Hirschsprung's disease
   Parkinson's disease
   Spinal cord tumors
   Trauma
SMOOTH MUSCLE/CONNECTIVE TISSUE DISORDERS
   Amyloidosis
   Scleroderma
DRUGS
   Antacids — aluminum- and calcium-containing compounds
   Anticholinergics
   Antidepressants
   Calcium channel blockers (especially verapamil)
   Cholestyramine
   Narcotics
   Sympathomimetics — pseudoephedrine
PSYCHOGENIC (especially depression)

especially if there is associated abdominal pain (see Chapter 26)
2. Physical examination
    a) Rectal examination useful to look for local lesions (Table 25.1) and to test stool for occult blood
    b) The general physical examination is usually not of help unless an abdominal mass is palpated or there are signs of a systemic or neurological illness associated with constipation
3. Endoscopy
    a) Anoscopy and flexible sigmoidoscopy should be done routinely if the cause of constipation is not obvious
    b) Even if proctosigmoidoscopy reveals a benign cause of constipation, a barium enema should be done, or, alternatively, the initial endoscopic procedure should be colonoscopy
        1) Inflamed hemorrhoids or fissures may be the cause or the result of constipation
        2) Melanosis coli, a spotty or diffuse brown pigmentation of the mucosa, indicates chronic laxative abuse
        3) Mass lesions may be identified
4. Radiological studies
    a) Primarily of help in detection of obstructing lesions
    b) Barium enema (or colonoscopy) should be performed in all patients whose constipation has begun within the last 6 months
    c) Repeated studies rarely of help
5. Other studies only for severely impaired patients, refractory to therapy
    a) Colonic motility studies — only available in specialized centers
    b) Colonic transit time
C. Treatment
    1. Correct underlying abnormality (Table 25.1) if possible
    2. Bowel retraining
        a) For patients whose constipation has no identifiable cause
        b) The patient is encouraged to attempt to defecate within 5–10 minutes after the same meal each day and to respond always to the urge to defecate
        c) May be initiated with enema or suppositories at the desired time for a few days only
    3. High-fiber diet (Table 25.2)
    4. Laxatives (Table 25.3)

DIARRHEA
A. Definition
    1. An increase in the frequency and fluid volume of defecation
    2. Usually diarrhea associated with stools in excess of 250 g/day (normal 100–200 g/day)
    3. A subset of patients will have frequent passage of small volumes of liquid stool
B. Pathophysiology
    1. Osmotic diarrhea, e.g., due to malabsorption, lactose intolerance, magnesium-containing laxatives
    2. Secretory diarrhea, e.g., due to toxin-producing bacteria, bile

Table 25.2.   Fiber Content of Various Foods

Type of Food	Dietary Fiber per Average Serving (g)
VEGETABLES	
Beans (navy, lima, kidney, baked)	8.5–10.0
Beans (string)	2.0
Broccoli	3.2
Brussels sprouts	2.3
Cabbage	2.0
Carrots	2.0
Celery	1.0
Corn	2.6
Corn on the cob	5.9
Lettuce	1.0
Potato (baked with skin)	3.0
Potato (french fried)	1.6
Peas (canned)	6.0
Rice	0.8
FRUIT	
Apple with peel	2.0
Apple juice	0.0
Banana	1.5
Grapefruit (fresh)	0.6
Orange	2.0
Peach	2.0
Raspberries	4.6
Strawberries	1.6
BREAD	
Whole wheat	1.3
White, rye, French	0.7
CEREAL	
All-Bran (100%)	8.4
Corn flakes	2.6
Wheaties	2.6
OTHER FOODS	
Meats: chicken, liver, fish, lamb	0.0
Cheese, milk, yogurt	0.0

salts, or long-chain fatty acids (e.g., postileal resection, Crohn's disease), anthraquinone laxatives

3. Exudative diarrhea, e.g., due to ulcerative colitis, Crohn's disease, invasive bacterial infections, or infiltrative diseases (e.g., Whipple's disease, lymphoma)

4. Motility disorders, e.g., irritable bowel syndrome or diabetes mellitus with autonomic neuropathy

C. Evaluation

1. Acute diarrhea

a) most cases are self-limited

b) Evaluation indicated if diarrhea persists for more than 72 hours or if there is hematochezia

c) History

1) Loose watery stools most commonly due to infection: toxins produce diarrhea within 6 hours of ingestion

2) Bloody diarrhea suggests invasive infections (*Shigella,*

Table 25.3. Laxatives

Classification and Active Ingredient	Examples	Dose	Average Onset of Action	Potential Adverse Effects
BULK				
Psyllium seed	Konsyl Effer-Syllium Perdiem (with senna) Metamucil	1 tsp to 2 tbsp/day	12–24 hours or more	Increased gas and bloating sensation; bowel obstruction if stricture present
Plus dextrose				
Bran		4+ tbsp/day		
Calcium polycarbophil	FiberCon	4–8 tablets/day		
EMOLLIENT (SOFTENERS)				
Dioctyl sodium (or calcium) sulfosuccinate (docusate sodium)	Colace, Peri-Colace (with casanthranol) Surfak	1–3 caps/day	24–48 hours	
STIMULANT				
Phenolphthalein	Correctol, Ex-Lax	1–2 tablets (100–200 mg)	6–8 hours	Dermatitis; electrolyte imbalance, melanosis coli
Bisacodyl	Dulcolax	2–3 tabs (10–15 mg)	6–12 hours	
Senna	Senokot, Perdiem (with psyllium)	1–4 tsp or 2–4 tabs	6–12 hours	
Cascara (casanthranol)	Peri-Colace (with dioctyl sodium)	1–2 tabs	8–12 hours	
CO_2	Ceo-two suppositories	1–2	10–30 minutes	
OSMOTIC				
Ricinoleic acid	Castor oil	1–2 tsp	24–48 hours	Electrolyte imbalance
Lactulose[a]	Cephulac, Chronulac	1–2 tbsp/day		Excessive gas production
Magnesium salts	Milk of Magnesia, magnesium citrate	2–4 tbsp	3–6 hours or less	Hypermagnesemia, hypocalcemia, hyperphosphatemia in chronic renal failure
Sodium salts	Phospho-Soda	2 tbsp in ½ glass of water	2–6 hours	
	Fleet enema (sodium phosphate)	120 ml	2–5 minutes	Dehydration; hypocalcemia; hyperphosphatemia in chronic renal failure

[a] Requires a prescription.

      Salmonella, Campylobacter, Yersinia), ulcerative colitis, or ischemic bowel disease

    3) Recently prescribed drugs should be asked about (Table 25.4)

    4) Campers and hikers may have been exposed to *Giardia*

    5) A number of HIV-associated intestinal disorders cause diarrhea (Chapter 20)

  d) Physical examination

    1) Generally unremarkable

    2) State of hydration an important measure of severity of diarrhea

    3) Abdomen may be slightly tender; bowel sounds are usually active or hyperactive

    4) Rectal examination is essential to look for rectal cancer and, in the elderly, fecal impaction

  e) Stool examination

    1) Look for blood

    2) Look for fecal leukocytes

      (a) Best seen by microscopic examination of liquid stool stained with methylene blue or with Gram's stain

      (b) Not seen in noninvasive processes (toxin-producing bacterial infection, viral enteritis)

      (c) Seen in invasive processes (*Salmonella, Shigella, Amoeba,* and *Campylobacter* infections or chronic inflammatory bowel disease)

    3) Culture — useful primarily in patients with fecal leukocytes

    4) Examination for parasites

Table 25.4.   Common Drugs That May Induce Diarrhea

ANTIBIOTICS[a]
  Clindamycin
  Ampicillin
  Cephalosporins
ANTACIDS
  Magnesium-containing
ANTIHYPERTENSIVE AGENTS
  Guanethidine
  Hydralazine
  Methyldopa
  Propranolol
  Reserpine
CARDIOVASCULAR AGENTS
  Digitalis
  Quinidine
ANTIMETABOLITES
  Colchicine
ALCOHOL
NUTRITIONAL SUPPLEMENTS
  Hyperosmolar solutions (enteral feedings)
POTENT DIURETICS
  Furosemide
  Ethacrynic acid
  Bumetanide

[a] All antibiotics can induce diarrhea (see Chapter 12).

        (a) Must be done immediately on prewarmed slide

        (b) Rectal biopsy sometimes necessary to demonstrate organisms

  f) Endoscopy

     1) Important in patients with fecal leukocytes if cause of diarrhea is not obvious

     2) Should be performed without a cleansing enema, which alters the appearance of the mucosa

     3) Flexible sigmoidoscopy preferable to colonoscopy (yield no greater)

  g) Radiographic studies

     1) Limited value, usually unnecessary

     2) Plain films may show "thumbprinting" due to mucosal edema in patients with inflammatory bowel disease or ischemic colitis

2. Chronic diarrhea

  a) Diarrhea of longer than 2 weeks duration

  b) History

     1) Diarrhea for many months or years without sequelae (e.g., weight loss, anemia, hypoalbuminemia) suggests irritable bowel syndrome (see Chapter 26)

        (a) Typically, several watery, at times explosive, bowel movements early in the morning, then no more the rest of the day

        (b) Abdominal pain may or may not be present

     2) Most common cause of chronic secretory diarrhea is laxative abuse

        (a) Apparently healthy patients with large volume diarrhea

        (b) Often associated with melanosis coli (see above)

     3) Large volume of frothy malodorous, nonbloody stools suggests small bowel diarrhea, often due to malabsorption

     4) Small volumes of poorly formed, bloody stools suggest inflammatory, exudative disorders of the colon, e.g., ulcerative colitis

     5) Presence of fat droplets suggests malabsorption, frequently due to pancreatic insufficiency

     6) Important to ask about association with dairy products or with drugs (Table 25.4)

     7) Arthritis and arthralgias may be associated with inflammatory bowel disease, Whipple's disease, Reiter's syndrome

     8) Weight loss, without anorexia, suggests malabsorption, hyperthyroidism, or a malignant tumor

     9) Abdominal pain may reflect the irritable bowel syndrome (left lower quadrant or suprapubic region), small bowel disease (periumbilical or right lower quadrant) or Zollinger-Ellison syndrome (epigastric)

  c) Physical examination

     1) Malabsorption may be associated with weight loss, peripheral neuropathy (vitamin deficiency)

     2) Inflammatory bowel disease may be associated with arthritis, erythema nodosum, pyoderma gangrenosum

    3) Whipple's disease and Addison's disease may be associated with hyperpigmentation

    4) Diabetic diarrhea is usually associated with other signs of autonomic dysfunction, e.g., postural hypotension

    5) Hepatosplenomegaly and lymphadenopathy suggest lymphoma or Whipple's disease

    6) A rectal examination may reveal perianal disease, a rectal tumor, or a fecal impaction

d) Endoscopy

    1) Proctoscopy should be performed at the initial visit (without cleansing enema)

    2) Rectal biopsy may reveal specific diagnosis; e.g., ulcerative colitis, Crohn's disease, amebiasis, Whipple's disease, amyloidosis

    3) Melanosis coli (see above) suggests laxative abuse

    4) Cultures, including gonococcal cultures, should be taken, and the stools should be examined for leukocytes, blood, fat, parasites

e) Radiological studies

    1) Plain film may reveal pancreatic calcifications (indicative of chronic pancreatitis), a dilated small bowel, or an abnormal bowel contour (such as in inflammatory bowel disease or lymphoma)

    2) In patients over 40 or if there is blood in the stool, barium enema (or colonoscopy) is indicated during the initial evaluation (barium enema should be delayed for 1 week after rectal biopsy)

    3) A small bowel series is of help in distinguishing celiac disease, Crohn's disease, Whipple's disease, etc.

f) 72-hour stool collection

    1) To measure stool volume (1000 ml/day suggests secretory diarrhea or malabsorption)

    2) To measure fecal fat (suggests malabsorption)

    3) To measure fecal osmolality and electrolyte concentration (to distinguish osmotic and secretory diarrhea, see above)

g) Evaluation of malabsorption in patients with steatorrhea

    1) D-Xylose test measures absorptive capacity of small bowel

    2) If D-xylose test normal, pancreatic insufficiency probable (can be confirmed by more sophisticated tests in a specialized laboratory, but therapeutic trial of pancreatic enzymes is often tried instead)

    3) Suction biopsy of the small intestine often useful in diagnosis; e.g., sprue, Whipple's disease, lymphoma, amyloidosis, giardiasis

    4) Schilling test or a bile salt breath test may demonstrate a disorder of the terminal ileum

h) Specific causes

    1) Lactose intolerance

       (a) A deficiency of lactase in the intestinal mucosa, causing an osmotic diarrhea and an irritant effect on the mucosa by the acid by-products of lactose metabolized by colonic bacteria

(b) Characterized by diarrhea, flatulence, bloating, abdominal cramps after ingestion of lactose

(c) Lactose intolerance may be inherited (50–80% African Americans, 75–100% Asians, 10–20% American whites) or acquired because of damage to the intestinal epithelium, e.g., infection

(d) Severity of symptoms highly variable and unpredictable

(e) Severity increased when another diarrheal disorder, e.g., irritable bowel syndrome, is present

(f) Diagnosis suggested by the history and by response to a lactose-free diet (3 weeks trial ordinarily sufficient)

(g) Specific diagnostic tests — lactose tolerance test, hydrogen breath test — widely available but usually not necessary

2) Fecal impaction

(a) Elderly sedentary people are most at risk

(b) Impaction is usually in the rectum or rectosigmoid region

(c) Leaking of fluid around impaction results in passage of frequent, small volume, watery bowel movements

(d) Often associated with sense of rectal fullness, vague lower abdominal pain, nausea

(e) Bimanual examination reveals firm stool in left lower quadrant of abdomen

(f) Impaction should be removed manually if possible; otherwise, through the sigmoidoscope

(g) Repeated fleet enemas (Table 25.3) may be of help after partial disimpaction

(h) Complications of impaction: recurrent urinary tract infection, urinary incontinence, intestinal obstruction, perforation of the colon, colonic ulceration

(i) Prevention of impaction: increase dietary fiber (Table 25.2); add a bulk laxative (Table 25.3) if necessary; drink 2 quarts of liquid each day in addition to that drunk with meals; obey the urge to defecate

3) Ulcerative colitis

(a) Affects any age, with peaks in third and seventh decades

(b) A mucosal disease that may be limited to the rectum or involve the entire colon

(c) Symptoms range from occasional rectal bleeding to profuse bloody diarrhea

(d) Severity of initial presentation a useful predictor of the course

(e) Most patients have mild disease, limited to the rectosigmoid region

(f) Patients with moderate or severe disease may have fever, fatigue, or weight loss

(g) Disease characterized by periodic exacerbations

(h) Patients with severe disease may develop dilated bowel ("toxic megacolon"), with high mortality

(i) Diagnosis made by symptoms, endoscopic and histological appearance of colon, and course of disease

(j) Treatment determined by severity of attack: sulfasalazine for mild disease, corticosteroids for more severe disease; 5-aminosalicylic acid for patients intolerant to sulfasalazine; colectomy for severe refractory disease

(k) Colon cancer: risk increased 5–10 times, proportionate to duration, extent of disease, and age of onset (onset under 25 years carries the greatest risk); high-risk patients who have had colitis for 8–10 years should have yearly colonoscopy

4) Crohn's disease

(a) Involves all layers of the intestine; most commonly, the terminal ileum is involved, but any part of intestinal tract from esophagus to anus can be involved

(b) Most often begins in early adolescence or in young adulthood

(c) Remains confined to initial site unless surgery is done

(d) May be associated with fistula formation, strictures, abscess formation

(e) Most common symptoms: diarrhea, abdominal pain, weight loss

(f) Treatment: as in ulcerative colitis, but sulfasalazine not of help in noncolonic disease; metronidazole for perianal fistulas; surgery for obstruction, removal of complicated fistulas, drainage of abscesses

(g) Highly variable course

5) Drug-induced diarrhea

(a) A variety of drugs may cause diarrhea (Table 25.4)

(b) Antibiotic-associated diarrhea

(1) Severity highly variable

(2) Occurs during administration (oral or parenteral) of antibiotic or up to 3 weeks after drug is discontinued

(3) Endoscopy may reveal pseudomembranes (raised yellowish plaques on edematous, friable mucosa) due to *Clostridium difficile* infection (toxin can be identified in stool)

(4) Treatment: stop antibiotic; if *C. difficile* infection, treat with metronidazole for 7 days; if relapse, treat with vancomycin orally for 7 days; Identification of toxin in stool in asymptomatic patients is not an indication to treat

6) Postsurgical diarrhea

(a) Extensive small bowel resection may require narcotics; home hyperalimentation may be needed

(b) Resection of the ileum: if limited, prescribe cholestyramine; if extensive, medium-chain triglycerides

(c) Gastric surgery with vagotomy may respond to cholestyramine

D. Symptomatic antidiarrheal therapy

1. Avoid in acute infectious diarrhea

2. Hydrophilic bulk-forming agents (Table 25.3), especially in irritable bowel syndrome
3. Adsorbents, e.g., bismuth salts — Pepto-Bismol — in traveler's diarrhea, cholestyramine after limited ileal resection
4. Opioid derivatives, e.g., after extensive small bowel resection or in minimal doses to prevent marked discomfort (loperamide, a synthetic opioid is commonly used; diphenoxylate-atropine, another synthetic, not as good a choice)
5. Oral rehydration with glucose-electrolyte solutions (but not Gatorade) is important for patients with acute diarrhea

26/ IRRITABLE BOWEL SYNDROME

DEFINITION AND EPIDEMIOLOGY
A. Abdominal pain and altered bowel habits in the absence of detectable organic disease
B. Onset usually in teen-age or early adulthood, with a 2:1 female to male predominance
C. Unlikely to begin after age 50

DIAGNOSIS
A. History
   1. Symptoms usually for months or years before medical attention is sought
   2. Symptoms typically intermittent
   3. Pain
      a) No consistent quality
      b) Usually relieved by bowel movement
      c) Does not awaken patient
      d) Location varies but is usually consistent in a given patient
   4. Altered bowel habits
      a) Constipation, diarrhea, or alternating constipation and diarrhea
      b) If diarrhea, first stool of day is often normal, followed by increasingly loose stools, with cramping relieved by defecation
      c) Some people have painless diarrhea — perhaps a variant, perhaps a different disease
   5. Upper gastrointestinal symptoms: up to one-half of patients have heartburn, epigastric discomfort, nausea
   6. Weight loss or bleeding suggests another disorder
   7. Psychological factors
      a) In 70% of patients (Table 26.1)
      b) History of sexual abuse common
B. Physical examination generally normal
C. Laboratory tests: do only those tests (e.g., flexible sigmoidoscopy) necessary to rule out organic disease with a reasonably high pretest probability

TREATMENT
A. Education and reassurance are critical
B. Diet
   1. A trial of a lactose-free diet for 3 weeks is worthwhile (Table 26.2)
   2. If certain foods cause symptoms, avoid them
   3. If constipation is a predominant symptom, increase fiber in the diet (see Chapter 25)
C. Drugs
   1. Hydrophilic colloids (see Chapter 25) may be useful for patients with alternating constipation and diarrhea
   2. Antispasmodic drugs, e.g., dicyclomine hydrochloride (Bentyl), may be useful for patients whose symptoms are induced by meals or who complain of tenesmus
   3. Synthetic opioids (Lomotil or Imodium) may be necessary for patients with significant diarrhea but should be stopped as soon as symptoms are controlled

Table 26.1. Psychological Features of Irritable Bowel Syndrome

Psychopathology	Diagnostic Features	Treatment
Depression	Sad, tearful, hopeless, fatigue, loss of interest, early morning awakening	Antidepressant medication, environmental manipulation
Anxiety	Symptoms increased by stress	Relaxation training; environmental manipulation; teach coping techniques
Gratification from illness behavior	Symptoms often interfere with work or socializing	Treat as a physical deformity; encourage maximal activity; discourage talking to others about illness; recognize chronic nature of disorder
Cancer phobia	Patient or family reports fear; patient describes similarity of his symptoms with a known cancer victim	Adequate early workup, then limit further investigation; discuss openly with patient

After Whitehead WE, Schuster MM: Psychological management of irritable bowel syndrome. *Pract Gastroenterol* 3:32, 1979.

Table 26.2. Lactose-Free Diet[a]

Type of Food	Food Allowed	Food to Be Avoided
Milk and milk products	Nutramigen and soya bean milk used in place of milk; nondairy "milk" that does not contain lactose; lactaid milk	All milk of any species and all products containing milk as skim, dried, evaporated, or condensed; yogurt, cheese;[b] ice cream, malted milk; sherbets
Meat, fish, fowl	Plain beef, chicken, fish, turkey, veal, pork, ham, liver, or other organ meats	Creamed or breaded meat, fish, or fowl; sausage products such as weiners, liver sausage; cold cuts that contain milk
Eggs	All	None
Vegetables	All	Creamed, breaded, or buttered vegetables; any vegetables to which lactose has been added during processing
Potatoes and substitutes	White potatoes, sweet potatoes, yams, macaroni, noodles, rice, spaghetti	Any creamed, breaded, or buttered potatoes or starch and instant potatoes if lactose has been added during processing
Breads and cereals	Any that do not contain milk or milk products	Prepared mixes such as muffins, biscuits, waffles, pancakes, dry cereals with added skim milk powder; instant cream of wheat and other instant hot cereals; read labels carefully
Fats	Margarines that do not contain milk or milk products; salad dressings that do not contain milk or milk products; bacon, salad oils, shortening	Margarines and dressings containing milk or milk products; butter, cream cheese
Soups	All except those listed under foods excluded	Cream soups, chowders, commercially prepared soups that contain lactose
Desserts	Water and fruit ices; Jello, angel food cake; homemade cakes, pies, cookies made without milk from acceptable ingredients; ice cream made with nondairy mix	Commercial cakes and cookies and mixes; custard, puddings, ice cream made with milk; any containing chocolate
Fruits	All fresh, canned, or frozen that are not processed with lactose	Any canned or frozen that are processed with lactose
Miscellaneous	Nuts and nut butter, unbuttered popcorn, olives, pure sugar candy, jelly or marmalade, sugar, Karo, chewing gum	Gravy, white sauce, coffee, powdered drink, caramels, molasses, molasses candies, most instant coffee (Folger's instant coffee and Tang are lactose free)

[a] In all instances labels should be carefully read, and any product that contains milk, lactose, dry milk solids, or curds should be omitted. Also avoid whey and sugar substitutes with lactose. For milk products use Coffee-mate, soy milk baby formulas, or Lactaid milk.

[b] Swiss, Jarlsberg, Edam, and sharp cheddar are the only cheeses allowed.

4. Codeine may be effective in patients with significant diarrhea uncontrolled by synthetic opioids; addiction is rare
5. Analgesic drugs should be avoided
6. Simethicone may be tried in patients with excessive gas

D. Psychological management
1. Anxiety: avoid or modify stress; teach relaxation techniques; occasionally, mild tranquilizing drugs (Chapter 2) must be prescribed
2. Depression: avoid or modify stress; antidepressants (Chapter 3) may be of help
3. Gratification from illness behaviors: instruct the patient and his or her family to avoid discussion of the illness

27/ DIVERTICULAR DISEASE OF THE COLON

NOMENCLATURE: TABLE 27.1
EPIDEMIOLOGY AND PATHOGENESIS
A. Prevalence strongly correlates with age (20% over 40, 50% over 60, 66% over 85)
B. Prevalence correlates with amount of fiber in the diet

ASYMPTOMATIC DIVERTICULOSIS
A. Most people with diverticulosis are asymptomatic
B. The more distal the position in the colon, the higher the prevalence of diverticula (although rectal diverticula are rare)
C. No evidence that adding fiber to the diet prevents the development of symptoms once diverticulosis has occurred

PAINFUL DIVERTICULAR DISEASE
A. Diagnosis
  1. Hallmark is lower abdominal pain without evidence of inflammation
  2. Pain may be colicky or steady, generally in left lower quadrant, made worse by eating, partially relieved by defecation or by passing flatus
  3. Constipation, diarrhea, or both are common during painful episodes
  4. Physical examination may reveal left lower quadrant tenderness; sometimes, a tender sigmoid can be palpated
  5. Proctosigmoidoscopy is normal but may cause painful spasms
  6. Barium enema is important in diagnosis and to exclude other conditions
B. Treatment
  1. High-fiber diet (see Table 25.2)
  2. Antispasmodic drugs (e.g., Bentyl) may be of help in relief of pain
C. Course
  1. Typically episodic
  2. High-fiber diet should be continued in patients with a history of painful diverticular disease

DIVERTICULITIS
A. Diagnosis
  1. Cardinal symptoms are abdominal pain and fever

Table 27.1. Nomenclature of Diverticular Disease of the Colon

Diverticulosis (presence of multiple diverticula)
  Asymptomatic
  Symptomatic (pain, altered bowel habits)
  Complicated by hemorrhage
Diverticulitis (necrotizing inflammation in one or more diverticula)
  With microperforation (local inflammation)
  With macroperforation, manifested by abscess, fistula, peritonitis, obstruction, or hemorrhage
Predivericular state: muscular thickening and shortening of colonic wall without recognizable diverticula

2. Pain may be severe, begin abruptly, persist and intensify, and localize to the left lower quadrant
3. Physical examination reveals abdominal tenderness and fever
   a) Localized peritonitis may be associated with marked direct and rebound tenderness
   b) Abdomen often distended and tympanitic; bowel sounds are decreased
   c) A mass may be felt at the site of inflammation
4. Laboratory findings: rectal bleeding in 25%, usually occult; leukocytosis; sometimes pyuria and/or hematuria
5. Plain films of abdomen important in detecting free air due to perforation, a surgical emergency
6. A limited flexible sigmoidoscopy indicated if diagnosis is in doubt
7. After process has been treated successfully, colonoscopy indicated to exclude other conditions
8. Computed tomography scanning may be of help in identifying abscesses

B. Treatment
1. Hospitalization usually indicated for hydration, antimicrobial therapy
2. Patients with relatively mild disease may be treated on an ambulatory basis with oral antibiotics (e.g., tetracycline 250 mg 4 times/day for 10–14 days)
3. Recurrence rate of 25%, mostly within 5 years

DIVERTICULAR BLEEDING

A. Commonest cause of hematochezia in adults
B. Occurs in right colon in two-thirds of people (though most diverticula are on the left)
C. Average age is 70
D. Dietary therapy does not reduce the risk of bleeding
E. Bleeding may be massive or occult
F. Requires hospitalization for stabilization, diagnosis, and treatment
G. Seventy percent stop bleeding spontaneously; recurrence rate is 20–25% and increases with each bleed

28/ DISEASES OF THE LIVER

HEPATITIS

A. Viral hepatitis
   1. Types and selected characteristics (Table 28.1)
      a) Type A is the most common
      b) The δ agent is transmitted by the same routes as type B, is manifest as a biphasic pattern of hepatitis when there is infection with type B or as an exacerbation of hepatitis in patients who are carriers of type B
      c) Type C accounts for the majority of cases of hepatitis acquired by blood transfusion
      d) Type E is a frequent cause of epidemics in developing countries, causes a high mortality in pregnant women
   2. Clinical presentation
      a) Symptoms of various types are similar
      b) Types B and C are usually more severe and have greater morbidity, mortality, and late sequelae
      c) Majority of cases are anicteric; patients have nonspecific symptoms (e.g., nausea, fatigue)
      d) In icteric disease anorexia, fatigue, abdominal discomfort, nausea usually precede jaundice; erythematous rash, urticaria, arthralgia, fever may also occur
      e) Jaundice follows prodromal symptoms by about 10 days, often with pruritus
      f) Physical examination: tender palpable liver in 70%; posterior cervical adenopathy and splenomegaly common
   3. Laboratory features
      a) Mild anemia, granulocytopenia, and mild absolute lymphocytosis are common
      b) Height of bilirubin (both direct and total) an index of severity
      c) Serum aminotransferase activity rises early, may reach several thousand units and stay elevated for several weeks
         1) Height of activity of no prognostic value
         2) Rapid fall in activity from peak to normal in less than a week may be a sign of fulminant hepatitis
      d) Serum alkaline phosphatase activity rises early, often remains elevated until after clinical recovery
      e) Serum albumin normal, serum γ-globulin often transiently elevated
      f) Prothrombin time usually normal; prolongation with no response to vitamin K suggests severe disease
   4. Immunological features (Table 28.1)
      a) Type B characterized by surface antigens and surface and core antibodies (Fig. 28.1)
      b) The e antigen is associated with type B and correlates with infectivity in chronic carriers of B
      c) Type D hepatitis (see above), characterized in early appearance of δ antigen; then immunoglobulin M (IgM), then IgG antibody

Table 28.1. Comparison of Selected Characteristics of Various Types of Viral Hepatitis

Characteristic	Type A	Type B	Type C	Type E
Hepatitis A antibody	Appearance of or increase in titer	Absent or no change in titer	Absent or no change in titer	Absent or no change in titer
Hepatitis B surface antigen	Absent	Present in early stage of illness	Absent	Absent
Hepatitis C antibody	Absent	Absent	Appears 4–32 weeks (mean of 15 weeks) after onset of hepatitis	Absent
Incubation period	15–50 days	50–160 days	15–160 days	35–40 days
Route of infection	Oral and parenteral	Usually parenteral, also oral or sexual	Usually parenteral, also oral or sexual	Oral
Age preference	Children	Any age	Any age	15–40 years
Seasonal incidence	Autumn-winter, epidemic outbreaks	All year	All year	Epidemic outbreaks
Severity	Usually mild	Often severe	Often severe	Mild, severe in pregnancy
Mortality	0.1%	1.0%	1.0%	0.5% (20% in pregnancy)
Prophylactic value of γ-globulin	Good	Good with hyperimmune hepatitis B globulin	Unclear	Unclear
Hepatitis B vaccine		90% efficacy		

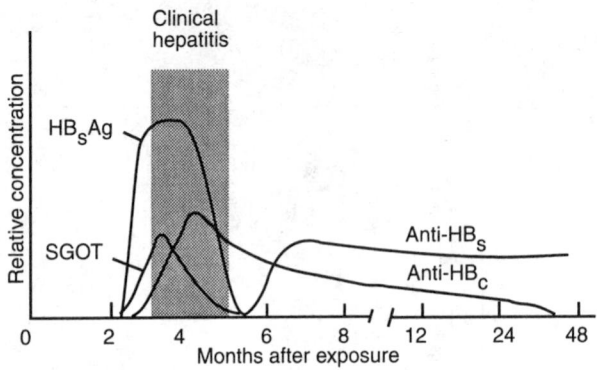

Figure 28.1. Pattern of appearance of hepatitis B surface antigen (HB$_s$Ag) and antibodies to hepatitis B surface antigen (anti-HB$_s$) and hepatitis B core antigen (anti-HB$_c$) in acute hepatitis B infection. SGOT is now properly called serum aspartate aminotransferase (AST). (From Mezey E: Specific liver diseases. In: Halsted JA, Halsted CH (eds): *The Laboratory in Clinical Medicine,* 2nd ed. Philadelphia, WB Saunders, 1981.)

      d) Anti-HC (hepatitis C virus antibody) detectable in most patients indefinitely

      e) No serological test for type E is available

  5. Management

      a) Acute viral hepatitis resolves completely in 1–3 months

      b) No specific treatment

      c) Strict isolation unnecessary

      d) Washing hands after contact with the patient and careful handling of stool and blood are mandatory

      e) Hospitalization for patients with uncertain diagnosis, those with severe nausea and vomiting or a change in mental status, those with prothrombin time prolonged more than 4 seconds

      f) Benadryl or Compazine for nausea; acetaminophen for abdominal discomfort; sedatives should not be given (risk of hepatic encephalopathy); corticosteroids are of no value

      g) Patients should be followed at 1–3-week intervals, discharged from care when asymptomatic and laboratory tests are normal

      h) No alcoholic beverages until 1 month after discharge from care

      i) Type B surface antigen should be measured after 6 months to detect carrier state

  6. Liver biopsy — only if the diagnosis is uncertain or the disease is prolonged beyond 6 months

  7. Prognosis

      a) Majority recover with no sequelae

      b) Principal cause of death is fulminant hepatitis; more common in type B hepatitis

      c) Older patients, patients with other systemic illnesses more likely to have a prolonged course

      d) Indicators of a poor prognosis

        1) Change in mental status

    2) Nonpalpable liver — small also on scan
    3) Liver that decreases rapidly in size
    4) Prothrombin time prolonged more than 4 seconds
  e) Chronic hepatitis and cirrhosis in 3–5% of patients with type
     B, 20–50% of patients with type C, do not occur after types A
     or E
     1) Suspect chronic course if there is still evidence of liver
        disease after 6 months
     2) Chronic carriers of B should have liver biopsy
  f) An increased incidence of hepatocellular cancer in carriers of B
     surface antigen and of anti-HC
8. Differential diagnosis
  a) Other viral hepatitides: cytomegalovirus, Epstein-Barr virus
  b) Leptospirosis if there has been contact with rodents
  c) Drug hepatitis (see below)
  d) Alcoholic hepatitis (see below)
  e) Extrahepatic biliary obstruction if there is persistent high
     bilirubin, high alkaline phosphatase activity, pruritus
9. Prevention
  a) Washing hands after contact with infected patient
  b) Patient's dishes and eating utensils can be shared only if
     heated above 120°C for 15–20 minutes in a dishwasher after
     use
  c) All excreta and blood-contaminated material should be handled
     with care
  d) Standard immune globulin
     1) Prevents clinical manifestations of type A in 80–90% if
        given within up to 6 months before to 2 weeks after
        exposure
     2) Not indicated for casual acquaintances or coworkers of
        patient with type A
     3) Role in prevention of type B, C, and E uncertain
  e) Hepatitis B immune globulin
     1) Prevents 75% of cases if given immediately after exposure
     2) Not indicated for casual acquaintances or coworkers of
        patient with type B
  f) Hepatitis B vaccine (see Chapter 18)
     1) For prevention of hepatitis B in people at high risk (e.g.,
        health care workers)
     2) Postexposure prophylaxis if exposure has been to persons
        with hepatitis B or who are known B carriers or if carrier
        status is unknown
B. Drug-induced hepatitis
  1. Cholestatic reactions
    a) A direct dose-related effect of anabolic steroids and of oral
       contraceptives
       1) Jaundice and pruritus are common
       2) Serum bilirubin principally direct fraction
       3) Serum alkaline phosphatase and cholesterol are elevated
       4) Serum aminotransferases are normal or only slightly
          elevated
       5) Cholestasis wanes soon after offending drug is withdrawn
    b) Large number of drugs cause cholestasis due to

hypersensitivity (e.g., phenothiazines, erythromycin, antithyroid drugs, hypoglycemic agents, chlorambucil)

1) Common features: fever, right upper quadrant abdominal pain, pruritus, rash, jaundice
2) Serum aminotransferase moderately elevated (<10 times normal)
3) Cholestasis usually subsides between 2 and 4 weeks after offending drug is withdrawn but sometimes persists for months or years
4) Severe pruritus treated with cholestyramine; response in 4–7 days

2. Hepatocellular reactions

a) Acetaminophen will produce hepatic necrosis in anyone if a dose of 10 g is ingested, usually as a suicide attempt
1) Alcoholics are at greater risk
2) Hepatotoxic effect first noted at about 48 hours
3) Patients known to have ingested a toxic dose should be hospitalized

b) Idiosyncratic hepatocellular reactions
1) Most common drugs: isoniazid or α-methyldopa, phenylbutazone, halothane
2) Asymptomatic increases in aminotransferase in 5–10% of people taking isoniazid or α-methyldopa
(a) Increases are transient; no need to stop drug or to monitor asymptomatic patients
(b) If fatigue, anorexia, nausea, or malaise develops, aminotransferases should be measured, and if they are elevated, the drug stopped
3) Women more at risk than men
4) Symptoms, laboratory tests, liver biopsy are indistinguishable from those of viral hepatitis (may need serological tests)
5) Hepatitis usually resolves in a few weeks after drug is stopped, but if the drug is continued, chronic liver disease can develop

C. Alcoholic hepatitis
1. Most frequently after prolonged heavy alcohol intake
2. Women more susceptible than men
3. Symptoms and signs are indistinguishable from viral hepatitis, but patients with alcoholic hepatitis more likely to have fever and leukocytosis
4. Activity of serum aminotransferases rarely more than 10 times normal, and aspartate aminotransferase (AST) characteristically higher than alanine aminotransferase (ALT)
5. Prothrombin time frequently prolonged
6. Jaundiced patients should be hospitalized, and a definite diagnosis established by liver biopsy
7. Illness often more severe than viral hepatitis, and morbidity and mortality risk is greater
8. About one-third develop cirrhosis, often in 6 months
9. If patients can abstain from drinking alcohol, one-half will recover completely, usually within a month

D. Chronic hepatitis

1. Definition: inflammatory liver disease, detected chemically or histologically, of 6 months or more duration
2. Liver histology essential both for diagnosis and to establish severity and the need for treatment
3. Principal causes are hepatitis virus B and C, autoimmune hepatitis, and drugs that cause hepatocellular necrosis (see above)
4. Chronic persistent hepatitis
   a) Characterized by portal inflammation and focal parenchymal necrosis with preservation of lobular architecture and with little or no fibrosis
   b) Patients are asymptomatic or have mild nonspecific symptoms
   c) Laboratory tests show aminotransferase activity 2–5 times normal; other liver tests are usually normal
   d) Forty percent have hepatitis B surface antigen (HB_sAg) in their blood
   e) If symptoms persist and aminotransferases stay elevated, liver should be rebiopsied after 2 or 3 years to rule out a sampling error on the initial biopsy
5. Chronic active hepatitis
   a) Characterized by extension of inflammation and necrosis from the portal area to adjacent hepatocytes (piecemeal necrosis), disruption of the lobular architecture, and bridging fibrosis
   b) Onset usually insidious: patients may be asymptomatic and found to have elevated serum aminotransferase activity or have malaise, fatigue, abdominal discomfort, anorexia, and jaundice
   c) In about one-third of patients disease evolves from overt acute hepatitis
   d) Physical examination reveals hepatomegaly and often spider angiomas, palmar erythema, gynecomastia
   e) Elevations of serum bilirubin, aminotransferases, globulins are the most sensitive indicators of degree of hepatocellular damage
   f) Decreases in serum albumin and prolongation of the prothrombin time reflect loss of hepatocellular function and a poor prognosis
   g) Autoimmune hepatitis
      1) More likely a woman
      2) Symptoms include acne, amenorrhea, arthralgia and arthritis, pleurisy or fever
      3) May be associated thyroiditis, Sjögren's syndrome, ulcerative colitis, glomerulonephritis, or hemolytic anemia
      4) Laboratory tests often show markedly elevated serum globulins, lupus erythematosus cells, and elevated titers of antinuclear antibodies (ANA) and smooth muscle antibodies
      5) A subset of patients have normal ANA but elevated titers of kidney-liver microsomal (anti-KM) antibodies
   h) Other diagnoses
      1) Wilson's disease (see below) should be explored in all patients with unexplained chronic hepatitis, particularly in patients under age 25
      2) α_1-Antitrypsin deficiency suggested by absent α_1-globulin on serum protein electrophoresis and confirmed by quantitative measurement

3) Primary bilirubin cirrhosis (see below)
   i) Variable course: some relatively asymptomatic; some progress to cirrhosis and death if untreated
   j) Treatment
      1) Corticosteroids useful if hepatitis B virus is not causative (40–60 mg/day, tapered slowly over 1–3 months to 15–20 mg/day)
         (a) Stopped if remission is attained
         (b) If remission not attained, no utility in continuing beyond 4 years
         (c) Asymptomatic patients are treated only if serum aminotransferases are more than 10 times normal and if histology shows severe disease
         (d) Contraindicated in patients with chronic hepatitis B
      2) α-Interferon effective in some patients with B or C infection; consultation with a hepatologist mandatory

UNEXPLAINED ELEVATIONS OF LIVER ENZYMES IN SERUM

A. Confirm by repeated testing
B. Evaluate possibility enzymes are being released from nonhepatic sites (e.g., aminotransferase from muscle, alkaline phosphatase from bone)
   1. If aminotransferase elevation is from muscle, creatine kinase will be elevated also
   2. If alkaline phosphatase is from bone, 5′-nucleotidase level will be normal
C. Persistent elevation of hepatic aminotransferase activity for 6 months or more warrants a liver biopsy to rule out chronic hepatitis
D. Persistent elevation of hepatic alkaline phosphatase warrants liver scan to rule out space-occupying lesions; liver biopsy warranted only if scan is positive or if granulomatous disease (sarcoid, tuberculosis) is suspected

ALCOHOLIC FATTY LIVER

A. Occurs in all people who ingest alcohol excessively
B. Manifested by
   1. Abdominal fullness due to hepatomegaly
   2. Elevation of serum aminotransferases (rarely more than twice normal)
   3. If marked infiltration, may be associated with malaise, weakness, anorexia, tender hepatomegaly, even jaundice; may require liver biopsy to distinguish from alcoholic hepatitis or cirrhosis
C. Treatment is abstinence from alcohol; fat disappears in 4–6 weeks
D. Fatty liver common in nonalcoholic obese patients
   1. Diagnosis can be confirmed by computed tomography scan
   2. Weight reduction effective

CIRRHOSIS

A. Chronic diffuse liver disease characterized by fibrosis and nodules of regenerated liver
B. Alcoholic (micronodular) and postnecrotic (macronodular)
   1. Onset: insidious, associated with nonspecific symptoms (fatigue, weight loss, nausea, abdominal discomfort)
   2. Course
      a) Jaundice, edema, ascites, spider angiomas, palmar erythema, gynecomastia, loss of axillary and pubic hair may develop

     b) Hepatomegaly and splenomegaly are common
     c) Most severe complications: encephalopathy, bleeding from esophageal varices, infection
     d) Patients with alcoholic cirrhosis may have fluctuating course dependent on alcohol intake
     e) Patients with postnecrotic cirrhosis have a steadily deteriorating course
     f) Rapid deterioration should raise the suspicion of hepatocellular cancer
     g) Most frequently abnormal liver function tests: serum bilirubin (high), serum albumin (low), serum globulins (high), prothrombin time (long)
     h) Anemia, slightly decreased white blood cell count, moderate thrombocytopenia are common
  3. Management
     a) High-protein, low-salt diet
     b) Abstinence from alcohol
     c) Avoidance of tranquilizers and sedatives
     d) Infection and gastrointestinal bleeding should be aggressively treated
     e) Trial of vitamin K 15 mg i.v. if prothrombin time prolonged
     f) Multivitamins and folic acid if diet is inadequate
     g) Potassium supplementation if serum potassium falls below 3.5 mEq/liter
     h) Treatment of edema-ascites
       1) Sodium restriction (500 mg NaCl a day)
       2) Diuretics
         (a) Aiming for loss of no more than 2.27 kg (5 lbs) of weight per week
         (b) Initiate with spironolactone 100 mg/day divided and increased to 200 mg/day
         (c) Thiazide diuretics or furosemide can be added if diuresis inadequate
         (d) Diuretic dosage must be decreased or diuretics stopped if hyponatremia or impaired renal function develops
     i) Restrict protein intake to 45 g/day (plus minimum of 400 g/day of carbohydrate) if encephalopathy is a concern; vegetable protein safer than animal protein
     j) Lactulose 20–30 g 3 or 4 times/day if there is chronic encephalopathy
     k) Consideration of liver transplant in decompensated patients
C. Cardiac cirrhosis
  1. Only after prolonged, severe heart failure, usually due to valvular disease
  2. Jaundice, hepatomegaly, and ascites are prominent features
  3. Diagnosis only established with certainty by liver biopsy
D. Primary biliary cirrhosis
  1. Progressive intrahepatic cholestasis, usually in middle-aged women
  2. Principal manifestations: jaundice, pruritus, hepatomegaly, hyperlipidemia, steatorrhea
  3. Antimitochondrial antibodies in 95% — virtually diagnostic

    4. Liver biopsy characteristic until end stage when indistinguishable from postnecrotic cirrhosis

E. Wilson's disease

    1. Inherited (autosomal recessive) disorder of copper metabolism

    2. Symptoms of hepatic and neurological dysfunction (latter predominant in adults)

    3. Kayser-Fleischer rings, greenish-brown cornea rings (visible by slitlamp), are diagnostic

    4. Serum ceruloplasmin, the copper-binding protein, is usually reduced

    5. Histology of liver is not diagnostic, but copper content of liver is

    6. Treatment is D-penicillamine

F. Hemochromatosis

    1. Inherited (autosomal recessive) disorder of iron metabolism, resulting in excessive body iron

    2. Characterized by cirrhosis, diabetes mellitus, grayish pigmentation of the skin

    3. Heart failure, arrhythmias, peripheral neuritis, arthritis, testicular atrophy may also occur

    4. Develops usually after age 40 in men earlier than in women

    5. High serum iron (>150 μg/dl), high saturation of iron-binding protein (>50%), and high serum ferritin are characteristic

    6. Treatment is repeated phlebotomy (1–2 units weekly)

G. Schistosomiasis

    1. Infection occurs in tropical areas by exposure to cercariae in infested water

    2. Ova deposited in portal area with resulting inflammation, granuloma formation, and fibrosis

    3. Jaundice uncommon on presentation

    4. Most common laboratory abnormalities: high serum alkaline phosphatase, mildly increased serum bilirubin and aminotransferases

    5. Diagnosis made by demonstrating ova on rectal biopsy or by liver biopsy

Section IV
Renal and Urological
Problems

29/ PROTEINURIA

ASSESSMENT OF PATIENTS WITH PROTEINURIA

A. Definitions of proteinuria
  1. Less than 150 mg of protein per 24 hours are normally present in urine (<300 mg/24 hours in adolescents)
  2. Most normal urinary protein is albumin
B. Methods for detecting proteinuria
  1. Dipstick
    a) Most practical, easiest test
    b) Increasingly green color as protein concentration increases
    c) One drop of strong acid (e.g., 1 N HCl) avoids false positive reactions that occur in alkaline urine (Table 29.1)
    d) Primarily sensitive to albumin (Table 29.1)
  2. Sulfosalicylic acid (SSA)
    a) Used most often to detect globulins or light chains
    b) False positive and negative results: Table 29.1
  3. Heat and acetic acid
    a) Use only if SSA unavailable (more time-consuming)
    b) Heat top of test tube that contains 10 ml of urine; when it is boiling, add 3 or 4 drops of diluted acetic acid (1 volume of glacial acetic acid to 2 volumes of water); reboiling causes protein to precipitate
    c) False positive and negative results: Table 29.1
  4. Microalbuminuria (see below)
    a) Micro-Bumintest
      1) One drop of urine is placed on a tablet, followed by 2 drops of water
      2) Bluish-green color in the presence of albumin
      3) False positive results: highly alkaline urine, contamination with skin cleaners containing chlorhexidine
    b) Micral test
      1) Monoclonal antibody immunoassay
      2) Reddish-brown color in the presence of albumin
C. Office assessment
  1. If individuals are otherwise healthy, test should be repeated 2 or 3

Table 29.1. Urinary Constituents That Alter the Results of Protein Screening Tests

Urinary Constituents	Dipstick	Sulfosalicylic Acid	Heat and Acetic Acid
Radiographic contrast media	No effect	False positive	False positive
Drugs and drug metabolites[a]	No effect	False positive	False positive
Bence Jones protein	False negative	No effect	False negative[b]
Highly alkaline urine	False positive	False negative	False negative
Urine turbidity	No effect	False positive	False positive
Vaginal or prostatic secretion	No effect	False positive	False positive

Modified from Bradley M, Schumann GB, Ward PCJ: Examination of urine. In: Henry JB (ed): *Todd-Sanford-Davidsohn Clinical Diagnosis and Management by Laboratory Methods*, 16th ed. Philadelphia, WB Saunders, 1979.

[a] Tolbutamide, tolmetin, chlorpromazine, sulfisoxazole, and high doses of cephalosporins and penicillin.
[b] Precipitated protein may disappear rapidly and be missed with continued heating.

times before further workup is begun (transient mild proteinuria may be associated with fever, exercise, etc.)

2. History
   a) Reports of abnormal urinalyses as part of previous screening examinations
   b) Detailed urological history (e.g., stones, x-rays, family history)
   c) History of edema, nocturia, hypertension
   d) Other evidence of systemic disease
3. Physical examination, looking for signs associated with renal disease (e.g., diabetic retinopathy, edema, hypertension)
4. Laboratory tests in patients with chronic proteinuria
   a) Urinalysis — microscopic examination to look for hematuria, casts, inflammatory cells
   b) Serum creatinine to assess renal function
   c) 24-hour collection for protein
      1) Refrigerate until brought to the laboratory (or add 1–2 g of boric acid)
      2) Nonnephrotic proteinuria: 200–3500 mg in 24 hours
      3) Nephrotic proteinuria: >3500 mg in 24 hours
   d) Protein:creatinine ratio
      1) Protein (mg/dl) divided by creatinine (mg/dl) determined in a random sample
      2) Ratio of >0.2 is abnormal; of >3.5 is nephrotic range
      3) Useful if 24-hour collection is difficult
      4) Protein excretion may be overestimated in diabetics after exercise or in frail persons whose creatinine excretion is low and may be underestimated in a first morning specimen
D. Nonnephrotic proteinuria
   1. Isolated proteinuria in apparently healthy persons (repeat measurement 5 or 6 times over several months)
      a) Intermittent
         1) Kidney biopsy not necessary
         2) Yearly measurement of urine protein, urinalysis, measurement of serum creatinine appropriate; if significant change, renal biopsy indicated
         3) Prognosis generally excellent
      b) Persistent (protein in 80% of specimens)
         1) Orthostatic proteinuria
            (a) Negligible after recumbent for 8 hours, significant after ambulatory for 8 hours
            (b) Renal biopsy not indicated, but yearly evaluation (see above) prudent
            (c) Prognosis excellent
         2) Constant proteinuria
            (a) Renal biopsy not indicated, but yearly evaluation (see above) including blood pressure measurement indicated
            (b) If proteinuria exceeds 2 g/day, sonogram or intravenous pyelogram (IVP) and collagen vascular screens may be appropriate
            (c) Course likely to be indolent: renal failure unusual, hypertension develops in 50%
   2. Nonisolated proteinuria

a) Renal biopsy may be indicated if an associated abnormality is present (e.g., hematuria, red cell casts, mild renal failure)
b) Other investigations may be indicated (see Table 29.2)
c) Microalbuminuria (see measurement above)
   1) In diabetics, small increases in albumin excretion are associated with an increased incidence of complications (see Chapter 56)
   2) Particular attention should be paid in such patients to control of blood pressure, dietary intake of protein, perhaps tight glucose control
E. Nephrotic proteinuria
   1. Causes: Table 29.3
   2. Some possible helpful laboratory tests are listed in Table 29.2
   3. Renal biopsy (by a nephrologist) is usually necessary if a specific diagnosis cannot be made by other tests

MANAGEMENT OF PATIENTS WITH PROTEINURIA

A. Nonnephrotic proteinuria
   1. No special treatment (treat any underlying disease)
   2. If a drug is involved, proteinuria may not resolve for several months after drug is discontinued
B. Nephrotic proteinuria
   1. Asymptomatic patients need no treatment unless renal biopsy dictates otherwise
   2. If there is edema
      a) Mild to moderate protein restriction
      b) Angiotensin-converting enzyme inhibitors and nonsteroidal anti-inflammatory agents
      c) No-salt-added diet
      d) Loop diuretics if necessary
      e) Potassium-sparing diuretics if loop diuretics have failed and there is no renal failure

Table 29.2.   Selected Investigations That May Be Appropriate in the Diagnosis of Proteinuria That Is Not Isolated or That Is Nephrotic

Antinuclear antibody if SLE is suspected
Antistreptolysin-O titer (ASO) if there is a possibility of poststreptococcal glomerulonephritis
Complement (C3,C4) if glomerulonephritis is suspected
Complete blood count to provide a baseline evaluation for subsequent use and to provide a clue to a systemic illness (such as leukemia)
Erythrocyte sedimentation rate if collagen vascular disease is suspected
Fasting blood sugar to consider the possibility of diabetes mellitus
Hepatitis B surface antigen if hepatitis-associated vasculitis may be present
IVP to provide evidence for structural renal disease (such as papillary necrosis)
Lupus erythematosus (LE) prep if SLE is suspected
Serum albumin if nephrotic range proteinuria is present
Serum electrolytes (Na^+, K^+, Cl^-, HCO_3^-, Ca^{2+}, PO_4^{2-}) to provide a screen for abnormalities subsequent to renal disease
Serum and urine protein electrophoresis if multiple myeloma is suspected
Uric acid to screen for urate-related renal disease
Urine culture if pyuria is present
X-ray of chest to provide evidence for systemic disease, e.g., sarcoidosis

SLE, systemic lupus erythematosus.

Table 29.3.   Cause of Nephrotic Syndrome in Adults[a]

MOST COMMON
  Diabetes mellitus
  Idiopathic membranous glomerulopathy
  Idiopathic lipoid nephrosis (including minimal change disease, mesangial proliferative
    glomerulonephritis, focal segmental glomerulosclerosis)
LESS COMMON
  Proliferative glomerulonephritis (crescentic glomerulonephritis)
  Membranoproliferative glomerulonephritis
  Collagen vascular disease
  Amyloidosis

[a] An extensive list of potential causes of nephrotic syndrome can be found in Glassock RJ, Adler SG, Ward HJ, Cohen AH: Primary glomerular disease. In: Brenner BM, Rector FC (eds): *The Kidney*, 4th ed. Philadelphia, WB Saunders, 1991, p 1213.

3. Tendency to venous thrombosis may be increased; avoid immobilization
4. Office visits every 1–4 months (weight, volume assessment, blood pressure, 24-hour urinary protein measurement or a protein: creatinine ratio, serum creatinine measurement, serum electrolyte measurement if diuretics are being used)

30/ HEMATURIA/ HEMATOSPERMIA

DETECTION AND FORMS OF HEMATURIA/HEMATOSPERMIA

A. Detection
1. Microscopy the most sensitive method (>1–3 red cells/high-power field)
2. Dipsticks are widely used as screening tests (for limits, see Table 30.1)
3. Lysis of red cells depends on duration of time in urine, concentration of urine

B. Pseudohematuria (red urine without red cells)
1. Caused by exogenous substances (Table 30.2) — negative microscopy and dipstick
2. Caused by endogenous substances — negative microscopy
   a) Porphyrins — negative dipstick
   b) Myoglobin
      1) Positive dipstick
      2) Indicates muscle disease or injury
   c) Hemoglobin
      1) Positive dipstick
      2) Indicates intravascular hemolysis

C. Innocent hematuria
1. After a pelvic or prostate examination, cystoscopy, bladder catheterization, or biopsy of prostate, bladder, or kidney
2. Sometimes after vigorous exercise

Table 30.1. Limits of Dipstick Method for Detection of Blood in the Urine

REASONS FOR A POSITIVE TEST
Hematuria — ≥5–10 RBCs/HPF
Hematuria with lysis of RBCs
   From hypotonic urine (specific gravity < 1.008)
   From highly alkaline urine (pH > 6.5–7.0)
Hemoglobinuria — from intravascular hemolysis
Myoglobinuria — from muscle injury
False positive reactions
   From hypochlorite (bleach) contamination of container
   From peroxidase (from heavy growth of bacteria)

REASONS FOR A FALSE NEGATIVE TEST
Vitamin C — ingestion by the patient of large amounts of vitamin C (>200 mg/day) results in diminished oxidation potential of the test material. The dipstick test may miss trace quantities of blood, although usually there is a quantitative decrease in the estimate of blood (such as 3+ to 2+). (This is of concern only if RBCs are observed but the dipstick test is negative.)
Formaldehyde — ingestion of bacterial suppressant agents (such as Mandelamine or Hiprex) that produce formaldehyde in acid urine or contamination of the container with formaldehyde will diminish the oxidizing potential of the reagent strips. This results in a quantitative estimate error or, if hematuria is minimal, false negative results.

RBCs/HPF, red blood cells per high-power field.

Table 30.2. Exogenous Substances That May Cause Pseudohematuria[a]

Medications
Analgesics: phenacetin; phenazopyridine (e.g., Pyridium)
Antimicrobials: nitrofurantoin; rifampin; sulfonamides
Antimalarials: chloroquine; primaquine
Laxatives: anthraquinones — cascara, senna, danthron (e.g., Modane or Dorbane)
Anticancer agents: doxorubicin, daunorubicin
Others: deferoxamine (an iron-chelating agent); levodopa; phenothiazines; methyldopa (rare)

Vegetable Dyes
Anthrocyanins: beets, blackberries
Paprika
Rhubarb
Fuscin (a reddish dye used in tropical agents)

Others
Antiseptics: mercurochrome, phenols, cresols, povidine-iodine (Betadine)
Urate crystals (in acid urine)

[a] Some of these agents cause hemoglobinuria.

---

a) Subsides in 24–48 hours
b) Sometimes accompanied by proteinuria, casts

D. Symptomatic hematuria
   1. Hematuria with pyuria
      a) Bacterial cultures should be obtained, and infections, treated appropriately (see Chapter 13)
      b) If cultures are sterile, a sexually transmitted disease (*Chlamydia* or gonorrhea, see Chapters 13 and 77), a viral infection (common in young women), or tuberculosis (now rare) should be suspected
      c) Noninfectious disorders of the bladder, including cancer, may present this way, especially over age 50; follow-up urinalysis on 2 or 3 occasions in next 4–6 weeks is appropriate
   2. Hematuria with proteinuria, red blood cell casts, or dysmorphic red blood cells
      a) Reflects either glomerulonephritis or interstitial nephritis (see Chapter 29 for evaluation of proteinuria)
      b) Glomerular disease likely associated with passage of deformed red cells
      c) Renal function (e.g., serum creatinine measurement) should be done
      d) Consultation with a nephrologist indicated; a renal biopsy often will be performed

E. Asymptomatic isolated microhematuria
   1. Selected findings: Table 30.3
   2. Measurement of 24-hour excretion of calcium and uric acid indicated; excess excretion (>300 mg of calcium or 750 mg of uric acid per 24 hours) is associated with hematuria and may respond to thiazides or to allopurinol (see Chapter 32)

Table 30.3. Distribution (%) of Selected Urological Findings in Asymptomatic Patients with Microhematuria[a]

Type Population	Urology Referral (500)	Urology Referral (246)	Young Israeli Men (636)[b]	Rochester, MN Population (781)[b]	Young Women Urology Referral (177)	Men >50 Years Old Screened for Hematuria (192)
Neoplasia	2.2	9.3	0.2	1.0	0	8.3
Other disorders						
Renal calculi	2.6	0	0.6	3.3	1.6	8.9
Ureteral calculi	0.4	1.0	0	0.9	0.6	
Nephritis/renal insufficiency	0	2.0	0.1	14.4	0	1.0
Benign prostatic hypertrophy	23.6	8.0	0	37.7		47.4
Urinary tract infection	3.6	2.0	0	0.5		2.6
Urethrotrigonitis-prostatitis	24.6	18.0	0.1	1.8	26.6	
Any finding[c]	56.0	47.6	[d]	62.5	63.0	84.9

[a] Numbers in parentheses are number of patients.
[b] Complete urological workup not performed on all patients.
[c] Includes those listed above, in addition to other findings that may or may not have been related to the hematuria. These include: hydronephrosis, renal cysts, polycystic kidney disease, vesicoureteral reflux, interstitial and radiation cystitis, diverticula, ureteropelvic junction obstruction, ureterocele, cystocele, neurogenic bladder, atrophic vagina, scarred kidney, cystitis cystica, polyps, papillary necrosis, calcified renal mass, trabeculated bladder. Some patients in all series had more than one disorder.
[d] Unable to determine from data.

Table 30.4. Examples of Drugs Causing Hematuria

Antimicrobials
   Penicillin analogs[a]
   Cephalosporin analogs[a]
   Sulfa analogs[a]
   Polymycin[a]
   Rifampin[a]

Analgesics and anti-inflammatory agents
   Aspirin[b]
   Phenacetin[b]
   Aminosalicylic acid[b]
   Nonsteroidal anti-inflammatory agents[a]

Diuretics
   Furosemide[a]
   Ethacrynic acid[a]
   Thiazides[a]

Anticoagulants
   Warfarin (Coumadin)[c]

Other
   Cyclophosphamide[d]
   Ifosfamide (Isex — an antineoplastic agent)[d]
   Danazol[d]

[a] Infrequent bleeding due to interstitial nephritis, usually occurring within days to weeks of taking drugs; usually reversible.
[b] Infrequent bleeding due to medullary/papillary necrosis, usually following many months or years of combination analgesic preparations; partially reversible.
[c] An underlying cause of hematuria is often found, and a workup should be considered.
[d] Bleeding due to hemorrhagic cystitis in 10–20% of patients; dose-related and usually reversible.

EVALUATION OF PATIENTS WITH HEMATURIA/HEMATOSPERMIA

A. Hematuria
   1. Rule out pseudohematuria (see above) and drug-induced hematuria (Table 30.4)
   2. History and physical examination to attempt to identify an underlying cause (e.g., prostate cancer)
   3. Urine culture if appropriate (see above)
   4. Complete blood count, serum creatinine measurement, sickle-cell preparation (in African Americans), urinary calcium and uric acid determinations (see above)
   5. Intravenous pyelogram with tomography if renal function normal
   6. In patients over 40 years, 2 or 3 fresh morning urine specimens should be evaluated for tumor cells by cytology laboratory
   7. In patients over 40 or in those with risk factors (occupational exposure to aromatic amines, dyes, or benzidine; prolonged daily use of analgesics; or heavy smoking), referral to a urologist for cystoscopy is appropriate
   8. If a tumor is not suspected, referral to a nephrologist for a renal biopsy should be considered
B. Gross hematuria
   1. Refer to a urologist
   2. Causes: Table 30.5

Table 30.5.   Diagnosis Established in 1000 Cases of Gross Hematuria

Diagnosis	% Patients	
Kidney	15.2	
Tumor		3.5
Pyelonephritis		3.0
Calculus		2.7
Trauma		2.0
Hydronephrosis		1.5
Polycystic disease		0.6
Chronic glomerulonephritis		0.6
Other		1.3
Ureter	6.5	
Calculus		5.3
Tumor		0.7
Other		0.5
Bladder	39.5	
Cystitis		22.0
Tumor		14.9
Calculus		1.2
Other		1.4
Prostate	23.6	
Benign hyperplasia		12.5
Chronic prostatitis		9.0
Carcinoma		2.1
Urethra	5.5	
Stricture		1.7
Calculus		1.3
Gonorrhea		0.4
Tumor		0.3
Other		1.8
Other causes	1.2	
Urinary tuberculosis		0.7
Hemophilia		0.2
Uremic syndrome		0.1
Thrombocytopenia		0.1
Dicumarol poisoning		0.1
"Essential" hematuria	8.5	
Total	100.0	

Adapted from Lee LW, Davis E: Gross urinary hemorrhage: a symptom, not a disease. *JAMA* 153:782, 1953. This study remains among the largest published series to date.

    3. If no cause found, re-evaluate every 6 months for several years, including urine cytology and cystoscopy if bleeding continues

C. Hematospermia

    1. Usually in men over 40 years of age

    2. Usually innocuous

    3. If history, physical examination (including prostate and seminal vesicle examination), urinalysis otherwise normal, no further evaluation necessary

31/ HYPOKALEMIA

A. Consequences
    1. Mild hypokalemia usually causes no symptoms
    2. Sequelae of severe hypokalemia: Table 31.1
B. History: diet, medications (especially diuretics, laxatives, β_2-adrenergic agonists), vomiting, diarrhea, urine output, hypertension, diabetes mellitus
C. Physical examination: volume status, blood pressure
D. Laboratory evaluation
    1. Diagnostic approach: Figure 31.1
    2. Transtubular potassium gradient (TTKG) (see Fig. 31.1)
        a) An index of potassium secretory processes

Table 31.1. Clinical Sequelae of Hypokalemia

CARDIOVASCULAR
  Predisposition to digitalis intoxication
  Abnormal electrocardiogram
  Ventricular ectopic rhythms
  Cardiac necrosis
  Increased blood pressure
NEUROMUSCULAR
  Gastrointestinal
    Constipation
    Ileus
  Skeletal muscle
    Weakness, cramps
    Tetany
    Paralysis (including respiratory)
    Rhabdomyolysis
RENAL
  Decreased renal blood flow
  Decreased GFR
  Renal hypertrophy
  Pathological alterations (interstitial nephritis)
  Predisposition to urinary tract infection
FLUID AND ELECTROLYTE
  Polyuria and polydipsia
    Renal concentrating defect
    Stimulation of thirst center
    ADH release (?)
  Increased renal ammonia production
    Predisposition to hepatic coma
    Altered urinary acidification
  Renal chloride wasting
  Metabolic alkalosis
  Sodium retention
  Hyponatremia (with or without concomitant diuretic therapy)
ENDOCRINE
  Decrease in aldosterone
  Increase in renin
  Altered prostaglandin metabolism
  Decrease in insulin secretion (carbohydrate intolerance)

Modified from Tannen RL: Potassium disorders. In: Kokko JP, Tannen RL (eds): *Fluids and Electrolytes*. Philadelphia, WB Saunders, 1986.
GFR, glomerular filtration rate; *ADH*, antidiuretic hormone.

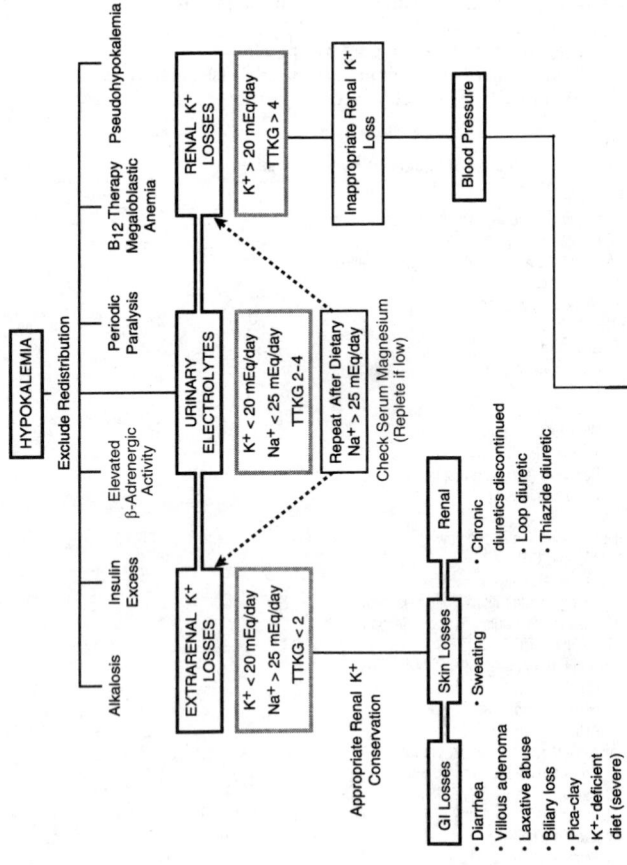

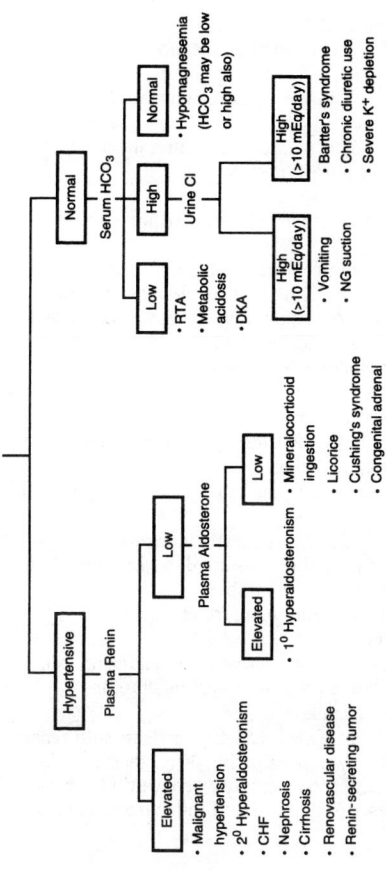

Figure 31.1. Diagnostic approach to hypokalemia. *CHF,* congestive heart failure; *DKA,* diabetic ketoacidosis; *GI,* gastrointestinal; *NG,* nasogastric; *RTA,* renal tubular acidosis; *TTKG,* transtubular potassium gradient. (Modified from Narins RG, Jones ER, Stom MC, et al: Diagnostic strategies in disorders of fluid, electrolyte and acid-base homeostasis. *Am J Med* 72:496, 1982.)

b) Calculation: $TTKG = [K]_{urine}/[K]_{plasma} \div U_{osm}/P_{osm}$

E. Causes

1. Gastrointestinal losses
   a) Diarrhea
      1) Usually associated with contracted volume: weight loss, poor skin turgor, tachycardia, orthostatic hypotension
      2) Urinary potassium excretion low (Fig. 31.1)
   b) Loss of gastric fluid
      1) Major loss is urinary (Fig. 31.1)
      2) Correction requires repletion of potassium and chloride (and sodium)

2. Diuretics (i.e., furosemide, ethacrynic acid, bumetanide, thiazides, chlorthalidone)
   a) Severe hypokalemia suggests excessive sodium intake or an unrecognized potassium-wasting state (e.g., hyperaldosteronism)
   b) Often accompanied by metabolic alkalosis, requires chloride repletion
   c) Monitor serum potassium concentration before and 1 and 4 weeks after starting diuretics or after increasing dose, then yearly if normal, more frequently if patient is taking digitalis
   d) Prevention: use of lowest effective dose of diuretic, moderate restriction of dietary sodium (<2 g/day)
   e) Treatment
      1) Indications (Table 31.2)
         (a) In general, mild hypokalemia (potassium > 3 mEq/liter) does not justify repletion
         (b) Nonspecific complaints (fatigue, myalgias) may respond to repletion
      2) Preparations (Table 31.3) vary greatly in expense, palatability and, if potassium-wasting diuretics continue to be used, may be relatively ineffective
      3) Potassium-sparing diuretics (e.g., spironolactone, triamterene, amiloride)
         (a) Often, a more effective alternative to potassium salts when given with a potassium-wasting diuretic
         (b) Risk of hyperkalemia
            (1) Especially in elderly, diabetics, patients with renal insufficiency, patients taking drugs that may also potentiate hyperkalemia (e.g., converting-enzyme inhibitors, nonsteroidal anti-inflammatory drugs, heparin)

Table 31.2.   Indications for Potassium Maintenance Therapy

1. Digitalis therapy
2. Predisposition to hepatic coma
3. Serum potassium < 3.0 mEq/liter
4. Development of glucose intolerance
5. Underlying cardiac disease
6. Symptoms attributable to hypokalemia

Used with permission from Tannen RL. Diuretic induced hypokalemia. *Kidney Int* 28:988, 1985.

Table 31.3. Commonly Available Potassium Chloride Supplements

Product	Amount/Dose
Extended-release tablets	
Micro-K Extentabs, Slow K, Klor-Con 8	8 mEq
K-Dur, K-Norm, K-Tab, Ten-K, Micro-K 10 Extentabs, Klor-Con 10	10 mEq
K-Dur	20 mEq
Powders for solution (flavored)[a]	
K-Lor (also 15 mEq), Kato, Klor-Con, Klor-Con 125 (25 mEq)	20 mEq/packet
Suspension (no taste)	
Micro-K LS	20 mEq/packet
Efflorescent granules or tablets (flavored)[a]	
Klorvess, Klor-Con/EF (25 mEq)	20 mEq
Solutions (flavored)[a]	
Klorvess 10%, Rum-K 15%	20–30 mEq/15 ml

[a]Taste generally improved by chilling.

       (2) Serum potassium concentration should be monitored after 1 and 4 weeks, then every 6–12 months

  3. Deficient potassium intake

    a) Unusual, requires failure to eat for prolonged periods

    b) If diet is inadequate during anabolic states (e.g., refeeding malnourished patients, treating vitamin B_{12}-deficient patients), severe hypokalemia may develop

  4. Excessive urinary losses other than induced by diuretics: see Table 31.1

32/ URINARY STONES

PRESENTATION

A. Acute colic
1. Symptoms
    a) Severe intermittent pain, most often in flank, radiates around groin and into testicles in men, into labia majora in women
    b) Nausea, vomiting may be associated with pain
2. Signs
    a) Uncomfortable, restless patient
    b) Costovertebral and deep abdominal tenderness may be present
    c) No signs of peritoneal irritation (guarding, rebound, or rigidity); no fever
3. Urinalysis
    a) Microscopic or gross hematuria almost always present
    b) Pyuria present if stone associated with chronic urinary tract infection (although may be absent if there is obstruction)
4. X-rays
    a) Abdominal x-ray
        1) 90% of stones radiodense
        2) Useful in identifying site of stone, monitoring progression
            (a) Stones of <5 mm usually pass spontaneously; stones between 5 and 10 mm have a 50% chance of passing; stones of >10 mm usually require surgical removal
            (b) An oblique view may help in visualization
    b) Intravenous pyelogram (IVP)
        1) Should be obtained as soon as possible
        2) Important in diagnosis (especially of radiolucent stones) and to establish severity
        3) Immediate urological referral indicated if a ureter is completely obstructed, partially obstructed and there is a solitary kidney, there is extravasation of urine, the stone is ≥10 mm (see above)
    c) Antegrade (catheter passed percutaneously into renal pelvis) or retrograde pyelogram may be considered if patient is allergic to radiological dye (ultrasonography is also an alternative)
5. Management
    a) Consultation and usually hospitalization necessary if stone is too large to pass spontaneously, is threatening kidney function, or has caused extravasation of urine (see above)
    b) The majority of patients can be managed at home
        1) Forced hydration of 2–3 liters/24 hours is necessary
        2) All voided urine should be strained (e.g., through an old stocking or filter paper) and collected so that when the stone is passed, it may be analyzed
        3) Analgesia
            (a) Oxycodone (5 mg), 1–3 tablets, or Tylox, 1–3 tablets, every 3–4 hours as necessary
            (b) Indomethacin 50 mg may be tried in combination with traditional analgesics if pain persists
        4) A phenothiazine (e.g., Phenergan 25 mg) may be needed to control nausea

5) If symptoms intermittent and well-controlled at home but stone has not passed, weekly abdominal x-rays should be done to determine progress of stone; if stone not passed in 6 weeks, referral to a urologist is indicated

c) Options for stone removal
   1) Lower ureteral stones may be removed with a basket through a cystoscope or ureteroscope
      (a) Requires spinal or general anesthesia
      (b) 95% success rate
   2) Percutaneous nephrolithotomy
      (a) A tube is passed percutaneously with help of fluoroscopy
      (b) Various devices employed to extract stone(s)
      (c) Most useful for renal or upper ureteral stones of 2.5 mm
      (d) 95% successful for renal stones, 85% for ureteral stones
      (e) Requires 4–5 days of hospitalization
   3) Extracorporeal shock-wave lithotripsy
      (a) Most often performed with intravenous sedation alone, but sometimes spinal anesthesia is needed
      (b) Usually done as an outpatient procedure
      (c) After procedure, stone fragments pass, may cause colic, usually causes hematuria
      (d) Procedure of choice for patients with renal stones of <2.5 mm, some upper ureteral stones
      (e) 90% successful

B. No colic: if stones are detected (after evaluation of, e.g., hematuria), workup is as in A

TYPES OF STONES

A. Calcium stones
   1. Majority (of all stones, calcium and otherwise) are composed of calcium oxalate (Table 32.1)
   2. Causes of calcium oxalate stones: Table 32.2
   3. Urine pH not a factor in calcium oxalate stone formation (calcium phosphate stones are promoted at a pH > 6)
B. Uric acid stones
   1. Associated factors
      a) Hyperuricosuria
      b) Highly acid urine

Table 32.1. Classification of Stone-Forming Patients by Type of Stone Passed

Type of Stone	Coe Series (1431 Patients)	Other Series Combined (1870 Patients)
Calcium oxalate (with or without phosphate)	69[a]	63.2[a]
Calcium phosphate	2	7.4
Calcium and uric acid	10	
Uric acid	2	5.4
Cystine	1	2.5
Struvite	7	21.5
Unknown	10	

From Coe FL: *Nephrolithiasis: Pathogenesis and Treatment*. Chicago, Year Book Medical Publishers, 1988.
[a] All values are expressed as percentages of patients in each category.

Table 32.2.   Metabolic and Clinical Disorders in 989 Calcium Oxalate Stone Formers

Disorder	No. of Patients (%)			
	Men		Women	
Systemic disease				
Primary hyperparathyroidism[a]	26	(4)	24	(10)
Sarcoid	6	(1)	1	(1)
Cushing's syndrome	5	(1)	1	(0.4)
Paget's disease	1	(0.1)	1	(0.4)
Renal tubular acidosis type I	7	(1)	4	(2)
Enteric hyperoxaluria[b]	39	(5)	13	(5)
No systemic disease				
Idiopathic (hereditary) hypercalciuria	213	(29)	121	(49)
Hyperuricosuria	126	(17)	9	(4)
Both disorders	120	(16)	22	(9)
No metabolic disorders[c]	186	(26)	52	(11)
Total	729		249	

From Coe FL: *Nephrolithiasis: Pathogenesis and Treatment.* Chicago, Year Book Medical Publishers, 1988.
[a] Seventeen additional patients had primary hyperparathyroidism; either their stones were admixed with uric acid, struvite, or cystine, they had stones with no calcium, or their stone type was unknown.
[b] Includes primary hyperoxaluria (three patients) and hyperoxaluria as a consequence of intestinal bypass for obesity.
[c] Urinary citrate data are not available. Hypocitraturia has been found alone or in combination with other disorders in 19% of hypercalciurias.

      c) Low urinary volume (severe dehydration)
  2. Causes
     a) Gout (see Chapter 53)
       1) Stones may long precede arthritis
       2) May be associated with calcium stones also (see Table 32.1)
     b) Asymptomatic hyperuricemia
     c) Hyperuricosuria without hyperuricemia
C. Struvite stones (infection stones)
  1. Almost always a complication of another primary stone disease in which infection has become superimposed
  2. Especially likely to grow into staghorn calculi
D. Cystine stones
  1. Most likely seen in young patients
  2. Inherited (autosomal recessive) defect in reabsorption of cystine
  3. May be associated with staghorn calculi
  4. Promoted in acid urine

DIAGNOSTIC WORKUP OF PATIENTS WITH URINARY STONE DISEASE

A. History
  1. Family history: useful as a clue to cystine stones, uric acid stones, some calcium stones (e.g., those associated with renal tubular acidosis)
  2. Dietary history
     a) Large intake of animal protein, tendency to eat one large meal a day may be associated with excess uric acid excretion
     b) May reveal excess consumption of calcium or oxalate
     c) Approximate fluid intake per day
  3. History of previous attacks: number of passed stones, frequency of attacks, history of infection, analyses of previous stones

4. Medication history
   a) Aspirin, >5 g/day, or probenecid are associated with increased uric acid excretion
   b) Calcium-containing antacids (e.g., Tums) as well as vitamins A and D increase calcium excretion
   c) Acetazolamide (Diamox) causes an alkaline urine and may promote calcium phosphate stone formation
   d) Vitamin C in high doses increases oxalate excretion
   e) Triamterene, itself, may precipitate in the urine
5. Occupational history: high ambient temperatures with associated fluid losses may favor stone formation

B. Physical examination
   1. During colic — see above
   2. Usually normal between attacks unless a systemic disease (e.g., one producing hypercalcemia, such as hyperparathyroidism or sarcoidosis; gout) is present

C. Urinalysis
   1. pH
      a) Usually acid in patients with a uric acid or cystine stone, invariably alkaline in patients with struvite stones
      b) First morning urine (usually acid) of 6 may reflect renal tubular acidosis
   2. May show hematuria (usually does not show between attacks), crystals, or pyuria

D. Stone analysis: important in determining evaluation and treatment

E. Laboratory assessment
   1. Table 32.3

Table 32.3.   Laboratory Assessment of Patients With Urinary Calculi[a]

	Day of Testing	
Measurement	1	2
24-hour urinary volume	✓	✓
24-hour urinary calcium[b]	✓	✓
24-hour urinary uric acid[c]		✓
24-hour urinary creatinine	✓	✓
24-hour urinary oxalate	✓	✓
24-hour urinary citrate	✓	✓
24-hour urinary sodium	✓	✓
Urinalysis	✓	
Urine cystine screen (cyanide-nitroprusside test)	✓	
Urine culture (if pyuria)	✓	
Urine pH (taken on first voided morning specimen collected under mineral oil)	✓	
Serum calcium	✓	✓
Serum phosphorus	✓	
Serum uric acid	✓	
Serum chloride	✓	
Serum bicarbonate	✓	
Serum creatinine	✓	
Serum urea nitrogen	✓	

[a] During evaluation, patients should follow their usual diet and life habits.
[b] The 24-hour urine container should contain 15 ml of concentrated HCl (with warning to avoid contact).
[c] The 24-hour urine container should contain a few crystals of thymol to retard bacterial overgrowth.

2. Intravenous pyelogram, if not done previously, to look for underlying structural disease
3. Parathyroid hormone assay if hypercalcemia (see Chapter 58), hypercalciuria, or hypophosphatemia is present
4. Urinary oxalate only if hyperoxaluria is suspected (see Table 32.4)
5. Hypercalciuria without hypercalcemia warrants referral to a nephrologist or urologist for consideration of an oral calcium tolerance test to distinguish a renal leak from excess absorption of calcium

PREVENTIVE TREATMENT OF URINARY CALCULUS DISEASE

A. General measures
   1. Usually all that is necessary if only a single stone has been passed and there is no evidence of stones on x-ray
   2. Diet: a dietician may be helpful, depending on nature of stone (see below)
   3. Fluid intake: regardless of type of stone, 3–4 liters/day are recommended (including 2 glasses before retiring, 2 in the middle of the night)
   4. Avoidance of dehydration
B. Specific therapy for formers of calcium stones
   1. Dietary
      a) Calcium restriction not recommended
      b) Probably helpful to limit animal protein intake to 1 g/kg
      c) High dietary potassium intake and avoidance of hypokalemia are of help; if supplementation is necessary, potassium citrate (see below) should be the salt
      d) Modest restriction of dietary sodium (no added salt to food)
   2. Thiazide diuretics
      a) Drugs of choice in patients with hypercalciuria
         1) To be avoided, however, in patients with hypercalcemia
         2) Avoid hypokalemia (see above and Chapter 30)
      b) Exact dose uncertain (equivalent of 25–50 mg of hydrochlorothiazide twice a day usually prescribed)
      c) Avoid triamterene (see above)
   3. Potassium citrate (e.g., Polycitra-K or Urocit-K)
      a) Useful in alkalinizing urine (see above), in increasing urinary citrate (low urinary citrate favors calcium stone formation), in decreasing calciuria
      b) Objective is urinary pH between 6 and 7 and normal citrate excretion (as close as possible to 640 mg/day — confirm by measurement initially and then every 6–12 months)
      c) Dose is 0.5–2.0 mEq/day in 2–4 doses/day

Table 32.4.   Situations in Which Hyperoxaluria May Be Expected

Hereditary overproduction — usually virulent stone disease with frequent recurrences and nephrocalcinosis often occurring before age 12 years
Methoxyflurane anesthesia — immediately after
Ethylene glycol ingestion — immediately after
Chronic inflammatory bowel disease affecting the ileum, ileal resection, or small bowel bypass
Cellulose phosphate ingestion — during entire period of ingestion
Oxalate gluttony (tea, spinach, rhubarb)

4. Orthophosphate (inorganic phosphate) and cellulose phosphate
   a) Reduces calciuria
   b) Not recommended without consultation
C. Therapy for patients with calcium or uric acid stones who have hyperuricosuria
   1. Reduce intake of purine-rich foods (e.g., liver, sweetbreads, fish, roe)
   2. Alkalinize urine to pH > 6.0
      a) Polycitra-K preparation of choice, 10 ml 3 times/day, modified according to urine pH
      b) Patient should measure urine pH during the first week and periodically thereafter
      c) Allopurinol (also see Chapter 53)
         1) For patients with recurrent stones whose urinary pH cannot be kept >6.5 or whose uric acid excretion is >650 mg/day
         2) Prescribed at 200 mg/day, raised to a dose that maintains uric acid excretion of <500–600 mg/day
D. Therapy for hyperoxaluria
   1. Reduction of intake of food with high oxalate content (spinach, rhubarb, chard, nuts, cocoa, chocolate)
   2. In patients with malabsorption, treatment may be complicated (reduce fat and oxalate intake, supplement calcium and magnesium, cholestyramine, potassium citrate), and consultation with a nephrologist is appropriate
E. Therapy for cystinuria: best managed in consultation with a nephrologist (alkalinization of urine usually necessary, D-penicillamine may be required)
F. Therapy for struvite or infection stones
   1. Because of high morbidity associated with staghorn calculi, these stones should be removed (see above)
   2. Suppressive therapy with antimicrobials indicated if infection is persistent
   3. Stone formation can sometimes be prevented by use of urease inhibitors, e.g., acetohydroxamic acid (Lithostat) 250 mg 3 or 4 times/day
      a) Only when urinary pH is high
      b) Not in pregnant women (teratogenic)
      c) Not effective in patients with renal failure
      d) High incidence of side effects — should be prescribed after consultation with a urologist
G. Therapy for patients who have no identifiable metabolic disorder; 10–15% may respond to thiazides and/or allopurinol as described above

33/ CHRONIC RENAL INSUFFICIENCY

DIAGNOSIS

A. History
1. Family history of polycystic disease, Alport's syndrome (nephritis and hearing loss), medullary sponge kidney, hypertension, diabetes mellitus, renal failure
2. Past history of a systemic illness associated with renal failure (e.g., hypertension, diabetes mellitus, collagen vascular disease, AIDS)
3. Symptoms associated with abnormalities of the urinary tract (dysuria, frequency, renal colic, hesitancy, urinary incontinence)
4. Symptoms of advanced renal failure (e.g., nausea, vomiting, fatigue, nocturia, itching)
5. Inventory of past and current drug use (Table 33.1)

B. Physical examination
1. Signs of systemic illness: e.g., high blood pressure, hypertensive or diabetic retinopathy, vascular bruits, vasculitic skin rashes)
2. Enlarged kidneys due to polycystic disease or to hydronephrosis
3. Pelvic and rectal examinations when lower urinary tract obstruction is suspected [residual urine of >100 ml in catheterized bladder also suggests bladder outlet obstruction (see Chapter 34) or neurogenic bladder (most common in diabetics)]

C. Laboratory evaluation
1. Urinalysis
   a) Red cells or red cell casts suggest glomerular disease
   b) White cells, with or without casts, are found in interstitial

---

Table 33.1. Some Commonly Used Drugs That May Adversely Affect Renal Function

Antibiotics
  Aminoglycosides (ATN)
  Penicillins (IN)
  Tetracyclines (increased azotemia and acidosis)
Analgesics
  Aspirin (PN and reduction in RBF)
  Phenacetin (PN and IN)
  Nonsteroidal analgesics (IN, nephrotic syndrome, and reduced RBF)
Diuretics
  Thiazides (volume depletion and IN)
  Loop agents (volume depletion and IN)
Miscellaneous
  Radiocontrast materials (ATN)
  Methysergide (retroperitoneal fibrosis causing obstructive uropathy)
  Penicillamine (NS)
  Gold (NS)
  H_2 receptor antagonists (interfere with secretion of creatinine and produce false elevations of the serum creatinine concentration)
  ACE inhibitors (precipitate renal failure in patients with renovascular disease)

ACE, angiotensin-converting enzyme; *ATN*, acute tubular necrosis; *IN*, interstitial nephritis; *NS*, nephrotic syndrome; *PN*, papillary necrosis; *RBF*, renal blood flow.

nephropathies (hyaline or granular casts have no specific diagnostic import)
    c) Urinary protein (see Chapter 29)
2. Complete blood count
    a) Severity of anemia roughly parallels blood urea nitrogen concentration (unless renal failure of recent onset or patient has polycystic disease or hydronephrosis)
    b) Examine blood smear for rouleaux formation (myeloma), microangiopathic hemolytic anemia (e.g., in accelerated hypertension, scleroderma, postpartum renal failure)
3. Measurement of blood glucose, serum electrolytes, uric acid
4. Measure of overall renal function
    a) Glomerular filtration rate (GFR), the standard, is almost always estimated by measurement of serum creatinine or endogenous creatinine clearance
    b) Creatinine production dependent on age and on muscle mass increases nonlinearly as renal function declines (Fig. 33.1)
5. Renal imaging
    a) Sonography
        1) Should be the initial technique in measuring the size of kidneys and in detecting hydronephrosis, which, if identified, dictates referral to a urologist to identify the site of the obstruction

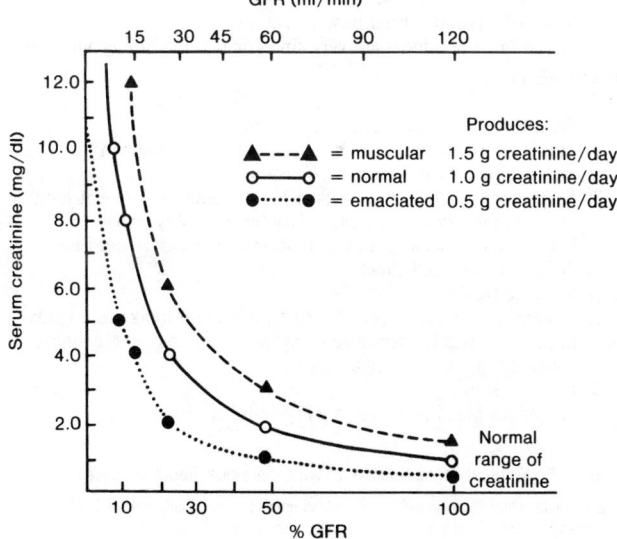

Figure 33.1. Relationship of serum creatinine concentration to GFR in patients with different muscle mass.

2) An abdominal x-ray will accurately estimate renal size but cannot detect hydronephrosis

3) Small kidneys indicate severe chronic renal disease, but the kidneys may also be large (e.g., in diabetics) or of normal size in patients in chronic renal failure

b) Intravenous pyelogram (IVP)

1) Most useful in determining etiology in those diseases that produce gross anatomical abnormalities (e.g., nephrolithiasis, polycystic kidneys)

2) Not useful in patients with parenchymal disorders not associated with gross anatomical defects

3) Should not be initial screening procedure because of increased risk of radiocontrast dye toxicity (maintenance of salt (6–8 g/day) and fluid (1–2 liters/day) intake appears to reduce risk)

c) CT scans: of limited usefulness

d) Radionuclide studies: no proven efficacy in patients with chronic renal failure because of bilaterally compromised blood flow

e) Arteriography

1) Should be obtained if index of suspicion of reversible bilateral renal vascular disease is high (Table 33.2)

2) Risk of acute tubular necrosis or atheromatous embolization warrants prior consultation with a vascular surgeon and a nephrologist

6. Renal biopsy

a) To estimate prognosis or help make therapeutic decisions if the diagnosis is uncertain

b) Usually requires brief hospitalization

c) Not done if kidneys are very small or renal failure is advanced

TREATMENT

A. Goals

1. Treat the underlying disease, if possible

2. Slow the progression of renal deterioration by modifying aggravating factors (e.g., hypertension)

3. Treat complications (e.g., acidosis) and attempt to prevent long-term complications (e.g., secondary hyperparathyroidism)

4. Refer to a dialysis and transplantation center before need for dialysis arises (see below)

B. Nonspecific treatment

1. Protein restriction: reasonable to limit protein intake to 40 g/day in patients with moderate renal insufficiency (serum creatinine concentration of 2–6 mg/dl)

2. Hypertension

a) Reduce blood pressure to <140 systolic, <90 diastolic

Table 33.2.   Clinical Presentations of Atheromatous Renal Disease

1. Acute renal failure following reduction in blood pressure (particularly with ACE inhibitors)
2. Progressive azotemia in a patient with known renovascular disease
3. Azotemia associated with new-onset hypertension or a change in severity of hypertension
4. Unexplained azotemia in an elderly patient with peripheral vascular disease
5. Progressive renal failure with evidence of cholesterol embolization

Adapted from Jacobson HR: Ischemic renal disease: an overlooked entity? *Kidney Int* 34:724, 1988.

      b) Antihypertensive therapy in patients with mild to moderate renal failure similar to that of hypertensives with normal renal function (see Chapter 46)

      c) Potassium-sparing diuretics contraindicated

      d) Diuretics progressively less effective as renal function worsens; other drugs can be used (see Chapter 46) with careful monitoring of orthostatic effects and renal function

C. Treatment of reversible causes of deterioration of renal function

   1. Extracellular volume depletion

      a) Most common cause

      b) May be related to an intercurrent illness (e.g., with fever, diarrhea, or vomiting), excessive salt restriction, or diuretic use

      c) Weight loss between visits usually the most important clue

   2. Congestive heart failure (Chapter 45)

   3. Drugs (Table 33.1)

      a) Diuretics and nonsteroidal anti-inflammatory agents are probably the most common offenders in an ambulatory setting [latter should probably be avoided entirely in patients with GFR < 50 ml/minute (Fig. 33.1)]

      b) Angiotensin-converting enzyme (ACE) inhibitors should be used cautiously in patients with bilateral renal vascular disease

   4. Obstruction

      a) Consider especially in elderly men with prostatic hypertrophy or in diabetics who may have autonomic neuropathy

      b) Drugs that reduce bladder tone (antidepressants, antispasmodics, anticholinergic, antiparkinsonian drugs) may reversibly impair renal function

   5. Orthostatic hypotension due to drugs or autonomic neuropathy (Chapter 64)

   6. Microcrystal deposition: reducing serum uric acid concentrations (often elevated) will not improve renal function when the original kidney disease was not due to gout

   7. Calcium phosphate deposits

      a) Commonly found in parenchyma of patients with end-stage kidney disease

      b) Recommend that dietary phosphorus be reduced to 800 mg/day once GFR falls below 30 ml/minute (Fig. 33.1)

D. Dietary management: Table 33.3

E. Use of diuretics (also see Hypertension, above): Table 33.4

F. Calcium and phosphorus

   1. Decreased synthesis of vitamin D leads to increased secretion of parathyroid hormone (PTH), which, in turn, leads to increasingly severe bone disease

   2. Periodic measurement (every 6 months in early disease, every month in more advanced disease) of serum calcium, magnesium, and phosphorus concentrations, serum alkaline phosphatase activity

   3. When PTH activity is measured, N-terminal or intact hormone assay should be used

   4. Derangement leads to bone pain, fractures, proximal myopathy, usually not until end-stage renal disease

   5. Treatment should begin early in the course of progressive renal disease (Table 33.5)

Table 33.3. Dietary Management of Renal Failure[a]

Therapy	Goals
Salt: 4–6 g/day	Maintain intravascular volume
Fluid: 1–3 liters/day	Avoid dehydration
Potassium: if [K] > 5.5 mEq/liter, restrict intake to 2–2.4 g/day	Prevent hyperkalemia
Protein: restrict intake to 0.55–0.6 g/kg/day (50% rich in essential amino acids)	Relieve uremic symptoms Retard progression of renal failure
Calories: provide 35–45 kcal/kg/day	Maintain nutrition
Calcium: provide 1–1.5 g/day	Maintain [Ca] = 9–10 mg/dl
Vitamins: multivitamin + folate	Replace vitamins lacking in protein-restricted diet
Phosphorus: restrict intake to 800 mg/day	Prevent secondary hyperparathyroidism

[a] A dietician should be consulted to teach the patient how to achieve these intakes.

    a) Other medications should not be given simultaneously with calcium binders, since their absorption may be increased or decreased
    b) Aluminum-containing antacids should be used cautiously in end-stage renal disease because dialysis dementia syndrome (myoclonus, seizures, dementia), anemia, or osteomalacia may develop
    c) Magnesium-containing antacids should be avoided because of risk of magnesium toxicity
G. Acidosis
  1. Mild hyperchloremic (normal anion gap) metabolic acidosis common in early renal failure (Fig. 33.2)
  2. Hypochloremic (abnormal anion gap) metabolic acidosis does not generally develop until GFR is <20 ml/minute
  3. Goal is to maintain a serum bicarbonate concentration of >20 mEq/liter
    a) Restrict dietary protein (see above)
    b) If necessary, sodium citrate 30–60 mEq/liter of base
    c) $CaCO_3$ may also be effective (Table 33.5)
H. Anemia
  1. Severity proportionate to degree of renal failure (Fig. 33.3)
  2. Multivitamins, including folate, should be given routinely
  3. Iron deficiency almost universal in patients on hemodialysis, should be diagnosed by measurement of serum ferritin (although higher in patients with renal failure than in persons with normal renal function)
  4. If hematocrit levels fall below 30% and patients are symptomatic, treatment with recombinant human erythropoietin 50–150 U/kg s.c. or i.v. is appropriate
    a) Need 300 mg ferrous sulfate a day, even if not iron deficient, and 1 mg folic acid a day
    b) Blood pressure may rise, should be monitored weekly for 6–8 weeks

DRUG USE IN RENAL FAILURE
A. General principles
  1. Incidence of adverse drug effects increased

Table 33.4. Diuretics in Renal Failure

Drug	Available Strengths (mg)	Dose	Route of Excretion	Comments
Thiazides (hydrochlorothiazide)	25, 50	50–200 mg/day	Renal	May induce volume depletion and hyperuricemia. Loses effectiveness if GFR < 30 ml/min but may be used in combination with loop diuretics in advanced renal failure.
Metolazone (Zaroxolyn)	2.5, 5, 10	5–20 mg/day	Renal	May induce volume depletion and hyperuricemia. Effective when GFR > 10 ml/min.
Furosemide (Lasix)	20, 40, 80	20–400 mg/day	Renal	May induce volume depletion and hyperuricemia. Effective when GFR > 5 ml/min. May produce ototoxicity and rarely interstitial nephritis. May increase nephrotoxicity of antibiotics.
Bumetanide (Bumex)	0.5, 1, 2	1–10 mg/day	Renal	May induce volume depletion and hyperuricemia. Side effects include ototoxicity and muscle pains and may also increase the risk of antibiotic nephrotoxicity.
Ethacrynic acid (Edecrin)		Avoid	Hepatic	Usually avoided in renal failure, since the risk of ototoxicity is significantly higher than with furosemide or bumetanide.
Spironolactone (Aldactone) Triamterene (Dyrenium) Amiloride (Moduretic)		Avoid	Hepatic	Avoid when GFR < 50 ml/min due to the risk of inducing serious hyperkalemia.

Table 33.5.   Steps in the Management of Calcium and Phosphorus Balance in Patients With Renal Failure

Therapy	Goals
GFR 50–30 ml/min	
Calcium supplements (1–1.5 g/day) (see text)	Maintain serum calcium concentration at 9–10 mg/dl
Vitamin D (Rocaltrol 0.25–0.5 µg/day, available in 0.25-µg tablets)	Maintain serum calcium concentration at 9–10 mg/dl
GFR < 30 ml/min	
Restrict phosphorus intake (800 mg/day)	Maintain serum phosphorus concentration at 4.0–6.0 mg/dl
Phosphorus-binding antacids (calcium carbonate, aluminum carbonate, or aluminum hydroxide taken with meals)	Maintain serum phosphorus concentration at 4.0–6.0 mg/dl

    2. Even over-the-counter drugs should not be taken without physician's approval
    3. Avoid drugs with marginal efficacy
B. Guidelines for drugs most commonly prescribed (Tables 33.6 and 33.7)
    1. An accurate measurement of GFR (e.g., by creatinine clearance) is important; serum creatinine measurement is not adequate
    2. Monitoring of serum drug levels often of help

CHRONIC RENAL FAILURE AND COEXISTING DISORDERS
A. Diabetes mellitus (see also Chapter 56)
    1. Up to 50% of type 1 and 10% of type 2 diabetics develop chronic renal failure (account for about one-third of dialysis populations)

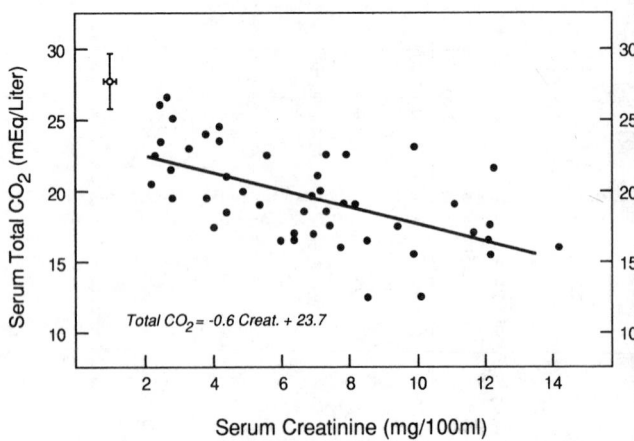

$$Total\ CO_2 = -0.6\ Creat. + 23.7$$

Figure 33.2. Relationship between serum bicarbonate and serum creatinine concentrations in patients with chronic renal insufficiency. (From Widmer B, et al: Serum electrolyte and acid-base composition. The influence of graded degrees of chronic renal failure. *Arch Intern Med* 139:1099–1102, 1979. Copyright 1979, American Medical Association.)

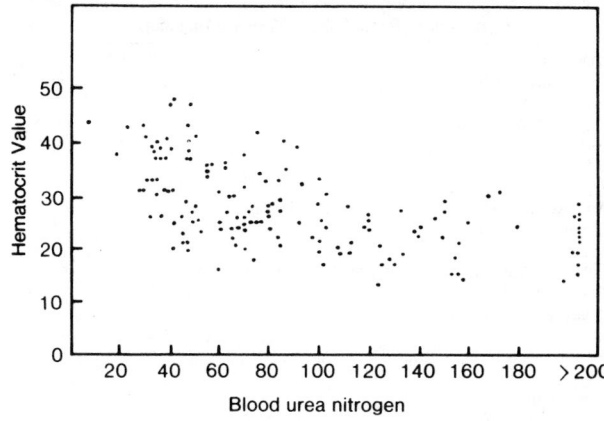

Figure 33.3. Relationship of blood urea nitrogen concentration to hematocrit value in patients with chronic renal failure. (From Erslev AJ: Erythrocyte function of the kidney. In: Wesson LG (ed): *Physiology of the Human Kidney.* New York, Grune & Stratton, 1969, p 521.)

    2. Proteinuria is the earliest clinical evidence of diabetic nephropathy [microalbuminuria (see Chapter 29)] and justifies an attempt at tighter control of blood glucose
    3. Control of hypertension important in retarding progress of disease
    4. Restriction of dietary protein important (see above)
    5. Dosage of insulin or of oral hypoglycemic agents may need to be modified (see Chapter 56)
    6. Critical that close attention be paid to eyes (Chapter 56) and feet (Chapter 85)
B. Heart disease
    1. Patients with congestive heart failure or symptomatic ischemic heart disease need more frequent monitoring
    2. Increased rate of atherogenesis in patients with chronic renal failure

Table 33.6.   Some Commonly Used Drugs That Require Dosage Reduction in Renal Failure (GFR < 30 ml/min)

Cardiovascular drugs	H₂ receptor antagonists
Digoxin (Lanoxin)	Cimetidine (Tagamet)
Nadolol (Corgard)	Ranitidine (Zantac)
Atenolol (Tenomin)	Hypoglycemic drugs
Procainamide (Pronestyl)	Insulin
Disopyramide (Norpace)	Acetohexamide
Antihypertensive drugs	Chlorpropamide
Captopril (Capoten)	Drugs used in the treatment of gout
Clonidine (Catapres)	Allopurinol (Zyloprim)
Guanethidine (Ismelin)	

Table 33.7.   Some Commonly Used Drugs That Should Be Avoided in Patients With Renal Failure (GFR < 30 ml/min)

Antimicrobials
 Cephaloridine (Loridine)
 Tetracyclines
 Nitrofurantoin (Macrodantin)
 Nalidixic acid (Negram)
Analgesics
 Aspirin
 Nonsteroidal anti-inflammatory agents (Motrin, Nalfon, etc.)
 Meperidine (Demerol)
Diuretics
 Potassium-sparing diuretics (Aldactone, Moduretics, Dyrenium)
 Ethacrynic acid (Edecrin)
 Thiazides (Diuril, etc.)
Antacids
 Magnesium-containing antacids (Maalox, Mylanta, etc.)
Hypoglycemic drugs
 Acetohexamide (Dymelor)
 Chlorpropamide (Diabinase)
Drugs used in the treatment of gout
 Phenylbutazone (Butazolidine)
 Sulfinpyrazone (Anturane)
 Probenecid (Benemid)

C. HIV infection (see Chapter 20)
  1. A progressive nephropathy characterized by renal failure and proteinuria may occur
  2. Advisability of dialysis in this population debatable

SYMPTOMATIC THERAPY OF ADVANCED RENAL INSUFFICIENCY

A. Gastrointestinal
  1. Nausea, vomiting, anorexia common
  2. Further restrict dietary protein (see above) and/or prescribe antiemetics (e.g., Compazine)
B. Itching
  1. Reduce serum phosphorus level to normal (see above)
  2. Use skin lubricants (Chapter 83)
  3. Prescribe antihistamines for a 1–3-week trial (e.g., Benedryl 25–50 mg 4 times/day)
C. Neuromuscular
  1. Myoclonus, restless legs, disturbed sleep are signs of advanced disease, predict more severe complications (seizures, coma)
  2. Dialysis should be considered when symptoms develop (usually at a serum creatinine of 10–12 mg/dl)

DIALYSIS AND TRANSPLANTATION

A. Hemodialysis
  1. Provisions for dialysis should be made, if possible, months in advance of need
  2. Not advisable to wait for signs and symptoms of far advanced uremia (e.g., pericarditis, seizures, coma, bleeding) before initiating

    3. Refer to a nephrologist associated with a dialysis center when creatinine clearance approaches 20 ml/minute

    4. Vascular access needed (e.g., arteriovenous fistula) and should be created several months before dialysis is anticipated

B. Peritoneal dialysis

    1. Continuous ambulatory peritoneal dialysis the preferred technique, provides a great degree of freedom

    2. Major complication is peritonitis, generally can be treated with antibiotics without hospitalization

    3. Choice of peritoneal versus hemodialysis depends on center and on patient's preference

C. Transplantation

    1. Success depends on antigenic similarity between donor and recipient (cadaveric transplants, the most common, have a 61% success rate at 2 years compared with 90% for transplants from living related donors)

    2. Patients require lifelong immunosuppression with cyclosporine, prednisone, and azathioprine

    3. Quality of life is the major determinant in choosing between dialysis and transplantation; the survivals are similar

34/ BLADDER OUTLET OBSTRUCTION

ASSESSMENT OF BLADDER OUTLET OBSTRUCTION
A. History
   1. Characteristic symptoms
      a) Urinary hesitancy, diminished force and caliber of the stream, postvoid dribbling
      b) Eventually, urinary frequency, urgency, nocturia (but without other symptoms, these symptoms suggest irritation rather than obstruction)
      c) Ultimately, when bladder decompensates, patients may develop residual urine, infection, hematuria, hydronephrosis, renal failure
   2. Urethral stricture usually associated with a history of prior urethral trauma, instrumentation, urethritis
   3. Carcinoma of the prostate may be associated with back or bone pain, anorexia, or weight loss; obstructive symptoms may be of relatively short duration
   4. Neurogenic bladder should be suspected when bowel or sexual dysfunction coexist with symptoms of bladder outlet obstruction or in the presence of a disease (e.g., diabetes mellitus) that can cause neurological bladder dysfunction
   5. Current and recently used medications should be reviewed (Table 34.1)
   6. Systems assessment tool: see Table 34.2
B. Physical Examination
   1. Abdominal: may reveal distended bladder, renal tenderness, renal mass, inguinal hernia
   2. Genital: may reveal phimosis, meatal stenosis, epididymal infection

Table 34.1. Pharmacological Agents With Known Influence on Bladder Function

Drugs that increase bladder tone and contractility
    Bethanecol (Urecholine)
Drugs that decrease bladder contractility
    Anticholinergic drugs (e.g., Pro-Banthine, Donnatal, Ditropan)
    Calcium antagonists (verapamil, nifedipine, diltiazam)
    Prostaglandin inhibitors (e.g., ibuprofen)
    Tricyclic antidepressants (e.g., imipramine, nortriptyline)
    β-Adrenergic antagonists (e.g., terbutaline)
Drugs that increase bladder outlet resistance
    Sympathomimetic drugs (e.g., ephedrine, Sudafed, Ornade)
    Antiparkinsonian drugs (e.g., levodopa, Sinemet)
    β-Adrenergic antagonists (e.g., propranolol)
    Estrogens
Drugs that decrease outlet resistance
    Antispasticity drugs (e.g., diazapam, Baclofen)
    α-Adrenergic antagonists (e.g., prazosin, phenoxybenzamine, terazosin)
Drugs that increase urinary volume
    Diuretics

Table 34.2. International Prostate Symptom Score (I-PSS)

	Not at All	Less Than 1 Time in 5	Less Than Half the Time	About Half the Time	More Than Half the Time	Almost Always	Your Score
1. Incomplete emptying Over the past month, how often have you had a sensation of not emptying your bladder completely after you finished urinating?	0	1	2	3	4	5	
2. Frequency Over the past month, how often have you had to urinate again less than 2 hours after you finished urinating?	0	1	2	3	4	5	
3. Intermittency Over the past month, how often have you found you stopped and started again several times when you urinated?	0	1	2	3	4	5	
4. Urgency Over the past month, how often have you found it difficult to postpone urination?	0	1	2	3	4	5	
5. Weak stream Over the past month, how often have you had a weak urinary stream?	0	1	2	3	4	5	
6. Straining Over the past month, how often have you had to push or strain to begin urination?	0	1	2	3	4	5	

Table 34.2. Continued

	None	1 time	2 times	3 times	4 times	5 or more times
7. **Nocturia** Over the past month, how many times did you most typically get up to urinate from the time you went to bed at night until the time you got up in the morning?	0	1	2	3	4	5

Total I-PSS Score =

Quality of Life Due to Urinary Symptoms

	Delighted	Pleased	Mostly Satisfied	Mixed (About Equally Satisfied and Dissatisfied)	Mostly Dissatisfied	Unhappy	Terrible
If you were to spend the rest of your life with your urinary condition just the way it is now, how would you feel about that?	0	1	2	3	4	5	6

From International Consensus Committee under patronage of the World Health Organization (R. 20). Handy cards containing this information are currently available at no cost from Merck and Co., Inc. (215)652-7300.

3. Neurological: especially anal sphincter tone; genital and perineal sensation; motor, sensory, and reflex activity of the lower extremities
4. Rectal: examination of the lateral and posterior lobes of the prostate (anterior and, usually, the median lobes are not palpable)

C. Preliminary laboratory assessment
  1. Urinalysis, measurement of urinary flow rate (see below), urine culture (if pyuria), measurement of serum creatinine
  2. Prostatic specific antigen (PSA)
     a) Elevated in blood of patients with prostate cancer, glandular hyperplasia, acute prostatitis, prostate abscess, mechanical (not digital) manipulation of the prostate
     b) Not clear that routine screening in asymptomatic men improves survival in patients with prostatic cancer
        1) Men over 50 years with a family history of prostate cancer should be screened yearly
        2) The most reliable marker for response to treatment of prostatic cancer
     c) If significant increase (e.g., PSA of >20 or an increase of 0.75 mg or more per year) is detected, transrectal ultrasound and prostatic biopsy (by a urologist) are warranted

D. Urodynamic assessment
  1. Uroflowmetry (urinary flow rate)
     a) Measure the volume of urine voided during a 5-second period
     b) Normal men have volumes in excess of 75 ml; men with urinary obstruction have volumes of <50 ml
  2. Cystometry
     a) Indicated in patients suspected of voiding dysfunction unrelated to bladder outlet obstruction, primarily patients with urgency and frequency
     b) Performed by a urologist

E. Urological investigation
  1. Indications when surgery is a consideration: Table 34.3
  2. Imaging
     a) Intravenous urography
        1) Limited primarily to patients with hematuria
        2) Serum creatinine concentration should be <1.8 mg/dl, and there should be no history of allergic reaction to radiocontrast media (nonionic media are less risky)
     b) Ultrasonography

Table 34.3.   Indications for Surgery in Patients With BPH and Bladder Outlet Obstruction

Urinary retention
Intractable symptoms due to obstruction
Recurrent or persistent urinary tract infection
Recurrent prostatic bleeding
Significant postvoid residual urine
Changes of the kidneys, ureters, or bladder caused by prostatic obstruction
Abnormally low urinary flow rate
Bladder calculi

BPH, benign prostatic hyperplasia.

      1) Procedure of first choice to evaluate upper urinary tract for hydronephrosis, stones, masses, anomalies

      2) Used to quantitate postvoid residual urine, identify bladder calculi, estimate size of prostate

   c) Transrectal ultrasonography

      1) To evaluate prostate in a patient with an elevated PSA

      2) Often done in combination with a prostatic biopsy

   d) Renal scan: to evaluate renal blood flow or delayed excretion suggestive of obstruction

   e) Retrograde ureteropyelogram

      1) Done in conjunction with cystoscopy (see below)

      2) To visualize the ureters, kidneys

      3) Radiocontrast dye rarely absorbed, can be used in patients with a history of allergy to contrast media

   f) Retrograde urethrogram if urethral stricture is suspected

3. Instrumentation

   a) Bladder catheterization for postvoid volume

      1) Inserting a urethral catheter immediately after a patient has voided (>100 mg of urine in bladder is abnormal)

      2) Generally replaced by ultrasonography (see above)

   b) Cystometrogram

      1) Similar to a catheterization for residual urine

      2) After catheter is placed, sterile saline is used to fill bladder, and then the detrusor response to the increasing volume is measured

   c) Cystourethroscopy: the urethra, prostate, and bladder are directly visualized

TREATMENT OF BLADDER OUTLET OBSTRUCTION

A. Benign prostatic hyperplasia (BPH)

  1. Indwelling or clean intermittent catheterization

   a) Associated with recurrent urinary tract infections

   b) Other options should always be considered first

  2. Surgical management

   a) Transurethral resection of the prostate

      1) Requires 2–3 days hospitalization

      2) Short-term complications: bleeding, infection, plasma hypo-osmolality

      3) Long-term complications: urethral stricture, bladder neck contracture, incontinence, retrograde ejaculation

      4) Should not affect potency

      5) Normal physical and sexual activity can be resumed within 4 weeks

   b) Open prostatectomy

      1) Performed when BPH associated with a coincidental bladder condition (diverticulum or stone) that requires surgery

      2) Organic erectile impotence occurs occasionally

      3) Residual prostatic tissue remains, so recurrent obstruction or cancer can develop

   c) Transurethral incision of prostate and bladder neck (TUIP)

      1) Fewer complications than with transurethral resection of prostate (TURP), including a lower incidence of retrograde ejaculation

       2) Shorter hospital stay, faster recovery
       3) Major disadvantage is the potential for missing major localized prostatic cancer (some believe biopsy of prostate should be done concurrently)
    d) Other procedures
       1) Balloon dilation: little benefit over instrumentation
       2) Urethral stent: limited to high-risk patients who are poor operative risks
       3) Transrectal or transurethral microwave hyperthermia: improvement in symptoms but no long-term reduction in volume of prostate
       4) Laser: may prove to be as effective as TURP, still being evaluated
  3. Nonsurgical management
    a) α-Adrenergic agonists, e.g., terazosin, 1-, 2-, 5-, 10-mg tablets (2–10 mg/day in 1 or 2 doses)
       1) Start 1 mg at bedtime, increase 2 mg in 3–7 days if no response, then twice a day
       2) Carefully monitor blood pressure if patient is taking another hypotensive drug or has a baseline low blood pressure
       3) Patients with minimal to moderate obstruction have excellent results
    b) Androgen deprivation (i.e., finasteride (Proscar) 5 mg once a day)
       1) No effect on testosterone levels
       2) Should be given for at least 6 months for trial to be considered adequate
       3) Effects reversible
    c) Estrogens: still being investigated
B. Urethral stricture: treated with dilation, incision, or open surgery, depending on length and location of stricture, patient's health, and urologist's experience
C. Prostatic carcinoma
  1. Most frequent sign is a prostatic nodule or induration discovered during routine rectal examination
    a) 30–40% will represent carcinoma
    b) Should be referred to a urologist for biopsy
  2. Stages (Table 34.4)

Table 34.4.   Staging of Prostatic Carcinoma

Stage	Description
A	Clinically undetectable; found on pathological examination after prostatectomy
A1	Focal and well differentiated
A2	Diffuse (>5%) or poorly differentiated
B	Limited to prostate on rectal examination
B1	Solitary nodule; <1.5 cm; one lobe
B2	One whole lobe or both lobes
C	Locally extending outside of prostatic capsule or into seminal vesicles
D	Metastatic disease
D1	Pelvic lymph node metastases
D2	Distant metastases, usually bone

Table 34.5. Survival With Appropriately Managed Prostatic Carcinoma

	% Survival		
Stage	5 yr	10 yr	15 yr
A1	Normal life expectancy		
A2	50–80	40–70	15–35
B	50–90	40–70	15–40
C	15–70	5–60	0–30
D	5–30	3–10	0–3

     a) Established usually by digital rectal examination, PSA levels, and bone scan

     b) Tissue obtained by biopsy will be graded by a Gleason Scoring System of 5 histological grades at 2 different sites: the most differentiated would be a score of 2; the least differentiated, a score of 10

  3. Treatment (Table 34.5)

     a) Stage A

        1) Men younger than 60 with A1 disease should have a radical prostatectomy (high risk of recurrence because of expected longevity)

        2) Men older than 60 can simply be observed

        3) Men with A2 disease should have a radical prostatectomy

     b) Stage B: if under age 75 and has an anticipated 10-year survival, should have radical prostatectomy

     c) Stage C: usually by definitive radiotherapy (risk of chronic prostatitis or cystitis)

     d) Stage D: best managed by androgen deprivation, castration or pharmacological treatment

        1) Diethylstilbestrol (3 mg/day) and orchiectomy both produce an 85–90% partial symptomatic response for an average of 18 months (no advantage in combining these therapies)

        2) Luteinizing hormone-releasing hormone (LHRH) analogs (Luprolide, Zoladex) are expensive but are as effective as estrogen (with far fewer side effects) and ordinarily have largely replaced estrogen in treatment of prostatic cancer (usually in combination with an antiandrogen, flutamide)

Section V
Hematological Problems

35/ ANEMIA

BASIC CONCEPTS

A. Definition: reduction of the proportion of red cells or of hemoglobin in the blood (Table 35.1)
B. Mechanisms
   1. Decreased effective production of blood
   2. Bleeding
   3. Hemolysis
C. Routine database (Table 35.2)
   1. Classify the anemia according to the mean corpuscular volume (MCV) (see below)
   2. Calculate reticulocyte index (Table 35.3), an assessment of marrow responsiveness to anemia (should be at least 3% in a patient with bleeding or hemolysis)
   3. Look for underlying disease: anemia is not a primary diagnosis

ANEMIA WITH LOW MEAN CORPUSCULAR VOLUME (TABLE 35.4)

A. Iron deficiency anemia
   1. History: search for history of bleeding; decreased intake of iron rarely a cause of iron deficiency
   2. Physical examination: if iron deficiency severe, patients may have sore tongue; brittle, ridged fingernails; spoon nails; cheilosis; otherwise, no characteristic findings
   3. Laboratory data reflect severity of process (Table 35.5)

Table 35.1. Representative Normal Values (Coulter S)

	Men	Women
Hemoglobin (g/dl of blood)	14–18	12–16
Hematocrit value (%)	42–54	37–47
MCV (fl)	82–98	82–98
MCH (pg)	27–32	27–32
MCHC (g/dl of red blood cells)	31.5–36	31.5–36

Hct, hematocrit; *MCV*, mean corpuscular volume; *MCH*, mean corpuscular hemoglobin; *MCHC*, mean corpuscular hemoglobin concentration.

Table 35.2. Routine Database for Anemic Patients

Hct value
Hemoglobin concentration
MCV
MCHC
Reticulocytic count (and calculation of reticulocytic index)
Evaluation of a peripheral blood smear (fingerstick)

Table 35.3. Reticulocyte Index

Reticulocyte index = reticulocyte count $\times \dfrac{\text{patient Hct}}{\text{normal Hct}}$

Example: reticulocyte count 6%, Hct 15%

Reticulocyte index = $6 \times \dfrac{15}{45} = 2\%$

Table 35.4.   Causes of Anemia With Low MCV

Iron deficiency
Thalassemia
Anemia of chronic inflammation (occasionally)
Sideroblastic anemia (rarely)
Aluminum toxicity

Table 35.5.   Representative Database at Various Stages in the Slow Development of Severe Iron Deficiency Anemia

Hct (%)	42	42	35	27	19
MCV (82–98 fl)	92	88	82	75	68
MCHC (32–36 g/dl)	33	33	33	31	29
SI (65–175 μg/dl)	70	60	35	20	20
TIBC (250–375 μg/dl)	300	300	300	400	450
Serum ferritin (10– 200 μg/ml)	60	30	5	3	1
Peripheral smear	Normal	Normal	Normal	1 + poikilocytosis 1 + hypochromia	4 + poikilocytosis 4 + hypochromia
Bone marrow iron stores	Present	Absent	Absent	Absent	Absent

SI, serum iron; *TIBC*, total iron-binding capacity; *numbers in parentheses*, range of normal values.

4. Treatment
   a) Standard: ferrous sulfate 300 mg p.o. 3 times/day on an empty stomach (avoid time-release and enteric-coated preparations)
   b) Usual response: maximal reticulocyte response in 7–10 days; normal hematocrit (Hct) within a few weeks
   c) Duration: 6 months to 1 year, depending on cause
   d) Parenteral iron indicated if patients have gastrointestinal (GI) inflammatory disease, malabsorption, rapid transit, or repeated noncompliance (use iron-dextran; instructions in *Physicians' Desk Reference*)
   e) Side effects
      1) 15% have GI side effects (constipation, cramping, diarrhea): give iron with food (absorption reduced by 50%) or lower dose (use pediatric liquid preps)
      2) Parenteral iron rarely needed to avoid side effects
B. Thalassemia, an inherited defect in globin chain production, most commonly β-chains (β-thal) or α-chains (α-thal)
   1. In the United States, β-thal seen primarily in African Americans, people from Southeast Asia, and people of Greek or Italian descent; α-thal has wider social distribution but is especially common in African Americans
   2. Most patients are heterozygous and have minimal or no symptoms
   3. Typical database: Table 35.6
   4. In the United States, β-thal usually associated with increased production of hemoglobin A_2 (demonstrated by electrophoresis), less often with increased production of hemoglobin F (demonstrated by alkali denaturation)

Table 35.6.   Heterozygous Thalassemia: Typical Database

Hct	37%
MCV	69 fl
MCH	20 pg
MCHC	32 g/dl
Reticulocyte count	2.5%
Red blood cell morphology	Microcytosis, poikilocytosis, stippling
Ferritin	Normal or increased

Table 35.7.   Differential Diagnosis of MCV > 100 fl

Spurious	Myelophthisis
Reticulocytosis (marked)	Drugs
Liver disease	Megaloblastic anemias
Alcoholism	Normal variant
Myelodysplastic syndromes	

    5. α-thal usually diagnosed presumptively (consistent laboratory data in the absence of iron deficiency and of β-thal)

ANEMIA WITH HIGH MEAN CORPUSCULAR VOLUME (TABLE 35.7)

A. Liver disease
    1. MCV usually < 115 fl
    2. Target cells common
    3. Alcoholics frequently have high MCVs even in the absence of overt liver disease
B. Megaloblastic anemia (Table 35.8)
    1. Laboratory data
        a) Peripheral blood: marked variation in size and shape of red cells; common cell is a macro-ovalocyte (large egg-shaped cell); nuclei of neutrophils often hypersegmented; neutropenia and thrombocytopenia common
        b) Bone marrow: megaloblastic changes of all cell lines, sideroblastic, hyperplastic
        c) Low reticulocyte index
        d) Mild indirect bilirubinemia and elevated serum LDH common
        e) Serum vitamin B_{12} level almost always low in vitamin B_{12} deficiency (Table 35.9)
        f) Serum folate level not useful (Table 35.9)
        g) Red blood cell (RBC) folate almost always low in folate deficiency (Table 35.9)
        h) Schilling test measures absorption of radioactive vitamin B_{12}; useful if other data do not allow a precise diagnosis (Table 35.10)
        i) Serum methylmalonic acid and homocysteine measurements: sensitive indices of B_{12} deficiency; expensive, usually unnecessary
    2. Vitamin B_{12} (cobalamin) deficiency
        a) Develops slowly (years)
        b) Pernicious anemia most common cause
        c) GI symptoms are common: sore tongue, indigestion, constipation or diarrhea

Table 35.8. Causes of Megaloblastosis due to Vitamin B_{12} and Folic Acid Deficiency

B_{12}
   Pernicious anemia (acquired and congenital)
   Gastrectomy
   Ileal resection
   Crohn's disease and tropical sprue
   Fish tapeworm infestation
   Blind loop syndrome
   Nutritional deficiency (strict vegetarian diet, rare)
   Familial selective malabsorption
Folic acid
   Dietary (old age, the alcoholic, chronic disease)
   Malabsorption (sprue)
   Hemodialysis
   Severe exfoliative skin disease (e.g., psoriasis)
   Drugs
      Interference with absorption or utilization (phenytoin, alcohol)
      Dihydrofolate reductase inhibitors (methotrexate, trimethoprim)
   Increased requirements
      Pregnancy
      Infancy
      Hemolysis (e.g., sickle cell anemia)

Table 35.9. B_{12} and Folate Concentrations

Serum B_{12} concentration
   1. Spuriously low in some patients with folate deficiency
   2. Spuriously low in some pregnant patients
   3. May be elevated for weeks after one injection of B_{12}
   4. Increased in myeloproliferative syndromes
RBC folate concentration
   1. Reflects chronic folate deficiency
   2. Falsely low in some patients with B_{12} deficiency
   3. Falsely high in patients with reticulocytosis
Serum folate concentration
   1. A measure of recent dietary intake of folate
   2. May be low, normal, or elevated in B_{12} deficiency

Table 35.10. Causes, Other Than Pernicious Anemia, of a Positive Schilling Test

1. Incomplete urine collection
2. Renal failure
3. Some patients with megaloblastic anemia before treatment
4. Gastric antibodies to intrinsic factor
5. Defective intrinsic factor
6. Drugs (alcohol, colchicine, neomycin, cholestyramine)
7. Pancreatic insufficiency

   d) Neuropsychiatric signs and symptoms are common:
      peripheral neuropathy, loss of position and vibration sense,
      change in affect; in severe disease, weakness and
      spasticity; *these signs and symptoms may be seen in some
      patients whose hematological values are
      normal*

       e) Treatment: 1000 μg/day i.m. in hospital; then 1000 μg/month for life
- 3. Folic acid deficiency
  - a) Can develop within months
  - b) Dietary deficiency most common cause (folate is in leafy vegetables, fruits, meats, liver)
  - c) Treatment: 1–5 mg/day p.o. until repleted
- 4. Myelodysplastic syndromes: acquired disorders of marrow stem cells; 25% terminate in acute nonlymphocytic leukemia (Table 35.11)

ANEMIA WITH NORMAL MEAN CORPUSCULAR VOLUME AND APPROPRIATE RETICULOCYTE INDEX

A. Think of bleeding and hemolysis; bleeding is usually obvious, but retroperitoneal or soft tissue bleeding may be occult

B. Approach to hemolysis
- 1. Intravascular
  - a) Look for hemoglobinemia, hemoglobinuria, reduced serum haptoglobin, urine hemosiderin (Table 35.12)
  - b) Causes: Table 35.13
- 2. Extravascular
  - a) Specific tests relatively insensitive or relatively difficult
  - b) Peripheral blood may give a clue, e.g., spherocytes, schistocytes
  - c) Tests for specific diseases (Table 35.14) may be more rewarding

C. Hemolysis with a positive Coombs test
- 1. Positive direct Coombs test: determine if due to complement (see below) or due to antibody adsorbed to RBCs; if antibody, is it an alloantibody or an autoantibody (Table 35.15)?
  - a) Alloantibody — induced by prior transfusions or pregnancies
  - b) Autoantibody — warm or cold reacting
- 2. Hemolysis due to warm antibodies
  - a) Usually immunoglobulin G (IgG)
  - b) Causes: Table 35.16
  - c) Spleen enlarged in 50% of patients
  - d) Peripheral smear shows polychromatophilia, spherocytosis, markedly elevated reticulocyte count
  - e) Treatment
    - 1) If hemolysis is due to a drug or a viral infection, process is self-limited (3–4 weeks)
    - 2) If it is chronic, corticosteroids should be prescribed
    - 3) Splenectomy necessary occasionally if corticosteroids are not effective
- 3. Cold agglutinin hemolysis
  - a) Usually IgM that fixes complement
  - b) Most commonly associated with a viral or mycoplasmal infection but may also be secondary to collagen vascular disease or lymphoma
  - c) Frequently refractory to corticosteroids or to splenectomy, but severe hemolysis is rare

D. Hemolysis with fragmented RBCs
- 1. Characterized by sharply pointed poikilocytes (schistocytes)

Table 35.11. Laboratory Features in Three Conditions Associated With an Elevated MCV

	Liver Disease	Megaloblastic Anemia	Myelodysplastic Syndrome
MCV	Usually < 115 fl	Frequently > 115 fl	Usually < 115 fl
WBC count	Variable	Frequently decreased	Frequently decreased
Platelet count	Variable	Frequently decreased	Frequently decreased
RBC morphology	Target cells, no poikilocytosis	Marked anisocytosis and poikilocytosis, macro-ovalocytes	Marked anisocytosis and poikilocytosis, may mimic megaloblastic anemia
Nucleated RBCs	Not common	Common	Common
WBC morphology	Normal	Hypersegmented nuclei of neutrophils	May have abnormal mononuclear cells, no nuclear hypersegmentation of neutrophils
Platelet morphology	Normal	Normal	Platelets may be large and degranulated
RBC folate	Depends on diet	Decreased in folate deficiency, normal or slightly decreased in B_{12} deficiency	Normal or elevated
Serum B_{12}	Normal	Decreased in B_{12} deficiency, may be slightly decreased in folate deficiency	Normal or elevated

RBC, red blood cell; *WBC*, white blood cell.

Table 35.12.   Appropriate Further Database When Intravascular Hemolysis Is Suspected

Observation of the color of the serum/plasma
Observation of the color of the urine
Measurement of free plasma hemoglobin
Heme pigment test of the urine if there are no RBCs in the urine sediment
Measurement of serum haptoglobin
Iron stain of urine sediment for hemosiderin several days after a presumed hemolytic event

Table 35.13.   Clinical States Associated With Intravascular Hemolysis

Acute hemolytic transfusion reactions
Severe and extensive burns
Physical trauma (e.g., march hemoglobinuria)
Severe microangiopathic hemolysis (e.g., aortic valve prosthesis)
G6PD deficiency
Paroxysmal nocturnal hemoglobinuria

Table 35.14.   Most Common Causes of Extravascular Hemolysis

Autoimmune hemolysis
Delayed hemolytic transfusion reactions
Hemoglobinopathies
Hereditary spherocytic and nonspherocytic anemias
Hypersplenism
Hemolysis with liver disease

Table 35.15.   Comparison of Alloantibody and Autoantibody

	Alloantibody	Autoantibody
Direct Coombs test	Frequently negative; may be positive if sensitized foreign RBCs are still circulating	Positive
Indirect Coombs test	Positive	Positive or negative
Antibody screen (panel)	Specificity is seen	Panagglutination, no specificity seen

  2. Hemolysis may be severe (and then is usually intravascular)
  3. Associated conditions: Table 35.17
E. Hemolysis with enlarged spleen ("hypersplenism")
  1. Degree of anemia (or leukopenia or thrombocytopenia) unpredictable
  2. Seen most often in association with chronic liver disease and portal hypertension
  3. Splenectomy rarely necessary
F. Glucose 6-phosphate dehydrogenase (G6PD) deficiency
  1. X-linked
  2. In the United States, seen mostly in African Americans (10% of males, hemizygotes; 20% of females, heterozygotes)
  3. Hemolysis provoked by an infection or by an oxidant drug (e.g., sulfonamides, nitrofurantoin, phenacetin)

Table 35.16.   Autoimmune Hemolysis Due to a "Warm Antibody": Differential Diagnosis

Idiopathic
Secondary
  Infection (particularly viral)
  Drugs
    α-Methyldopa
    Penicillin
    Quinine/quinidine
  Collagen vascular disease (systemic lupus erythematosus)
  Lymphoproliferative disorders
  Miscellaneous (thyroid disease, malignancy, etc.)

Table 35.17.   Hemolysis With Fragmented RBCs on Peripheral Smear: Differential Diagnosis

Aortic valve prosthesis
Arteritis (malignant hypertension, polyarteritis, etc.)
Disseminated intravascular coagulation
Thrombotic thrombocytopenic purpura
Hemolytic-uremic syndrome
Malignancy
Giant hemangiomas
Renal transplant rejection
Eclampsia

    4. Screening tests may be normal after a hemolytic event for several weeks (young cells have more G6PD)

G. Sickle cell disorder
    1. Hemoglobin S changes shape when oxygen is reduced, distorting RBC shape, causing clumping that occludes small blood vessels and leads to tissue ischemia and infarction
    2. In the United States, 8% of African Americans are affected, diagnosed by hemoglobin electrophoresis
    3. Heterozygotes (sickle cell trait) are usually asymptomatic, and blood looks normal
      a) May become symptomatic when at high altitude or after vigorous exercise
      b) All patients have hyposthenuria, some have severe hematuria
    4. Homozygotes (sickle cell anemia) are usually severely affected
      a) Have recurrent painful crises (mostly severe limb and abdominal pain)
      b) Have chronic severe anemia
        1) Persistent hyperbilirubinemia, reticulocytosis, leukocytosis
        2) Severely distorted RBCs in peripheral smear, including sickled cells
      c) Abnormal bone x-rays due to repeated infarctions
      d) Spleen small in adults (autosplenectomy) with increased propensity to bacterial (especially pneumococcal) infection
      e) Gallstones common
      f) Venous thromboembolic events common
      g) Cerebrovascular accidents more common

**Table 35.18.   Anemia With a Normal MCV and Low Reticulocyte Index:
Differential Diagnosis**

Renal failure
Anemia of chronic disease (inflammatory disease and malignancy)
Anemia of hypoendocrine states (hypothyroidism, etc.)
Mild (early) iron deficiency
Combined iron deficiency and megaloblastic anemia
Drug-induced marrow depression
Primary bone marrow disorders
Bone marrow infiltration (myelophthisis)
Bleeding or hemolysis plus one of the above

- h) Retinopathy common
- i) Chronic leg ulcers common
5. Sickle cell disease and S-thalassemia, double heterozygotes with usually milder disease than sickle cell anemia
6. Treatment
    - a) Painful crises often require use of narcotics, but limit amount in ambulatory practice; hospitalize if high doses are needed
    - b) Pneumococcal vaccine
    - c) Aggressive treatment of infections
    - d) Folate 1 mg/day

ANEMIA WITH NORMAL MEAN CORPUSCULAR VOLUME AND AN INAPPROPRIATELY LOW RETICULOCYTE COUNT

A. Differential diagnosis: Table 35.18
B. Anemia of renal failure
    1. Hct value related to degree of renal failure
    2. Responsive to administration of recombinant human erythropoietin
C. Anemia of chronic disease (chronic inflammatory or malignant disease)
    1. Seek another explanation if Hct < 25%
    2. Occasionally macrocytic (see above)
    3. Serum iron and total iron-binding capacity low; serum ferritin normal or high; bone marrow iron normal or increased

36/ DISORDERS OF HEMOSTASIS

EVALUATION OF PATIENTS
A. Disorders of long standing are associated with excessive bleeding in response to minor trauma or to surgery
B. Most patients who bleed *do not* have defective hemostasis; there is a bleeding lesion (e.g., a gastrointestinal (GI) lesion)
C. Even patients with defective hemostasis tend to bleed from local lesions
D. Screening laboratory tests are essential (Table 36.1)

DISORDERS OF BLOOD VESSELS
A. Relatively rare except from trauma
B. No reliable screening test
C. Primary lesion is purpura
D. Cutaneous lesions
   1. Unexplained bruises are common
   2. Senile purpura (persistent intracutaneous lesions on the dorsum of the hands and forearms) not indicative of a generalized hemostatic dysfunction
   3. Allergic purpura
      a) A vasculitis (a drug or infection only sometimes can be incriminated)
      b) Symmetrical, petechial, slightly raised rash
      c) No hemostatic dysfunction
      d) Sometimes associated with arthralgias, fever, abdominal pain, GI bleeding, or focal glomerulonephritis
      e) No specific treatment
      f) Most recover in 3–4 weeks, but disease sometimes lingers for months
   4. Autoerythrocyte sensitization
      a) Apparently spontaneous painful bruises, usually on the lower extremities and anterior trunk
      b) Patients, most of them women, are psychoneurotic or even psychotic
      c) Lesions are probably self-inflicted
   5. Cryoglobulinemia
      a) Purpura, especially on the lower extremities
      b) Cryoglobulins are monoclonal proteins or immune complexes

Table 36.1. Laboratory Evaluation of Hemostatic Function

System	Screening Tests	Specific Tests
Blood vessels	None	Depends on suspected underlying disorder (see the text)
Platelets		
Quantitative	Scanning of a stained smear of the peripheral blood	Platelet count
Qualitative	Bleeding time	Platelet aggregation
Coagulation	Partial thromboplastin time, prothrombin time, thrombin time	Factor assays

sometimes associated with drugs, proteinuria, lymphoma, or collagen vascular disease

   c) Sometimes, there is also glomerulonephritis

   d) No effective treatment

6. Hyperglobulinemic purpura of Waldenström

   a) Purpura, especially on the lower extremities

   b) Polyclonal increase of immune complexes

   c) High erythrocyte sedimentation rate

   d) May be primary or (especially after 40) may be associated with a collagen vascular disease

   e) Primary disorder untreatable

E. Mucocutaneous lesions

  1. Amyloidosis

    a) Periorbital bleeding and bleeding in skin folds especially common

    b) Amyloid deposits are sometimes palpable

    c) Diagnosis made by skin biopsy plus serum and urine electrophoresis

  2. Dysproteinemia: myeloma or macroglobulinemia

  3. Vitamin C deficiency (scurvy)

    a) Large ecchymoses, bleeding gums, perifollicular hemorrhages on lower extremities and anterior trunk (highly suggestive of diagnosis)

    b) Occasional hemarthroses

    c) Seen in chronic alcoholics, in chronically debilitated people, and in food faddists

    d) Therapeutic trial of vitamin C (250 mg/day) is appropriate if diagnosis is suspected (assays usually unnecessary)

  4. Hereditary hemorrhagic telangiectasia

    a) Inherited condition (autosomal dominant)

    b) Small flat red or purple telangiectases that blanch on pressure, especially on lips, tongue, inside of nose, hands; may bleed when traumatized

    c) Epistaxes the most common symptom, but recurrent GI bleeding is the most troublesome problem

    d) Pulmonary arteriovenous fistulas in up to one-third of patients; may be associated with high output heart failure

    e) Variable course; no definitive treatment

DISORDERS OF PLATELETS

A. Evaluation

  1. Petechia is the hallmark of disorders of platelets; epistaxis, menorrhagia, GI bleeding also common

  2. Observation of a stained blood smear (normally, a clump of platelets in each oil immersion field)

  3. Automated platelet count

  4. Bleeding time if qualitative defect is suspected

  5. If patient is asymptomatic, platelet count is over 50,000/mm^3, and no underlying disease is suspected, follow-up with monthly platelet counts is sufficient

  6. If patient is symptomatic, bone marrow aspiration to evaluate number of megakaryocytes is important (decreased in disease

affecting marrow except cobalamin or folate deficiency; increased in destructive thrombocytopenias)
B. Decreased production of platelets
    1. Causes
        a) Viral infections (e.g., upper respiratory infections, childhood exanthemas)
        b) Drugs (cytotoxic drugs, thiazides questionably, many others anecdotally)
        c) Diseases primarily affecting the bone marrow (e.g., leukemia, myeloma)
    2. Management
        a) Stop administration of drugs, if possible
        b) If process severe, consider referral for platelet transfusion
C. Increased destruction of platelets
    1. Causes
        a) Autoimmune: usually primary, sometimes associated with lymphoproliferative disease, systemic lupus, or HIV infection; diagnosis usually presumptive (when no other apparent cause, consider destructive thrombocytopenia)
        b) Drugs: most common are quinidine and quinine, but all drugs should be discontinued if the process is suspected; gold and heroin associated rarely also; process is immunological
        c) Alcohol: occurs after a binge, rapidly reversible
    2. Management
        a) If an immunological cause is suspected and the patient is symptomatic or platelet counts are below 20,000/mm^3, consider beginning prednisone 60 mg/day and hospitalization
        b) Decisions about splenectomy or other kinds of treatment should be made in consultation with a hematologist
D. Increased sequestration of platelets — big spleen syndromes: most commonly associated with portal hypertension; splenectomy only if there is a clear-cut hemorrhagic diathesis
E. Increased utilization of platelets — disseminated intravascular coagulation: patients have coagulation defects; hospitalization indicated
F. Qualitative disorders of platelets
    1. Platelet counts usually normal
    2. May be inherited (rare) or acquired (e.g., aspirin, uremia)
    3. Bleeding time prolonged
G. Thrombocytosis
    1. High platelet counts only associated with bleeding or clotting if a manifestation of a myeloproliferative disease
    2. Reactive thrombocytosis most often associated with inflammatory disease or malignancy; platelets appear normal
    3. Myeloproliferative disease (polycythemia vera, chronic myeloid leukemia, myelofibrosis): platelets appear large, distorted; there is other physical and laboratory evidence of the disease

COAGULATION DISORDERS
A. Symptoms: extensive soft tissue bleeding or major hemorrhage in response to trauma
B. Hereditary disorders (e.g., hemophilia) are rare, usually diagnosed in childhood, but von Willebrand's disease (long bleeding time, low

concentration of antihemophilic globulin) may first present in adults (GI bleeding)
C. Acquired disorders (more common than inherited ones) usually characterized by multiple hemostatic abnormalities (e.g., disseminated intravascular coagulation or response to anticoagulant drugs)
D. Screening tests (prothrombin time, partial thromboplastin time) are abnormal, depending on disorder, in symptomatic patients

ADVICE TO GIVE PATIENTS WITH A DISORDER OF HEMOSTASIS: TABLE 36.2

Table 36.2.   Advice to Give Patients With a Disorder of Hemostasis

Take only medicine prescribed by your doctor. Do not take aspirin or cold remedies. You may take Tylenol instead of aspirin for pain, colds, etc.

Do not drink any alcoholic beverage.

Avoid any activity that might expose you unnecessarily to trauma, e.g., contact sports.

Wear a bracelet (prescribed by the physician) identifying you as a "bleeder" and giving the name of your disorder.

Call your physician:

Whenever you experience any abnormal bleeding (including excessive menstrual bleeding)

Before you visit your dentist

Before seeing any other physician

If you are hospitalized for any reason without your physician's knowledge

37/ THROMBOEMBOLIC DISEASE

VENOUS THROMBOEMBOLISM

A. Risk factors
1. Stasis of blood (e.g., sedentary people)
2. Oral contraceptive agents (less of a risk with current preparations, which contain less estrogen than older ones)
3. Malignancy (sometimes occult)
4. Inherited deficiency of a naturally occurring anticoagulant (protein C, protein S, or antithrombin)
5. Inherited abnormality of fibrinolysis or of fibrinogen (requires specialized laboratory to detect)
6. Antibodies to phospholipid (including lupus anticoagulants)
   a) Detected by prolonged partial thromboplastin time (PTT) or by immunoassay (concordance limited between the two tests)
   b) Risk highest in patients with systemic lupus, in whom spontaneous abortion, thrombocytopenia are also common
   c) Patients at risk seem to be those with highest titers

B. Presentation
1. Superficial thrombophlebitis
   a) Visible, tender, often palpably thrombosed vein
   b) No risk of embolism unless deep vein is involved
   c) Anticoagulant drugs not indicated; prescribe moist, local heat and a nonsteroidal anti-inflammatory drug
2. Deep vein thrombosis (DVT)
   a) May present with signs and symptoms of pulmonary embolism
   b) Most patients have swelling, pain, tenderness of involved extremity
   c) Impossible to distinguish DVT from other processes by signs and symptoms alone
   d) Test of reference is contrast venography, but noninvasive tests are ordinarily sufficient
   e) Favored noninvasive test is Doppler ultrasonography, but many laboratories still do impedance plethysmography (more false positives and, perhaps, false negatives)
   f) Noninvasive tests not sensitive to thrombosis of leg veins, but these clots are unlikely to embolize
   g) If DVT is suspected, do noninvasive test: hospitalize if positive; repeat test on days 5 and 10 if negative

C. Treatment
1. Warfarin
   a) Takes approximately 5 days to reach stable therapeutic level
   b) Effect monitored by prothrombin time, properly reported in terms of an international normalized ratio (INR)
   c) Goal is an INR of 2–3
   d) During first few weeks, measure prothrombin time every few days; then, if stable, every month
   e) Avoid traumatic activities, intramuscular injections
   f) Factors affecting response: Table 37.1

Table 37.1.   Some Factors That May Affect a Patient's Response to Warfarin

Enhanced Response	Reduced Response
Vitamin K deficiency	Antacids
Liver disease	Antihistamines
Drugs	Barbiturates
Anabolic steroids	Cholestyramine
Antibiotics	Griseofulvin
Cimetidine[a]	Rifampin
Clofibrate	Spironolactone
Disulfiram (Antabuse)	Foods[b]
Heparin	Fish
Metronidazole (Flagyl)	Broccoli
Phenylbutazone	Spinach
Phenytoin	Cabbage
Quinidine	Kale
Tamoxifen	Cauliflower

[a] The effect of other H_2 blockers is uncertain.
[b] Rich in vitamin K.

    g) Risk of untoward bleeding increased by intensity of treatment, comorbid conditions
    h) Local cause of gastrointestinal or genitourinary bleeding or of menorrhagia *must be investigated*
    i) Major or uncontrolled bleeding should be treated by giving 25 mg of vitamin K i.v. (5 mg/minute); effect in 4–6 hours; prothrombin time in a safe range by 12–24 hours
    j) Contraindicated in pregnant women because of teratogenicity
    k) Hemorrhagic fat necrosis a rare complication
    l) Advice to patients: Table 37.2
  2. Heparin
    a) Rare necessary alternative to warfarin for outpatients (e.g., pregnant women)
    b) Give subcutaneous heparin every 12 hours to maintain the PTT at 1.5–2 times control
    c) Low-dose heparin (5000 units twice a day) inadequate
    d) Low-molecular-weight heparins are becoming available, can be given once a day with apparently comparable efficacy
    e) Some patients develop thrombocytopenia — probably by an immunological mechanism — within a week or two; platelet counts only indicated if there is untoward bleeding
    f) Prolonged use of heparin (4 months or more) may cause osteoporosis, but degree of risk is unknown
    g) Aminotransferase activity commonly reversibly increased — not an indication to stop heparin
  3. Aspirin
    a) May be of some use as prophylaxis in patients at risk
    b) No justification for using it for patients with DVT
D. Course
  1. Unless there is continuing risk, standard practice is to give anticoagulant drug for 3 months, although 4–6 weeks may be enough

Table 37.2. Advice to Be Given Patients Taking a Coumarin Anticoagulant

Take only medicines prescribed by your doctor. Do not take mineral oil, laxatives, aspirin (or any product such as a cold remedy that contains aspirin), or other proprietary anti-inflammatory agent (e.g., Advil) or any multivitamin preparation that contains vitamin K. You may take acetaminophen (e.g., Tylenol) instead of aspirin for pain.

Take your coumarin at the same time each day.

Avoid wide variation in the kinds and amounts of food you eat, especially fish, broccoli, spinach, cabbage, kale, or cauliflower.

Do not drink more than 1 or 2 glasses of beer or wine or the equivalent of more than 1 ounce (1 "shot") of whiskey a day.

Avoid any activity that might expose you unnecessarily to trauma, e.g., contact sports.

Call your doctor immediately:

If you experience any abnormal bleeding

Before you visit the dentist

Before seeing any other physician

If you cannot keep your scheduled appointment

Before leaving on a trip

If you are hospitalized for any reason without your doctor knowing about it

2. When anticoagulant drug is to be stopped, it can be stopped abruptly (no "rebound")
3. Recurrent DVT: difficult to diagnose; Doppler ultrasonography probably the best test (if it normalized after initial treatment); if situation equivocal, reinstitute anticoagulation
4. Postphlebitic syndrome
    a) Chronic edema and discoloration of the leg and ankles
    b) Sometimes associated with stasis ulcers
    c) Use support hose and elevate the lower extremities for several hours a day; see Chapter 71 for treatment of stasis ulcers

ARTERIAL THROMBOEMBOLISM

A. Risk Factors
    1. Atherosclerosis
    2. Malignancy, rarely
    3. Hereditary defect in fibrinolysis (see above)
B. Presentation: abrupt onset, associated with necrosis of tissue
C. Treatment
    1. Aspirin
        a) Effective in secondary prevention of arterial thromboembolic disease in patients with a history of atherosclerotic disease
        b) Dose: 325 mg/day is as effective as higher doses
        c) Major risk is gastrointestinal bleeding — not a major problem at recommended dose
        d) Adding dipyridamole to the regimen not necessary
        e) No compelling evidence that aspirin is useful in the primary prevention of arterial thromboembolic disease
    2. Ticlopidine (Ticlid)
        a) Effective in secondary prevention of cerebral vascular events in patients with a history of cerebral vascular disease
        b) Dose: 250 mg twice a day
        c) Diarrhea common; 1% get severe reversible neutropenia, so use aspirin preferentially if possible
    3. Fish oil: no current justification for using it

38/ SELECTED ILLNESSES AFFECTING LYMPHOCYTES

INFECTIOUS MONONUCLEOSIS

A. Epidemiology and pathogenesis
   1. Epstein-Barr virus (EBV) is the cause
   2. Primarily affects age groups between 15 and 25 years; rare in people over 30
   3. Spread by oral contact
B. Signs and symptoms (Table 38.1)
   1. First week characterized by nonspecific symptoms
   2. Adenopathy, splenomegaly, pharyngitis usually appear at about 1 week
C. Laboratory features
   1. Elevated white blood count reaching a height within 2nd and 3rd week
   2. Absolute lymphocytosis with >10% *atypical lymphocytes* (large lobulated or indented nuclei and vacuolated and/or bluish cytoplasm)
   3. Platelet count often slightly, sometimes markedly, reduced
   4. Mild hepatic dysfunction common
   5. Serological (Table 38.2)
      a) Heterophil antibodies usually elevated; highest titer during first week (antibodies absorbed by beef red cells, not by guinea pig kidney)
      b) Rapid slide tests (e.g., Mono-Test) quite sensitive for detection of heterophil antibodies but specificity only moderate

Table 38.1. Signs and Symptoms of Infectious Mononucleosis

Common Symptoms	%	Common Signs	%	Less Common Signs and Symptoms	%
Malaise	100	Adenopathy	100	Jaundice	10
Sore throat	85	Fever	90	Arthralgia	5
Warmth, chilliness	70	Pharyngitis	85	Skin rash	5
Anorexia	70	Splenomegaly	60	Diarrhea	5
Headache	50	Bradycardia	40	Photophobia	5
Cough	40	Periorbital edema	25		
Myalgia	25	Palatal enanthem	25		

Table 38.2. Serological Evidence of EBV Infection

1. IgM antibody to viral capsid antigen (IgM anti-VCA) appears early in primary infection and disappears within 3–6 months.
2. IgG antibody to viral capsid antigen (IgG anti-VCA) appears slightly later than IgM anti-VCA and remains detectable for life.
3. Antibodies to the early antigen complex of EBV of the diffuse (D) type (anti-D) appear early in primary infection and disappear by 2–3 months.
4. Antibodies to EB nuclear antigen (anti-EBNA) appear very late (months) after primary infection and are detectable for life.

From Evans AS, et al: Seroepidemiologic studies of infectious mononucleosis with EB virus. *N Engl J Med* 279: 1121, 1968.
IgG, immunoglobulin G; *IgM,* immunoglobulin M.

**Table 38.3. Etiologies Other Than EBV for the Mononucleosis Syndrome —
Serological Diagnosis of Recent Infection**

CMV	Four- to 8-fold rise in complement fixation titer. Elevated IgM or cytolytic antibodies to CMV antigen, if available, are more helpful.
Toxoplasmosis	Dye test (DT) or immunofluorescent antibody (IFA) titers of >1:1000 plus an IgM-IFA titer of >1:64.
Hepatitis A	Elevated titer of IgM antibody to hepatitis A antigen (IgM anti-HAAg).
Hepatitis B	Elevated hepatitis B surface antigen (HB$_s$Ag). Chronic carrier state identification will require follow-up measurement of HB$_s$Ag, HB$_e$Ag, and lack of rise of anti-HBs.
Rubella	The hemagglutination inhibition antibody (HIA) titer is the most widely used. The antibody is first detected after onset of the rash, and the titer rises rapidly for 1–2 weeks thereafter. If one does not catch this rise with acute and convalescent sera, the titer usually remains high for several months, so a single high titer is not meaningful. However, a low titer (<1:16) 2 weeks after the rash is strongly against the diagnosis.
HIV infection	Serological evidence of infection may follow by weeks signs and symptoms of the mononucleosis syndrome.

D. Complications rare (neurological problems, superinfection, splenic rupture)
E. Treatment
  1. No specific treatment
  2. Avoid contact sports if spleen is tender or enlarged
  3. Surgery for splenic rupture
  4. Corticosteroids for severe pharyngitis and impending airway obstruction

OTHER CAUSES OF THE MONONUCLEOSIS SYNDROME (TABLES 38.3 AND 38.4)
A. Cytomegalovirus (CMV) infection
  1. Devastating illness in immunocompromised host; otherwise, syndrome resembles mononucleosis, except exudative pharyngitis unusual
  2. Usually occurs in people over 25–30 years
  3. Diagnosis depends on serological tests
B. Toxoplasmosis
  1. No pharyngitis
  2. Splenomegaly and lymphadenopathy less prominent
C. Other infections: Table 38.3
D. Chronic fatigue syndrome
  1. Cause unknown
  2. Criteria: Table 38.5
  3. Psychiatric symptoms (depression, somatoform disorder, anxiety) very common
  4. Minor immunological dysfunction also common
  5. Treatment: support the patient, not the symptoms; do not overprescribe, overdiagnose, or overrefer; encourage gradual increase in activity and decrease in sleep

CHRONIC LYMPHOCYTIC LEUKEMIA
A. Most common leukemia
B. Primarily a disease of older men

Table 38.4.   Stepwise Serological Testing in the Diagnosis of the Etiology of the "Mononucleosis Syndrome"

1. Typical clinical features with a positive heterophil slide test. This essentially establishes a diagnosis of infectious mononucleosis, usually due to EBV.
   Recommendation: No further testing is needed.
2. Typical clinical features with a negative heterophil slide test at the time the patient first presents to the physician.
   Recommendation: Draw acute serum samples (save frozen in two containers) for pertinent serological testing for EBV, toxoplasmosis, CMV, hepatitis A, hepatitis B, and rubella (see Table 38.3). Repeat heterophil slide test during the third week of clinical illness. If positive, no further testing is necessary. If negative, repeat EBV serology (at least 2 weeks after acute sample) and send with one of the acute serological samples for EBV IgM anti-VCA testing (and anti-D testing if available). If the EBV serologies are diagnostic of recent infection, no further testing is necessary.
3. Typical clinical features, negative heterophil test at week 3 of clinical illness, and negative EBV serology (IgM anti-VCA or anti-D).
   Recommendation: Draw convalescent sera for testing for toxoplasmosis, CMV, hepatitis A, hepatitis B, and rubella and send with acute sera for appropriate serological testing (see Table 38.3). Consider HIV infection in patients at risk.
4. Typical or atypical clinical features with negative serologies for all of the above. Consider other etiologies (leukemia, lymphoproliferative disease, granulomatous disease, collagen vascular disease, etc.).
   Recommendation: Consider lymph node biopsy and other tests (e.g., bone marrow aspiration and biopsy).

Table 38.5.   Chronic Fatigue Syndrome

Persistent or relapsing fatigue (that reduces average daily activity by 50%)
Failure to identify medical and psychosocial conditions that may produce chronic fatigue
Presence concurrently of 4 or more of the following symptoms:
   Impaired memory or concentration
   Sore throat
   Tender cervical or axillary nodes
   Muscle pain
   Multijoint pain
   New headaches
   Unrefreshing sleep
   Postexertion malaise

Adapted from Fukada K, Straus SE, Hickie I, et al: *Ann Intern Med* 121:953, 1994.

C. Many patients are asymptomatic when diagnosed, but malaise and fatigue are common
D. Eventually, most patients develop splenomegaly and generalized adenopathy
E. Hallmark is absolute chronic lymphocytosis (>10,000/mm³ for 3 months or more)
F. As disease progresses, hypogammaglobulinemia, anemia, granulocytopenia, thrombocytopenia may develop
G. Treatment and course
   1. Survival correlates with extent of disease at diagnosis
   2. Current treatment probably does not prolong survival, may control signs and symptoms

Table 38.6.   When to Recommend Lymph Node Biopsy in the Teenager and Young Adult

Features against early biopsy
1. Mononucleosis syndrome, especially when proven serologically
2. Ear-nose-throat symptoms (earache, sore throat, coryza, tonsillar or dental infection)
3. Lymph nodes < 2 cm in diameter
4. Normal chest x-ray, especially when associated with one of the above

Features for early biopsy
1. Systemic illness with atypical features of the mononucleosis syndrome and without serological proof of a cause of the mononucleosis syndrome (see Table 38.4)
2. Lymph nodes > 2 cm in diameter and an abnormal chest x-ray, absence of ear-nose-throat symptoms, or no proof of a typical mononucleosis syndrome
3. Localized supraclavicular lymphadenopathy, which may be seen in the mononucleosis syndrome but in its absence is suggestive of mediastinal (right supraclavicular) or abdominal (left supraclavicular) granulomatous or neoplastic disease

UNDIAGNOSED PATIENT WITH LYMPHADENOPATHY

A. Primarily seen in younger patients
B. When to biopsy: Table 38.6

Section VI
Pulmonary Problems

39/ COMMON PULMONARY PROBLEMS

COUGH (TABLE 39.1)
A. Acute cough syndromes
   1. Productive coughs suggest bacterial infection
   2. Older patients as a group have more difficulty clearing secretions than younger patients
   3. Environmental pollutants may cause either a productive or a nonproductive cough
B. Chronic cough syndromes
   1. Cigarette smoking is the commonest cause
   2. In nonsmokers, postnasal drip is the commonest cause
C. Evaluation
   1. Evaluation of acute and chronic cough syndromes is similar
   2. A history and physical examination will usually yield a presumptive diagnosis
   3. If, after history and physical examination, there is no diagnosis, a chest x-ray is indicated
   4. If the chest x-ray is normal and the cough is productive, the sputum should be examined
   5. Use spirometry (see Chapter 40) if there is a suspicion of chronic obstructive lung disease
   6. If still no diagnosis, the patient should be re-evaluated every 1–2 months
   7. Bronchoscopy usually unrevealing if chest x-ray is normal
D. Treatment
   1. Specific therapy depends on the cause
   2. Viral tracheobronchitis requires only symptomatic treatment
   3. Persistent cough and a history compatible with bronchospasm

Table 39.1. Causes of Cough

Causes	Examples
COMMON CAUSES	
Acute	
Inflammation	Tracheitis, bronchitis, pneumonia
Irritation	Environmental pollutants
Bronchospasm	Infection
Chronic	
Inflammation	Bronchitis, pollution, cigarettes, bronchiectasis, aspirated foreign body, chronic pneumonia (e.g., PCP, Tbc)
Irritation	Cigarettes, cancer, postnasal drip
Bronchospasm	Asthma, heart failure
LESS COMMON CAUSES	
Drug-induced	Angiotensin converting enzyme inhibitor
Irritation	Aortic aneurysm, chronic aspiration (including gastroesophogeal reflux), auditory canal stimulation (cerumen, hair)
Inflammation	Sarcoid, alveolitis
Psychogenic	

PCP, phencyclidine; Tbc, tuberculosis.

Table 39.2. Nonnarcotic Antitussives

Drug	Brand Name	Usual Dose	Site of Action	Comment
Dextromethorphan	Many preparations	15–30 mg 4 times/day	Central	Considered most effective central agent
Benzonatate	Tessalon	100–200 mg 4 times/day	Peripheral	Considered most effective peripheral agent

Table 39.3. Pulmonary Causes of Hemoptysis

COMMON
Inflammatory   Bronchitis, bronchiectasis, tuberculosis, pneumonia, lung abscess
Neoplasm   Lung cancer
Vascular   Pulmonary embolus/infarction
LESS COMMON
Inflammatory/   Goodpasture's syndrome, idiopathic pulmonary hemosiderosis,
  immunological   cavitary disease (with a "fungus ball"), parasites, broncholithiasis,
                      cystic fibrosis
Neoplasm   Bronchial adenoma, metastatic cancer
Vascular   Arteriovenous malformation, sequestration, mitral stenosis,
                      anticoagulation
Chest trauma

(postviral infection, allergic airway disease, early obstructive lung disease) may benefit from bronchodilators (Chapter 40)
4. Cessation of cigarette smoking and avoidance of polluted air are critical
5. After specific therapy or if no specific therapy is possible, antitussives should be considered
   a) If cough is productive, total suppression is to be avoided
   b) Preparations that combine an antitussive and an expectorant work at cross-purposes and should be avoided
   c) Nonnarcotic antitussives (Table 39.2)
      1) Dextromethorphan should be prescribed first
      2) If cough persists, benzonatate
   d) Codeine, 15–20 mg every 3–6 hours, can be tried if nonnarcotic antitussives are ineffective

HEMOPTYSIS
A. Causes (Table 39.3)
   1. Chronic bronchitis is cause 50–60% of time
   2. Lung cancer is cause 10–20% of time (dependent on prevalence of smokers in the population)
   3. Bacterial infection (pneumonia, abscess) causes hemoptysis mixed with pus
   4. Cause remains unknown 5–15% of the time
B. Evaluation
   1. Aimed at the cause, site, and amount of bleeding
   2. >25–50 ml of blood in 24 hours warrants hospitalization
   3. Massive hemoptysis (>600 ml of blood during 24 hours) is an emergency

Table 39.4.   Causes of Dyspnea

Dyspnea	Acute	Chronic
COMMON		
Pulmonary		
Obstructive airways disease	Asthma, bronchitis	Chronic obstructive pulmonary disease
Restrictive lung disease	Pneumothorax	Pleural effusions, cancer, diffuse interstitial lung disease
Inflammatory	Pneumonia	
Vascular	Pulmonary embolism	
Cardiac	Heart failure (ischemic)	Heart failure (myopathic)
Other	Psychogenic, acute blood loss or hemolysis	Obesity, chronic anemia
LESS COMMON		
Pulmonary		
Upper airway obstruction	Epiglottitis, aspiration (foreign body)	Goiter
Restrictive lung disease		Diaphragm paralyses, kyphoscoliosis
Vascular		Pulmonary hypertension
Cardiac		Heart failure (pericardial disease)
Other	CO intoxication	

4. Chest x-ray is essential, although aspiration of blood or bilateral pulmonary disease may complicate its interpretation
5. If chest x-ray normal, endobronchial malignancy must be excluded, but bronchitis (or bronchiectasis) is the likely diagnosis
   a) Patients under 40 (even smokers) or who have hemoptysis for less than a week are unlikely to have cancer — evaluation can be limited to analysis of sputum for tuberculosis and to cytological examination of 3 sputum samples for malignant cells
   b) In patients over 40 who smoke, both sputum cytology and bronchoscopy are indicated

DYSPNEA
A. Causes (Table 39.4)
   1. Major causes in ambulatory practice are obstructive airways disease and left-sided heart failure (atherosclerotic and hypertensive heart disease primarily)
   2. More serious causes tend to present abruptly and must be evaluated quickly, often in a hospital, whereas chronic dyspnea can be evaluated in an ambulatory setting
B. Acute dyspnea
   1. History, physical examination, and chest x-ray are the foci of evaluation
   2. Acute tracheobronchitis: consider in a middle-aged smoker with cough, dyspnea, purulent sputum, normal chest x-ray

3. Spontaneous pneumothorax: presents with sudden, sharp chest pain and dyspnea
   a) Small pneumothorax can be missed on chest x-ray, sensitivity of which is increased by expiration
   b) May be first evidence of interstitial lung disease, bullous lung disease, or cystic fibrosis
4. Pneumonia: symptoms include fever, cough
5. Heart failure: paroxysmal nocturnal dyspnea, rales, cardiomegaly usually associated
6. Psychogenic dyspnea: anxiety is usually obvious
7. Foreign body aspiration: aspiration was usually recognized; physical examination may demonstrate decreased breath sounds over that part of the lung supplied by the occluded bronchus
8. Carbon monoxide intoxication: in heating season or in certain industrial settings should be suspected as a cause of dyspnea and headache
9. Pulmonary embolism
   a) Risks: recent peripheral venous disease, prolonged immobilization, right-sided heart failure, women using oral contraceptives
   b) Symptoms: dyspnea, chest pain commonly; hemoptysis, cough, apprehension less commonly
   c) Physical examination: usually not of help
   d) Chest x-ray: nonspecific (localized infiltrates, atelectasis, elevated hemidiaphragm, pleural effusion)
   e) Arterial blood gasses often abnormal (reduced PaO_2 and $PaCO_2$) but not of help diagnostically
   f) Most useful procedure is ventilation/perfusion scan of the lungs
      1) 100% sensitive: if normal, diagnosis of pulmonary embolism can be excluded
      2) Low-probability scan: 15–20% have embolized
      3) Moderate-probability scan: 30–35% have embolized
      4) High-probability scan: 80–90% have embolized
      5) Patients with low-, moderate-, or high-probability scan should be hospitalized
   g) If there are signs and symptoms suggestive of embolism and peripheral thrombosis, Doppler duplex scan of the lower extremities should be performed; if possible, patient should be hospitalized
C. Chronic or progressive dyspnea
   1. Chest x-ray most useful test; if negative, likeliest diagnosis is obstructive lung disease
   2. Spirogram is a useful screen, since, if it is normal, significant parenchymal or airways disease is unlikely
   3. Hemoglobin concentration or hematocrit value important, since anemia or erythrocytosis may be associated with dyspnea
   4. Complete the pulmonary function tests; pulmonologist may recommend other tests if spirometry is abnormal (e.g., total lung capacity, functional residual capacity, diffusing capacity)
   5. Arterial blood gas analysis
      a) Normal studies do not exclude pulmonary disease
      b) Should be drawn during exercise in a dyspneic patient

Table 39.5. Causes of Chest Pain

COMMON CAUSES	
Chest wall (musculoskeletal)	Nonspecific (smokers, nonsmokers with increased exertion)
	Costochondritis (Tietze's syndrome)
Cardiac	Angina
Pulmonary	Tracheitis, cough, pleuritis, pneumonia
Neurological	Radicular pain of cervical spine disease
LESS COMMON CAUSES	
Chest wall (musculoskeletal)	Thoracic outlet syndrome, herpes zoster, fractured rib, tumor
Cardiac	Aneurysm, pericarditis
Pulmonary	Pneumothorax, pulmonary embolus, pulmonary hypertension, cancer
Gastrointestinal	Stomach disease, duodenal ulcer, abdominal infection, peritonitis, esophageal reflux

6. Cardiovascular testing: if heart disease is suspected (Chapter 44 and 45)
7. Exercise tests
   a) If patient is dyspneic on exercise and baseline studies are normal
   b) Cardiac stress test (Chapter 42)
   c) Cardiopulmonary stress test: cardiac function, pulmonary gas exchange, ventilation, fitness are assessed

NONCARDIAC CHEST PAIN
A. Causes (Table 39.5)
   1. Usually fleeting, sharp pain
   2. Smokers have chest pain more than nonsmokers
   3. Musculoskeletal pain is very common in young people who increase exercise abruptly
   4. Pain of tracheitis or tracheobronchitis is a distinctive substernal burning precipitated by coughing
   5. Pain of pneumonia is sharp, stabbing pleuritic
   6. Costochondritis (Tietze's syndrome) causes anterior localized pain associated with tenderness over one or more costochondral junctions
   7. Herpes zoster causes dermatomal aching or itching, sometimes before vesicles appear
   8. Pulmonary hypertension causes heavy aching pain
   9. Spontaneous pneumothorax (see above)
B. Evaluation
   1. History and physical examination can often establish diagnosis; latter more useful than in diagnosis of dyspnea or hemoptysis
   2. Laboratory studies and chest x-ray often not necessary

ABNORMAL CHEST X-RAY
A. Specific patterns
   1. Air bronchogram
      a) Indicative of a collapsed or consolidated part of the lung but not universally so
      b) Presence more significant than absence
   2. Silhouette sign

Table 39.6.   Causes of Diffuse Alveolar Pulmonary Disease

Disorder	Common	Uncommon
Infection (pus)	Pneumonia	
Edema (fluid)	Cardiac and noncardiac pulmonary edema	
Hemorrhage (blood)		Anticoagulant therapy
		Trauma
		Hemoptysis with aspiration
		Goodpasture's syndrome
		Idiopathic pulmonary siderosis
Cells	Sarcoidosis	Bronchoalveolar cell cancer
		"Eosinophilic" infiltrative disorders
Foreign material		Lipoid pneumonia
Protein		Alveolar proteinosis

      a) Obliteration of the margin of a normally opaque structure in the chest by an abnormal pulmonary density

      b) Can be used to localize abnormalities within the lung parenchyma

   3. Collapse mechanisms

      a) Bronchial obstruction (intrinsic or extrinsic)

      b) Compression of the lungs from a pleural effusion or a pneumothorax

      c) Peripheral bronchial plugging

      d) Contraction of the lung secondary to chronic inflammatory disease

B. Common problems

   1. Infiltrates

      a) Alveolar

         1) Fluffy margins, "rosette" formations, occasional "butterfly" appearance involving hilar and central zones of the lung and the presence of air bronchograms

         2) Causes of diffuse disease (Table 39.6): most common are infection, edema, hemorrhage, characterized by rapid progression and regression

      b) Interstitial

         1) Linear or discrete nodular

         2) Honeycombing is pathognomonic of interstitial disease and pulmonary fibrosis

         3) Causes (Table 39.7)

            (a) Bilateral lower lobe infiltrates are a common pattern and usually represent one of the following diseases: bronchiectasis, aspiration, collagen vascular disease, asbestosis, sarcoidosis, idiopathic pulmonary fibrosis

            (b) Specialized pulmonary function testing (lung volume, diffusing capacity) is necessary to establish severity

            (c) Transbronchial biopsy may be necessary to make a diagnosis

      c) Slowly resolving or recurrent infiltrates

         1) Obstructing cancer must be considered

         2) Patients with chronic obstructive airways disease may retain

Table 39.7. Causes of Diffuse Interstitial Pulmonary Disease

Disorder	Common	Uncommon
KNOWN CAUSES		
Infection		Miliary tuberculosis
		Fungal
		Viral and atypical pneumonia
		Pneumocystis infection
Collagen vascular disease	Scleroderma	
	Rheumatoid arthritis	
	Systemic lupus erythematosus	
Occupational (pneumoconiosis)	Asbestosis	
	Silicosis	
	Coal miner's pneumoconiosis	
Hypersensitivity and drug reactions	Extrinsic allergic alveolitis	Nitrofurantoin
		Cytotoxic drugs
Physical agents		Radiation
Vascular	Early heart failure	
Neoplastic		Lymphoma
		Lymphatic metastasis
UNKNOWN CAUSES		
Idiopathic pulmonary fibrosis	Sarcoidosis	Eosinophilic granuloma

Table 39.8. Causes of Pleural Effusion

Effusion	Common	Uncommon
Vascular	Congestive heart failure[a]	
	Pulmonary infarction	
Metabolic		Hypoproteinemia[a]
		Cirrhosis[a]
		Nephrotic syndrome[a]
		Glomerulonephritis[a]
Malignancy	Metastatic disease	Mesothelioma
Infection	Bacterial (parapneumonic and empyema)	*Mycoplasma* (and other atypical pneumonias)
	Tuberculosis	Fungal
		Viral
Trauma	Hemothorax	Chylothorax
Gastrointestinal		Pancreatitis
		Esophageal rupture
		Subphrenic abscess
Collagen vascular disease		Systemic lupus erythematosus
		Rheumatoid arthritis
Miscellaneous		Asbestos exposure
		Drug hypersensitivity
		Postmyocardial infarction syndrome
		Meig's syndrome[a]
		Lymphoma and lymphatic abnormalities

[a] Usually transudative pleural effusion.

secretions and recover from heart failure or pneumonia slowly

    3) A younger patient should be suspected of having an altered pulmonary defense, e.g., cystic fibrosis or HIV infection

2. Pleural effusion

    a) Thoracentesis is almost always necessary to evaluate the fluid (except if it forms during acute left-sided heart failure)

    b) Fluid is transudative or exudative (latter characterized by pleural fluid protein concentration of 50% of concentration of serum protein)

    c) Causes: Table 39.8

40/ OBSTRUCTIVE AIRWAYS DISEASES

ASTHMA

A. Characteristics
1. Recurrent bronchospasm in response to specific (e.g., allergic) and nonspecific stimuli that cause airways inflammation
2. Attacks of cough, chest tightness, shortness of breath, wheezing, and limitation of airflow
3. Obstruction is variable
4. Most asthmatics have no symptoms between attacks
5. One-half of asthmatics develop symptoms in childhood
6. Childhood asthmatics are usually allergic to common aeroantigens; in adult-onset asthma, such allergies are less common

B. Clinical presentations
1. Extrinsic asthma
   a) Closely associated with exposure to a specific allergen (Table 40.1)
   b) Diagnosis requires a history of asthma on exposure to an allergen, improvement when allergen is removed, and positive wheal and flare to offending allergen on skin testing
2. Intrinsic asthma
   a) Etiology unclear: no clear association with exposure to a specific allergen
   b) Acute episodes may be triggered by viral respiratory illness
   c) In half the cases, asthma persists or worsens throughout life, leading to incompletely reversible abnormalities of pulmonary function
3. Occupational asthma
   a) Characterized by cough, wheezing, bronchospasm after occupational exposure
   b) Common substances that cause occupational asthma are listed in Table 40.2
   c) Prognosis good if exposure is stopped
4. Reactive airways dysfunction syndrome
   a) Follows an intensive short-term exposure to a toxic, nonallergic substance (such as acid fumes)

Table 40.1. Common Triggers for Asthma

Exercise	Viral respiratory infections
Cold air	Strong odors/irritants
Seasonal aeroallergens	Cigarette smoke
Ragweed pollen	Perfume
Tree pollen	Detergents
Grass pollen	Oxidant air pollutants
Indoor aeroallergens	Psychological stress
Dust mite feces	
Cockroaches	
Warm-blooded pets	
Mold spores	

Table 40.2. Occupational Exposures Causing Asthma

Agent	Specific Examples	Occupation
Birds	Pigeons, chickens	Pigeon breeders, poultry workers
Chemicals	Hexachlorophene, formalin, ethylene diamine, metabisulfite	Hospital workers, photographers, food preparation workers, water purification workers
Crustaceans	Crabs, shrimp	Food processing workers
Drugs	Antibiotics, sulfa derivatives	Workers in pharmaceutical industry, agricultural feed mixing
Enzymes	*Bacillus subtilis*, trypsin, papain	Detergent handlers, pharmaceutical industry workers
Epoxy resins	Anhydride compounds	Workers in manufacturing, auto body repair
Laboratory animals	Rats, mice, rabbits, guinea pigs	Laboratory workers, veterinarians
Metals	Platinum, nickel, chromium, cobalt, vanadium	Workers in metal plating, leather tanning, hard metal industry
Plants	Grain dust, flour	Grain handlers, bakers, millers
Plastics and rubber	TDI (toluene diisocyanate)	Polyurethane plastic, paint, varnish, and rubber workers
	DDI (diphenylmethane diisocyanate),	
	Azodicarbonamide	
Soldering fluxes	Colophony, aminoethylethanolamine	Electronics, aluminum fabrication workers
Vegetable products	Gum acacia	Printing workers
Wood dust	Cedar, redwood	Carpenter, construction workers, woodmill workers

Adapted from Chan-Yeung M: Occupational asthma. *Chest* 98:148S–161S, 1990.

b) After exposure, there is chronic airways hyperreactivity to physical-chemical agents (e.g., tobacco smoke, cold air)
5. Exercise-induced bronchospasm
    a) Present in the majority of asthmatics
    b) Worse in cold weather
    c) Can be prevented by an inhaled β-agonist or sodium cromolyn (see below)
6. "Triad" asthma
    a) Syndrome of nasal polyps, asthma, aspirin sensitivity
    b) Removal of polyps may help, but they tend to recur
    c) Asthma often severe, chronic
    d) Aspirin, other nonsteroidal anti-inflammatory drugs are contraindicated
7. Cough-variant asthma
    a) Cough is the major complaint: about 30% of patients with persistent cough of >8 weeks duration have airways hyperreactivity
    b) Other symptoms minimal
8. Allergic bronchopulmonary aspergillosis
    a) Caused by local allergic reaction to noninvasive *Aspergillus fumigatus* or to other fungi
    b) Criteria
        1) Recurrent atelectasis
        2) Pulmonary infiltrates
        3) Blood and sputum eosinophilia
        4) Immediate skin test reactivity to *Aspergillus*
        5) Serum precipitants to *Aspergillus*
        6) Elevated serum immunoglobulin E (IgE)
        7) IgG and IgE antibodies to *Aspergillus*
        8) Proximal bronchiectasis on chest computed tomography (CT) scan
    c) Treatment: systemic corticosteroids for at least 6 months
    d) Consider screening for cystic fibrosis, an underlying disease in 10%
C. Evaluation
    1. History
        a) Determine duration, frequency, severity of attacks
        b) Nocturnal asthma is typical; its absence should make one ask about trigger factors (Table 40.1), occupational exposures, medication use, and adherence to prescribed medicines
    2. Physical examination
        a) Acute attack
            1) Patients appear anxious, fatigued
            2) Deep, slow respirations with prolonged expiratory phase
            3) Breathing that becomes rapid and shallow with expiratory grunting may herald respiratory failure
            4) Speech difficult
            5) Chest appears hyperinflated
            6) Sternomastoid muscles contract with each inspiration
            7) Tachycardia
            8) Pulsus paradoxus in severe attacks

　　　　9) Diffuse polyphonic expiratory wheezes (inspiratory wheezing suggests upper airway obstruction)
　　b) Chronic asymptomatic asthma
　　　　1) Examination may be normal
　　　　2) There may be mild expiratory wheezing, a nonspecific finding
　3. Laboratory testing
　　a) Spirometry in all asymptomatic asthmatics periodically to establish a baseline and to monitor therapy: may be abnormal in asymptomatic patients, always abnormal in symptomatic patients
　　b) Chest x-ray in asymptomatic asthmatics is normal, shows hyperinflation during acute attacks
　　c) Eosinophilia common, correlates with severity
　　d) Charcot-Leyden crystals (spear-shaped) and Curschmann spirals (mucus casts of small airways) in sputum are characteristic
　　e) Skin testing for specific allergies is of help if there is a compatible history
　　f) Methacholine challenge (in a pulmonary function laboratory) is of help if diagnosis is uncertain
D. Treatment
　1. Monitoring
　　a) Peak flow meters for home use are important in monitoring asthmatics who require bronchodilators more than once or twice a week
　　b) Diaries of peak flow, symptoms, and use of bronchodilators are of help
　2. Control of environmental triggers
　　a) Identify and remove nonspecific irritants and specific allergens from environment
　　b) If there are symptoms of gastroesophageal reflux, treat appropriately (Chapter 21) — asthma may be triggered by reflux
　　c) Dehumidification in the home to control house dust mite and mold exposure; remove carpeting and stuffed furniture from the bedroom to reduce house dust mite exposure
　　d) Wash bedding in hot water weekly to eliminate house dust mites
　　e) Remove furry animals from house if they exacerbate asthma
　　f) Stay indoors at times of high pollen counts or when air pollution is high
　　g) Avoid aspirin, other nonsteroidal anti-inflammatory drugs, β-blockers
　3. Education
　　a) General components of program: Table 40.3
　　b) Proper use of a metered dose inhaler: Table 40.4
　　c) Action plans for acute and chronic management: Tables 40.5 and 40.6
　4. Drug treatment
　　a) Inhaled β-agonists for mild asthma (Table 40.7)
　　　　1) Frequency of use should be monitored
　　　　2) Most common side effects are tremor and arrhythmias; hypokalemia occurs with chronic use

Table 40.3.   Components of Asthma Education

Description of asthma
What asthma medicines do
Community resources for asthma patients and their families
Correct use of metered dose inhaler and nebulizer
How to use a peak flow meter
How to record an asthma diary
Warning signs of asthma attacks
Asthma trigger control plan
Steps to manage an asthma attack
School, work, and exercise activity plans

Table 40.4.   Proper Use of Metered Dose Inhaler (MDI)

Action	Reason for Action
Shake MDI gently.	Disperses drug evenly with vehicle. Check that canister is full.
Hold the MDI 4–6 finger breadths from the widely opened mouth.	Larger droplets will rain out in the air rather than impact in the mouth. This prevents mouth and throat irritation with some vehicles and thrush with inhaled corticosteroids.
Breathe normally and pause at quiet end-expiration.	Inhaling from a low lung volume allows greater peripheral penetration of the drug.
Actuate the MDI at the onset of inspiration and slowly inhale over 4–6 seconds.	Slow inspiratory flow rates enhance deposition of particles in the peripheral airways and reduce turbulence and impaction in the upper airway.
Hold the breath for 5–10 seconds at total lung capacity.	Small respirable particles will be allowed to settle in the smaller airways during the breath-hold.
Exhale slowly.	Slow expiration reduces exhalation of drug from the lung.

Adapted from Newhouse MT, Dolovitch MB: Control of asthma by aerosols. *N Engl J Med* 315:870, 1986.

Table 40.5.   Self-Management of Acute Exacerbations

Monitor peak flow and symptoms.
Use inhaled β-adrenergic agonist every 20 minutes for 3 doses, then every 3–4 hours for 6–12 hours as needed.
Contact physician or visit emergency department if there is incomplete response to initial treatment and peak flow is 50–70% of baseline.
Go to emergency department if poor response to initial therapy or if peak flow is <50% of baseline.

    b) Inhaled nonsteroidal antiallergy drugs (cromolyn or nedocromil) if inhaled β-agonists are being used more than 3–4 times/day
      1) Two sprays 4 times/day
      2) Maximum effect over several weeks
      3) Virtually no side effects
    c) Inhaled corticosteroids: highly effective if other regimens do not control symptoms
      1) Four sprays twice a day, increasing to 8 sprays 4 times/day as needed
      2) Systemic effects are minimal at conventional doses
      3) Local effects (i.e., oral candidiasis) can be avoided by use of spacer/reservoir devices or by rinsing the mouth with water after each use

Table 40.6.   Typical Action Plans for Management of Chronic Asthma

Condition	Indicators	Action
Stable (mild asthma)	Brief symptoms < 1–2/week Nocturnal asthma < 2/month Asymptomatic between exacerbations Peak flow > 80% baseline	Continue prescribed program Use inhaled bronchodilator prior to exercise or known provocative exposure
Possibly unstable (moderate asthma)	Symptoms more often than 1–2/week Nocturnal asthma > 2/month Nearly daily use of bronchodilator to treat symptoms Peak flow 60–80% baseline 20–30% variability in peak flow	Consult physician on routine basis Observe for new environmental triggers Physician should consider use of new or increased dose of inhaled anti-inflammatory agents and long-acting oral bronchodilator
Unstable (severe asthma)	Symptoms do not resolve completely between attacks, usual activity level limited, nearly daily nocturnal symptoms Peak flow < 60% baseline More than 30% variability in peak flow	Consult physician on urgent basis Start or increase oral corticosteroids Review new environmental exposures Physician should consider increasing inhaled corticosteroids, continuing short-term oral steroids, daily or alternate-day long-term steroids, and long-acting oral bronchodilator

Table 40.7.   β-Sympathomimetic Agonists

Generic Name	Trade Name	β₂ Selectivity	Onset of Action (min)	Inhalation Peak Effect (min)	Duration of Effect (hr)	Dosage Form
Isoetharine	Bronkosol Bronkometer	β₂>	5	5–15	2–3	Metered dose inhaler, 340 μg/puff Nebulized solution, 1%
Metaproterenol	Alupent	β₂>>>	1–5	30–60	2–5	Metered dose inhaler, 650 μg/puff Nebulized solution, 5% Tablets, 10 and 20 mg
Terbutaline	Brethine Bricanyl Brethaire	β₂>>>	1–5	30–60	2–5	Metered dose inhaler, 200 μg/puff Injection, 1 mg/ml Tablets, 2.5 and 5 mg
Bitolterol	Tornalate	β₂>>>	3–5	30–60	4–8	Metered dose inhaler, 370 μg/puff
Pirbuterol	Maxair	β₂>>>	5	30–60	4–5	Metered dose inhaler, 200 μg/puff
Albuterol	Proventil Ventolin	β₂>>>>	5–15	60–90	3–6	Metered dose inhaler, 90 μg/puff Nebulized solution, 0.5% Tablets, 2 and 4 mg
Fenoterol[a]	Berotec	β₂>>>>	1–5	60	4–8	Metered dose inhaler, 200 μg/puff
Salmeterol[a]	Serevent	β₂>>>>>	10–20	180	12+	Metered dose inhaler, 25 μg/puff

[a]Not available in the United States.

    d) Long-acting oral theophylline preparations (e.g., Theo-Dur 200 mg every 12 hours) if corticosteroids ineffective
      1) Should be started at low dose and titrated upward
      2) Side effects include anorexia, nausea, gastroesophageal reflux, anxiety, palpations
      3) Serious side effects occur at serum levels >20 μg/ml: seizures, tachyarrhythmias
      4) Interactions with other drugs (e.g., erythromycin, ciprofloxacin, cimetidine) increase levels
    e) Oral β-agonists (long-acting preparations of terbutaline, metaproterenol, and albuterol): an alternative to theophylline preparations; side effects of tremor and nervousness abate with use
    f) Inhaled anticholinergic drugs (ipratropium bromide) may augment effects of β-agonists
    g) Oral corticosteroids if other drugs fail
      1) Typically, a 14-day course of prednisone 30–60 mg/day and either stopping abruptly or tapering
      2) Some cases require tapering over months or require long-term daily or every-other-day use; side effects are common in such cases
  5. Emergency treatment of an acute asthmatic attack
    a) Risk factors for fatal asthma: Table 40.8
    b) If home treatment fails, patient should be sent to an emergency facility for more aggressive treatment
E. Course and prognosis
  1. Asthma that begins in childhood generally improves, degree of improvement related to severity at onset
  2. Asthma that begins in adulthood often causes progressive, fixed airway obstruction

CHRONIC OBSTRUCTIVE PULMONARY DISEASE (COPD)

A. Definition: abnormal tests of expiratory flow that do not change markedly over several months observation
  1. Emphysema: abnormal dilatation of the terminal airspaces with destruction of alveolar septa in the absence of interstitial fibrosis
    a) Panacinar: all of the airspaces in an acinus are equally dilated, typically bases more than apices (e.g., α_1-antitrypsin deficiency)
    b) Centriacinar: the respiratory bronchiole at the proximal end of the acinus is more dilated than the other portions, typically apices more than bases (e.g., peripheral airways disease)
  2. Chronic bronchitis: chronic cough and sputum production for the

---

Table 40.8.   Risk Factors for Fatal Asthma

Previous episode of mechanical ventilation for asthma
Hospitalization for asthma in previous year
Steroid-dependent asthma
Nonadherence to medical treatment
Overuse of inhaled β-adrenergic agonists
Recent steroid taper or abrupt withdrawal
Lack of objective measures of asthma severity
Psychiatric disorder
Inner-city residence, poverty

Table 40.9. Risk Factors for Developing COPD

Established risk factors
Cigarette smoking
Age
Male sex
Reduced lung function
Accelerated decline in lung function
Occupational dust exposure
α_1-Antitrypsin deficiency (Pi-ZZ phenotype)
Probable and possible risk factors
Air pollution
Childhood respiratory infections
Allergic diathesis
Airways reactivity
Low socioeconomic status
Poor nutrition
ABO blood type
ABH nonsecretor status
Family members with COPD

Adapted from Burrows B: Airways obstructive diseases: pathogenetic mechanisms and natural histories of the disorders. *Med Clin North Am* 74:547, 1990; and from Higgins M: Risk factors associated with chronic obstructive lung disease. *Ann N Y Acad Sci* 624:7, 1991.

majority of days of the week for at least 3 months of the year for at least 2 years in a row (not explained by a specific disorder such as bronchiectasis)

   a) Common in cigarette smokers

   b) Not necessarily associated with major physiological impairment

B. Natural history

  1. Symptoms typically in late middle-age or in the elderly

  2. Over half of patients with emphysema die within 10 years of diagnosis; 15% of patients with chronic asthmatic bronchitis (chronic bronchitis with prominent reversible airflow obstruction)

C. Pathogenesis: Table 40.9

D. Evaluation

  1. History (Table 40.10)

    a) Smoking history critical

    b) Symptoms of cough, sputum production, exertional dyspnea should be quantified

  2. Physical examination (Table 40.10)

    a) Absence of physical abnormalities is not sensitive enough to exclude diagnosis of COPD

    b) In far-advanced disease there are signs of right-sided heart failure: neck vein distention, peripheral edema, hepatomegaly, pronounced cardiac impulse in the epigastrium, epigastric systolic murmur that increases with inspiration

  3. Additional studies

    a) Chest x-ray: abnormal only in advanced disease

      1) Hyperinflation with flattening of the diaphragm

      2) Increased retrosternal airspace on lateral view

      3) Narrow cardiac silhouette

      4) Paucity and tapering of peripheral blood vessels

      5) Bullae

Table 40.10.   Sensitivity and Specificity of History and Physical Findings
for Diagnosis of Moderate COPD

HISTORICAL ITEMS

Historical Finding	Cutoff	Sensitivity (%)	Specificity (%)
Age	≥75 years	13	99
Previous diagnosis of COPD	Yes vs. no	80	74
Smoking history	≥70 pack-years	40	95
Dyspnea severity (5-point scale)	≥4	60	75
Phlegm	2 oz or more in A.M. when present	20	95
Theophylline use	Yes vs. no	60	71
Steroid use	Yes vs. no	40	87
Inhaler use	Yes vs. no	27	94
Home oxygen	Yes vs. no	20	96

PHYSICAL EXAMINATION ITEMS

Physical Finding	Cutoff	Sensitivity (%)	Specificity (%)
Initial impression[a]	Yes vs. no	25	95
Diaphragm excursion	<2 cm TLC vs. RV	12	98
Chest percussion	Increased resonance	32	94
Cardiac dullness	Decreased area	16	99
Blow out a match	≤10 cm	53	88
Wheeze	Yes vs. no	9	100
Reduced breath sounds	Yes vs. no	65	96
Forced expiratory time	>10 seconds	12	99
Cardiac point of maximum impulse	Abdominal	27	98
Final overall opinion	Yes vs. no	51	93

Adapted from Badgett RG, Tanaka DJ, Hunt DK, et al: Can moderate chronic obstructive pulmonary disease be
diagnosed by historical and physical findings alone? *Am J Med* 94:188, 1993.
RV, residual volume; *TLC*, total lung capacity.
[a] Based on general inspection.

  b) High-resolution CT: the standard for evaluation of emphysema
     but rarely necessary
  c) Spirometry: should be performed initially during routine visits
     and during exacerbations (Fig. 40.1)
  d) Bronchodilator testing: postbronchodilator FEV_1 is best overall
     predictor of life expectancy
  e) Carbon monoxide diffusing capacity: of help in distinguishing
     emphysema (capacity below 70%) from chronic asthmatic
     bronchitis (capacity normal)
  f) Exercise testing
     1) Indicated in individuals with diffusing capacity of <50–60%
        predicted who are not hypoxemic at rest, to evaluate for
        supplemental oxygen therapy (see below)
     2) Performed in a monitored facility
  g) Measurement of arterial oxygen tension in patients at rest with
     FEV_1 of <1.5 liters who are at higher risk of chronic
     hypoxemia and cor pulmonale
  h) Screening for severe α_1-antitrypsin deficiency by serum protein
     electrophoresis (reduced α_1-globulin level) if there is a strong
     family history of premature emphysema, there is evidence of

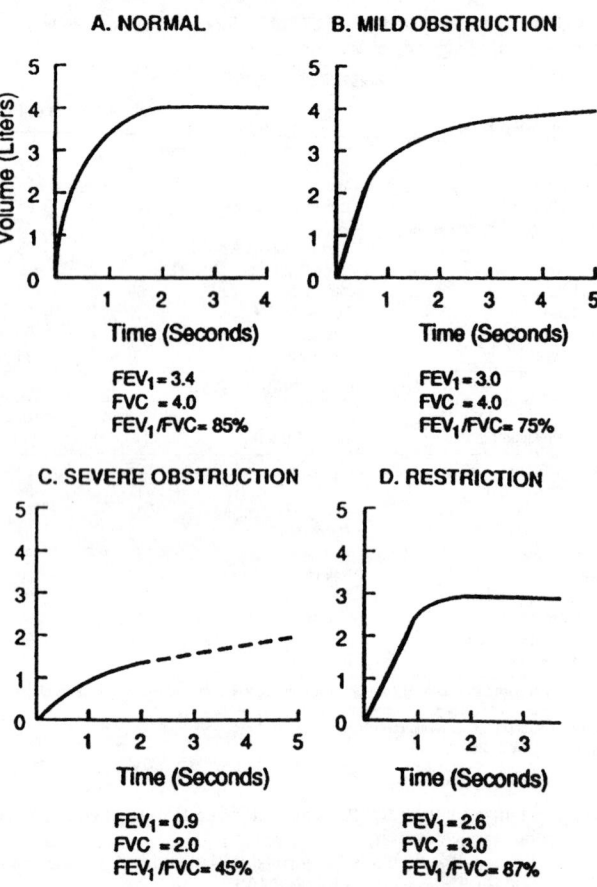

Figure 40.1. Spirographic tracings of forced expiration. Exhaled volume is plotted against time. Forced vital capacity *(FVC)* is represented by the total volume expired. One-second forced expiratory volume *(FEV₁)* is the volume of air expired during the first second. **A.** Normal spirogram. **B.** Spirogram from a patient with mild obstructive airways disease. **C.** Spirogram from a patient with a severe obstructive defect. If the spirogram were incorrectly terminated after 2 seconds, the FVC would be artificially reduced. When it is performed correctly *(dotted lines),* it is obvious that there is airway obstruction and no restrictive disease. **D.** Spirogram showing restrictive pulmonary disease (FEV₁/FVC is normal, but FVC is reduced).

panacinar emphysema (see below), or if the patient has severe COPD and is young

i) Screening for cystic fibrosis (sweat chloride analysis) if there is x-ray evidence of bronchiectasis, a family history of childhood lung disease, allergic bronchopulmonary aspergillosis (see above), or persistent *Pseudomonas* in the sputum

j) Electrocardiography: can confirm right ventricular dilatation and/or tricuspid insufficiency
1) Indeterminate or vertical axis
2) If cor pulmonale, enlarged P waves, right-axis deviation, signs of right ventricular hypertrophy

k) Sputum examination
1) During exacerbations, neutrophil or eosinophil predominance can be of help in deciding between antibiotics and corticosteroids
2) Culture unnecessary unless there is pneumonia

E. Management
1. Education: the natural course; available aids, appropriate use of medications and of oxygen, advanced directives
2. Prevention of disease progression
a) Help with smoking cessation: behavioral modification techniques (most communities have smoking cessation programs), use of nicotine gum or patch
b) Avoidance of environmental air pollutants
c) Pneumococcal vaccination every 6 years and influenza vaccination annually
3. Treatment of complications
a) Tracheobronchial infections
1) Heralded by a change in quantity, viscosity, or color of sputum
2) Broad spectrum antibiotics (tetracycline, erythromycin, amoxicillin, trimethoprim-sulfamethoxazole) may shorten duration of symptoms
b) Chronic hypoxemia
1) Oxygen therapy prolongs survival and improves functioning in hypoxemic patients
2) Oxygen available for home use; portable systems allow mobility out of home
3) Oxygen prescribed at lowest level necessary to maintain oxygen saturation at 90% (usually 1–4 liters) for a minimum of 18 hours/day
c) Pulmonary hypertension and cor pulmonale
1) Treatment with continuous oxygen and diuretics
2) Digitalis not useful in absence of left ventricular failure
d) Supraventricular tachyarrhythmias (see Chapter 43)
e) Mucus hypersecretion: iodinated glycerol (Organidin or IoTuss) may be of help
f) Hypercapnia
1) Respiratory stimulants and sedatives should be avoided
2) Bronchospasm (see below), obesity (Chapter 60), and sleep apnea (Chapter 68) can contribute to hypercapnia and should be treated

g) Malnutrition: common, should be looked for and treated with caloric supplementation

4. Drug therapy
   a) Minimum number of agents and least frequent dosing schedule should be the goal
   b) Start with ipratropium bromide (Atrovent)
      1) Inhaled anticholinergic that causes 4–8 hours of bronchodilation
      2) Particularly effective in chronic asthmatic bronchitis
      3) Two inhalations 3 times/day to start, can be increased to 6 inhalations 4 times/day
      4) Local side effects (irritation and cough) can be reduced by good technique (Table 40.4) or by use of a spacer
   c) β-Adrenergic agonists: Table 40.7
   d) Theophylline: best taken in a long-acting preparation (e.g., Theo-Dur 200 mg every 12 hours)
      1) A second-line drug most useful for prevention of nocturnal symptoms
      2) Probably has effects (improvement in respiratory muscle function) beyond that of bronchodilation
   e) Oral corticosteroids
      1) Only 10–20% of patients show substantial response (increase in FEV_1 of ≥25%)
      2) Some benefit in nonsmokers or in patients with asthmatic bronchitis

5. Pulmonary rehabilitation
   a) Education about COPD
   b) Support group discussions
   c) Energy conservation training
   d) Aerobic exercise conditioning
   e) Respiratory muscle training
   f) Consideration of intermittent respiratory muscle rest with an external ventilator

6. Surgery
   a) Resection of bullae rarely indicated
   b) Lung transplantation not well established

41/ LUNG CANCER

RISKS
A. Lung cancer caused by tobacco smoke in 80–90%
   1. Risk proportionate to number of cigarettes smoked per day (not to the tar in each cigarette)
   2. Risk falls to that of nonsmokers within 10 years of cessation of smoking
B. Other exposures that impose risk (Table 41.1)
   1. Asbestos exposure especially important to identify: increased incidence of mesothelioma and, in smokers, markedly increased risk of bronchogenic cancer
   2. Radon, a naturally produced radioactive gas, a risk for miners, but risk in general population is unclear

SCREENING
No proven benefit of periodic chest x-ray or sputum cytologies

HISTOLOGY BY SMOKING HABITS: TABLE 41.2

HISTORY
A. Pulmonary symptoms
   1. Most patients are symptomatic at diagnosis
      a) Cough in almost all patients
      b) Hemoptysis
         1) Warrants investigation in patients over 40, in smokers, in patients with abnormal chest x-rays, in patients with a

Table 41.1. Occupational Agents Associated With Lung Cancer

Known carcinogens	Probable carcinogens
Arsenic	Acrylonitrile
Asbestos	Beryllium
Bis(chloromethyl)ether	Cadmium
Chromium, hexavalent	Formaldehyde
Nickel and nickel compounds	Possible carcinogens
Polycyclic aromatic compounds	Acetaldehyde
Radon	Synthetic fibers
Vinyl chloride	Silica
	Welding fumes

Modified from Coultas DB, Samet JM: Occupational lung cancer. *Clin Chest Med* 13:341, 1992.

Table 41.2. Histological Type of Lung Cancer by Smoking Habits

Type	Never Smoked (%)	Pipe/Cigar (%)	Current Cigarette Smoker (%)	Ex-Cigarette Smoker (%)
Non-small cell carcinoma				
Squamous cell		33.3	45.9	15.5
Adenocarcinoma	30.0	20.0	8.5	25.2
Large cell	10.0	13.3	13.0	9.7
Bronchioloalveolar	50.0	33.3	9.8	26.2
Small cell carcinoma			15.4	2.0
Other types	10.0		7.4	21.4
No. of patients	10	15	377	103

Modified from Auerbach O, Garfinckel L: The changing pattern of lung carcinoma. *Cancer* 68:1973, 1991.

chronic cough, in patients with hemoptysis persisting for a week or more, in patients with anemia or weight loss
2) Hemoptysis usually blood-streaked sputum rather than massive
c) Chest pain: usually a dull pain on side of tumor
B. Extrapulmonary symptoms
1. Superior vena cava syndrome
a) Edema and rubor of the upper trunk and face, sometimes with syncope
b) Chest x-ray usually shows right upper lobe mass, widened mediastinum, and (in 25%) right pleural effusion
2. Pancoast syndrome: shoulder pain, arm pain, paresthesias caused by a pulmonary apical tumor
3. Horner's syndrome: miosis, ptosis, enophthalmos, facial blushing, anhidrosis on affected side
4. Hoarseness
a) Suggests recurrent laryngeal nerve involvement
b) Warrants a flow-volume loop to evaluate degree of upper airway obstruction
C. Extrathoracic symptoms
1. Metastatic disease found in majority of patients
2. Anorexia, cachexia, weight loss, and fever are common
3. Paraneoplastic syndromes
a) May precede other symptoms, may mimic metastatic disease, usually responds to treatment of primary tumor
b) Endocrine syndromes
1) Hypercalcemia: usually due to a squamous cell tumor
2) Inappropriate antidiuretic hormone syndrome and ectopic adrenal corticotropic hormone secretion (mild hypertension, hyperglycemia, hypokalemia, alkalosis): usually due to a small cell cancer
c) Clubbing and hypertrophic pulmonary osteoarthropathy (pain, swelling, positive bone scan): lung cancer is the leading, but not the only, cause
d) Neurological syndromes: rare
e) Migratory thromboembolic disease

PHYSICAL EXAMINATION
A. Usually unrevealing, but see above
B. Supraclavicular adenopathy should be looked for particularly; a positive needle aspiration cytology is a simple way of diagnosing the tumor

DIAGNOSTIC PROCEDURES
A. Chest x-ray
1. A mass with a doubling time of <30 or >450 days is unlikely to be malignant (see Solitary Pulmonary Nodule, below)
2. Squamous cell and small cell tumors tend to be central; adenocarcinoma and large cell carcinomas tend to be peripheral
a) Central tumors more likely to present with symptoms and signs of obstruction: atelectasis, pneumonia, dyspnea
b) Small cell tumors may be revealed by hilar adenopathy without visible tumor mass

    c) Squamous cell tumor is the most likely to cavitate (uncommonly)

    d) Bronchoalveolar cancer usually presents peripherally and is often multifocal

B. Chest computed tomography (CT) scan

  1. Useful to determine extent of primary tumor and to guide diagnostic and therapeutic procedures

  2. Useful to quantitate calcification of a nodule (densely calcified nodules are more likely benign)

  3. Presence and size of mediastinal or hilar nodes can be evaluated

C. Sputum cytology

  1. Three early morning sputum samples should be obtained after deep inhalations

  2. If sputum is not being produced spontaneously, induction with nebulized saline (by experienced personnel) should be attempted

  3. Squamous cell tumors diagnosed 80% of the time; adenocarcinomas, <5% of the time

D. Bronchoscopy

  1. Useful for diagnosis and staging and to evaluate vocal cord function

  2. Also allows transbronchial biopsy, brushing for cytology, lavage, and transtracheal needle aspiration of lymph nodes

  3. Diagnostic yield high for large (>2 cm) tumors and for tumors in the central airways

E. Needle biopsy

  1. Most useful when a mass is peripheral near the pleura or in the apex

  2. Most useful in diagnosis of metastatic tumors

  3. Done under CT guidance

F. Mediastinoscopy and mediastinotomy

  1. Indicated when enlarged nodes cannot be sampled by less invasive techniques

  2. Require hospitalization

STAGING

A. Non-small cell cancer (Table 41.3): diagnostic scans not indicated in the absence of symptoms

B. Small cell cancer

  1. Either confined to the hemithorax and regional lymph nodes or not

  2. Two-thirds of patients have distant metastases at presentation

  3. Staging includes cranial and abdominal CT scans, bone scans, possibly bone marrow examination

TREATMENT

A. Non-small cell cancer

  1. Surgery is the treatment for patients without evidence of mediastinal or metastatic disease

    a) If preoperative spirometry shows lobectomy or pneumonectomy is feasible (FEV_1, >2 liters)

    b) Patients with clinical stage I or II disease (Table 41.3) have, respectively, 50% and 30% 5-year survivals

    c) Patients with stage III disease may tolerate surgery: survival is 15% at 5 years

Table 41.3. Staging System for Lung Cancer

Tumor (T)	
TX	Occult carcinoma (malignant cells in sputum or bronchial washings, but tumor not visualized by imaging studies or bronchoscopy)
T1	Tumor ≤ 3 cm in greatest diameter, surrounded by lung or visceral pleura, but not proximal to lobar bronchus on bronchoscopy
T2	Tumor > 3 cm in diameter, or with involvement of main bronchus at least 2 cm distal to carina, visceral pleural invasion, or associated atelectasis or obstructive pneumonia extending to the hilar region but not involving the entire lung
T3	Tumor invading chest wall, diaphragm, mediastinal pleura, or parietal pericardium; or tumor in main bronchus within 2 cm of but not invading the carina; or atelectasis or obstructive pneumonitis of entire lung
T4	Tumor invading mediastinum, heart, great vessels, trachea, esophagus, vertebral body, or carina; or ipsilateral malignant pleural effusion
Nodes (N)	
N0	No regional lymph node metastases
N1	Metastases to ipsilateral peribronchial or hilar nodes
N2	Metastases to ipsilateral mediastinal or subcarinal nodes
N3	Metastases to contralateral mediastinal or hilar nodes or to any scalene or supraclavicular nodes
Distant metastases (M)	
M0	No distant metastases
M1	Distant metastases
Stages	
Occult	TXN0M0
Stage I	T1-2N0M0
Stage II	T1-2N1M0
Stage IIIa	T3N0-1M0
	T1-3N2M0
Stage IIIb	T4N0-2M0
	T1-4N3M0
Stage IV	TX-4N0-3M1

Reprinted, by permission of The New England Journal of Medicine, from Ihde DC: Chemotherapy of lung cancer. N Engl J Med 327:2434, 1992.

2. Definitive radiotherapy
   a) A small potential for prolonged survival when surgery is not an option
   b) May cure 15–20% of patients with stage I or II disease and is an option for selected patients with stage III disease
3. Postoperative radiation: does not improve survival but is indicated if margins of resection are positive for tumor
4. Palliative therapy for patients who are not candidates for surgery or definitive radiotherapy
   a) Radiotherapy often relieves hemoptysis, superior vena cava syndrome, and dyspnea; atelectasis seldom relieved
   b) Laser therapy and brachytherapy
      1) Require hospitalization
      2) Indicated for treatment of symptomatic obstruction of a major airway
B. Small cell cancer
   1. Chemotherapy standard treatment
      a) Increases survival

b) Usually 2–3 drugs every 3–4 weeks for 6–8 courses
2. Surgery, radiation usually ineffective

PLEURAL EFFUSIONS (SEE ALSO CHAPTER 39)

A. Carcinomatous involvement of the pleura
  1. Usually exudative
  2. Usually serosanguineous but may be bloody
  3. May have a lymphocytosis, a low pH, and a low glucose concentration
B. Paramalignant effusion
  1. Exudative or transudative
  2. May be due to mediastinal carcinoma obstructing lymph drainage
  3. May be secondary to postobstructive pneumonia or atelectasis
C. Not curable: most patients die within 6 months
D. Diagnosis by pleural fluid cytology and by blind pleural biopsy; thoracoscopy is a more sensitive procedure but requires hospitalization

SOLITARY PULMONARY NODULE

A. Definition: a spherical density of <4 cm in diameter
B. Forty to fifty percent are malignant, of which 80% are resectable (5-year survival, 40%)
C. Evaluation
  1. Risks of malignancy
    a) Age: small under 35 years, increase rapidly thereafter
    b) History of exposure to tobacco or to other substances (Table 41.1)
    c) History of a previous malignancy (80% will be metastatic or a new primary cancer)
    d) CT densitometry: the degree of calcification inversely correlates with risk of malignancy
    e) Size: of >3 cm is more likely malignant
    f) Shape: an irregular lesion with poorly defined borders is suggestive of malignancy
    g) Although nodules that grow relatively slowly (double in size in more than 2–5 years, depending on other risk factors) are less likely to be malignant, many oncologists do not believe diagnosis should be deferred unless there is no suspicion of cancer
  2. Percutaneous transthoracic needle aspiration or bronchoscopy is the initial procedure
    a) Needle aspiration has a higher yield (70–90%), especially for nodules of <2 cm but has a higher risk of complications
    b) Bronchoscopy has a 30–70% diagnostic yield
    c) If lesion appears benign, adequacy of sample, clinical scenario dictate whether a more invasive procedure or serial x-rays should be recommended

42/ ANGINA PECTORIS

RISK FACTORS
A. Enumeration of factors: Table 42.1
B. Modification of risk: Table 42.2

DIAGNOSIS
A. Onset: time can often be precisely established
B. Character and location
   1. Variously described: usually squeezing, crushing, burning, smothering; typically diffuse
   2. Usually begins and ends gradually
   3. Typically midline and substernal
   4. Often radiates to shoulder, arm, hand — usually the left — and may radiate to the neck, lower jaw, and intrascapular region
C. Initiation
   1. Predictable relationship to exertion or to emotional stress
   2. More likely in cold or windy weather
   3. If pain occurs at rest and is due to cardiac ischemia, likely to be unstable angina (see below), variant angina (see below), or myocardial infarction
   4. Nocturnal angina may be due to left heart failure or to unstable angina
   5. Increased level of carboxyhemoglobin (heavy traffic or inhalation of tobacco smoke)

Table 42.1. Risk Factors for Coronary Artery Disease

Factor	Comment	Documentation
Blood pressure (Chapter 46)	Risk is directly proportionate to increase of systolic or diastolic blood pressure	Excellent
Blood lipids (Chapter 59)	Risk is directly proportionate to increase in concentration of total cholesterol and of low-density lipoprotein (LDL) and inversely proportionate to concentration of high-density lipoprotein (HDL)	Excellent
Diabetes mellitus (Chapter 56)	Risk is 2 times control in diabetic men, 3 times control in diabetic women	Excellent
Cigarette smoking	Proportionate to number of cigarettes smoked per day (3 times control at a pack or more per day)	Excellent
Oral contraceptives (Chapter 76)	Risk is much greater in women over age 35 and when higher doses of estrogen are taken (see Chapter 76)	Excellent
Personality type	A competitive, driving person (so-called type A personality) is more prone to coronary artery disease	Good
Sedentary living	Individuals who do not exercise regularly may have a greater risk of myocardial infarction than do individuals who exercise regularly	Fair
Diet[a] (Chapter 59)	High lipid content of diet may potentiate coronary artery disease	Good in humans Excellent in animals

[a] Alcohol and caffeine, although claimed by some in the past to be independent risk factors, have not been established to be so. However, obesity, by increasing the severity of hypertension, hyperlipidemia, and diabetes mellitus, may have an important influence on the development of coronary artery disease.

Table 42.2. Primary Prevention of Coronary Artery Disease: Recommended Actions

Demonstrated risk factors that can be modified
  Discontinue cigarette smoking
  Control hypertension
  Control blood lipids
  Monitor use of oral contraception (see Chapter 76)
Demonstrated risk factors that cannot or probably cannot be modified
  Identify ECG abnormalities
  Identify type A behavior
  Identify diabetes mellitus and gout
Factors that are not established risks
  Encourage regular physical activity
  Monitor intake of alcohol and coffee

Modified from American Heart Association: Risk factors and coronary disease: a statement for physicians. *Circulation* 62:449A, 1980.

D. Relief
  1. With cessation of exertion or of emotional stress, occurs within minutes (longer duration suggests infarction)
  2. Nitroglycerin: a nonspecific diagnostic test
E. Physical examination
  1. Measurement of blood pressure [may be high or (an ominous sign) may be low], signs of chronic hypertension (e.g., cardiomegaly), evidence of peripheral vascular disease (Chapter 70)
  2. Listen for S_4, paradoxical splitting of S_2, murmur of mitral insufficiency (Chapter 44) — all may disappear when pain abates
F. Electrocardiogram (ECG)
  1. Often normal between attacks; important to get ECG during attack
  2. Q wave is a reliable sign of old infarction
  3. Nonspecific ST-T wave changes or arrhythmias are not of help in diagnosis
  4. ST depression with a flat or down-sloping ST segment indicates subendocardial ischemia
  5. ST elevation at rest during an attack suggests variant angina (see below)
  6. T wave inversion is nonspecific
  7. Left bundle branch block (see Chapter 43) correlates with organic heart disease; right bundle branch block does not
G. Exercise stress tests
  1. Positive test is down-sloping or horizontal ST depression of 1 mm (65% sensitivity but 90% specificity — more sensitive with extensive disease)
  2. False positive tests common in patients taking certain drugs (e.g., digitalis), in women, in patients with left ventricular hypertrophy or mitral valve prolapse
  3. Indications
    a) To clarify cause of chest pain
    b) To assess prognosis in patients with known ischemic disease
    c) To ascertain the effects of medical and surgical management of coronary artery disease

   d) To evaluate a previously sedentary asymptomatic middle-aged or elderly person prior to the initiation of a vigorous exercise program; the number of false positive tests will be increased in this population
   e) To document the response of a patient with an arrhythmia to exercise
  4. Contraindications
   a) Recent onset of unstable angina
   b) Uncontrolled hypertension
   c) Uncontrolled heart failure
   d) Significant ventricular arrhythmias
   e) Severe valvular disease
   f) Myocarditis, acute pericarditis, severe pulmonary hypertension, recent pulmonary hypertension, uncontrolled atrial fibrillation, acute systemic illness
   g) Neurological or orthopedic disease (may make exercise difficult)
H. Radioisotopic (thallium-201) imaging
  1. To assess myocardial regional blood flow, ordinarily as part of an exercise stress test
  2. Permanent cold spots indicate likely infarcted myocardium; transient cold spots likely transiently ischemic myocardium
  3. More sensitive and specific for detection of occlusive coronary artery disease than standard exercise stress testing
  4. Especially useful if ECG interpretation is difficult (e.g., diffuse ST-T changes, bundle branch block), for detecting recent or remote infarction
  5. If patients cannot exercise, thallium imaging after intravenous dipyridamole or adenosine is useful
 I. Ambulatory electrocardiography ("Holter monitoring")
  1. Not a good screening test
  2. To evaluate the number of episodes of painful ischemia and of "silent" ischemia in patients with known coronary artery disease
 J. Coronary arteriography
  1. Indications
   a) To determine suitability for revascularization of patients who have failed medical therapy (see below)
   b) To detect left main or severe three-vessel disease (indication for early bypass), e.g., suspected by positive stress test on submaximal exercise
   c) To make decisions about management in young patients with coronary artery disease
   d) To evaluate patients with equivocal standard and thallium stress tests
  2. Complications: major ones are infarction, stroke, and death — reduced in active laboratories, increased in elderly patients with poor left ventricular function

PROGNOSIS
A. Mortality
  1. Without infarction, about 5% a year; worse the more abnormal the exercise stress test

    2. Most important determinants are location and extent of coronary artery disease and left ventricular ejection fraction

B. Morbidity
    1. Risk of myocardial infarction at 5 years: 25% in men, 12.5% in women
    2. Reduction of functional capacity: a reflection of extent of disease, degree of usual activity, response to treatment

TREATMENT

A. General considerations
    1. Treatment of hypertension
    2. Smoking cessation
    3. Sensitivity to possibility of hyperthyroidism
    4. Treatment of anemia
    5. Treatment of heart failure
    6. Modification of risk factors (Table 42.2)
    7. Physician-supervised physical conditioning

B. Medical (Table 42.3)
    1. Initial treatment should be a nitrate preparation or a β-blocker, then both if necessary
    2. Calcium channel blocker for patients with unpredictable chest pain [possibility of variant angina (see below)] or who have failed β-blockers
    3. Aspirin, e.g., 325 mg/day, is beneficial

C. Percutaneous transluminal coronary angioplasty
    1. In patients who have failed medical therapy or who have left main or extensive three-vessel disease and have accessible lesions
    2. Risk (low) of coronary dissection, myocardial infarction, or death; dissection dictates immediate bypass
    3. Restenosis rate of about 30%
    4. Especially attractive option in patients 50 or younger

D. Coronary bypass surgery
    1. For patients with incapacitating angina who have failed medical therapy or who have left main coronary artery disease
    2. Risk of perioperative infarction and stroke, especially in older patients
    3. About 80% of patients will have complete or significant resolution of symptoms, but 50% will have recurrence within 5 years
    4. Postpericardiotomy syndrome in 30% within 2–4 weeks: fever, pleuritic chest pain, pleural and pericardial effusions — will respond to diuretics, nonsteroidal anti-inflammatory drug (sometimes, prednisone)

UNSTABLE ANGINA

A. Angina that is becoming more intense, more frequent, relieved less readily by nitroglycerin
B. Patients should be hospitalized (increased risk of infarction or sudden death) and treated aggressively

VARIANT ANGINA

A. Occurs usually at rest (not on exertion or in response to stress)
B. ECG shows ST elevation during attacks
C. Coronary spasm often plays a role: associated with atherosclerotic disease in 85%, with anatomically normal arteries in 15%

Table 42.3. Selected Drugs Used in the Treatment of Angina[a]

Class	Brand Name	Available Strengths	Usual Starting Dose	Usual Maximum Dose	Onset	Duration
Short-acting nitrates						
Nitroglycerin						
Sublingual tablet[b]	Nitrostat and others	0.15-, 0.30-, 0.40-, 0.60-mg tablets, sublingual	1 tablet (0.4 mg) at time of, or in anticipation of, pain	2-3 tablets at time of pain	30 sec	3-5 min
Topical ointment	Nitro-Bid, Nitrol	2% ointment	½-inch every 4-6 hr as needed	4-5 inches every 3-4 hr	30-60 min	3-6 hr
Patch[c]	Transderm Nitro, Nitro-Dur, and Nitrodisc	2.5-, 5-, 10-, 15-mg/24 hr rated release (0.1, 0.2, etc., mg/hr)	5 mg	2-3 patches that deliver 15 mg/24 hr	30 min	24 hr
Long-acting nitrates						
Erythrityl[b] tetranitrate	Cardilate	5-, 10-, 15-mg tablets, oral or sublingual; 10-mg tablets, chewable	5 mg sublingually in anticipation of pain or 10 mg orally or chewed 3 times/day	100 mg/day in divided doses	5 min (sublingual and chewed)	4 hr
Isosorbide[b] dinitrate	Isordil, Sorbitrate, and others	5-, 10-, 20-mg tablets, oral; 40-mg tablets or capsules, oral	10 mg every 4-6 hr	60-80 mg every 4 hr	15-30 min	4-6 hr
Isosorbide mononitrate	Ismo	20 mg	20 mg b.i.d. given 7 hr apart	40 mg b.i.d. given 7 hr apart	60 min	5 hr after 2nd dose
β-Adrenergic blockers[b]						
Propranolol[b]	Inderal	10-, 20-, 40-, 80-mg tablets, oral	10-20 mg 3 or 4 times/day	320 mg/day in divided doses	1-1.5 hr	4-6 hr
Nadolol	Corgard	40-, 80-, 120-mg tablets, oral	40 mg once a day	240 mg	1-2 hr	24 hr
Tenormin	Atenolol	50-, 100-mg tablets, oral	50 mg once a day	100-150 mg	1-2 hr	24 hr
Metoprolol	Lopressor	50, 100 mg	100 mg in 2 divided doses; in older	200 mg b.i.d.	1-2 hr	24 hr

persons, 25 mg b.i.d.

Calcium channel blockers						
Nifedipine	Procardia	10-mg capsule	10 mg 3 or 4 times/day; 10 mg at time of pain if sublingual	40 mg every 6 hr	20–30 min	8 hr
Nifedipine, extended release	Procardia XL	30, 60, 90 mg	30 mg q.d. (for converting from t.i.d. to XL, add up mg dose, e.g., 30 mg t.i.d. = 90 mg XL)	90 mg q.d.	1–2 hr	> 24 hr
Verapamil	Calan, Isoptin	80-, 120-mg tablets	80 mg 3 or 4 times/day	120 mg 4 times/day	30–45 min	6–8 hr
Verapamil SR	Isoptin SE, Calan SR	120, 180, 240 mg	120–180 mg q.d.	240 mg b.i.d.	1–2 hr	24 hr
Diltiazem	Cardiazem	30-, 60-mg tablets	30 mg 4 times/day	60 mg every 6 hr	30–45 min	6–8 hr
Diltiazem CD	Cardizem CD	180, 240, 300 mg	180–240 mg q.d.	360 mg q.d.	1–2 hr	24 hr
Nicardipine	Cardene	20-, 30-mg capsules	20 mg 3 times/day	40 mg 3 times/day	30–120 min	8 hr
Amlodipine	Norvasc	2.5, 5, 10 mg	5 mg q.d., increase dose after 3–5 days; start small or elderly on 2.5 mg q.d.	10 mg q.d.	Several hours	24 hr

aOther drugs, other doses of the drugs listed, and combinations of different drugs are marketed. The drugs and dosages shown are the ones most often used.
bGeneric available. Table 43.2 provides information on the pharmacology of all six of the currently available β-blockers.
cThe brand name of these preparations is followed by a number (5, 10, 15, 20). It is important to know whether that number refers to milligrams per 24 hours (Transderm Nitro or Nitrodisc) or to square centimeters of the patch (Nitro-Dur). Nitro-Dur contains 4 mg/cm² of patch, reported now as release per hour.

D. Coronary arteriography important to exclude those patients with normal arteries from consideration for bypass

E. Calcium channel blockers are the drug of choice (Table 42.3)

ANGINA WITH NORMAL CORONARY ARTERIES

A. Coronary artery spasm (see above)

B. Abnormal coronary reserve (e.g., hypertension, aortic stenosis or regurgitation, hypertrophic cardiomyopathy)

C. Cocaine abuse

D. Prognosis generally favorable: antianginal drugs are effective

43/ ARRHYTHMIAS

DIAGNOSIS
A. History
  1. May be asymptomatic
  2. Appreciation of irregular rhythm (palpitations)
  3. Symptoms of reduced cardiac output: light-headedness, dizziness, syncope, dyspnea, chest pain
  4. Trigger factors: coffee, smoking, exercise, emotional stress
  5. Symptoms of underlying disease: heart failure, angina, thyrotoxicosis
  6. Taking of stimulant drugs
  7. Taking of prescription drugs that may cause arrhythmias (e.g., digitalis, theophylline, β-blockers, β-agonists, antidepressants, antihypertensives)
B. Physical examination
  1. Jugular pulse: cannon waves [atrioventricular (AV) dissociation, complete heart block, or supraventricular tachycardia]; "a" waves of atrial tachycardia
  2. Arterial pulse: ventricular rate and rhythm of conducted beats
  3. Auscultation of the heart: ventricular rate and rhythm; S_1 variation during regular tachycardia suggests AV dissociation; during regular bradycardia, heart block; loud S_1 suggests short P-R interval; soft S_1 suggests long P-R interval
  4. Electrocardiogram (ECG)
     a) Surface resting ECG for atrial and ventricular activity
     b) Ambulatory (Holter) ECG to evaluate suspicious symptoms when resting ECG is normal, to assess whether patients with known heart disease are having episodic arrhythmias, to assess the effectiveness of antiarrhythmic therapy
     c) Exercise ECG to evaluate symptoms suggestive of arrhythmia during exercise

MANAGEMENT
A. Antiarrhythmic drugs
  1. Characteristics: Tables 43.1 and 43.2
  2. Adverse effects (Table 43.3)
     a) Proarrhythmia effects usually seen within a few days, usually in patients with ejection fractions of <40%
     b) Drug levels (Table 43.1) should be checked at steady state and then 1–3 times/year (about 8 hours after last oral dose)
B. Pacemaker therapy
  1. Treatment of choice for patients with symptomatic bradyarrhythmias and heart block
  2. Also may be used to terminate certain tachyarrhythmias
C. Cardioversion
  1. For rapid conversion of tachyarrhythmias
  2. Usually anticoagulated for 3 weeks, pretreated with quinidine
  3. Requires hospitalization
D. Referral for an electrophysiological study
  1. History of cardiac arrest with ventricular fibrillation in absence of myocardial infarction
  2. Sustained ventricular tachycardia

Table 43.1.   Characteristics of Antiarrhythmic Drugs

Drug	Common Brand Name	Effects on ECG	Half-Life (hr)	Time to Steady State (days)	Available Strength (mg)	Usual Oral Dose	Maximal Daily Dose (mg)	Therapeutic Plasma Levels
Class IA								
Quinidine	Generic	Prolongs QRS, QT, and (±) PR	6	1–2	200 (s) 342 (g)	200–600 mg every 6–8 hr	1800 (s) 2400 (g)	3–7 μg/ml
Procainamide	Pronestyl	Prolongs QRS QT, and (±) PR	3–4	1	250, 500 500, 750 (SR)	500–1000 mg every 3–4 hr or every 6 hr (SR)	4000	3–8 μg/ml[a]
Disopyramide	Norpace	Prolongs QRS QT, and (±) PR	6–9	1–2	100, 150	150 mg 4 times/day	1200	2–4 μg/ml
Class IB								
Tocainide	Tonocard	Shortens QT	15	1.5–3	400	400–600 mg every 8 hr or 600 mg every 12 hr	2400	4–10 μg of base/ml
Mexiletine	Mexitil	Shortens QT	10–12	2–3	150, 200, 250	200–300 mg every 8 hr	1200	0.5–2 μg/ml
Phenytoin (diphenylhydantoin)	Dilantin	Shortens QT	24–36	3–5	30, 100	300–400 mg/day	600	10–20 μg/ml
Class IC								
Flecainide	Tambocor	Prolongs PR, QRS, QT, bradycardia	12–27	2–3	100	200 mg every day	400	0.2–1.0 μg/ml
Propafenone	Rythmol	Prolongs PR, QRS, but not QT	2–10 (90% of patients) 10–32 (10% of patients)	Depends on genetically determined metabolic rate	150, 300	450–900 mg in 3 divided doses	900	0.2–1.5 μg/ml

Class II Propranolol[b]	Inderal	Prolongs (±) PR, shortens QT	6	10, 20, 40, 60, 80 and 60, 80, 120, 180 (long acting)	10–40 mg every 6 hr or 60–180 mg (long acting) once or twice a day	640	50–100 ng/ml
Class III Amiodarone	Cordarone	Prolongs PR, QRS	53	200	200–600 mg once daily	800	Not useful
Sotalol	Betapace	Slows HR, prolongs QTc, no effect on QRS	12	80, 160	80–160 mg 2–3 times/day	320[c]	Not useful
Class IV Verapamil	Calan, Isoptin	Prolongs PR	4.5–12	40, 80, 120 or 120, 180, 240 SR	40–120 mg every 8 hr or 120–360 mg SR once a day	480	125–400 ng/ml
Diltiazem	Cardizem	Prolongs PR	3.5	30, 60, 90, 120 or 180, 240, 300 CD	30–120 mg 3–4 times/day or 120–480 mg CD once a day	480	Not useful

s, sulfate; g, gluconate; SR, sustained release; CD, continuous delivery.

[a] It may also be important to measure, especially in patients in cardiac or renal failure, the level of the active metabolite of procainamide, N-acetylprocainamide (NAPA).

[b] Other β-blockers are equally effective (see text).

[c] Elimination is mainly in the urine. Doses should be lowered in patients with renal insufficiency.

Table 43.2. Currently Available β-Blockers

Agent	β-Blocking Plasma Levels	Elimination Half-Life (hr)	Active Metabolites	Predominant Route of Elimination	β₁-Blockade Potency Ratio (Propranolol = 1.0)	Relative β₁-Selectivity	Available Strengths (mg)	Usual Maintenance Dose
Acebutolol (Sectral)	0.2–2.0 μg/ml	3–4	Yes	HM	0.3	+	200, 400	200–600 mg twice daily
Labetalol (Normodyne, Trandate)	0.7–3.0 μg/ml	5–6	No	HM	0.3	0	100, 200, 300	100–600 mg twice daily
Atenolol (Tenormin)	200–500 ng/ml	6–9	No	RE (mostly unchanged)	1.0	+	50, 100	50–100 mg daily
Metoprolol (Lopressor and Toprol XL)	50–100 ng/ml	3–4	No	HM	1.0	+	50, 100 or 50, 100, 200 XL	50–100 mg twice daily or 50–200 mg XL once daily
Nadolol (Corgard)	50–100 ng/ml	14–24	No	RE	1.0	0	40, 80, 120, 160	40–50 mg every day
Pindolol (Visken)	50–100 ng/ml	3–4	No	RE (40% unchanged and HM)	6.0	0	5, 10	5–20 mg 3 times/day
Propranolol (Inderal)	50–100 ng/ml	3.5–6	Yes	HM	1.0	0	10, 20, 40, 60, 80 and 60, 80, 120, 180 mg long acting	40–80 mg 4 times/day or 120–160 mg long acting once a day
Timolol (Blocadren)	5–10 ng/ml	4	No	RE (20% unchanged and HM)	6.0	0	10	20 mg twice daily

Modified from Frishman WH: Beta-adrenoceptor antagonists: new drugs and new indications. *N Engl J Med* 305:550, 1981.
HM, hepatic metabolism; *RE*, renal excretion.

Table 43.3. Adverse Effects of Antiarrhythmic Drugs

Drug	Cardiac		Noncardiac	
	Common	Uncommon	Common	Uncommon
Class IA				
Quinidine	Decreased digoxin excretion (may precipitate digitoxicity)	Ventricular arrhythmias, myocardial depression, hypotension	Nausea, diarrhea, tinnitus, vertigo, rash, fever	Hepatic dysfunction, thrombocytopenia, hemolytic anemia
Procainamide	None	Myocardial depression	Nausea, vomiting	Agranulocytosis, lupus-like syndrome
Disopyramide	Myocardial depression (should be used with caution in patients with severe or poorly compensated congestive heart failure)	Severe hypotension in absence of known heart disease	Anticholinergic effects, especially urinary retention, dry mouth, blurred vision, constipation, aggravation of narrow angle glaucoma	Acute psychoses, cholestasis
Class IB				
Tocainide	None	Ventricular arrhythmias	Dizziness, paresthesias, tremor, nausea, vomiting, and sweating	Rashes, convulsions
Mexiletine	None	Increased frequency of ventricular arrhythmias	Nausea, vomiting, indigestion, dizziness, tremor	Sleep disturbances, fatigue
Phenytoin (diphenylhydantoin)	None	Heart block	Cerebellar-vestibular effects, especially ataxia, nystagmus, vertigo; nausea, lethargy, seizures, rashes	Pseudolymphoma, megaloblastic anemia, peripheral neuropathy
Class IC				
Flecainide	Increased frequency of ventricular arrhythmias, myocardial depression; use with caution in patients with ejection fraction < 40%	New supraventricular arrhythmias, congestive heart failure	Dizziness, visual disturbances, dyspnea, nausea, tremor	Constipation, edema, abdominal pain
Propafenone	Conduction delay	?Congestive heart failure	Unusual taste, constipation	Nausea, blurred vision, dizziness

Table 43.3. Continued

Drug	Cardiac Common	Cardiac Uncommon	Noncardiac Common	Noncardiac Uncommon
Class II Propranolol[a]	Bradycardia, myocardial depression	Anginal syndrome may worsen if drug suddenly discontinued	Fatigue, nausea, vomiting, depression, impotence; potentiates bronchospasm in patients with asthma	Peripheral vascular insufficiency, hyperglycemia, alopecia
Class III Amiodarone	Bradycardia, increased heart block, increased digoxin concentration	Ventricular arrhythmias	Nausea, corneal microcrystallization, thyroid function abnormalities, decreased pulmonary diffusing capacity	Blue tint of exposed skin, pulmonary fibrosis
Sotalol	Bradycardia, fatigue, increased QTc	Torsades de pointes in 3-5%	Dyspnea	
Class IV Verapamil	Bradycardia, prolongation of P-R interval, peripheral edema, increased digoxin level	Precipitation of congestive heart failure or pulmonary edema, severe hypotension, heart block	Dizziness, headache, constipation, nausea	Confusion, sleep disorders
Diltiazem	Bradycardia, prolongation of P-R interval	Heart block, increased digoxin level	Dizziness, headache, constipation	Rash, itching

[a] Other β-blocking agents have the same adverse effects, although bronchospasm and peripheral vascular insufficiency may be less likely with use of β-specific agents (see Table 43.2).

3. Frequent episodes of supraventricular tachycardia, thought due to pre-excitation (see below)

SPECIFIC ARRHYTHMIAS

A. Sinus tachycardia
  1. Sinus rhythm at a rate of >100 beats/minute
  2. Usually reflects an increased cardiac output to meet increased metabolic demands
  3. Regular rapid pulse and heart rate
  4. ECG: P wave is normal and precedes each QRS complex; P-R interval is normal for rate
  5. Treatment: none, or treat underlying condition

B. Sinus bradycardia
  1. Sinus rhythm at a rate of <60 beats/minute
  2. Can reflect good physical conditioning, increased vagal tone, hypersensitive carotid sinus, parasympathomimetic drugs (e.g., tranquilizers, phenothiazines, digitalis), sympatholytic drugs (e.g., reserpine, methyldopa, clonidine, β-blockers)
  3. Regular slow pulse and heart rate
  4. ECG: P wave is normal and precedes each QRS complex; P-R interval is normal for rate
  5. Treatment: none, or if symptomatic (e.g., syncope), stop offending drugs, if any, or implant pacemaker

C. Sick sinus syndrome
  1. Periods of inappropriate sinus bradycardia that may precede or follow supraventricular tachyarrhythmias; also varying degrees of sinoatrial block
  2. Much more common over age 60
  3. Many patients asymptomatic; symptoms, if present, are palpitations, light-headedness, syncope
  4. Cardiac examination normal unless done during bradyarrhythmia or tachyarrhythmia
  5. ECG: normal or sinus bradycardia; often, there are varying degrees of sinoatrial block (varying P-P intervals); sometimes, sinus arrest (absent P waves with a junctional escape rhythm); symptomatic patients with normal ECGs need ambulatory ECGs
  6. Treatment: symptomatic patients from bradyarrhythmias need a pacemaker; symptomatic patients from tachyarrhythmias need, in addition, digitalis or a β-blocker; patients with uncontrolled tachyarrhythmias need anticoagulation

D. Premature atrial and junctional contractions
  1. Commonly seen in well people, may be induced by exertion or stress but may progress to atrial flutter or fibrillation in patients with underlying heart or lung disease
  2. Patients usually unaware of contractions but may be noted as palpitations
  3. May cause slight irregularity in pulse or heart beat
  4. ECG: premature atrial contractions are characterized by morphologically abnormal P waves followed by premature morphologically normal QRS complex, but often, premature impulse not conducted or aberrantly conducted; premature junctional contractions are characterized by retrograde P waves

(negative in leads II, III, aVf) that may follow, be hidden in, or precede morphologically normal but premature QRS complexes

5. Treatment: usually no treatment necessary; rarely digitalis or a β-blocker needed if there are frequent annoying palpitations or if there is a concern (see above) about progression to atrial fibrillation

E. Paroxysmal supraventricular tachycardia (SVT)
   1. Heart rates of 120–220/minute triggered by a premature impulse generated between sinus node and AV node
   2. In 50%, heart is otherwise normal; if there is heart disease, most common forms are pre-excitation syndrome (see below), mitral valve prolapse (Chapter 44), atrial septal defect; nonparoxysmal atrial tachycardia with block a common manifestation of digitoxicity
   3. Patients are almost always aware of rapid heart rate; if coexistent heart disease, may be associated with dyspnea or chest pains
   4. Attacks may be spontaneous or follow exertion, stress, caffeine, or nicotine
   5. Frequency quite variable
   6. Rapid regular pulse and heart rate
   7. ECG: rapid regular heart rate, a fixed relationship between a P wave and the QRS complex (P wave may be buried in or follow QRS)
   8. Treatment: increase vagal tone (e.g., Valsalva); then try carotid sinus massage (if no carotid bruits) one side at a time; then try drugs (e.g., adenosine 6–12 mg i.v.) — best done in an emergency facility
   9. Prevention: digoxin in most; verapamil or β-blocker in hypertensives or patients with hypertrophic cardiomyopathy

F. Multifocal atrial tachycardia
   1. Chaotic supraventricular arrhythmia, usually seen in patients with serious underlying disease, especially chronic obstructive pulmonary disease (COPD)
   2. ECG: varying P wave morphology, varying P-R intervals, heart rate 100–200/minute; normal QRS complex, preceded by a P wave
   3. Treat underlying disease; verapamil or diltiazem may be used to control heart rate

G. Atrial fibrillation
   1. Rapid uncoordinated atrial impulses (300–500/minute) with ventricular rate, untreated, between 150 and 200 beats/minute
   2. May occur paroxysmally in otherwise-normal people; often induced by sinus tachycardia, premature atrial contractions, SVT, exertion, stress, alcohol, nicotine, or caffeine
   3. Major associated noncardiac illness is hyperthyroidism
   4. Predisposing heart disease: hypertensive, atherosclerotic, rheumatic heart disease; sick sinus syndrome
   5. Common symptoms: palpitations, fatigue
   6. Irregularly, irregular heart beat and pulse with variation in intensity of sounds
   7. ECG: irregular fibrillatory atrial activity at rates between 300 and 500/minute; irregularly, irregular ventricular rhythm at rates at onset between 150 and 200/minute (unless there is AV nodal disease, in which case rates are slower)

8. All patients should have thyroid function studies (Chapter 57) and a two-dimensional (2-D) echocardiogram
9. Treatment
   a) Remove precipitating factors (e.g., alcohol)
   b) Specific treatment indicated if there is a rapid ventricular response, especially associated with symptoms; if there is underlying severe heart disease, hospitalize for cardioversion
   c) If there is a rapid ventricular response and patient is asymptomatic or mildly symptomatic, digitalize; if rate is still too high, prescribe verapamil (80 mg 3–4 times/day), diltiazem (30–60 mg 3–4 times/day), or propranolol (20–30 mg 4 times/day)
   d) If there is a slow ventricular response, specific therapy (pacemaker) is not needed unless there is evidence of heart failure and bradycardia
   e) Patients with chronic atrial fibrillation should be anticoagulated with warfarin (Chapter 37)

H. Atrial flutter
   1. Relatively coordinated rapid atrial activity with rates of about 300/minute with regular ventricular response, usually at about 300/minute
   2. Almost always seen in association with underlying disease: ischemic or rheumatic heart disease, congestive cardiomyopathy, atrial septal defect, mitral value disease, COPD, thyrotoxicosis
   3. Patients are usually aware of rapid heart rate; heart rate and pulse are rapid and regular
   4. ECG: rapid regular sawtooth flutter waves at about 300/minute; no P waves; rapid regular ventricular rate, usually at about 300 minute; QRS complex normal
   5. Treatment
      a) Hospitalize for cardioversion
      b) Digitalis to prevent recurrence; if not effective alone, add propranolol (20–40 mg every 6 hours) or quinidine (200–300 mg every 6 hours)

I. Ventricular premature beats
   1. Occur commonly in healthy people but are also associated with underlying heart disease
   2. Frequency may be increased by caffeine, alcohol, sympathomimetic drugs, tricyclic antidepressants, phenothiazines, hypokalemia, hypoxia, stress
   3. Usually abolished by exercise in otherwise-normal people
   4. Patients may be asymptomatic or experience palpitations
   5. ECG: premature ventricular response with a morphologically abnormal QRS complex
   6. Treatment
      a) Healthy, asymptomatic young people need no treatment
      b) Healthy, symptomatic young people need reassurance, possibly a trial of β-blockers
      c) Symptomatic patients with ischemic heart disease should be referred to a cardiologist for consideration of amiodarone or sotalol or an implantable defibrillator
      d) Patients in heart failure should be treated before prescribing antiarrhythmic therapy

J. Heart block
  1. Right bundle branch block (RBBB)
     a) Modest prolongation (0.12 second) of the QRS complex (the terminal vector)
     b) RBBB sometimes seen in normal people, more often associated with, e.g., interatrial septal defect or hypertensive or ischemic disease
  2. Left bundle branch block (LBBB)
     a) Marked prolongation (0.12–0.16 second) of the QRS complex
     b) Almost always signifies heart disease, usually ischemic or cardiomyopathy
  3. Hemiblocks
     a) Left anterior (LAH): marked left-axis deviation on the ECG; normal duration of QRS complex; same causes as LBBB
     b) Left posterior (LPH): marked right-axis deviation on the ECG; normal duration of QRS complex; same causes as LBBB, LAH
  4. Bifascicular blocks
     a) RBBB with LAH or RBBB with LPH
     b) Refer patient with a history of syncope or light-headedness to a cardiologist to determine need for electrophysiological study or for a pacemaker
  5. First-degree heart block
     a) Prolonged P-R interval
     b) Usually due to degenerative, ischemic, or inflammatory changes in AV conducting system or to digitalis
     c) No associated symptoms; first heart sound increased in intensity
     d) No treatment
  6. Second-degree AV block
     a) Some, but not all, P waves are followed by QRS complexes
     b) Mobitz type I or Wenckebach: progressive lengthening of the P-R interval until P wave blocked completely
        1) May be caused by anything that increases vagal tone; may be seen transiently in normal people or due to some conditions that cause first-degree block
        2) Patients often asymptomatic, but if vagal tone is increased, symptomatic bradycardia may ensue
        3) Asymptomatic patients need no treatment; if symptomatic from bradycardia, drugs such as digitalis and propranolol should be stopped; if symptoms continue, consider a pacemaker
     c) Mobitz type II: failure to conduct a P wave, either randomly or in a fixed ratio
        1) No influence of vagal tone
        2) Asymptomatic or symptomatic bradycardia
        3) All patients should have a permanent pacemaker
  7. Third-degree (complete) heart block: total failure of conduction of impulses from the atria through the AV junction; QRS complexes may be normal or abnormal; rate is slow, dependent on site of block
     a) Most commonly due to congenital cardiac defects in young; in older people, to degenerative changes in the conduction

system; also may be due to infiltrative, inflammatory, or ischemic disease

b) Heart block a subcategory of AV dissociation in which atria and ventricles are depolarized independently (if no complete heart block, ventricular rate usually greater than atrial rate)

c) Major symptom is sudden loss of consciousness, the result of asystole or of ventricular tachyarrhythmia — usually patient awakens quickly, but occasionally seizures or even death occurs

d) Physical findings: slow rate; variation in intensity of first heart sound, in systolic blood pressure, in intensity of murmur; appearance of jugular cannon waves

e) Treatment: permanent pacemaker

K. Pre-excitation syndrome
1. Associated with accessory pathways of impulse conduction into the ventricles [e.g., Wolff-Parkinson-White (WPW) syndrome]
2. Patients may be asymptomatic or have episodic supraventricular arrhythmias
3. ECG: typically short P-R interval; WPW syndrome characterized also by wide QRS complex initiated by a delta wave
4. Treatment
   a) None for asymptomatic patients; treat symptomatic patients (tachyarrhythmias) by vagal maneuvers (e.g., Valsalva)
   b) If QRS complex normal during arrhythmia, treat with atenolol 50–100 mg/day or
   c) Amiodarone 100–200 mg/day, the most effective drug for WPW
   d) Patients with symptomatic supraventricular arrhythmias with wide QRS complexes should be hospitalized for intravenous antiarrhythmics and for catheter ablation of the accessory pathway

L. Long Q-T interval syndrome
1. Inherited: autosomal recessive (with deafness) or dominant
2. Predisposes to ventricular tachyarrhythmias, which often cause syncope and may cause sudden death
3. Treatment is β-blockade

44/ COMMON CARDIAC DISORDERS REVEALED BY AUSCULTATION OF THE HEART

AORTIC STENOSIS
A. Epidemiology and etiology
1. Below age 30, most likely a congenitally stenotic unicuspid valve
2. Between ages 30 and 65, most commonly a bicuspid valve that has calcified
3. Rheumatic heart disease accounts for a minority of cases
4. Most cases in patients over age 65 are due to degeneration and sclerosis of the valve
5. More common in women except in the elderly, where prevalence the same in both sexes

B. Symptoms
1. Usually asymptomatic until late in course
2. Earliest symptoms are easy fatigability and excessive dyspnea after unusual exertion
3. Syncope or near-syncope with effort, angina, or dyspnea on usual exertion are indicative of severe obstruction
4. Sudden death in a minority
5. Once symptoms develop, death occurs within a few years unless problem is corrected

C. Physical findings (Table 44.1)
1. Absent S_2 when the valve is rigid
2. Paradoxical splitting of S_2 (in the absence of left bundle branch block), a sign of severity
3. Small pulse pressure (<30 mm Hg) also a sign of severity
4. S_4 indicates severe obstruction in patients under age 40
5. Early diastolic murmur of aortic insufficiency heard in 30–40%

D. Management
1. Reassess asymptomatic patients yearly
2. Avoid undue exertion
3. Antibiotic prophylaxis before dental or surgical procedures (Chapter 69)
4. Treat atrial arrhythmias (uncommon) aggressively
5. When to refer: Table 44.2
6. Value replacement usually recommended in all symptomatic patients and in asymptomatic patients with severe obstruction

HYPERTROPHIC CARDIOMYOPATHY
A. Definition: disease of cardiac muscle in which ventricular septum is thickened disproportionately compared with free wall of left ventricle
1. Asymmetry, one of differences from aortic stenosis (Table 44.1)
2. Left ventricle hypercontractile

B. Epidemiology and etiology
1. Inherited (usually autosomal dominant) in 60%
2. Men and women affected equally

Table 44.1. Comparison of Valvular Aortic Stenosis and Hypertrophic Cardiomyopathy

	Valvular Aortic Stenosis	Hypertrophic Cardiomyopathy
Symptoms	Dyspnea, angina, syncope, or near-syncope	Dyspnea, angina, syncope, or near-syncope
Signs	Systolic ejection murmur loudest at aortic area or at apex; louder if patient squats	Systolic ejection murmur loudest at left lower sternal border; louder if patient stands or performs a Valsalva maneuver
	A_2 may not be audible	A_2 is usually audible
	S_4 is common	S_4 is very common
	Ejection sounds are common	Ejection sounds are uncommon
	Carotid upstroke is delayed	Carotid upstroke is brisk
ECG	LVH and strain pattern	LVH and strain pattern; Q waves in inferior and lateral leads are common
Chest x-ray	LVH is a late sign	LVH may occur but unpredictably
	Aortic valve is always calcified (may be seen only on fluoroscopy)	Aortic valve is not calcified
	Ascending aorta may be dilated	Ascending aorta is not dilated
Echocardiogram	Characteristic echoes of valvular calcification and of valvular stenosis	Disproportionate septal hypertrophy, systolic anterior displacement of mitral valve

LVH, left ventricular hypertrophy.

Table 44.2. Indications for Referral of Patients With Aortic Stenosis

If there is a question about the diagnosis
If the patient is symptomatic
If the asymptomatic patient has signs of severe obstruction:
    Physical signs
        Small pulse pressure (<30 mm Hg)
        Late peak to systolic murmur
        Diminished A_2
        Paradoxical splitting of A_2
    ECG
        Left ventricular hypertrophy
        ST depression, T-wave inversion
    Chest x-ray
        Concentric left ventricular hypertrophy
    Echocardiogram
        Concentric left ventricular hypertrophy
        Calcification of aortic valve in patients under 60
        Doppler-calculated gradient > 50 mm Hg or valve area < 1.0 cm²

C. Symptoms (Table 44.1)
    1. Most patients asymptomatic (and have an excellent prognosis)
    2. Dyspnea most common symptom
    3. Much more likely to be induced by exertion
    4. Sudden death in 3–4% a year of symptomatic patients — no way to identify patients at risk
D. Physical findings: Table 44.1
E. Laboratory findings: Table 44.1
F. Management

1. Reduce hypercontractile state of left ventricle: verapamil 80–120 mg 4 times/day unless there is evidence of heart failure; alternatively, prescribe a β-blocker (e.g., propranolol 10–80 mg 4 times/day)
2. Avoid digitalis, vasodilators, β-adrenergic stimulants, diuretics
3. Avoid undue exertion (even if asymptomatic)
4. Antibiotic prophylaxis before dental and surgical procedures (Chapter 69)
5. Symptomatic patients refractory to drugs should be referred to a cardiologist for consideration of dual chamber pacing

ATRIAL SEPTAL DEFECT

A. Epidemiology and etiology
   1. Inherited
   2. Female:male ratio of 1.5–3.5:1
   3. Occasionally associated with other cardiac abnormalities
B. Symptoms
   1. Usually asymptomatic until third or fourth decade; virtually all patients are symptomatic by age 60
   2. Usually dyspnea on exertion, fatigue, palpitations
   3. Eventual pulmonary hypertension in 15%; cyanosis at that point
C. Physical findings
   1. Wide fixed split of second heart sound
   2. Soft-blowing systolic pulmonic ejection murmur; also a middiastolic flow murmur is common
   3. Precordium may be hyperdynamic with a palpable S_3
   4. Clubbing and cyanosis and accentuated P_2 if there is pulmonary hypertension
   5. Late in disease, signs of right-sided heart failure (edema, distended neck veins, hepatomegaly)
D. Laboratory findings
   1. ECG: incomplete right bundle branch block in 90–95%; atrial fibrillation common
   2. Chest x-ray: increased pulmonary vascularity with a prominent main pulmonary artery and increased heart size
   3. Echocardiogram: right ventricular enlargement and paradoxical motion of the ventricular septum; Doppler echocardiogram will show defect
E. Management
   1. Refer to a cardiologist for cardiac catheterization (surgical repair indicated if pulmonary blood flow is more than 1½ times systemic flow)
   2. Endocarditis prophylaxis unnecessary

MITRAL REGURGITATION

A. Chronic
   1. Epidemiology and etiology: rheumatic fever in only 5–15%; otherwise, papillary muscle necrosis is due to ischemic heart disease, an inherited (e.g., Marfan's syndrome) or acquired (e.g., lupus) disease of connective tissue, to idiopathic valvular calcification, or to congenital maldevelopment of the valve
   2. Symptoms
      a) Patients may be asymptomatic for years
      b) Appear gradually: dyspnea, fatigue, palpitations

3. Physical findings
   a) High-pitched holosystolic murmur, loudest at apex, radiates to the axilla, sometimes to the back and to the base of the heart
   b) Murmur diminished on standing or during Valsalva, intensified on squatting
   c) Precordium hyperdynamic, usually with an S_3 and a soft S_1, if regurgitation severe
   d) S_4, loud P_2, right ventricular heave if there is pulmonary hypertension
   e) Late in disease: edema, hepatomegaly, distended neck veins, hepatojugular reflux
4. Laboratory findings
   a) ECG: signs of left atrial enlargement, sometimes atrial fibrillation; if process is severe, signs of left ventricular hypertrophy; signs of right ventricular hypertrophy less often
   b) Chest x-ray: left ventricular and left atrial enlargement
   c) Echocardiogram: left atrial and left ventricular enlargement; two-dimensional (2-D) echocardiogram can define etiology; Doppler echocardiogram can detect regurgitation and estimate severity
5. Management
   a) Antibiotic prophylaxis before dental and surgical procedures (Chapter 41)
   b) If atrial fibrillation, attempt to restore sinus rhythm if possible (Chapter 43)
   c) Arteriolar vasodilator (see Chapter 45) useful
   d) When to refer: Table 44.3
   e) Valve replacement likely to be recommended in symptomatic patients

B. Acute
   1. Epidemiology and etiology: most often due to rupture of the chordae tendineae, usually due to myxomatous degeneration of the valve
   2. Symptoms: severe dyspnea at rest
   3. Physical findings
      a) Harsh holosystolic murmur, loudest at apex
      b) Sometimes, an early or middiastolic murmur
      c) S_3 almost always; S_4 commonly
      d) Rales, edema, distended neck veins
   4. Laboratory findings
      a) Chest x-ray: marked pulmonary congestion

Table 44.3. Indications for Referral of Patients With Mitral Regurgitation

Progressive dyspnea or fatigue

Development of supraventricular arrhythmia

Mildly symptomatic or asymptomatic patient with progressive cardiac enlargement

Uncertainty about the diagnosis

Acute mitral regurgitation

Patients with mitral valve prolapse who have symptomatic arrhythmias, symptomatic mitral regurgitation, infectious endocarditis, or transient ischemic attacks

   b) Echocardiogram: increased systolic motion of the valve; 2-D
      echocardiogram may show flailing chordae or marked prolapse
5. Management: hospitalization, consideration for early repair

MITRAL VALVE PROLAPSE

A. Epidemiology and etiology
   1. Occurs in women more than in men
   2. In most people appears to be inherited (autosomal dominant)
   3. "Secondary prolapse:" associated with coronary artery disease,
      hypertrophic cardiomyopathy, atrial septal defect
   4. Associated with inherited disorders of connective tissue
B. Symptoms
   1. Most patients are asymptomatic; less often they have palpitations,
      dyspnea, or chest pain (usually sharp, lancinating, left-sided,
      unrelated to exertion)
   2. If associated with mitral regurgitation (15% of cases), symptoms
      of that (see above)
   3. Sudden death, rare
C. Physical findings
   1. Midsystolic click, best heard lower left sternal border
   2. Very often click is followed by a crescendo left systolic murmur
   3. If mitral regurgitation, signs of that (see above)
   4. Common association with skeletal abnormalities (e.g., scoliosis,
      pectus excavatum)
D. Laboratory findings
   1. ECG: usually normal, may show nonspecific ST-T changes,
      sometimes, long Q-T interval; a variety of arrhythmias may occur
      (premature ventricular contractions, paroxysmal supraventricular
      tachycardia)
   2. Echocardiogram: M mode usually diagnostic
E. Management
   1. Asymptomatic patients need no treatment
   2. Symptomatic patients should receive antibiotic prophylaxis before
      dental or surgical procedures if there is evidence of mitral
      regurgitation
   3. If symptoms suggest arrhythmia, ambulatory ECG (Holter) to
      determine severity, need for treatment (often a β-blocker)
   4. If chest pain, β-blocker (e.g., atenolol 25–50 mg/day)

MITRAL STENOSIS

A. Epidemiology and etiology
   1. Most common cause is rheumatic fever (but history of rheumatic
      fever in only 50%)
   2. Two-thirds are women
B. Symptoms
   1. Usually not before fourth decade
   2. Variable
   3. Pulmonary congestion causes many symptoms: dyspnea,
      orthopnea, paroxysmal nocturnal dyspnea, hemoptysis
   4. Pulmonary hypertension eventually develops: edema, distended
      neck veins, tender liver, ascites
   5. Atrial fibrillation in 40–50%
C. Physical findings

    1. Middiastolic rumbling murmur with presystolic accentuation —
       best heard at apex
    2. Loud S_1 and opening snap
    3. Loud P_2 and right ventricular heave late
D. Laboratory findings
    1. ECG: left atrial enlargement, signs of right ventricular
       enlargement late
    2. Chest x-ray: left atrial enlargement, right atrial and ventricular
       enlargement late
    3. Echocardiogram: diagnostic; severity can be assessed by 2-D and
       Doppler echocardiograms
E. Management
    1. Asymptomatic patients need only prophylaxis for endocarditis
       (Chapter 69)
    2. Mildly symptomatic patients: diuretics and sodium restriction
       (Chapter 45)
    3. Atrial fibrillation: see Chapter 43
    4. When to refer: Table 44.4
    5. Symptomatic patients usually will be offered mitral
       commissurotomy, a prosthetic valve, or nonsurgical valvulotomy

AORTIC REGURGITATION

A. Epidemiology and etiology
    1. Rheumatic fever accounts for 29% of cases
    2. Congenital disease due to a bicuspid valve
    3. Endocarditis the most common cause of acute regurgitation
    4. Dilation of the aortic root: idiopathic in 12% of chronic cases; if
       acute, usually a dissecting aneurysm
    5. Less commonly, rheumatoid disorders
B. Symptoms
    1. If chronic regurgitation, no symptoms for up to 20 years or only
       mild dyspnea on excitation; when symptoms develop (e.g., more
       severe dyspnea, orthopnea, paroxysmal nocturnal dyspnea),
       situation is ominous
    2. Marked dyspnea and weakness of rapid onset if there is acute
       regurgitation
C. Physical findings
    1. Chronic regurgitation
       a) High-frequency early diastolic decrescendo murmur, best heard

---

Table 44.4. Indications for Referral of Patients With Mitral Stenosis

Progressive dyspnea or recurrent attacks of pulmonary edema
Symptomatic disease of the aortic and/or tricuspid valve
Women, whether symptomatic or not, who wish to become or who are pregnant
Patients whose symptoms have developed recently who have no history of rheumatic fever
    (to rule out an atrial myxoma)
Patients with chronic obstructive lung disease
Patients with angina pectoris
Patients with evidence of pulmonary hypertension (including right ventricular hypertrophy)
Patients with new onset of atrial fibrillation

Modified from Brandenburg RO, Fuster V, Giuliani ER: Valvular heart disease. When should the patient be referred? *Pract Cardiol* 5:50, 1979.

Table 44.5.   Indications for Referral of Patients With Aortic Regurgitation

Uncertainty about the diagnosis
Symptomatic chronic aortic incompetence (dyspnea, fatigue, angina)
Acute aortic incompetence
Asymptomatic patients with evidence of severe chronic aortic incompetence: widened pulse
    pressure, holodiastolic murmur, left ventricular hypertrophy, progressive cardiac
    enlargement

Modified from Brandenburg RO, Fuster V, Giuliani ER: Valvular heart disease. When should the patient be referred? *Pract Cardiol* 5:50, 1979.

Table 44.6.   Indications for Referral of Patients With Prosthetic Valves

Progressive symptoms of congestive heart failure
Progressive cardiac enlargement
Changes in prosthetic heart sounds
Pregnancy or the desire to become pregnant
Embolization
Endocarditis

at aortic area and at left sternal border (duration correlates
with severity)
b) Often a harsh systolic ejection murmur at base
c) Possibly a loud apical diastolic murmur (Austin-Flint murmur)
d) Wide pulse pressure
e) Changes in the peripheral pulse (e.g., water-hammer pulse,
"pistol shot" over femoral artery) and bobbing of head with
heartbeat
2. Acute regurgitation
a) Regurgitant diastolic murmur is lower pitched and shorter
b) Pulse pressure normal
c) Signs of left and right heart failure
D. Laboratory findings
1. ECG: if chronic regurgitation, signs of left ventricular
hypertrophy; if acute regurgitation, nonspecific ST-T wave changes
2. Chest x-ray: degree of enlargement of heart depends on duration
and severity of process
3. Echocardiogram: can assess left ventricular function and
hypertrophy, degree of dilation of the aortic root, severity of
stenosis (also assessable by Doppler echocardiogram)
E. Management
1. Asymptomatic patients need not be treated
2. Prophylaxis for endocarditis during dental or surgical procedures
(Chapter 69)
3. If heart failure, digitalis, diuretics, afterload reducing agents
(Chapter 45)
4. When to refer: Table 44.5
5. Valve replacement indicated in symptomatic patients

PATIENT WITH A PROSTHETIC VALVE
A. Complications
1. Thromboembolic phenomena
2. Perivalvular leakage resulting in regurgitation
3. Tissue valve degeneration

      4. Prosthetic valve endocarditis
B. Physical and laboratory findings
      1. Mechanical findings produce loud opening and closing clicks: in aortic position, loud metallic S_2; in mitral position, loud S_1
      2. All valves produce systolic ejection murmurs; Bjork-Shiley mechanical valve produces diastolic murmur in the mitral position
      3. Change in baseline sounds a reliable sign of valvular dysfunction
      4. Echocardiogram (including Doppler) often of help in assessment
C. Management
      1. Patients with mechanical valves must be anticoagulated indefinitely; with tissue valves, for 6 weeks postoperatively
      2. Endocarditis prophylaxis (Chapter 69)
      3. When to refer: Table 44.6

45/ HEART FAILURE

DIAGNOSTIC PROCESS

A. Causes
1. Selected examples of basic mechanisms: Table 45.1
2. Precipitating causes: Table 45.2
3. Systolic versus diastolic dysfunction (see below)
   a) Systolic: inability of the ventricles to eject a normal volume of blood [reduced ejection fraction (EF)]
   b) Diastolic: inability of the ventricles to accept a normal volume of blood (increased left ventricular end-diastolic pressure)

B. Assessment of functional capacity: Table 45.3

C. History
1. Most common symptom is dyspnea, often with orthopnea
2. Dry hacking cough common
3. Paroxysmal nocturnal dyspnea characteristic of poorly compensated chronic heart failure
4. Fatigue a common complaint
5. Edema and/or weight gain
6. Chest pain (due to myocardial ischemia)
7. Nocturia
8. Mild anxiety and depression common
9. Swelling and tenderness in the right upper quadrant of the abdomen (hepatic congestion)

D. Physical findings

Table 45.1. Causes of Heart Failure

Increased workload to which the heart cannot accommodate

High output states
  Hyperthyroidism[a]
  Anemia[a]
  Systemic arteriovenous fistulas[a]
  Certain dermatological disorders (e.g., psoriasis, erythroderma)[a]
Valvular regurgitation or left to right shunts[a]
Increased impedance to injection
  Systemic hypertension[a]
  Pulmonary hypertension
  Pulmonic or aortic stenosis[a]

Disorder of myocardium so that the heart is unable to accommodate normal workloads

Cardiomyopathies [viral, familial, drug-induced (cytotoxic chemotherapy, chronic use of amphetamines, cocaine)]
Myocardial infarction

Restriction of ventricular filling

Pericardial constriction or effusion[a]
Atrial myxoma
Mitral and tricuspid valvular stenosis[a]
Increased ventricular stiffness
  Infiltrative myocardial disease (e.g., amyloid, hemochromatosis)
  Ventricular hypertrophy
  Hypertrophic cardiomyopathy

Adapted from Weisfeldt ML: Congestive heart failure: pathophysiology and the evaluation of ventricular function. In: Harvey AM, Johns RJ, McKusick VA, et al (eds): *The Principles and Practice of Medicine*. New York, Appleton-Century-Crofts, 1984.
[a] Indicates causes of heart failure that are potentially treatable by specific therapy.

Table 45.2.   Precipitating Causes of Heart Failure

Factors decreasing myocardial efficiency
   Myocardial infarction
   Ischemia
   Arrhythmia
   Hypoxia
   Alcohol and other toxic substances
   Recent initiation of a β-blocking drug
   Discontinuation of a cardiac glycoside
   Myocardial depressant drugs [e.g., verapamil, disopyramide (Norpace), adriamycin]
   Pericardial tamponade
   Myocardial infections (e.g., bacterial endocarditis, myocarditis, parasitic infection)
   Vasculitis
Factors increasing cardiac load
   Noncompliance with low salt diet
   Uncontrolled systemic hypertension
   Systemic infection
   Psychological stress
   Exercise, especially in extremes of heat or humidity
   Discontinuing diuretics, antihypertensive drugs, or afterload-reducing agents
   Drugs that retain or contain sodium
   Infection
   Anemia
   Pulmonary embolism
   Thyrotoxicosis
   Acute valvular dysfunction

   1. Uncompensated heart failure
      a) Increased heart size
      b) Sinus tachycardia
      c) S_3 the most specific sign
      d) Rales
      e) Neck vein distention and hepatojugular reflux
      f) Peripheral pitting edema
   2. Compensated heart failure
      a) Increased heart size
      b) S_4
      c) Soft systolic murmur at point of maximal impulse is
         commonly heard
E. Laboratory findings
   1. Chest x-ray
      a) Cardiac enlargement
      b) Pulmonary congestion
         1) Cephalization of blood flow
         2) As severity increases, interstitial edema, then alveolar edema
            and pleural effusion
   2. ECG
      a) No diagnostic changes
      b) May reflect underlying disease (e.g., hypertensive or ischemic
         heart disease)
      c) Signs of left ventricular hypertrophy common
      d) Conduction abnormalities (Chapter 43) are common, especially
         left bundle branch block

Table 45.3.   Assessment of Functional Capacity

New York Heart Association Classification[a]	Severity of Symptoms[b]	Maximum Oxygen Uptake (ml/mm/kg)[b]	Goldman's Specific Activity Scale (METs)[c]
I Patients with cardiac disease but without resulting limitations of physical activity. Ordinary physical activity does not cause undue fatigue, palpitations, dyspnea, or anginal pain.	None to mild	>20	10 METs
II Patients with cardiac disease resulting in slight limitation of physical activity. They are comfortable at rest. Ordinary physical activity results in fatigue, palpitations, dyspnea, or anginal pain.	Mild to moderate	16–20	5–6 METs
III Patients with cardiac disease that results in marked limitation of physical activity and causes fatigue, palpitations, dyspnea, or anginal pain.	Moderate to severe	10–16	3.6–4.2 METs
IV Patients with cardiac disease that results in inability to carry on any physical activity without discomfort. Symptoms of cardiac insufficiency or of the anginal syndrome may be present even at rest. If any physical activity is undertaken, discomfort is increased.	Severe	<10	2–2.3 METs

METs, metabolic equivalents of activity where 1 MET equals 3.5 mg of O_2/kg/minute at rest.
[a] The Criteria Committee of the New York Heart Association, Inc: *Diseases of the Heart and Blood Vessels, Nomenclature and Criteria for Diagnosis*, 6th ed. Boston, Little, Brown, 1964.
[b] Adapted from Weber KT, Janiski JS: *Cardiopulmonary Exercise Testing*. Philadelphia, WB Saunders, 1986.
[c] Adapted from Goldman L, Hashimoto B, Cook EF, Loscalzo A: Comparative reproducibility and validity of systems for assessing cardiovascular functional class: advantages of new specific activity scale. *Circulation* 64:1227, 1981.

3. Echocardiogram
   a) Reliable technique [two-dimensional (2-D)] for determining ventricular size and thickness, presence of valvular abnormalities and of pericardial effusion
   b) EF can be estimated
   c) Useful in distinguishing diastolic from systolic dysfunction (see above) — 2-D echocardiogram with pulsed Doppler evaluation of mitral flow velocity
4. Radionuclide angiography ["gated blood pool scan" or multigated acquisition study (MUGA)]
   a) Technique for visualizing the cardiac chambers throughout the cardiac cycle
   b) Precise determination of EF
   c) Effective in distinguishing between cardiac and pulmonary causes of dyspnea, in evaluating left ventricular wall motion abnormalities, and in estimating diastolic compliance
5. Cardiac catheterization and muscle biopsy
   a) Catheterization considered in any patient in whom an etiological and anatomical diagnosis has not been made
   b) Biopsy may be useful in young patients suspected of having a cardiomyopathy
6. Exercise testing: the most precise determination of functional classification (Table 45.3)

MANAGEMENT

A. General
   1. Treat underlying disease (Table 45.1) if possible
   2. Same measures used in ambulatory patients (Table 45.4)
   3. Life-style: stop smoking, avoid stress, get adequate rest
   4. Diet: avoid sudden increases in salt intake; 2–4 g of sodium/day (no-added-salt diet) usually suffices

B. Drugs
   1. Diuretics (Table 45.5)
      a) First-line drugs in treatment of heart failure
      b) Goal is to reach patient's dry weight (edema free, no significant increase in weight loss thereafter)
      c) Hydrochlorothiazide, lowest effective dose, is first choice; if patient becomes resistant or complications ensue, *loop diuretics* are prescribed

Table 45.4.   Measures Used in Ambulatory Treatment of Heart Failure

Increasing capacity of heart to do work
Digitalis
Antiarrhythmic drugs (Chapter 43)
Pacemaker (Chapter 43)
Decreasing amount of work that heart has to do
Rest
Low-sodium diet
Diuretics
Vasodilator drugs
Home oxygen

Table 45.5. Characteristics of Selected Diuretic Drugs

Generic Name	Brand Name	Available Preparations	Usual Daily Dose (per day)	Frequency of Dose (per day)	Onset of Effect	Peak Effect	Duration
Hydrochlorothiazide	Generic, Hydro-Diuril, Esidrix	25-, 50-, 200-mg tablet	25–100	1–2	2 hr	4 hr	12 hr or more
Chlorthalidone	Generic, Hygroton	50-, 100-mg tablet	50–100	1	2 hr	6 hr	24 hr
Metolazone	Zaroxolyn	2.5-, 5-, 10-mg tablet	2.5–10	1	1 hr	2 hr	12–14 hr
Furosemide	Lasix	20-, 40-, 80-mg tablet	20–160	1–2	1 hr	1–2 hr	6 hr
Ethacrynic acid	Edecrin	50-mg tablet	50–100	1–2	30 min	2 hr	6–8 hr
Bumetanide	Bumex	0.5-, 1-mg tablet	0.5–2	1	30 min to 1 hr	1–2 hr	4 hr
Triamterene	Dyrenium	100-mg capsule	100–300	1–2	2 hr	6–8 hr	12–16 hr
Spironolactone	Aldactone	25-mg tablet	50–400	1–2	Gradual onset	2–3 days after initiation of therapy	2–3 days after cessation of therapy
Amiloride	Midamor	5-mg tablet	5–10	1	2 hr	6–10 hr	24 hr
Indapamide	Lozol	2.5-mg tablet	2.5–5.0	1	1 hr	2 hr	28 hr

Modified from Frazier H, Yager H: The clinical use of diuretics. *N Engl J Med* 288:246, 455, 1973.

    d) Side effects
       1) Hypokalemia
       2) Contraction of extracellular volume (postural hypotension)
       3) Acid-base disturbance (usually metabolic alkalosis)
       4) Hyponatremia
       5) Hyperuricemia
       6) Hyperglycemia
       7) Ototoxicity (loop diuretics)
       8) Lipid abnormalities (thiazides may increase serum triglyceride levels)
       9) Small-vessel vasculitis (thiazides)

2. Digitalis
    a) Indication: patients in heart failure with dilated hearts
    b) Recommendations
       1) Use only digoxin (Lanoxin preferred)
       2) Digitalize by early administration of maintenance dose (average 0.25 mg/day; 0.125 mg/day over age 65 or if renal function impaired)
       3) Follow heart size and serum level to ensure effect and compliance
       4) Be aware of drug interactions; e.g., quinidine, verapamil, diltiazem may increase serum digitalis level
    c) Toxicity
       1) Most frequent cardiac toxic effect is nodal rhythm, frequent premature ventricular contractions
       2) Gastrointestinal effects: especially anorexia, nausea
       3) Changes in sensorium: mild confusion most often
       4) If suspected, stop drug, measure serum level

3. Vasodilator therapy (Table 45.6)
    a) Should be considered for all patients whose heart failure is due to systolic dysfunction (see above)
    b) Venodilators
       1) Most useful in patients with evidence of pulmonary congestion on exercise
       2) Should not be used in patients with restriction to ventricular filling (e.g., hypertrophic cardiomyopathy)
    c) Arteriolar vasodilators
       1) Most effective in patients with severe peripheral and central congestion who have signs of peripheral hypoperfusion (e.g., cool hands, cyanosis)
       2) Converting-enzyme (CE) inhibitors the most effective vasodilators available for long-term use
       3) If CE inhibitor cannot be used, hydralazine plus a long-acting nitrate gives equivalent effect
       4) Patient weight and signs of congestion should be assessed at each visit
       5) CE inhibitors should be used cautiously in patients with signs of overdiuresis or evidence of renal insufficiency

4. β-Blocker therapy
    a) Cautious use may be beneficial in patients with dilated cardiomyopathy

Table 45.6.   Vasodilators Useful in Treating Heart Failure

Site of Action	Drugs	Venodilation/Arteriolar Dilation	Available Tablet Strength	Usual Dose	Effectiveness After 1 Year
Smooth muscle	Isosorbide dinitrate (Isordil)	+++/+	10, 20, 40 mg	20–60 mg every 6 hr	?
	Nitroglycerin dermal patches[a]	+++/+	0.1, 0.2, 0.4, and 0.6 mg/hr	0.2–0.6 mg/hr	?
	Hydralazine (Apresoline)	0/+++	10, 25, 50, 100 mg	25–50 mg every 6 hr	1+
	Hydralazine plus long-acting nitrate	+++/+++		As above, in combination	+++
Calcium channel blockers	Nifedipine (Procardia)	+/+++	10, 20 mg	10–30 mg every 6 hr	?
	Felodipine (Plendil)	+/+++	5, 10 mg	5–10 mg every 24 hr	?
	Amlodipine (Norvasc)	+/+++	2.5, 5, 10 mg	5–10 mg every 24 hr	?
	Diltiazem (Cardizem)[b]	+/++	30, 60 mg	30–60 mg every 6 to 8 hr	?
	Verapamil (Calan, Isoptin)[b]	+/+	40, 80, 120 mg	80–120 mg every 8 hr	?
Converting-enzyme inhibitors	Captopril (Capoten)	++/+++	12.5, 25, 50 mg	6.25–50 mg every 6 hr	+++
	Enalapril (Vasotec)	++/+++	2.5, 5, 10, 20 mg	5–20 mg every 24 hr	+++
	Lisinopril (Zestril, Prinivil)	++/+++	5, 10, 20 mg	5–20 mg every 24 hr	+++

[a] To avoid development of tolerance, an 8–12-hr period without topical nitrates should be scheduled daily. Usually, this means applying nitroglycerin patches upon awakening and removing them at bedtime.
[b] Should be used only in patients with heart failure due to diastolic dysfunction or when ischemia is a major reason for left ventricular decompensation. These drugs are available in sustained release preparations, which can be used if compliance is an issue.

b) Should be considered if symptoms do not respond to diuretics, digitalis, vasodilators
c) Metoprolol, the β-blocker of choice, should be started at 12.5 mg twice a day and titrated to 50–100 mg twice a day
d) Useful also in thyrotoxicosis, severe hypertension, hypertrophic cardiomyopathy, failure due to ischemia

46/ HYPERTENSION

DIAGNOSTIC EVALUATION

A. Classification: Table 46.1
B. Definitions
   1. Labile hypertension: blood pressure is high (Table 46.1) at some times, normal at others
      a) Should be repeated within a week or two if high at first visit
      b) Increased risk of sustained hypertension
   2. Chronic hypertension: most people present at stage 1 or 2 (Table 46.1)
   3. Accelerated hypertension: hypertension with retinal hemorrhages and/or fresh exudates or papilledema or renal insufficiency attributable to hypertension
   4. Hypertensive emergency: hypertensive encephalopathy (e.g., headache, confusion) or thoracic aortic dissection
C. Baseline evaluation (Table 46.2)
   1. Target organ status (Table 46.3)
   2. Secondary hypertension
      a) Chronic alcoholism
      b) Use of a medication that may cause high blood pressure (Table 46.2, Footnote a)
      c) Renovascular hypertension
         1) In patients under 40, usually due to fibromuscular hyperplasia of renal artery; over 40, atherosclerosis of renal artery

Table 46.1. Classification of Blood Pressure (BP) for Adults Aged 18 Years and Older[a]

Category	Systolic BP (mm Hg)	Diastolic BP (mm Hg)
Normal[b]	<130	<85
High normal	130–139	85–89
Hypertension[c]		
Stage 1 (mild)	140–159	90–99
Stage 2 (moderate)	160–179	100–109
Stage 3 (severe)	180–209	110–119
Stage 4 (very severe)	≥210	≥120

From The Fifth Report of the Joint National Committee on Detection, Evaluation, and Treatment of High Blood Pressure (JNC V). *Arch Intern Med* 153:154, 1993.

[a] Not taking antihypertensive drugs and not acutely ill. When systolic and diastolic pressures fall into different categories, the higher category should be selected to classify the individual's blood pressure status. For instance, 160/92 mm Hg should be classified as stage 2, and 180/120 mm Hg should be classified as stage 4. *Isolated systolic hypertension* is defined as a systolic blood pressure of ≥140 mm Hg and a diastolic blood pressure of <90 mm Hg and staged appropriately (e.g., 170/85 mm Hg is defined as stage 2 isolated systolic hypertension).

In addition to classifying stages of hypertension on the basis of average blood pressure levels, the clinician should specify presence or absence of *target organ disease and additional risk factors*. For example, a patient with diabetes and a blood pressure of 142/94 mm Hg, plus left ventricular hypertrophy (LVH), should be classified as having "stage 1 hypertension with target organ disease (LVH) and with another major risk factor (diabetes)." This specificity is important for risk classification and management.

[b] Optimal blood pressure with respect to cardiovascular risk is <120 mm Hg systolic and <80 mm Hg diastolic. However, unusually low readings should be evaluated for clinical significance.

[c] Based on the *average of two or more readings* taken at each of two or more visits after an initial screening.

Table 46.2. Recommended Baseline Evaluation of the Patient With Sustained Hypertension

Information	Reason for Obtaining Information				
	End-Organ Status	Etiology Screening	Selecting Treatment	Factors Modified by Treatment	Additional Cardiovascular Risk Factors
INTERVIEW, OLD RECORDS					
Age and race		x	x		
Blood pressure levels		x	x	x	
Hypertension treatment, results, side effects		x	x		
Family history		x	x		x
Congestive heart failure	x		x		
Angina	x		x		
Transient ischemic attack or cerebrovascular accident	x				
Renal disease	x	x	x		
Comprehension of hypertension			x	x	
Diet (Na, K, fats)		x	x	x	x
Exercise habits			x		x
Current medications[a]		x	x	x	x
Alcohol use		x	x		
Tobacco use					x
Current life stresses		x	x		x
Coexisting conditions		x	x		
Periodic sympathetic symptoms		x			
PHYSICAL EXAMINATION					
Weight		x	x	x	
Blood pressure (right, left, resting, standing)		x	x	x	
Heart rate and rhythm		x	x	x	
Eye grounds	x		x		
Peripheral pulses	x	x	x		

Table 46.2. Continued

Information	Reason for Obtaining Information				
	End-Organ Status	Etiology Screening	Selecting Treatment	Factors Modified by Treatment	Additional Cardiovascular Risk Factors
Heart	X				
Lungs			X		
Abdomen (mass, bruit)		X			
Neurological	X				
LABORATORY					
Complete blood count		X		X	
Calcium level		X		X	
Creatinine level	X	X	X	X	
Potassium level		X	X	X	
Sodium level		X	X	X	
Fasting glucose level			X	X	
Cholesterol (total, high-density lipoprotein) level[b]				X	X
Uric acid level			X	X	
Urinalysis		X			
Electrocardiogram (ECG)	X				

[a] Identify medications that may cause hypertension or may counteract antihypertensive drugs (e.g., oral contraceptives, tricyclic antidepressants, sympathomimetic decongestants, appetite suppressants, corticosteroids, nonsteroidal anti-inflammatory drugs, cyclosporine, erythropoietin, monoamine oxidase inhibitors).

[b] Recommendations of the National Cholesterol Education Program: nonfasting total and high-density lipoprotein (HDL) cholesterol. If total cholesterol ≥ 240 mg/dl or if HDL ≤ 35 mg/dl, obtain fasting lipoprotein analysis (see Chapter 59).

Table 46.3.   Manifestations of Target Organ Disease

Organ System	Manifestations
Cardiac	Clinical, ECG, or radiological evidence of coronary artery disease; LVH or "strain" by ECG or LVH by echocardiography; left ventricular dysfunction or cardiac failure
Cerebrovascular	Transient ischemic attack or stroke
Peripheral vascular	Absence of one or more major pulses in extremities (except for dorsalis pedis), with or without intermittent claudication; aneurysm
Renal	Serum creatinine $\geq$ 130 μmol/liter (1.5 mg/dl); proteinuria (1+ or greater); microalbuminuria
Retinopathy	Hemorrhages or exudates, with or without papilledema

From The Fifth Report of the Joint National Committee on Detection, Evaluation, and Treatment of High Blood Pressure (JNC V). *Arch Intern Med* 153:154, 1993.

Table 46.4.   Clinical Index of Suspicion (Pretest Probability) for Renovascular Hypertension

Moderate suspicion (5–15%)
Very severe diastolic hypertension ($\geq$120 mm Hg) at baseline
Change over 1–2 years from normal blood pressure to severe diastolic hypertension ($\geq$110 mm Hg) in patients <20 or >50 years old
Hypertension refractory to pharmacological treatment
High suspicion ($\geq$25%)
Severe diastolic hypertension ($\geq$110 mm Hg) with either progressive renal insufficiency or grade 3 or 4 hypertensive retinopathy plus resistance to aggressive pharmacological treatment
Severe diastolic hypertension ($\geq$110 mm Hg) with incidentally detected asymmetry of kidney size

Adapted from Mann SG, Pickering TG: Detection of renovascular hypertension: state of the art — 1992. *Ann Intern Med* 117:845, 1992.

2) Index of suspicion: Table 46.4
3) First attempt to control with drugs (see below); then, if not controlled, evaluate for renal artery sclerosis:
   (a) Captopril scintirenography best noninvasive test
   (b) Renal arteriography definitive test
d) Kidney disease: suspect if a history of hematuria, stones, recurrent infection, if urinalysis shows heavy proteinuria or red cell casts, or if kidneys are large
e) Pheochromocytoma
   1) Clues: hypermetabolic state, paroxysmal hypertension, positive family history
   2) Screening tests (only if clinical suspicion is high): measurement of 24-hour urinary catecholamines, metanephrines, or vanillylmandelic acid
   3) Diagnostic tests: radioisotopic screening with iodobenzylguanidine followed by computed tomography scanning or magnetic resonance imaging
f) Coarctation of the aorta
   1) Clues: young patient, decreased blood pressure in extremities, collateral circulation on inspection of the chest or by chest x-ray
   2) Definitive test: arteriogram

TREATMENT
A. Goals
   1. If possible, to restore normal blood pressure within 1–3 months (drug treatment) or 1 year (nonpharmacological)
   2. If not possible (stage 3 or 4 hypertension) to restore normal blood pressure, partial reduction of pressure is acceptable
   3. Control of other treatable cardiovascular risk factors
B. Initiation of treatment
   1. Stage 1 (Table 46.1): try nonpharmacological approach for 1 year in the absence of, and for several months in the presence of, cardiovascular risk factors or target organ disease (Table 46.2)
   2. Stage 2 and above: drug treatment
C. Nonpharmacological treatment
   1. Weight reduction: even modest reduction, e.g., 10 lbs, may be of help
   2. Sodium restriction: diet should be limited to 1.5–2 g of sodium (4–6 g of salt) per day
   3. Exercise: all patients who can should exercise regularly, e.g., walking 3 miles 4 or more times a week
D. Pharmacological treatment
   1. Initial therapy with a low dose of diuretic (e.g., 25 mg of hydrochlorothiazide per day) or a β-blocker (e.g., 20 mg of propranolol twice a day) is appropriate for most patients
      a) Assess response in 2–4 weeks
      b) Approximately 50% will respond
      c) In general, whites respond better to β-blockers; African Americans, to diuretics
   2. Angiotensin-converting enzyme (ACE) inhibitors probably are initial drugs of choice in diabetics
   3. Properties of individual drugs
      a) Diuretics (Table 46.5)
         1) Major antihypertensive response in 1–2 weeks
         2) Increased urination, transient orthostasis are common
         3) Metabolic effects (hypokalemia, hyponatremia, hyperuricemia, impaired glucose tolerance, mild hyperlipidemia) may occur
         4) No absolute contraindications
      b) Nondiuretics (Table 46.6)
         1) β-blockers
            (a) Should not be stopped abruptly (risk of angina, acute blood pressure rebound, symptoms of anxiety)
            (b) Most common side effects: nausea, abdominal cramps, diarrhea, sedation, fatigue, nightmares
            (c) Absolute contraindications: heart rate of <50, dilated cardiomyopathy, symptomatic asthma or chronic obstructive pulmonary disease, severe peripheral vascular disease
         2) Central-acting adrenergic inhibitors
            (a) Rebound hypertension a risk if abruptly discontinued
            (b) Most common side effects: sedation, dry mouth, constipation, orthostasis
            (c) No absolute contraindications
         3) α_1-Adrenergic inhibitors

Table 46.5. Diuretic Drugs Used for Hypertension

Class/Name of Drugs[a]	Available Strengths (mg)	Dose Range for Hypertension (mg/day)
THIAZIDES AND RELATED SULFONAMIDE DIURETICS		
Bendroflumethiazide (Naturetin)	2.5, 5, 10	2.5–5
Benzthiazide	25, 50	25–50
Chlorothiazide sodium (Diuril)[b]	250, 500	250–500
Chlorthalidone (Hygroton)[b]	25, 50, 100	25–50
Cyclothiazide (Anhydron, Fluidil)	2	1–2
Hydrochlorothiazide[b]	25, 50	25–50
Hydroflumethiazide (Diucardin, Saluron)[b]	50	25–50
Indapamide (Lozol)	2.5	2.5–5
Methyclothiazide[b]	5	2.5–5
Metolazone (Diulo, Zaroxolyn)	2.5, 5, 10	2.5–5
Polythiazide (Renese)	1, 2, 4	2–4
Quinethazone (Hydromox)	50	50–100
Trichlormethiazide (Metahydrin, Naqua)[b]	2, 4	2–4
LOOP DIURETICS		
Bumetanide (Bumex)	0.5, 1	0.5–10
Ethacrynic acid (Edecrin)	50	50–200
Furosemide (Lasix)[b]	20, 40, 80	20–480
POTASSIUM-SPARING DIURETICS		
Amiloride hydrochloride (Midamor)	5	5–10
Spironolactone (Aldactone)[b]	25, 50, 100	50–100
Triamterene (Dyrenium)	50, 100	50–100
COMBINATIONS		
Hydrochlorothiazide/spironolactone (Aldactazide)[b]	25/25, 50/50	See above
Hydrochlorothiazide/triamterene (Dyazide)[b,c]	25/50	See above
Hydrochlorothiazide/amiloride (Moduretic)	50/5	See above

[a] If more than two proprietary formulations are available, names are not listed.
[b] Generic is available.
[c] Also Maxide: hydrochlorothiazide/triamterene 50/75 mg; and Maxide-25, which contains 25/37.5 mg.

      (a) Common side effects: postural hypotension, headache, drowsiness, dry mouth, palpitations
      (b) No absolute contraindications
  4) α-β-Blockers
      (a) Common side effects: fatigue, nausea, dyspepsia, dizziness, nasal stuffiness, rash, impotence
      (b) Contraindicated in patients with second- or third-degree heart block
  5) Peripheral-acting adrenergic inhibitors
      (a) Common side effects: depression, slight decrease in alertness, nasal stuffiness, dyspepsia
      (b) Contraindicated in patients with peptic ulcer or depression
  6) Guanadrel and guanethidine
      (a) Use severely limited by exaggerated orthostasis; male sexual dysfunction and diarrhea are also common
      (b) No reason to prescribe
  7) ACE inhibitors
      (a) Common side effects: rash, altered taste, nonproductive cough

Table 46.6. Pharmacological Characteristics of Nondiuretic Antihypertensive Drugs

Class/Name of Drug	Available Strengths (mg)	Dose Range (mg/day)	Schedule (Alternative)	Major Action Onset/Duration (hr)	Metabolism and Elimination
ADRENERGIC INHIBITORS					
β-Blockers					
Acebutolol (Sectral)[a,b]	200, 400	200–1200	Once daily (twice daily)	3–8/≤24[c]	L, K
Atenolol (Tenormin)[a,d]	25, 50, 100	25–100	Once daily	2–4/24–48[c]	K
Betaxolol (Kerlone)[a]	10, 20	10–20	Once daily	?/?	K
Carteolol (Cartrol)	2.5, 5	2.5–10	Once daily	?/?	K
Metoprolol (Lopressor)[a]	50, 100	50–300	Once daily (twice daily)	2–4/24–48[c]	L
Metoprolol (long acting) (Toprol XL)	50, 100, 200	50–200	Once daily	?/?	L
Nadolol (Corgard)	40, 80, 120	20–120	Once daily	2–4/24–48[c]	K
Penbutolol (Levatol)[b]	20	20–80	Once daily	1–3/20–24	L
Pindolol (Visken)[b]	5, 10	20–60	Twice daily	?	L
Propranolol (Inderal)[d]	10, 20, 40, 60, 80	40–≥480	Twice daily	2–4/24–48[c]	L
Propranolol (long acting) (Inderal LA)[d]	80, 120, 160	80–>480	Once daily	24/24	L
Timolol (Blocardren)	5, 10, 20	20–60	Twice daily	?	L
Centrally acting sympatholytics					
Clonidine (Catapres)[d]	0.1, 0.2, 0.3	0.2–2.4	Twice weekly	1–2/8–12	K
Clonidine patch (Catapres TTS-1, TTS-2, TTS-3)	0.1, 0.2, 0.3/day	0.1–0.3	Once weekly	3 days/7 days	K
Guanabenz (Wytensin)	4, 8	8–32	Twice daily	2–4/12	
Guanfacine (Tenex)	1, 2	1–3	Once daily	?/24	K
Methyldopa (Aldomet)[d]	250, 500	250–3000	Twice daily (once at bedtime)	4–6/24–48	K
α₁-Blockers					
Doxazosin (Cardura)	1, 2, 4, 8	1–16	Once daily	2–3/24	L
Prazosin (Minipress)[d]	1, 2, 5	2–40	Twice daily (3 times/day)	1–2/12–24	L
Terazosin (Hytrin)	1, 2, 5, 10	1–20	Once daily	2–3/24	L
α-β-Blocker					
Labetalol (Trandate, Normodyne)	100, 200, 300	200–≥2400	Twice daily (3 times/day)	1–3/8–24	L, K
Peripherally acting sympatholytics					
Guanadrel (Hylorel)	10, 25	20–75	Twice daily	2–6/?	K

Drug	Available strengths (mg)	Dosage range (mg)	Frequency	Onset/duration	Metabolism
Guanethidine (Ismelin)	10, 25	10–200	Every day	3–5 days/≥1 wk	K
Reserpine[d]	0.1, 0.25	0.1–0.25	Once daily	1–2 wk/≥1 wk	K
ACE INHIBITORS					
Benazepril (Lotensin)	5, 10, 20, 40	10–80	Once daily (2 times/day)	3–4/24	K
Captopril (Capoten)[d]	12.5, 25, 50, 100	25–≥150	Twice or 3 times/day	1–3/8–12	K
Enalapril (Vasotec)	2.5, 5, 10, 20	5–20	Once daily (2 times/day)	3–4/24	K
Fosinopril (Monopril)	10, 20	20–≥40	Once daily (2 times/day)	3–4/24	L
Lisinopril (Prinivil, Zestril)	5, 10, 20, 40	10–40	Once daily	3–4/24	K
Quinapril (Accupril)	5, 10, 20, 40	10–≥40	Once daily (2 times/day)	3–4/24	K
Ramipril (Altace)	1.25, 2.5, 5, 10	2.5–≥10	Once daily (2 times/day)	3–4/24	K
CALCIUM CHANNEL BLOCKERS					
Diltiazem (Cardizem)[d]	30, 60, 90	90–360	3 times/day	1–3/8–12	L, K
Diltiazem (long acting) (Cardizem SR)[d]	60, 90, 120	120–≥240	Twice daily	24/24	L, K
(Cardizem CD)	180, 240, 300	180–360	Once daily	24/24	L, K
(Dilacor XR)	180, 240	180–480	Once daily	24/24	L, K
Verapamil (Calan, Isoptin)[d]	40, 80, 120	240–360	3 times/day	1–3/8–12	L, K
Verapamil long acting[d] (Calan SR, Verelan)	120, 180, 240	120–480	Once daily (2 times/day)	24/24	L, K
DIHYDROPYRIDINES					
Amlodipine (Norvasc)	2.5, 5, 10	5–10	Once daily	24/24	L
Felodipine (Plendil)	5, 10	5–20	Once daily	24/24	L
Isradipine (DynaCirc)	2.5, 5	5–20	Twice daily	2–3/12–24	L, K
Nicardipine (Cardene)	20, 30	60–120	3 times/day	1–2/8–12	L
(Cardene SR)	30, 45, 60	60–120	Twice daily	2–4/12–24	L
Nifedipine (Procardia, Adalat)[d]	10, 20	30–180	3 times/day	1–2/8–12	K
Nifedipine (long acting) (Procardia XL)	30, 60, 90	30–≥90	Once daily	24/24	K
DIRECT VASODILATORS					
Hydralazine (Apresoline)[d]	10, 25, 75, 100	20–≥300	Twice daily (3 times/day)	1–4/12–24	K
Minoxidil (Loniten)[d]	2.5, 10	5–≥40	Once daily (twice daily)	1–3/24–48	L

L, liver; K, kidney.
[a] Cardioselective β-blockade.
[b] Has intrinsic sympathomimetic activity.
[c] Refers to cardioinhibitory action (principal antihypertensive effect may be delayed 1–7 days).
[d] Generic is available.

Table 46.7. Differential Diagnosis of Instability in Blood Pressure Control

COMMON CAUSES	UNCOMMON CAUSES
Noncompliance	Concurrent medications[a]
Increased salt consumption	Tolerance
Weight gain	Refractory hypertension
Psychological stress	
Increased use of or withdrawal from ethanol	

[a] See Table 46.8.

Table 46.8. Medications That May Attenuate Response to Antihypertensive Drugs

PROMOTES POSITIVE SODIUM BALANCE	MECHANISM NOT ESTABLISHED
Nonsteroidal anti-inflammatory drugs	Tricyclic antidepressants
Corticosteroids	Phenothiazines
Estrogens	Monoamine oxidase inhibitors
Sodium-containing antacids	Nonsteroidal anti-inflammatory drugs
SYMPATHOMIMETIC	Oral contraceptives
Decongestants (oral)	Cyclosporine
Amphetamines	Erythropoietin
Bronchodilators	

   (b) May cause acute renal failure in patients with bilateral renal stenosis or in a patient with a transplanted kidney and a stenotic renal artery
  8) Calcium channel blockers
   (a) Common side effects: nausea, flushing, headache, tachycardia
   (b) Contraindicated in patients with bradycardia, atrioventricular conduction disturbance, uncontrolled heart failure
  9) Direct vasodilators
   (a) Hydralazine: most common side effects are headaches, palpitations, tachycardia
   (b) Minoxidil: most common side effects are fluid retention, hirsutism
E. Problems in the course of treatment
 1. Instability in blood pressure (Tables 46.7 and 46.8)
 2. Resistant hypertension
  a) Resistance should be confirmed by observation in office for several hours after medication is taken
  b) Effective regimens
   1) Minoxidil or nifedipine with a β-blocker
   2) ACE inhibitors with a calcium channel blocker
   3) High-dose furosemide with potent nondiuretic drugs
   4) High-dose prazosin or terazosin

Section VIII
Musculoskeletal Problems

47/ SHOULDER PAIN

ANATOMY (FIG. 47.1)
A. Superficial layer
   1. Deltoid (abducts)
   2. Pectoralis major and minor (adduct)
   3. Trapezius (elevates and rotates)
   4. Acromion, coracoacromial ligament, and deltoid: form a roof over deeper structures
B. Subacromial or subdeltoid bursa: assists free movement of underlying structures
C. Rotator cuff
   1. Supraspinatus superiorly, infraspinatus and teres minor posteriorly, subscapularis anteriorly
   2. Stabilizes the humeral head during abduction, rotation
D. Ligamentous capsule, glenohumeral joint space, articulation of humeral head with glenoid fossa

DIAGNOSTIC APPROACH
A. History
   1. Perceived location of pain usually not of help in establishing cause, but pain confined to the joint of the shoulder suggests a lesion of the acromioclavicular joint
   2. Ask about recent trauma; review patient's problem list, medication list, past medical history
      a) Dislocation of shoulder should be suspected if there has been major trauma to the arm
      b) Injury to or separation of the acromioclavicular joint usually results from a direct blow to the acromion
   3. Ask what precipitates or worsens the pain
      a) Referred pain is not exacerbated by movement of the shoulder
      b) Pain with movement of the shoulder suggests an articular or periarticular problem
   4. Inquire about occupational and athletic activities
B. Physical examination (use uninvolved shoulder as a control)
   1. Inspection: may reveal atrophy or displacement of bony landmarks
   2. Active motion
      a) Have the patient elevate the arm as far as possible
      b) Assess external and internal rotation with the patient's elbow at his or her side, with the forearm held at a right angle in the anteroposterior plane (normally, 40–45° and 55–60°, respectively)
      c) Assess adduction by having the patient place his or her hands on the opposite shoulder
   3. Passive range: compare to active motion
   4. Resisted movements, i.e., those made without movement of the shoulder joint, with the elbow at the patient's side, with the forearm at a right angle in the anteroposterior plane
      a) Test abduction by having the patient press outward against the examiner's braced hand
      b) Test adduction by having the patient press in, flexion forward and extension backward against the examiner's hand

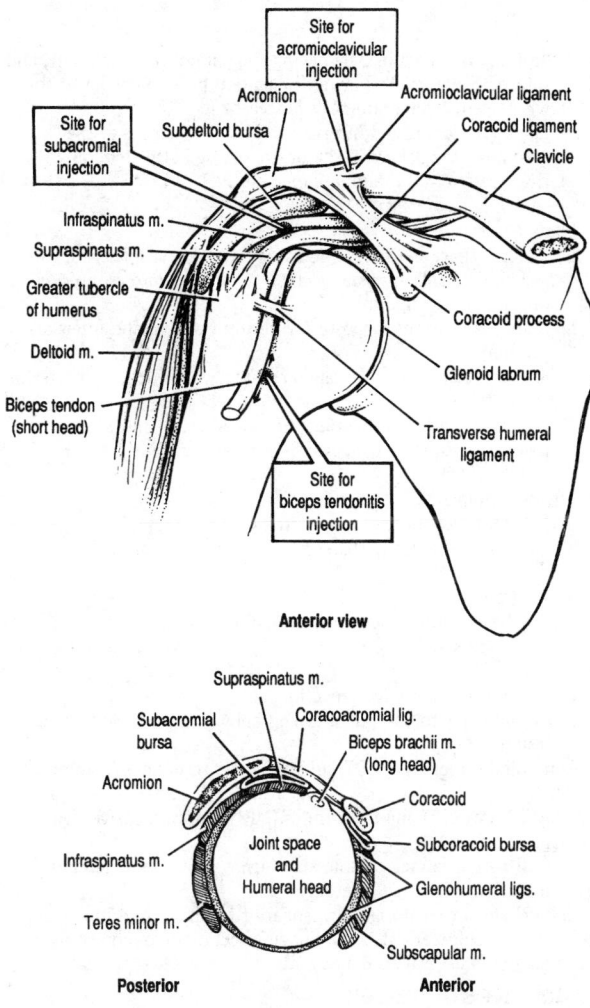

Anterior view

Sagittal view

Figure 47.1.   Structures of the shoulder and their relationships. Note that the subdeltoid bursa lies next to the supraspinatus tendon but separate from the shoulder joint. Note the acromion and the coracoacromial ligaments, which may impinge on the supraspinatus tendon on abduction of the arm. Note the location for subacromial injection into the bursa and about the rotator cuff tendons. (Sagittal section adapted from Pansky B: *Review of Gross Anatomy*. New York, Macmillan, 1979.)

        c) Test external rotation, by having the patient press laterally, and internal rotation, by having the patient press medially, at the wrist against the examiner's braced hand

        d) Palpation: less useful but may confirm problem is at the acromioclavicular joint, the bursa, or the biceps tendon

        e) Interpretation of examination: Table 47.1

C. Additional diagnostic tests

  1. Plain x-rays

      a) Order if there has been trauma, if there is a suspicion of arthritis, neoplasm, osteonecrosis, or if there are chronic unexplained symptoms

      b) Standard view: anteroposterior film in external and internal rotation

      c) Axillary lateral view or scapular "Y" view will detect a posterior dislocation

      d) Caudal tilt view can help identify subacromial spurs

      e) Insensitive to early osteonecrosis, rotator cuff tear, other soft tissue injuries

  2. Ultrasonography

      a) 1.2–2.5 times more expensive than plain x-rays

      b) Much more sensitive than plain x-rays to rotator cuff tears

  3. Arthrography

      a) 3–4 times more expensive than plain x-rays

      b) Very high sensitivity and specificity for detecting rotator cuff tears

      c) Can confirm adhesive capsulitis

      d) Combined with computed tomography can detect soft tissue lesions

  4. Computed tomography (CT) and magnetic resonance imaging (MRI)

      a) 5–7 times (CT) and 9–10 times (MRI) more expensive than plain x-rays

      b) MRI better defines capsule anatomy, supraspinatus tendon integrity, and bursal anatomy

      c) MRI equal to arthrography, superior to ultrasound in detecting rotator cuff tears; it is the imaging technique of choice in diagnosis of early osteonecrosis

MANAGEMENT STRATEGIES

A. Physical activity and physical therapy

  1. Putting patient's arm in sling for 2–3 days may help to relieve acute pain

  2. Range of motion exercises are important, and prolonged immobilization should be avoided to prevent adhesive capsulitis

  3. When acute pain subsides, specific exercises should be prescribed (Fig. 47.2) for 5–10 minutes 2–4 times/day if the glenohumeral range of motion is restricted

  4. Effectiveness of heat or ultrasound not established, but they are often recommended

  5. Local cooling often recommended after acute injury

Table 47.1. Muscles Acting on the Shoulder Joint

Flexion	Extension	Abduction	Adduction	Medial Rotation	Lateral Rotation
Pectoralis major (clavicular head)	Latissimus dorsi	Deltoid (as whole)	Pectoralis major (as whole)	Pectoralis major (as whole)	Infraspinatus[a]
Deltoid (anterior fibers)	Teres major	Supraspinatus[a]	Latissimus dorsi	Latissimus dorsi	Teres minor
Coracobrachialis	Deltoid (posterior fibers)		Teres major	Teres major	Deltoid (posterior fibers)
Biceps[a] (long head)	Triceps (long head)		Subscapularis	Subscapularis[a]	
			Triceps (long head)	Deltoid (anterior fibers)	

Modified from Pansky B: *Review of Gross Anatomy*, 4th ed. New York, Macmillan, 1979.
[a] Muscles (rotator cuffs and biceps) most commonly associated with shoulder pain.

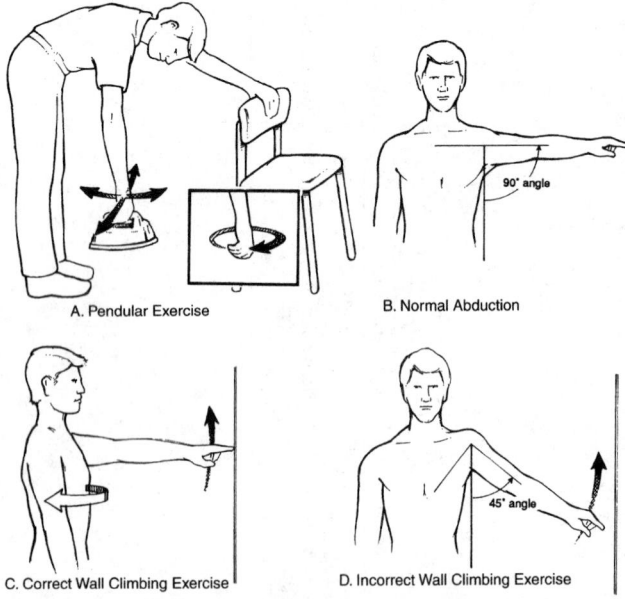

A. Pendular Exercise

B. Normal Abduction

C. Correct Wall Climbing Exercise

D. Incorrect Wall Climbing Exercise

Figure 47.2.   Range of motion exercises of the shoulder. **A.** *Pendular exercises* can be done with a weight, which will help increase the pendular movement. The arm is moved back and forth in the sagittal and frontal planes, then circumducted in the clockwise and counterclockwise directions in increasingly large circles. **B** and **C.** *Wall-climbing exercise done correctly.* The wall climb can be started facing the wall. The body is then turned until the patient is at a right angle to the wall. The shoulder movement is at the glenohumeral joint. **D.** *Wall-climbing exercise done incorrectly* with "shrugging" of the scapula. (Redrawn from Cailliet R: *Shoulder Pain.* Philadelphia, FA Davis, 1981.)

     6. Referral to a physical therapist recommended if a supervised exercise program is indicated

B. Medication

     1. Nonsteroidal anti-inflammatory agents (NSAIDs) are more effective than placebo, but whether they are more effective than acetaminophen is not clear

     2. NSAIDs (see Chapter 54) usually prescribed for 2 weeks for an acute problem

C. Injection therapy

     1. Injections of depocorticosteroid (Kenalog, Celestone, or Depo-Medrol) more effective than oral medication or physical therapy in relieving pain and speeding recovery after rotator cuff injury or bursitis

     2. Two or three injections often required

     3. Avoid injecting more than 1–2 ml at a time or injecting a solution

4. Rotator cuff lesions and subdeltoid bursitis are generally treated with a subacromial injection of 20–40 mg of triamcinolone or its equivalent in 4–6 ml of local anesthetic
5. Adhesive capsulitis is treated with intra-articular injection of 20–40 mg of triamcinolone or its equivalent in local anesthetic
6. Bicipital tendinitis treated with injection of 20 mg of triamcinolone or its equivalent in local anesthetic
7. Acromioclavicular joint problems may be treated with injections of 4–10 mg triamcinolone in local anesthetic
8. Full activity should not be resumed for several weeks after pain is relieved
D. Referral indicated for dislocation, fracture, functionally significant rotator cuff tear, suspected tumor, inability to give steroid injections, unresponsiveness to treatment, chronic or recurrent symptoms, uncertainty about diagnosis or treatment

PERIARTICULAR DISORDERS
A. Rotator cuff tendinitis
  1. Most common cause of shoulder pain
  2. Risk factors: repetitive overhead work or activities and increasing age
  3. Physical examination: pain on resisted abduction, lateral rotation, and/or medial rotation
    a) Often a painful arc, i.e., pain between 60° and 120° of shoulder abduction
    b) Normal muscle strength usually
    c) Normal passive range of motion
  4. X-rays: usually unnecessary (see above), usually normal, may show periarticular calcification of uncertain significance
  5. Management (see above): usually responds to injection
B. Subdeltoid (subacromial) bursitis
  1. Onset often abrupt
  2. Characterized by pain, often severe, with limitation of both active and passive motion (abduction more limited than lateral or medial rotation)
  3. Bursa tender
  4. Treatment: see above
C. Rotator cuff tear
  1. Trauma the usual cause, but by the sixth decade, degenerative changes allow spontaneous rupture
  2. Small tears may be indistinguishable from rotator cuff tendinitis (see above) in physical examination
  3. Larger tears characterized by weakness on resisted abduction; in complete tears, the patient is unable to initiate abduction or lower the arm to the side smoothly
  4. X-ray: narrowing of the space between the acromion and humerus suggests a tear, as does proximal subluxation of the humeral head and erosive changes in the anterior acromion
  5. Arthrography, CT, MRI, ultrasonography are all more useful than plain x-rays
  6. Treatment
    a) Consult an orthopedist, at least by telephone
    b) Small tears can be treated conservatively (see above)

c) Large tears often require surgical repair

D. Bicipital tendinitis
1. More common in later life
2. Pain on resisted flexion and supination of the elbow are characteristic findings
3. Active and passive ranges of motion of the shoulder are painless and full
4. X-rays not necessary
5. Treatment (see above): injection
6. Rupture of the biceps tendon: rare
    a) A mass of contracted muscle midway between shoulder and elbow
    b) Rupture accompanied by sudden painful popping sensation, usually during lifting
    c) Except in athletes (who may want surgical repair), conservative management is acceptable (with an ultimate loss of movement of 5–10%)

E. Acromioclavicular disorders
1. Osteoarthritis common by middle age
2. Trauma may cause subluxation or dislocation
3. Pain usually localized to exact site
4. Physical examination
    a) Active and passive ranges of motion usually normal
    b) Full passive adduction of the arm across the front of the upper chest often the most painful movement
    c) In complete dislocations, acromion displaced inferiorly and anteriorly
5. X-rays indicated after severe trauma (having the patient hold weights in both hands may help reveal separations)
6. Treatment
    a) Analgesics (see above)
    b) Use of a sling until pain subsides
    c) Surgery if occupation is dependent on overhead activity and if conservative treatment has failed

GLENOHUMERAL DISORDERS

A. Adhesive capsulitis
1. Cause unknown but often preceded by an underlying painful condition of the shoulder, a stroke, a myocardial infarction, or cervical radiculopathy (prolonged immobility of the arm a common factor)
2. Generally occurs in fifth decade or later
3. Patient complains of insidious onset of diffuse pain in and limitation of motion of the shoulder, especially tasks that require overhead arm motion
4. Physical examination: pain at the extremes of motion and markedly reduced active and passive ranges of motion of the glenohumeral joint (see above)
5. Plain x-ray generally normal
6. Arthrography usually not necessary but is diagnostic
7. Treatment
    a) If only analgesics are prescribed, most patients recover in 2–3 years

     b) Weekly injections of corticosteroids (see above) for several weeks with a progressive exercise program (see above) results in recovery in 4–8 weeks

B. Trauma
1. Dislocation occurs most frequently in active young to middle-aged adults
   a) Anterior dislocation (95% of dislocations)
      1) Usually follows a fall on an outstretched hand
      2) Physical examination: contour of the shoulder, normally convex below the acromion, is flattened; a noticeable prominence is seen and felt inferior to the clavicle
      3) Standard x-rays confirm the diagnosis
   b) Posterior dislocation
      1) Follows trauma that forces the humeral head posteriorly out of the glenoid fossa, may follow an electrical shock or convulsion
      2) Physical examination: arm held adducted and fixed in internal rotation; anteriorly, flattening of the shoulder contour and prominence of the coracoid process; posteriorly, prominence and rounding of the shoulder
      3) Standard x-ray findings are subtle (slight increase in space between anterior glenoid rim and medial humeral head); scapular "Y" view reveals the displacement
   c) Treatment of dislocations: immediate referral to an orthopedist for prompt reduction and, after a variable period of immobilization, a postreduction intensive physical therapy program
2. Fractures
   a) Occur most commonly in the elderly, usually after a fall
   b) Usually involve the proximal humerus
   c) Plain x-rays establish the diagnosis
   d) Referral to an orthopedist indicated

C. Arthritic and other conditions
1. Pain and limitation of active and passive range of motion
2. X-rays may show arthritic changes or osteonecrosis (see below) but may be normal in early or acute arthritis
3. Osteonecrosis (avascular or aseptic necrosis) of the humeral head
   a) Should be suspected in patients with a history of fracture or of prolonged corticosteroid therapy
   b) Diagnosis confirmed by plain x-ray or, occasionally, by MRI
   c) Treatment (see above): range of motion exercises, analgesics or NSAIDs, and limitation of stress; nonresponsive patients are candidates for replacement of the humeral head or of the total joint

REFERRED PAIN

A. When to suspect
1. Initial physical examination reveals another source for the pain
2. Active, passive, and restricted movements and palpation of the shoulder fail to elicit or exacerbate pain
3. Pain is in an atypical distribution

B. Causes
1. Visceral (e.g., subdiaphragmatic abscesses; ruptured viscus;

diseases involving the mediastinum, pericardium, liver, spleen, gallbladder; ischemic heart disease; apical or superior sulcus tumors of the lung)

2. Reflex sympathetic dystrophy (shoulder-hand syndrome): see Chapter 66
3. Nerve compression
   a) May be associated with paresthesias, numbness, weakness, or muscle atrophy
   b) Cervical nerve root irritation a common cause of shoulder pain, characteristically exacerbated by movement of the neck but not the shoulder
   c) Carpal tunnel syndrome (Chapter 67)
4. Thoracic outlet syndrome relatively less common
   a) Caused most frequently by muscle weakness, obesity, heavy breasts or arms, poor posture, the carrying of heavy loads on the shoulder, prolonged overhead work
   b) Caused less frequently by an anatomical condition such as a cervical rib
   c) If primarily neural compression, patient complains of pain from neck or shoulder to forearm or hand, accompanied by paresthesias or numbness; weakness and muscle atrophy may be noted
   d) If primarily vascular compression, patient may complain of an alteration in color or temperature, swelling of the affected hand, or a Raynaud-like phenomenon (see Chapter 50)
   e) Physical examination
      1) A decrease or obliteration of the radial pulse when the extended neck is rotated toward the symptomatic side, when the patient's arm is abducted 180° in external rotation, when the patient assumes an exaggerated military posture with the shoulder braced posteriorly and inferiorly (all accompanied by reproduction of symptoms)
      2) Only a minority of patients show reddening, warmth, or swelling of the hand
   f) Doppler flow studies may be of help if vascular impingement is suspected; subclavian arteriography occasionally necessary
   g) Management depends on underlying cause, but identification and elimination of aggravating factors and implementation of an exercise program provide relief for most patients
   h) Patients with severe refractory pain may need surgery

48/ NECK PAIN

ANATOMY OF THE NECK AND SOURCES OF PAIN: FIGURE 48.1 (PAGE 346)

EVALUATION OF NECK PAIN

A. History
   1. Date of onset of symptoms
   2. Description of specific activity in which patient was engaged at onset of symptoms
   3. Whether there has been prolonged extension (e.g., overhead work) or flexion (e.g., computer operation) of neck or a twisting injury or trauma to the neck
   4. Whether the pain is reproduced or increased by neck motion (if not, may be referred pain) (Table 48.1)
   5. Whether the pain is felt outside the neck (Table 48.2)
   6. Whether there is sensory loss in the hands (and if so, in which fingers)

B. Physical examination
   1. Inspection of the head, neck, shoulders, upper extremities, looking for abnormal posture (e.g., torticollis or wryneck) or muscle atrophy
   2. Have patient extend neck to look directly above, touch chin to chest and to each shoulder and bend each ear to shoulder
   3. Compress top of head with hands (may produce pain in patients with degenerative disc disease)
   4. Palpate the posterior neck muscles to determine if they are in spasm
   5. Move the shoulders in all directions to see if pain is elicited
   6. Neurological tests
      a) Evaluating deep tendon reflexes of upper and lower extremities
      b) Muscle and sensory testing of upper extremities

C. Laboratory assessment
   1. Cervical spine x-rays
      a) If pain is severe, if there has been recent trauma, or if neurological examination is abnormal
      b) Should include views of C1 through C7-T1, with oblique and open-mouth odontoid views
      c) To look for fracture or evidence of metastasis
      d) Not a good correlation between evidence of degenerative disease (common in asymptomatic persons after age 40) and signs and symptoms
   2. Computed tomography (CT) useful in evaluation of the upper cervical spine
   3. Magnetic resonance imaging (MRI) useful in patients suspected of having soft tissue abnormalities (e.g., metastatic cancer) or disc disease

SELECTED SYNDROMES ASSOCIATED WITH NECK PAIN (TABLE 48.3)

A. Pain with neurological findings (see above)
   1. Due to nerve root compression
      a) Symptoms and signs
         1) Patients present with acute or gradual onset of posterior

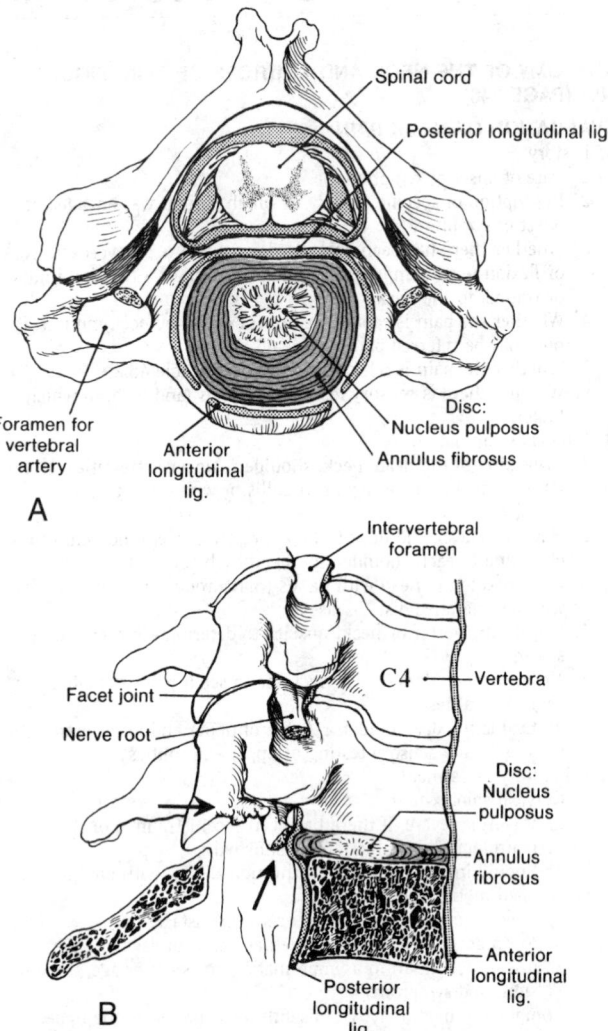

Figure 48.1. Anatomy of disc and ligaments of the cervical spine. **A.** Superior view. Note relationship of anterior and posterior longitudinal ligament to the intervertebral disc. **B.** Lateral view. Note relationship of intervertebral foramen to the intervertebral disc and facet joint. Bulging of the intervertebral disc and bone spurs forming from the facet joint may cause compression of the nerve root within the intervertebral foramen *(arrows)*.

Table 48.1.   Sources of Referred Pain in the Neck[a]

Source	Referred Location
Disorders of the head	
Migraine or tension headache	Anterior or posterior
Sinus infection	Most often anterior but occasionally posterior
Temporomandibular joint problem	Usually anterolateral
Oral problems (see Chapter 84) such as a pharyngeal or tonsillar abscess	Middle of the neck
Distant lesions	
Irritation of the surface of the diaphragm innervated by the phrenic nerve (C3, C4, and C5)	Frequently shoulder as well as low neck pain, but medial diaphragmatic lesion may be associated with neck pain
Shoulder problems (see Chapter 47) such as arthritis or periarticular inflammation	May be referred to the lateral part of the neck
Thoracic outlet syndrome from the compression of vascular and neural structures between the rib and the clavicle or between the scalene muscles	May be noticed in the lateral aspect of the neck
Lung problems such as superior sulcus tumor (Pancoast's tumor)	Initially may be located in the lateral aspect of the neck and shoulder
Cardiovascular problems such as a heart attack or an aneurysm of the thoracic aorta	May be localized to the base of the neck

[a] The clue to referred pain is the absence of any tenderness in the neck or of exacerbation of symptoms with manipulation of the neck.

Table 48.2.   Characteristic Findings at Individual Cervical Nerve Root Levels

Nerve Root	Disc Level	History	Examination
C3	(C2–3)	Pain into the back of the neck to the pinnae and the angle of the jaw	No reflex changes
C4	(C3–4)	Pain into the back of the neck to the levator scapulae to anterior chest	No reflex changes
C5	(C4–5)	Pain into the side of the neck to the superior lateral shoulder, numbness over deltoid muscle	Deltoid muscle atrophy and weakness of shoulder abduction
C6	(C5–6)	Pain to the lateral aspects of the arm and forearm and into the thumb and index finger with numbness of thumb and dorsum of hand	Weak biceps and brachioradial muscles and decreased biceps and brachioradial tendon reflexes
C7	(C6–7)	Pain into the midforearm to middle and ring fingers	Triceps muscle weakness with decreased triceps muscle reflex
C8	(C7–T1)	Pain to the medial aspect of the forearm into the ring and small fingers with numbness of the ulnar border and small finger	Triceps weakness with weakness of intrinsic muscles of the hand

Table 48.3.   Selected Problems of the Neck That May Result in Neck Pain

Problem	Comment
Arthritis	Especially rheumatoid (see Chapter 54) and degenerative joint disease (see text and Chapter 52).
Disc disease	See text.
Fibromyalgia	See Chapter 50.
Infection	Osteomyelitis or soft tissue infection — look for point tenderness (see Chapter 17).
Neoplasia	Myeloma or metastatic disease is associated with point tenderness and x-ray (or bone scan in the case of metastases) abnormalities.
Neuritis	Any nerve may be involved. A relatively common one is the spinal accessory nerve. Look for tenderness over the nerve — lateral aspects of upper one-third of sternomastoid muscle.
Platybasia	A congenital disorder that may not manifest symptoms before age 40 or a complication of Paget's disease; x-rays show characteristic changes (i.e., invagination of the base of the skull)
Sprain	Cervical sprain syndrome due to whiplash and other forms of trauma (see text)
Structures in neck	Any organ or structure located in the neck may become a source of neck pain. Careful examination will detect abnormalities such as thyroiditis, lymphadenitis, pharyngitis, sialadenitis, or tender carotid artery (carotodynia).
Tendinitis	Any tendon may be involved, but occipital and sternomastoid are particularly common. Local tenderness is a clue.
Torticollis (wryneck)	Diagnosis is usually obvious by observation. An underlying structural problem could produce reflex muscle spasm; therefore, with an initial episode an underlying problem (such as tumor or infection) should be considered.
Trauma	Because of the danger of cord injury, trauma associated with neck pain should be carefully evaluated.
Vascular	Arteritis or dissection may cause neck pain.

neck pain that radiates to the shoulder, down one arm, often to the hand

2) Pain worse on movement of the neck

3) May be associated with decreased sensation and with paresthesias in the arm and hand

4) Neurological symptoms and signs may occur without pain

b) Causes

1) In persons under age 50, most commonly cervical disc impingement on the nerve

2) In persons over age 50, most commonly osseous proliferation, compressing the nerve as it exits from the foramen

c) Management

1) If symptoms and signs are relatively mild, a soft cervical collar (basically a reminder to restrict neck motion) may be sufficient

2) If symptoms or signs are relatively severe

(a) Bed rest may be necessary, with a small pillow used under the nape of the neck to provide the proper position

(b) A nonsteroidal anti-inflammatory agent (see Chapter

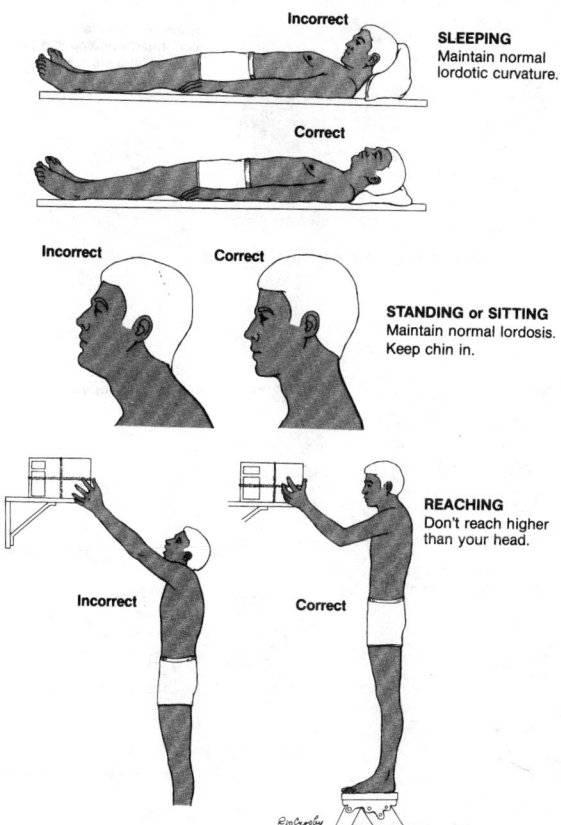

SLEEPING
Maintain normal lordotic curvature.

STANDING or SITTING
Maintain normal lordosis. Keep chin in.

REACHING
Don't reach higher than your head.

Figure 48.2. Position to prevent recurrence of neck pain.

54) or acetaminophen may help, or if necessary, codeine, 30–60 mg 3 or 4 times/day, may be prescribed
(c) A muscle relaxant (see Chapter 49) may be of help if symptoms persist beyond 3 or 4 days
(d) If symptoms recur or persist beyond 2–3 weeks, cervical traction may be of help (initially performed by a physical therapist after x-rays have shown neck to be stable; later, patient can be instructed to apply traction at home)
(e) If symptoms and signs persist, referral to an orthopedist or neurosurgeon is warranted for further evaluation (CT or MRI) and consideration of surgery (usually discectomy and anterior interbody fusion)
3) To prevent recurrence patient should be taught about positions to avoid (Fig. 48.2) and exercises to do (Fig. 48.3)

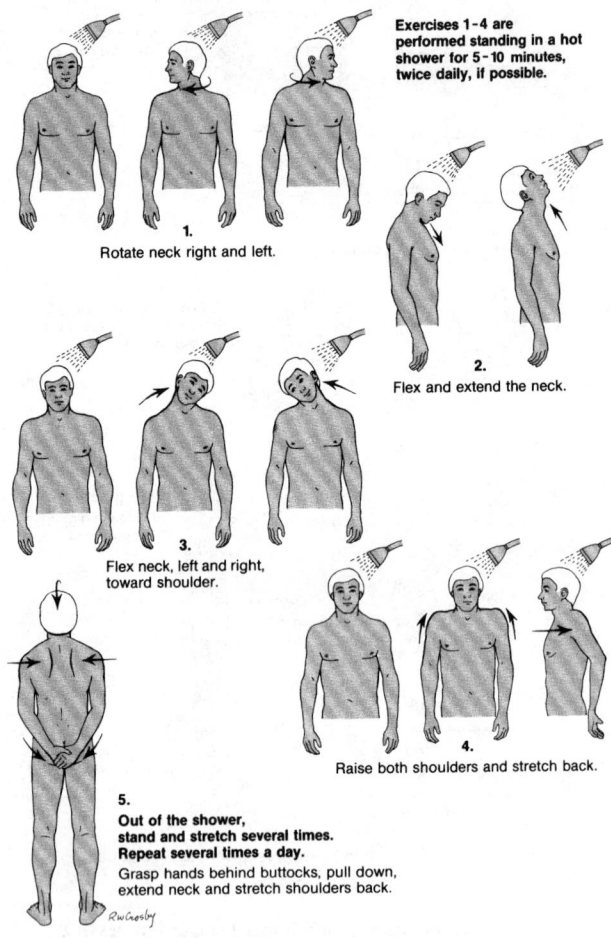

Exercises 1-4 are performed standing in a hot shower for 5-10 minutes, twice daily, if possible.

1.
Rotate neck right and left.

2.
Flex and extend the neck.

3.
Flex neck, left and right, toward shoulder.

4.
Raise both shoulders and stretch back.

5.
Out of the shower, stand and stretch several times. Repeat several times a day.
Grasp hands behind buttocks, pull down, extend neck and stretch shoulders back.

Figure 48.3. Exercises to rehabilitate the neck.

2. Due to spinal cord compression
   a) Symptoms and signs
      1) May present with numb, clumsy hands or spastic paraparesis
      2) Neck pain may be minimal
   b) Causes
      1) Medical disorders (e.g., multiple sclerosis) should be considered in younger persons
      2) Cervical disc or cervical spondylosis, as above
   c) Management: refer promptly to a neurologist or neurosurgeon

to establish etiology and to decide on therapy (e.g., laminectomy or anterior cervical fusion)

B. Pain without neurological findings
   1. Signs and symptoms: except for absence of neurological signs and symptoms, the same as above
   2. Causes
      a) Acute onset of pain usually due to disc herniation
      b) Gradual onset of pain usually due to osteoarthritis
   3. Management: as above for patients with neurological signs and symptoms

C. Cervical sprain syndrome
   1. Cause: acute extension of the cervical spine ("whiplash")
   2. Diagnosis
      a) Pain in the posterior and/or anterior neck, commonly radiating to the occiput, sometimes to the shoulders
      b) Because of risk of disc herniation, fracture, or subluxation, cervical x-rays are essential (if normal, flexion-extension x-rays should be taken)
      c) Any neurological abnormalities warrant urgent referral to a neurosurgeon or an orthopedist
   3. Treatment
      a) Soft cervical collar, analgesics, moist or dry heat
      b) Avoid neck extension
   4. Course: if pain and spasm severe, symptoms usually last 4–6 weeks; if no neurological deficits, conservative therapy can be continued without further evaluation for up to a year

49/ LOW BACK PAIN

EVALUATION OF LOW BACK PAIN

A. History
1. Prior episodes, onset, duration, frequency, location, radiation, time of day, quality, intensity, aggravating and alleviating factors
2. Weakness, sensory abnormalities, bladder or sexual dysfunction
3. Occupational history
4. Presence of systemic symptoms (e.g., fever, weight loss)

B. Physical examination
1. Of lumbosacral spine and associated musculoskeletal structures
   a) Patient standing, in a gown, barefoot or wearing only socks
      1) Check for kyphosis, scoliosis, or excessive lordosis
      2) Palpate the paravertebral muscles and each vertebral spine (isolated tenderness suggests a localized problem such as tumor, infection, fracture)
      3) Assess mobility of the spine
         (a) Have patient bend forward to attempt to touch his or her toes (normal 50–80°) and note if normally smooth reversal of lumbar lordosis occurs (if not, an abnormality of the apophyseal joints or of paraspinous structures may be present)
         (b) Lateral flexion normally to about 30° (if not, may indicate a joint problem of the spine)
         (c) Extension normally to about 30° (if not, suggests disease of apophyseal joints or spinal stenosis)
      b) Patient bent forward over the examining table: palpate the inferior part of the sacroiliac joints, ischial tuberosities, sciatic notch
      c) Observe gait: may be stiff, or one leg may be favored if there is radiculopathy
      d) Patient sitting with legs dangling
         1) Test deep tendon reflexes of knees and ankles
         2) Extend patient's knees (may incite radiating radicular pain, a positive "distracted" straight leg raising (SLR) test)
      e) Patient supine
         1) Standard SLR test: fully extend knee, slowly flex at hip; positive test manifested by radicular pain radiating below knee(s) after elevation of 30°
         2) Crossed SLR: repeat test on side that is unaffected; symptoms often reproduced on affected side
         3) Sensory and motor examination of lower extremities
         4) Assess range of motion of hip and knee joints
         5) Assess sacroiliac joint: put lateral malleus of tested leg on patella of opposite leg and press down on knee while with the other hand applying pressure on the contralateral anterior superior iliac spine (positive reaction is pain in the lateral lumbar spine)
      f) Patient on side
         1) Pressure applied to iliac wing: pain in sacroiliac joints suggests intra-articular disease or strain of posterior iliac ligaments

        2) Elevate upper leg against pressure applied below knee to test muscles of hip abduction

    g) Patient prone

        1) Assess symmetry of buttocks

        2) Extend hip joint: pain in anterior thigh or medial leg suggests herniated disc

    h) Signs of malingering

        1) Overreaction during examination

        2) Positive response (back pain) to pressure applied to top of head or to standing with feet together and arms at side and having torso passively rotated (leg pain may be incited if there is radiculopathy)

        3) Observe patient's movements when he is not aware of being observed

        4) Superficial, nonanatomical or variable tenderness

        5) Nonphysiological motor or sensory findings

  2. Of other regions: particularly important if pain cannot be attributed to a local process in back, if pain is of recent onset, if patient is 50 years or older

C. Laboratory evaluation

  1. Radiographic tests

    a) Plain films of lumbar spine need not be obtained routinely

        1) Positive and negative findings do not correlate well with symptoms

        2) Obtain only after conservative therapy has failed, if there is reflex asymmetry, if there is vertebral point tenderness, or if patients are elderly and have new onset of pain

    b) Perform other radiographic tests preferably only after consultation with a neurosurgeon or orthopedist

        1) Bone scan: to detect infection, tumor (not myeloma), arthritis, fracture

        2) Computed tomography (CT): to detect herniated disc, spinal stenosis, myeloma and to evaluate retroperitoneal structures

        3) Magnetic resonance imaging (MRI): most sensitive test

  2. Other tests: not necessary unless there is suspicion of systemic disease

D. Approach

  1. Most patients with acute onset of low back pain have a mechanical cause (see below) and respond to conservative therapy

  2. Follow-up visit should be scheduled 3–4 weeks after initial contact, at which point patients with persistent or progressive symptoms should be further evaluated

COMMON MECHANICAL BACK SYNDROMES

A. Lumbosacral strain

  1. Epidemiology

    a) Most common cause of low back pain

    b) Persons aged 20–40 years are at greatest risk

    c) Predisposing factors: failure to lift properly, obesity, abnormal forward pelvic tilt, leg length discrepancy

  2. Diagnosis

    a) See Table 49.1

Table 49.1. Information Useful in the Differential Diagnosis of Mechanical Low Back Pain

Diagnosis	Age (years)	Pain Characteristics						Straight Leg Raising Test	Walking	Plain X-ray
		Location	Onset	Standing	Sitting	Bending				
Lumbosacral strain	20–40	Back (unilateral)	Acute	+	–	+		–		–
Herniated nucleus pulposus	30–50	Back and leg (unilateral)	Acute (prior episodes)	–	+	–		+		–
Osteoarthritis	>50	Back (bilateral)	Insidious	+	–	–		–		+
Spinal stenosis	>60	Leg (bilateral)	Insidious	+	–	–		+	Stress, i.e., after walking — see text	+

Adapted from Borenstein DG, Wiesel SW: *Low Back Pain: Medical Diagnosis and Comprehensive Management*. Philadelphia, WB Saunders, 1989.
+, exacerbating; –, alleviating.

       b) Pain usually follows recent increase in activity (e.g., lifting, shoveling) by 12–36 hours
       c) Muscle spasm common
       d) No evidence of nerve root impingement
  3. Management
       a) Reduce physical activity
          1) Strict bed rest for 2 days often effective
          2) ⅝-inch board between mattress and springs is of help
       b) Physical therapy
          1) Initially ice massage
          2) Subsequently, heating pad (low or medium setting with a towel between pad and back) or moist heat for 20–30 minutes several times a day
       c) Nonnarcotic analgesics
          1) For nonelderly, a nonsteroidal anti-inflammatory agent (see Chapter 54) for a limited time (2–6 weeks)
          2) For elderly, acetaminophen or, if necessary, a small dose of narcotic
       d) Muscle relaxants
          1) If there is significant muscle spasm
          2) Flexeril (10 mg once a day), Robaxin (750 mg 4 times/day), Parafon DSC (500 mg 4 times/day), or Norflex (100 mg 2 times/day) for 7–10 days
          3) Valium not effective
       e) As improvement occurs (usually 3–4 days), gradually increase physical activity, avoiding lifting, pushing, etc. and prescribe exercises (Figs. 49.1 and 49.2) for a few minutes 4–6 times/day
       f) Lumbosacral supports (corsets, etc.) for patients who must remain active while symptomatic
          1) Should be fitted by an orthotist or physical therapist
          2) Should be taken off when patient is not working
          3) Patients should be weaned gradually but steadily to avoid weakening of back muscles
B. Herniated intervertebral disc
  1. Diagnosis
       a) See Tables 49.1 and 49.2
       b) Sharp, lancinating pain radiating down back of leg in the distribution of the affected nerve
       c) Bilateral radiating pain, especially with bowel or bladder dysfunction or progressive muscle weakness, suggests cauda equina syndrome, a surgical emergency
       d) Herniated disc most likely diagnosis if there is sensory or motor loss or loss of deep tendon reflexes
       e) If symptoms persist for 3–4 weeks despite conservative treatment (see below), MRI is probably best test to document disc herniation
  2. Management
       a) Limit physical activity: patient in bed with hips and knees flexed, supported by pillows for several days
       b) Nonsteroidal anti-inflammatory drugs (see Chapter 54), muscle relaxants (see above), and narcotic analgesics if necessary (but if narcotics still necessary after 2–3 days, an orthopedist or neurosurgeon should be consulted)

Pelvic tilt
© 1981 THE JOHNS HOPKINS UNIVERSITY

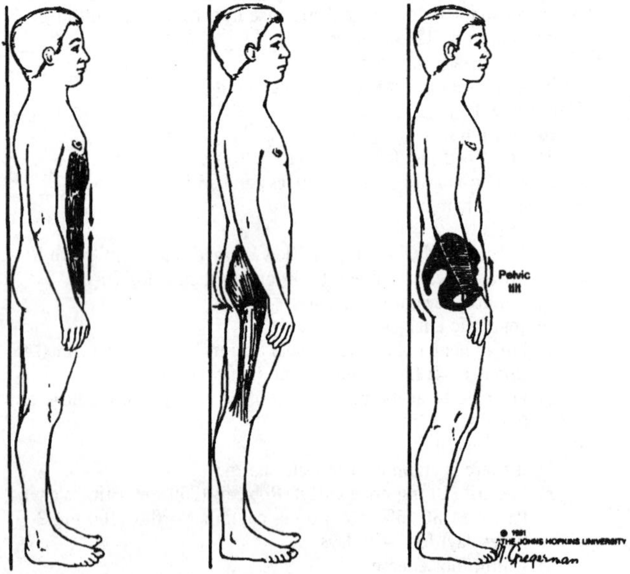

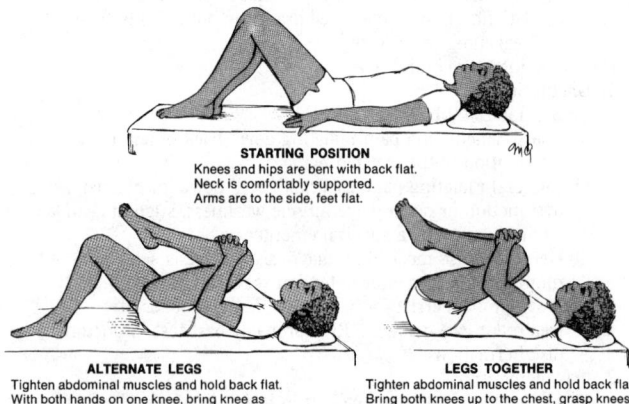

CONTRACT the abdominal muscles (pull umbilicus toward spine as hard as possible). Relax.

CONTRACT the gluteal muscles. Relax.

COMBINE abdominal and gluteal contractions, (produces a pelvic tilt with flexion of the lumbar spine). Relax.

Figure 49.1. Exercises — abdominal muscles and pelvic tilt.

STARTING POSITION
Knees and hips are bent with back flat.
Neck is comfortably supported.
Arms are to the side, feet flat.
ALTERNATE LEGS
Tighten abdominal muscles and hold back flat.
With both hands on one knee, bring knee as near chest as possible.
Return slowly to starting position. Relax.
Repeat, alternating legs, 10 times.
LEGS TOGETHER
Tighten abdominal muscles and hold back flat.
Bring both knees up to the chest, grasp knees with hands, and hold position for 30 seconds.
Return slowly to starting position. Relax.
Repeat 5 times.

Figure 49.2. Knee-chest exercises.

Table 49.2.   Common Findings in Lumbar Disc Herniations

Level of Disc Herniation	Nerve Root Compressed	Pain	Numbness[a]	Weakness	Reflexes (Decreased or Absent)
L3–4	L4	Sacroiliac joint, hip, posterolateral thigh, anterior aspect of leg	L4 dermatome	Extension of knee (quadriceps)	Knee jerk
L4–5	L5	Sacroiliac joint, hip	L5 dermatome (includes great toe)	Dorsiflexion of great toe (extensor hallucis longus)	
L5–S1	S1	Lateral aspect of leg and foot	S1 dermatome (includes lateral toes)	Unusual (plantar flexion of foot)	Ankle jerk
Massive midline lumbar disc herniation	Multiple roots in dural sac	Midline of back, posterior aspect of both thighs and legs	Perineum, posterior thighs, plantar aspect of feet	Paralysis of feet and sphincters	Absent ankle jerk
Cauda equina syndrome (usually L4 or L5)					

Adapted from Vanden Briuk KD, Edmonson AS: The spine. In: Edmonson AS, Crenshaw AH (eds): *Campbell's Operative Orthopaedics*. St Louis, CV Mosby, 1980.

Table 49.3.   Causes of Referred Low Back Pain

Absence of any tenderness, limitation of motion, or aggravation of pain or spasm during the physical examination is suggestive of referred pain

Lower thoracic and upper lumbar pain — from an upper abdominal disease process (e.g., pancreas)

Low lumbar pain — from a lower abdominal disease process (e.g., aortic aneurysm)

Sacral pain — from a pelvic problem (e.g., endometriosis, prostate cancer)

Table 49.4.   Dermatome to Which Pain From Various Visceral Structures May Be Referred

Dermatome	Viscera
L1	Kidney, ureter, body of uterus, abdominal aorta, small intestine
L2	Bladder, abdominal aorta, ascending colon
L3	Abdominal aorta
L4	Abdominal aorta
L5, S1, S2	
S3	Rectum, anus, lower portion of bladder, cervix, upper vagina, prostate
S4	Rectum, anus, base of bladder, cervix, upper vagina, prostate
S5	—

Modified from Borenstein DG, Wiesel SW: *Low Back Pain.* Philadelphia, WB Saunders, 1989, p. 33.

    c) Not needed: physical therapy, ultrasound, diathermy, heat or cold packs, traction
    d) If symptoms persist beyond 3–4 weeks, consider surgical decompression

C. Osteoarthritis and/or spinal stenosis
  1. Diagnosis
    a) See Table 49.1
    b) Pain typically relieved by back flexion, exacerbated by hyperextension
    c) Pain may mimic that of arterial peripheral vascular disease
    d) Neurological deficits may not emerge until patient walks for several minutes
    e) Plain x-rays show degenerative changes in facet joints and decreased anteroposterior canal diameter
    f) CT best technique to show spinal stenosis
  2. Management
    a) Avoid activities that incite pain
    b) Nonsteroidal anti-inflammatory drugs (see Chapter 54)
    c) Conservative management should be tried for 2–3 years, unless pain is incapacitating, before considering corrective surgery

MEDICAL (SYSTEMIC) BACK PAIN SYNDROME

A. Spondyloarthropathies (see Chapter 55)
  1. Morning stiffness a major component
  2. Other symptoms and signs (e.g., iritis, conjunctivitis, skin rash) may be present
  3. Percussion tenderness over the axial skeleton or the sacroiliac joints (see above) may be present

B. Infections, i.e., osteomyelitis, discitis, or septic arthritis (see Chapter 17)

SITTING
Avoid leaning forward.
Support spine with backrest and armrests.
Straight standing is preferable to unsupported sitting.

STANDING
Eliminate work done at slight flexion.
To avoid this posture, the height of the work area may be raised.

LIFTING
Avoid back flexion.
Flex knees, keep spine straight.
Hold objects close to the body.

SLEEPING
Avoid the prone position.
Rest on one side, with pillow under head, knees flexed.

© 1981
THE JOHNS HOPKINS UNIVERSITY

Figure 49.3.   Incorrect and correct postural attitudes.

C. Vertebral fractures
  1. Most common in elderly, often associated with osteoporosis
  2. Most common in thoracic spine
  3. Pain often associated with local tenderness
  4. Bone scan often useful (plain films may miss defect)
  5. CT or MRI often indicated if neurological defects have developed

      6. Management: rest, analgesia, gradual ambulation, lumbosacral support if necessary

      7. Pain may persist for several months, although severe pain usually abates after a few weeks

D. Tumors

      1. Commonly increased pain when patient recumbent

      2. Localized tenderness

      3. Often neurological dysfunction

      4. Radiographic evaluation (see above) useful: in general, benign tumors in the posterior elements of vertebrae; malignant, in anterior

      5. Most effective treatment, if possible, is excision; otherwise, radiation, chemotherapy, corticosteroids must be considered

E. Referred pain: see Tables 49.3 and 49.4

PREVENTION OF RECURRENCE: FIGURE 49.3 (PAGE 359)

50/ NONARTICULAR RHEUMATIC DISORDERS

BURSITIS

A. Etiology
   1. Most often, minor trauma (e.g., repetitive throwing of a ball or prolonged kneeling on a hard floor), particularly in the middle-aged or elderly
   2. Less often, rheumatoid arthritis, gout, sepsis
B. Manifestations
   1. Acute onset of aching pain: precisely localized if affected bursa is superficial, imprecisely localized if affected bursa is deep, often after some repetitive physical activity
   2. There may be swelling, redness, tenderness over bursa (redness, heat, fever suggest infection but not reliably)
   3. No pain on passive motion of joint
C. Aspiration of bursae
   1. Technique: Table 50.1
   2. Primarily to rule out infection
   3. Laboratory tests: Table 50.2
D. Treatment
   1. If septic

Table 50.1. Technique for Aspiration of Superficial Bursae (or Joints) and of Analysis of Bursal (or Synovial) Fluid

1. Determine by palpation the area of maximal tenderness and/or fluctuance and outline with indelible pen.
2. Clean the skin with iodine solution such as povidone (Betadine).
3. Anesthetize the skin with lidocaine in the area of planned aspiration.
4. Use an 18-gauge needle to aspirate.
5. Grossly inspect the fluid and analyze for the following:
   a. Cell count and differential — fluid needs to be in a tube containing heparin or ethylenediaminetetraacetic acid (EDTA)
   b. Type of crystals (see Chapter 53)
   c. Gram stain and culture, using transport media (even in the absence of a high white cell count)

Table 50.2. Patterns of Bursal (or Joint) Fluid Findings in Common Problems

	Normal	Trauma	Sepsis	Rheumatoid Inflammation	Microcrystalline Inflammation
Color of fluid	Clear yellow	Bloody, xanthochromic	Yellow to cloudy	Clear yellow to cloudy	Clear yellow to cloudy
WBC, RBC	0–200/0	<1,000/many	1,000–200,000/ few	1,000–20,000[a]/ few	1,000–20,000[a]/ few
Crystals	–	–	–	–	+[b]
Culture	–	–	+	–	–

WBC, white blood cell count; RBC, red blood cell count.
[a] Cell count in noninfected inflammatory fluid may sometimes be as high as it is with sepsis, thus the need for culture.
[b] Gout: negatively birefringent sodium urate (see Chapter 53). Pseudogout: positively birefringent sodium pyrophosphate (see Chapter 53).

Table 50.3. Treatment of Bursitis

1. Splint where feasible (especially effective in the hand and fingers).
2. Application of heat or cold may be of benefit in some patients.
3. Anti-inflammatory agents: a nonsteroidal anti-inflammatory agent with rapid onset of action is preferred (see Chapter 54 for a full discussion of NSAIDs).
4. Improvement is usual in several days, but the anti-inflammatory agent should be continued an additional 4–5 days to prevent recurrence.
5. If no significant response is noted in 5–7 days and if sepsis has been ruled out, the bursa may be injected with lidocaine and/or a steroid preparation (see Table 50.4).

NSAIDs, nonsteroidal anti-inflammatory drugs.

Table 50.4. Methods of Injection of Bursae or Joints With Lidocaine and/or Depoglucocorticoid Preparations[a]

1. Be certain sepsis has been ruled out (Tables 50.1 and 50.2).
2. Prepare the skin carefully with an iodine-containing solution such as povodone (Betadine).
3. Anesthetize the skin with intradermal 1–2% lidocaine.
4. Mix 2–3 ml of 1–2% lidocaine with 20–40 mg of a depoglucocorticoid (such as Celestone, Aristocort, or Kenalog) and inject the bursa with 1–3 ml of this mixture using a 22-gauge needle.

[a] *Notes of caution:* (*a*) injection into the skin will cause atrophy and thus should be avoided; the patient should understand that there is a possibility of this complication; and (*b*) injection into tendons themselves may cause degeneration and, in time, rupture; these structures should be avoided by careful palpation.

      a) If Gram stain is negative or Gram-positive organisms are seen, prescribe a penicillinase-resistant antistaphylococcal drug
      b) If Gram-negative organisms are seen, do blood cultures, seek an extrabursal source of infection
      c) Hospitalize if there is high fever, chills, surrounding intense cellulitis, extrabursal or deep bursal infection, infection with an unusual organism, a compromised patient (e.g., diabetes mellitus, alcoholism, HIV infection)
      d) Repeat aspirations (usually 2–3 times/week) until fluid stops accumulating
  2. If not septic, follow the procedures and methods described in Tables 50.3 and 50.4

E. Specific forms
  1. Olecranon bursitis
      a) A "goose-egg" swelling just behind the olecranon process of the ulna
      b) Movement of the elbow is nearly painless
      c) Frequently associated with systemic disease (e.g., rheumatoid arthritis or gout)
      d) Symptoms frequently chronic (often present for several weeks before patient sees a physician)
      e) Should be aspirated (see Tables 50.1 and 50.2)
      f) Therapy: see "Treatment," above; if process has been present for more than 2 weeks, obtain elbow x-ray to rule out osteomyelitis or a foreign body
  2. Prepatellar bursitis
      a) Most often caused by excessive kneeling
      b) Should always be aspirated to rule out sepsis
      c) Treatment: see above

3. Anserine bursitis
   a) At anterior medial aspect of the knee just below joint space
   b) Most often seen in people with arthritis, especially overweight, middle-aged women with osteoarthritis of the knee
   c) Pain worse when the knee is flexed, particularly bothersome at night
4. Ischial bursitis
   a) Over ischial tuberosity
   b) Often induced by prolonged sitting on a hard surface (e.g., bicycling)
   c) Pain usually begins abruptly but may develop insidiously; worse when sitting or lying supine
   d) May be associated with sciatica
   e) Aspiration not recommended (difficult to localize bursa, may cause nerve injury)
   f) Treatment: see above; if symptoms persist, patient should be referred to a rheumatologist or orthopedist for aspiration, injection
5. Semimembranosus-gastrocnemius bursitis (Baker's cyst)
   a) Posterior medial knee: best seen and felt when patient is standing
   b) Commonly associated with other knee problems (e.g., internal derangements, rheumatoid or degenerative arthritis)
   c) Frequently asymptomatic unless cyst ruptures (then, acute pain, swelling, redness of calf and lower leg; must be distinguished from thrombophlebitis)
   d) Treatment
      1) Aspiration and injection (Tables 50.3 and 50.4)
      2) Minimize weight bearing for several days
      3) If cyst ruptures, bed rest, heat, elevation
6. Iliopectineal bursitis
   a) Between inguinal ligament and iliopsoas muscle just lateral to femoral artery
   b) Pain in anterior pelvis, groin, thigh
   c) Swelling may be mistaken for femoral hernia
   d) Extension of legs (e.g., walking) intensifies the pain
   e) May be associated with irritation of adjacent anterior crural nerve with associated neuritic thigh pain and, possibly, weakness of anterior thigh
   f) May compress femoral vein, causing edema
   g) Treatment: refer to an orthopedist for aspiration and injection
7. Trochanteric bursitis
   a) Lateral thigh over greater trochanter of femur
   b) Primarily in elderly
   c) Onset acute, subacute, or chronic
   d) Pain may radiate to knee or groin
   e) Pain accentuated by moving from sitting to standing position, going up or down stairs, sleeping on affected side
   f) Point tenderness over bursa and pain on external rotation combined with abduction of hip
   g) Treatment: see above
8. Subdeltoid bursitis: see Chapter 47

TENOSYNOVITIS

A. Etiology
   1. Usually from repetitive unaccustomed exercise
   2. Occasionally part of a generalized inflammatory process
B. Manifestations
   1. Pain and swelling over tendon, intensified by stretching of the tendon
   2. Occasionally, a friction rub is felt or heard when the muscle is contracted
C. Treatment
   1. If due to trauma, a nonsteroidal anti-inflammatory drug (see Chapter 54)
   2. If in wrist, fingers should be splinted in position of function
   3. If symptoms persist for more than 3 or 4 days, the peritenon should be injected with lidocaine and a corticosteroid (Table 50.4) — no more than 0.5 ml of each
   4. See also Chapters 47 ("Shoulder Pain"), 51 ("Exercise-Related Musculoskeletal Problems"), and 85 ("Common Problems of the Feet")

STENOSING TENOSYNOVITIS

A. Etiology
   1. Not a complication of tenosynovitis
   2. A response to severe, localized, usually repeated, trauma (e.g., using a screwdriver)
   3. Occasionally associated with rheumatoid arthritis, pregnancy, amyloidosis, myxedema
B. Manifestations
   1. Tendon "sticks" painfully in fixed position
   2. If flexor tendons of finger affected, called "trigger finger"
   3. If abductor or extensor tendon of thumb affected, called De Quervain's disease
C. Treatment
   1. See Tables 50.3 and 50.4
   2. Splinting of help if hand and fingers affected
   3. If no response after several weeks, surgical release may be necessary

DUPUYTREN'S CONTRACTURE

A. Etiology: unknown, more common in epileptics and alcoholics
B. Manifestations
   1. Flexion contracture of digits, most commonly fourth and fifth
   2. Primarily affects middle-aged and older men; bilaterally in 40%
C. Treatment
   1. Anti-inflammatory agents, injections not effective
   2. If functional disability has occurred, patient should be referred to an orthopedist for possible surgery

GANGLIONS

A. Manifestations
   1. Cystic swellings arising from the synovium of a joint or tendon sheath
   2. More frequently occur in women from teens through age 50
   3. Onset may be sudden or gradual
   4. Cysts may disappear, then recur

5. Most common site is dorsum of the wrist between thumb and index finger
6. May ache

B. Treatment
1. If asymptomatic, do not treat
2. If symptomatic, aspirate and/or inject with cortisone; recurrent ganglions may need to be excised

FIBROMYALGIA

A. Manifestations
1. Widespread soft tissue aching and stiffness: of variable severity, occurring usually daily for months or years
2. Other symptoms are common: fatigue, headaches, sore throat, depression, insomnia, difficulty concentrating, constipation and diarrhea, swollen glands, subjective sense of fever or joint swelling
3. Ninety percent of affected persons are women
4. Only positive physical findings are tender points (Fig. 50.1); 90% will have tenderness of at least 11 of 18 points
5. Laboratory tests are normal; should be ordered sparingly

B. Treatment
1. Evaluation: explanation that process is not progressive
2. One-third of patients respond to antidepressants (e.g., Elavil 10–50 mg at bedtime) or to muscle relaxants (e.g., Flexeril 5–30 mg at bedtime)
3. Anti-inflammatory drugs are not of help
4. Supportive therapy: talking to patient for structured periods of

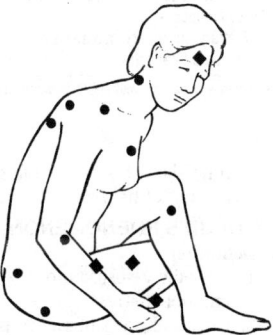

● = PAIRED TENDER POINTS (9)

1. Insertion of Nuchal Muscles into Occiput
2. Upper Trapezius (midpoint)
3. Pectoralis Muscle – just lateral to second costochondral junction
4. 2 cm below Lateral Epicondyle
5. Upper Gluteal Region
6. 2 cm posterior to Greater Trochanter
7. Medial Knee in area of Anserine Bursa
8. Paraspinous, 3 cm lateral to midline at the level of midscapula
9. Above the scapular spine near medial border

◆ = 4 CONTROL POINTS

1. Middle of forehead
2. Volar aspect of midforearm
3. Thumbnail
4. Muscles of anterior thigh

Figure 50.1. The tender point locations in fibromyalgia are remarkably constant from patient to patient. Multiple locations have been described; the 9 paired tender points with fibrositis usually have 11 or more tender points. Control points are not unduly tender; their examination should be interspersed with the tender points. (Modified from Bennett RM: Fibrositis. In: Kelly WN, Harris ED, Rudy S, Sledge CB (eds): *Textbook of Rheumatology,* 4th ed. Philadelphia, WB Saunders, 1993.)

Table 50.5.   Classification of Raynaud's Phenomenon

Primary: Idiopathic Raynaud's, Raynaud's disease	
Secondary: Disorders associated with Raynaud's phenomenon	
Connective tissue diseases	
Systemic sclerosis	90[a]
Systemic lupus erythematosus	20[a]
"Mixed" connective tissue disease	75[a]
Dermatomyositis/polymyositis	20[a]
Rheumatoid arthritis	10[a]
Neurovascular compression	
Thoracic outlet syndrome (e.g., cervical ribs, scalenus anticus syndrome)	
Carpal tunnel syndrome	
Arterial disease	
Arteriosclerosis	
Arteritis (thromboangiitis obliterans)	
Hematological disorders	
Paraproteinemia	
Cryoglobulinemia	
Polycythemia	Unknown[a]
Hyperviscosity syndrome	
Occupational	
Vibratory tools (white finger syndrome)	
Polyvinyl chloride exposure	
Drugs	
Ergot-containing drugs (e.g., ergotamine)	
β-Adrenergic blockers	
Sympathomimetic agents (e.g., Actifed)	
Methysergide (Sansert)	
Chemotherapy (bleomycin, vinblastine)	
Miscellaneous	
Primary pulmonary hypertension	30[a]
Migraine headache	10[a]

[a] Percentages of patients with stated disorder who also have Raynaud's phenomenon.

time about his or her life situation without dwelling on symptoms is often of help

RAYNAUD'S PHENOMENON

A. Definition
1. Episodic vasospasm of the digital vessels in response to cold or emotional stress
2. Classically, a triphasic response: pallor from fingertips to midfinger, then mottling and cyanosis persist until hand is rewarmed, then intense hyperemia over 15–20 minutes

B. Classification (Table 50.5)
1. About 40% of patients who present with Raynaud's phenomenon will have an underlying condition
2. Secondary form suggested by childhood onset, male sex, onset in women after age 40, unilateral symptoms, fingertip ulcers or gangrene, signs of a systemic disorder

C. Evaluation
1. Focused history and physical examination to look for associated disease
2. Look for digital ulcers

Table 50.6.   Nonpharmacological Management of Patients With Raynaud's Phenomenon

Education and reassurance

    Establish precipitating factors (such as refrigerator/freezer, air conditioning, emotional stress).

    Provide emotional support; e.g., assurance of the mild nature of the disease in most patients may reduce some of the stress that can precipitate attacks.

Avoidance of precipitating factors

    Wear gloves before reaching into refrigerator or freezer.

    Wear warm body clothing to avoid cold exposure when dressing.

    Keep head covered to avoid heat loss.

    Keep extremities warm and body well covered in cool weather or in air-conditioned environments.

    Be aware that stress can cause Raynaud's attacks.

Avoid certain drugs that precipitate attacks:

    β-Blockers (e.g., propranolol)

    Ergot-containing drugs (i.e., ergotamine)

    Sympathomimetic agents (e.g., isoproterenol, Actifed, or other cold remedies)

    Nicotine (smoking)

    Oral contraceptives

3. Looking at the nail bed through an ophthalmoscope with a 20+ diopter may reveal abnormal capillaries suggestive of an underlying connective tissue disease

4. If symptoms are unilateral, consider neurovascular compression syndrome (Chapter 47), chest x-ray, and Doppler studies or digital plethysmography

5. Carpal tunnel syndrome may be associated with Raynaud's phenomenon and should be evaluated (Chapter 67) if symptoms and signs are compatible

6. If primary disease likely, laboratory evaluation can be limited (e.g., complete blood count, urinalysis)

D. Treatment

  1. Nonpharmacological (Table 50.6): the approach for most of the patients with primary disease

  2. Nifedipine (the first choice) and diltiazem are effective

    a) Give 10 mg nifedipine in office, then measure sitting and standing blood pressure and pulse every 15 minutes for 30–45 minutes; if systolic pressure does not fall ≥20 mm (or <90 mm Hg), may prescribe 10 mg 3 times/day and may increase dose every 3 or 4 days by 10 mg, if necessary, to 30 mg 3 times/day

    b) If nifedipine fails or is not tolerated, diltiazem 30 mg 4 times/day may be tried, then advanced if necessary by 30 mg/day every 3–4 days to 120 mg 4 times/day

  3. No other drugs are clearly effective; in intractable situations, sympathectomy may give short-term relief

51/ EXERCISE-RELATED MUSCULOSKELETAL PROBLEMS

PROBLEMS OF THE KNEE

A. Knee structure: Figure 51.1, *A* and *B*
B. General evaluation of knee injuries
   1. If no history of acute trauma, ask about any recent change in physical activity and look for problems elsewhere in the extremity that might increase stress on the knee (e.g., excessive pronation of the feet — Chapter 85)
   2. Also consider nonarticular rheumatism (Chapter 50) or arthritis (Chapters 52–54)
C. Meniscal and ligamentous injuries
   1. Symptoms and signs
      a) Meniscus injury
         1) Twisting flexion injury followed by pain, inability to flex knee fully or to bear weight
         2) Usually associated with an effusion, tenderness over the joint line medially (medial meniscus injury) or laterally (lateral meniscus injury)

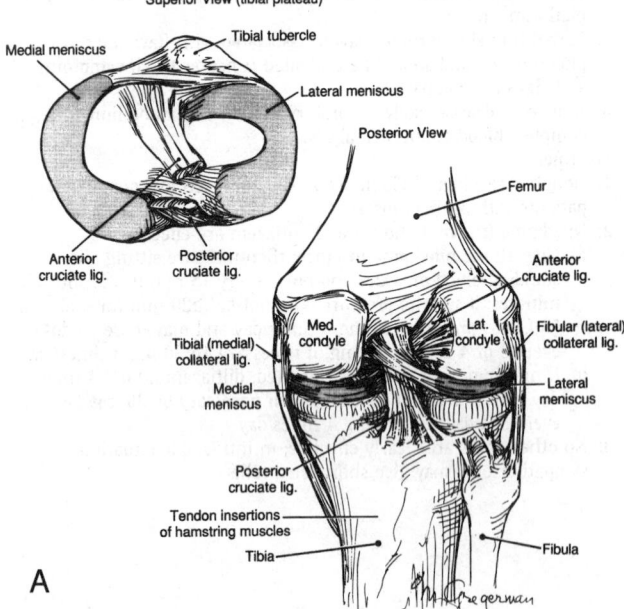

Figure 51.1. **A.** Important structures of the knee.

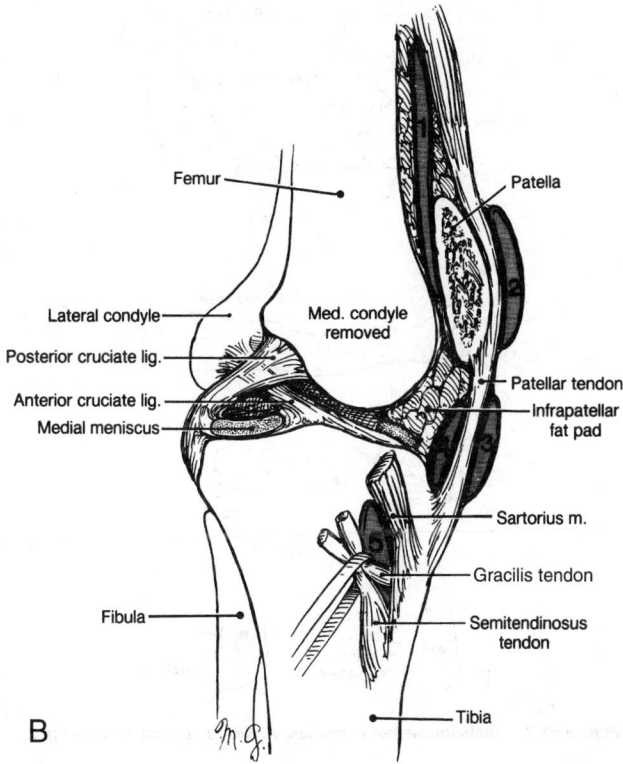

Figure 51.1. B. Five bursae of the knee: *1,* suprapatellar; *2,* prepatellar; *3,* superficial patellar tendon; *4,* retropatellar tendon; *5,* pes anserinus.

3) Onset sometimes insidious with episodic effusion or clicking or locking of knee, minimal tenderness, and perhaps disuse atrophy of quadriceps
4) In acute situations, certain maneuvers may produce pain (Fig. 51.2)
  b) Ligament injuries
1) A sprain (a strain is a milder injury — see Sprains and Avulsion Fractures, below) causes pain at the time of injury and then stiffness of the knee, tenderness, fullness over the ligament, sometimes a serous joint effusion
2) Stability of ligaments should be assessed (compare with uninjured knee) (Fig. 51.3)
2. Additional evaluation
  a) X-rays of the knee (anteroposterior, lateral, tunnel, and sunrise patellar views) to exclude other problems
  b) Aspirate large effusions

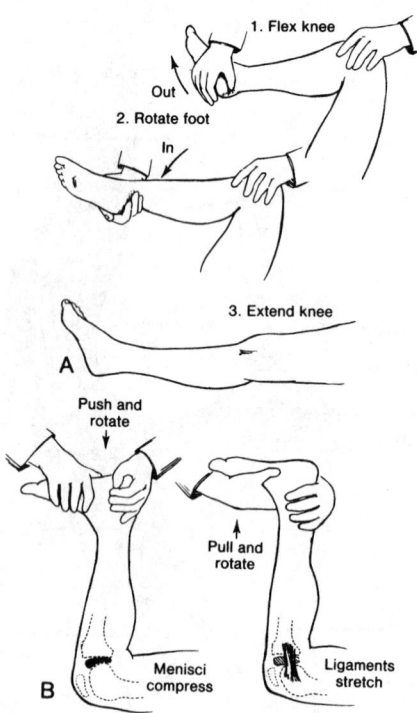

Figure 51.2.   Tests for meniscus injuries. **A.** McMurray test. **B.** Apley test.

    1) To relieve discomfort
    2) If there is hemarthrosis, may indicate more serious injury,
       and referral to an orthopedist is indicated
3. Treatment
    a) Meniscus injuries
        1) Immobilization of the knee with an immobilizer (available
           from large pharmacies or orthopedic appliance stores)
        2) Patient should use crutches (proper use should be taught by
           physician, nurse, or therapist)
        3) Injured extremity should be elevated when the patient lies
           down
        4) Ice packs for 15 minutes several times a day
        5) Isometric quadriceps-strengthening exercises as soon as
           they can be done comfortably (Fig. 51.44)
        6) If symptoms persist beyond 2 weeks or if they recur, refer to
           an orthopedist for consideration for magnetic resonance
           imaging or arthroscopic repair
    b) Ligament injuries
        1) If a ruptured ligament is suspected (unstable joint),
           immobilize the knee as described above with a posterior
           splint and refer immediately to an orthopedist

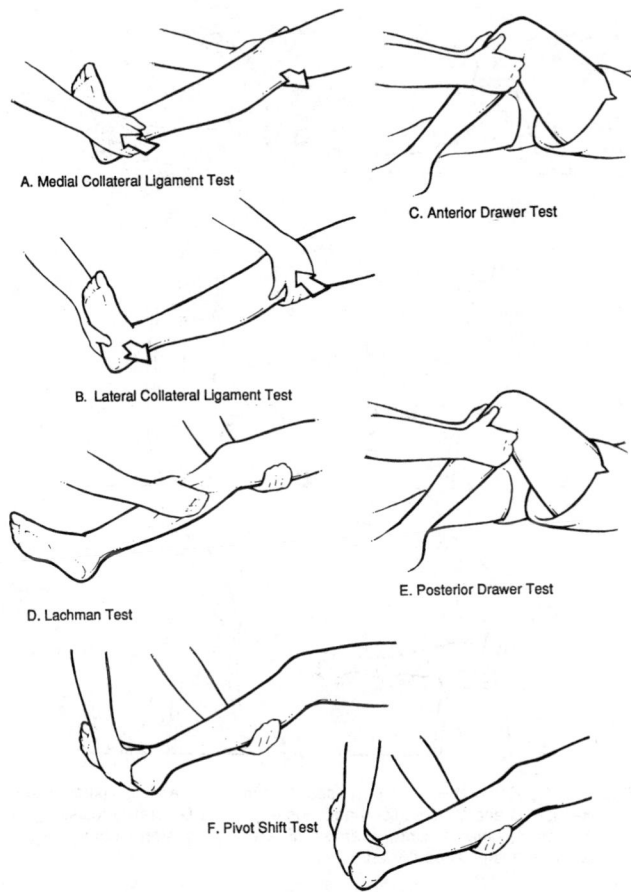

A. Medial Collateral Ligament Test

B. Lateral Collateral Ligament Test

C. Anterior Drawer Test

D. Lachman Test

E. Posterior Drawer Test

F. Pivot Shift Test

Figure 51.3. Examination for collateral and cruciate ligament injuries (see text). **A.** Medial collateral ligament test. **B.** Lateral collateral ligament test. **C.** Anterior drawer test. **D.** Lachman test. **E.** Posterior drawer test. **F.** Pivot shift test. (Modified and redrawn from Scott WN, Nisonson B, Nicholas JA (eds): *Principles of Sports Medicine.* Baltimore, Williams & Wilkins, 1984.)

       2) If there is a sprain and symptoms are relatively mild, increase activity gradually over 1–2 weeks
       3) If there is a sprain and symptoms are relatively severe, treat as for meniscus injuries (see above), and when brace is removed, progressively increase activity and begin isotonic quadriceps exercises (Fig. 51.4, *B* and *C*)
D. Patellofemoral arthralgia and other causes of anterior knee pain
   1. Causes

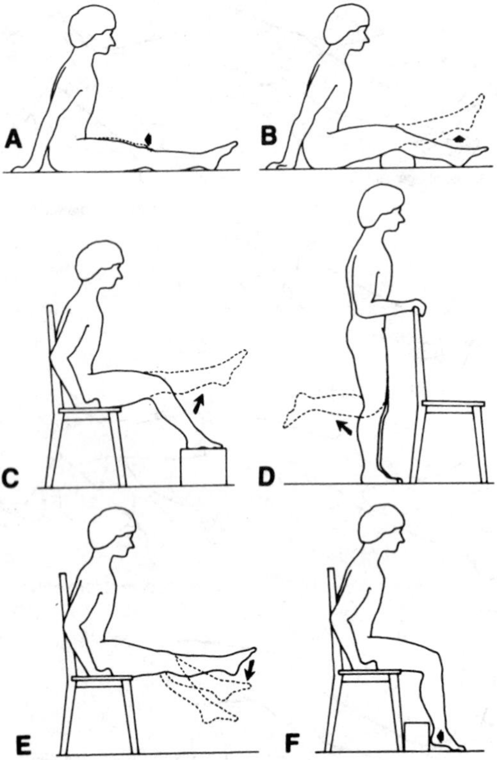

Figure 51.4. Restorative knee exercises. **A.** Isometric quadriceps (knee extensor) exercise. **B** and **C.** Isotonic quadriceps exercises. **D.** Gravity-resisted isotonic hamstring (knee flexion) exercise. **E.** Gravity-assisted isotonic flexion exercise. **F.** Isometric knee flexion exercise.

    a) Chondromalacia — breakdown of cartilage
    b) Hypermobility of the patella
       1) Due to increased angle between quadriceps and patellar tendon, sometimes associated with excessive pronation of feet
       2) Due to patella alta, variant in which patella is more proximal than usual, identified by a patellar tendon length exceeding length of patella by >1 cm
    c) Overuse, e.g., quadriceps strain
    d) Abnormal hip joint causing compensatory changes in knee that displace the patella
  2. Symptoms and signs
    a) Soreness or aching around or under the patella, aggravated by

running up hills, climbing or descending stairs, kneeling or hyperextending the knee
  b) Pain and/or crepitus with patellofemoral manipulation
  c) Effusion can be present
  d) Patellar displacement, as above
3. X-rays of knee should be done routinely
4. Differential diagnosis: exclude bursitis (Fig. 51.1*B* and Chapter 50), meniscal or ligamentous injury (see above), arthritis, hip or pelvic disease with referred pain, and osteochrondritis dissecans (necrosis within the condylar epiphysis, confirmed by x-ray, characterized by insidious onset of knee aching at rest, worsened by weight bearing)
5. Treatment
  a) Crutches for up to 7 days
  b) Application of ice packs for 15 minutes several times a day
  c) Analgesics, e.g., aspirin, 600 mg 4 times/day, or nonsteroidal anti-inflammatory agents (see Chapter 54)
  d) After acute inflammation has subsided, referral to a physical therapist for exercises to strengthen quadriceps (Fig. 51.4)
  e) If symptoms persist, referral to an orthopedist for advice about corticosteroid injections, use of orthotics to correct excessive pronation of feet, use of a knee brace, etc.

PROBLEMS OF THE LEG

A. Apophysitis of the tibial tubercle (Osgood-Schlatter's disease)
  1. Common cause of knee pain in adolescents
  2. Usually self-limited
  3. Insidious onset of pain over the tibial tubercle with activity, often bilateral
  4. Tubercle and adjacent tendon often enlarged and tender
  5. Quadriceps may be atrophied, quadriceps and hamstrings may be tight
  6. Treatment: have patient avoid climbing, running, kicking until symptoms abate (usually 6–8 weeks), do stretching exercises (see below); if pain persists, refer to an orthopedist for evaluation for surgical correction
B. Shin splints
  1. Definition: pain over the anteromedial aspect of the middle to distal portion of the lower leg, usually due to overuse in poorly conditioned persons
  2. Symptoms and signs: pain and tenderness during or just after exercise; onset usually gradual
  3. Other evaluation: bone scan is more sensitive than x-ray
  4. Treatment
    a) Ice packs for 15 minutes several times a day
    b) If pain is severe, have patient avoid exercise
    c) Elastic wraps on lower leg may be of help
    d) Analgesics (see above) or nonsteroidal anti-inflammatory agents (Chapter 54)
    e) After symptoms resolve, stretching exercises (see below) before returning to activity that generated symptoms
C. Compartment syndromes

1. Signs and symptoms
    a) Anterior compartment syndrome
        1) Pain in the extensor muscles of the leg and in the lower leg, ankle, foot during or just after exercise
        2) Tenderness and often swelling over the midlateral aspect of the lower leg
        3) Sometimes, weakness of toe extensors and ankle dorsiflexors
    b) Lateral compartment syndrome — pain in the posterolateral ankle above and behind the lateral malleolus
2. Treatment
    a) Ice packs for 15 minutes several times a day
    b) Abstain from exercise for 3–4 weeks
    c) Nonsteroidal anti-inflammatory agents (see Chapter 54)
    d) Pre-exercise stretching (see below) once symptoms subside
    e) After lateral compartment syndrome, consideration of orthotics (on consultation with an orthopedist or podiatrist)

PROBLEMS OF THE ANKLE AND FOOT

A. Injuries of the ankle joint
    1. Signs and symptoms
        a) Sensation or sound of tearing followed immediately by pain
        b) If a sprain (rather than a strain), instability of joint on weight bearing
        c) Local tender swelling within 1 hour, perhaps followed by diffuse swelling of the foot and ecchymosis if ligaments are torn
    2. Treatment
        a) Immobilize ankle (no walking, elastic bandage); elevate leg
        b) Ice packs for 15 minutes several times a day
        c) If symptoms relatively mild and no instability of ankle, weight bearing can be gradually increased over 2–4 weeks
        d) If symptoms relatively severe or if joint is unstable, referral to an orthopedist for definitive diagnosis and treatment is warranted; rigid splints, crutches will be required, perhaps even surgical repair
B. Achilles tendinitis
    1. Symptoms and signs
        a) Common in runners
        b) Burning pain early in run, which then lessens, recurs after completion of the run
        c) Local or diffuse tenderness in tendon; if condition chronic, there may be a tender nodule in the tendon, crepitus and swelling
    2. Treatment
        a) Ice packs for 15 minutes several times a day
        b) Analgesic agents or nonsteroidal anti-inflammatory agents, as above
        c) Rest for several days, then reduced mileage on run, avoiding hills, until symptoms have abated for 3–4 weeks
        d) Ultrasound may be of help in resistant cases
        e) Removable heel lift may help
C. Plantar fascitis: see Chapter 85
D. Retrocalcaneal bursitis: see Chapter 85
E. Tarsal tunnel syndrome: see Chapter 67

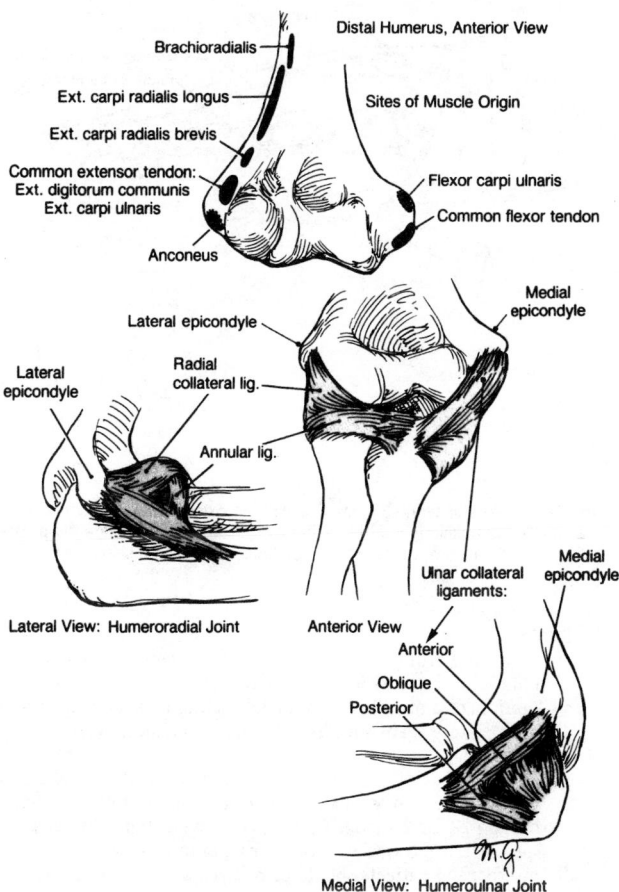

Figure 51.5. Important structures of the elbow.

PROBLEMS OF THE ELBOW
A. Elbow structures: Figure 51.5
B. Lateral epicondylitis (tennis elbow)
   1. Definition: inflammation in the region of the lateral epicondyle of the humerus, caused by activities that combine excessive pronation and supination of the forearm with an extended wrist (e.g., tennis, bowling, repetitive use of a screwdriver)
   2. Symptoms and signs
      a) Gradual onset of pain
      b) Tenderness over the lateral epicondyle or over the radiohumeral joint (Fig. 51.5)
      c) See Figure 51.6

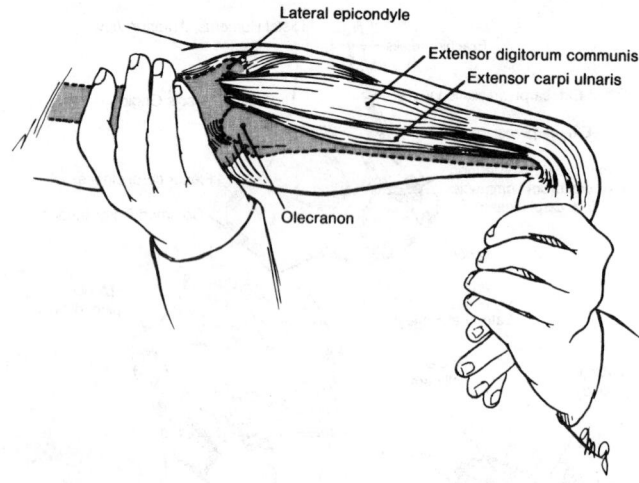

Figure 51.6. Test for tennis elbow. The wrist is extended against resistance from a fully flexed position, and the patient will notice pain at the lateral epicondyle. This usually mimics the patient's symptoms if the diagnosis is correct.

   3. Treatment
      a) Immobilize arm in a sling or, if symptoms severe, a long arm splint with the wrist in dorsiflexion
      b) Aspirin, acetaminophen, or a rapidly acting nonsteroidal anti-inflammatory agent such as naproxen or piroxicam (see Chapter 54)
      c) Injection at point of tenderness with a mixture of 3 ml of 1–2% lidocaine and 1 ml glucocorticoid (e.g., Aristocort or Kenalog) through 22- or 25-gauge needle may provide dramatic relief of pain; repeat in 3 weeks if symptoms continue to recur
      d) Unresponsive patients should be referred to an orthopedist; surgery will occasionally be required
C. Medial epicondylitis (golfer's elbow)
   1. Definition: inflammatory in the region of the medial epicondyle, caused by repetitive pronation (e.g., golf, carrying objects with elbows flexed)
   2. Symptoms and signs: as with lateral epicondylitis (see above) but medially
   3. Treatment: as with lateral epicondylitis, above

SPRAINS AND AVULSION FRACTURES (SEE ALSO PROBLEMS OF THE KNEE AND PROBLEMS OF THE ANKLE AND FOOT, ABOVE)
A. Definitions
   1. Strain — overstretching of a muscle (or a tendon or ligament) without disruption of tissue
   2. Sprain — partial or complete rupture of fibers of a ligament, as well as a stress injury to a joint capsule

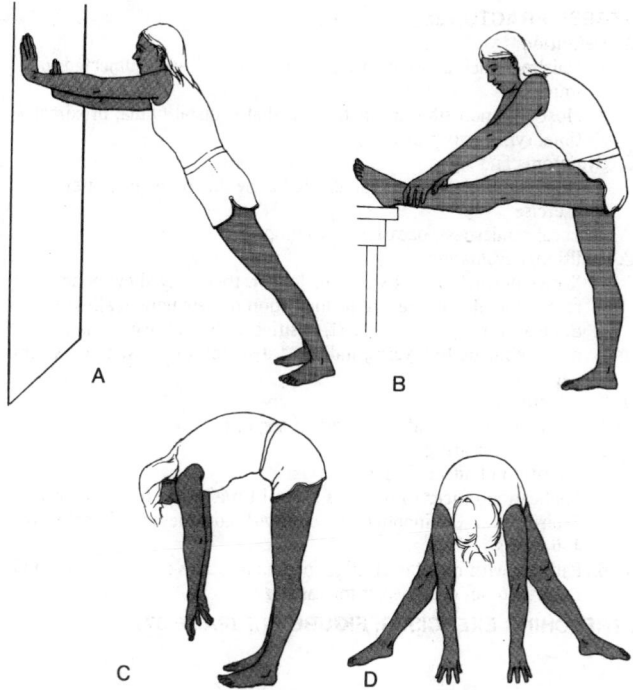

Figure 51.7. **A.** Stretch the Achilles tendon by leaning forward with the feet flat and placed at least 4 feet from the wall. **B.** Stretch the hamstring and gastrocnemius muscle groups by elevating the leg and bending forward as far as possible. **C.** Stretch the hamstring and back muscles by touching the toes slowly; bouncing should be avoided. **D.** Stretch the adductor muscle by gradually spreading the legs as far as possible; place the fingers on the floor for support.

    3. Avulsion fracture — avulsion of a chip of bone from the insertion of a ligament; most common around knee, elbow, fingers

B. Symptoms and signs
    1. Pain in the area of the injury
    2. Stiffness, tenderness, and swelling of the involved joint with increased pain on use of the joint
    3. Joint may be unstable if ligament has ruptured

C. Additional evaluation
    1. X-ray to diagnose avulsion fracture
    2. If joint is unstable, refer to an orthopedist

D. Treatment
    1. Immobilization with a splint (if finger, in the position of function for no more than 3 weeks), elevation of affected part, application of ice for 15 minutes several times a day
    2. Aspirin or acetaminophen, alone or with codeine, 30–60 mg every 4–6 hours
    3. Crutches if injury is to knee or ankle (see above)

STRESS FRACTURES

A. Definition
   1. Hairline crack in a bone that has been repetitively subjected to impact
   2. Most common sites are metatarsal shafts, distal fibula, proximal tibia, symphysis pubis
B. Symptoms and signs
   1. Gradual onset of aching of affected bone during or just after exercise
   2. Local tenderness, occasional swelling
C. Additional evaluation
   1. X-rays normal for 2–4 weeks or longer, then may show bone resorption at fracture site or formation of new bone (callus)
   2. Bone scan most sensitive test, positive early and may remain positive for up to 2 years; indicated if symptoms persist and x-rays negative
D. Treatment
   1. Immobilization of affected part in a splint
   2. No weight bearing
   3. Elevation of affected part
   4. Application of ice, 15 minutes several times a day for a day or two
   5. Aspirin or acetaminophen alone or with codeine, 30–60 mg every 4–6 hours
   6. Patients with metatarsal, tibial or fibular stress fractures should be referred to an orthopedist for casting

STRETCHING EXERCISES: FIGURE 51.7 (PAGE 377)

52/ OSTEOARTHRITIS

EVALUATION
A. Prevalence
   1. Increases with advancing age, ubiquitous by seventh or eighth decade as detected by x-ray
   2. Poor correlation between symptoms and radiographic evidence of osteoarthritis (but 35–40% over age 65 have osteoarthritic symptoms)
B. Predisposing factors: Table 52.1
C. General clinical features
   1. History
      a) Distribution of joint involvement: Table 52.2
      b) Aching in and around joint, increasing in severity with use of joint, relieved by rest
      c) Morning stiffness or stiffness at rest, absent or present for no more than 15–20 minutes (but may last longer if disease is far advanced)
      d) If joint destruction is marked, pain may occur at rest, and pieces of cartilage may be shed into joint, causing joint to lock or give way
      e) No systemic symptoms

Table 52.1. Factors Contributing to Development of Osteoarthritis

Aging
  Diminished proteoglycan aggregation
  Diminished resistance of cartilage to fatigue fracture (?defective collagen network)
  Decreased resiliency of soft tissues
  Loss of normal anatomical relationship (hip)
Heredity
  Heberden's nodes
  Primary generalized osteoarthritis
  Postural or developmental defects (e.g., scoliosis, slipped capital femoral epiphyses, Legg-Calvé-Perthes disease, etc.)
  Procollagen gene (COL2A1) defects
  Metabolic defects (ochronosis, Wilson's disease)
Abnormal distribution of mechanical stress
  Postural or developmental defects
  Joint instability or hypermobility
  Local incongruity of joint surfaces posttrauma, after meniscectomy, after prolonged immobilization
  Obesity (abnormal stress on knees due to adiposity)
Excessive repetitive stress
  Occupational
  Sports related
  Associated with neuropathy
Crystalline deposit disease
  Calcium pyrophosphate
  Hydroxyapatite
Previous inflammatory joint disease
Metabolic abnormalities
  Ochronosis
  Wilson's disease
  Acromegaly

Table 52.2.   Distribution of Joint Involvement in Osteoarthritis

Commonly affected
Hands
Distal interphalangeal (Heberden's nodes)
Proximal interphalangeal (Bouchard's nodes)
Carpometacarpal of the thumb (joints between first metacarpal and greater multangular and between greater multangular and navicular)
Knees
Hips
Spine
Cervical
Lumbar
Thoracic
Feet
Metatarsophalangeal (especially first)
Usually spared
Ankles
Hands
Metacarpophalangeal
Carpometacarpal (except first)
Wrists
Elbows
Shoulders

    2. Physical examination
      a) Most symptomatic patients have some pain on passive motion of involved joints or on motion against resistance
      b) Frequently crepitus as the joint is moved
      c) Tenderness along the joint line is common but not invariable
      d) Soft tissue swelling absent or minimal
      e) Bony enlargement common, especially in distal interphalangeal joints (Heberden's nodes)
      f) Joint effusions not common but may occur, especially in knees
      g) No heat or redness over joints (in advanced disease, there may be some warmth due to chronic synovitis)
    3. Laboratory findings
      a) Normal laboratory tests, including measures of inflammation
      b) If effusion is present, white blood cell count < 2000/mm^3, protein content < 4 g/dl, glucose concentration normal
    4. Imaging
      a) Radiographic findings: Table 52.3
      b) Computed tomography and magnetic resonance imaging
        1) May be of help in patients with spinal osteoarthritis who have not responded to conservative management (see Chapters 48 and 49)
        2) For imaging of peripheral joints, considerable experience in interpretation is necessary; best utilized by rheumatologist or orthopedist for patients with uncertain diagnosis
  D. Clinical patterns of osteoarthritis
    1. Heberden's nodes (see Physical examination, above)
      a) More frequent in women
      b) Commonly appear in fourth or fifth decade of life
      c) Often asymptomatic, but worrisome to patient

Table 52.3.   X-ray Findings in Osteoarthritis

Earliest
  No abnormality
Early
  Slight loss of articular cartilage thickness (narrowing of radiological joint space)
Moderate
  Marginal osteophyte formation
Late
  Loss of cartilage space (often focal in weight-bearing joints)
  Sclerosis of subchondral bone
  Subchondral cyst formation
  Loose bodies
  Subluxation or deformity

2. Primary generalized osteoarthritis
   a) Involvement of the distal and proximal interphalangeal joints, carpometacarpal joint of thumb, and multiple other joints (hips, knees, metatarsophalangeal, and spine)
   b) Affects mostly middle-aged women with a family history of this disorder
   c) Early, may be episodic, be associated with an elevated erythrocyte sedimentation rate; must be distinguished from rheumatoid arthritis and other polyarticular diseases
3. Erosive osteoarthritis of hands
   a) Severe osteoarthritis of hands (distal and proximal interphalangeal joints) with erosion of subchondral bone, eventual deformity and limitation of motion of fingers
   b) X-rays show erosions and subchondral cyst formation that may be mistaken for rheumatoid arthritis or gout (sparing of metacarpophalangeal joints and wrists establishes diagnosis)
4. Hip
   a) More often unilateral
   b) Obesity not a major causal factor
   c) Pain, first with weight bearing and movement, then at rest as process becomes more severe
   d) Patient may limp or have an abnormal gait
   e) On physical examination, pain and limitation of motion during internal rotation and extension are early signs; later, pain and restricted movement with any motion
   f) Progression may be rapid
5. Knee (see Chapter 51)
   a) Most common symptomatic joint
   b) Slowly progressive pain with ambulation
   c) Relationship to obesity
6. Spinal syndromes
   a) See Chapters 48 and 49
   b) Diffuse idiopathic skeletal hyperostosis
      1) Radiological criteria: Table 52.4
      2) Motion and function relatively maintained, as opposed to ankylosing spondylitis (Chapter 52)
7. "Acute" exacerbations of osteoarthritis
   a) Actively swollen, painful, hot joint in a patient with osteoarthritis

Table 52.4.   X-ray Abnormalities in Diffuse Idiopathic Skeletal Hyperostosis

Spinal

Laminated calcification and ossification along the anterior lateral aspect of at least four contiguous vertebral bodies continuing across the disc spaces and varying in thickness from 1 to 20 mm with relative preservation of the height of the disc space

Bumpy spinal contour appearance from increased bone deposition located at the anterior disc space margins

Radiolucent disc extension (i.e., L-, F-, or Y-shaped lucencies within the bone deposition along the anterior disc margin)

Radiolucency beneath deposited bone linearly located between the anterolateral calcification and the vertebral bodies

Absence of apophyseal joint anklyosis or of sacroiliac joint erosions

Extraspinal[a]

Bony proliferation

Ligament calcification, ossification

Para-articular osteophytes

Adapted from Resnick D, Shapiro RF, Wiesner KB, et al.: Diffuse idiopathic skeletal hyperostosis (DISH) (ankylosing hyperostosis of Forestier and Rotes-Querol). *Semin Arthritis Rheum* 7:153, 1978.

[a] Frequent and distinctive features that permit a diagnosis even without spinal x-rays. These changes are always present in the pelvis and in approximately 75% of cases in the heel and foot and less commonly in the elbows, knees, shoulders, humerus, wrist, and hands.

Table 52.5.   Differential Diagnosis of Osteoarthritis: Extra-articular Causes of Pain or Restricted Movement

Bone disease

Osteopenia or osteoporosis (see Chapter 58)

Malignancy: myeloma, metastatic Paget's disease

Osteomyelitis (see Chapter 17)

Periarticular soft tissue abnormalities

Soft tissue contractures (Dupuytren's, postcerebrovascular accident, or debilitating disease with disuse)

Tendinitis or bursitis (see Chapters 47 and 50)

Ligament strain (see Chapter 51)

Reflex sympathetic dystrophy

Neuromuscular diseases

Neuropathy (diabetes, alcoholism, B_{12} deficiency) (see Chapter 67)

Parkinsonism (see Chapter 65)

Tardive dyskinesias (see Chapters 4 and 65)

Senile dementia with rigidity (see Chapters 5 and 65)

Vascular diseases (see Chapter 70)

Atherosclerosis

Diabetes

Vasculitis

b) Often the result of calcium pyrophosphate or hydroxyapatite crystal deposition (see Chapter 53), occasionally the result of sepsis

c) Joint should be aspirated, fluid analyzed to rule out microcrystalline or infectious arthritis

8. Differential diagnosis of osteoarthritis: Table 52.5

MANAGEMENT

A. General measures

1. Patient education: explaining that other joints not likely to be involved, that disease progresses slowly, that function is likely to be preserved

2. Rest: short periods of rest during day are important, especially when weight-bearing joints are involved

3. Use of canes, crutches, walkers, to rest a weight-bearing joint and to provide stability when walking
   a) Cane should be used on opposite side simultaneously with the affected limb; cane should be held tightly, close to body
   b) Crutch should be used on affected side (or 2 crutches should be used)
   c) Walker should be used for greater stability

4. Correction of postural or mechanical strain
   a) Patients with pronated feet, genu varum, or genu valgum will stress the compartments of the leg (see Chapter 85)
   b) Instruction in proper lifting and avoidance of unnecessary strain on muscles (see Chapters 48 and 49)

5. Physical therapy: at home for patients with mild disease; by a therapist for patients with more advanced disease
   a) Heat
      1) Moist or dry heat 15–20 minutes several times a day
      2) Paraffin wax baths (available from large pharmacies) may help osteoarthritic hands
      3) Avoid temperatures over 110°F (43°C); avoid prolonged application of heat
   b) Exercise: gradual conditioning important, best done after consultation with a physical therapist

6. Diet: control of obesity important (Chapter 60)

B. Drug therapy
1. Analgesic and nonsteroidal anti-inflammatory drugs (NSAIDs)
   a) Do not alter course
   b) If disease is mild, analgesic doses are sufficient (e.g., aspirin, 1.2–2.4 g/day, or acetaminophen, 1 g/day
   c) In advanced disease, inflammation is more likely, and NSAIDs (see also Chapter 54) may be useful
      1) Side effects more likely in elderly (see Chapter 54)
      2) Choice of an NSAID influenced by cost, frequency of administration (e.g., naproxen and piroxicam can be given less often than many other preparations), and side effects
      3) Combinations of NSAIDs not beneficial; increase dose of a single agent over 2–6 weeks until symptoms are relieved, side effects occur, or lack of efficacy is established

2. Corticosteroids
   a) Intra-articular injection useful when osteoarthritis is associated with effusion in large joints (e.g., knees) — see Chapter 50; if several months relief is not realized after 1 or 2 injections, no more should be given
   b) Systemic steroids should not be given

3. Orthopedic surgery
   a) Consultation warranted if patient has malalignment or major instability in weight-bearing joints, if loose bodies are in joint, if there is intractable pain with advanced disease of hips or knees
   b) Osteotomy, arthroplasty, arthroscopic surgery, fusion, joint replacement are options, depending on the problem

53/ CRYSTAL-INDUCED ARTHRITIS

CRYSTAL IDENTIFICATION (TABLE 53.1)

A. Monosodium urate
1. Place a drop of aspirated fluid on a glass slide and examine through a microscope under polarized light
2. Fluid may be preserved overnight in a refrigerated test tube
3. Pathognomonic of gout; if absent, strongly against diagnosis

B. Calcium pyrophosphate dihydrate (CPPD)
1. False negative reports from unspecialized observers common (crystals harder to see than urate crystals)
2. May dissolve within a few hours, even if refrigerated

GOUT

A. Pathophysiology: gout is due to hyperuricemia with deposition of urate crystals in various tissues, including joints
1. Normal serum urate level 7–8 mg/dl in males; 6–7 mg/dl in females
2. Normal urinary urate: <600 mg/day
3. Causes: Table 53.2

Table 53.1. Identification of Crystals in Synovial Fluid

Monosodium urate
  Morphology
    Rod or needle shaped
    Length often approaches diameter of polymorphonuclear (PMN) leukocyte
  Polarized light
    Stand out brightly when field is dark
    Strongly negatively birefringent
  Red plate compensator
    Yellow crystals parallel and blue crystals perpendicular to axis
Calcium pyrophosphate dihydrate
  Morphology
    Rhomboid, rod, or irregular rhomboid shape
    Length variable, often smaller than one lobe of a PMN nucleus
  Polarized light
    No increase in refractile appearance when field is dark
    Weakly positively birefrigent
  Red plate compensator
    Blue crystals parallel and yellow crystals perpendicular to axis
Hydroxyapatite and basic calcium phosphates (BCPs)
  Not usually seen with ordinary or polarized light microscopy except as large aggregates that are not birefringent
  Aggregates of BCP may occasionally be seen as "shiny coin" refractile bodies
  Stain nonspecifically with alizarin red S dye (available in histology laboratories) as clusters of crystalline material; useful as a screening test
Requires electron microscopy, x-ray diffraction, or microprobe analysis for more definite identification
Calcium oxalate
  Morphology
    Polymorphic, irregular squares, short rods, bipyramidal; may appear in clumps
  Polarized light
    Variable, most not birefringent, some strongly positively birefringent

Table 53.2. Causes of Hyperuricemia

With Increased Urinary Uric Acid	With Normal or Low Urinary Uric Acid
10% of primary gout (defect unknown)	90% of primary gout (defect unknown)
Specific enzyme defects with primary gout	
Secondary causes	Secondary causes
Myeloproliferative disease	Renal insufficiency
Lymphoproliferative disease	Lead nephropathy
Obesity	Drugs
Glycogen storage disease	Salicylates (low dose, i.e., <2.4 g/day)
Exercise	Diuretics
Psoriasis	Pyrazinamide
	Ethambutol
	Nicotinic acid
	Alcohol
	Others
	Obesity
	Sarcoidosis
	Starvation

Modified from Wyngaarden JB, Kelley WN: *Gout and Hyperuricemia.* New York, Grune & Stratton, 1976.

Table 53.3. Clinical Features of Gout

Epidemiology
  Sex: males 10:1; rare in premenopausal women
  Age: usually middle age or older (peak age 60)
Acute gout
  History
    Acute attacks, recurrent, with disease-free intervals
    Rapid progression to peak severity within 24 hours
  Physical findings
    Usually monoarticular with swelling, tenderness, erythema, and intense inflammation
    Big toe metatarsophalangeal joint commonly involved (podagra)
    Forefeet, heels, ankles, knees, wrists, fingers, elbows, and other joints may be affected
    Occasionally polyarticular
    Fever may occur
  Laboratory
    Joint aspiration with leukocytosis and identification of urate crystals is diagnostic
Intercritical gout
  No symptoms or findings except hyperuricemia
Chronic gout
  Often polyarticular
  Symptoms may persist between attacks
  Tophi are common (approximately 90–95%)
  Deformities may develop

B. Epidemiology: Table 53.3
C. Clinical features (Table 53.3)
  1. Attacks may be triggered by trauma, an acute illness, dietary
    indiscretion, excess intake of alcohol, starvation, recent
    administration of drugs that lower serum urate concentration (see
    below)
  2. Family history of gout in some patients with primary gout
  3. Attacks are self-limited, subside even without treatment in days to
    weeks
  4. Urate crystals often demonstrable in joints, especially if they have
    previously been inflamed, in intercritical gout

        5. Chronic gout is uncommon
        6. Extra-articular manifestations
           a) Chronic gouty nephropathy
               1) Interstitial nephritis from deposition of urate crystals
               2) Prevalence is low; dysfunction relatively mild
           b) Uric acid nephrolithiasis (see Chapter 32)

D. X-rays
    1. Normal early in course except for acute soft tissue swelling
    2. Ultimately, lucent areas of urate deposits in bone adjacent to joints

E. Management
    1. Acute attack
        a) Nonsteroidal anti-inflammatory drugs (NSAIDs): rapid relief almost always achieved (e.g., indomethacin 50 mg every 6 hours for 6–8 doses)
           1) Reduce dose if probenecid (see below) has been prescribed
           2) Be cautious in elderly, especially if renal function is impaired
        b) Colchicine
           1) Because of side effects when given by mouth (diarrhea, nausea, vomiting), largely replaced by NSAIDs
           2) Usual dose is 0.6 mg every 1 or 2 hours up to 16 doses or until relief or side effects occur
           3) Intravenous colchicine does not cause gastrointestinal side effects; used (2 mg diluted with 20 ml of saline, given over 10 minutes) when oral drugs cannot be given, relief within 6–8 hours; up to 4 mg/24 hours can be given
               (a) Reduce dose if hepatic or renal impairment
               (b) If extravasated, may cause necrosis
               (c) After full dose, no more colchicine for 7 days
               (d) Diagnostic therapeutic trial of limited value, should be discouraged
        c) Aspiration and intra-articular injection of corticosteroid are useful when a single large joint is involved; oral corticosteroids (prednisone 30–60 mg/day tapered over 7–10 days) are also effective if NSAIDs cannot be used
    2. Intercritical gout
        a) Prophylactic colchicine
           1) Should be given (0.6 mg 1, 2, or 3 times/day — dose frequency depends on control) to all patients who have had more than one attack of acute gout
           2) Use cautiously if renal function is impaired (reversible myopathy and neuropathy have been reported)
           3) If serum urate concentration is >9 mg/dl, it should be lowered
        b) Probenecid (Benemid)
           1) Promotes urinary excretion of urate
           2) For patients with nontophaceous gout with normal renal function, uric acid excretion is <750–800 mg/24 hours
           3) Initial dose of 0.5 g twice a day increased to a maximum of 2 g/day to achieve a serum urate level of <6.5 mg/dl
           4) Should not be initiated for 1 week after an acute attack has

subsided, only after colchicine prophylaxis has been given for 3 or 4 days

  5) Have patient drink 2–3 liters of fluid per day and take sodium bicarbonate or Polycitrate, 0.5–1 mEq/kg of body weight in 5 or 6 doses/day, to keep a urine pH of >6.0–6.5 for the first week of treatment

c) Allopurinol
1) Decreases production of urate
2) For persons with a history of urinary calculi; with renal insufficiency, chronic tophaceous gout, basal urate excretion of >750–800 mg/24 hours, hyperuricemia, and secondary gout
3) Initial dose 200 mg/day (100-, 300-mg tablets) increased over 2–3 weeks until serum urate level is <6 mg/dl
4) Side effects (<2% of patients): rash, fever, leukopenia, hepatitis, vasculitis — all likely to occur within first 2 months; risk of toxicity enhanced by thiazides

d) Diet: avoid alcohol, fasting beyond 24 hours, purine-rich foods (liver, kidney, roe), especially if urate excretion is >1100 mg/24 hours

F. Asymptomatic hyperuricemia (>7 mg/dl in males, >6 mg/dl in females)
1. If urate excretion elevated (>600 g/day on low-purine diet, >750–800 g/day on a normal diet), a cause should be sought (Table 53.2), and a consideration should be given to use of allopurinol (see above)
2. If urate excretion not elevated, therapy not warranted

G. Hyperuricemia secondary to diuretics
1. Reversible dose-related rise of serum urate level secondary to thiazides (average 1–2 mg/dl)
2. Furosemide also frequently raises serum urate level; ethacrynic acid, acetazolamide less commonly
3. No treatment necessary unless gout develops

CALCIUM PYROPHOSPHATE DIHYDRATE (CPPD)-INDUCED ARTHRITIS (PSEUDOGOUT)

A. Pathophysiology: deposition of CPPD in fibrocartilage (chondrocalcinosis), joints, ligaments, tendons, occasionally with an inflammatory response

B. Epidemiology
1. Increases in frequency with age
2. Affects males more than females (1.5:1)

C. Associated diseases: Table 53.4
D. Clinical features: Table 53.5
E. Laboratory evaluation
1. Synovial fluid contains polymorphonuclear leukocytes in a range of 15,000–25,000/mm^3 usually (occasionally ≥50,000/mm^3)

Table 53.4. Diseases Associated With CPPD Deposition Disease

Hemochromatosis — hemosiderosis	Hereditary hypophosphatasia
Gout	Hypothyroidism
Hyperparathyroidism	Neurogenic arthropathy
Hypomagnesemia	

Table 53.5.   Clinical Features of CPPD Deposit Disease

Epidemiology
　Age: middle-aged or elderly
Site
　Knee and wrist most common joints involved
　Metacarpophalangeal joints, hips, shoulders, elbows, ankles may be affected
　Arthritis usually monoarticular
Pattern
　Acute gout-like attacks with symptom-free intervals in 25%
　Osteoarthritis-like disease in 50%, with superimposed acute attacks in half of these
　　patients
　Rheumatoid-like polyarthritis in 5%
　Neuropathic-like arthritis without neurological damage (rare)
　Asymptomatic chondrocalcinosis in 20% (found on x-ray)
Laboratory
　Synovial fluid shows leukocytosis and characteristic CPPD crystals

　　2. Because of association with other disorders (Table 53.4), the
　　　 following studies are indicated: serum calcium, phosphorus,
　　　 magnesium, alkaline phosphatase, uric acid, ferritin
　F. X-rays
　　1. Punctate and linear calcifications in fibrocartilage, especially of
　　　 the knees
　　2. Similar calcifications in hyaline cartilage
　　3. Absence of calcifications does not exclude diagnosis if typical
　　　 crystals are in joint fluid
　G. Management
　　1. No therapy influences deposition or resolution of tissue deposits of
　　　 CPPD
　　2. Aspiration of fluid for diagnosis may provide relief
　　3. Local injection of corticosteroid often effective (see Chapter 50)
　　4. NSAIDs (Chapter 54) effective during acute attack (early use may
　　　 abort an attack), but caution must be exercised with use in the
　　　 elderly (see Chapter 33)
　　5. Colchicine may be effective, but is not recommended over NSAIDs

HYDROXYAPATITE-INDUCED ARTHRITIS
A. May be associated with acute inflammation of joints in patients with
　 osteoarthritis
B. Sometimes found in association with deposition of other basic
　 calcium salts; term basic calcium phosphate (BCP) deposit disease
　 used to describe these conditions
C. Hydroxyapatite crystals appear as red clumps after staining with
　 alizarin red S dye (available from scientific supply houses); BCP
　 crystals do not stain
D. Relief of symptoms may be provided by aspiration of joint (Chapter
　 50), injection of a lidocaine/corticosteroid solution (Chapter 50), or
　 use of a NSAID (Chapter 54)

ARTHRITIS ASSOCIATED WITH CALCIUM OXALATE
A. In patients on chronic hemodialysis or peritoneal dialysis for end-
　 stage renal disease
B. Management difficult: NSAIDs, corticosteroids, colchicine may
　 provide incomplete relief

54/ RHEUMATOID ARTHRITIS

EVALUATION

A. Epidemiology
   1. Prevalence increases with age
   2. Prevalence and incidence 2–3 times greater in women than in men
   3. Most commonly begins in third to sixth decade
   4. Articular disease worse in women; extra-articular disease more common in men
   5. Seropositive disease (see below) aggregates in families

B. History
   1. Symptoms and signs: Table 54.1
   2. Onset typically insidious over weeks to months but occasionally acute over 1–2 days
   3. Extra-articular symptoms common but not invariable
   4. Number of involved joints highly variable, but process is almost always polyarticular
   5. Predilection for peripheral joints with relative sparing of the axial skeleton

C. Physical examination
   1. General: complete examination initially and a limited examination every 6 months
   2. Joints
      a) Swelling
         1) Soft tissue swelling first; eventually increased amounts of fluid within joint spaces
         2) Almost always symmetrical
      b) No redness (in contrast to most other inflammatory arthritides)
      c) Tenderness and pain on passive motion: most sensitive indices of inflammation
      d) Range of motion: may be limited by inflammation or by structural deformity
      e) Permanent deformity
         1) May be an end stage of inflammatory process

Table 54.1. Symptoms and Signs of Rheumatoid Arthritis

Symptoms		Signs	
Extra-articular	Articular[a]	Extra-articular	Articular
Fatigue	Morning stiffness	Rheumatoid nodules	Pain on passive motion
Depression	Pain and tenderness	Lymphadenopathy	Tenderness
Malaise	Swelling	Splenomegaly	Swelling
Anorexia		Ocular disease	Heat
		Entrapment neuropathies	Typical deformity

[a] Persistence (6 weeks or more) and symmetrical nature of signs and symptoms are important, but not invariable, diagnostic features.

2) Flexion contractures and subluxation (incomplete dislocation), especially of fingers and toes
   f) Synovial cysts: common, readily seen and palpated over affected joints
D. Laboratory tests
   1. Hematology
      a) Anemia (hematocrit values 30–34%) in 25–35% of patients
         1) Usually anemia of chronic disease: low level of serum iron, low serum iron-binding capacity, normal or increased serum ferritin concentration
         2) Iron deficiency may occasionally develop because of blood loss: especially important to recognize in patients over age 40
      b) White blood cell count
         1) Usually normal
         2) Occasionally elevated in patients with extensive inflammation
         3) Rarely depressed (except as in, e.g., Felty's syndrome — rheumatoid arthritis, splenomegaly, leukopenia)
      c) Erythrocyte sedimentation rate: usually elevated and may be useful in following disease activity
   2. Serology
      a) Rheumatoid factor
         1) Antibodies [for clinical purposes, immunoglobulin M (IgM)] that react with IgG
         2) Not pathognomonic of rheumatoid arthritis but detectable in 70–80% of patients with the disease
         3) Significant titer: ≥1:80
         4) Usually becomes positive within the first 6 months of disease
         5) Does not correlate with disease activity but is usually very high in patients with severe erosive arthritis or extensive extra-articular disease
      b) Antinuclear antibodies (ANA)
         1) Present in 20–30% of patients with rheumatoid arthritis
         2) More common in patients with extra-articular disease and in patients with high titers of rheumatoid factor
      c) Serum complement
         1) Generally normal or increased
         2) Occasionally low in severe disease
         3) May be of use in distinguishing rheumatoid arthritis from systemic lupus erythematosus where serum complement is often markedly decreased
   3. Synovial fluid
      a) Extraction technique: Chapter 50 (Table 50.1)
      b) Arthrocentesis important in ruling out infection if a single joint flares up, especially if fever develops, or a recent procedure (e.g., tooth extraction) has been done
      c) Findings in comparison to normal and to various arthritides (Table 54.2)
         1) Mucin clot evaluated by adding 1 ml of joint fluid to 4 ml of 2% acetic acid

Table 54.2. Synovial Findings in Various Arthritides*

	Color	Clarity	White Cells (per mm³)	Polymorpho-nuclear Leukocytes (%)
Normal	Clear	Transparent	<150	<25
Rheumatoid arthritis	Yellow	Turbid	3,500–50,000	>70
Noninflammatory arthritis	Clear yellow	Transparent	<3,000	<25
Septic arthritis	Variable	Opaque	50,000–100,000	>75

*See Table 50.2.

     2) Fluid often clots spontaneously (as opposed to normal fluid)
  4. Radiology (x-rays)
    a) Not necessary in making diagnosis
    b) Lag behind other clinical signs of disease
    c) Should be obtained if there is suspicion of structural or traumatic damage to bone or joint
    d) Findings vary depending on severity and duration of disease (soft tissue swelling to periarticular osteoporosis to narrowing of joint space and juxta-articular erosions to cystic erosions of bone and structural deformity)
  5. Biopsies: histology of synovium or of rheumatoid nodules (see below) is diagnostic, but biopsies are usually not necessary
E. Extra-articular disease
  1. Usually in patients with relatively more severe disease
  2. Rheumatoid nodules
    a) Most characteristic extra-articular lesion
    b) Occur in 20–30% of cases
    c) Located most commonly at extensor surfaces of arms but also prone to develop at pressure points on the feet and on the knees and rarely may arise in visceral organs
    d) Usually asymptomatic but may erode into bone or ulcerate
  3. Systemic manifestations (Table 54.3): usually warrant subspecialty consultation
F. Course
  1. Usual pattern is one of persistent and progressive disease that waxes and wanes in intensity
  2. Patients with persistent signs of inflammation will develop radiological signs of joint narrowing within 2 years
  3. Patients with indolent onset, high-titer rheumatoid factor, and nodules, particularly men, tend to have more severe disease
G. Differential diagnosis of polyarthritis: Tables 54.4–54.6

MANAGEMENT
A. Serial observations: Table 54.7
B. Use of self-report questionnaires: Table 54.8
C. Reduction of joint stress
  1. Achieve and maintain ideal body weight
  2. Adequate rest: 8–9 hours of sleep at night, 2-hour rest period in middle of day

Table 54.3.   Systemic Manifestations of Rheumatoid Arthritis (Rheumatoid Disease)

General
  Fever
  Fatigue, malaise, diffuse stiffness
  Adenopathy
  Splenomegaly
Pulmonary
  Pleuritis (±effusion)
  Intrapulmonary nodules
  Interstitial pneumonitis
  Rheumatoid pneumoconiosis (Caplan's syndrome)
  Pulmonary fibrosis
  Arteritis (rare)
Cardiovascular
  Heart
    Pericarditis, effusion, tamponade, constriction
    Myocarditis
    Endocarditis, including valvulitis
    Rheumatoid nodule (conduction defects)
  Peripheral
    Vasculitis or arteritis
Nervous system
  Peripheral neuropathy (mononeuritis multiplex) (sensory, motor, or both)
  Central nervous system
    Spinal cord lesion
      Vascular thrombosis
      Rheumatoid nodule
    Intracranial
      Arteritis (rare)
      Rheumatoid nodule (rare)
Ocular
  Keratoconjunctivitis (Sjögren's syndrome)
  Episcleritis (simple or nodular)
  Scleritis
    Diffuse
    Nodular (scleromalacia perforans)
    Necrotizing
Hematological
  Anemia (chronic disease)
  Neutropenia (Felty's syndrome)
  Thrombocytosis
  Eosinophilia
Skin
  Palmar erythema
  Nodules
  Vasculitic lesions
  Leg ulcers (Felty's syndrome)
Others
  Sjögren's syndrome
  Osteoporosis
  Hyperviscosity
  Lymphoma (Sjögren's syndrome)
  Secondary amyloidosis (controversial)

Table 54.4. Differential Diagnosis of Polyarthritis Based on Age and Sex

	Male	Both Sexes	Female
Childhood (1–15)	Juvenile ankylosing spondylitis (Chapter 55) Kawasaki's syndrome[a] Hemophilia (Chapter 36)	Juvenile rheumatoid arthritis — systemic onset ("Still's disease")[a] Rheumatic fever[a] Leukemia[a]	Juvenile rheumatoid arthritis[a] Pauciarticular arthritis[a] Juvenile rheumatoid arthritis — polyarthritis onset[a]
Young adult (15–30)	Ankylosing spondylitis (Chapter 55) Reiter's syndrome (Chapter 55) "Reactive" arthritis[a] Behçet's syndrome[a]	Psoriatic arthritis (Chapter 83) Lyme disease (Chapter 16) Inflammatory bowel disease (Chapter 25)	Systemic lupus erythematosus[a] Gonococcal arthritis (Chapter 13) Scleroderma[a]
Middle years (30–60)	Gout (Chapter 53) Palindromic rheumatism[a] Whipple's disease[a]	Seronegative polyarthritis (Chapter 54) Hypersensitivity reactions (Chapter 9) Vasculitic syndromes[a] Relapsing polychondritis[a]	Rheumatoid arthritis Sjögren's syndrome Sarcoidosis[a] Polymyositis[a] Erosive osteoarthritis (Chapter 52)
Elderly (60+)	Diffuse idiopathic skeletal hyperostosis (Chapter 52) Hypertrophic pulmonary osteoarthropathy (Chapter 41)	Pseudogout (Chapter 53) Polymyalgia rheumatica (Chapter 62) Tumor-related syndromes Secondary osteoarthritis (Chapter 52) Metabolic disorders	Primary generalized osteoarthritis (Chapter 52)

[a]These conditions are not discussed in this book.

Table 54.5.   Assessment of Joint Involvement

NUMBER		
Monarthritis	*Oligoarthritis* (2–4)	*Polyarthritis* (≥5)
Septic arthritis[a]	Reiter's syndrome	Rheumatoid arthritis
Gout	Inflammatory bowel disease	Systemic lupus erythematosus[a]
Pseudogout	Psoriatic arthritis	Serum sickness
Other crystals	Rheumatic fever[a]	Psoriatic arthritis
Local tumor[a]	Juvenile rheumatoid arthritis[a]	Tophaceous gout

PATTERNS	
Symmetrical	*Asymmetrical*
Rheumatoid arthritis	Psoriatic arthritis
Serum sickness	Reiter's syndrome
Systemic lupus erythematosus[a]	Gout, pseudogout

INTENSITY OF PAIN	
Severe	*Moderate*
Septic arthritis[a]	All others, including
Microcrystalline arthritis	rheumatoid arthritis

COURSE	
Acute	Infection, gout, pseudogout
Chronic	Psoriatic arthritis, rheumatoid arthritis, ankylosing spondylitis
Additive	Rheumatoid arthritis
Migratory	Rheumatic fever,[a] systemic lupus erythematosus[a]
Evanescent	Systemic lupus erythematosus,[a] viral[a]
Episodic	Gout, pseudogout, palindromic rheumatism[a]

[a] These conditions are not discussed in this book.

Table 54.6.   Diagnostic Clues Provided by Arthritis of Specific Joints

First metatarsal (podagra)	Gout
Knee (acute, episodic)	Pseudogout
Distal interphalangeal	Psoriatic arthritis
	Osteoarthritis
Metacarpals, wrist, metatarsals	Rheumatoid arthritis
Sausaged digits	Reiter's syndrome
	Psoriatic arthritis
	Sarcoidosis
Sacroiliac	Ankylosing spondylitis
	Reiter's syndrome
	Psoriatic arthritis
	Inflammatory bowel disease
Sternoclavicular	Septic arthritis
	Polymyalgia rheumatica
Heel/ankle	Reiter's syndrome

  3. Avoid vigorous activity but maintain modest activity to prevent joint laxity, muscle atrophy
  4. Splinting, use of walking aids, specially designed furniture, and utensils on recommendation of consulting rheumatologist, orthopedist, or physiatrist
D. Physical and occupational therapist
  1. Should be seen early in illness

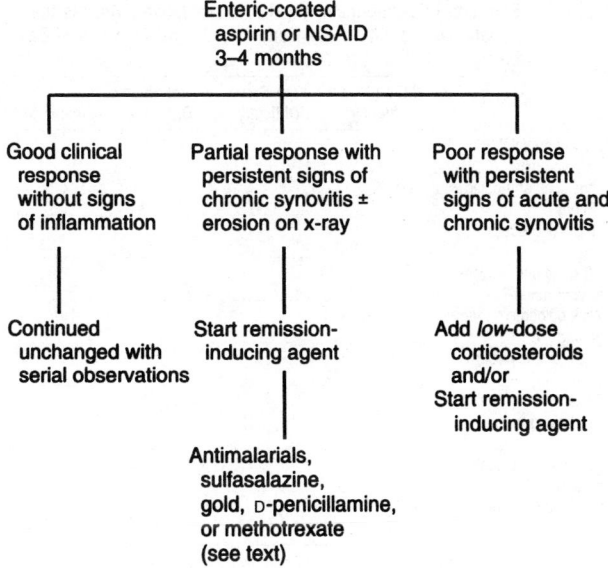

Figure 54.1. Suggested approach to drug treatment in rheumatoid arthritis. *NSAID,* nonsteroidal anti-inflammatory drug.

Table 54.7. Measurements to Be Made Serially in Patients With Rheumatoid Arthritis

Duration of morning stiffness
Time of onset of fatigue
NSAID need per day
Grip strength
Number of joints that are tender or are painful on passive motion
Degree of swelling of affected joints
Erythrocyte sedimentation rate (Westergren)

Adapted from McCarty DJ: Clinical assessment of arthritis. In: McCarty DJ (ed): *Arthritis and Allied Conditions,* 9th ed. Philadelphia, Lea & Febiger, 1979.

    2. To design a balanced program of rest and activity appropriate for stage of disease

E. Drug treatment (Fig. 54.1)

    1. Anti-inflammatory drugs

        a) Aspirin and other salicylates (Table 54.9)

            1) Nonacetylated preparations are less potent, have fewer side effects

            2) Enteric-coated preparations preferable to reduce otherwise-high incidence of gastrointestinal (GI) side effects

            3) Measure salicylate level before assuming medication is ineffective; should be 20–25 mg/dl

        b) Nonsteroidal anti-inflammatory drugs (NSAIDs)

Table 54.8.   Self-report Questionnaire Used to Quantitatively Assess the Functional Capacity of the Patient to Do the Activities of Daily Living

	Without Any Difficulty	With Some Difficulty	With Much Difficulty	Unable to Do
A. Dress yourself, including tying shoelaces and doing buttons?				
B. Get in and out of bed?				
C. Lift a full cup or glass to your mouth?				
D. Walk outdoors on flat ground?				
E. Wash and dry your entire body?				
F. Bend down to pick up clothing from the floor?				
G. Turn regular faucets on and off?				
H. Get in and out of a car?				

Table 54.9.   Salicylates

Preparations	Product Names	Available Strengths (mg)[a]
Acetylated preparations		
Regular aspirin	Multiple brands	300–800
Buffered aspirin	Multiple brands	300–650
Enteric-coated aspirin	Ecotrin, Encaprin	325–500
	Cosprin	325–650
	APF	500
	Easprin	950
Nonacetylated preparations		
Salicylsalicyclic acid	Disalcid, Mono-Gesic, Salflex	500, 750
Choline-magnesium trisalicylate	Trilisate	500, 750
Salicylate derivative		
Diflunisal	Dolobid	250–500

[a] The usual dose varies widely, based on individual tolerance. It is best to start with low doses and build the dose every week until symptoms are improved, a satisfactory salicylate level in the blood has been achieved, or symptoms of intolerance or toxicity develop. The elderly generally tolerate only lower doses.

      1) Preparations: Table 54.10
      2) Side effects: Table 54.11
      3) Drug interactions: Table 54.12
    c) Corticosteroids
      1) A low dose (5–15 mg once a day) of prednisone can be used as a "bridge" between aspirin or a NSAID and a remission-inducing agent (see below)
      2) Daily treatment usually required
      3) High doses are to be avoided

Table 54.10. Nonsteroidal Anti-inflammatory Drugs (NSAIDs)

Generic Name	Trade Names	Available Strengths (mg)	Recommended Dosage and Schedule	Maximal Daily Dosage (mg/day)
PROPIONIC ACID DERIVATIVES				
Ibuprofen[a]	Motrin, Rufen, IBU Nuprin, Advil	300, 400, 600, 800 200	600–800 mg 3–4 times/day	3200
Naproxen[a]	Naprosyn Anaprox	250, 375, 500 275	500 mg twice a day	1000
Fenoprofen[a]	Nalfon, Fenopron	200, 300, 600	600 mg 3 times/day	2400
Ketoprofen[a]	Orudis	50, 75	50 mg 3–4 times/day or 75 mg 3 times/day	300
Flurbiprofen[a]	Ansaid	100	100 mg 2–3 times/day	300
Oxaprozin	Daypro	600	600–1200 mg once daily	1200
OXICAMS				
Piroxicam[a]	Feldene	10, 20	10–20 mg/day	20
ACETIC ACIDS				
Indomethacin[a]	Indocin	25, 50 75 (slow release)	50 mg 3–4 times/day 1–2 times/day	150–200
Sulindac[a]	Clinoril	150, 200	150–200 mg twice a day	400
Tolmetin[a]	Tolectin	200, 400	400 mg 3–4 times/day	2000
Diclofenac[a]	Voltaren	25, 50, 75	50 mg 2–3 times/day or 75 mg twice a day	150
Etodolac[a]	Lodine	200, 300	200–400 mg 3 times/day	1200
Nabumetone[a]	Relafen	500, 750	1000–2000 mg once daily	2000
FENAMATES				
Meclofenamate[a]	Meclomen	50, 100	50–100 mg 3–4 times/day	400
Mefenamic acid	Ponstel	250	250 mg every 6 hours	(Use only short periods)
PYRAZOLES				
Phenylbutazone	Butazolidin	100	100 mg 3 times/day	300 for no more than 7 days
Ketorolac tromethamine	Toradol	10	10 mg every 4–6 hours	(Use only short periods)

[a] Approved for use in rheumatoid arthritis.

Table 54.11.   NSAID Side Effects

	Approximate Incidence
Gastrointestinal	10–20%
Epigastric pain, nausea	
Anorexia, dyspepsia, peptic ulceration	
Overt or occult bleeding	<1%
Hypersensitivity reactions	1–5%
Rashes, rarely Stevens-Johnson syndrome	
Very rarely, anaphylactoid reactions	
Aggravation of allergic rhinitis or asthma	10% of sufferers
Renal effects	>5%
Transient renal failure	
Water and salt retention	
Hypokalemia, inhibition of diuretic action	
Interstitial nephritis, nephrotic syndrome	>1%
Hepatic effects	5–15%
Cholestatic hepatitis	
Central nervous system	>5%
Tinnitus/deafness	(Primarily aspirin)
Headache, vertigo, confusion	(Higher with indomethacin)
Others	
Agranulocytosis, aplastic anemia	<1% (phenylbutazone)
Diarrhea	10–15% (mefenamic acid, other fenamates)
Aggravation of congestive heart failure, angina	>1%
Parotitis	<1% (phenylbutazone)
Toxic amblyopia	<1% (ibuprofen)

Table 54.12.   NSAID Interactions

Antacids	Reduce rate and extent of absorption of NSAIDs; variable effect.
Anticoagulants	Phenylbutazone and oxyphenbutazone enhance the activity of warfarin. Aspirin and, potentially, all NSAIDs increase the risk of bleeding of an anticoagulant patient.
Oral hypoglycemic drugs	Aspirin, phenylbutazone, and oxyphenbutazone may potentiate the activity of sulphonylurea drugs. Other NSAIDs do not.
Digoxin	Aspirin or ibuprofen may increase serum concentration.
Antihypertensive/diuretics	NSAIDs may attenuate the effect of diuretics, β-blockers, hydralazine, prazosin, angiotensin-converting enzyme inhibitors.
Lithium	Elevation of plasma lithium level may occur, particularly with indomethacin and diclofenac.
Methotrexate	Salicylate inhibits the renal clearance of methotrexate, and toxic levels may occur.
Phenytoin	Phenylbutazone inhibits the metabolism of phenytoin. Salicylates displace phenytoin from albumin and increase the concentration of free drug.
Probenecid	Inhibits renal clearance of several NSAIDs.
Combination of NSAIDs	Should be avoided.

   4) Intra-articular injections (e.g., 40 mg triamcinolone in a knee) are effective for controlling a local flare; do not inject the same joint more than twice a year
2. Remission-inducing agents (agents with delayed onset of action): Tables 54.13 and 54.14
   a) Consider only after consultation with a rheumatologist
   b) Consider if swelling, warmth, tenderness persist despite an anti-inflammatory regimen for at least 2–3 months or the development of erosions on x-ray
   c) Antimalarials (hydroxychloroquine is the preferred drug)
      1) Relatively low toxicity and so used first
      2) Usually used in combination with an NSAID or low-dose corticosteroids (see above)
      3) Delayed response typical with increasing improvement (usually not total) for 6 months
      4) Best used in patients with relatively mild disease
   d) Methotrexate
      1) Most popular agent for patients with persistent, relatively aggressive inflammatory disease
      2) Less toxic than gold or D-penicillamine, other choices for patients with aggressive disease (see below)
   e) Gold salts
      1) Oral preparations ineffective
      2) Intramuscular injections, because of toxicity, used only if methotrexate fails to sustain a remission

Table 54.13. Remission-Inducing Agents

Drugs	Brand Name	Available Strengths (mg)	Recommended Dosage and Schedule	Maximal Dosage (mg)
Sulfasalazine	Azulfidine en-tabs	500	Begin at 500 g/day, increase every week to 2 g/day	2000–3000/day
Hydroxychloroquine	Plaquenil	200	Begin at 6 mg/kg for 2–3 months; then lower to 200 mg/day	400/day
Methotrexate		2–5	Begin with 7.5 mg once a week, increase to 15 mg every week if necessary in 6–8 weeks	25/week
Gold	Myochrysine or Solganal	25 or 50 mg/ml or 50 mg/ml	Begin at 10 mg i.m.; if tolerated, 25 mg the next week; if tolerated, 50 mg weekly until 1 g has been given, then 50 mg/month indefinitely	
D-Penicillamine	Cuprimene, Depen	125, 250	Begin with 25 mg 1½ hr after a meal once a day, increase by 125–250 mg/day every 3 months until benefit or toxicity is observed	750–1000/day

Table 54.14.   Side Effects of Remission-Inducing Agents

Drug	Side Effect	Approximate Incidence
Sulfasalazine	GI (most common), headache, dizziness, bone marrow suppression, mucocutaneous reactions, hepatotoxicity, hypersensitivity	30%
Hydroxychloroquine	Ocular toxicity (baseline eye examination, repeated every 6 months), GI upset, leukopenia, various neurological reactions	Rare
Methotrexate	Hepatotoxicity	Rare if no pre-existing liver disease
	GI upset	10%
	Bone marrow suppression	3%
Gold salts	Dermatitis	35%
	Proteinuria	10%
	Hematological reactions	Rare
	Flushing, dizziness, fainting	Rare
D-Penicillamine	Skin rash, loss of taste, GI upset	Dose related
	Thrombocytopenia, nephrotoxicity, skin rash, unusual autoimmune syndromes (after 3–4 months)	30%

     f) D-Penicillamine
       1) Relatively toxic
       2) Prescribed primarily for patients who have failed methotrexate (and then gold)
     g) Cytotoxic drugs (other than methotrexate, e.g., azathioprine, cyclophosphamide) for very aggressive, otherwise-unresponsive disease
  3. Analgesic drugs
     a) Pain caused by inflammation best treated with a NSAID (see above), although acetaminophen may be prescribed concurrently
     b) Narcotics should not be prescribed
F. Surgery
  1. To correct structural or mechanical derangement
  2. The patient, primary physician, rheumatologist, and orthopedist must be involved in the decision

55/ SACROILIITIS, ANKYLOSING SPONDYLITIS, AND REITER'S SYNDROME

SACROILIITIS (TABLE 55.1)

A. May be an isolated problem or a component of another chronic rheumatic disorder
B. The sine qua non of early primary ankylosing spondylitis (only diagnosable after other parts of the axial skeleton are involved)
C. May complicate course in 10% of patients with inflammatory bowel disease, 5–10% of patients with psoriatic arthritis, 20% of patients with Reiter's syndrome
D. Strong hereditary component marked by histocompatibility antigen, HLA-B27 (Table 55.1)

ANKYLOSING SPONDYLITIS

A. History
   1. Typical patient: Table 55.2
   2. Initial symptoms in women may be peripheral or cervical arthritis and may lead to misdiagnosis
   3. Symptoms begin insidiously
   4. Progressive limitation of motion of spine

Table 55.1. Classification of Spondylitis and Frequency of HLA-B27[a]

Classification	HLA-B27 Positive
Primary	
Isolated sacroiliitis	70–90%
Ankylosing spondylitis	90%
Secondary	
Spondylitis of inflammatory bowel disease	50%
Psoriatic spondylitis	50%
Reiter's disease with spondylitis	90%
Infectious	
Sacroiliitis	Not increased
Discitis	Not increased
Osteomyelitis	Not increased
Degenerative spondylosis	Not increased

[a] Found in 8–10% of normal white Americans and 2–4% of African Americans.

Table 55.2. Clues to Early Ankylosing Spondylitis

A young man
Pain and/or stiffness in buttocks, low back, chest wall
   Worse with rest
   Better with exercise
Sciatic-like pains
Family history of spondylitis
History of iritis

Table 55.3. Physical Examination in Ankylosing Spondylitis

Sacroiliac joints	Thoracic spine
Tenderness	Increased kyphosis
Pain with compression and/or stress	Tenderness
Lumbar spine	Pain with rib cage compression
Tenderness	Decreased chest expansion (<3 cm)
Paravertebral muscle spasm	Cervical spine
Loss of lordosis	Tenderness
Decreased flexion: Schober test (<5 cm)	Pain on motion
(see text)	Muscle spasm
Abnormal finger-to-floor distance	Decreased motion
Decreased lateral motion and extension	Kyphosis, decreased lordosis
Hips, shoulders	Occiput to wall movement (see text)
Pain on motion	
Decreased range	

Table 55.4. Extra-articular Manifestations and Complications of Ankylosing Spondylitis

Cardiac	5%
First-degree AV block	
Second- and third-degree AV block	
Aortic regurgitation	
Ocular	25%
Acute iritis	
Chronic iritis	
Neurological	Rare
Cauda equina syndrome	
Cord injury due to fractures	
Renal	Rare
IgA nephropathy	
Amyloidosis	4%
Pulmonary fibrosis	Rare

AV, atrioventricular; IgA, immunoglobulin A.

5. Hips and shoulders are symptomatic in 50% of patients
B. Physical examination
    1. Should be performed initially and every 4–6 months and should include not only joints but also eyes, heart, skin, gastrointestinal tract
    2. Articular features (Table 55.3)
        a) Early in disease, examination may be normal or the sacroiliac joints may only be tender, despite symptoms
        b) Schober test: patient erect, a horizontal line is drawn at L5-S1, and another line is drawn 10 cm above that; with forward flexion the distance between these two lines should normally increase to 15 cm
    3. Extra-articular features (Table 55.4)
        a) Cardiac abnormalities: see Chapters 43 and 44
        b) Iritis: see Chapter 82
        c) Cauda equina syndrome: see Chapter 49
C. Laboratory tests
    1. Radiological studies

Table 55.5.   New York Diagnostic Criteria for Ankylosing Spondylitis[a]

Clinical

1. Limitation of motion of the lumbar spine in all three planes — anterior flexion, lateral flexion, and extension
2. History or presence of pain at the dorsolumbar junction *or* in the lumbar spine
3. Limitation of chest expansion to 2.5 cm (1 inch) or less, measured at the level of the fourth intercostal space

Radiographic

1. Sacroiliitis: grade 3 (sclerosis and erosions of the joint margins) or grade 4 (fusion across the joint)

From Bennett PH, Burch TA: New York Symposium on Population Studies in the Rheumatic Diseases: New Diagnostic Criteria. *Bull Rheum Dis* 17:453, 1967, copyright 1967. Used by permission of the Arthritis Foundation.

[a] Definite ankylosing spondylitis equals grade 3 or 4 bilateral sacroiliitis with at least one clinical criterion *or* unilateral grade 3 or 4 or bilateral grade 2 (sclerosis or joint margins) sacroiliitis with clinical criterion 1 *or* with both clinical criteria 2 and 3.

        a) Radiological evaluation of the sacroiliac joints is the most specific test
           1) A single anteroposterior view of the pelvis is usually adequate; at times, oblique views are necessary
           2) Earliest change is bony sclerosis on both sides of the joint margins; then bony erosions occur; eventually, there is fusion across the joint space
        b) An early radiological sign is "squaring" of the vertebral bodies, especially of the lumbar spine; later, apophyseal joints become fused and osteoporosis ensues; ultimately, the ligamentous structures between the vertebrae become calcified and ossified
        c) Computed tomography and magnetic resonance imaging are more sensitive than plain x-rays in detecting early disease but are much more expensive
    2. Histological studies usually normal; erythrocyte sedimentation rate usually elevated
    3. Serological studies usually normal
    4. Tissue typing
        a) HLA-B27 in 90% of patients and in 8–10% of normals
        b) Testing not usually needed to support diagnosis; most useful when x-rays are not yet diagnostic
D. Diagnostic criteria: summarized in Table 55.5
E. Course
    1. Disease may remain confined to sacroiliac joints or may ascend into lumbar, thoracic, cervical spine
    2. Duration of time from onset to fusion of spine highly variable
    3. Continued medical surveillance important
F. Management
    1. Pharmacological
        a) Anti-inflammatory drugs
           1) To relieve pain, stiffness and to promote ability to perform exercises (see below)
           2) Aspirin may be tried as the initial drug, 3 enteric-coated tablets 4 times/day
               (a) Salicylate levels should be measured; goal is 15–25 mg/dl

          (b) Usually not adequate to control symptoms
      3) Indomethacin
          (a) Especially effective in dosages up to 75–150 mg/day
          (b) Side effects: see Chapter 54
          (c) Tolmetin or sulindac (two other indole nonsteroidal
              anti-inflammatory agents [NSAIDs]) may be tried if
              patient is intolerant of Indocin
          (d) If indoles are ineffective, then other NSAIDs may be
              tried (see Chapter 54)
      4) Sulfasalazine (Azulfidine) is effective
          (a) Enteric-coated preparation, 500 mg twice a day for 1
              week; then 1 g 2–3 times/day
          (b) Adverse reactions are common (see Chapter 54),
              especially gastrointestinal, and consultation with a
              rheumatologist is warranted before prescribing
  2. Physical measures
      a) Encourage an erect posture
      b) Advise use of a bed board, sleeping prone without a pillow
      c) Refer to a physical therapist to design an active exercise
         program to maintain mobility
      d) Encourage spondylitic patients to wear soft cervical collars
         when riding in cars to avoid whiplash injuries

REITER'S SYNDROME
A. Definition: a reactive arthritis that follows certain genitourinary or
   gastrointestinal infections
B. Epidemiology
   1. May be the most common cause of arthritis in young men
   2. Eight or nine times more common in men than in women
   3. Much more common in whites than in African Americans
C. Presentation
   1. May follow diarrhea caused by *Shigella, Salmonella, Yersinia,* or
      Campylobacter (see Chapter 12) — 15% of cases
   2. May follow venereal infection, especially *Chlamydia trachomatis*
      (see Chapters 13 and 27) including HIV infection, the bulk of the
      cases
   3. Urethritis classically the first symptom; usually painless or with
      mild dysuria and mucopurulent discharge; lasts 1–2 weeks
   4. Conjunctivitis follows shortly; usually mild with redness, weeping,
      crusting; lasts a few days
   5. Arthritis appears last — from days to 1 month after onset of
      urethritis
      a) Typically lower extremity oligoarthritis (most commonly knees,
         ankles, feet)
      b) Pain, swelling, heat, redness over joints
      c) Fifty percent will have nonarticular musculoskeletal pain (heel
         pain very common)
      d) Diffuse swelling (sausaging) of digits occurs commonly
      e) Forty percent of cases have only arthritis
   6. Mucocutaneous features: highly variable when present, lasts for
      days to months
      a) Often asymptomatic
      b) Painless shallow oral ulcers

      c) Circinate balanitis: shallow moist painless ulcers on glans penis in uncircumcised men or a dry scaling eruption on the glans in circumcised men

      d) Keratoderma blennorrhagica, a papulosquamous eruption beginning on the palms and soles

      e) Onychodystrophy

    7. Other features: fever, weight loss, uveitis (see Chapter 82) may occur

D. Laboratory tests

    1. Hematological studies

      a) Mild normocytic normochromic anemia (hematocrit value 30–35%)

      b) Modest granulocytosis (up to 15,000/mm^3)

      c) Thrombocytosis in one-third of patients

      d) Erythrocyte sedimentation rate usually elevated

    2. Serological studies

      a) Rheumatoid factor, antinuclear antibody negative

      b) Serum complement normal or elevated

      c) HLA-B27 in 75%, but testing rarely warranted

      d) Antibodies to *C. trachomatis* in up to 50% of cases

    3. Radiological studies

      a) Normal early in disease

      b) Eventually, periostitis involving the calcaneus or along the shafts of swollen digits

      c) Sacroiliitis in 20%, typically unilateral in this disease

    4. Synovial fluid findings

      a) Poor mucin clot

      b) White cell count from 5,000–50,000/mm^3

      c) Elevated protein content

      d) Normal glucose concentration

      e) High complement titer (as opposed to low titer in rheumatoid arthritis)

    5. Urinalysis

      a) To detect urethritis

      b) *C. trachomatis* can be cultured in 30–50% of cases

E. Course

    1. Resolves in majority of cases in 3 months to 1 year

    2. Fifteen percent chance of recurrence

    3. Uncommonly, a chronic progressive disease develops with joint destruction and fusion

    4. Cardiac complications (atrioventricular block, aortic regurgitation) and visual loss due to uveitis develop rarely

F. Management

    1. If *C. trachomatis* has been cultured from urine or if serum antibodies to chlamydia are identified, treat with tetracycline (250 mg 4 times/day) or doxycycline (100 mg 2 times/day) for 3 months

    2. If syndrome occurs after dysentery, not clear that antimicrobial treatment is effective in shortening course

    3. Indole NSAIDs are effective in suppressing inflammation, reducing pain in majority of cases (see Ankylosing spondylitis, above)

    4. Systemic corticosteroids may be necessary for patients with severe uveitis or arthritis unresponsive to NSAIDs but should be prescribed in consultation with a rheumatologist

5. Intra-articular injection of corticosteroids may be useful if systemic treatment has failed; usually done by a rheumatologist
6. Physical therapy is important when arthritis is active (see Ankylosing spondylitis, above)
7. Nonarthritic manifestations usually require no specific treatment (although chlamydial urethritis should be treated, as above, and patients with uveitis should be treated by an ophthalmologist)

Metabolic and Endocrinological Problems

56/   DIABETES MELLITUS

CHARACTERISTICS: TABLE 56.1
DIAGNOSIS
A. History
   1. Many patients asymptomatic at diagnosis
   2. Symptoms, when present
      a) Polyuria, polydipsia
      b) Polyphagia and weight loss in severe disease
      c) Other: blurred vision, vaginitis, skin infections
      d) Often insidious
B. Blood glucose concentration
   1. Elevation is the hallmark of the disease
   2. Elevation should be repeatedly demonstrated
   3. Urine glucose concentration not as reliable
   4. Normal values: Table 56.2
   5. Diagnostic values: fasting and during glucose tolerance test (Table 56.3)
      a) Levels between normal and diabetic *(impaired glucose tolerance)* associated with development of diabetes in 1–5% a year
      b) Repeatedly elevated fasting glucose level does not warrant a glucose tolerance test
      c) Two-hour postprandial blood glucose as a screening test is unreliable
      d) Glucose tolerance test mostly done in people with positive family history and normal fasting glucose or in pregnant women (see below)
      e) Drug effects on glucose tolerance: Table 56.4

TREATMENT
A. Education
   1. Impact of the diet
   2. Implications for normal activities
   3. Recognition of the signs of worsening of the disease
   4. Importance of foot care
   5. Correct administration of insulin
   6. Recognition and treatment of hypoglycemia
B. Diet
   1. Weight reduction in non-insulin-dependent diabetes mellitus (NIDDM)
      a) Can prevent or eliminate symptoms and need for drug treatment
      b) Prevention of atherosclerotic complications by control of hyperlipidemia (Chapter 59)
   2. Ideal composition: Table 56.5
   3. Importance of constancy in distribution of amount of food each meal each day in insulin-dependent diabetes mellitus (IDDM)
   4. Recognition that exercise will modify insulin requirements
C. Selection of drug therapy
   1. NIDDM: Table 56.6
   2. IDDM
      a) Always requires insulin

Table 56.1. Classification and Clinical Characteristics of Diabetes Mellitus and Other States of Glucose Intolerance

Type of Diabetes	Former Terminology	Clinical Characteristics
Insulin-dependent type (IDDM, type I)	Juvenile diabetes Juvenile-onset type diabetes Ketosis-prone diabetes Brittle diabetes	Onset usually in youth but occurs at any age. Insulin deficiency requires exogenous insulin to prevent ketosis-acidosis. Non-insulin-dependent phases may occur during natural history. 10–12% of all cases.
Non-insulin-dependent types (NIDDM, type II) Nonobese NIDDM Obese NIDDM	Adult-onset diabetes, maturity-onset diabetes (MOD); stable diabetes, nonketosis-prone diabetes; in young people was called maturity-onset diabetes of youth (MODY)	Onset generally after age 40 but may occur in young; not insulin dependent or ketosis prone but may need insulin for control of persistent hyperglycemia; periods of ketosis-acidosis may occur during stress of illness; weight control of obese subtypes may ameliorate disease. 80–90% of all cases.
Other types *Diabetes mellitus associated with* Pancreatic disease Hormone excess due to endocrine disease or hormone treatment (steroids of glucocorticoid type) Drug use (e.g., diuretics, nicotinic acid) Insulin receptor abnormalities	Secondary diabetes	Diagnosis demands usual abnormalities of glucose handling and documentation of associated condition.
Impaired glucose tolerance (IGT) Nonobese IGT Obese IGT IGT associated with certain conditions Drug (chemical) induced Insulin receptor abnormalities Genetic syndromes	Asymptomatic diabetes; chemical diabetes; subclinical diabetes; borderline diabetes; latent diabetes	Diabetes is based on abnormality of glucose handling; may represent a stage of development of diabetes, although most remain in this class for years or revert to normal glucose tolerance. Usually associated with acanthosis nigricans; rare, familial
Gestational diabetes mellitus (GDM)	Gestational diabetes	Glucose intolerance has onset during pregnancy; does not include diabetic who becomes pregnant; increased risk of perinatal complications and future diabetes.

IDDM, insulin-dependent diabetes mellitus; NIDDM, non-insulin-dependent diabetes mellitus.

Table 56.2.   Normal Values for Plasma Glucose and for the Glucose Tolerance Test[a]

Fasting state (10–16 hr postprandial)	
Venous plasma	<115 mg/dl
Venous whole blood	<100 mg/dl
Capillary whole blood	<100 mg/dl
2 Hr oral glucose tolerance test	
Venous plasma	<140 mg/dl
Venous whole blood	<120 mg/dl
Capillary whole blood	<140 mg/dl

Values between those that are diagnostic (see Table 56.3) and those that are normal should be considered nondiagnostic. Impaired glucose tolerance (IGT) is considered present when three criteria are met: (a) fasting level is below diagnostic, (b) 2-hr value is intermediate, and (c) some other value (0.5, 1, 1.5) is elevated to:

Venous plasma	>200 mg/dl
Venous whole blood	>180 mg/dl
Capillary whole blood	>200 mg/dl

[a] To express values as millimoles per liter, multiply glucose in milligrams per deciliter ×0.056. Serum and plasma values are the same.

Table 56.3.   Diagnosis of Diabetes: Diagnostic Value of Glucose and of the Glucose Tolerance Test[a]

Fasting state (10–16 hr postprandial)	
Venous plasma[a]	>140 mg/dl
Venous whole blood	>120 mg/dl
Capillary whole blood	>140 mg/dl

Oral glucose tolerance test preparation: fasting 10–16 hr during which no caffeine-containing drinks or smoking is permitted.

75 g glucose (40 g/m[2])

Use in nonpregnant adults: (1.75 g/kg for children, up to 75 g maximum). Dosage form: flavored water, 25 g of glucose/100 dl. Drink over 5 min. Obtain blood samples at 0, 0.5, 1, 1.5, 2 hr.

Test positive for diabetes mellitus: both the 2-hr sample and at least one other sample must meet following criteria:

Venous plasma	>200 mg/dl
Venous whole blood	>180 mg/dl
Capillary whole blood	>200 mg/dl

100 g glucose

Use only in pregnant adults: obtain blood samples at 0, 1, 2, 3 hr. Test positive for diabetes mellitus: two or more of the following values must be met or exceeded:

	Venous Plasma (mg/dl)	Venous Whole Blood (mg/dl)	Capillary Whole Blood (mg/dl)
Fasting	105	90	90
1 hr	190	170	170
2 hr	165	145	145
3 hr	145	125	125

[a] Serum and plasma values are the same.

    b) "Tight control" of blood sugar important to prevent atherosclerotic complications

        1) Requires considerable effort by patient and physician, including multiple doses of insulin (or infusion pump) and multiple tests of blood glucose each day

        2) In patients unable or unwilling to make the effort, near-normalization of blood glucose is the goal (see below)

Table 56.4. Drugs Associated With Abnormal Glucose Tolerance or Diabetes Mellitus

Hormones and related agents
  Adrenocorticotropic hormone
  Catecholamines (epinephrine, isoproterenol, levodopa)
  Dextrothyroxine
  Estrogens (oral contraceptives)
  Glucocorticoids (cortisone and derivatives)
  Thyroxine and triiodothyronine (toxic doses)
Diuretics and antihypertensive drugs
  Bumetanide (Bumex)
  Chlorthalidone (Hygroton, Combipres, Regroton)
  Clonidine (Catapres, Combipres)
  Ethacrynic acid (Edecrin)
  Furosemide (Lasix)
  Prazosin (Minipress)
  Propranolol (Inderal)
  Thiazides (Diuril, Hydrodiuril, etc.)
Psychoactive agents
  Chlorprothixene (Taractan)
  Haloperidol (Haldol)
  Lithium (Lithane, Eskalith)
  Phenothiazines (Thorazine, Trilafon, Etrafron, Triavil, etc.)
  Tricyclic antidepressants
    Amitriptyline (Elavil, Endep, Triavil, etc.)
    Desipramine (Norpramin, Pertofrane)
    Doxepin (Adapin, Sinequan)
    Imipramine (Presamine, Tofranil)
    Nortriptyline (Aventyl)
Miscellaneous
  Antineoplastic drugs (L-asparaginase, streptozotocin)
  Dilantin (Phenytoin)
  Indomethacin
  L-Dopa (Sinemet)
  Morphine; marijuana
  Nicotinic acid (niacin)

D. Insulin
  1. Types
    a) Regular (crystalline zinc)
      1) Used in mixtures for ambulatory patients
      2) Rapid onset (20 minutes when given subcutaneously)
      3) Short-acting (4–6 hours)
    b) Protamine zinc
      1) Long-acting (over 24 hours)
      2) Not commonly used
    c) Neutral protamine Hagedorn (NPH)
      1) Intermediate-acting
      2) Duration of action generally of <24 hours
    d) Lente
      1) Semilente — equivalent to regular
      2) Ultralente — equivalent to protamine zinc
      3) Lente — intermediate-acting, but duration of action is longer than that of NPH if a single injection is desired; lente is the choice

Table 56.5.   Distribution of Major Nutrients in Typical, Traditional, Diabetic, and Current Diabetic Diets (United States)

	Nutrients (Percentage of Total Calories)						
	Starch and Other Complex Polysaccharides	Sugars and Dextrins	Total Carbohydrates	Fat		Protein	Alcohol
				Total	% Mono- or Polyunsaturated		
"Typical" diet	25–35	20–30	45–50	35–45	30	12–20	1–10
Traditional diabetic diet	25–30	10–15	35–40	40–50	30	15–20	0
Current diabetic diets[a]	40[b]	40	50	30	20	20	

Modified from West KM: Diet therapy of diabetes: an analysis of failure. *Ann Intern Med* 79:425, 1973.
[a] The recommended diet of the American Diabetic Association additionally provides <300 mg cholesterol and 28 g dietary fiber.
[b] Even higher levels of starch and lower levels of fat might be desirable but are seldom possible in Western societies because they differ too much from the traditional diets of these cultures.

Table 56.6.   Therapeutic Approach to Patients With NIDDM[a]

Fasting Plasma Glucose (mg/dl)	Age of Patient (yr)			
	20	40	60	80
Obese patient (initial dietary treatment)				
115–139	DIET	DIET	DIET	diet or do nothing
140–199	ORAL AGENT or insulin	ORAL AGENT or insulin	ORAL AGENT	oral agent or diet
200	INSULIN or oral agent	INSULIN or ORAL AGENT	ORAL AGENT or insulin	oral agent or insulin or diet
Nonobese patient (initial dietary treatment)				
115–139	INSULIN or oral agent	ORAL AGENT or insulin	ORAL AGENT	oral agent or diet
140–199	INSULIN	INSULIN or ORAL AGENT	ORAL AGENT or INSULIN	ORAL AGENT or INSULIN
200	INSULIN	INSULIN or ORAL AGENT	INSULIN or oral agent	INSULIN or oral agent

Modified from: *ADA Physician's Guide to Non-insulin Dependent (Type II) Diabetes. Diagnosis and Treatment*, 2nd ed. Alexandria, VA, American Diabetes Association, 1988.

[a] This table presents results of a poll involving specialists in diabetes. However, it does not represent the opinion of all experts. Treatment must be *individualized* for all patients. When two therapeutic approaches are listed, if both are capitalized, slight preference is given to the first one listed. If the second approach is in lower case letters, the first approach is strongly preferred. If both approaches are in lower case letters, no clear-cut preference can be stated.

e) Mixtures: regular and NPH or lente; or semilente and lente
2. Commercial preparations
   a) Standard animal
      1) From pig and/or beef pancreas
      2) Least expensive
      3) Generally satisfactory
   b) Purified animal
      1) From pig pancreas
      2) Expensive
   c) Human
      1) Recombinant or semisynthetic
      2) Expensive
      3) Intermediate- and long-acting preparations often have a maximal duration of action of <24 hours, so single-dose control not possible
3. Allergic reactions
   a) Local, at injection site: redness, heat, swelling, itching
   b) Systemic (rare): urticaria, angioedema, anaphylaxis
      1) First response is to use a purer insulin
      2) Second response is desensitization (kits and instructions from manufacturer)
      3) Antihistamines or corticosteroids may help
4. Injections
   a) Alcohol wipe unnecessary
   b) Always subcutaneously in ambulatory patients
   c) Sites should not be rotated (absorption varies by site)
5. Possible goals of therapy
   a) Minimal therapy
      1) Avoidance of extremes of symptomatic hyperglycemia and hypoglycemia
      2) Use of least amount of insulin, in a single dose
      3) Minimal testing of blood or urine
      4) Hemoglobin A_{1C} (HbA_{1C}) of 9.5–12% (normal is 3.8–6.3%)
   b) Average therapy
      1) An attempt to approach a nearly normal fasting blood sugar
      2) One or two doses of intermediate insulin, usually mixed with regular insulin
      3) Urine testing before meals and at bedtime; testing of blood glucose when no glucose is detected in urine; HbA_{1C} of 7.5–9.5%
   c) Intensive therapy
      1) An attempt to normalize blood sugar
      2) Requires maximal effort by the patient and a health care team (physician, trained nurse, dietician)
      3) An insulin pump (regular insulin) or 3 or 4 daily doses of insulin (long-acting insulin plus bolus of regular insulin before meals)
      4) Frequent testing of blood glucose (by the patient), including a weekly 3:00 A.M. sample
      5) HbA_{1C} of 7.2%
      6) Adrenergic symptoms of hypoglycemia (e.g., sweating, tachycardia) may be lost

6. Factors affecting insulin requirement
   a) Insulin resistance
      1) Obesity
      2) Insulin antibodies
         (a) A slow increase in requirement for insulin
         (b) Use of purified preparation may help
         (c) Short course of corticosteroids may be necessary
   b) Decreased requirement
      1) Vigorous exercise
      2) First trimester of pregnancy
      3) Renal failure
      4) Chronic heart failure
      5) Adrenal or pituitary insufficiency
      6) Hypoglycemia
         (a) May be due to erratic diet
         (b) May be due to loss of counterregulatory mechanisms
         (c) Nocturnal: Somogyi effect — rebound fasting hyperglycemia, induced by release of epinephrine by hypoglycemia — must be distinguished from effect of inadequate insulin dosage
         (d) Treated with ingestion of sugar (e.g., candy) by conscious patient; glucagon 1 mg s.c. given to a patient with impaired consciousness
E. Oral hypoglycemic drugs (sulfonylureas)
   1. Candidates for therapy: Table 56.6
   2. Available agents: Table 56.7
   3. One-half of patients will have an optimum response; one-third, no response
   4. Monitoring: overnight urine glucose once a week, fasting blood glucose every few months
   5. Drug interactions
      a) A wide variety of drugs interact with oral hypoglycemic agents
      b) Be aware of a change in effect of oral hypoglycemics whenever a regimen is changed

COMPLICATIONS

A. Hypertension
   1. Accelerates retinopathy and nephropathy
   2. Requires aggressive treatment (Chapter 46)
B. Peripheral neuropathy
   1. Peripheral sensory neuropathy
      a) "Stocking glove:" symmetrical, with a proximal-distal gradient of dysfunction
      b) Common symptoms: hyperesthesia, dysesthesia (tingling and burning), stabbing leg pains
      c) Symptoms often respond to amitriptyline or desipramine, 100 mg/day; analgesics sometimes needed
   2. Peripheral motor neuropathy
      a) Less common
      b) Intrinsic muscles of the feet are most commonly involved
   3. Mononeuropathies
      a) Lower extremities more commonly involved
      b) Sudden onset, with intense pain

Table 56.7.   Characteristics of Hypoglycemic Drugs (Sulfonylureas)

Compound	Generic Available	Trade Name	Tablet Size	Daily Dose Range	Duration of Action (hr)	Doses/Day	Route of Inactivation
Tolbutamide	Yes	Orinase	0.5 g	1–3 g	12	2–3	100% in liver
Chlorpropamide	Yes	Diabinese	0.1 g 0.25 g	0.1–0.5 g	36+	1	100% excretion by kidney: as intact drug, 30%, plus less-active metabolites, 70%
Acetohexamide		Dymelor	0.25 g 0.5 g	0.25–1.5 g	12–18	1–2	100% kidney excretion of active metabolites from liver plus unchanged drug
Tolazamide	Yes	Tolinase	0.1 g 0.25 g 0.5 g	0.25–1.0 g	12–24	1–2	Partial liver metabolism; partial excretion via kidney
Glyburide	No	Micronase Diabeta	1.25 mg 2.5 mg 5 mg	1.25–20 mg	16–24	1–2	100% metabolized to inactive compounds
Glipizide	No	Glucotrol	5 mg 10 mg	2.5–40 mg	12–24	1–2	100% metabolized to inactive compounds

        c) Typically worse at night

        d) Reversible cranial and oculomotor neuropathies may occur

    4. Neuropathic foot ulcers

        a) A late consequence of sensory neuropathy most often

        b) Typically plantar

        c) Podiatric care critical

C. Autonomic neuropathy

    1. Abnormal sweat production

        a) Typically, heat intolerance, an increased sweating of upper half of body with decreased sweating of lower half

        b) Predisposition to hyperthermia

    2. Cardiovascular

        a) Painless infarctions are common

        b) Resting sinus tachycardia

        c) Postural hypotension (Chapter 64)

    3. Digestive system dysfunction

        a) Gastric atony: may be associated with anorexia, early satiety, postprandial bloating, occasionally vomiting

        b) Diarrhea: typically nocturnal

    4. Neurogenic bladder

        a) Insidious onset

        b) Usually associated with other neuropathic syndromes

        c) First manifest by increased intervals between voiding

        d) Also associated with dribbling, sensation of incomplete voiding

        e) Residual urine is the hallmark

    5. Sexual dysfunction: impotence common

    6. Neuropathic arthropathy

        a) Preceded by a sensory neuropathy

        b) A progressive degeneration of the bones of the foot, most often the tarsal and metatarsal joints

        c) Presents with sudden deformed foot, usually warm and red

D. Diabetic nephropathy (Chapter 33)

    1. Earliest sign is microalbuminuria (Chapter 29)

    2. Even slight elevation of serum creatinine associated with increased risk of acute renal failure from radiographic contrast media

E. Infection

    1. Urinary tract: more complications than in nondiabetics (e.g., papillary necrosis)

    2. Skin: *Candida* infections are common

    3. Soft tissue: usually lower extremity, especially feet

F. Retinopathy

    1. A leading cause of blindness

    2. Prevented in IDDM by intensive insulin treatment (see above)

    3. Types

        a) Nonproliferative and preproliferative

            1) Earliest lesions are perimacular: microaneurysms, punctate hemorrhages, hard exudates, soft exudates, intraretinal microvascular anomalies

            2) Ophthalmologist needed to evaluate severity, including presence or absence of macular edema

        b) Proliferative: new vessel formation, fibrosis

    4. Treatment

418 Section IX Metabolic and Endocrinological Problems

Table 56.8. Reasons for Referral of Patients With Diabetes Mellitus to an Ophthalmologist

High-risk patients
Neovascularization covering more than one-third of optic disc
Vitreous or preretinal hemorrhage with any neovascularization, particularly on optic disc; or macular edema (suspect from hard exudates in macula)

Symptomatic patients
Blurry vision persisting for more than 1–2 days or not associated with a change in blood glucose; suspect macular edema
Sudden loss of vision in one or both eyes; *or*
Black spots, cobwebs, or flashing lights in field of vision

Asymptomatic patients
Yearly examinations (an optometrist can check pressures if there are no retinal changes or if only background diabetic retinopathy is present)
Hard exudates near macula
Any preproliferative or proliferative characteristics; or pregnancy

Modified from: *ADA Physician's Guide to Non-insulin Dependent (Type II) Diabetes. Diagnosis and Treatment,* 2nd ed. Alexandria, VA, American Diabetes Association, 1988.

  a) Photocoagulation (Argon laser)
    1) Reduces visual loss in preproliferative and proliferative disease
    2) Used also to treat macular edema
  b) Vitrectomy
    1) Usual indication is vitreous hemorrhage
    2) Also used to treat retinal detachment that has resulted from traction bands in the vitreous
    5. When to refer: Table 56.8

57/ THYROID DISORDERS

LABORATORY TESTS (TABLE 57.1)

A. Plasma T_4 and T_3
  1. T_4 is the single most important measurement in evaluation of thyroid disease
  2. Interpretation of T_4 requires assessment of binding of T_4 to plasma proteins
B. Estimates of thyroxine-binding globulin (TBG)
  1. T_3 uptake test (T_3U) provides an indirect estimate of TBG
  2. Multiplying T_4 and T_3U gives free T_4 index, a reflection of "free T_4"
  3. Factors affecting TBG: Table 57.2
C. Thyroid-stimulating hormone (TSH)
  1. Increased level is the most sensitive index of hypothyroidism (see below)
  2. Sensitive assays now permit measurement in support of diagnosis of hyperthyroidism when other tests are equivocal
D. Thyrotropin-releasing hormone (TRH) tests
  1. Measures release of TSH after injection of TRH
  2. Obsolete in diagnosis of hyperthyroidism
  3. Occasionally useful in diagnosis of hypothyroidism
E. Thyroidal radioiodide uptake (RAIU) tests
  1. Largely replaced by more sensitive tests
  2. Still useful in patients with hyperthyroidism associated with thyroiditis (see below)
F. Effects of nonthyroidal illness and of drugs on thyroid function tests: Tables 57.3 and 57.4

Table 57.1. Thyroid Function Tests[a]

	Plasma T_4 (μg/dl)	Plasma T_3 (ng/dl)	T_3U (%)	T_3UR	TSH (μU/ml)	FT_4 (ng/dl)	FTI[b]
Normal mean	8	120	30	1		1.5	8.0
Normal range	5–12	80–160	25–35	0.85–1.15	0.3–5	1.0–2.0	5.8–10.6
Confidence limits	±1	±20	±2	±0.05		±0.3	

T_3U, T_3 resin uptake; T_3UR, T_3 resin uptake ratio; *TSH*, thyroid-stimulating hormone; *FT₄*, free T_4; *FTI*, free T_4 index.
[a] See the text for limitations of interpretation of normal ranges. Confidence limits (95%) of a single value are approximate and depend on both the laboratory and the level within the range.
[b] The FTI on any sample is calculated as $T_4 \times T_3UR$, but the normal range for the FTI is determined empirically. The units of the FTI depend on whether the percentage T_3U or the T_3UR is multiplied by T_4.

Table 57.2. Factors Affecting TBG

TBG INCREASED	TBG DECREASED
Estrogens	Androgens
Exogenous	Anabolic steroids
Pregnancy	Cirrhosis
Hypothyroidism	Glucocorticoids
Acute hepatitis	Nephrotic syndrome
Cirrhosis	Severe chronic nonthyroidal illness
Genetic TBG excess	Cushing's syndrome
Acute intermittent porphyria	Genetic TBG deficiency
Perphenazine (Trilafon)	

Table 57.3. Nonthyroidal Illness: Effects on T$_4$, Free T$_4$, TBG, and TSH in Plasma[a,b]

	T$_4$	Free T$_4$	TGB	TSH
LIVER DISEASE				
Active hepatitis	↑	↔↑	↑	
Cirrhosis, other chronic disease	↑↓	↔↑	↑↓	↔↑
Cholangitis	↑	↔↑	↑	
RENAL DISEASE				
Nephrotic syndrome	↔↓	↔	↔↓	
Uremia, chronic	↔↓	↔↓	↔↓	
INFECTIONS	↓	↑	↔	
MALNUTRITION	↔↓	↔↑	↔↓	
SEVERE ACUTE ILLNESS[c]	↔↑	↔↑	↔	↓

[a] Most illnesses and even such minor alterations of physiological state as decreased food intake will produce a decrease of plasma T$_3$.
[b] Changes of TSH not likely in ambulatory patients.
[c] Not likely to be seen in ambulatory patients.

Table 57.4 Drug and Hormone Effects on T$_4$, Free T$_4$, TBG, and TSH

Gonadal Hormones	T$_4$	Free T$_4$	TBG	TSH
ESTROGENS	↑	↔↓	↑	
Exogenous				
Pregnancy				↓
ANDROGENS	↓	↔		
Testosterone		↑		
Anabolic steroids				
GLUCOCORTICOIDS	↓	↔	↓	
Cushing's syndrome				
Pharmacological uses				
PSYCHOTROPIC DRUGS				
Perphenazine (Trilafon)	↑	↔	↑	
Amphetamines	↑	↑	↔	
ANTICONVULSANTS				
Phenytoin (Dilantin)	↓	↔↓	↔	↔↑
HEPARIN	↔	↑	↔	
ADRENERGIC BLOCKERS				
Propranolol (Inderal)	↔(↓T$_3$)	↔	↔	
ANTIARRHYTHMIC DRUGS				
Amiodarone	↑	↑	↔	
GALLBLADDER DYES				
Iopanoic acid	↑↔(↓T$_3$)	↔↑	↔↑	↔↑
Ipodate	↑↔(↓T$_3$)	↔↑	↔	↔↑
OPIATES	↑		↑	
MISCELLANEOUS				
Clofibrate	↑		↑	
5-Fluorouracil	↑		↑	

HYPERTHYROIDISM

A. Causes: Table 57.5
B. Graves' disease (diffuse toxic goiter)
    1. Signs and symptoms: Table 57.6
    2. Laboratory tests
        a) T$_4$ and the free T$_4$ index are usually elevated
        b) Only T$_3$ is elevated in about 5% of cases

Table 57.5.   Causes of Hyperthyroidism[a]

COMMON
  Graves' disease
  Toxic nodular goiter
    Multinodular
    Uninodular
  Hyperthyroidism in association with thyroiditis
  Iodide-induced (iodide, iodine-containing drugs, and contrast media)
RARE TO VANISHINGLY RARE
  Thyrotoxicosis due to TSH or TSH-like stimulator
    Choriocarcinoma or hydatidiform mole
    Embryonal cell carcinoma of testis
    Pituitary tumor with TSH excess
    Idiopathic TSH excess
  Toxic thyroid carcinoma
  Hyperthyroidism due to exogenous thyroid hormone
    Factitia
    Medicamentosa (iatrogenic)
  Toxic struma ovarii

[a] Listed in approximate decreasing order of frequency.

Table 57.6.   Signs and Symptoms of Hyperthyroidism

Organ or System	Signs and Symptoms
Adrenergic manifestations	Excess sweating, heat intolerance, palpitations, tachycardia, tremor, lid lag, stare, nervousness, and excitability
Hypermetabolism and catabolism	Increased appetite, weight loss
One system predominance	
Eyes[a]	Periorbital edema, exophthalmos (proptosis), chemosis, ophthalmoplegia, papilledema
Cardiac	Arrhythmia, congestive heart failure
Muscle	Fatigue and weakness, muscle wasting, proximal myopathy, periodic paralysis
Gastrointestinal	Increased frequency of bowel movements, pernicious vomiting
Bone	Acropachy, osteoporosis, hypercalcemia
Reproductive	Infertility, abortion, scanty menses, testicular atrophy, gynecomastia
Mental	Anxiety, irritability, psychosis, insomnia
Skin	Onycholysis, "pretibial" myxedema, hyperpigmentation

[a] Graves' disease only.

  c) TSH measurement (low) or serial studies are sometimes
      needed to make diagnosis
  3. Treatment
    a) Antithyroid drugs: propylthiouracil and methimazole
      1) Takes 4–8 weeks for euthyroidism to be restored
      2) Preferred treatment in children, some uncomplicated young
          adults, pregnant patients
      3) Adjunctive treatment before thyroidectomy and before and
          after use of radioiodide
      4) If primary treatment, given for 12–24 months before
          discontinued and thyroid function monitored (relapses are
          50% within 6–12 months)

422 Section IX Metabolic and Endocrinological Problems

            5) Side effects
                (a) Rash the commonest
                (b) Dose-related leukopenia
                (c) Non-dose-related agranulocytosis: rare
        b) Adjunctive drug therapy
            1) Iodide — only for patients with severe illness: one drop of
               saturated solution of potassium iodide in juice once a day
            2) β-Adrenergic antagonists
                (a) For patients with severe tremor, tachycardia, sweating,
                    agitation
                (b) Most patients require equivalent of 160 mg of
                    propranolol a day
        c) Radioiodide (iodine-131) therapy
            1) Preferred treatment
            2) Improvement in few weeks; euthyroidism in a few months
            3) Commonly causes hypothyroidism
            4) No risk of thyroid cancer or other neoplastic processes
        d) Surgery: rarely necessary
    4. Ophthalmopathy (Table 57.6)
        a) Eye disease and thyroid disease usually, but not always,
           coincide
        b) Severe inflammation and edema require an ophthalmologist
C. Hyperthyroidism and thyroiditis
    1. Subacute thyroiditis (see below) may be associated with transient
       (a few months) hyperthyroidism
    2. Lymphocytic thyroiditis
        a) Nontender enlarged thyroid gland
        b) RAIU very low; T_4 and T_3 high
        c) Often postpartum
    3. RAIU should be done in all patients with hyperthyroidism who do
       not clearly have Graves' disease (i.e., no eye findings) or toxic
       nodular goiter (see below)
    4. Propranolol may be adequate therapy; if not, an antithyroid drug
       may be of use
D. Hyperthyroidism associated with multinodular goiter (toxic nodular
   goiter)
    1. Disease of middle or old age
    2. More insidious onset than that of Graves' disease
    3. Best treated with iodine-131
    4. Posttreatment hypothyroidism more common than in Graves'
       disease
E. Hyperthyroidism due to excessive secretion of T_3: "T_3 toxicosis"
    1. May occur (5% of time) in Graves' disease or with toxic goiter
    2. T_3 should be measured in patients who appear thyrotoxic but
       whose T_4 is normal
F. Hyperthyroidism (or hypothyroidism) due to iodide
    1. Amiodarone (an antiarrhythmic agent) is most common iodine-
       containing drug that causes thyroid dysfunction
    2. Hyperthyroidism: cannot be treated with iodine-131 (low uptake)
       and may be resistant to antithyroid drug therapy (combination
       may be necessary)
G. Thyroid storm
    1. Now rare

Table 57.7. Clinical Classification of Hypothyroidism[a]

HYPOTHYROIDISM WITHOUT GOITER (DECREASE OF THYROID TISSUE MASS)
   Postablative for hyperthyroidism (radioiodide therapy or surgery)
      Idiopathic atrophy
      Postpartum
      Developmental defect (congenital)
      Pituitary or hypothalamic disease
HYPOTHYROIDISM WITH GOITER
   Chronic thyroiditis (Hashimoto's disease, etc.)
   Postpartum
   Drug induced (antithyroid drugs, iodide, lithium,[b] sulfonylureas, etc.)
   Iodide deficiency (remote geographic areas)
   Genetic biosynthetic defects

[a] Hypothyroidism in the United States is now most commonly the consequence of therapy for hyperthyroidism. Hypothyroidism due to idiopathic atrophy of the thyroid is second in frequency. Developmental defects (e.g., lingual thyroid) are rare. Hypothyroidism with goiter is nearly always due to Hashimoto's thyroiditis, rarely to a drug. Genetic biosynthetic defects are rare and usually become manifest in childhood.
[b] Hypothyroidism due to chronic lithium therapy may occur without goiter.

   2. Follows stress in a patient with uncontrolled hyperthyroidism
   3. Fever, marked tachycardia, diarrhea, hypotension
   4. May progress to coma
   5. Warrants hospitalization

HYPOTHYROIDISM

A. Definition
   1. Myxedema: severe form that results in deposition of mucopolysaccharides in the skin and other tissues
   2. Primary hypothyroidism: results from a disease of the thyroid gland
   3. Secondary hypothyroidism: results from lack of TSH secretion
B. Causes (Table 57.7)
   1. Thyroidectomy or effect of iodine-131, used in the treatment of hyperthyroidism, may be commonest cause
   2. Autoimmune thyroiditis
      a) Commonest cause of idiopathic hypothyroidism
      b) Associated with high titers of antibodies to thyroid antigens
   3. Hashimoto's thyroiditis
      a) Commonest cause of goitrous hypothyroidism
      b) Also associated with high titers of antibodies to thyroid antigens
   4. Drug-induced: Table 57.7
C. Clinical features
   1. Insidious onset of easy fatigability, lethargy, increased sleep requirement, cold intolerance, muscle aching, constipation, hearing loss, paresthesias, menorrhagia
   2. Physical findings: dry skin; hair loss; puffy face; low-pitched, hoarse voice; depression, especially in the elderly
   3. Most commonly symptoms are nonspecific; physical findings are few; T_4 normal but TSH is elevated (see below)
   4. Myxedema
      a) In spontaneous hypothyroidism, only after longstanding disease
      b) In addition to findings listed above, skin is cool, thickened; "water bags" beneath eyes, tongue sometimes large, heart rate

slow; slow relaxation of deep tendon reflexes, slow mentation (with slow speech)
c) Pleural effusions and ascites may be present
d) Dilutional hyponatremia may be present
e) Myxedema coma
1) Typically in an elderly patient
2) Often precipitated by systemic infection
3) Demands hospitalization
D. Laboratory findings
1. Low plasma T_4, low free T_4 index (or free T_4), and high TSH are diagnostic
2. Measurement of T_3 not useful
3. In secondary hypothyroidism, TSH is low (but may be low in severe nonthyroidal illness)
4. Muscle enzymes (e.g., creatine kinase) often elevated
5. Hyperlipoproteinemia of all types (Chapter 59) may be seen
6. Nonspecific electrocardiogram changes are seen
7. Anemia reflects severity of process
E. Treatment
1. Best preparation is T_4
2. Usual patient can be started on full replacement (125 μg/day on average)
a) Elderly patients or patients with pre-existing heart disease should be started on a lower dose (12.5–25 μg/day)
b) Goal is plasma T_4 at middle to upper range of normal and, ideally, normal TSH, but "fine tuning" usually unnecessary

POSTPARTUM THYROID DYSFUNCTION
A. Common — both hyperthyroidism and hypothyroidism
B. Occurs within 8 months usually, lasts up to 4 months
1. Transient cases associated with thyroid-blocking antibodies (e.g., antimicrosomal antibodies)
2. Thirty percent of cases of hypothyroidism are permanent

GOITER
A. Definition: an enlarged thyroid gland
B. Diagnosis
1. Physical finding best confirmed by ultrasonography
2. Pain not usual but can develop during cyst formation or hemorrhage
3. Dysphagia or hoarseness not common; latter suggests malignancy
4. Clinical and laboratory assessment of thyroid function should be made routinely (see above)
C. Treatment
1. Suppression with T_4 (thyroxine, 125 ± 25 μg/day) or T_3 (Cytomel, 25 ± 5 μg/day)
2. Given for cosmetic reasons or to prevent obstructive symptoms in a relatively young person
3. Plasma T_4 should be monitored so that it does not rise above normal (if T_3 is given, a T_4 below normal is evidence of suppression)
4. Diffuse glands regress by 6 months in 50% of patients; nodular glands are less likely to respond; no glands will enlarge further

THYROID NEOPLASMS

A. Benign solitary nodules
1. Very common: noted in 4% of people by palpation; in up to 50% by ultrasound
2. Hyperthyroidism should be excluded by T_4 index (and, if necessary, T_3)
3. Hashimoto's thyroiditis should be excluded by measurement of thyroid autoantibodies
4. Sonography establishes whether or not there are, in fact, multiple nodules; whether the palpated nodule is cystic
5. Scintiscan
   a) If uptake is greater than that of surrounding gland ("hot" nodule), nodule can be considered benign
   b) If uptake is same as that of surrounding gland ("warm" nodule), nodule is very likely benign
   c) If uptake is less than that of surrounding gland ("cold" nodule), nodule is benign 75–95% of the time
6. Needle biopsy
   a) Usually with a fine needle
   b) Many believe it should be the first diagnostic procedure if diagnosis is believed necessary (see below)
7. Management
   a) Hot or warm nodules
      1) If associated with hyperthyroidism, treat with iodine-131 or surgery (see above)
      2) If associated with euthyroidism, patient should be followed periodically with thyroid function tests
      3) Suppression unwarranted
   b) Cold nodules
      1) Some will biopsy first; some will do sonography first; some will simply initiate suppression therapy
      2) Even those patients with a malignant nodule (see below) will generally do well with suppression
B. Thyroid carcinomas
1. Papillary
   a) Commonest thyroid cancer, by far
   b) Low-grade are rarely fatal
   c) Near-total thyroidectomy is usually performed, and visible nodes are removed
   d) Postoperative suppression with full replacement doses of thyroxine (see above) are routine
   e) If lesion was large and locally invasive, postoperative iodine-131 in ablative doses is given
2. Follicular
   a) More aggressive than papillary tumors
   b) Most important prognostic feature is invasion, through the tumor capsule or into blood vessels
   c) Same surgical approach as for papillary cancer
   d) Postoperative ablative iodine-131 probably warranted
3. Anaplastic
   a) Uncommon, but incidence increases with age
   b) Aggressive; quickly produces pain, dysphagia, hoarseness and is fatal in 6–12 months

        c) Surgery may be curative if tumor can be resected
- 4. Medullary
    - a) Produce thyrocalcitonin
    - b) May be part of a multiple endocrine adenomatosis syndrome
    - c) If tumor is resectable, chance of cure is good

THYROIDITIS

A. Pyogenic: rare
B. Riedel's: rare
C. Hashimoto's (see above): common
1. Painless, associated with modest glandular enlargement, often nodular
2. Distinguished from nontoxic nodular goiter by high titers of thyroid autoantibodies in serum
D. Subacute: common
1. Often an antecedent upper respiratory infection
2. Earliest symptoms may be referred pain, usually to the ear
3. Thyroid becomes tender in a few days
4. Usually abates in a week or 2, may persist for months
5. RAIU depressed; T4 may be elevated (see above)
6. Aspirin is treatment of choice, but severe cases may require corticosteroids

58/ SELECTED ENDOCRINE PROBLEMS

PITUITARY DISEASE

A. General presentation
   1. Disturbance of function (hypersecretion or hyposecretion of tropic hormones)
   2. Anatomical encroachments on adjacent structures (enlargement of tumors)
B. Evaluation of the sella turcica
   1. Best evaluated by computed tomography (CT) (cheaper) or magnetic resonance imaging (MRI) (more sensitive)
   2. Empty sella syndrome
      a) Enlarged sella of unknown cause
      b) Pituitary function should be evaluated but is usually normal
      c) MRI is definitive study
C. Chromophobe adenomas
   1. Most common pituitary tumors
   2. May be part of a multiple endocrine adenomatosis (MEA) syndrome
      a) MEA I: pituitary adenomas with parathyroid and/or pancreatic islet cell adenomas and sometimes with gastrinomas (Chapter 23)
      b) MEA II: no pituitary adenoma but pheochromocytoma, medullary thyroid carcinoma and, occasionally, parathyroid adenoma
   3. If hypopituitarism develops, hypogonadism is usually first sign, but hypothyroidism also occurs early; hypoadrenalism occurs late
   4. Many chromophobes secrete prolactin
      a) Galactorrhea common
      b) May be associated with hypogonadism (e.g., impotence and amenorrhea)
      c) High levels of prolactin (>200 ng/ml) suggest tumor; low levels (<50 ng/ml) suggest a functional disorder
      d) Treatment
         1) Most cases respond to bromocriptine
         2) Large tumors should be removed; with transsphenoidal surgery even microadenomas can be removed
D. Acromegaly
   1. From pituitary tumors that produce excess growth hormone
   2. Presentation
      a) Most common feature is insidious (over years) alteration of face
         1) Enlargement of the mandible, sometimes with separation of the teeth
         2) Coarsening of facial features
         3) Widening of nose, protrusion of lips
      b) Enlargement of hands and feet
      c) Skin thickening; sebaceous gland enlargement
      d) Carpal tunnel syndrome
      e) Large tumors may cause headache, visual field defect

3. Laboratory diagnosis
   a) Best screening test is determination of insulin-like growth factor (IGF-1)
   b) Definitive test is measurement of 24-hour integrated serum growth hormone
   c) If fasting serum growth hormone is elevated (>10 ng/ml), failure of ingestion of glucose to suppress activity is also highly suggestive of tumor (e.g., during course of a glucose tolerance test)
4. Treatment
   a) Irradiation is standard treatment, but response is slow
   b) Transsphenoidal surgery if rapid response is needed (e.g., cosmetic consideration in a young woman, visual field loss)

E. Hypopituitarism
   1. Causes
      a) Idiopathic: some eventually proved to have infiltrative disease (e.g., sarcoidosis, histiocytosis)
      b) Postpartum failure (Sheehan's syndrome)
      c) Pituitary apoplexy: most often hemorrhagic infarction of a pituitary tumor
      d) Tumors (see above)
   2. Hormone replacement: end-organ hormones as needed to restore function
   3. Pituitary dysfunction due to nonendocrine disease
      a) Malnutrition (e.g., anorexia nervosa)
      b) Marked obesity
      c) Severe chronic infections
      d) Severe emotional disturbances

ADRENAL DISEASES

A. Adrenocortical insufficiency (Addison's disease)
   1. Causes
      a) Commonly an autoimmune disease, sometimes with hypothyroidism (Schmidt's syndrome)
      b) Tuberculosis, now a rare cause
   2. Clinical presentation
      a) Common symptoms: anorexia, weight loss, weakness, decreased endurance
      b) Other symptoms: vomiting, abdominal pain, irritability, symptoms of postural hypotension or of hypoglycemia, darkening of skin; loss of pubic or axillary hair
      c) Physical examination
         1) Often, postural hypotension
         2) Pigmentation diffuse but most evident in creases of the hands, the areolae, over pressure areas, in new scars, and, in whites, on buccal mucosa
      d) Laboratory evaluation
         1) Hyponatremia and hyperkalemia are result of severe disease — not likely seen in ambulatory practice
         2) Diagnosis made by measuring plasma cortisol
            (a) Solidly normal value (15–25 μg/dl) excludes the diagnosis
            (b) Intermediate or low value requires remeasurement after

Table 58.1.   Adrenocortical Hyperfunction

GLUCOCORTICOID EXCESS PREDOMINATES
   Adrenal hyperplasia (60–70% of all cases)
     1. Pituitary microadenoma secreting ACTH (most cases of adrenal hyperplasia)
     2. Endocrine tumor [pheochromocytoma, medullary carcinoma of thyroid, others
       secreting ACTH in addition to other hormone(s) (rare)]
     3. Nonendocrine tumor secreting ACTH (rare)
   Adrenal neoplasm (30–40% of all cases)
     1. Adrenal adenoma
     2. Adrenal carcinoma (about equal in frequency)
ADRENAL ANDROGEN EXCESS PREDOMINATES (HIRSUTISM/VIRILISM)
   Some adrenal adenomas
   Some adrenal carcinomas
   Partial adrenogenital syndrome[a]
ALDOSTERONE EXCESS
   Primary aldosteronism
     1. Adrenal adenoma
     2. Adrenal nodular hyperplasia
   Secondary aldosteronism
     1. Salt and volume depletion, including diuretic use and various disease states causing
       increased production of renin
     2. Juxtaglomerular cell hyperplasia or tumor (rare)

[a] Complete enzymatic defects in steroid synthesis are rare and are invariably manifest early in life as adrenal insufficiency and abnormalities of genital development. In ambulatory adults, partial defects of synthesis of cortisol lead to compensatory adrenal hyperplasia with production of excessive quantities of adrenal steroids with weak androgenic activity. Hirsutism, with or without virilism, ensues (see Chapter 61).

        adrenocorticotropic hormone (ACTH) stimulation (e.g., 0.25 mg ACTH i.v.; plasma cortisol measured 2–3 hours later)
     3) Measurement of urinary steroid metabolites an unreliable way of making the diagnosis
   3. Treatment
     a) Steroid replacement
       1) Cortisol 15–20 mg/day is standard regimen, although there are many variations
       2) Requirement increased by stress (cortisol 50–100 mg/day in divided doses)
       3) Mineralocorticoid usually prescribed also (0.1 mg fludrocortisone a day is a standard initial dose; 0.05 mg/day is a common maintenance dose)
     b) Patient education
       1) Symptoms of crisis; how to respond in emergencies
       2) Identification bracelet
       3) Dietary instructions: liberal salt intake (100–150 mEq/day of sodium)
B. Adrenocorticol hyperfunction (Table 58.1)
   1. Glucocorticoid excess (Cushing's syndrome)
     a) Presentation
       1) Severity depends on magnitude of excess, rapidity of onset, degree of increase of androgen production
       2) "Moon facies," "buffalo hump," truncal obesity
       3) Telangiectasia over face, thinning of skin with easy bruising, purplish abdominal striae

        4) Proximal muscle weakness
        5) Eventually, osteoporosis with back pain, often crush fractures of vertebrae
        6) Hypertension, diabetes mellitus common
        7) Hypokalemia may occur
        8) Psychiatric disorders common (e.g., depression, mania)
        9) Androgenic effects: hirsutism, acne common; true virilization suggests tumor
    b) Differential diagnosis
        1) Obesity: can be distinguished by measurement of steroids (see below)
        2) Psychiatric illness: screening test (see below) may not distinguish; signs and symptoms respond to treatment of psychiatric illness
    c) Laboratory diagnosis
        1) Screening
            (a) Random determination of plasma cortisol or of urinary steroids not of help
            (b) Best test is a dexamethasone suppression test; e.g., 1 mg between 11:00 P.M. and midnight, measure plasma cortisol between 8:00 and 9:00 P.M.
            (c) Measurement of 24-urinary cortisol an alternative test
    d) Treatment
        1) Surgery the preferred treatment for an adrenal or pituitary adenoma
        2) Medical therapy with inhibition of adrenal steroid synthesis for recurrent tumors, best done by an endocrinologist
  2. Adrenal androgen excess
    a) If there is clinical evidence for, measure 24-hour urinary 17-ketosteroids and 17-hydroxycorticoids
    b) Hirsutism without virilism (Chapter 61) is common; hirsutism with virilism warrants consultation
C. Other adrenal diseases
  1. Mineralocorticoid excess (see Chapter 31)
  2. Mineralocorticoid deficiency
    a) As part of Addison's disease (see above)
    b) Hyporeninemic hypoaldosteronism (Chapter 33)
D. Adrenal mass lesions incidentally discovered
  1. In general, tumors producing biochemical products should be removed
  2. If no biochemical abnormality, tumors 6 cm are more likely malignant
    a) Risk is still small
    b) Follow-up with CT scan at 2, 6, 18 months: progressive enlargement dictates removal

HYPOCALCEMIC STATES

A. Causes: Table 58.2
B. Clinical manifestations
  1. Primarily neuromuscular
  2. Mild symptoms: irritability, mood changes, paresthesias, muscle cramps
  3. Severe symptoms: delirium, psychosis, tetany, seizures

Table 58.2.   Causes of Hypocalcemia[a]

HYPOCALCEMIA WITH HIGH SERUM PHOSPHATE
    Renal failure
    Postablative hypoparathyroidism (postthyroidectomy)
    Idiopathic hypoparathyroidism
HYPOCALCEMIA WITH LOW OR NORMAL SERUM PHOSPHATE
    Malabsorption (vitamin D deficiency)
    Magnesium deficiency (alcoholism)
    Renal rickets (renal tubular acidosis; phosphate diabetes; cystinosis; Fanconi's syndrome;
       vitamin D-resistant rickets)
    Medullary carcinoma of thyroid

[a] The serum alkaline phosphatase activity is elevated whenever severe metabolic bone disease is present. Parathyroid hormone levels are depressed in magnesium deficiency. Parathyroid hormone levels are regularly elevated in renal failure and in pseudohypoparathyroidism. Urine calcium is depressed in most hypocalcemic states, except when the rare renal tubular calcium-wasting syndromes are responsible for the hypocalcemia.

    4. Chvostek's sign: contraction of the perilabial facial muscles when the facial nerve is tapped anterior to the ear
    5. Trousseau's sign: spasm of the hand within 3 minutes when the blood pressure cuff is elevated above the systolic pressure
    6. Signs of chronic hypocalcemia: hair loss, scaling of skin, brittle fingernails, cataracts, candidiasis
C. Laboratory findings
    1. Hypocalcemia defined as a serum calcium of <8.5 mg/dl
    2. Remember that reduction of serum albumin by 1 g/dl lowers serum calcium by 0.8 mg/dl
    3. Serum magnesium level should be measured if serum calcium is low
    4. Plasma parathyroid hormone (PTH) levels often useful (see below)
D. Selected entities
    1. Idiopathic hypoparathyroidism
       a) Rare, occasionally not diagnosed until adulthood
       b) Autoimmune, may be associated with adrenal insufficiency, Hashimoto's thyroiditis, pernicious anemia
    2. Postthyroidectomy hypoparathyroidism
       a) Most common cause of hypoparathyroidism
       b) May be evident immediately or over many years
    3. Pseudohypoparathyroidism
       a) X-linked dominant inheritance
       b) Associated skeletal developmental defects
       c) Elevated PTH (end-organ resistance)
E. Treatment of hypoparathyroidism and pseudohypoparathyroidism
    1. Calcium supplements only, 1–2 g/day, in a few patients
    2. Vitamin D: either dihydrotachysterol, 0.2–2 mg/day, or 1,25-dihydroxyvitamin D_3, 0.25–1 μg/day
    3. Goal is serum calcium of 8.5–9.5 mg/dl

HYPERCALCEMIC STATES
A. Causes: Table 58.3
    1. Most common cause of minimal asymptomatic hypercalcemia is use of thiazide diuretics
    2. Hyperparathyroidism: see below
    3. Malignancy: suspect especially if hypocalcemia associated with anorexia, weight loss, etc.

Table 58.3 Causes of Hypercalcemia

Condition	Comment
COMMON CAUSES	
Thiazide drugs	Mild elevation (not >12.5 mg/dl); requires 2 or more weeks to subside
Hyperparathyroidism	Frequently asymptomatic; commonly discovered on routine blood test
Malignancy (including myeloma)	Commonest cause in hospitalized patients; may lead to initial encounter in ambulatory patients
Spurious	Inappropriate technique while drawing blood (venous stasis produces hemoconcentration)
RARE CAUSES	
Milk alkali syndrome	Requires use (abuse) of both alkali ($NaHCO_3$) and large quantities of milk or calcium salts
Hypervitaminosis D	Usually 50,000 units or more daily
Thyrotoxicosis	Severe disease is evident
Paget's disease of bone	Immobilization is necessary
Immobilization	Body cast in adolescent males; patients with Paget's disease of bone; quadriplegia
Sarcoidosis	Hyperglobulinemia usually present
Chronic renal failure	Very uncommon; may exacerbate after transplantation or during hemodialysis
Adrenal insufficiency	Hemoconcentration present
Idiopathic elevation	Mild elevation in postmenopausal women; may revert to normal with physiological estrogen therapy

Table 58.4. Symptoms and Signs of Hypercalcemia

SHORT-TERM (READILY REVERSIBLE)
  General: weakness, anorexia, weight loss, fatigue
  Gastrointestinal: nausea, vomiting, constipation
  Genitourinary: polyuria, azotemia
  Musculoskeletal: bone aches
  Neurological: lethargy, sleepiness, difficulty concentrating, confusion, psychosis
  Cardiovascular: bradycardia, electrocardiographic abnormalities (short QT, arrhythmias, digitalis toxicity)
  Ophthalmological: difficulty focusing
  Dermatological: pruritus
LONG-TERM (IRREVERSIBLE OR SLOWLY REVERSIBLE)
  Gastrointestinal: peptic ulcer, pancreatitis
  Genitourinary: renal calculi (colic, hematuria); nephrocalcinosis; polyuria
  Skeletal: bone loss (osteopenia); subperiosteal resorption, bone cysts, pseudogout
  Neuromuscular: muscle atrophy
  Ophthalmological: band keratopathy; conjunctival calcifications (usually require slitlamp examination)

B. Primary hyperparathyroidism
  1. Usually due to a single benign adenoma
  2. May be part of MEA syndrome (see above)
  3. Diagnosis
    a) Hypercalcemia (10.5 mg/dl on multiple measurements) often detected by routine automated analysis of blood
    b) Symptoms and signs of hypercalcemia: Table 58.4
    c) Assay of PTH in blood (immunoradiometric assays are the most sensitive)
    d) Serum phosphorus often low

Table 58.5. Calcium Content of Some Foods

Food	Serving Size	Calcium Content (mg)
Sardines, canned in oil	8 medium	354
Spinach, frozen chopped, cooked	½ cup	113
Turnip greens, cooked	½ cup	246
Cheddar cheese (American)	1 ounce	211
Creamed cottage cheese	1 cup	211
Muenster cheese	1 ounce	203
Milk, whole	1 quart	1152
Milk, skim	1 quart	1212
Yogurt (low fat, fruit flavored)	1 cup	345
Chocolate fudge	3½ ounces	100

From: Calcium for postmenopausal osteoporosis. *Med Lett* 24:105, 1982.

  e) Bone x-ray not useful for screening
  f) Steroid suppression test (30–40 mg prednisone a day for 10–14 days); hypercalcemia will reverse in 50% of patients with malignancy, in many other patients with diseases other than hyperparathyroidism
  g) Urinary calcium ultimately should be measured to exclude *benign familial hypercalcemia* (parathyroid hyperplasia causing mild hypercalcemia without hypercalciuria)
 4. Treatment
  a) Truly asymptomatic patients can be followed
  b) Surgery for symptomatic patients who can tolerate the operation
  c) Oral phosphate salts (e.g., K-Phos or Neutra-Phos) for symptomatic patients who cannot be operated on

OSTEOPOROSIS
A. Generalized decrease in bone mass
B. Major etiologies
 1. Estrogen deficiency in women
 2. Aging
C. Risk factors
 1. Sedentary life-style
 2. Chronic cigarette smoking
 3. Nulliparity
 4. Diabetes mellitus
 5. Caucasian race
 6. Chronic glucocorticoid therapy
D. Prevention
 1. Bone density measurements may be useful in patients at risk who are deciding whether or not to initiate therapy
 2. Estrogen begun at or within 5 years of menopause (see Chapter 61)
 3. Calcium (Tables 58.5 and 58.6), after age 40: 1200 mg/day for premenopausal women and estrogen-treated women and 1500 mg/day for women not treated with estrogen and for men
 4. Modest weight-bearing exercise
E. Treatment
 1. Estrogen (e.g., 0.625 mg/day of Premarin)

Table 58.6.   Commercially Available Calcium Supplements

Drug	Tablet Size (mg)	Equivalent of 1 g of Calcium/Day (tablets)
Calcium carbonate (40% calcium)		
Generic (Lilly)	600	4
(Rugby)	600	4
Alka-2 (Miles)	500	5
Amitone (Norcliff Thayer)	350	7
Equilet (Mission)	500	5
Diacarbosil (Norcliff Thayer)	500	5
Mallamint (Mallard)	420	6
OsCal-500 (Marion)	1250	2
TUMS (Norcliff Thayer)	500	5
Calcium gluconate (9% calcium), generic	600	18.5
	1000	11
	930	12
Calcium lactate (13% calcium), generic	600	12
Dibasic calcium phosphate (31% calcium), generic	500	7
Chelated calcium (20% calcium)		
Generic (Arco)	750	7
(Nature's Bounty)	750	7

Adapted from: Calcium for postmenopausal osteoporosis. *Med Lett* 24:105, 1982.

Table 58.7.   Causes of Polyuria[a]

Disorder	Mechanism
Glucosuria (diabetes mellitus)	Osmotic diuresis
Excessive intake of water	Psychogenic
Various drugs	Often due to anticholinergic effects producing dryness of mouth; possible central effects
Decreased ADH effect	Deficiency of ADH secretion (idiopathic diabetes insipidus or due to pituitary-hypothalamic disease); nephrogenic diabetes insipidus
Renal disease plus renal effects of potassium depletion, hypercalcemia, and lithium therapy	In all of these disorders, impairment of renal concentrating ability is present
Hyperthyroidism	Impairment of urinary concentrating ability; decreased salivary flow

ADH, antidiuretic hormone.
[a] Disorders associated with increased urine volume.

    2. Calcitonin, especially for relief of pain, but expensive, requires injection
    3. Biphosphonates (e.g., etidronate)
    4. Calcium
    5. Vitamin D

DISORDERS OF WATER METABOLISM

A. Polyuria
    1. Causes: Table 58.7
    2. History
       a) History of polydipsia and polyuria
       b) Psychiatric history
       c) Drug history

Table 58.8.   Causes of Hypoglycemia in Ambulatory Adults

POSTPRANDIAL STATE
   Reactive (idiopathic)
   Early diabetes mellitus
   Ethanol ingestion
   Postgastrectomy state
FASTING STATE
   Insulin excess
     1. Insulin injection
     2. Sulfonylurea ingestion[a]
     3. Miscellaneous drugs and poisons[b]
     4. Insulinoma
     5. Autoimmune hypoglycemia (very rare)
   Alcohol ingestion
   Hormonal deficiencies
     1. Glucocorticoid
     2. Growth hormone
   Fasting in normal young women (24–48 hr)
   Malnutrition
   Liver disease
   Extrapancreatic tumors
   Renal failure (chronic end stage)
   Congestive heart failure

[a] Many drugs, including such diverse compounds as anti-inflammatory agents, antibiotics, and lipid-lowering agents, potentiate the effects of sulfonylureas and may cause hypoglycemia.
[b] Haloperidol, propoxyphene, salicylates, etc.

   3. Laboratory evaluation
     a) Morning serum glucose, sodium, potassium, urea nitrogen, creatinine measurements
     b) Urine collection for 24 or 48 hours: volume, osmolality, total glucose, creatinine measurements
     c) Distinction between psychogenic polydipsia and diabetes insipidus made by water deprivation followed by injection of antidiuretic hormone (ADH)
   4. Treatment
     a) Psychogenic polydipsia requires psychiatric therapy
     b) Diabetes insipidus requires ADH [e.g., intranasal desmopressin (DDAVP)]
B. Inappropriate secretion of ADH
   1. Causes
     a) Tumors, especially small cell lung cancer
     b) Myxedema
     c) Intracranial disease
     d) Drugs (e.g., morphine, barbiturates, chlorpropamide)
   2. Hyponatremia is hallmark with inappropriately high urine sodium concentration or osmolality
   3. Treatment
     a) Stop offending drug
     b) Water restriction (hospitalize if necessary)
     c) Lithium, demeclocycline sometimes useful

HYPOGLYCEMIA
A. Causes: Table 58.8
B. Diagnosis

1. History
   a) Adrenergic symptoms
      1) Rapid onset, lasting 15–30 minutes
      2) Sweating, tremor, hunger, anxiety
      3) Mainly postprandial (2–5 hours after eating)
   b) Neuroglycopenic symptoms
      1) Headache, dullness, fatigue
      2) If severe hypoglycemia, confusion, visual disturbances, possibly coma and seizures
      3) Mainly after fasting
2. Laboratory evaluation
   a) Postprandial
      1) Glucose tolerance test (GTT) (30-minute sampling up to 5 hours), correlating symptoms with blood sugar values
      2) Early diabetes mellitus: diagnostic values in 2 hours in GTT, hypoglycemia in 3–4 hours
      3) Postgastrectomy: high value in 1 hour in GTT, lowest value in 2–3 hours
      4) Idiopathic: lowest values in about 3 hours in GTT
   b) Fasting
      1) Serum glucose measurement after patient has fasted overnight
      2) Prolonged fasting (24, 48, or 72 hours) before glucose measurement is sometimes necessary
      3) In patients with suspected insulinoma, measurement of plasma insulin activity is important
      4) Specialized tests require an endocrinologist
      5) If self-administration of insulin suspected, insulin C-peptide measurement (low) will establish insulin is exogenous
C. Management
   1. Early diabetes mellitus
      a) Weight reduction in obese patients
      b) Diet containing complex carbohydrates rather than simple sugars
      c) Up to five small meals
      d) Avoidance of alcohol
   2. Postgastrectomy
      a) Frequent small meals
      b) Restriction of simple sugars
      c) Anticholinergic drug (i.e., Pro-Banthine) may be of help
   3. Idiopathic: course and management unclear
   4. Insulinoma: surgery

59/ CLINICAL IMPLICATIONS OF ABNORMAL LIPOPROTEIN METABOLISM

LIPOPROTEIN NOMENCLATURE: TABLE 59.1

PLASMA LIPOPROTEINS IN ATHEROSCLEROSIS

A. Risk factors
   1. Levels of low-density lipoprotein (LDL) correlate positively with risk
   2. Levels of high-density lipoprotein (HDL) correlate negatively with risk
   3. Levels of triglyceride and of its major transporter, very low density lipoprotein (VLDL), correlate positively with risk

HYPERLIPOPROTEINEMIA

A. Classification
   1. Primary (genetic) or secondary (Table 59.2)
   2. Pathophysiological and genotypic (Table 59.3)
B. Clinical manifestations: Table 59.3
C. Diagnosis
   1. Screening: measure total cholesterol (TC) and HDL every 5 years in adults 20 and older
      a) HDL: <35 mg/dl is low
      b) TC: <200 mg/dl is desirable, 200–239 is borderline, and ≥240 is high
      c) Combination of borderline TC and low HDL or two or more risk factors for coronary artery disease (CAD) (Table 59.4) equates to high level
   2. Evaluation of patient with hypercholesterolemia: measure triglyceride, LDL, and evaluate CAD risk
      a) LDL: <130 mg/dl is low, 130–159 is intermediate, and ≥160 is high
      b) If patient has CAD or two or more risk factors for CAD, 130–159 mg/dl equates to high level
      c) Low HDL an independent risk
      d) Triglycerides: <200 mg/dl is normal, 200–400 is borderline high, 401–1000 is high, and >1000 is very high
D. Treatment
   1. If a cause of secondary hyperlipoproteinemia is present, treat it
   2. If TC borderline–high, HDL > 35 mg/dl, and fewer than two CAD risk factors, patient should be educated about diet (see below), exercise, life-style (e.g., smoking) and re-evaluated in 1–2 years
   3. If TC normal and HDL low, patient should be educated about diet etc. (see above) and re-evaluated in 5 years
   4. If TC borderline–high and HDL low or there are two or more CAD risk factors or if TC high, prescribe diet first, then consider drugs if necessary

Table 59.1. Classification of Plasma Lipoproteins by Physical and Chemical Characteristics

Lipoprotein Fraction (Ultracentrifugation)	Density (g/ml)	Migration (Electrophoresis)	Composition as Percentage of Total Mass			
			Cholesterol	Triglyceride	Apoprotein	Phospholipid
Chylomicron	0.95	Origin	2–7	80–90	2 (A, B-48, C, E)	3
Very low density (VLDL)	<1.006	Pre-β	10–22	50–70	6 (B-100, C, E)	14
β-Very low density (β-VLDL or VLDL₂)	<1.006	β	30–40	45	12 (B-100, B-48, C, E)	15
Intermediate density or remnant (IDL)	1.006–1.019	Slow pre-β	30–40	40	18 (B, E)	22
Low density (LDL)	1.019–1.063	β	45–50	5–10	21 (B-100)	22
High density (HDL)	1.063–1.21	α	15–25	3–5	50 (A, C, E)	28

Table 59.2.   Causes of Secondary Lipoprotein Disorders

Exogenous	Alcohol, oral contraceptives, estrogens, androgens, corticosteroids, diuretics (thiazides, chlorthalidone), β-adrenergic blocking agents, obesity, nutrition (diet high in cholesterol/saturated fat)
Endocrine-metabolic	Diabetes mellitus, hypothyroidism, Cushing's disease, Addison's disease, acromegaly, hypopituitarism, growth hormone deficiency
Hepatic	Obstructive or parenchymal disease, hepatoma
Renal	Nephrotic syndrome, chronic renal failure, hemodialysis
Acute stress situations	Acute myocardial infarction, sepsis, burns
Pregnancy	
Pancreatitis	
Dysgammaglobulinemias	Multiple myeloma, macroglobulinemia
Systemic lupus erythematosus	
Gout	
Viral infections, including AIDS	
Other	Glycogen storage disease, lipodystrophies, progeria, acute intermittent porphyria, anorexia nervosa, Klinefelter's syndrome

5. Diet (Table 59.5)
   a) Goals: LDL of <160 mg/dl if no CAD or fewer than two CAD risk factors; LDL of <130 mg/dl if no CAD but two or more CAD risk factors; LDL of <100 mg/dl if CAD
   b) Monitoring effects: measure LDL or TC after 4–6 weeks of Step-one diet (Table 59.5), and again at 3 months; if goals not met, monitor again at 6 months or initiate Step-two diet
   c) Elderly patients should not receive Step-two diet (to avoid malnutrition)
   d) Triglyceride reduction: diet and avoidance of alcohol often sufficient
   e) Chylomicron reduction: reduction of dietary fat to 5–20% of total calories; medium-chain triglycerides (15 ml 3–4 times/day) may be of help
6. Exercise
   a) Thirty minutes or more of continual effort at 75–85% of maximal heart rate at least 3 times/week
   b) HDL rises in mostly everyone; LDL falls up to 10% in people with elevated TC and LDL
   c) Changes appear to be more striking in men
7. Smoking cessation: reduces CAD risk; HDL rises
8. Drugs (Table 59.6)
   a) Indications: see diet, above
   b) Goals: same as with diet (see above)

Table 59.3.   Classification of Lipoprotein Disorders by Phenotypes and Genotypes and Corresponding Clinical Manifestations

Phenotype	Lipoprotein in Excess	Plasma Lipid Levels Cholesterol	Plasma Lipid Levels Triglyceride	Plasma Appearance[a]	Genotype	Age of Onset (Primary Form)	Xanthomas[b]	Other Clinical Manifestations
I	Chylomicrons	Normal or ↑	↑↑↑ lipemia	Clear plasma, creamy supernatant	Familial lipoprotein lipase deficiency, apo C-II deficiency	Infancy or childhood	Eruptive, tuberoeruptive	Recurrent abdominal pain, other gastrointestinal symptoms, lipemia retinalis, hepatosplenomegaly
IIA	LDL	↑↑↑	Normal	Clear	FHC Familial combined hyperlipidemia Polygenic and sporadic hypercholesterolemia	Childhood for homozygous FHC, late childhood to middle age for heterozygous FHC, adulthood for others	Tendinous, xanthelasma, tuberous; planar (homozygous)	Premature CAD, arcus cornealis, aortic stenosis (homozygous FHC), arthritic symptoms
IIB	LDL + VLDL	↑↑	↑	Clear	Familial combined hyperlipidemia FHC			
III	β-VLDL, IDL	↑↑	↑↑	Slightly turbid	Familial dysbetalipoproteinemia	Adulthood (occasionally late adolescence)	Planar (especially palmar), tuberous	Premature CAD and peripheral vascular disease, male > female, obesity, abnormal glucose tolerance, hyperuricemia, aggravated by hypothyroidism, good response to therapy
IV	VLDL	Normal or ↑[c]	↑↑	Turbid	Familial hypertriglyceridemia Familial combined hyperlipidemia Sporadic	Early to late adulthood	Usually none; rarely eruptive, or tuberoeruptive	CAD and peripheral vascular disease, obesity, abnormal glucose tolerance, hyperuricemia, arthritic

	Chylomicrons + VLDL		Turbid plasma, creamy supernatant	Homozygous familial hypertriglyceridemia	Childhood to middle age, usually adulthood	Eruptive, tuberoeruptive	symptoms, gallbladder disease
V	Normal or ↑	↑↑↑	Turbid plasma, creamy supernatant	Homozygous familial hypertriglyceridemia	Childhood to middle age, usually adulthood	Eruptive, tuberoeruptive	Recurrent abdominal pain, other gastrointestinal symptoms, lipemia retinalis, hepatosplenomegaly, peripheral paresthesias, abnormal glucose tolerance, hyperuricemia

hypertriglyceridemia

CAD, coronary artery disease; FHC, familial hypercholesterolemia.
[a] Plasma obtained after 12 hours of fasting, left undisturbed in refrigerator overnight.
[b] Seen only in a minority of patients, but the frequency increases as plasma lipid levels rise.
[c] Cholesterol normal if triglycerides < 400 mg/dl.

Table 59.4. CAD Risk Factors as Defined by the 1993 NCEP Adult Treatment Guidelines

POSITIVE RISK FACTORS
Age
    Male ≥ 45 yr
    Female ≥ 55 yr or premature menopause without estrogen replacement therapy
    Family history of premature CHD (definite myocardial infarction or sudden death before 55 yr of age in father or other male first-degree relative, or before 65 yr of age in mother or other female first-degree relative)
    Current cigarette smoking
    Hypertension (blood pressure ≥ 140/90 mm Hg or taking antihypertensive medication)
    Low HDL cholesterol [<35 mg/dl (0.9 mmol/liter)]
    Diabetes mellitus
NEGATIVE RISK FACTOR
    High HDL cholesterol [≥35 mg/dl (1.6 mmol/liter)]

From: Summary of the Second Report of the National Cholesterol Education Program (NCEP) Expert Panel on Detection, Evaluation, and Treatment of High Blood Cholesterol in Adults (Adult Treatment Panel II). *JAMA* 269: 3015–3023, 1993.
CHD, congenital heart disease.

Table 59.5. Dietary Therapy of High Blood Cholesterol

Nutrient	Recommended Intake	
	Step-One Diet	Step-Two Diet
Total fat	<30% of total calories	
Saturated fatty acids	<10% of total calories	<7% of total calories
Polyunsaturated fatty acids	Up to 10% of total calories	
Monounsaturated fatty acids	10–15% of total calories	
Carbohydrates	50–60% of total calories	
Protein	10–20% of total calories	
Cholesterol	<300 mg/day	<200 mg/day
Total calories	To achieve and maintain desirable weight	

From The Expert Panel: Report of the National Cholesterol Education Program Expert Panel on Detection, Evaluation and Treatment of High Blood Cholesterol in Adults. *Arch Intern Med* 148:36–69, 1988.

Table 59.6. Commonly Used Lipid-Lowering Drugs

BILE ACID SEQUESTERING RESINS (cholestyramine, colestipol)

Mechanism: Anion exchange resins bind bile acids, resulting in increased hepatic synthesis of cholesterol and bile acids, increased apo B catabolism, increased fecal excretion of cholesterol, increased LDL receptor activity, and usually a net reduction of plasma cholesterol levels.

Efficacy: Decreases total and LDL cholesterol up to 25–40% (onset 4–7 days, maximal effect within 1–3 weeks). In the LRC trial, mean reductions in experimental group of total and LDL cholesterol were 13.4 and 20.3%. Apo B level falls, while HDL level rises slightly. VLDL is unchanged or increased.

Pharmacokinetics: Not absorbed, but may bind other drugs (e.g., thiazides, digitalis preparations, anticoagulants, phenobarbital, thyroxine, phenylbutazone, propranolol, iron). *Side effects:* (a) Common — unpleasant sandy/gritty preparations, GI (constipation in 10–20%, nausea, heartburn, abdominal discomfort, flatulence, etc., often resolve with continued therapy and/or treatment of constipation), lowered serum folate levels; (b) uncommon — GI (steatorrhea), hyperchloremic acidosis (small patients on high doses), fat-soluble vitamin deficiency; increased alkaline phosphatase and aminotransferase (usually transient).

Administration: (a) Cholestyramine — 12–32 g/day given 2–4 times/day before or during meals, supplied as Questran in 9-g packets, each containing 4 g of active drug; (b) colestipol — 15–30 g/day, given 2–4 times/day before or during meals, supplied as Colestid in 5-g packets or 500-g bottles.

Preparations should be taken in water or juice to prevent esophageal irritation or blockage. Other medicines should be taken 1 hour before or 4 hours after dosage. Monitor serum folate levels and consider supplemental multivitamins with folic acid.

Clinical use: Drugs of first choice in the treatment of hypercholesterolemia because of their relative safety and efficacy. Well tolerated in combination with niacin or lovastatin. Contraindications include marked hypertriglyceridemia and severe constipation.

NICOTINIC ACID (niacin, and preparations such as Nicobid (time-released), 125, 250, or 500 mg, Slo-Niacin, 250, 250, 500 and 750 mg, or Nicolar, 500 mg)

Mechanism: Diverse effects on lipid metabolism; decreases LDL and apo B synthesis by decreasing hepatic synthesis of VLDL, increases synthesis of HDL, inhibits lipolysis in adipose tissue, increases lipase activity.

Efficacy: Decreases VLDL triglycerides within 1–4 days (mean 26% in Coronary Drug Project), range up to 80% depending on pretreatment levels); decreases LDL cholesterol, onset 5–7 days, maximal effect 3–5 weeks (mean decrease of 10% in total cholesterol in Coronary Drug Project, range up to 30%). Favorable impact on total and LDL cholesterol, triglyceride, VLDL, HDL (increases up to 35%), apo A-1 and apo B.

Pharmacokinetics: Absorbed by mouth; peak concentrations in 20–70 minutes; in the high doses used it is partially metabolized in liver and partially excreted unchanged in urine; plasma half-life is about 45 minutes.

Side effects: (a) Common — cutaneous flushing and pruritus, which diminish after several weeks of therapy; GI (nausea, diarrhea, abdominal pain, abnormal liver function); (b) less common — dermatological disorders (e.g., increased pigmentation); activation of peptic ulcer; dysrhythmia; gout; urinary frequency and dysuria; glucose intolerance, etc.

Administration: 100-, 250-, 300-, 400-, and 500-mg tablets. Gradual increase over 1–3 weeks from 100 to 200 mg/day to 2–9 g/day; given in 3 daily dosages; given with meals to diminish side effects. Flushing may be ameliorated by pretreatment with aspirin, one-half to one 325-mg tablet 30 minutes before each dose. Generic form is inexpensive compared

Table 59.6.   Continued

with time-release form (Nico-Bid); the latter may reduce the frequency of flushing but increase the frequency of GI side effects. Nicotinic acid should be administered with caution in the presence of coronary artery disease.

Clinical use: First-line (despite side effects) effective drug in the treatment of elevated LDL cholesterol or VLDL triglyceride. Well tolerated in combination with bile acid-binding resins and statins. Contraindications include peptic ulcer disease, dysrhythmia, liver disease, diabetes mellitus, hyperuricemia, and gout.

HMG-CoA REDUCTASE INHIBITORS (lovastatin, pravastatin, simvastatin)

Mechanism: Competitively inhibits HMG-CoA reductase, the rate-limiting enzyme in the synthesis of cholesterol, decreases production of LDL, increases LDL receptor activity in the liver and the rate of removal of LDL from the plasma.

Efficacy: Decreases total cholesterol (20–37%), LDL cholesterol (20–37%), LDL apo B (20–48%), VLDL cholesterol (27–40%), and triglycerides (7–27%). Provides variable and modest increases in HDL cholesterol (4–12%) and apo A-I and A-II.

Pharmacokinetics: Incompletely absorbed (average 30%); extensive first-pass extraction by the liver with <5% reaching systemic circulation: inactive lovastatin converted to several active metabolites; peak plasma concentrations of active metabolites within 2–6 hours; steady-state concentrations of total inhibitors achieved within 2–3 days; 83% of radiolabeled dose eliminated in feces (represents unabsorbed drug and active and inactive metabolites excreted in bile) and 10% in urine (as inactive metabolites).

Side effects: (a) Generally well tolerated, discontinuation required in 1–2% of patients due to adverse effects; reasonable safety now established; (b) occasional — headache (9% of patients), GI (flatulence, abdominal pains or cramps, diarrhea, constipation, nausea, dyspepsia — usually mild and transient (4–6%)); elevation in liver aminotransferases and, uncommonly, alkaline phosphatase usually within 3–16 months (≥3 times increase in 2%), reverses over several weeks after discontinuation of drug; mild increase in creatinine kinase (11%); myalgias (3%); rash and pruritus (5%); (c) uncommon — GI (heartburn, dysgeusia), dizziness, insomnia, malaise, fatigue, myopathy (0.5%, but up to 30% in patients taking immunosuppressant drugs or gemfibrozil — also reported in patients taking nicotinic acid or erythromycin), renal failure due to rhabdomyolysis; (d) unknown — (?) cataracts.

Administration: Lovastatin (Mevacor, 20 mg, 40 mg). 20–80 mg/day once daily with evening meal or twice daily with meals (administration with food results in 50% higher plasma concentrations of total inhibitors, effectiveness greater when given as evening dose, perhaps because cholesterol synthesis occurs mainly at night); provastatin (Pravachol, 10 and 20 mg), 10–40 mg once a day at bedtime; simvastatin (Zocor, 5, 10, 20, and 40 mg), 5–40 mg once a day in the evening. Obtain baseline liver function tests, then every 4–6 weeks for first 12–15 months, then every 3–4 months thereafter. Discontinue if aminotransferase rises ≥3 times normal. Because of the development of cataracts in animals on very high doses, baseline and yearly slitlamp examinations are currently recommended.

Clinical use: First-line drugs, very effective and well-tolerated drugs for the treatment of hypercholesterolemia. When response to a single drug is inadequate, statins are effective in combination with a bile acid-sequestering agent or nicotinic acid. Each drug contributes separately to reductions in lipoprotein concentrations.

FIBRIC ACID DERIVATIVES (gemfibrozil)

Mechanism: Increases clearance of VLDL by enhancing lipolysis, may increase lipoprotein lipase activity, reduces hepatic cholesterol synthesis, and increases cholesterol excretion in the bile.

Efficacy: Gemfibrozil lowers triglycerides to a greater extent, raises HDL more consistently, and is less likely to raise LDL than clofibrate. In familial combined hyperlipoproteinemia, however, use of any fibric acid analog is likely to raise LDL cholesterol.

Pharmacokinetics: Gemfibrozil — completely absorbed; peak concentration within 2 hours; half-life, 1.5 hours; undergoes enterohepatic circulation, metabolized in liver, and excreted in urine. May enhance action of oral anticoagulants, phenytoin, and hypoglycemic agents, and of furosemide by displacing them from albumin-binding sites.

Side effects: (a) Usually — well tolerated; (b) occasional — (6-fold) increase in the incidence of cholelithiasis (may be less with gemfibrozil and newer analogs); other GI (nausea, abdominal pain, diarrhea, weight gain); reduced libido, impotence; unusual flu-like syndrome; (c) uncommon — rash, alopecia, breast tenderness, reversible abnormality in liver function, hepatomegaly, myositis, increased plasma glucose, etc.; (d) unknown — (?) thromboembolism, (?) intermittent claudication, (?) dysrhythmia, (?) neoplasia.

Administration: Gemfibrozil (Lopid, 300 and 600 mg), 600 mg twice daily ½ hour before meals). Some recommended periodic monitoring of asparate aminotransferase (formerly SGO-T), alanine aminotransferase (formerly SGP-T), and creatinine kinase (formerly CPK).

Clinical use: Gemfibrozil is the drug of choice in the treatment of elevated VLDL triglyceride; it can also be used to lower total and LDL cholesterol and to raise HDL cholesterol, of particular utility in type III. Use with caution in the presence of hepatic or renal insufficiency.

GI, gastrointestinal; *HMG-COA reductase,* human menopausal gonadotropin-coenzyme A reductase; *LRC,* Lipid Research Clinics.

DEFINITION

A. Excess of total body fat
B. Methods for quantifying obesity
   1. Hydrodensitometry: cumbersome
   2. Dual energy x-ray absorptiometry (DEXA): an emerging "gold standard"
   3. Determination of weight relative to tabulated standards (e.g., Metropolitan's height and weight table — see Table 60.1); body mass index (BMI) (weight/height^2) has best correlation with total body fat
   4. Skin fold thickness: less reliable than weight-height correlation
   5. Waist:hip ratio (WHR): correlates with central adiposity (see below)
C. Morbid obesity: 50–100% or 100 lbs above "ideal" weight (see Table 60.1) or a BMI > 39

NATURAL HISTORY

A. Age of onset: childhood onset tends to be more severe and persistent than adult onset
B. Possible medical consequences: Table 60.2

EVALUATION

A. Age of onset
B. Usual diet and level of activity
C. Physical examination
   1. WHR of >0.85 indicates upper body obesity, a greater risk than lower body obesity with WHR of <0.75
   2. Measurement of BMI
D. Associated illnesses
   1. Fasting blood sugar
   2. Free thyroxine index (Chapter 57)
   3. Total lipid analysis (Chapter 59)
   4. Evaluate possibility of hypercortisolism (if associated plethora, hypertension, glucose intolerance) — see Chapter 58
   5. Evaluate possibility of sleep apnea (Chapter 68)

MANAGEMENT

A. Mild to moderate obesity
   1. Moderate diet (Table 60.3), regular exercise
   2. No justification for anorexigenic drugs
   3. Lay organizations (e.g., Weight Watchers) are as effective as physicians
B. Morbid obesity
   1. Diet
      a) Total fasting: requires hospitalization; useful only if rapid weight loss (e.g., presurgical) is desired
      b) Supplemented fasting (1–1.5 g of protein per kg per day of desirable weight, i.e., 300–500 calories, plus adequate water, potassium salts, vitamins, and minerals): can be an ambulatory regimen but is associated with a number of complications, including sudden death; results in rapid weight loss, hard to sustain

Table 60.1. Comparison of the Weight for Height Tables From Actuarial Data (*Build Study*, 1979): Non-Age-Corrected Metropolitan Life Insurance Company and Age-Specific Gerontology Research Center Recommendations

Height		Metropolitan 1983 Weights (lbs)[a]		Gerontology Research Center[a]				
		Men	Women	Age-Specific Weight Range for Men and Women (lbs)				
Feet	Inches	25-59 yr		25 Yr	35 Yr	45 Yr	55 Yr	65 Yr
4	10		100–131	84–111	92–119	99–127	107–135	115–142
4	11		101–134	87–115	95–123	103–131	111–139	119–147
5	0		103–137	90–119	98–127	106–135	114–143	123–152
5	1	123–145	105–140	93–123	101–131	110–140	118–148	127–157
5	2	125–148	108–144	96–127	105–136	113–144	122–153	131–163
5	3	127–151	111–148	99–131	108–140	117–149	126–158	135–168
5	4	129–155	114–152	102–135	112–145	121–154	130–163	140–173
5	5	131–159	117–156	106–140	115–149	125–159	134–168	144–179
5	6	133–163	120–160	109–144	119–154	129–164	138–174	148–184
5	7	135–167	123–164	112–148	122–159	133–169	143–179	153–190
5	8	137–171	126–167	116–153	126–163	137–174	147–184	158–196
5	9	139–175	129–170	119–157	130–168	141–179	151–190	162–201
5	10	141–179	132–173	122–162	134–173	145–184	156–195	167–207
5	11	144–183	135–176	126–167	137–178	149–190	160–201	172–213
6	0	147–187		129–171	141–183	153–195	165–207	177–219
6	1	150–192		133–176	145–188	157–200	169–213	182–225
6	2	153–197		137–181	149–194	162–206	174–219	187–232
6	3	157–202		141–186	153–199	166–212	179–225	192–238
6	4			144–191	157–205	171–218	184–231	197–244

From Andres R: Mortality and obesity. The rationale for age-specific height-weight tables. In: Andres R, Hazzard WR, Bierman E (eds): *Principles of Geriatric Medicine*. New York, McGraw-Hill, 1985.
[a] Values in this table are for height without shoes and for weight without clothes.

Table 60.2. Possible Medical Consequences of Obesity

ENDOCRINE-METABOLIC
  Hyperglycemia, hyperinsulinemia, insulin resistance
  Hypertriglyceridemia, hypercholesterolemia (↑ VLDL, ↑ LDL, ↓ HDL)
  ↑ Cortisol production but normal plasma cortisol, diurnal rhythm, urine free cortisol, and
    overnight dexamethasone suppression
  Early menarche, menstrual abnormalities, hirsutism
  ↓ Sympathoadrenal activity
  ↓ HBG and ↑ total and/or free androgens
  ↓ Growth hormone, basally and after provocative stimuli
  Hyperuricemia, gout
CARDIOVASCULAR
  Hypertension
  Coronary artery disease
  Congestive heart failure
  Varicose veins
  Cerebrovascular disease
PULMONARY
  Hypoventilation (e.g., pickwickian) syndromes
  Sleep apnea syndrome
  Chronic respiratory infections
GALLBLADDER
  Cholelithiasis (cholesterol gallstones)
MUSCULOSKELETAL
  Osteoarthritis
  Chronic orthopedic problems
  ↓ Ambulation
RENAL
  Nephrotic syndrome (normal or nonspecific biopsy)
ONCOLOGICAL
  Endometrial, breast carcinoma (postmenopausal women), prostate, colon
DERMATOLOGICAL
  Acanthosis nigracans
  Chronic skin infections
PSYCHOSOCIAL
  Depression, loss of self-esteem
  ↓ Employability
PREGNANCY
  Worsen underlying hypertension, diabetes mellitus
  ↑ Maternal mortality
SURGERY (especially under general anesthesia)
  Increased perioperative morbidity and mortality

HBG, hormone-binding globulin; *VHDL,* high-density lipoprotein; *LDL,* low-density lipoprotein; *VLDL,* very low density lipoprotein.

    c) Liquid protein diets: to be avoided; risk of sudden death
    d) Safest diets are balanced and contain >800 calories daily
    e) Only 10–20% of patients who lose weight maintain that loss
2. Exercise: aerobic, at least 30 minutes 3 times/week, and resistive are useful
3. Behavior modification: individual and group therapy equally effective
4. Drugs (Table 60.4)
    a) No reliably effective drug that does not have side effects
    b) Can be used appropriately in selected patients in medically supervised, comprehensive programs

Table 60.3. Recommended Dietary Guidelines

1. Reduce total fat intake to ≤30% of calories, saturated fatty acid intake to <10% of calories, and cholesterol intake to <300 mg daily. The intake of fat and cholesterol can be reduced by substituting fish, poultry without skin, lean meats, and low-fat or nonfat dairy products for fatty meats and whole-milk dairy products; by choosing more vegetables, fruits, cereals, and legumes; and by limiting oils, fats, egg yolks, and fried and other fatty foods.
2. Every day eat five or more servings of a combination of vegetables and fruits, especially green and yellow vegetables and citrus fruits. Also, increase intake of starches and other complex carbohydrates by eating six or more daily servings of a combination of breads, cereals, and legumes. An average serving is equal to a half cup for most fresh or cooked vegetables, fruits, dry or cooked cereals or legumes, one medium piece of fresh fruit, one slice of bread, or one roll or muffin.
3. Maintain protein intake at moderate levels (<1.6 g/kg body weight for adults).
4. Balance food intake and physical activity to maintain appropriate body weight.
5. The committee does not recommend alcohol consumption. For those who drink alcoholic beverages, the committee recommends limiting consumption to the equivalent of <1 ounce of pure alcohol in a single day. This is the equivalent of two cans of beer, two small glasses of wine, or two average cocktails. Pregnant women should avoid alcoholic beverages.
6. Limit total daily intake of salt to ≤6 g. Limit the use of salt in cooking and avoid adding it to food at the table. Salty, highly processed salty, salt-preserved, and salt-pickled foods should be consumed sparingly.
7. Maintain adequate calcium balance. The potential benefits of calcium intakes above the RDAs to prevent osteoporosis or hypertension are not well documented and do not justify the use of calcium supplments.
8. Avoid taking dietary supplements in excess of the RDA in any one day.
9. Maintain an optimal intake of fluoride, particularly during the years of primary and secondary tooth formation and growth.

Adapted from Committee on Diet and Health, Food and Nutrition Board. Commission on Life Sciences. National Research Council: *Diet and Health. Implications for Reducing Chronic Disease Risk.* Washington, DC, National Academy Press, 1989.
RDA, recommended daily allowance.

5. Surgery
   a) Jejunoileostomy: no longer advised because of unacceptable side effects
   b) Gastric bypass (and gastroplasty)
      1) For well-informed, motivated, severely obese patients in whom the operative risks are acceptable
      2) Patients should be selected after evaluation by a multidisciplinary team

Table 60.4. Appetite-Suppressing Drugs

Generic and Proprietary Names	Common Trade Names	Dosage (mg)	Administration (mg)	Peak Blood Concentration (Hours After Oral Dose)	Half-Life in Blood (hr)	Percentage Excreted Unchanged in Acidic Urine
Schedule IV						
Diethylpropion	Tenuate, Propion	25, 75	25 before meals (t.i.d.) 75 in morning	1–2	8–13	24
Fenfluramine	Pondimin	20	20–40 before meals	1	20	20
Mazindol	Sanorex, Mazanor	1, 2	1 before meals	2	13	22
Phentermine	Ionamin resin	15, 30	2 in morning 15 (t.i.d.) 30 in morning	1	Free 7–8 20–24	75
Schedule III[a]						
Phendimetrazine	Plegine, Obalan	35	35 before meals		4	??
Benzphetamine	Didrex	25, 50	25–50 before meals	1–2	2	??
Schedule II[a]						
Dextroamphetamine	Dexedrine	5, 10, 15	5–10 before meals (t.i.d.)	1–2	5	55
Methamphetamine	Desoxyn	5, 10, 15	2.5 or 5 before meals (t.i.d.) 10 or 15 in morning	1–2	13	45
Phenmetrazine	Preludin	25, 50, 75	25 (b.i.d. or t.i.d.)			19

[a] The Federal Controlled Substance Act of 1970 places the prescription anorexiants into three of five schedule categories. Appetite suppressants in schedule IV have little or no risk of abuse. The schedules of the Controlled Substance Act are numbered in order of decreasing potential for abuse; drugs in schedule II (amphetamine, methamphetamine, and phenmetrazine) are the most restricted. (From Weintraub M, Bray, GA: Drug treatment of obesity. *Med Clin North Am* 73:237, 1989.)

61/ COMMON PROBLEMS IN REPRODUCTIVE ENDOCRINOLOGY

SEXUAL AND REPRODUCTIVE DYSFUNCTION IN MEN

A. Hypogonadism
   1. Classification (Table 61.1)
      a) Central
         1) Kallmann's syndrome: characterized by hyposmia or anosmia
         2) Hypothalamic or pituitary disease (e.g., neoplastic, granulomatous, or infectious disease)
      b) Gonadal
         1) Genetic (e.g., Klinefelter's syndrome)
         2) Trauma, infection (e.g., mumps)
         3) Autoimmune (sometimes part of multiendocrine failure)
      c) Peripheral, always genetic: androgen insensitivity
   2. Evaluation
      a) History
         1) Questions about pubertal progression; loss of libido, erections, ejaculations; slowing of beard growth and thinning of body and pubic hair; breast swelling or tenderness
         2) Questions about headache, double vision, reduced peripheral vision
         3) Elicitation of symptoms suggestive of hypothyroidism, adrenal failure, acromegaly, etc.
         4) Questions about urological problems, episodes of orchitis
         5) Family history may be revealing
      b) Physical examination
         1) Body habitus and facies: apparent maturity, apparent gender

Table 61.1. Classification of Male Hypogonadism

Classification	Criteria
ACCORDING TO LOCATION OF LESION	
Central (hypothalamic or pituitary)	Gonadotropins ↓ or → Testosterone ↓
Gonadal (testis)	Gonadotropins ↑ Testosterone ↓
Peripheral (failure of end-organ response)	Gonadotropins ↑ Testosterone ↑ or →
ACCORDING TO ETIOLOGY	
Genetic	History (especially family history) Buccal smear, karyotype
Acquired	History, physical examination, radiology Evidence of infection, trauma, neoplasia, etc.
ACCORDING TO TIME OF ONSET	
Primary (failure of pubertal development) Secondary (loss of previously developed libido and secondary sex characteristics)	History, physical examination

451

Table 61.2.   Additional Investigations Useful in the Evaluation of Hypogonadism

Type of Failure	Radiological Procedure	Hormone Measurements	Other Tests
Central	Skull film	Prolactin	Visual fields (formal)
	Computed tomography scan with contrast	T_4	Clomiphene test
	Magnetic resonance scan	Thyroid-stimulating hormone	Luteinizing hormone-releasing hormone test
	Cerebral angiogram	Cortisol (morning)	
		Growth hormone (with glucose tolerance test)	
Gonadal	Bone age (if primary)	T_4	Buccal smear
		Cortisol (morning)	Karyotyping
			Gonad biopsy

2) Upper body segment greater than lower body segment and arm span greater than height are "eunuchoid" proportions suggestive of pubertal or prepubertal hypogonadism
3) Male pattern baldness, comedones indicate androgen activity
4) Look for signs of adrenal failure (e.g., hyperpigmentation — see Chapter 58) and of hypothyroidism (Chapter 57)
5) Hypertension may reflect adrenal enzyme defect or Cushing's disease
6) Limitation of extraocular movements, papilledema, or restricted visual fields suggest an intracranial tumor
7) Look for gynecomastia (see below) and galactorrhea (prolactinoma — see Chapter 58)
8) Size and appearance of genitalia and appearance of pubic hair are important

c) Laboratory tests
1) Most informative tests are serum testosterone and gonadotropin [luteinizing hormone (LH) and follicle-stimulating hormone (FSH)] (Table 61.1)
2) Additional tests: Table 61.2
3) Testicular biopsy sometimes useful (e.g., infection or Klinefelter's syndrome)

3. Treatment
a) Suppress or remove any intracranial mass whose size threatens vision or cerebral function
b) Suppress abnormal hormone secretion (e.g., bromocriptine for prolactinomas — see Chapter 58)
c) Replace deficient androgen: injection of testosterone enanthate the only approved method, e.g., 200 mg i.m. every 2–4 weeks

B. Gynecomastia
1. Causes
a) Common in normal adolescence
b) Mild idiopathic forms (<5 cm) increasingly more common with age (60% in the fifties)
c) Benign or malignant adrenal or testicular tumor or pituitary prolactinoma
d) Hypothyroidism or hyperthyroidism

       e) Exogenous estrogens or drugs that have estrogenic activity (e.g., diazepam, cimetidine, spironolactone, digitalis)

       f) Liver failure

  2. Evaluation

    a) History

       1) Duration and age of onset

       2) History of galactorrhea

       3) Symptoms of hypogonadism (see above) or of Cushing's disease (Chapter 58)

       4) Drug and sexual history

    a) Physical examination: same as for hypogonadism

       1) Signs of Cushing's disease or of hypothyroidism should be emphasized

       2) Palpation for adrenal tumor

       3) Bimanual palpation of the testes

       4) Examination of the breast to distinguish breast tissue from fat from tumor and to elicit discharge

    c) Laboratory tests

       1) If cause is unclear, measure serum levels of estradiol, testosterone, LH, FSH, prolactin, human chorionic gonadotropin (hCG β-subunit)

       2) Evaluate thyroid function (Chapter 57)

       3) Suspected breast tumors warrant mammography and/or biopsy

    d) Treatment

       1) Drug-induced gynecomastia responds over months to discontinuation of drug

       2) Primary endocrine disease warrants referral to an endocrinologist

       3) Idiopathic gynecomastia may warrant cosmetic surgery

C. Impotence

  1. Causes

    a) Psychological (Chapter 6)

    b) Vascular (e.g., atherosclerosis)

    c) Neuropathic (e.g., autonomic neuropathy as in diabetes mellitus or disease of the spinal cord)

    d) Toxic (e.g., due to alcohol or sympatholytic antihypertensives)

    e) Debilitative

    f) Endocrine (e.g., hypogonadism, thyroid disease, Cushing's syndrome, acromegaly)

  2. Evaluation

    a) History

       1) Duration of symptoms, percent of attempts ending in erectile failure, whether or not libido has been maintained

       2) Marital situation, number of partners, whether there is impotence with one partner and not another

       3) Preservation or not of morning erections

       4) Medication and alcohol use

       5) Symptoms of thyroid disease (Chapter 57), Cushing's disease (Chapter 58), peripheral neuropathy (Chapter 67), peripheral vascular disease (Chapter 70)

    b) Physical examination: look especially for signs of hypogonadism (see above), thyroid or adrenal disease (Chapters 57 and 58),

peripheral neuropathy (Chapter 67), peripheral vascular disease (Chapter 70)
- c) Laboratory tests
  1) Hormone determination if endocrine dysfunction suspected (see above)
  2) Fasting blood sugar: always
  3) Consider nocturnal penile tumescence study in a sleep laboratory to distinguish psychogenic from organ impotence
  4) Doppler flow studies if peripheral vascular disease suspected (Chapter 70)
- d) Treatment
  1) Psychogenic impotence (Chapter 6)
  2) Organic impotence: according to cause (see above)
  3) Urological procedures — penile prostheses, injection of papaverine with or without phentolamine, occlusive ring plus suction device — all require referral

SEXUAL AND REPRODUCTIVE DYSFUNCTION IN WOMEN
A. Hirsutism and virilization
  1. Definitions
    a) Hirsutism is the male distribution of hair (face, limbs, chest, superior pubic triangle, linea alba, back, possibly male pattern baldness)
    b) Virilization is characterized by increased muscle mass, redistribution of fat from hips and breasts to abdomen, clitoral enlargement, deepening of the voice, male pattern baldness, acne, malodorous perspiration
  2. Causes
    a) Hirsutism without virilization
      1) May be an early sign of Cushing's syndrome or of an adrenal or ovarian tumor
      2) Usually "idiopathic"
      3) Stein-Leventhal syndrome (central obesity, acne, amenorrhea or oligomenorrhea, polycystic ovaries) or ovarian hyperthecosis (overgrowth of interstitial tissue)
      4) Pregnancy, menopause (transitory)
      5) Drugs (phenytoin, glucocorticoids, minoxidil, phenothiazines)
      6) Congenital adrenal hyperplasia
    b) Hirsutism with virilization
      1) Rare
      2) Almost always due to adrenal or ovarian tumor, congenital adrenal hyperplasia, male pseudohermaphroditism, use of exogenous androgen
  3. Evaluation
    a) History
      1) Ethnic and family
      2) Temporal evolution
      3) Menstrual history
    b) Physical examination
      1) Distribution and density of terminal hairs on face, periareolar and midsternal regions, over back and buttocks; particular attention to pubic hair pattern

Table 61.3.   Causes of Abnormal Vaginal Bleeding in the Premenopausal Woman

1. Dysfunctional uterine bleeding (hypothalamic idiopathic anovulation)
2. Perineal causes: bladder pathology, hemorrhoids
3. Vulvar causes: infection, laceration, tumor
4. Vaginal causes: infection, laceration, tumor, foreign body
5. Cervical causes: infection, erosion, polyp, carcinoma
6. Uterine causes: infection, polyp, leiomyomata, carcinoma, intrauterine device
7. Ovarian causes: infection, polycystic ovary (Stein-Levinthal syndrome)
8. Pregnancy: threatened abortion, complete abortion, ectopic pregnancy
9. Oral contraceptives
10. Systemic medical conditoins: e.g., bleeding diathesis (especially thrombocytopenia), thyroid disease

        2) Look for signs of virilization (see above)
        3) Look for signs of Cushing's syndrome (Chapter 58)
    c) Laboratory tests
        1) Depend on severity of hirsutism
        2) Plasma testosterone is measured first
           (a) If normal, no further workup
           (b) If between 85 and 200 ng/dl, a diagnosis of ovarian hyperthecosis or of polycystic ovaries is likely (latter revealed by sonography)
           (c) If >200 ng/dl, ovarian neoplasm is suggested; referral to a gynecologist is warranted
  4. Treatment
    a) Local therapy usually sufficient: bleaching, wax stripping, shaving, plucking, use of depilatories, electrolysis
    b) Medical therapy: slow (6–18 months)
        1) Low-dose corticosteroids [e.g., dexamethasone 0.1–0.3 mg (pediatric solution) at bedtime]: effective in one-third of patients
        2) Oral contraceptive: effective in one-half of patients
        3) Spironolactone, 25 mg twice a day, in more severe cases, unresponsive to ovarian and adrenal suppression
B. Dysmenorrhea
  1. Primary: within a year or 2 of menarche
  2. Secondary: nearly always a result of a specific disorder — e.g., fibroids, endometriosis, pelvic inflammatory disease, intrauterine contraceptive device — and warrants referral to a gynecologist
  3. Treatment
    a) Mild dysmenorrhea: mild analgesics (e.g., aspirin, acetaminophen)
    b) More severe dysmenorrhea: nonsteroidal anti-inflammatory agents effective in one-half of patients
    c) Very severe dysmenorrhea: oral contraceptives and referral as above
C. Premenstrual tension syndrome
  1. Symptoms: irritability, food cravings, depression, mood swings, headaches, fatigue
  2. No accepted treatment; in severe cases, steroid hormone replacement after gynecological consultation
D. Abnormal vaginal bleeding before menopause (Table 61.3)

1. Evaluation
    a) History
        1) Description of the bleeding
            (a) Menorrhagia: consistent with dysfunctional uterine bleeding (DUB) of unknown cause, fibroids, endometrial polyps, underlying medical disease (e.g., hypothyroidism)
            (b) Metrorrhagia: consistent with fibroids, polyps, local vulvovaginal problems, cancer of the cervix or endometrium
            (c) Polymenorrhagia or oligomenorrhea: often associated with dysfunctional bleeding
        2) Evidence of ovulation
            (a) Mittelschmerz
            (b) Increased midcycle mucus
            (c) Premenstrual fullness, headaches, irritability
            (d) Dysmenorrhea
            (e) Diphasic basal body temperature pattern
        3) Contraceptive history
        4) Symptoms suggestive of pregnancy (possibility of threatened abortion, spontaneous abortion, ectopic pregnancy)
        5) Symptoms suggestive of pelvic infection (Chapter 77)
        6) Symptoms suggestive of hemostatic dysfunction (Chapter 36)
        7) Recent changes in health or activity that might have precipitated DUB (change in diet or physical activity, new stress, sleep loss, intercurrent disease, use of alcohol, etc.)
    b) Physical examination: pelvic examination but also a general examination to look for signs of systemic illness
    c) Laboratory tests
        1) Hematocrit value or hemoglobin concentration
        2) Papanicolaou smear (Chapter 78)
        3) Pregnancy test in sexually active women
        4) Hemostatic testing (Chapter 36) if indicated
        5) Pelvic sonography if ectopic pregnancy suspected
    d) Treatment
        1) Anatomical causes: most cases should be referred to a gynecologist; vaginitis and cervicitis (Chapter 77) and medical conditions (e.g., hypothyroidism) can be treated by a generalist
        2) Dysfunctional uterine bleeding
            (a) If severe, a trial of an oral contraceptive may be warranted
            (b) If persistent, should be referred to a gynecologist
E. Oligomenorrhea and hypogonadism (Table 61.4)
    1. Primary, before puberty: if *central,* genetic gonadotropin deficiency; if *gonadal,* most likely Turner's syndrome (XO sex chromosomes); if maturation is normal, may be anatomical (e.g., imperforate hymen or uterine agenesis)
    2. Secondary, after puberty: if *central,* often idiopathic but may have tumor or anorexia nervosa; if *gonadal,* may be due to infection

Table 61.4. Classification of Female Hypogonadism (i.e., Oligomenorrhea)

Classification	Criteria
ACCORDING TO TIME OF ONSET	
Primary (no onset of menses)	History
Secondary (cessation of established menses)	
ACCORDING TO SOMATOTYPE	
Maturation failure (juvenile)	Physical examination
Feminized (normal secondary sex)	
Masculinized (hirsute, deep voice, increased muscle mass, clitoromegaly)	
ACCORDING TO LOCATION OF LESION	
Central (hypothalamic or pituitary)	Gonadotropins ↓ or →
Without galactorrhea	
With galactorrhea	
Gonadal (ovarian failure)	Gonadotropins ↑
Exogenous (disruption of menses by drugs, stress, or illness of other than reproductive organs)	History, physical examination, various laboratory and radiological tests
ACCORDING TO ETIOLOGY	
Genetic (chromosomal or familial)	History, buccal smear, karyotype
Acquired (infectious, neoplastic, traumatic, surgical, hemorrhage or infarction, autoimmune)	History, physical examination, radiology, other special procedures

    (e.g., tuberculosis), tumor, trauma, or an autoimmune disorder (often polyglandular — see Chapter 58)

   3. Exogenous: e.g., thyroid disease, hepatic or renal failure, weight loss, morbid obesity, overly rigorous exercise, substance abuse

   4. Galactorrhea: in 15% of patients with secondary central amenorrhea; 40% of these due to prolactinoma (Chapter 58 and above); drugs (e.g., isoniazid, phenothiazines); hypothyroidism; idiopathic

F. Diagnosis of female reproductive dysfunction

   1. History

      a) Chronicle of pubertal events

      b) Menstrual history

      c) Pregnancy and nursing history

      d) History of gynecological surgery

      e) History of hirsutism and symptoms of virilization (see above)

      f) Symptoms of estrogen deficiency (hot flashes, vaginitis, dyspareunia, breast atrophy)

      g) Medication use

      h) History of weight loss or gain, strenuous exercise

      i) Symptoms of diabetes mellitus, of thyroid disease, or of another systemic illness

   2. Physical examination

      a) Body habitus

      b) Pubic hair pattern and distribution of hair elsewhere on the body

      c) Breast development; presence of galactorrhea

      d) Pelvic examination (?clitoromegaly, state of the vaginal mucosa, ?ovarian enlargement)

      e) General examination, especially for signs of intracranial mass lesions or of systemic disease

    3. Laboratory tests
- a) hCG assay for pregnancy in all women with secondary amenorrhea
- b) Assessment of estrogen status (vaginal cytology, provocation of withdrawal bleeding, serum estrogen level)
- c) Measurement of serum or urinary gonadotropins to distinguish central from gonadal hypogonadism
- d) Prolactin measurement, especially if galactorrhea

G. Treatment of women with oligomenorrhea
1. Absence of menses: if idiopathic, oral contraceptives; if fertility an issue, see below
2. Galactorrhea (see Chapter 58): bromocriptine 2.5 mg 2 or 3 times/day; removal of prolactinoma; or treat proximal cause (e.g., stop offending drug)
3. Intracranial tumor: if small, follow with visual fields, computed tomography scan every 6 months and replace any hormonal deficiency; if large, refer for bromocriptine, surgery, or radiation

H. Sexual dysfunction (frigidity and dyspareunia) (see also Chapter 6)
1. Organic causes: endocrinopathies, other systemic illness, diseases of the reproductive system
2. History
- a) Same questions as asked of women with hypogonadism
- b) Dyspareunia: whether with initial (vulvovaginal disease) or deep penetration (pelvic disease); history of previously satisfactory sexual activity
- c) Symptoms of systemic disease; medication history; history of substance abuse
3. Physical examination: as for patients with hypogonadism (see above)
4. Laboratory tests: if evidence of hypogonadism or of systemic disease
5. Treatment: see above; estrogen deficiency should be corrected (see below)

I. Problems of menopause
1. Psychological symptoms
- a) Highly variable: minor irritability and lability to severe depression
- b) No clear-cut effectiveness of estrogen replacement
- c) Low doses of androgen (e.g., 30 mg testosterone enanthate i.m. every 3 weeks) may increase libido but should be prescribed only if situation is extreme
- d) Significant problems (e.g., anxiety, depression) treated as in Chapters 1 and 3
2. Estrogen deficiency state
- a) Hot flashes
- b) Genital and breast atrophy
- c) Estrogen replacement: see below
3. Osteoporosis (see also Chapter 58)
- a) Risk factors: family history, fine body structure, sedentary lifestyle, cigarette smoking, alcohol abuse, nulliparity, diabetes mellitus, chronic glucocorticoid therapy
- b) Crush fractures of vertebrae initially predominate; later, hip and forearm fractures are common

Table 61.5. Regimens of Estrogen Replacement Therapy

Type	Method	Advantages	Disadvantages
Continuous estrogen[a]	Estrogen given daily without interruption	Easily remembered No regular menses No progestogen lipid effect	Risk of endometrial cancer increased Irregular bleeding frequent
Cyclic estrogen	Estrogen for 21–24 days; off for 7 days	Less risk of endometrial cancer No progestogen lipid effect	Risk of endometrial cancer increased Withdrawal bleeding may occur
Cyclic progestogen[b] Opposed estrogen	Estrogen for 21–24 days; add progestogen for last 10–12 days; then off both for 4–7 days	No excess risk of endometrial cancer Irregular bleeding infrequent	Regular withdrawal bleeding Progestogen effect on lipids
Interrupted progestogen Opposed estrogen	Estrogen for 90–180 days; add progestogen for last 12–14 days; off both for 7 days	Probably less risk of endometrial cancer Withdrawal bleeding less frequent Progestogen lipid effect insignificant	Level of cancer protection unknown Irregular bleeding may occur
Continuous progestogen Opposed estrogen	Estrogen and progestogen[c] both given daily without interruption	Probably no excess cancer risk No withdrawal bleeding Easily remembered	Level of cancer protection unknown Irregular bleeding frequent, especially in first 3 months Progestogen effect on lipids

[a]Conjugated estrogens (e.g., Premarin) 0.625–1.25 mg/day; micronized estradiol (e.g., Estrace) 1–2 mg/day; transdermal estradiol (e.g., Estraderm) 50–100 μg/day.
[b]Medroxyprogesterone acetate (e.g., Provera) 5–10 mg/day; norethindrone 350 μg/day.
[c]Medroxyprogesterone acetate (e.g., Provera) 2.5 mg/day, increase to 5 mg/day for bleeding.

      c) Dual x-ray photon absorptiometry (DEXA) scanning can identify women at high risk of fractures if done serially

      d) Prevention: see below

  4. Atherosclerosis and blood lipids: low-density lipoprotein (LDL) levels (see Chapter 59) rise significantly in estrogen-deficient women

  5. Endometrial hyperplasia and carcinoma: often manifest by postmenopausal bleeding (see below)

  6. Estrogen replacement

    a) Benefits

      1) Predictably relieves hot flashes, genital atrophy, dyspareunia

      2) Effective in prevention of osteoporosis and of fractures

      3) Significant reduction (40–60%) in risk of coronary events, in part because of effect on plasma lipids (rise in high-density lipoprotein (HDL), fall in LDL — see Chapter 59)

    b) Risks

      1) Endometrial cancer only an increased risk if estrogen is prescribed without interruption and without progesterone

      2) Breast cancer: risk unclear, perhaps slightly increased

    c) Regimens: Table 61.5

J. Postmenopausal bleeding

  1. Definition: any vaginal bleeding after 1 year of amenorrhea (in a woman who is not taking cyclic estrogen replacement)

  2. History

    a) Duration, frequency, characteristics (color, amount, flow)

    b) History of cyclic hormone therapy (heavy or unexpected bleeding should still be investigated)

    c) Physical examination: abdominal and pelvic examination

    d) Laboratory tests

      1) Analysis of stool and urine for blood

      2) Referral to gynecologist to biopsy vulvovaginal or cervical lesions, to evaluate adrenal function, to do a dilatation and curettage (D&C) as appropriate

Section X
Neurological Problems

62/ HEADACHES AND FACIAL PAIN

GENERAL APPROACH TO THE PATIENT WITH HEADACHE

A. History
  1. Associated factors, e.g., prodrome, inciting factors, drugs
  2. Temporal features: rapidity of onset, time of day, duration, frequency
  3. Character and location of pain
  4. Aggravating and alleviating factors
  5. Environmental exposures
  6. Associated neurological symptoms
  7. Prior evaluation
  8. Family and household history
B. Physical and laboratory examination (see below)
C. Principles of initial treatment
  1. If history consistent with tension or migraine (see below) and physical examination normal, treat presumptively
  2. If presumptive treatment fails or if symptoms or physical findings change, more extensive workup (see below) indicated
  3. Total relief should not be promised or anticipated

SPECIFIC HEADACHE SYNDROMES

A. Tension headache
  1. Classification
    a) Episodic: often controlled by over-the-counter analgesics
    b) Chronic daily: often associated with depression and/or anxiety; refractory to analgesics and to migraine prophylaxis (except antidepressants)
  2. Presentation
    a) Characteristics of headaches: Table 62.1

Table 62.1. Characteristics of Migrainous and Tension Headaches

	Migraine (%)	Tension (%)
Age at onset		
<20 years	55	30
>20 years	45	70
Premonitory symptoms	60	10
Frequency		
Daily	3	50
<Weekly	60	15
Duration		
Constant, daily	0	20
1–3 days	35	10
Throbbing pain	80	30
Location		
Unilateral	80	10
Bilateral	20	90
Vomiting with attacks	50	10
Family history of headache	65	40

Adapted from Raskin NH, Appenzeller O: *Headache*. Philadelphia, WB Saunders, 1980, as modified from Friedman AP, et al: *Neurology* 4:773, 1954.

b) Physical examination: normal or neck, scalp, muscle tenderness

3. Treatment
   a) Nonpharmacological: attempt to identify and relieve stress; teach massage of scalp and neck muscles
   b) Pharmacological
      1) Aspirin or acetaminophen 650 mg every 4–6 hours; if ineffective, a nonsteroidal anti-inflammatory drug (NSAID) other than aspirin is indicated
      2) Codeine or combination analgesics should be avoided
      3) Prophylaxis with amitriptyline 50–100 mg at bedtime if headaches very severe or frequent

B. Migraine headache
   1. Classification
      a) Migraine with aura (premonitory sensory, motor, or visual disturbances)
      b) Migraine without aura
   2. Presentation
      a) Characteristics of headaches (Table 62.1)
         1) Premenstrual period, oral contraceptives (especially off days), menopause are associated with migraine
         2) Common initiating substances or circumstances: vasodilators, alcohol, chocolate, cheeses, monosodium glutamate, withdrawal of caffeine, unusually prolonged sleep
      b) Physical examination: often scalp vessels are tender, attacks may be attenuated somewhat by pressure on temples
   3. Treatment
      a) Nonpharmacological: avoid trigger factors (see above)
      b) Pharmacological (see Table 62.2)
         1) Mild attacks: acetaminophen, aspirin, or another NSAID
         2) Moderate to severe attack: a NSAID, ergotamine, or sumatriptan (either of the latter two can be given as a therapeutic trial to establish diagnosis)
            (a) Ergotamine: to avoid side effects, do not give more than recommended dose; give early for optimum effect; do not give to patients with arterial vascular disease
            (b) Sumatriptan: can be effective even hours after onset; contraindicated in patients with hemiplegic or basilar artery migraine or with coronary artery disease
            (c) If unresponsive to a NSAID, ergotamine, or sumatriptan, consider codeine 60 mg
            (d) Sumatriptan or Compazine suppository, 25 mg: use to treat nausea and vomiting
      c) Prophylaxis (Table 62.3)
         1) Effective in 50% of patients during first year, compared with untreated controls
         2) Improvement consists of decrease in frequency or severity of headaches
         3) Each class of drugs in Table 62.3 equally effective; failure of a drug from one class does not predict response to a drug from another class
         4) Failure to give an adequate dose is a common reason for failure of prophylaxis

Table 62.2. Drugs for Acute Migraine Attacks

Drug	Route	Trade Name	Dose[a]
Nonprescription Analgesic			
Aspirin	p.o.		650 mg 2 q4h p.r.n.
Acetaminophen	p.o.	Tylenol	650 mg q4h p.r.n.
Ibuprofen	p.o.	Advil, Nuprin, etc.	200 mg 1–4 q4–8h p.r.n.
Prescription Analgesics			
Naproxen (or other NSAID)[b]	p.o.	Anaprox DS	550 mg q8h p.r.n.
		Naprosyn	500 mg q8h p.r.n.
Ketorolac	p.o., i.m.	Toradol	10-mg tablets: 2 initially, then 1 q6h
			Prefilled syringes: 15, 30 mg
			30–60 mg, then 30 mg q6h
Isometheptene, acetaminophen, and dichloralphenazone	p.o.	Midrin	2 capsules, then 1 qh (up to 5 capsules/12 h)
Butalbital, acetaminophen	p.o.	Phrenilin	1–2 q4h p.r.n. (up to 6/day)
Butalbital, acetaminophen, and caffeine	p.o.	Fioracet, Esgic	2 q4h p.r.n. (up to 6/day)
Butalbital, aspirin, and caffeine	p.o.	Fiorinol	2 q4h p.r.n. (up to 6/day)
Butorphanol	Nasal spray	Stadol NS	1 mg (1 spray), may repeat in 1–1.5 h
Prescription Nonanalgesics			
Ergotamine	p.o.[c]	Cafergot, Wigraine	2 mg at onset, 1 mg q0.5h (up to 6 tablets/day; 10 tablets/wk)
	Suppository[c]	Cafergot	3 mg at onset, may repeat in 1 h (up to 5/wk)
	Sublingual	Ergostat	2 mg at onset and q0.5h (up to 3 tablets/day, 5/wk)
Dihydroergotamine	i.m. or i.v.	D.H.E. 45	1 mg i.m. or i.v. and q1h (2/day, 6/wk)
Sumatriptan	s.c.	Imitrex	6 mg s.c. may repeat in 1 h (up to 2/24 h)
			(available as 6 mg/ml unit-dose syringes or SELF dose systems containing
			2 6-mg unit-dose syringes and self-injector device)

[a] Information given in quantities of available strengths unless otherwise described in parentheses.
[b] See list of NSAIDs and available strengths in Chapter 54.
[c] These ergotamine products also contain caffeine (100 mg/dose), which enhances gastrointestinal absorption.

Table 62.3. Prophylactic Therapy for Migraine[a]

Drugs	Dose/Day (mg)
β-Blockers	
Propranolol	80–320
Metoprolol	100–250
Atenolol	50–100
Timolol	10–60
Nadolol	40–240
Calcium channel blockers	
Verapamil	240–480
Tricyclic antidepressants	
Amitriptyline	10–150
Nortriptyline	10–150
Doxepin	10–100

[a] Most of these drugs are now available in generic forms. All are available in forms that can be taken once per day. Information is found for tricyclic antidepressants in Table 3.3.

C. Cluster headache
   1. Occurs predominantly in middle-aged men, often thin smokers
   2. Characteristics
      a) Sudden excruciating stabbing or burning pain in the eye, orbit, and cheek on one side
      b) Patients usually agitated (in contrast to patients with migraine headache)
      c) Ipsilateral lacrimation, rhinorrhea, conjunctival injection; ipsilateral ptosis and miosis may also occur
      d) Attacks last 30 minutes to 2 hours
      e) Attacks occur in clusters over days to weeks (from many a day to one a week, usually at same time of day) with months to years between attacks
   3. Treatment
      a) Acute attacks
         1) Oxygen, 100%, 15 minutes at 7 liters/minute preferred
         2) Ergotamine, sublingual, and sumatriptan also effective (Table 62.2)
      b) Cluster
         1) Prednisone 60–80 mg/day, tapered over 2–4 weeks, is drug of choice
         2) Also effective: indomethacin, ergotamine, propranolol, amitriptyline, verapamil, cyproheptadine
      c) Daily cluster (chronic paroxysmal hemicrania): lithium carbonate (see Chapter 3) plus, if necessary, ergotamine (Table 62.2) or methysergide
D. Sinus headache: see Chapter 14
E. Acute exertional headache (orgasmic, cough, sneeze)
   1. Features
      a) Sudden onset
      b) Directly related to exertion
      c) Lasts minutes up to, but rarely longer than, one-half hour
      d) Benign in 90%; indicates significant intracranial disease (e.g., arteriovenous malformation, tumor, subarachnoid hemorrhage) in 10%

    2. Evaluation: computed tomography (CT) scanning indicated, with and without contrast, or magnetic resonance imaging (MRI) when headaches first experienced

    3. Treatment: prophylaxis with a NSAID (Table 62.2) or a β-blocker (Table 62.3) may be effective

F. Temporomandibular joint syndrome (see Chapter 84)

G. Headache due to drugs (e.g., indomethacin, nalidixic acid, trimethoprim-sulfamethoxazole, oral contraceptives, vasodilators): try alternate therapy if possible; prophylaxis (e.g., β-blocker) if headaches severe

H. Giant cell arteritis (GCA) and polymyalgia rheumatica (PMR)

    1. Definitions

      a) GCA: large-vessel vasculitis, sometimes called temporal arteritis because of most typical presentation (see below)

      b) PMR: diagnosis by symptoms primarily (see below); overlaps in 50% of patients with GCA but occurs in 75–80% of patients without GCA

    2. Manifestations

      a) GCA

        1) A disease of the middle-aged and elderly

        2) Uncommon in African Americans

        3) Headache not clearly distinguishable from other headaches, but one-half are temporal; headaches usually not throbbing, often worse at night

        4) Associated findings: see Table 62.4

      b) PMR

        1) Insidious onset of aching, stiffness of shoulder girdle, less often of thighs

        2) Commonly associated with low-grade fever, weight loss, anorexia

    3. Diagnosis

      a) GCA

        1) Erythrocyte sedimentation rate (ESR) is best screening test; very high level (>100) in most

        2) Temporal artery biopsy is definitive diagnostic test (examine serial sections; sometimes, both sides must be biopsied if one side is not diagnostic)

      b) PMR

        1) Typical symptoms

        2) High ESR, as above

    4. Course

      a) Both GCA and PMR are self-limited, last up to 2 years

      b) In GCA, unilateral or bilateral blindness in 20–30% of untreated patients, due to ischemic optic neuropathy

    5. Treatment

      a) GCA: treat immediately (biopsy can be done within 4 days) with prednisone 40–60 mg/day for 4–6 weeks, then taper by 10% a week until 10–15 mg/day, then taper according to response of symptoms and ESR (may need to treat for 2 years or longer)

      b) PMR: prednisone 10–20 mg/day, tapered in a few weeks to 5–7.5 mg/day, continued for about 2 years regardless of symptoms or ESR

Table 62.4.   Clinical Features of Giant Cell Arteritis

Common Features	Approximate % of Patients With Features at Initial Evaluation	Less Common but Characteristic Features
Headache	85	Raynaud's phenomenon of limbs or tongue
Temporal artery tenderness	70	
Jaw claudication	65	Tender scalp nodules
Lingual, limb, or swallowing claudication	20	Thick, tender occipital arteries Necrotic lesions of scalp, tongue
Brachiocephalic bruits	50	
Thickened or nodular temporal artery	45	Carotid artery tenderness Swelling of the hands
Pulseless temporal artery	40	Taste, smell disturbances
Visual symptoms	40	Distended, beaded retinal veins
Fixed blindness, partial or complete	15	Diminished or absent radial artery pulses
Polymyalgia rheumatica	50	
Weight loss > 6 kg	40	Mononeuropathy — median, peroneal, cervical root
Erythrocyte sedimentation rate		
>50 mm/hr	95	
>100 mm/hr	60	
Fever (>37.7°C)	20	
Abnormal liver function	50	
Anemia (hematocrit level < 35%)	50	

Adapted from Raskin NH, Appenzeller O: *Headache*, Philadelphia, WB Saunders, 1980.

I. Benign intracranial hypertension (pseudotumor cerebri)
   1. Manifestations
      a) Prototypically occurs in an obese young woman who develops progressively more severe generalized headaches, nausea, vomiting, dizziness, transiently blurred vision
      b) Headaches precede usual symptoms
      c) Papilledema without focal neurological signs
   2. Diagnosis of exclusion after, e.g., intracranial mass lesion, hydrocephalus, hypertensive encephalopathy, or venous sinus thrombosis has been excluded
      a) Contrast CT or MRI should be done
      b) If scan negative, a lumbar puncture (LP) should be done (high cerebrospinal fluid pressure; otherwise, normal)
   3. Course: recovery usual in weeks to months
   4. Treatment
      a) Obese patients should lose weight
      b) At initial LP, enough fluid should be removed (usually 25–30 ml) to reduce closing pressure to ≤100 mm H_2O
      c) Acetazolamide (Diamox) 500-mg sustained release capsules twice a day; can be stopped if symptoms abate, papilledema disappears
      d) If symptoms and/or papilledema continues, repeated LPs are indicated

       e) If condition refractory, referral to a neurologist or a neurosurgeon is warranted

J. Posttraumatic (postconcussive) headache
1. Manifestations
   a) Occurs after head trauma that may not have been severe
   b) May be associated with vertigo (Chapter 64), light-headedness, poor concentration and memory, fatigue, irritability, anxiety
   c) Headache begins within 24 hours of trauma as a dull constant generalized ache that may wax and wane, may transiently concentrate at different points on the head
   d) May throb when intense, may be associated with nausea, vomiting, may be exacerbated by exertion
   e) Typically worsens over days to weeks, then resolves over weeks to months, but 15% of patients may develop typical migraine headaches
2. Diagnosis: electroencephalogram, vestibular function tests, auditory and visual evoked potentials may or may not be abnormal
3. Treatment: in some patients, the same treatment as is used for migraine (Tables 62.2 and 62.3) may be necessary

K. Low-pressure headache (post-LP)
1. Brought on by sitting or standing, relieved by lying down, commonly associated with nausea and dizziness
2. Problem usually resolves in a few days, occasionally in a few weeks
3. Persistent headache warrants referral to an anesthesiologist for epidural instillation of autologous blood (clots at site of leak)
4. Occasionally follows blunt trauma to head or spine; persistent headache warrants referral to a neurologist or neurosurgeon

L. Headache caused by a mass lesion
1. Characteristics
   a) Suspect more strongly if headache and focal neurological signs or a change in mental status develops simultaneously
   b) Typically becomes more intense and continuous, less responsive to treatment
   c) May awaken the patient from sleep or be present on awakening every day (but tension or migraine headache may do the same)
   d) May be aggravated by exertion (as may migraine headache)
2. Diagnosis: CT with contrast or MRI
3. Treatment: refer to a neurologist or neurosurgeon

FACIAL PAIN SYNDROMES

A. Idiopathic trigeminal neuralgia (tic douloureux)
1. Manifestations
   a) Limited to persons over age 40, usually elderly
   b) Pain severe, paroxysmal, lancinating, lasting seconds to a minute
   c) Frequency of paroxysms highly variable
   d) Pain typical in lips, gums, cheek, chin; almost always unilateral
   e) Trigger points frequently identified that, when touched, precipitate an attack
2. Differential diagnosis: consider other diagnoses (e.g., multiple sclerosis, acoustic neurinoma, etc.) if patient is under age 40, has

pain in forehead or eye, has bilateral pain, or has sensory loss or weakness
3. Diagnosis: typical patient requires no diagnostic tests; if treatment fails, refer to a neurologist
4. Treatment
   a) Initially, carbamazepine (Tegretol) 1/2 tablet (100 mg) twice a day with meals, increasing every 2–3 days to a typical total dose of 100–200 mg 3 times/day
      1) Some patients may need up to 1200 mg/day
      2) 60–70% of patients get relief
      3) Benign side effects: nausea, vomiting, ataxia, vertigo, transient leukopenia
      4) Serious side effects: persistent leukopenia, aplastic anemia (do serial complete blood counts after 1 week, 6 weeks, 3 months, periodically thereafter)
      5) Attempt to discontinue drug use every 3 months if there is response
   b) If carbamazepine does not help or is toxic, try amitriptyline (progressing from 25–150 mg at bedtime) for at least several weeks or baclofen (progressing from 10 mg twice a day to 70 mg twice a day) for several weeks
B. Atypical facial pain
   1. Pain that fits into no specific diagnostic category
   2. Persists if untreated
   3. Warrants evaluation by a dentist and an otolaryngologist
   4. Many patients will respond to a tricyclic antidepressant (see above)

63/ SEIZURE DISORDERS

CLINICAL MANIFESTATIONS

A. Generalized tonic-clonic (grand mal) seizures
   1. Sudden loss of consciousness, then trembling, tonic extension of the extremities, then clonic limb jerking, followed by flaccidity, stupor, labored breathing
   2. Seizures of less than 2 minutes, lethargy lasts minutes to hours
   3. No meaningful movements or speech, no memory of attacks
   4. No sensory, autonomic, psychic, or motor prelude
   5. May be accompanied by incontinence; sweating; tachycardia; elevated blood pressure; biting of lips, cheek, or tongue
   6. Electroencephalogram (EEG) typically shows lateral synchronous spike-and-wave discharges
   7. Onset rare after age 35
   8. Frequency varies greatly
B. Generalized absence (petit mal) seizures
   1. Onset between ages 4 and 12
   2. Lapses of vigilance or awareness typically lasting 3–20 seconds, up to 100/day
   3. No tonic-clonic phase nor loss of posture
   4. Slight twitching of mouth common
   5. Amnesia for event but rapid recovery of awareness
   6. EEG during seizure shows a characteristic pattern, normal between attacks
   7. Attacks may be induced by hyperventilation or flashing lights
   8. Attacks usually remit by age 20, but about half of patients develop tonic-clonic seizures
C. Myoclonic seizures
   1. Synchronous, involuntary, nonrhythmic jerking of limbs, trunk, or head; usually bilateral
   2. No alteration of consciousness
   3. May be due to abnormal discharges from the brain or the spinal cord
   4. Seen most frequently after severe diffuse cortical injury, cerebral ischemia, or anoxia but may occur also during course of a metabolic insult (e.g., hypoglycemia, renal or hepatic failure, drug toxicity)
   5. Attacks may last seconds to hours
   6. EEG abnormal during attacks only if abnormal discharge is in cortex
D. Partial (focal) seizures without impairment of consciousness
   1. Symptoms depend on focus of abnormal discharge, most often in motor cortex
   2. May be followed by focal weakness of a limb, usually lasting a few hours
   3. EEG may or may not show focus
E. Partial complex seizures (also called "temporal lobe" or "psychomotor" seizures)
   1. Often begin with an aura, usually poorly described visceral sensations or malaise

2. Aura may blend into the seizure itself, with distorted visual or auditory sensations or vertigo or unsteadiness
3. Arrest of motor activity, rapid posturing, slow repetitive limb movements may occur
4. Fluctuating heart rate or blood pressure, flushing, sweating, salivation may occur
5. Consciousness variably impaired; patients may feel in a "dream" or experience intense fear or strange serenity
6. EEG abnormal in less than half of patients, but sleep tracings very often abnormal when electrodes are applied over temporal lobes
7. Majority of patients experience seizures before age 20; in all cases, a treatable structural lesion should be excluded by computed tomography (CT) scanning or magnetic resonance imaging (MRI)

F. Secondarily generalized tonic-clonic seizures
1. Focal seizures (see above) that spread to produce tonic-clonic movements
2. Consciousness maintained early, then lost

NATURAL HISTORY

A. Risk of recurrence
1. After first seizure, the cumulative risk of another one is 50–70%
2. Role of treatment in reducing risk is unclear
B. Remission rates
1. Fifty to eighty-two percent of patients are in remission after 2–5 years
2. At 20 years, remission rate is 80–85% for primary generalized seizures, 65% for partial complex seizures
C. Prognostic factors: age of onset, severity, history of status epilepticus, number of antiseizure medicines, length of time before control was obtained, presence of other neurological or psychological problems

ETIOLOGY

A. Overview: Table 63.1 lists causes in order of frequency from top down, except for Idiopathic, at bottom
B. Posttraumatic
1. More likely after severe head injury (e.g., with intracranial hematoma, focal neurological signs, unconsciousness for more than 24 hours)
2. If one seizure occurs within 2 weeks of injury, long-term treatment not indicated; if more than one seizure, long-term treatment should be considered (with phenytoin, see below)
3. If seizure occurs more than 2 weeks after injury, seizure should not be attributed to trauma unless other causes excluded
C. Alcohol-related seizures
1. Alcohol withdrawal a common cause of seizures
2. Twenty-five percent are focal
3. If history imprecise and findings equivocal or if there is a fever or granulocytosis, lumbar puncture and EEG are indicated
4. If focal signs or evidence of head trauma, CT scan is indicated
5. Short term: patient should be hospitalized
6. Long term: treatment with anticonvulsants not indicated
D. Seizures and brain tumors
1. Brain tumors are uncommon causes of seizures, but seizures are common symptoms of brain tumors

Table 63.1.   Etiological Factors for Seizures With Onset at Various Ages

Adolescent (12–21 yr)	Adult (21–65 yr)	Elderly (65+ yr)
COMMON CAUSES		
Genetic (g)	Alcohol withdrawal (g)	Cerebrovascular (m)
Mesial temporal sclerosis (f)	Toxins or drugs (g)	Thrombotic
Infection (m)	Drug withdrawal (g)	Embolic
Meningitis	Tumor (f)	Hemorrhagic
Viral encephalitis	Trauma (f)	Cardiac arrhythmia
Abscess	Scar	Trauma (f)
TORCHS	Subdural hematoma	Scar
Parasites	Mesial temporal sclerosis (f)	Subdural hematoma
Psychogenic (m)	Genetic (g)	Tumor (f)
Toxins or drugs (g)	Psychogenic (m)	Infection (m)
Drug withdrawal (g)	Infection (m)	Meningitis
	Meningitis	Viral encephalitis
	Viral encephalitis	Abscess
	Abscess	Syphilis
	Syphilis	Parasites
	Parasites	
OCCASIONAL CAUSES		
Metabolic (g)	Metabolic (g)	Alcohol withdrawal (g)
Hypoglycemia	Hypoglycemia	Toxins or drugs (g)
Hyponatremia	Hyponatremia	Drug withdrawal (g)
Hypocalcemia	Hypocalcemia	Hypoxia (g)
Porphyria	Hypomagnesemia	Metabolic (g)
Trauma (f)	Hypoxia (g)	Hypoglycemia
Scar	Cerebrovascular (m)	Hyponatremia
Subdural hematoma	Thrombotic	Hypocalcemia
Tumor (f)	Embolic	
Arteriovenous malformation	Hemorrhagic	
(f)	Cardiac arrhythmia	
Subarachnoid hemorrhage	Renal failure (g)	
(m)	Eclampsia (m)	
Eclampsia (m)		
Renal failure (g)		
RARE CAUSES		
Collagen disease (m)	Collagen disease (m)	Hypertensive encephalopathy
Hepatic failure (g)	Hypertensive encephalopathy	(m)
Multiple sclerosis (f)	(m)	Hyperosmolar (m)
	Hyperosmolar (m)	Renal failure (g)
	Multiple sclerosis (f)	Hepatic failure (g)
	Degenerative	Degenerative (g)
		Factitious (m)
Idiopathic	Idiopathic	Idiopathic

f, usually focal; *g*, usually generalized; *m*, often mixed; TORCHS, toxoplasmosis, rubella, cytomegalovirus, herpes, syphilis.

   2. Young and middle-aged adults with new onset of focal seizures
      have greatest chance of having a brain tumor
   3. Seizures may be generalized tonic-clonic or partial
E. Seizures and cerebrovascular disease
   1. Relatively uncommon
   2. More likely to be focal than generalized
   3. Early-onset seizures after a stroke usually do not recur; late-onset
      seizures often do and warrant therapy

EVALUATION
A. History: see above
B. Physical examination, including detailed neurological examination

C. Laboratory tests
   1. No routine tests are recommended; tests should be done only
      because of suspicion of a specific diagnosis (e.g., serum glucose
      measurement if hypoglycemia suspected)
   2. Serum prolactin level may occasionally be of help to distinguish
      epileptic from psychogenic seizure (rises 2–3 times baseline for
      10–60 minutes after an epileptic attack)
D. Electroencephalography (EEG)
   1. Most useful test in diagnosis of seizure disorders
   2. Epileptiform discharges within a week of first seizure predicts an
      83% recurrence rate within 2 years versus 41% if no discharges
   3. Should be used to confirm, not make, diagnosis (patients without
      a history of seizures should not be treated on the basis of EEG
      alone, nor does a normal EEG exclude the diagnosis of seizures)
   4. Ordinarily, antiepileptic medicine need not be stopped before
      doing EEG
E. Cerebrospinal fluid examination
   1. Not routinely recommended
   2. Should be done if meningitis or subarachnoid hemorrhage is
      suspected
   3. Seizure alone may cause transient pleocytosis of up to 100 cells
F. Cerebral imaging
   1. CT with contrast or MRI for patients with new-onset focal or
      secondarily generalized seizures or with an abnormal neurological
      examination
   2. MRI has a higher diagnostic yield than CT but is much more
      expensive

TREATMENT
A. General principles (Table 63.2)
   1. Single seizure does not necessarily warrant chronic treatment
   2. Selecting the proper drug: Table 63.3
   3. Characteristics of individual drugs: Table 63.4
   4. Ninety percent of seizures can be controlled with one drug
   5. When to refer or hospitalize: Table 63.5

SOCIAL ISSUES AND PATIENT EDUCATION
A. Restriction of activity
   1. Avoid identifiable precipitants (e.g., sleep deprivation, flashing
      lights, alcohol)
   2. Limits on hazardous activities (e.g., flying a plane, scuba diving)
   3. Driving: low but real risk; decision should be left to licensing
      authorities (i.e., accurate information should be transmitted)

Table 63.2.   Principles of Drug Therapy

Decide whether to treat.
Select the proper drug for the particular form of epilepsy.
Start drugs slowly and build up levels gradually, to avoid toxicity.
Start with one drug and use it to effect or toxicity before adding another.
Choose the simplest regimen possible.
Suspect compliance problems in treatment failures.
Monitor blood levels in problem cases.
Withdraw medications gradually.
Decide how long to treat.

Table 63.3.   Drugs of Choice According to Seizure Type

Seizure Category	Drugs of Choice	Alternatives
Primary generalized, tonic-clonic	Valproic acid	Carbamazepine Phenytoin Primidone Phenobarbital
Primary generalized, absence	Ethosuximide Valproic acid	Clonazepam
Primary myoclonic	Valproic acid Clonazepam	Phenytoin Phenobarbital
Partial simple and complex and secondarily generalized epilepsy	Carbamazepine Phenytoin	Valproic acid Phenobarbital Primidone
Mixed forms	Valproic acid Clonazepam	Carbamazepine Phenytoin Phenobarbital

B. Employment
   1. Illegal to discriminate against epileptic persons
   2. Epilepsy Foundation of America can help
C. Pregnancy
   1. Seizures may complicate pregnancy
   2. Many antiseizure medicines have teratogenic potential (especially phenytoin, carbamazepine, valproic acid), but risk is relatively low
D. Family education
   1. Do not force patient's mouth open during seizure
   2. Move the patient with a seizure away from sharp corners, heights; turn patient on his or her side
   3. Do not forcibly restrain
   4. Teach importance of patient compliance with medications

Table 63.4. Major Antiseizure Medications

Medication[a] (Brand Name)	Available Strength (mg)	Typical Adult Dose, Schedule, Range	Half-life (hr)	Target Levels (mg/liter)[b]	Major Side Effects
Phenytoin (Dilantin)[c]	30, 100 capsules 30/5 ml and 125/5 ml suspension 50 chewable tablets	300 mg 1 time/day[d,e] (200–500 mg)	22[e]	10–20	Ataxia Cosmetic changes (gum hyperplasia, hirsuteness)
Phenobarbital[c] (Luminal)	15, 30, 60, 100 tablets	100 mg 1 time/day	72	15–40	Sedation Hyperactivity Confusion Mood change
Primidone (Mysoline)	50, 250 scored tablets and suspension	250 mg 3 or 4 times/day (500–1500 mg)	3–12[f] 72[g]	6–12[f] 15–40[g]	Sedation Hyperactivity Mood change
Carbamazepine[c] (Tegretol)	200 tablets (100 chewable) 100/5 ml suspension	200 mg 3 or 4 times/day (400–2000 mg)	10–25	4–12	Gastrointestinal (GI) distress Ataxia Blurred vision Blood changes Hepatotoxicity
Ethosuximide (Zarontin)	250 capsules 250/5 ml syrup	250 mg 2–4 times/day (500–1500 mg)	30	50–100	GI distress Sedation Headache Dizziness
Valproic acid[c] (Depakene) (Depakote)	250 capsules 250/5 ml syrup 125, 250, 500 tablets 125 sprinkles	50–4000 mg 250 mg 2–4 times/day (500–4000 mg)	8–12	50–100	GI distress Drowsiness Ataxia Alopecia Tremor Blood changes

Table 63.4.   Continued

Medication[a] (Brand Name)	Available Strength (mg)	Typical Adult Dose, Schedule, Range	Half-life (hr)	Target Levels (mg/liter)[b]	Major Side Effects
Clonazepam (Klonopin)	0.5, 1, 2 tablets	2 mg 3 times/day (2–20 mg)	20–40	0.05–0.7	Rare liver toxicity Rare pancreatitis Drowsiness Ataxia Behavior changes Dizziness

[a] Generic products are available, but there have been reports of bioinequivalence between brand name and generic products.
[b] Laboratory may report same figures as micrograms per milliliter.
[c] Generic product available.
[d] These doses are usually attained gradually over days to weeks. The ranges are relatively rough guidelines; because absorption varies, serum levels are better guides to dosage.
[e] Only for Dilantin capsules (Kapseals).
[f] For primidone.
[g] For phenobarbital.

Table 63.5. When to Refer or Hospitalize the Patient With Seizures

DIAGNOSTIC ISSUES FOR REFERRAL
Question about whether a seizure took place
Abnormal physical examination
Questionable focal neurological findings
Focal seizures
Focality on the EEG
Need for special diagnostic investigations (e.g., lumbar puncture, CT or MRI scan)
Uncertainty about etiology
THERAPEUTIC ISSUES FOR REFERRAL
Complex medication adjustments
Patient does not respond to a drug of choice
Patient has significant medication side effects
Patient wishes to become pregnant
Patient wishes to taper off medication
Significant change in the pattern of seizures
WHEN TO HOSPITALIZE
Most new-onset seizures
New focal signs on examination
Obtunded or prolonged "postictal" patients
Febrile patients
Crescendo pattern of seizures
All cases of status epilepticus
Barbiturate and benzodiazepine withdrawal seizures
Possibility of rapidly expanding mass lesion
Seizures after recent head trauma
Need for special inpatient studies
Consideration for neurosurgery
Monitoring of compliance

64/ DISORDERS OF SPATIAL ORIENTATION

VERTIGO

A. Definition: an illusion of movement, either that the environment is moving or that the patient is turning in place

B. History
   1. General: onset, severity, duration, frequency of symptoms; inciting-relieving factors; associated symptoms (e.g., nausea or vomiting)
   2. Auditory symptoms: hearing, tinnitus, aural pressure, history of ear infection, trauma, or exposure to ototoxic drugs (e.g., aspirin, aminoglycosides, loop diuretics)
   3. Neurological symptoms: numbness, weakness, clumsiness, alteration of consciousness, slurring of speech, difficulty swallowing, headache

C. Physical examination
   1. Auditory canal and tympanic membrane (Chapter 79)
   2. Observation for nystagmus, an involuntary rhythmic movement of the eyes
      a) Pendular (to-and-fro movements equal in amplitude and speed): usually due to disturbance of central vision
      b) Jerk nystagmus (slow and quick component): usually a sign of vestibular disease
      c) Spontaneous
         1) May be due to peripheral or central vestibular dysfunction (Table 64.1)
         2) With eyes in midposition, head upright
         3) Usually present during attack of vertigo if due to vestibular disease
         4) Increases in amplitude with gaze in direction of quick phase, decreases in opposite direction
         5) If not observed, have patient close eyes, look for nystagmus through the patient's closed lids (fixation may suppress spontaneous nystagmus of peripheral vestibular disease)
         6) If present with eyes open, ask patient to fix on a distant object: suppression again favors peripheral vestibular disease
      d) Gaze evoked
         1) Elicited when eyes are held eccentrically in the orbit

Table 64.1. Features of Spontaneous Nystagmus, According to Anatomical Location of the Cause

Feature	Peripheral	Central
Direction	Usually horizontal-rotatory Never purely vertical	Any direction May be purely vertical
Direction of fast component	Away from side with disease	Toward side with disease (or direction changing)
Effect of visual fixation	Suppressed	Not suppressed
Usual anatomical location of problem	Labyrinth or vestibular nerve	Brainstem or cerebellum

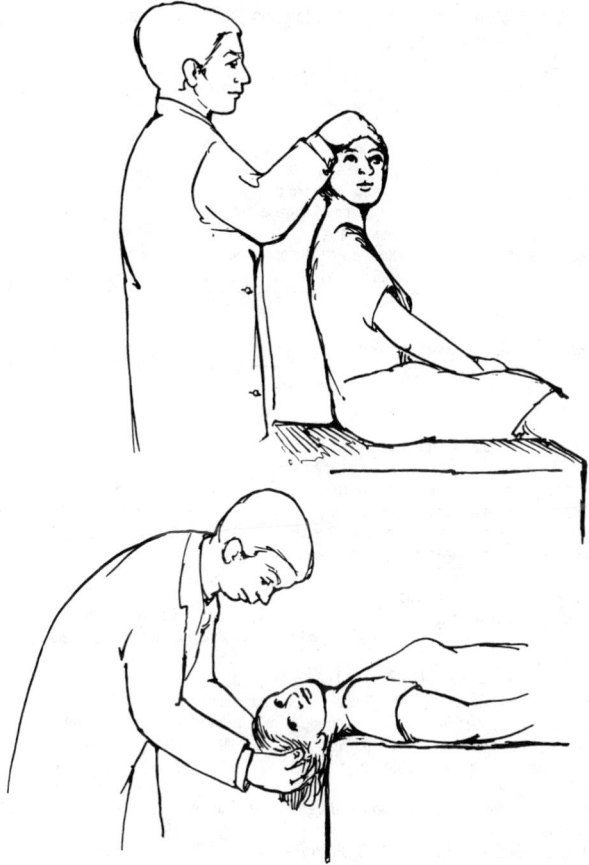

Figure 64.1. Bárány maneuver for testing a patient for positional vertigo and nystagmus (see text).

   2) Most frequently due to drugs, less often to brainstem or
    cerebellar lesions
  e) Positional
   1) May be due to peripheral or central disease (Table 64.2)
   2) Produced by sudden change in head position
   3) Elicited by Bárány maneuver (Fig. 64.1)
D. Causes (Table 64.3)
 1. Peripheral
  a) Benign positional vertigo (BPV)
   1) Most common type of vertigo in adults
   2) Occurs at all ages but most commonly after fourth decade
    and in persons with recent head trauma (up to weeks
    before)

Table 64.2. Features of Positional Nystagmus Elicited by the Bárány Maneuver (See Text)

Feature	Peripheral (BPV)	Central
Time to onset after quick position change (latency)	3–20 seconds	Immediate
Duration	Less than 1 minute (often only a few seconds)	Persists longer than 1 minute
Fatigability	Marked (may not be present on immediate repetition)	None
Subjective vertigo	Often marked	Often minimal or absent
Nystagmus direction	Upward and torsional toward abnormal ear	Changing with change in head position

Table 64.3. Major Causes of Vertigo

PERIPHERAL CAUSES OF VERTIGO
   Benign positional vertigo
   Posttraumatic vertigo
   Peripheral vestibulopathy (labyrinthitis, vestibular neuronitis)
   Vestibulotoxic drug-induced vertigo (aminoglycosides)
   Ménière's syndrome (endolymphatic hydrops)
   Inflammatory labyrinthitis (syphilis, vasculitis)
   Other focal peripheral disease (acute and chronic otitis media, cholesteatoma, tumor, fistula, genetic anomalies, rarely focal ischemia and others)
CENTRAL CAUSES OF VERTIGO
   Brainstem ischemia and infarction
   Cerebellopontine angle tumor (acoustic neurinoma, meningioma, metastatic tumor, etc.)
   Demyelinating disease (multiple sclerosis, postinfectious demyelination, remote effect of carcinoma)
   Cranial neuropathy with focal involvement of eighth nerve
   Intrinsic brainstem lesions (tumor, arteriovenous malformation, trauma)
   Other posterior fossa lesions (primarily intrinsic or extra-axial masses of the posterior fossa, such as meatoma, metastatic tumor, and cerebellar infarction)
   Seizure disorder (temporal lobe epilepsy)
   Migraine
   Heredofamilial disorders (spinocerebellar degenerations: Friedreich's ataxia, olivopontocerebellar atrophy, etc.)
SYSTEMIC CAUSES OF VERTIGO AND DIZZINESS
   Drugs (anticonvulsants, hypnotics, antihypertensives, alcohol, analgesics, tranquilizers)
   Infectious disease (meningitis and systemic infection)
   Endocrine disease (diabetes mellitus and hypothyroidism particularly)
   Vasculitis (systemic lupus erythematosus, giant cell arteritis, and drug-induced vasculitis)
   Other systemic conditions (erythrocytosis, anemia, dysproteinemia, Paget's disease of the bone, sarcoidosis, granulomatous disease, and systemic toxins)

Adapted from Troost BT: Dizziness and vertigo in vertebrobasilar disease. *Curr Concepts Cerebrovasc Dis* 14:21, 1979.

   3) Symptoms often first noted in bed
   4) Episodes usually last less than 1 minute
   5) Typically no auditory symptoms
   6) No spontaneous nystagmus (see above)
   7) Positive Bárány maneuver (see above) with quick phase of nystagmus upward and torsionally toward the affected ear
   8) Usually self-limited but may persist for months, may recur;

if so, referral to a neurologist or otolaryngologist is reasonable

b) Posttraumatic
   1) After either blunt head trauma or whiplash injury to the neck
   2) Immediate vertigo
      (a) Spontaneous nystagmus, nausea, vomiting, hearing loss suggest temporal bone or occiput fracture, computed tomography (CT) scan warranted, as is immediate evaluation by an otolaryngologist
      (b) If vertigo and hearing loss induced by Valsalva maneuver (e.g., coughing), may be due to a perilymph fistula; majority heal spontaneously
      (c) Majority of patients improve spontaneously over 6–12 weeks
   3) Delayed onset (days to weeks after trauma)
      (a) Most typical of BPV (see above)
      (b) Tends to be self-limited
c) Peripheral vestibulopathy (acute viral labyrinthitis and vestibular neuronitis)
   1) Most common in third to fifth decades
   2) Typically, sudden-onset moderate to severe spontaneous vertigo
   3) Often with nausea, vomiting; symptoms made worse by change in position
   4) Hearing loss, tinnitus common with labyrinthitis, not with vestibular neuronitis
   5) On examination, spontaneous nystagmus with peripheral features (see above); Bárány maneuver (see above) may show the same response as in BPV
   6) Usually at maximum severity for several days; vertigo resolves usually within 6 weeks
   7) No specific treatment; antivertigo drugs (see below) may be of help
d) Vertigo due to vestibulotoxic drugs
   1) Streptomycin, gentamycin are vestibulotoxic
      (a) Symptoms may appear after patient has been discharged from the hospital
      (b) Usually, no frank vertigo but unsteadiness, difficulty walking in dark
      (c) Symptoms are permanent
   2) Mild vertigo that abates when drug is stopped may be a side effect of a number of drugs (Table 64.3)
e) Ménière's syndrome (endolymphatic hydrops) (see Chapter 79): distinguished from other causes of vertigo by
   1) Spontaneous onset of recurrent attacks
   2) Duration of attacks of no more than minutes to hours
   3) Associated tinnitus, ear discomfort, sensorineural hearing loss
d) Inflammatory labyrinthitis
   1) Secondary or tertiary syphilis: rare
      (a) Associated with sensorineural hearing loss
      (b) Impaired ability to understand speech

        (c) Peripheral-type vertigo
     2) Various vasculitides (e.g., lupus, polyarteritis)
  2. Central (see Table 64.3): less likely to be encountered by a generalist, usually warrants referral to a specialist
    a) Cerebellopontine (CP) angle tumor
      1) Acoustic neuroma is the commonest CP angle tumor (see Chapter 79)
      2) Vertigo and nystagmus seen infrequently
      3) Unsteadiness a symptom in 50% of patients
      4) Unilateral hearing loss and tinnitus common
      5) Onset insidious
    b) Vertebrobasilar arterial disease
      1) Vertigo caused in one of two ways
        (a) Ischemia of the brainstem or cerebellum, associated with other signs and symptoms of brainstem disease (e.g., clumsiness, weakness, visual loss, ataxia, dysarthria)
        (b) Ischemia only of the labyrinth, usually associated with unilateral hearing loss, but no evidence of brainstem involvement
E. Symptomatic treatment of vertigo (Table 64.4)
  1. For peripheral vertigo, an "antivertigo" antihistamine
    a) Prescribe for a week, then try discontinuing
    b) Major side effects are dry mouth, sedation
  2. If nausea and vomiting are pronounced, an antiemetic
    a) Major side effect is sedation
    b) Prochlorperazine may produce acute dystonia (see Chapter 4)

MOTION SICKNESS

A. Manifestations
  1. Malaise, nausea always; vomiting commonly
  2. Other symptoms occur variably: drowsiness, yawning, salivation, hyperventilation, headache, flushing, diaphoresis
  3. Adaptation usually after a few days (e.g., at sea)
B. Treatment (see Table 64.4)

Table 64.4. Drugs for Symptomatic Treatment of Vertigo

Type of Action	Generic (Trade Name)	Available Preparation	Dose and Schedule
Labyrinthine suppressants			
Antihistamines	Meclizine (Antivert, Bonine)	12.5- and 25-mg tablets	12.5–25 mg 3 or 4 times/day
	Dimenhydrinate (Dramamine)	50-mg tablets	50 mg 3 or 4 times/day
Anticholinergic	Transderm scopolamine	1.5-mg disc	1 disc every 3 days
Antiemetic	Prochlorperazine (Compazine)	5- and 10-mg tablets	5-10 mg every 4 hours as needed
		10- and 25-mg suppositories	10 mg 4 times/day or 25 mg 2 times/day
Sedative	Diazepam (Valium)	5, 10 mg	3 times/day

1. Much more effective if taken in anticipation of, rather than after onset of, symptoms
2. Antihistamines (best taken 1 hour before experience)
3. Scopolamine (best applied 8 hours before exposure)

SYNCOPE AND NEAR-SYNCOPE

A. Definition
    1. Syncope is a sudden transient (a few seconds to a few minutes) loss of consciousness with concurrent loss of postural tone
    2. Near-syncope is a transient sensation of imminent loss of consciousness

B. History
    1. Situation immediately before the attack: e.g., psychological stress, exercise, micturition, coughing, defecation
    2. Position at time of attack: syncope usually does not occur unless patient is upright; syncope in seated or recumbent position suggests hypoglycemia, cardiac arrhythmia, hyperventilation, or seizure
    3. Associated symptoms may suggest a specific diagnosis: e.g., chest pain, headache, incontinence and tonic-clonic movements, focal neurological symptoms
    4. Frequency of attacks

C. Physical examination
    1. General examination: blood pressure after recumbent for 5 minutes, standing for 2 minutes; pulse and heart rate; character and timing of carotid pulse; cardiac examination (murmur, clicks, gallops); abdominal examination (large bladder, signs of an acute abdomen)
    2. Neurological examination: orientation, speech, memory, evidence of focal deficits
       a) Slight focal weakness, reflex asymmetries, or pathological reflexes may be found for a minute after syncope due to any cause; if they persist, search for an anatomical lesion in the brain
       b) Postsyncopal seizures (usually a tonic convulsion) may occur after syncope due to any cause but should prompt a search for a seizure focus (see Chapter 63)
    3. Carotid massage
       a) For patients with episodes that suggest carotid hypersensitivity (see below) or for older patients with recurrent syncope of unknown cause
       b) Should only be done in a hospital or in an emergency facility

D. Diagnostic tests
    1. Electrocardiogram (ECG) with a rhythm strip if cause is not obvious
    2. Ambulatory ECG (Holter) monitoring
       a) If standard ECG is normal or nondiagnostic
       b) Twenty-four-hour monitoring ordinarily sufficient
    3. Tilt-table testing
       a) Requires referral
       b) To help in diagnosis of vasovagal (neurocardiogenic) syncope (see below)
       c) Low specificity in young people without heart disease

484 Section X Neurological Problems

4. Other tests (EEG, CT of head, blood tests) have a low yield if there are no clues to a specific diagnosis
E. Features of common causes (Table 64.5)
   1. Hypotension (see Table 64.5)
      a) Vasovagal (neurocardiogenic) syncope
         1) Occurs in setting of anxiety, fatigue, pain

Table 64.5. Differential Diagnosis of Syncope/Near-Syncope

HYPOTENSION	CARDIAC DISEASE
Vasovagal or neurocardiogenic syncope	*Arrhythmia (heart block, bradyarrhythmia,*
Vasodilating drugs	*and tachyarrhythmia)*
1. Angiotensin-converting enzyme	*Outflow obstruction*
inhibitors	1. Aortic stenosis
2. Calcium channel blockers	2. Idiopathic hypertrophic subaortic
3. Nitroglycerin preparations	stenosis
4. Vasodilator antihypertensives	3. Aortic dissection
Drugs affecting autonomic function	4. Myxoma
1. Sympatholytic antihypertensives	*Acute myocardial infarction*
2. Neuroleptics	*Mitral valve prolapse*
3. Tricyclics and monoamine oxidase	*Cyanotic congenital heart disease*
inhibitors	*Cardiac tamponade*
4. Levodopa	METABOLIC CONDITIONS
5. Cholinergic agents	*Hypoglycemia or hyperglycemia*
Autonomic neuropathy	*Hyponatremia, hypokalemia, or*
1. Peripheral neuropathy	*hypocalcemia*
2. Postsympathectomy	*Hypocapnia (hyperventilation)*
3. Tabes dorsalis and diabetic	*Hypoxia*
pseudotabes	1. Anemia
4. Parkinsonism (Shy-Drager	2. Airway obstruction
syndrome)	3. Carbon monoxide
5. Idiopathic	4. Change to moderate/high altitude
Decreased blood volume	*Hyperviscosity*
1. Hemorrhage	*Drug overdose (sedatives and ethanol)*
2. Salt and water deficit	INTRACRANIAL CONDITIONS
3. Fasting	*Seizure disorder*
4. Adrenal insufficiency	*Subarachnoid hemorrhage*
5. Hypoalbuminemia	*Cerebral embolism or thrombosis*
Venous pooling	*Migraine*
1. Prolonged immobility while standing	*Acutely increased intracranial pressure*
2. Severe varicose veins	1. Tumor
3. Late pregnancy	2. Trauma
4. After exercise	3. Ventricular obstruction
Mobilization after bed rest	4. Hypertensive encephalopathy
Orthostasis of aging	*Brainstem compression*
Valsalva maneuver	1. Cervical or odontoid fractures
1. Tussive	2. Metastasis
2. Micturition	3. Cysts or anomalies of the posterior
3. Defecation (with straining)	fossa
4. Intermittent positive-pressure	4. Platybasia
breathing	PSYCHIATRIC DISORDERS
Compromise of cerebral blood flow due	*Panic disorder*
to cervical osteoarthritis or	*Generalized anxiety disorder*
subclavian steal	*Major depression*
Carotid sinus hypersensitivity	*Somatization disorder*
Pulmonary embolism	*Conversion disorder*

Modified from Lee JE, Killip T, Plum F: Episodic unconsciousness. In: Baron JA (ed): *Diagnostic Approaches to Presenting Syndromes*, Baltimore, Williams & Wilkins, 1971.

2) Occurs at any age
3) Nearly always occurs when patient is upright (occasionally when seated), terminated when patient lies (or falls) down
4) Typically, a prodrome of up to 5 minutes, characterized by dizziness, flushing, nausea, with pallor and cold hands just before faint
5) Bradycardia after faint; patient should remain recumbent (up to 30 minutes) while heart rate is slow
6) If recurrent, may be prevented by β-blockers, transdermal scopolamine, supportive stockings, fludrocortisone (see Chapter 67)

b) Autonomic impairment
1) Always associated with orthostatic hypotension
2) Most commonly due to use of antihypertensive drugs (see Table 64.5)
3) Autonomic neuropathy, if suspected, can be evaluated by noting size and reactivity of pupils, distribution of sweating, response to a Valsalva maneuver (Table 64.6)

c) Orthostasis of aging
1) Especially common after meals
2) Standing blood pressure should be taken in all elderly with even mild orthostatic symptoms

2. Cardiac abnormalities (see Table 64.5)
a) Arrhythmias
1) Should be suspected in older people, people with known heart disease, with palpitations, people who faint while sitting or lying down
2) ECG, with ambulatory monitoring if appropriate (see above), is mandatory
3) Electrophysiological testing may be warranted (requires a specialized laboratory)

b) Outflow obstruction often with exertion

3. Metabolic abnormalities (see Table 64.5)
a) Hypoglycemia: see Chapters 56 and 58
b) Hypocapnia: anxiety the commonest cause (see Chapter 2)

Table 64.6. Four Phases of a Normal Valsalva Maneuver

ONSET		*Phase I:* A *sharp rise* in systolic pressure caused by an abrupt increase in intrathoracic pressure and emptying of the pulmonary bed during forced expiration against a closed glottis.
	(20–30 seconds)	*Phase II:* A *gradual fall* in systolic pressure and a concomitant narrowing of peripheral pulse pressures caused by decrease in pulmonic and systemic venous return. *Heart rate* increases during this phase.
RELEASE		*Phase III:* A sudden *further drop* in blood pressure occurs. Pulse pressure may be very narrow for the few beats during refilling of pulmonary venous reservoir.
		Phase IV (overshoot): Cardiac output increases with the increase in ventricular filling. Within 30 seconds of release of intrathoracic pressure, blood pressure *rises above its original level* because of reflex vasoconstriction initiated by small pulse pressure during phase III. The pressoreceptor stimulation in phase IV results in *transient bradycardia.*

       c) Hypoxemia: if acute, may cause seizures

    4. Intracranial abnormalities (see Table 64.5)

F. Selected conditions that may mimic syncope

    1. Hysterical faint (see Chapter 1): injury always avoided

    2. Drop attack: sudden fall to the ground, usually in older men, without loss of consciousness, probably due to brainstem ischemia (see Chapter 66)

    3. Cataplexy: sudden fall to the ground due to loss of extensor motor tone, without loss of consciousness

       a) Usually provoked by a sudden startle

       b) Part of the narcolepsy syndrome (see Chapter 68)

65/ COMMON DISORDERS OF MOVEMENT

TREMOR

A. Definition and classification
   1. Involuntary rhythmic or semirhythmic oscillation of a body part
   2. Major types: Table 65.1
B. Evaluation: Table 65.2
C. Common conditions presenting with tremor
   1. Physiological tremor
      a) Barely perceptible postural tremor that may be transiently exacerbated by illness, stress, certain drugs, alcohol (Table 65.1)
      b) Remove offending cause if possible; resolution may take 1–2 weeks
      c) If acute stress and tremor anticipated, propranolol 20–40 mg 1 hour before an anxiety-producing situation may be of help
   2. Essential tremor
      a) Onset insidious, usually after age 50
      b) Family history often positive (autosomal dominant)
      c) Alcohol, although its regular use should be discouraged, will suppress

Table 65.1. Conditions Associated With the Three Major Types of Tremor

Resting Tremor

Parkinson's disease

Secondary parkinsonism; postencphalitic, toxic (neuroleptics, reserpine, carbon monoxide, manganese, carbon disulfide, MPTP), tumor, trauma, vascular, metabolic (hypoparathyroidism, chronic hepatocerebral degeneration)

Heterogeneous disorders with parkinsonian features: striatonigral degeneration, olivopontocerebellar atrophy, progressive supranuclear palsy, Wilson's disease

Postural Tremor

Exaggerated physiological tremor
    Anxiety, fright, fatigue, exercise

Endocrine: thyrotoxicosis, hypoglycemia, pheochromocytoma

Drugs: any sympathomimetics, caffeine, theophylline, L-dopa, lithium, tricyclic antidepressants, neuroleptics, thyroid hormone, hypoglycemic agents, withdrawal from alcohol and sedative-hypnotic drugs

Essential tremor
    Familial (autosomal dominant)
    Sporadic
    With other neurological disorders: parkinsonism, torsion dystonia, spasmodic torticollis, neuropathy

Kinetic or Intention Tremor (Cerebellar Dysfunction)

Cerebellar degeneration, infarction

Multiple sclerosis

Wilson's disease

Drugs and toxins: phenytoin, barbiturates, lithium, alcohol, mercury, 5-fluorouracil
Miscellaneous cerebellar and cerebellofugal lesions

Adapted from Jankovic J, Fahn S: Physiologic and pathologic tremors: diagnosis, mechanism, and management. *Ann Intern Med* 93:460, 1980.

Table 65.2.　Principal Features of Different Tremor Types and Their Treatment

	Resting (Parkinsonian)	Postural (Essential)	Kinetic or Intention (Cerebellar)
History			
Age at onset	Age 60 and older	All ages, more common after age 60	All ages
Family history	Negative	Often positive (autosomal dominant)	Rarely positive
Response to alcohol	No effect	Often suppresses tremor	No effect
Physical Examination			
Frequency	3–6 Hz	6–12 Hz	3–5 Hz
Symmetry	Almost always begins unilaterally	Symmetrical	Either symmetrical or asymmetrical
Body part(s) affected	Arms > legs	Hand > head > voice	Arms > legs > trunk/head
Associated signs	Bradykinesia, rigidity, postural instability	None	Dysarthria, nystagmus, broad-based gait
Treatment	Anticholinergics	Primidone	Stereotactic surgery
	Amantadine	Propranolol	
	Sinemet	Alprazolam	
	Bromocriptine	Stereotactic surgery	
	Pergolide		
	Stereotactic surgery		

Hz (Hertz), cycles per second.

      1) Propranolol 10 mg twice a day, gradually increased, if necessary and if tolerated, to 320 mg/day (at a stable dose, Inderal LA can be prescribed)

      2) Primidone 25 mg/day, gradually increased as tolerated to 250 mg 3 times/day

      3) Propranolol and primidone can be prescribed together, if necessary, beginning at low doses, increasing in small increments

      4) Alprazolam (Xanax) 0.25–1.0 mg 3 times/day is effective

      5) If tremor is uncontrolled and is disabling, stereotactic thalamotomy should be considered

3. Tremor due to cerebellar dysfunction (kinetic or intention tremor)
   a) Rarely the only sign of cerebellar dysfunction; underlying disease (Table 65.1) usually known
   b) Unless an offending drug can be stopped, referral to a neurologist is warranted for management (stereotactic thalamotomy a possible solution)

PARKINSON'S DISEASE AND "PARKINSONISM"

A. Diagnosis
   1. Signs: tremor at rest, bradykinesia, muscular cogwheel rigidity, postural instability
   2. Symptoms: impaired handwriting, trouble walking, falling, poor coordination, trouble arising from a rested position, drooling, trouble turning in bed
   3. Associated manifestations: seborrhea, excessive perspiration, dysphagia (late), sialorrhea, autonomic dysfunction (most often orthostatic hypotension and constipation)
   4. Common unexpressed problems: impotence, concern about loss of independence, depression, embarrassment, fears of the future
   5. Differential diagnosis: Tables 65.3 and 65.4

B. Natural history: slowly progressive; life span rarely shortened; most patients remain functional

C. Treatment
   1. Education of patient and caregivers
   2. Encouragement of physical activities, especially walking
   3. Avoidance of falling (encourage walking with hands clasped behind back, use of a walker if necessary, removal of obstacles in the home)
   4. Drugs (Table 65.5)
      a) Withhold until there is significant impairment of function
      b) Begin treatment with either an anticholinergic or amantadine
         1) Anticholinergics take 2–4 weeks to maximum effect; of help early when tremor is a predominant sign
         2) Amantadine takes 2 weeks to maximum effect; benefit generally no longer than 6 months
      c) Almost all patients eventually require L-dopa; add to regimen when disease further impairs function, gradually reduce dose of anticholinergics or amantadine
      d) As disease progresses, bromocriptine, pergolide, or deprenyl should be added
   5. Surgical treatment
      a) Stereotactic thalamotomy or pallidotomy effective for

> > unresponsive disabling tremor or for severe fluctuations with
> > dyskinesias
> >
> > b) Fetal implantation still experimental

D. Dementia and depression
1. Dementia develops in 15–20% of patients; if complicated by
hallucinations, agitation, psychosis, sleep disturbance may require
a neuroleptic or a mild sedative (Chapter 4)
2. Depression develops in up to 50% of patients; responds to
tricyclics (Chapter 3)

Table 65.3   Differential Diagnosis of Parkinsonism

Toxins
  Manganese
  Carbon monoxide
  Carbon disulfide
  Cyanide
  Methanol
  MPTP
Drug-Induced
  Neuroleptics
  Metoclopramide (Reglan)
Multisystem degenerations
  Progressive supranuclear palsy
  Shy-Drager syndrome
  Olivopontocerebellar atrophy
  Striatonigral degeneration
Primary dementing illnesses
  Alzheimer's disease
  Creutzfeldt-Jakob syndrome
Heredofamilial diseases
  Wilson's disease
  Juvenile Huntington's disease
  Hallervorden-Spatz disease
Multi-infarct state
Calcification of the basal ganglia
  Idiopathic
  Hypoparathyroidism
Postencephalitic
Trauma
  Dementia pugilistica

Table 65.4.   Clinical Features Suggesting a Parkinsonian Syndrome Rather Than Idiopathic Parkinson's Disease

Little or no response to L-dopa
Young onset
Early-onset dementia
Rapid progression
Early-onset dysarthria or dysphagia
Prominent and early dysautonomia
Early falling
Impaired ocular motility
Positive family history
Lower motor neuron, cerebellar, or pyramidal signs

Table 65.5. Drugs Used for Parkinson's Disease

Drug	Available Preparation (mg)	Schedule	Starting Dose (mg)	Maintenance Drug (mg)
Anticholinergic Agents (representative examples)				
Trihexyphenidyl (Artane)	Scored tablets (2, 5) Elixir (2 mg/5 ml) Time-release capsules (5)	3–4 times daily Once daily	2 (May be substituted for regular Artane after maintenance dose is determined)	2–10 (May be substituted for regular Artane after maintenance dose is determined)
Benztropine mesylate (Cogentin)	Tablets (0.5, 1, 2)	Once or twice daily	1	0.5–6
Dopaminergic Agents				
Carbidopa L-dopa (Sinemet)	Scored tablets (10/100, 25/100, 25/250)	2–4 times daily	50/200 in 2 divided doses	400–500 L-dopa
Sinemet CR	Scored tablets (50/200)	2–4 times daily	50/200 twice daily	500–1000 L-dopa
Bromocriptine (Parlodel)	Scored tablets (2.5) Capsules (5.0)	2–3 times daily	1.25 daily	7.5–30
Pergolide (Permax)	Scored tablets (0.05, 0.25, 1.0)	3 times daily	0.05 daily	1–3
Deprenyl (Eldepryl)	Tablets (5.0)	2 times daily	5 daily	10
Anticholinergic and/or Dopaminergic Agents				
Amantadine (Symmetrel)	Capsules (100)	2 times daily	200 daily	200

66/ CEREBROVASCULAR DISEASE

OVERVIEW

A. Epidemiology
1. Eighty percent due to thrombotic or embolic infarction; 12% due to cerebral hemorrhage, 8% due to subarachnoid hemorrhage
2. Seventy percent in people over age 65

B. Risk factors
1. Previous stroke (10% recurrence in 1 year, 20% in 5 years)
2. Transient ischemic attacks (TIAs): see below
3. Hypertension (treatment reduces risk — see Chapter 46)
4. Cardiac impairment
   a) Embolic infarction highly associated with cardiac arrhythmias, especially atrial fibrillation (Chapter 43)
   b) Nonembolic infarction more likely in persons with left ventricular hypertrophy or with coronary artery disease
5. Other factors: family history, diabetes mellitus, hyperlipidemia, cigarette smoking, oral contraceptive use

C. Asymptomatic carotid disease
1. Usually detected by presence of a cervical bruit; no consensus on whether further evaluation is indicated
2. Carotid stenosis demonstrated by a noninvasive test, usually a duplex scan
3. Not yet clear what treatment is indicated, although risk of stroke is increased

CLASSIFICATION OF CEREBROVASCULAR EVENTS

A. Type of event
1. TIA: episode of focal cerebral dysfunction in which maximal symptoms develop in less than 5 minutes and which usually lasts 5–15 minutes but always resolves within 24 hours
2. Reversible ischemic neurological deficit (RIND): episode of focal cerebral dysfunction that lasts longer than 24 hours but always resolves within 3 weeks

B. Vascular territory
1. Symptoms and signs of events referable to the two major vascular territories (Table 66.1)
2. Lacunar syndromes: occlusion of penetrating nonanastomosing branches of major cerebral arteries
   a) Pure motor hemiparesis
   b) Pure sensory stroke
   c) Homolateral ataxia and crural paresis (ataxia and weakness on same side)
   d) Dysarthria-clumsy hand syndrome (with facial weakness, slight imbalance, positive Babinski on affected side)
   e) Multi-infarct dementia characterized by stepwise progression (see Chapter 5)

Table 66.1. Clinical Features of Ischemia Involving the Major Vascular Territories

CAROTID ARTERIAL DISEASE
  Monoparesis or hemiparesis
  Sensory loss or monoparesthesia or hemiparesthesia
  Speech or language disturbances
  Loss of vision in one eye or part of one eye (amaurosis fugax)
  Homonymous hemianopsia
  Cognitive impairment
VERTEBROBASILAR ARTERIAL DISEASE
  Vertigo, diplopia, dysphagia, or dysarthria when two occur together or when one occurs with any of the following:
  Paresis (any combination of the extremities)
  Sensory loss or paresthesias (any combination of the extremities)
  Ataxia
  Homonymous hemianopsia (unilateral or bilateral)

SYMPTOMATIC PATIENTS
A. Evaluation
  1. In hospital if within hours to a few days of event; in ambulatory setting if more than a few days from event
  2. History
    a) Identify risk factors: see above
    b) Classify focal symptoms: Table 66.1
  3. Physical examination: assess blood pressure, cardiac function, cerebrovascular function, peripheral blood vessels, fundi
  3. Brain computed tomography (noncontrast) scanning or magnetic resonance imaging (more expensive) to assess evidence of previous events, exclude lesions other than those of cerebral vascular disease
  4. If there is suspicion of heart disease, transthoracic echocardiogram to look for source of emboli (transesophageal echocardiogram if no source found); ambulatory (Holter) monitoring to look for arrhythmia
  5. Persons with carotid territory events (Table 66.1) should have a noninvasive carotid evaluation (preferably a duplex scan)
B. Early management
  1. Atherothrombotic events
    a) Medical treatment
      1) Risk factors (see above) reduction
      2) Anticoagulant therapy: no proved efficacy, although often prescribed for patients with high-grade intracranial stenosis or preocclusive extracranial carotid bifurcation disease who are not surgical candidates
      3) Antiplatelet drugs (see Chapter 37)
    b) Carotid endarterectomy
      1) For symptomatic patients with carotid occlusion of 70% or more
      2) For symptomatic patients with carotid occlusion of less than 70%, efficacy not yet known
  2. Cardioembolic events
    a) Anticoagulation with warfarin (Chapter 37) for patients with

atrial fibrillation, recent myocardial infarction, dilated
cardiomyopathy, rheumatic or prosthetic heart valves
b) Value of aspirin in patients with atrial fibrillation unknown

STROKE PROGNOSIS AND MANAGEMENT

A. Prognosis
1. Worse with advancing age
2. Worse after hemorrhage than after thrombotic or embolic events
3. Spontaneous improvement most rapid in the first few months,
rare after 2 years
4. Approximately 50% are independent at 2 years
5. Depression common, especially after right frontal damage
6. High mortality: 50–60% by 5 years, most in first year; leading
cause is cardiovascular disease

B. Management
1. Role of the family
a) Divide duties
b) Allow patient to take responsibility for as much as, but not for
more than, he or she can
c) Do not isolate patient
2. Role of rehabilitation
a) Offer whenever possible
b) Should begin as soon as possible
c) Rehabilitation begun in hospital should be continued in the
patient's home or in ambulatory care facilities
3. Management of psychological and behavioral sequelae: see Table
66.2
4. Management of late complications
a) Shoulder problems
1) See Chapter 47
2) Shoulder-hand syndrome
(a) Painful shoulder associated with stiffness and swelling of
hands and fingers in 5%
(b) Onset may be acute or symptoms may develop over 6
months
(c) Ultimately, atrophy of the muscles of the hand,
demineralization of the carpal bones occur
(d) Treatment: nonsteroidal anti-inflammatory drugs, heat
to the shoulder, abduction and rotation exercises
(Chapter 47); refer to a neurosurgeon for consideration
of a stellate block if no improvement in a month
b) Complications of inactivity (thrombophlebitis and pressure
sores): use elastic stockings, reposition immobile patients
frequently
c) Neurological complications
1) Peripheral neuropathy from prolonged pressure on a
paralyzed limb: difficult to recognize, responds to physical
therapy (Chapter 67)
2) Seizure in 2.5–5% of patients (see Chapter 63)
3) Transient worsening of stroke-related deficits in course of
major intercurrent illness

Table 66.2.   Recommendations for Dealing With Behavioral Problems Associated With Permanent Loss of Higher Functions in Stroke Patients

LEFT HEMISPHERE DAMAGE

Right hemiplegics will often have difficulties with speech and language. They also tend to be somewhat cautious, anxious, and disorganized when attempting a new task. Keep in mind the following suggestions:
1. Do not underestimate the patient's ability to learn and communicate even if he cannot use speech.
2. If he cannot use speech, try other forms of communication. Pantomime and demonstration are often useful.
3. Do not overestimate his understanding of speech and overload him with "static."
4. Do not shout. Keep messages simple and brief.
5. Do not use special voices.
6. Divide tasks into simple steps.
7. Give much feedback and many indications of progress.

RIGHT HEMISPHERE DAMAGE

If the patient is having difficulty with self-care activities, you can expect spatial-perceptual deficits. He will tend to talk better than he can actually perform. He may be impulsive or careless. Remember, when working with the patient who has significant spatial-perceptual deficits:
1. Do not overestimate his abilities. Spatial-perceptual difficulties are easy to miss.
2. Use verbal cues if he has difficulty with demonstration.
3. Break tasks into small steps and give much feedback.
4. Watch to see what he can do safely rather than taking his word for it.
5. Minimize clutter around him.
6. Avoid rapid movement around the patient.
7. Highlight visual reference points.

ONE-SIDED NEGLECT

One-sided neglect is a problem that involves more than a simple visual field cut or hearing loss. It can occur in both right and left hemiplegics but seems to be more common and more persistent among left hemiplegics. When dealing with a neglect problem, you should:
1. Keep the unimpaired side toward the action unless specifically working with the neglected side.
2. Avoid trapping the patient in an unnecessarily confined environment.
3. Avoid nagging but give frequent cues to aid orientation.
4. Provide reminders of the neglected side.
5. Arrange the environment to maximize performance.

MEMORY PROBLEMS

Some memory problems can be expected in most stroke patients. When working with memory deficits, you can often increase the patient's ability to perform if you:
1. Establish a fixed routine whenever possible.
2. Keep messages short to fit his retention span.
3. Present new information one step at a time.
4. Allow the patient to finish one step before proceeding to the next.
5. Give frequent indications of effective progress; he may forget his past "successes."
6. Train in settings that resemble, as much as possible, the setting in which the behavior is to be practiced.
7. Use memory aids such as appointment books, written notes, and schedule cards whenever possible.
8. Use familiar objects and old associations when teaching new tasks.

Adapted from: *Strokes: Why Do They Behave That Way?* American Heart Association.

67/ PERIPHERAL NEUROPATHY

DEFINITIONS

A. Mononeuropathy: lesions of individual nerve roots or peripheral nerves
B. Mononeuropathy multiplex: lesions of two or more named nerves, usually sequentially and not contiguously
C. Polyneuropathy: lesions of many peripheral nerves, often symmetrically

APPROACH TO THE PATIENT

A. Symptoms
  1. Hyperesthesia, paresthesias, dysesthesias, weakness, muscle cramps
  2. If autonomic nerves are involved, the following symptoms are common: impotence, urinary retention or overflow incontinence, constipation or diarrhea, diminished sweating, orthostatic hypotension
  3. Innocuous stimuli may be perceived as painful
  4. Heaviness or coldness of extremities is common
  5. Unsteady gait possible if there is loss of position sense
B. Signs
  1. Sensory loss, weakness, muscle atrophy, reduced or lost tendon reflexes, and, if autonomic involvement, trophic skin changes
  2. Loss of pain, vibration sense in a stocking-glove distribution is characteristic of polyneuropathy
  3. Distal weakness characteristic of polyneuropathies may eventually lead to atrophy of the small vessels of the feet and hands
C. Causes
  1. Of mononeuropathy and mononeuropathy multiplex: Table 67.1
  2. Of polyneuropathy: Table 67.2 (differential diagnosis: Table 67.3)

INVESTIGATIONS

A. Clinical laboratory
  1. If cause not obvious, measure erythrocyte sedimentation rate, fasting blood glucose level, serum creatinine concentration, complete blood count, chest x-ray, serum and urine protein electrophoresis

---

Table 67.1. Common Causes of Mononeuropathy and Mononeuropathy Multiplex

MONONEUROPATHY
  Trauma — direct (occupational, recreational, e.g., ulnar or peroneal nerve), compression and entrapment (e.g., carpal tunnel, root compression, etc.)
  Infection — herpes zoster
  Toxins (e.g., penicillin injection into a sciatic nerve)
  Vascular — vasculitis, diabetes mellitus
  Neoplasm — neurofibroma, lymphoma
MONONEUROPATHY MULTIPLEX
  Diabetes mellitus
  Vasculitis

Table 67.2. Polyneuropathy: Etiology and Mode of Predominant Involvement

	Predominant Involvement
METABOLIC	
Diabetes mellitus	
Polyneuropathy	S,SM,A
Mononeuropathy	SM
Lumbar plexopathy (diabetic amyotrophy)	M>S
Alcohol and vitamin deficiency	SM
Uremia	SM
Porphyria	M>S
TOXIC (see Table 67.5)	
Lead	M>S
Pyridoxine	S
cis-Platinum	S
Most other toxic agents	SM
INFECTIOUS	
Diphtheria	M
Leprosy	S
Lyme disease	SM
HIV	S,SM,M
INFLAMMATORY AND COLLAGEN-VASCULAR	
Guillain-Barré syndrome	M
Chronic inflammatory demyelinating polyneuropathy	M
Systemic lupus erythematosus	SM
Polyarteritis nodosa	SM
Sjögren's syndrome	SM,S
Rheumatoid arthritis	SM
NEOPLASTIC	
Carcinomatous	S,SM
Paraproteinemia, plasma cell dyscrasias	S,SM,A
Benign monoclonal gammopathy	S,SM
Waldenström's macroglobulinemia	SM,M
Cryoglobinemia	SM
HEREDITARY	
Hereditary motor and sensory neuropathies	M>S
Amyloidosis	S>M,A
Dysautonomia (Riley-Day)	S,A
Tangier (Bassen-Kornzweig)	S
Fabry	S

A, autonomic; *M*, motor; *S*, sensory.

    2. If no clues to diagnosis, extensive screening to look for an unusual condition not warranted

B. Nerve conduction studies
    1. To distinguish axonal from demyelinating processes (Table 67.3)
    2. To establish a baseline
    3. Measures latency of response, conduction velocity, amplitude of response by stimulating a nerve at one point and recording response (motor or sensory) at another

C. Electromyography (EMG)
    1. Principal use is to help define entrapment neuropathies and distinguish them from more proximal radicular compression
    2. Not usually of help in patients with polyneuropathy
    3. Can be of help in distinguishing neuropathic from myopathic disorders (Table 67.4)

Table 67.3.   Polyneuropathy: Differential Diagnosis[a]

TIME COURSE
  Acute (days)
    Guillain-Barré syndrome
    Porphyric neuropathy
    Vasculitis neuropathy
    Some toxins (e.g., triorthocresyl phosphate)
  Subacute (weeks)
    Many toxins (see Table 67.5)
    Nutritional neuropathies
    Carcinomatous neuropathies
    Diabetic amyotrophy
    Uremic neuropathy
  Relapsing
    Chronic inflammatory demyelinating polyneuropathy
    Refsum's disease
    Porphyria
  Chronic (many months or years)
    Diabetic motor and sensory neuropathy
    Alcoholic neuropathy
    Chronic inflammatory demyelinating polyneuropathy
  Very chronic (childhood onset)
    Hereditary, motor and sensory neuropathies (e.g., Charcot-Marie-Tooth disease)
SELECTIVE FUNCTIONAL INVOLVEMENT[b]
  Predominantly motor
    Guillain-Barré syndrome
    Chronic inflammatory demyelinating polyneuropathy
    Acute intermittent porphyria
    Lead neuropathy
    Hereditary motor and sensory neuropathies (e.g., Charcot-Marie-Tooth)
    Diphtheritic neuropathy
  Predominantly sensory
    Global sensory loss
    Diabetes mellitus
    Carcinomatous sensory neuropathy (ganglioradiculitis)
    Paraproteinemic and cryoglobulinemic neuropathy
    Tabes dorsalis
  Dissociated loss of pain and thermal sensibility
    Diabetes (small fiber type)
    Amyloidosis
    Hereditary sensory neuropathies
    Lepromatous leprosy
  Dissociated loss of joint position and vibration sensibility
    Subacute combined degeneration
    Friedreich's ataxia
  Autonomic neuropathy
    Diabetes
    Amyloid
    Acute, chronic, and relapsing pandysautonomia
    Dysautonomia (Riley-Day)
DISTRIBUTION[c]
  Proximal weakness
    Guillain-Barré syndrome
    Porphyria
    Diabetic amyotrophy
    Carcinomatous neuropathy with proximal weakness ("carcinomatous neuromyopathy")
    Spinal muscular atrophies
  Proximal sensory loss
    Porphyria
    Tangier disease (analphalipoproteinemia)
  Temperature-related distribution
    Lepromatous leprosy

Modified from Griffin, JW, Cornblath DR: Peripheral neuropathies. In: Harvey, AM, et al (eds): *Principles and Practice of Medicine*, ed 22. New York, Appleton & Lange, 1988.
[a] The most common etiologies are set in *italics*.
[b] Most polyneuropathies produce sensory and motor disturbances.
[c] Most polyneuropathies produce distal involvement.

Table 67.4. Electromyography: Patterns Typical of Nerve and Muscle Disorders

Disorder	Insertional Activity	Complete Rest (Spontaneous Activity)	Action Potentials	Recruitment
Denervation[a]	Increased	Fibrillations, positive waves, fasciculations	High amplitude, long duration, polyphasic	Reduced
Myopathic				
Myopathy	Normal	Normal or rare fibrillations	Small amplitude, short duration, polyphasic	Early
Myositis	Increased	Fibrillations, positive waves	Small amplitude, short duration, polyphasic	Early

[a] Neuropathy, radiculopathy, disc disease.

D. Nerve biopsy
   1. Only for patients in whom a specific histological diagnosis (e.g., amyloidosis, vasculitis) would be useful in deciding about management
   2. Always leads to fixed numbness in distribution of biopsied (sensory) nerve

COMMON PROBLEMS

A. Guillain-Barré syndrome
   1. An acute (Table 67.3) polyradiculoneuropathy characterized by rapidly progressive symmetrical paralysis usually moving from lower to upper extremities
   2. Most cases follow a mild viral illness by 10–12 days, but the syndrome may also be associated with pregnancy, surgery, influenza vaccination, or HIV infection
   3. Sensory loss mild
   4. Cranial nerve palsies may be present
   5. Spinal fluid may show an increased protein concentration and normal cell counts
   6. Warrants hospitalization for monitoring and support
   7. Most patients (90%) recover completely or nearly completely in up to 18 months
B. Diabetic neuropathy: see Chapter 56
C. Alcoholic neuropathy
   1. Often a distal symmetric sensorimotor neuropathy
   2. Examination frequently reveals diminished ankle reflexes and a stocking-glove pattern of decreased sensation
   3. Treatment includes improved nutrition, vitamin replacement, and effective rehabilitation for addiction (see Chapter 7)
   4. Usually partial recovery if it occurs
D. Carcinomatous neuropathy
   1. Distal sensorimotor
      a) Usually affects feet first
      b) Progressive over weeks to months
      c) May improve if cancer responds to therapy
   2. Carcinomatous sensory
      a) Begins subacutely, with pain and paresthesias of lower and upper extremities
      b) A severe loss of position sense develops over weeks, so that patient may be unable to stand
      c) Underlying tumor often small cell cancer but may originate in breast, ovary, uterus, or gastrointestinal tract
      d) Usually progressive
   3. Paraproteinemic
      a) Often characterized by burning sensations, autonomic dysfunction (see above)
      b) May respond to treatment of underlying disease
E. Toxic neuropathy
   1. Causes: see Table 67.5
   2. Classically associated with chronic low-dose exposure over months to years but may occur more rapidly if dose of toxin is high
   3. No distinct pattern of involvement

Table 67.5. Toxins Associated With Peripheral Neuropathies

INDUSTRIAL
  Pesticides — organophosphates, dichlorophenoxyacetate (2,4-D), Vacor rodenticide
  Metal work — lead, arsenic, mercury, thallium, methyl bromide
  Plastics, synthetic fabrics — *n*-hexane, methyl, *n*-butyl ketone, acrylamide, carbon disulfide,
    perchlorethylene, trichlorethylene, dimethylaminoproprionitrile
  Gases — carbon monoxide, ethylene oxide
EUPHORIANTS
  Glue sniffing — *n*-hexane, solvents
  Nitrous oxide inhalation — whipped cream dispensers, dental offices
PHARMACOTHERAPEUTIC AGENTS
  Antimicrobial — isoniazid, nitrofurantoin, metronidazole
  Cardiovascular — hydralazine, procainamide, amiodarone
  Other — phenytoin, colchicine, disulfiram, pyridoxine, vincristine, *cis*-platinum, taxol,
    thalidomide

    4. May resolve if exposure stops
  F. HIV infection
    1. A painful sensory neuropathy develops late in 30% of patients;
       treatment symptomatic (see below)
    2. Multiple mononeuropathies have been reported in infected
       patients who do not yet have AIDS
    3. Acute and chronic polyneuropathies of Guillain-Barré type (see
       above) occurring early in infection have been described
  G. Compression and entrapment neuropathies
    1. Median nerve (carpal tunnel syndrome)
      a) Causes
        1) Decrease in size of tunnel, e.g., Colles' fracture,
          rheumatoid arthritis
        2) Enlargement of the nerve, e.g., amyloid, neuroma, edema
          in diabetics
        3) Increase in volume of other structures in tunnel, e.g.,
          tenosynovitis, ganglion, lipoma, urate deposits in gout,
          hematoma, fluid retention in pregnancy
        4) Repetitive movements of wrist, e.g., meat processing, fruit
          packing, typing, or repeated stress over the base of the
          palm, e.g., use of various tools, or vibration exposure, e.g.,
          use of air-powered tools
      b) Manifestations and evaluations
        1) Symptoms
          (a) Onset usually insidious, nocturnal
          (b) Episodic tingling and numbness in hand progressing
             to burning, aching, painful numbness, feeling of
             clumsiness
          (c) Often an accompanying dull ache in the forearm,
             sometimes reaching the shoulder
          (d) At first, relief may be gotten by hanging the arm out
             of bed or shaking the hand
          (e) Symptoms may occur without signs for many years
        2) Signs
          (a) Ultimately, sensory loss over the first three and one-
             half digits, then thenar atrophy, weakness of thumb

        (b) Pressure over flexor wrist or prolonged hyperflexion of wrist may reproduce sensory symptoms (Phalen's sign)

        (c) Percussion of the nerve at the wrist may cause sharp pain and tingling (Tinel's sign)

    3) Nerve conduction studies often needed to confirm diagnosis

  c) Treatment

    1) Immobilization with an anterior splint from fingers to upper forearm will often alleviate symptoms

    2) If symptoms persist or if there is thenar atrophy, surgery is indicated

2. Ulnar nerve

  a) Causes

    1) Compression of the nerve at the cubital tunnel at the elbow during anesthesia, intoxication, coma, trauma or by activities that require repeated or sustained flexion of the elbow

    2) Ganglion, rheumatoid arthritis, trauma distal to cubital tunnel

  b) Manifestations and evaluation

    1) Symptoms: elbow pain, often nocturnal; shooting pain in the hand or fifth digit, paresthesias and hyperesthesia of fourth and fifth fingers; ultimately, weakness of grasp or pinch

    2) Signs: sensory loss over symptomatic areas, decreased grip and pinch strength, atrophy of the muscles to the fourth and fifth fingers

    3) Nerve conduction studies abnormal in one-third to one-half of patients

  c) Treatment

    1) If symptoms intermittent or mild, wearing elbow pads and splinting the elbow (wrap a pillow around it at night) may help

    2) If compression is at the wrist, a splint is usually adequate

    3) Surgery if symptoms progressive or intolerable

3. Radial nerve

  a) Causes

    1) Prolonged hyperabduction of the arm (surgery or sleep)

    2) Incorrect use of a crutch (axillary pressure)

    3) Compression of the nerve against the humerus (e.g., by sleeping with the arm draped over a chair)

    4) Compression of the nerve in the forearm from a lipoma, fibroma, or callus from a fracture

  b) Manifestations (depend on location of compression) and evaluation

    1) Elbow flexion and supination may be slightly affected

    2) Wrist drop, finger drop

    3) High lesions may produce sensory loss over the dorsum of the hand

    4) Nerve conduction study and EMG may be of help in localizing and quantifying compression

  c) Treatment

       1) Splinting by an occupational therapist usually results in recovery within weeks to a few months

       2) If finger drop alone, surgery should be considered if no recovery in 1–3 months

4. Peroneal nerve
   a) Causes
      1) Improperly applied casts, tight stockings, falling asleep with the side of the leg against a protruding object
      2) Prolonged leg crossing, squatting, or kneeling
   b) Manifestations and evaluations
      1) Painless weakness of ankle dorsiflexion (foot drop) and foot eversion and sensory loss over lateral calf and dorsum of foot
      2) Nerve conduction studies and EMG may be useful
      3) If no clear history of trauma, the popliteal fossa should be imaged to rule out a mass lesion
   c) Treatment
      1) Most patients recover within weeks to months; surgical exploration should be considered in severe cases with no clear-cut etiology
      2) Avoid leg crossing, squatting
      3) A custom-fitted ankle-foot orthotic is recommended

5. Tibial nerve (tarsal tunnel syndrome)
   a) Causes: fracture or dislocation at the ankle, tenosynovitis
   b) Manifestations and evaluation
      1) Pain and dysesthesia in sole; pain worsens with rest, worse at night
      2) Percussion over tarsal tunnel may produce shooting pain to the sole (Tinel's sign)
      3) Sensory loss, if present, is localized to sole, tips of toes
      4) Weakness of intrinsic muscles may impair walking
      5) Nerve conduction studies very useful; EMG demonstrates denervation
   c) Treatment
      1) Remove any external pressure
      2) Definitive treatment is surgical

6. Femoral nerve
   a) Causes
      1) Stab wounds to groin or hip, pelvic fractures, inguinal surgery, angiography
      2) Stretch injuries from prolonged lithotomy position or with hyperextension during exercise
      3) Pressure from hematoma or abscess
   b) Manifestations and evaluation
      1) Buckling of the knee, frequent falls
      2) Pain in the groin radiating into the thigh
      3) Sensory loss in the anteromedial thigh and medial leg
      4) Weakness of knee extension, loss of knee jerk
      5) Must be distinguished from diabetic lumbar plexopathy (see Chapter 56)
   c) Treatment: depends on cause, e.g., drainage of abscess

7. Saphenous nerve
   a) Causes: vein stripping and knee surgery

       b) Manifestations
         1) Pain and numbness of medial knee
         2) Pain may worsen with walking, climbing
         3) Pressure at Hunter's canal (10 cm proximal to medial condyle of the femur) produces radiating pain
       c) Treatment: injection of local anesthetic if pain severe
    8. Sciatic nerve
       a) Causes
         1) Hip fractures, dislocation, arthroplastic surgery
         2) Compression of nerve in chronically bedridden patients or after sitting on a hard edge
         3) Hematoma, endometriosis, lipoma, aneurysms of gluteal artery
         4) Misplaced injections into buttocks
       b) Manifestations and evaluation
         1) Mimics pain of L5-S1 radiculopathy (Chapter 49)
         2) EMG may be useful
    9. Lateral femoral cutaneous nerve
       a) Causes: obesity, acute abdominal enlargement (pregnancy, ascites), external trauma, diabetes mellitus
       b) Manifestations and evaluation
         1) Burning pain, paresthesia, decreased sensation over lateral thigh
         2) No motor involvement
       c) Treatment
         1) Weight loss
         2) Local injection of anesthetic for severe pain
   10. Bell's palsy
       a) Causes
         1) Usually unknown
         2) Lyme disease
         3) HIV infection
       b) Manifestations and evaluation
         1) Unilateral facial paralysis within hours of onset
         2) Less commonly, loss of taste on anterior two-thirds of tongue, accentuation of sounds in affected ear, pain behind ear
       c) Treatment
         1) If recent onset (<4 days) and no contraindications, 10-day course of prednisone (60 mg for 3 days, tapering by 10 mg each day thereafter)
         2) Surgical decompression no longer done
       d) Prognosis
         1) 85% recover completely within weeks to months; remainder recover incompletely, but severe residual weakness is rare
         2) Synkinesis, contraction of all facial muscles on affected side when one or a few muscles are moved, may occur

OTHER PROBLEMS

A. Restless leg syndrome
   1. An aching or painful crawling sensation in the calf at rest, especially in bed; walking provides some relief

2. Restricting caffeine use and exercising before bedtime may be of help, as may aspirin or acetaminophen
3. Clonazepam (0.5–2.0 mg) or triazolam (0.125 mg) may relieve nocturnal symptoms
4. In severe cases, carbidopa/L-dopa combinations (1–2 25/100 tablets) at bedtime may be effective

B. Muscle cramps
1. Localized involuntary painful contractions that produce a visibly palpable, hard bulging muscle
2. Ordinary cramps may be stopped by stretching the affected muscle
3. Frequent cramps associated with denervating diseases, fatiguing exercises, salt depletion, dehydration, pregnancy, hypothyroidism, alcoholism, uremia, hypomagnesemia
4. Daytime cramps, if no correctable condition exists, may respond to carbamazepine (100–500 mg twice a day), phenytoin (300–500 mg/day), or amitriptyline (25–75 mg at bedtime)
5. Nocturnal cramps often respond to quinine sulfate, 300 mg, or clonazepam, 0.25–0.5 mg, at bedtime

68/ SLEEP DISORDERS

HISTORY (TABLE 68.1)

A. Insomnia, the perception of not sleeping well
  1. Transient
    a) Lasts no more than a few days
    b) Often associated with a recognizable stimulus (e.g., grief, anxiety, anticipation)
  2. Short term
    a) Up to 3 weeks
    b) Environmental stressors may be evident but often more severe than those associated with transient insomnia
  3. Chronic
    a) Lasts longer than 3 weeks
    b) Causes
      1) Psychiatric disorders (e.g., depression, anxiety, dementia)
      2) Medical disorders, especially if associated with pain or dyspnea
      3) Neurological disorders (e.g., Parkinson's disease, stroke, seizures)
      4) Medications, especially stimulants, overuse of sedatives, also bronchodilators, corticosteroids, some antihypertensives, antiarrhythmics, anticonvulsants, antidepressants
      5) Substance abuse (e.g., cocaine, opiates, alcohol)
      6) Circadian rhythm disturbance (e.g., constantly changing work shifts, permanent night work, or delayed sleep phase syndrome, i.e., normal deviation of sleep but out of phase with the day/night cycle)
      7) Other sleep disorders: see below
      8) Environmental factors (e.g., living near an airport, high ambient temperature)

Table 68.1. Sleep History

Questions for the patient
Nighttime
  What time do you go to bed?
  Are you sleepy at that time?
  How long does it take you to fall asleep?
  Once you fall asleep, do you sleep soundly through the night?
  Do you feel restless during the night?
  Have you been told that you snore?
  Have you been told that you move in your sleep?
Daytime
  What time do you awaken? (Work days, weekends, and vacations?)
  Do you use an alarm clock?
  Do you feel rested when you get up?
  Do you awaken with a headache?
  Are you tired during the daytime?
  Do you nap? (What time? How long?)
  Do you fall asleep at undesired times?
Questions for the sleep partner
  Does your bed partner move?
  Does your bed partner seem to stop breathing at times?
  Does your bed partner kick or jerk his/her legs during sleep?

Table 68.2.   Symptoms Associated With the Complaint of Excessive Daytime Sleepiness

Sleepiness	Increased aggressive behavior
Fatigue	Depression
Decreased motivation	Frequent motor vehicle accidents or near-accidents
Forgetfulness	Accidents at work
Poor concentration	

Table 68.3.   Sleepiness Scale

Severity	Falls asleep while
Mild	Watching television
	Reading
	Attending lectures
	Riding in car
	Sitting in church
Moderate	Visiting family and friends
	At work
	During extended driving
Severe	During local driving or at stop light
	Eating a meal

      9) Poor sleep hygiene (see below)
B. Excessive daytime sleepiness (EDS)
  1. Symptoms: Table 68.2
  2. Indices of severity: Table 68.3
  3. Causes
    a) Drugs (e.g., alcohol, benzodiazepines, antidepressants, neuroleptics, antihistamines)
    b) Medical conditions (e.g., chronic renal or hepatic disease)
    c) Disturbed nocturnal sleep (see Insomnia, above)
    d) Sleep apnea (see below)
    e) Chronic insufficient sleep
      1) Most common causes are personal life-styles (e.g., shift workers, house staff) and poor sleep habits (e.g., watching TV until late, getting up early)
      2) Eight-hour sleeping pattern needs to be established, and patients should then keep a written record for a month of when they fall asleep and when they awaken
        (a) If patient is sleeping 8 hours and daytime sleepiness has abated, problem is solved
        (b) If patient is sleeping 8 hours and still sleepy during day, referral to a sleep center is indicated
    f) Chronic fatigue syndrome: see Chapter 38
    g) Narcolepsy, having the following clinical features (Table 68.4)
      1) In addition to excessive daytime sleepiness, loss or absence of muscle tone and strength is an important part of the syndrome
        (a) Cataplexy — the loss of muscle tone or strength while awake, precipitated by sudden burst of emotion — occurs only with narcolepsy
        (b) Sleep paralysis — total inability to move or speak for up

Table 68.4.   Clinical Features of Narcolepsy

Altered levels of alertness and attentiveness	REM-related disturbances
Sleepiness	Cataplexy
Poor concentration	Sleep paralysis
Memory difficulty	Hypnagogic hallucinations
Automatic behavior	**Sleep disturbances**
Blurred or poorly focused vision	Frequent awakenings
	Vivid dreams
	Sleep terrors

REM, rapid eye movement.

Table 68.5.   Disorders Associated With Sleep Apnea

Obstructive sleep apnea
  Narrowing of upper airway
    Nasal abnormalities (deviation, polyps)
    Oral abnormalities (tonsillar hypertrophy, acromegaly)
    Bony abnormalities (micrognathia)
    Shy-Drager syndrome
    Myotonic dystrophy
  Hypothyroidism
Central sleep apnea
  Cerebral disorders (stroke)
  Brainstem-spinal disorder (polio, infarction, neoplasia, surgery)
  Congestive heart failure (increased circulation time)

        to a few minutes just before falling asleep or just after
        awakening — may occur without narcolepsy or EDS
    2) Hypnagogic hallucinations and EDS despite normal
       nocturnal sleep
C. Breathing problems during sleep (sleep apneas)
  1. Definitions
    a) Central apnea: cessation of respiratory effort
    b) Obstructive apnea: associated with occlusion of upper airway
       and continued respiratory effort
  2. Epidemiology
    a) Twice as common in men
    b) More prevalent in obese people
    c) Central apnea more common in elderly
    d) Various associated conditions: Table 68.5
  3. Presentation
    a) Snoring: loud, intermittent, punctuated by respiratory efforts
       without obvious airflow
    b) Sleep is fragmented, leading to daytime sleepiness of varying
       severity (Table 68.3)
    c) Physical examination may be normal (central apnea in elderly)
       or reveal neurological impairment or obvious evidence of
       airway obstruction (e.g., large tonsils)
    d) Course
      1) Obstructive: chronic, progressive, occasionally leading to
        cor pulmonale, life-threatening arrhythmias
      2) Central: dependent on underlying disease; if no obvious
        disease, course and prognosis unknown

e) Diagnosis: to be definitive requires a sleep study at a sleep center

D. Sleep-associated leg discomfort and movements
   1. Restless leg syndrome (RLS) and periodic leg movements (PLM) of sleep are the major complaints
      a) Etiology usually not known
      b) More common in elderly
      c) RLS sometimes associated with iron deficiency anemia, dialysis, dopamine agonists and antagonists
      d) PLM sometimes associated with use of antidepressants
      e) RLS or PLM may be associated with disorders of spinal cord or peripheral nerves
   2. Components of RLS
      a) Sensory
         1) Deep uneasy feeling (not pain) of one or both legs
         2) Compulsion to move a part or all of the leg (akathisia), worse in late evening
         3) Discomfort worsens with rest, improves with movement
      b) Motor
         1) Brief periodic movements of one or both legs during sleep (PLM) may cause awakening
         2) PLM and the sensory components of RLS may occur independently

E. Abnormal behaviors emanating from sleep (parasomnias)
   1. Arousal disorders
      a) General characteristics
         1) Tend to occur during first third of night
         2) Frequency may range from several times a night to less than once a year
         3) Commonly, amnesia for the event
         4) Affected individual typically will not awaken during event
      b) Sleepwalking: usually without danger to the affected individual
      c) Sleep terrors: often associated with screaming, an attempt to avoid perceived danger
      d) Confusional arousal: disorientation and incomplete awakening following an arousing stimulus; likelihood of an event increased by sleep deprivation, sedation
   2. Nightmares: usually result in full awakenings, tend to occur toward end of night
   3. Rapid eye movement behavior disorder: may be associated with violent physical activity (e.g., kicking out, punching), more common in elderly

MANAGEMENT

A. Insomnia
   1. Sleep hygiene measures: Table 68.6
   2. Behavioral management
      a) Relaxation techniques (see Chapter 2)
      b) Stimulus control therapy, minimizing the time the patient is sleepless in bed (as detailed in Table 68.6)
      c) Sleep restriction therapy, limiting time in bed to specific hours

Table 68.6.   Sleep Hygiene Measures

1. Try to maintain a regular sleep/wake schedule. It is particularly important to get up at about the same time every day.
2. Avoid afternoon or evening napping if you have difficulty getting to sleep at night.
3. Allow yourself enough time in bed for adequate sleep duration (e.g., 11:00 P.M. to 7:00 A.M.). Don't spend excessive time in bed, hoping to get more sleep.
4. Spend some idle time reflecting on the day's events before going to bed. Make a list of concerns and how you might solve them.
5. Avoid alcohol and caffeine in the evening.
6. Reserve the bed for sleep and sex. Don't do homework or pay bills in bed.
7. Avoid stressful activities at bedtime. Develop a relaxing and enjoyable routine prior to retiring to bed (e.g., reading, television).
8. Minimize annoying noise, light, or temperature extremes.
9. Consider a light snack before bedtime.
10. Exercise regularly, but not late in the evening.
11. Don't try harder and harder to fall asleep. If you are unable to sleep, do something else instead.
12. Avoid smoking.

Table 68.7.   Benzodiazepine and Related Hypnotic Medications

Generic Name	Brand Name	Available Strengths and Dose Ranges (mg)
Shorter acting		
Triazolam	Halcion	0.125–0.25
Zolpidem[a]	Ambien	5–10
Intermediate acting		
Estazolam	ProSom	1–2
Temazepam	Restoril	7.5–15–30
Longer acting		
Flurazepam	Dalmane	15–30
Quazepam	Doral	7.5–15

[a] A nonbenzodiazepine agent.

3. Circadian manipulations
   a) When traveling across time zones, follow the day/night pattern of the new time zone as quickly as possible
   b) Become exposed to bright light soon after awakening in morning; avoid bright light late in the day
4. Hypnotic medications
   a) Only indicated for short-term use, of help mostly for transient insomnia
   b) Most commonly prescribed drugs
      1) Benzodiazepines and related drugs (Table 68.7)
         (a) Sleep onset insomnia may respond well to a short-acting agent
         (b) Sleep continuity problems may respond well to short- or intermediate-duration preparations
      2) Sedating antidepressants especially for depressed persons (see Chapter 5)
      3) Over-the-counter antihistamines (Table 68.8): limited efficacy compared to benzodiazepines but relatively safe
B. Narcolepsy and idiopathic hypersomnolence

Table 68.8. Constituents of Commonly Used Over-the-Counter Sleep Remedies

Product Name	Constituent	Dose (mg)
Miles Nervine[a]		
Sleep-Eze		
Sominex[c]	Pyrilamine maleate[b]	25
Nytol		
Unisom Nighttime Sleep Aid	Doxylamine succinate[d]	25
Benadryl	Diphenhydramine	25

[a] This product no longer contains bromine.
[b] Antihistamine of the ethylenediamine class.
[c] This product no longer contains scopolamine.
[d] Antihistamine of the ethanolamine class.

Table 68.9. Nonpharmacological Treatment of Narcolepsy

Brief daytime naps as needed
Light meals during the day
Remain active if at all possible
If sleepy, get up, walk around, take a break
Avoid sedative medication
Use caffeinated beverages as needed
Add exercise to the daily routine

Table 68.10. Stimulant Medication

Generic Name	Brand	Initial Dose (mg)	Maximum Dose (mg)	Available Strengths (mg)
Pemoline	Cylert	18.75 q.d.	37.5 b.i.d.	18.75, 37.5, 75
Methylphenidate	Ritalin	5 t.i.d.	30 q.i.d.	5, 10, 20
Dextroamphetamine	Dexedrine	5 b.i.d.	40 t.i.d.	5, 10, 15

1. Narcolepsy
   a) Nonpharmacological: Table 68.9
   b) Pharmacological: Table 68.10
      1) Stimulants
         (a) Should be targeted for specific use (e.g., driving, concentrating while at work)
         (b) Drug holiday on weekends for amphetamine or methylphenidate
         (c) Pemoline may rarely increase liver enzyme activity in blood, should be monitored once or twice a year
      2) Cataplexy may respond to antidepressants (e.g., protriptyline, 5 mg in the morning, increased if necessary to 10 mg/day, or fluoxetine, 10 mg/day)
      3) Tricyclics can also be used to treat sleep paralysis and hypnagogic hallucinations (e.g., protriptyline 5 mg before bedtime)
2. Idiopathic hypersomnia: same treatment as for narcolepsy but with less clear-cut results
C. Sleep apnea and other breathing disorders (Table 68.11)
   1. Correct associated medical conditions including obesity

Table 68.11.   Approaches to Management of Obstructive Sleep Apnea

Most effective	Least effective
General	Medications
Avoid CNS depressants	Medroxyprogesterone
Weight loss	Protriptyline
Upper airway measures	Oxygen
CPAP	
Tracheostomy	
Palatopharyngoplasty	

2. Discontinue central nervous system (CNS) depressants if they have been prescribed
3. Continuous positive airway pressure (CPAP), the mainstay of treatment for moderate to severe disease, requires referral to a sleep center
4. Surgical procedures (Table 68.11) should be considered only if medical treatment has failed
5. Medications
   a) Which patients will respond is unclear
   b) Protriptyline (5–10 mg at bedtime) generally more effective than medroxyprogesterone
6. Oxygen: only for persons with waking hypoxemia and/or cor pulmonale

D. RLS and PLM
1. Nonpharmacological approaches (e.g., exercise) generally of limited benefit
2. Dopamine agonists
   a) Start with one-half tablet of Sinemet 25/100
      1) Increase if necessary by one-half tablet every 3 or 4 days
      2) Most common side effect is "rebound," i.e., RLS symptoms occurring earlier in the day; may respond to Sinemet CR, ½–2 tablets at bedtime
   b) Other dopamine agonists are best prescribed at a sleep center because their use is complicated

E. Sleep walking, sleep terrors, and confusional states
1. Minimize sleep loss
2. Minimize stress
3. Severe cases may respond to benzodiazepines (e.g., clonazepam 0.5 mg at bedtime)

69/ PREOPERATIVE PLANNING FOR AMBULATORY PATIENTS

OVERVIEW

A. General guidelines on eligibility for same day surgery: Table 69.1
B. The objective, potential complications and expected outcome of surgery should be discussed with the patient by the referring physician
C. General evaluation: Tables 69.2–69.5
D. Recommendations to the surgeon about patient's regular medications: Table 69.6

SPECIFIC SURGICAL PROBLEMS

A. Surgery in the elderly
   1. Mortality risk: 1% under age 65, 9% between ages 65 and 80, 8–10% over age 80
   2. High mortality: unresectable lesions (e.g., infarcted bowel) with coexistent heart disease, systemic infection, renal or pulmonary disease
   3. Comprehensive workup (Table 69.2)
      a) Patient may be infected and not show classic signs
      b) Routine spirometry
      c) Baseline mental status examination
B. Surgery in the pregnant patient
   1. Women of childbearing age should be routinely screened for pregnancy before surgery

---

Table 69.1. General Guidelines on Patient Eligibility for Ambulatory Surgery Based on Medical Condition (Not Considering Type of Surgery)

1. American Society of Anesthesiologists class 1–2 (some class 3 for minor procedures).
   Class 1: There is no physiological, biochemical, or psychiatric disturbance. The pathological process for which operation is to be performed is localized and not conducive to systemic disturbance. Examples: A fit patient with inguinal hernia; fibroid uterus in an otherwise-healthy woman.
   Class 2: Mild to moderate systemic disturbance caused either by the condition to be treated surgically or by other pathophysiological processes. Examples: Presence of mild diabetes mellitus, essential hypertension, or anemia.
   Class 3: Rather severe systemic disturbance from whatever cause, even though it may not be possible to define the degree of disability with finality. Examples: Severe diabetes mellitus with vascular complications; moderate to severe degrees of pulmonary insufficiency; angina pectoris or healed myocardial infarction.
2. Stable chronic medical problems well controlled by medicines; absence of acute medical problems.
3. No recent myocardial infarction or unstable cardiac disease.
4. No decompensated lung disease.
5. If diabetic, not taking insulin; if taking insulin, stable and patient capable of self-monitoring (insulin-dependent diabetics should be operated on in the morning).

Adapted from Kammerer WS, Gross RJ (eds): *Medical Consultation: The Internist on Surgical, Obstetric, and Psychiatric Services,* 2nd ed. Baltimore, Williams & Wilkins, 1990, p 620.

Table 69.2. Two Types of General Preoperative Evaluation

Component of Workup	Limited Workup[a]	Comprehensive Workup[a]
History	HPI, past medical history, allergies, medications, heart, lungs, hemostasis, endocrine, family history of surgical/anesthesia problems and new symptoms (especially upper respiratory infection)	HPI, past medical history, social history, family history, allergies, medications, brief review of all systems
Physical examination	Vital signs, oral cavity, chest, heart, and abdomen	Complete physical examination
Laboratory[a]	Hematocrit, urinalysis, ECG (some cases over age 35), serum potassium concentration some cases, pregnancy test[b]	Chest x-ray, ECG (over age 35), complete blood count, serum urea nitrogen or serum creatinine, serum glucose, serum electrolytes, urinalysis, pregnancy test[b]

ECG, electrocardiogram; HPI, history of present illness.
[a] Basic evaluation for screening and baseline data. Other tests may be added to evaluate known disease in a patient or to follow up findings in the preoperative history and physical examination; see also Table 69.4.
[b] Women in childbearing age group.

Table 69.3. Guidelines for Selecting the General Preoperative Evaluation

Limited Workup	Comprehensive Workup
Age < 40 yr	Age > 40 yr (especially > 60 yr)
Recent comprehensive physical examination	No, old, or inadequate database
Well patient	Patient with moderate-to-severe major organ disease
Local, regional, or spinal anesthesia	General anesthesia
Established patient; previously examined by physician	New patient, unknown to physician
Minor procedure	Major procedure (especially thoracic, abdominal, neurosurgical)

2. Physiological alterations in pregnancy and their relevance to surgery: Table 69.7
C. Patient with cardiovascular disease
  1. Ischemic heart disease
    a) Overall, mortality risk increased 2–3 times, dependent on cardiac status (Table 69.8)
    b) Coronary artery bypass surgery, if indicated, should be done before elective noncardiac surgery
    c) Comprehensive preoperative workup: Table 69.2
  2. Hypertension
    a) Degree of risk not established
    b) Comprehensive preoperative workup: Table 69.2
    c) Antihypertensive medication should be continued, except for guanethidine and monoamine oxidase inhibitors
    d) If diastolic blood pressure > 110 and surgery is elective, attempt better control for 1–2 weeks before surgery
  3. Valvular heart disease

Table 69.4. Additional Preoperative Screening Tests for Common High-Risk Situations

High-Risk Situations	Screening Tests
Patient undergoing neurosurgical, cardiac, vascular, or major abdominal procedure	Tests of hemostasis: platelet count, prothrombin time, partial thromboplastin time
Patient on diuretics, with vomiting/diarrhea, other abnormal fluid loss, cardiac disease, renal disease	Electrolytes
Patient with increased risk of active liver disease (e.g., alcoholism, drug addiction, homosexuality, dialysis patient, high-risk medications) who is undergoing general or spinal anesthesia	Liver function tests; serum aminotransferases, alkaline phosphatase, bilirubin, hepatitis-associated antigen
Patient with increased risk of chronic pulmonary disease (e.g., smoker with ≥10 pack-years) who is undergoing general anesthesia	Pulmonary function tests (spirometry)
Patient with increased risk of tuberculosis (e.g., known exposure, HIV positive, underprivileged population)	Chest x-ray, purified protein derivative skin test
Patient with increased risk of coronary artery disease (i.e., smoker, hypertensive, strong family history, diabetic, hyperlipidemia)	ECG
Malnourished patient or prolonged inability to eat	Nutritional assessment

Table 69.5. Commonly Forgotten or Underestimated Items in the Office Evaluation and Management of the Surgery Patient

A. Evaluation
1. One disease (review the problem list)
2. Generally sick patient
3. Inquiry about current medications (include aspirin and other OTC medications)
4. Blood tests indicated by specific medical diseases or medications (e.g., drug levels, potassium for diuretics)
5. Inquiry about abnormal bleeding or knowledge that the patient is a bleeder
6. Inquiry about prior history of transfusion or of transfusion reactions
7. Inquiry about previous problems with anesthesia
8. Inquiry about current use of alcohol or illicit drugs
9. Pregnancy test (serum qualitative human chorionic gonadotropin)
10. Spirometry (smoker who may have unrecognized COPD)
11. Echocardiogram (evaluation of murmur regarding subacute bacterial endocarditis prophylaxis)

B. Management
1. Tell patient to report even minor intercurrent illnesses between physical examination and day of surgery
2. Stop smoking, alcohol, illicit drugs, OTC medications (no new OTC medications)
3. Medications (see Table 69.6) — whether to take medications the morning of surgery and when to restart postoperatively; discontinuing certain medications (such as aspirin, coumadin); coverage for corticosteroids if indicated
4. Subacute bacterial endocarditis prophylaxis
5. Teach patient what to expect preoperatively and postoperatively; call if unexpected problems arise
6. Tell the patient about, and plan several weeks in advance, banking one or more units of blood for autologous transfusion

Adapted from Kammerer WS, Gross RJ (eds): *Medical Consultation: The Internist on Surgical, Obstetric, and Psychiatric Services*, 2nd ed. Baltimore, Williams & Wilkins, 1990, p 622.
OTC, over the counter; *COPD*, chronic obstructive pulmonary disease.

Table 69.6. Recommendations to the Surgeon Regarding the Patient's Regular Medications[a]

Drug Class	Anticipated Problems	Recommendations to Surgeon for Perioperative Period
CARDIOVASCULAR		
Antihypertensives[b]	Interaction with anesthetics, hypotension	Inform anesthesiologist of use
	Inability to give orally	Plan postoperative regimen with alternative agents if needed
Antiarrhythmics[b]	Inability to give orally	ECG monitor in operating room and postoperatively, use alternative parenteral agents
β-blockers	Myocardial depression, bradycardia	Continue intravenously, taper to lower dose, or discontinue depending on circumstances
Digitalis[b]	Toxicity	Obtain serum levels preoperatively
	Inability to give orally	Give 75% of daily oral dose of digoxin intravenously each day
Long-acting oral nitrates[b]	Inability to give orally	Substitute transdermal nitroglycerin
GASTROINTESTINAL		
Antacids[b]	Inability to give orally	Intravenous H_2 blockers, nasogastric suction (if patient has active peptide ulcer disease)
ANTIBIOTICS		
Tetracycline	Risk of renal failure if given with methoxyflurane	Use alternative antibiotic or anesthetic
CORTICOSTEROIDS[b]	Adrenal insufficiency	Plan coverage (with intravenous corticosteroids) adequate for the stress of surgery
	Poor wound healing	Discuss with surgeon
NEUROLOGICAL		
Levodopa/carbidopa[b]	Interaction with anesthetics (hypertension or hypotension), inability to give orally	Inform anesthesiologist of use; resume orally as soon as possible after surgery
Barbiturates	Increased CNS depression by anesthesia, inability to give orally	Inform anesthesiologist of use; give daily dose intramuscularly
Dilantin	Inability to give orally	Give daily dose slowly intravenously (or substitute phenobarbital before admitting patient for surgery)
BRONCHODILATORS		
Theophylline[b]	Inability to give orally	Switch to intravenous aminophylline
β$_2$-Sympathomimetics[b]	Inability to give orally	Switch to aerosolized or subcutaneous β$_2$-agent

Table 69.6. Continued

Drug Class	Anticipated Problems	Recommendations to Surgeon for Perioperative Period
PSYCHIATRIC		
Antidepressants[b]	Hypotension or hypertension, arrhythmias	Inform anesthesiologist of use; withhold monoamine oxidase inhibitors 2 weeks preoperatively; selectively withhold other agents 24 hours preoperatively
Neuroleptics (i.e., phenothiazines and haloperidol)[b]	Arrhythmias, enhancement of neuromuscular blocking agents, hypotension	Inform anesthesiologist of use; withhold 24 hours preoperatively in some cases
Benzodiazepines	Increased CNS depression by anesthesia	Inform anesthesiologist of use
Lithium[b]	Myocardial depression, hypernatremia	Inform anesthesiologist of use; determine blood levels; withhold 24 hours preoperatively; avoid diuretics and NSAIDs; follow electrolytes closely
ANALGESICS		
Narcotics	Decreased cough reflex, increased CNS depression by anesthesia, hypotension	Inform anesthesiologist of use
Aspirin compounds[b]	Intestinal bleeding	Discontinue 1–2 weeks before surgery
NSAIDs	Gastrointestinal tract bleeding	Discontinue one or more days preoperatively
ANTICOAGULANTS		
Warfarin[b]	Increased bleeding	Discontinue 48 hours before surgery, vitamin K, if needed, check prothrombin time before operation
DIURETICS	Electrolyte abnormalities, hypotension, inability to give orally	Obtain electrolytes and check blood pressure (lying, standing) within 24 hours preoperatively, use intravenous furosemide if needed
GOUT		
Benemid, allopurinol	Inability to give orally	Observe, treat acute gout with intravenous colchicine
DIABETES		
Oral hypoglycemics[b]	Inability to give orally	Switch to insulin preoperatively in selected patients
Insulin[b]	Risk of hyperglycemia or hypoglycemia	Give one-third to one-half usual dose preoperatively

THYROID THERAPY		
Thyroid hormone[b]	Inability to give orally	Usually can be discontinued for up to 7–10 days
Antithyroid drugs[b]	Inability to give orally	Use parenteral iodides or propranolol if necessary
LIPID LOWERING		
Lovastatin, other hydroxymethylglutaryl-CoA reductase inhibitors	Rhabdomyolysis	? Discontinue preoperatively
Gemfibrozil	Rhabdomyolysis	? Discontinue preoperatively
TOPICAL DRUGS FOR GLAUCOMA		
Timolol	Systemic β-blockage	Notify anesthesiologist preoperatively
Phospholine iodide	Prolonged muscle relaxant activity	Discontinue 7–10 days preoperatively
RECREATIONAL DRUGS		
Alcohol	Affect drug metabolism, drug interactions, withdrawal syndrome, impaired respiratory function	If possible, have patient discontinue use 1 or more weeks before admission for surgery. If a shorter interval is crucial, a maintenance drug can be given with less than 1 ounce of water several hours before anesthesia (e.g., 6 A.M.), and the drug can be resumed orally after surgery.
Illicit drugs		
Tobacco		

CNS, central nervous system; *CoA*, coenzyme A; *ECG*, electrocardiogram; *NSAIDs*, nonsteroidal anti-inflammatory drugs.

[a] If the patient will be able to take medication orally within 12 hours postoperatively, most maintenance drugs can be given at that time. If a shorter interval is crucial, a maintenance drug can be given with less than 1 ounce of water several hours before anesthesia (e.g., 6 A.M.), and the drug can be resumed orally after surgery.

[b] See additional details in subsequent section of this chapter.

Table 69.7.   Physiological Alterations in Pregnancy and Their Relevance to the Surgical Patient

System	Change	Clinical Implications
Cardiovascular	Uterine compression of vena cava and aorta in supine position	Decreased cardiac output and uterine perfusion; avoid supine recumbency; tilt hip 15° in perioperative period
	Decrease in blood pressure in early to mid gestation	Altered criteria for diagnosis of hypotension
	Presence of dyspnea, third heart sound, and edema	No known increased risk, and such findings are not an indication for diuretic therapy or delay of surgery
Respiratory	Decreased arterial pO_2 when patient is in the supine position	Avoid supine recumbency
	Decreased pulmonary functional residual capacity and increased O_2 consumption	Increased risk of hypoxia perioperatively; avoid hypoventilation and increase inspired O_2 content prior to procedures inducing apnea (intubation or tracheal suctioning)
	Arterial pCO_2 and serum HCO_2 decrease to 30 mm Hg and 20 mmol/liter, respectively	Maternal and fetal acidosis may occur in pregnancy; normal values of arterial pCO_2 for pregnancy should be used to guide diagnosis and therapy of acid-base disturbances
Hematological	Decreased venous flow in legs and increased levels of clotting factors	Increased risk of thromboembolism; avoid supine position and consider use of support stockings, or pneumatic compression device
	Proximity of fetal and maternal circulations	Risk of isoimmunization; $Rh_0(D)$ immune globulin should be considered when uterine trauma is likely
Gastrointestinal	Decreased gastric motility and reduced competency of gastroesophageal sphincter	Increased risk of aspiration; preoperative antacids should be considered
Renal	Dilatation of urinary collection system	Increased risk of urinary infection, and hence catheterization should be avoided when possible
	30-50% increase in glomerular filtration rate and renal plasma flow with a concomitant decrease in serum creatinine and urea nitrogen to 0.5 and 9 mg/dl, respectively	Serum creatinine above 0.8 mg/dl may reflect impaired renal function; the clearance of many drugs is increased, and dosage schedules may require alteration

From Barron WM: The pregnant surgical patient: medical evaluation and management. *Ann Intern Med* 101:683, 1984.

Table 69.8   **Summary of Perioperative Cardiovascular Risk in Patients With Ischemic Heart Disease**

Patient Status (Preoperative)	Mortality (Range)		Postoperative Myocardial Infarction (%)
	Total (%)	Cardiac (%)	
No "cardiac disease"[a]	3 (0.2–10)	?[b]	0.8 (0.1–2)
"Cardiac disease" present[a]	11 (5–20)	?	5 (2–8)
Angina (stable)	4 (4–12)	?	4 (?)
Past myocardial infarction			
All	5–15	5	7
Within 3 months	25–40 } 15–25[c]	?	35 } 25[d]
Between 3 and 6 months	5–20	?	17
More than 6 months	2.5	?	5
Unknown	?	?	10

From Kammerer WS, Gross RJ: *Medical Consultation: The Internist on Surgical, Obstetric, and Psychiatric Services*, 2nd ed. Baltimore, Williams & Wilkins, 1990, p 108.
[a] Cardiac disease data based mostly on patients with ischemic heart disease.
[b] ?, data not available or uncertain.
[c] Recent figures show postoperative mortality may be less.
[d] Recent studies indicate current risk of reinfarction may be about 2–6%, using modern hemodynamic monitoring and anesthesia.

      a) Major risks are cardiac death and heart failure
      b) Aortic stenosis of any degree imposes a very high risk; other aortic or mitral lesions less risky unless they are hemodynamically severe (Chapter 44)
      c) Endocarditis prophylaxis important (see Table 69.9)
   4. Congestive heart failure
      a) Risks of developing: Table 69.10
      b) Patients with compensated failure warrant a comprehensive preoperative evaluation (Table 69.2)
      c) A history of heart failure probably warrants preoperative digitalization (Chapter 45)
   5. Arrhythmias
      a) Risk is increased but not quantified
      b) Comprehensive preoperative workup: Table 69.2
      c) Patients with supraventricular arrhythmias should have their rates controlled or rhythms converted to more stable forms (Chapter 43)
      d) Patients with ventricular premature beats or with heart block or sick sinus syndrome (see Chapter 43)
D. Patient with pulmonary disease
   1. Chronic obstructive pulmonary disease (COPD)
      a) Risk increased in moderate or severe disease (4% mortality rate)
      b) History of smoking, dyspnea, cough, or abnormal spirometry increases risk of postoperative atelectasis or pulmonary infection
      c) Preoperative FEV_1 of <1.5 liters increases risk of postoperative respiratory failure; FEV_1 of <1.0 liter defines a very high risk group
      d) Nonpulmonary factors that increase pulmonary risk during surgery: Table 69.11
      e) Comprehensive preoperative workup: Table 69.2

Table 69.9. Prevention of Bacterial Endocarditis in Patients With Valvular Heart Disease, Prosthetic Heart Valves, and Other Abnormalities of the Cardiovascular System

Endocarditis Prophylaxis[a]	Dosage for Adults
DENTAL AND UPPER RESPIRATORY PROCEDURES[b]	
Oral[c]	
Amoxicillin[d]	3 g 1 hr before procedure and 1.5 g 6 hr later
Penicillin allergy:	
Erythromycin	1 g 2 hr before procedure and 500 mg 6 hr later
Parenteral[c,e]	
Ampicillin	2 g i.m. or i.v. 30 min before procedure
Plus gentamicin	1.5 mg/kg i.m. or i.v. 30 min before procedure
Penicillin allergy:	
Vancomycin	1 g i.v. infused *slowly over 1 hr* beginning 1 hr before procedure
GASTROINTESTINAL AND GENITOURINARY PROCEDURES[b]	
Oral[c]	
Amoxicillin[d]	3 g 1 hr before procedure and 1.5 g 6 hr later
Parenteral[c,e]	
Ampicillin	2 g i.m. or i.v. 30 min before procedure
Plus gentamicin	1.5 mg/kg i.m. or i.v. 30 min before procedure
Penicillin allergy:	
Vancomycin	1 g i.v. infused *slowly over 1 hr* beginning 1 hr before procedure
Plus gentamicin	1.5 mg/kg i.m. or i.v. 30 min before procedure

From *Med Lett* 31:112, 1989 (omits information for children).

[a] For patients with previous endocarditis, valvular heart disease, prosthetic heart valves, most forms of congenital heart disease (but uncomplicated secundum atrial septal defect), idiopathic hypertrophic subaortic stenosis, and mitral valve prolapse with regurgitation. Viridans streptococci are the most common cause of endocarditis after dental or upper respiratory procedures; enterococci are the most common cause of endocarditis after gastrointestinal or genitourinary procedures.

[b] For a review of the risk of bacteremia and endocarditis with various procedures, see Durack D: Prophylaxis of infectious endocarditis. In: Mandell GL, et al (eds) *Principles and Practice of Infectious Disease*, 3rd ed. New York, Churchill Livingstone, 1990, p 716.

[c] Oral regimens are more convenient and safer. Parenteral regimens are more likely to be effective; they are recommended especially for patients with prosthetic heart valves, those who have had endocarditis previously, or those taking continuous oral penicillin for rheumatic fever prophylaxis.

[d] Amoxicillin is recommended because of its excellent bioavailability and good activity against streptococci and enterococci.

[e] A single dose of parenteral drugs is probably adequate, because bacteremia after most dental and diagnostic procedures is of short duration. An additional dose may be given 8 hours later in patients judged to be at higher risk.

    f) Indications for pulmonary function testing: Table 69.12
2. Asthma
    a) Major risks (severe bronchospasm and inspissation of thick mucus) occur immediately postoperatively
    b) Comprehensive preoperative workup including spirometry: Table 69.2
E. Patient with renal disease
    1. Risk is proportionate to severity (2–4% in patients with severe renal disease, appropriately managed)
    2. Major risks are electrolyte abnormalities, volume contraction or overload, worsening renal function due to use of nephrotoxic agents, and bleeding
    3. Comprehensive preoperative workup: Table 69.2
F. Patient with endocrine disease

Table 69.10. Risks of Developing CHF in the Perioperative Period[a]

Patient Characteristics	Size of Risk	
	All CHF (%)	Pulmonary Edema (%)
No prior CHF	4	2
Past CHF		
All — now compensated	16	6
Past pulmonary edema (regardless of current status)	32	23
Decompensated CHF preoperatively	21	16
Preoperative physical findings		
S_3 gallop	47	35
Jugular venous distention	35	30
NYHA class preoperatively (see Table 45.3)		
Class 1	5	3
Class 2	7	7
Class 3	18	6
Class 4	31	25

Adapted from Goldman L, Caldera DL, Southwick FS, et al: Cardiac risk factors and complications in non-cardiac surgery. *Medicine (Baltimore)* 57:357, 1978.

CHF, congestive heart failure; *NYHA*, New York Heart Association.

[a] Based upon 1001 consecutive patients undergoing general surgery, orthopedic surgery, or urological surgery (transurethral resection of the prostate omitted because of existing evidence of its safety even in elderly patients).

Table 69.11. Nonpulmonary Factors That Increase Pulmonary Risks During General Surgery

MOST IMPORTANT
  Age > 60
  Upper abdominal or thoracic operation
  Repeat operations within 1 year
OTHER
  General anesthesia lasting more than 3 hours
  Obesity
  Abnormal ECG
  Poor patient effort/cooperation
  Narcotic analgesics
  Upper respiratory infection

Table 69.12. Indications for Pulmonary Function Test in Preoperative Patients With Pulmonary Disease

SPIROMETRY ONLY (FEV_1 and FVC)
  Smokers (>10 pack-years)
  Any pulmonary symptoms (e.g., dyspnea, wheezing, cough, or sputum production)
  Upper abdominal surgery
  Age > 60
  Repeat surgery within 1 year
  Multiple other risk factors (obesity, recent upper respiratory infections, narcotics abuse, abnormal ECG)
SPIROMETRY, LUNG VOLUMES, AND ARTERIAL BLOOD GASES
  Thoracic surgery
  Upper abdominal surgery and pulmonary disease
  Patients with restrictive lung disease
  Patients with COPD with FEV_1 < 1.0 liter

1. Diabetes mellitus
   a) Mortality rate of about 2–4%
   b) Comprehensive preoperative evaluation: Table 69.2
   c) Management on day of surgery: Table 69.13
2. Adrenal insufficiency and chronic steroid therapy
   a) Patients who have taken pharmacological dose of corticosteroids (hydrocortisone >20–30 mg/day) for 2 or more weeks in the past year or who are receiving replacement therapy for adrenal insufficiency should receive additional corticosteroids in the perioperative period
   b) Comprehensive preoperative workup: Table 69.2
3. Hypothyroidism
   a) Major risks are increased sensitivity to anesthetic agents, hypoventilation and respiratory arrest, hyponatremia, myxedema coma
   b) Comprehensive preoperative workup (Table 69.2) and measurement of serum T_4 [also thyroid-stimulating hormone if hypothyroidism recently diagnosed]
4. Hyperthyroidism
   a) If uncontrolled, risk of thyroid storm (Chapter 57)
   b) T_4 before surgery plus comprehensive workup (Table 69.2)
5. Obesity
   a) Massive obesity increases mortality risk considerably (perhaps 10-fold), but lesser degrees of obesity do not
   b) Even moderate obesity may make ventilation more difficult during and after surgery
   c) For elective surgery, gradual preoperative weight reduction (Chapter 60) warranted
G. Patient with gastrointestinal disease
   1. Peptic ulcer disease
      a) No data on risk
      b) If disease active, elective nonulcer surgery should be delayed until ulcer heals (Chapter 23)
      c) Comprehensive preoperative workup: Table 69.2
   2. Hepatitis
      a) High morbidity and mortality associated with general anesthesia and surgery
      b) Comprehensive preoperative workup (Table 69.2), liver function tests, and, if not known, serological tests for hepatitis B antigen and hepatitis C antibody
      c) Surgery should be postponed, if possible, for 6–12 months after liver function tests have returned to normal
   3. Cirrhosis
      a) Risk dependent on severity (Table 69.14)
      b) Perioperative complications include encephalopathy, jaundice, gastrointestinal bleeding, infection, and hepatorenal syndrome
      c) Even regional or spinal anesthesia associated with some risk
      d) Comprehensive preoperative workup (Table 69.2) plus liver function tests
H. Patient with iatrogenic impairment of hemostasis
   1. Coumarin derivatives

Table 69.13. Management of Diabetes on Day of Surgery

		Treatment Required to Control Glucose Preoperatively	
Surgical Procedure	Diet Only	Oral Hypoglycemic Agent	Insulin
Minor	Observe	Withhold until after procedure	Withhold until after procedure, or use "major" protocol
Major	Observe	Change to long-acting insulin (achieve control with insulin before operation)	*Preferred regimen:* One-half to two-thirds total long-acting insulin dose preoperatively; regular insulin only if needed
			or
			One-third total long-acting insulin dose preoperatively; one-third postoperatively; regular insulin only if needed
			or
			Continuous low-dose infusion of regular insulin
			or
			Regular insulin in each liter of dextrose 5% in water (D_5W)

Table 69.14.   Child's Classification of Operative Risk in the Cirrhotic Patient

Risk Group by Severity of Liver Disease	Bilirubin (mg/ 100 ml)	Serum Albumin (g/100 ml)	Ascites	Encephalopathy	Nutrition	Operative Mortality (%)
"A" minimal	<2.0	>3.5	None	None	Excellent	0
"B" moderate	2.0–3.0	3.0–3.5	Controlled	Minimal	Good	9
"C" advanced	>3.0	<3.0	Poorly controlled	Coma	Poor ("wasted")	53

Adapted from Siefkin AD, Bolt RJ: Preoperative evaluation of the patient with gastrointestinal or liver disease. *Med Clin North Am* 63: 1309, 1979.

      a) Stop anticoagulation 48–96 hours preoperatively, if possible; otherwise, give vitamin K 10 mg p.o., s.c., or slowly i.v.; response usually in 24–36 hours

      b) If high risk of thromboembolic disease (e.g., patient with prosthetic plastic heart valves), stop anticoagulation 24–36 hours preoperatively, give vitamin K

    2. Aspirin: discontinue 1 week preoperatively

I. Patient with a chronic infection

    1. Skin infection: suppress or eradicate if possible (Chapter 11)

    2. Tuberculosis (Tbc)

      a) Evaluate all patients for active Tbc who have an unexplained chronic cough or a history of Tbc

      b) Patients with active disease should be stable and have negative sputum cultures before elective surgery

    3. HIV infection (see Chapter 20)

J. Patient with neuropsychiatric disease

    1. Cerebrovascular accident

      a) Risk of uncertain proportion of worsening focal deficits and in deterioration of mental status

      b) Comprehensive preoperative workup (Table 69.2) should include a complete assessment of neurological status and mental state

      c) In general, delay elective surgery for 6 weeks after a completed stroke

    2. Asymptomatic cervical bruit

      a) No increased risk

      b) Value of noninvasive tests (e.g., duplex carotid ultrasound) in predicting risk of postoperative stroke not established

    3. Parkinson's disease

      a) Rigidity may impair postoperative voluntary ventilation, mobilization, and swallowing

      b) Antiparkinsonian regimen should be optimum (Chapter 65)

    4. Dementia and organic brain syndrome

      a) Increased risk of morbidity and mortality

      b) Mental state should be formally documented (Chapter 5)

    5. Other psychiatric problems

      a) Major problems are potential interaction between psychotropic drugs and anesthetic agents and possible lack of cooperation

      b) Mental state should be formally documented (Chapter 5)

      c) Operation should be planned in consultation with a psychiatrist if problems are severe (e.g., psychosis)

70/ PERIPHERAL VASCULAR DISEASE AND ARTERIAL ANEURYSMS

ACUTE PERIPHERAL ARTERIAL OCCLUSION
A. Etiology
   1. Emboli
      a) The majority originate in the heart, mostly associated with atherosclerotic disease and arrhythmia, mural thrombosis (recent infarct), or ventricular aneurysm (old infarct)
      b) Responsible for 75% of acute lower extremity arterial occlusions, essentially all of acute upper extremity arterial occlusions
   2. Thrombi in situ
      a) Account for 25% of acute lower extremity arterial occlusions
      b) Most likely to occur at arterial bifurcations
B. Symptoms and signs
   1. Depend on adequacy of pre-existing collateral circulation (scant collaterals likely in patients who have emboli), site of occlusion, degree of occlusion
   2. Six "Ps": pulselessness, pallor, poikilothermia, pain (75% of patients), paralysis, paresthesias (20% complain of numbness first)
   3. Cardiac examination may be abnormal: e.g., arrhythmia or signs of heart failure
C. Laboratory and x-ray studies
   1. Not required before hospitalization
   2. Arteriography not performed routinely
   3. Noninvasive evaluation (i.e., Doppler ultrasonography) often superfluous
D. Treatment
   1. Immediate intravenous administration (in the physician's office) of heparin 100–150 units/kg body weight
   2. Urgent vascular surgery consultation
   3. After operation (clot removal through a catheter), patients are ordinarily given warfarin (see Chapter 37) for life
E. Prognosis
   1. Limb salvage in 95% or more, dependent on rapidity of restoration of blood flow
   2. Overall mortality, related to complications of cardiovascular disease, 10–40% in postoperative period

CHRONIC ARTERIAL OCCLUSIVE DISEASE
A. Etiology
   1. Atherosclerosis in the majority of patients
   2. Thrombi that form at lower extremity arterial bifurcations
   3. Often accelerated by diabetes mellitus (see Chapter 56)
   4. Thromboangiitis obliterans (Buerger's disease): a panarteritis (and venitis) of small vessels of the lower and upper extremities, affecting young male heavy smokers
B. Symptoms and signs
   1. Intermittent claudication common, reflects a relatively good

prognosis (only one-third deteriorate); distance walked before pain ensues and the location of pain should be documented

2. Men should be asked about impotence
3. Physical examination: status of peripheral pulses, presence or absence of peripheral or abdominal bruits, palpation for peripheral arterial aneurysms, blood pressure in both upper extremities, appearance of skin, hair, and nails of lower extremities
   a) Diminished but palpable pulses suggest mild disease
   b) Trophic changes suggest severe disease
   c) Lack of peripheral pulses, blanching of the elevated extremity, dependent rubor suggest severe disease
   d) Ischemic ulcers may occur over the calcaneus, lateral malleolus, or dorsum of foot

C. Laboratory and x-ray studies
   1. Doppler flow studies to demonstrate distribution and severity of disease
   2. Arteriography important if patient is an operative candidate

D. Treatment
   1. Indications for operation: Table 70.1
   2. General recommendations: Table 70.2
   3. Drugs
      a) No benefit from vasodilators or anticoagulants
      b) Aspirin (e.g., 325 mg/day) is used routinely, but effectiveness unclear

Table 70.1. Indications for Operation

Claudication that is intolerable in a good-risk patient
Ischemic rest pain
Impending gangrene
Nonhealing ulceration

Table 70.2. Advice That Should Be Given to Patients With Arterial Insufficiency

QUITE SMOKING — Use NO tobacco in ANY form
If overweight, lose weight.
Exercise (walk) to the point of discomfort at least 2 miles a day.
Keep feet very clean. Bathe at least daily in LUKEWARM water.
Gently apply lanolin or mild hand cream to feet after bathing.
Use a night light to avoid hitting toes or shins.
Wear clean, preferably cotton socks daily (cotton does not retain moisture).
Avoid injury to feet. Wear properly fitting shoes to prevent calluses, corns, blisters. Avoid shoes made of synthetic material that doesn't "breathe." Wear slippers at night and use a night light after going to bed.
Place lamb's wool (available from pharmacies) between overriding toes.
Avoid extremes of temperature. Do not put feet in hot water or use heating pads on lower extremities. In cold weather, wear socks to bed to warm feet. Do not get feet cold or wet.
If feet hurt at night, raise head of bed 6–10 inches (15–25 cm) on blocks.
For any sudden change in symptoms, such as prolonged pain, numbness or tingling, or inability to move foot or leg, consult your physician *immediately*.

   c) Pentoxifylline (Trental) 400 mg 3 times/day may increase
      distance to claudication within 1–2 months
   d) Amputation may be needed in patients with gangrene or with
      severe unremitting rest pain in whom an operation is not
      possible

ABDOMINAL AORTIC ANEURYSMS

A. Etiology and epidemiology
   1. Most are due to arteriosclerosis
   2. Men affected 10 times more than women; incidence increases with
      age
B. History
   1. Most patients are asymptomatic at the time of diagnosis
   2. Abdominal, flank, or back pain is a harbinger of rupture
   3. Symptoms of rupture range from syncope and pain to collapse,
      associated with a free (intraperitoneal) bleed
   4. Large aneurysms may compress adjacent structures (e.g., ureter,
      duodenum, vena cava)
   5. Emboli may dislodge and cause acute lower extremity ischemia
      (see above)
C. Physical examination
   1. Epigastric or left upper quadrant abdominal laterally pulsatile
      mass
   2. Palpation not an accurate way to assess size
   3. Look for other evidence of occlusive arterial disease (carotids,
      peripheral arteries)
D. Laboratory and x-ray studies
   1. Ultrasonography is the definitive test
   2. Computed tomography and magnetic resonance imaging usually
      unnecessary
   3. Anteroposterior and cross-table lateral plain films will show
      aneurysm in 70–80% of patients (dependent on calcification of the
      aneurysmal wall)
E. Treatment
   1. Large aneurysms (>6 cm) should be resected semiurgently
   2. Smaller aneurysms should be electively resected, unless risk is
      prohibitive; age of patient not a deterrent

PERIPHERAL ARTERIAL ANEURYSMS

A. Etiology and epidemiology
   1. Most are due to arteriosclerosis
   2. Over 90% involve either popliteal or femoral arteries
   3. Multiple aneurysms common
B. History
   1. Many patients are asymptomatic
   2. Approximately 50% present with thrombosis, embolism, or
      rupture
C. Physical examination
   1. An enlarged artery with a very prominent pulse
   2. Occasionally, popliteal aneurysms present only with small
      punctate necrotic areas of skin over the anterior tibial region or
      with small gangrenous areas of the tips of the toes ("blue toe"
      syndrome)

D. Laboratory and x-ray studies
1. Ultrasonography if diagnosis uncertain
2. Once diagnosis is made, arteriography is mandatory to confirm anatomy and patency of vessels
E. Treatment
1. All aneurysms should be repaired
2. If patients cannot be operated on, risk of complications is high

71/ LOWER EXTREMITY ULCERS AND VARICOSE VEINS

LOWER EXTREMITY ULCERS

A. History
1. Associated illnesses: arteriosclerotic cardiovascular disease, diabetes mellitus, sickle cell disease, collagen vascular disease
2. Pay specific attention to
   a) Duration of ulceration and previous treatment
   b) Symptoms of peripheral vascular disease (see Chapter 70)
   c) History of thrombophlebitis, ulceration, or injury to the lower extremities
   d) History of edema
B. Physical examination
1. General: signs of chronic hypertension and of heart disease; evidence of abdominal aortic aneurysm or of abdominal or groin masses; needle tracks
2. Lower extremities
   a) Examine both legs while the patient is supine
   b) Look for pitting or nonpitting edema (latter a sign of lymphatic obstruction)
   c) Look for hemosiderin deposits in the skin of the ankles (a sign of venous insufficiency)
   d) Examine the skin and hair for evidence of arterial insufficiency (Chapter 70)
   e) Look for evidence of fungal infection (e.g., scaling)
   f) Examine and grade all the pulses of the lower extremities
   g) Measure the capillary refill time after pressure on the toes with the legs elevated 45° (normally less than 5 seconds)
   h) Compare the temperature of the legs
   i) Observe venous filling time with the patient sitting and the presence or absence of dependent rubor
3. Ulcers
   a) Site
   b) Size
   c) General characteristics: e.g., regular or irregular; raised, heaped, everted, or flat; undermined or not; evidence of healing; clean or covered with exudate; vascularity of the base (an important index of potential to heal)
   d) Tenderness
   e) Changes in adjoining skin: e.g., adjacent areas of purulence, callosities, pigment deposition, or edema
4. Presence or absence of edema and/or varicose veins with patient standing
C. Types (Table 71.1)
1. Ulcers associated with venous insufficiency
   a) Commonest leg ulcers
   b) Usually superficial, irregular, exudative, movable, tender
2. Ulcers associated with arterial insufficiency

Table 71.1. Characteristics of Common Leg Ulcers

Type of Ulcer	Usual Location	Edema	Pigmentation	Evidence of Arterial Insufficiency
Varicose	Medial leg	0 to +	0 to +	0
Stasis	Medial leg	++ to ++++	+++	0 to +
Arterial	Lateral leg, foot	0 to +	0	++++
Dystrophic	Sole, tip of toe	++	0	0
Traumatic	Midleg, toe	0	0	0 to ++++
Diabetic	Toes, dorsum, or foot	++	0	+ to +++
Factitious	Anywhere	+	0	0

       a) Second most common leg ulcers
       b) Associated with peripheral arterial disease (see Chapter 70)
       c) Usually begin with trauma
       d) Quite painful
    3. Dystrophic ulcers
       a) Usually associated with peripheral or autonomic neuropathy
       b) Usually insensitive to touch
       c) May be undermined; there may be subcutaneous tracking of infection
    4. Posttraumatic ulcers
       a) Usually associated with neurological or vascular impairment of the leg
       b) Major trauma, e.g., fractures, may cause ulceration even in previously healthy legs
    5. Diabetic ulcers
       a) Have features of dystrophic, traumatic, and arterial ulcers
       b) Fairly insensitive, often infected and undermined
       c) X-rays of bone underlying the ulcer should be done routinely to look for osteomyelitis (see Chapter 17)
    6. Factitious ulcers
       a) Especially common in addicts
       b) Distribution usually bizarre
       c) May also be seen in patients with psychiatric disorders or chronic disorders associated with pruritus
    7. Neoplastic ulcers
       a) Usually basal cell or squamous cell carcinoma
       b) Elevated or rolled edges
       c) Anesthetic
    8. Hypertensive ulcers
       a) Rare, most frequently found in women
       b) Extremely painful
    9. Miscellaneous ulcers: sickle cell disease, polyarteritis, brown recluse spider bite, cytomegalovirus infection (in HIV-infected patients)
D. Laboratory aids
    1. Bacteriology: if apparently infected, cultures of the ulcer bed are useful
    2. Biopsy if neoplastic or fungal disease is suspected (a chronic ulcer in a scar should always be biopsied)

3. Noninvasive vascular testing (Chapter 70) when arterial disease is suspected

E. Management
   1. Indications for hospitalization
      a) Extent of ulcer requires absolute bed rest and elevation of leg that are not possible at home
      b) Invasive infection: e.g., cellulitis, lymphangitis, evidence of systemic infection
   2. Ulcers associated with venous insufficiency
      a) Bed rest with leg elevated
      b) Compression wraps whenever leg is dependent
      c) After culture, topical antibacterial preparations (e.g., silver-sulfadiazine cream)
      d) When edema and infection are controlled, usually in 48–72 hours, apply:
         1) Wet-to-dry dressing (sterile gauze pad moistened with normal saline is secured with a rolled bandage over the ulcer, allowed to dry, and removed): useful when there is substantial exudate
         2) Wet-to-wet dressing (same as above but moistened again before removal): useful for ulcers with less exudate
         3) Unna boot: for 48 hours; if no problems, can be reapplied and changed weekly
         4) Hydrocolloid dressing (e.g., Duoderm) under an elastic bandage: for clean or shallow ulcers
   3. Ulcers associated with arterial insufficiency
      a) Surgical evaluation important: if correction of vascular impairment not possible, debridement (by surgeon) every 2 or 3 days
      b) Short course of a proteolytic enzyme (e.g., Travase) 3–5 times/day, followed by wet-to-dry dressing
      c) Foot protection, elevation of leg, avoidance of weight
   4. Dystrophic ulcers
      a) Bed rest, debridement, wet-to-wet dressings
      b) "Total contact" casting (plastic cast directly applied for 1 week)
   5. Traumatic ulcers
      a) Avoidance of weight, elevation of leg, appropriate dressings (see above)
      b) Surgical consultation if no progress within 2–3 weeks
   6. Diabetic ulcers
      a) Hospitalization usually warranted
      b) Absolute bed rest, elevation of leg, consideration of total contact casting (see above)
   7. Factitious ulcers
      a) Control cause
      b) Apply occlusive dressing to prevent manipulation
   8. Hypertensive ulcers
      a) Control hypertension
      b) Treatment the same as for venous stasis ulcers
   9. Ulcers associated with chronic administration of corticosteroids: vitamin A 25,000 U/day and A and D ointment
   10. Neoplastic ulcers: refer to surgeon

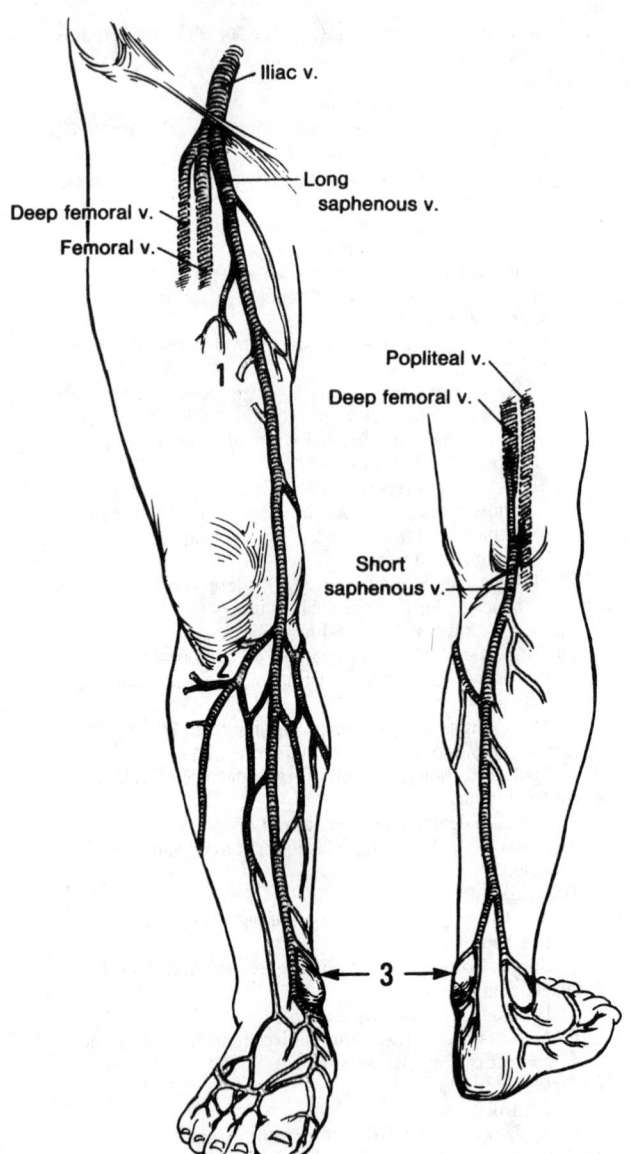

Figure 71.1. Venous circulation of the lower extremity. *1,* Hunter's canal perforator; *2,* anterior communicating vein of the leg; and *3,* ankle perforators.

VARICOSE VEINS
A. Causes and epidemiology
   1. Occur in women more than men
   2. Aggravated (and may be caused) by elevated intra-abdominal pressure (e.g., pregnancy), abdominal tumors, chronic straining at defecation)
B. Symptoms
   1. Heaviness and aching, sometimes mild edema
   2. Cosmetic complaints
   3. Occasionally, symptoms of superficial thrombophlebitis
C. Physical examination (Fig. 71.1)
   1. Telangiectasia ("sunburst" varices): cosmetic problems but otherwise asymptomatic
   2. Varicosities of long saphenous system
      a) Most common type of varicosities
      b) Clearly visible when patient stands
   3. Varicosities of short saphenous system: best seen with the patient standing with his or her back to the examiner
   4. Perforator varicosities: usually seen in the long saphenous vein where the ankle perforators and the above-the-knee perforator join the vein (Fig. 71.1)
D. Testing to determine level of incompetence
   1. Trendelenburg's test: leg elevated; tourniquet applied; patient stands; tourniquet released; if veins fill from above, incompetent; if from below, competent; tourniquet first applied 7.7 cm (3 inches) below inguinal ligament; repeated at successively lower levels until level of incompetence identified
   2. Noninvasive vascular testing
      a) Enables precise diagnosis
      b) Requires referral to a vascular laboratory (e.g., for Doppler ultrasonography)
E. Treatment
   1. Conservative
      a) Observation if asymptomatic
      b) Telangiectases, if large enough, can be injected with a sclerosing solution (see below)
      c) Use of masking creams
      d) Support hose: worn continuously when out of bed
   2. Sclerotherapy
      a) For segmental subcutaneous varicosities that are not associated with greater or lesser saphenous incompetence
      b) Several sittings may be required
      c) Solutions (e.g., morrhuate or sodium tetradecyl sulfate) are injected antiseptically with a tourniquet at the thigh to make the vein prominent
   3. Surgery: symptomatic patients should be referred for consultation

72/ DISEASES OF THE BREAST

EVALUATION OF THE BREAST
A. Screening procedures
  1. No evidence that self-examination is effective
  2. Yearly physical examination and mammography over the age of 50 universally recommended
  3. Value of mammography under age 50 is controversial
B. Clinical characteristics
  1. Fibroadenoma
     a) Most common cause of a unilateral discrete mass in the 15–35-year-old group
     b) No pain or discharge
     c) Lesion firm, not rock hard; smooth, well-circumscribed, nontender, movable
     d) Mammography not recommended
     e) Excisional biopsy usually recommended
  2. Cystosarcoma phyllodes
     a) Malignancy rate of 20–30%
     b) Wide excision if benign; modified radical mastectomy if malignant
  3. Intraductal papilloma
     a) Often present with serosanguineous discharge
     b) Not palpable
     c) A small segment of that part of the breast producing the discharge must be excised to exclude the diagnosis of cancer
  4. Fibrocystic disease
     a) Patient usually complains of dull, aching pain that is worse just before menses
     b) Breast feels "lumpy" and is tender
     c) Mammography often difficult to interpret
     d) Biopsy often necessary: majority benign, but if there is hyperplasia plus atypia, risk of cancer increased; annual physical examinations, mammography indicated
     e) Sometimes, prophylactic mastectomy may be considered
     f) Duct ectasia (usually evidenced by thick gray-green discharge) warrants biopsy if associated with fibrocystic disease (estrogen administration may stop discharge if there is no fibrocystic disease)
  5. Premature hyperplasia
     a) Concentric unilateral swelling beneath nipple before puberty in girls
     b) Biopsy contraindicated
  6. Gynecomastia: see Chapter 61
  7. Cancer
     a) Often detected by physical examination (painless hard mass) or by mammography
     b) Advanced cases: skin changes, fixed axillary nodes, mass fixed to the chest wall
C. Evaluation of a breast mass

1. Risk factors for cancer: Table 72.1
2. Symptoms suggestive of cancer: mass (commonest symptom) and nipple discharge (second most common symptom)
3. Physical examination: see above
4. Initial management
   a) Ages 25–30: most likely fibroadenoma (see above)
   b) Ages 30–50: cystic mass might warrant sonography early; if the mass persists beyond one or two menstrual cycles, do mammography, consider biopsy
   c) Ages 50 and over: mammography, then biopsy

MANAGEMENT OF A BREAST MASS

A. Follow-up management of a benign breast mass
   1. Fibroadenoma: routine follow-up as defined by risk factors for cancer and age
   2. Fibrocystic disease
      a) With normal or proliferative epithelium: no special follow-up
      b) Atypia
         1) With no other risk factors for cancer: physician examination twice a year, annual mammogram
         2) With other risk factors: consider prophylactic bilateral mastectomies with reconstruction
      c) If pain persists, patient should wear a brassiere day and night; danazol 100–400 mg/day for 4–6 months is often effective
B. Cancer
   1. Staging
      a) Resectable: tumors not fixed to the chest wall and no fixed axillary nodes
         1) Do chest x-ray, liver function studies, serum calcium level
         2) If symptoms compatible with bone metastases, do bone scan, x-rays of symptomatic bones
      b) Locally advanced, unresectable: tumors fixed to the chest wall or fixed axillary nodes or inflammatory skin changes but no evidence of metastases
      c) Metastatic tumors
   2. Surgery
      a) Radical mastectomy no longer performed
      b) Modified radical mastectomy (preservation of the pectoral muscles) a common choice
         1) Reconstructive surgery should be planned preoperatively
         2) Attention should be paid to minimizing edema in the ipsilateral arm: e.g., avoid prolonged dependency of the arm;

Table 72.1.   Risk Factors for Carcinoma of the Breast

Factors	Relative Risk
Positive family history	1–5
Early menarche and late menopause (cyclic ovarian activity for more than 40 years)	Slight
Nulliparity	Slight
Previous breast cancer	5
Benign disease of the breast	1–4 (see the text)
Radiation	Dependent on dose

Table 72.2 Survival of Patients With Breast Cancer Relative to Status of the Axillary Lymph Nodes[a]

Status of Nodes	Crude Survival (%)		5-Year Disease-Free Survival (%)
	5-Year	10-Year	
All patients	63.5	45.9	60.3
Negative axillary lymph nodes	78.1	64.9	82.3
Positive axillary lymph nodes	46.5	24.9	34.9
1–3 positive axillary lymph nodes	62.2	37.5	50.0
≥4 positive axillary lymph nodes	32.0	13.4	21.1

[a] National Surgical Adjuvant Breast Project.

        aggressively treat infection of the arm; consider a Jobst sleeve (commercially available) if edema persists
- c) Simple excision of intraductal tumors
    1) Concern about a high relapse rate
    2) May be considered for tumors of <0.5 cm, tumors detected by mammographic microcalcifications, or tumors in older women
- d) Radiotherapy combined with surgery ("lumpectomy")
    1) As effective as radical surgery for tumors of ≤4 cm
    2) Cosmetic results poorer with larger tumors or tumors close to the nipple
    3) Risk of recurrence in radiated breast relatively high (5–15%), but survival unaffected
3. Multimodal therapy
    a) For unresectable tumors
    b) Systemic chemotherapy followed by surgery or radiation
4. Prognosis
    a) Intraductal (noninvasive): close to 100% cure rate
    b) Invasive: Table 72.2
5. Adjuvant therapy
    a) For 6 months for all premenopausal women with metastases to axillary nodes
    b) Tamoxifen (for 5 years) for all postmenopausal women with metastases to axillary nodes and with tumors that have significant estrogen receptors
    c) Decision should be made in consultation with an oncologist
6. Follow-up
    a) Physical examination every 3 months; mammography yearly
    b) Screening for metastatic disease is of no value in prolonging life

73/ DISEASES OF THE BILIARY TRACT

CHOLELITHIASIS

A. Epidemiology
   1. Ninety percent in the United States are cholesterol stones; 10% are pigment stones
   2. Prevalence greater in women, increases with age (e.g., 20% of women, 10% of men between ages 55 and 65)
   3. Particularly high prevalence in native Americans of Southwest
B. Risk factors: Table 73.1
C. Natural history
   1. Fifty percent of patients asymptomatic when detected
      a) About 18% become symptomatic some time in their lives
      b) No way to predict course on basis of size, number of stones, sex or age of the patient
      c) Patients with calcified gallbladder and native Americans with gallstones should have cholecystectomies (higher risk of gallbladder cancer)
      d) If no risk factors for gallbladder cancer, cholecystectomy unwarranted
   2. Fifty percent of patients are symptomatic, i.e., present with pain of acute or chronic cholecystitis (see below)

CHOLECYSTITIS

A. Acute
   1. Signs and symptoms
      a) Severe persistent abdominal pain — often epigastric at onset, then localizing in right upper quadrant — usually within 1–3 hours of eating but may awaken patient from sleep
      b) Usually nausea, less often vomiting

Table 73.1. Risk Factors for Gallstones

CHOLESTEROL STONES

Demography: Northern Europe, North and South America more than the Orient; Native Americans; probably familial predisposition

Obesity

High-calorie diet

Drugs used in the treatment of hyperlipidemia: clofibrate, cholestyramine, and colestipol

Gastrointestinal disorders involving major malabsorption of bile acids; ileal disease, resection or bypass; cystic fibrosis, with pancreatic insufficiency

Female sex hormones: women more at risk than men, use of oral contraceptives and other estrogenic medications

Age, especially among men

Probable but not well established: pregnancy, diabetes mellitus, and polyunsaturated fats

PIGMENT STONES

Demography: oriental more than occidental; rural more than urban

Chronic hemolysis

Alcoholic cirrhosis

Biliary infection

Age

After Bennion LJ, Grundy SM: Risk factors for the development of cholelithiasis in man. *N Engl J Med* 299:1161, 1978.

      c) Fever (99–102°F)
      d) Patient restless, with guarding of abdominal wall; gallbladder palpable in one-third of patients; occasionally, mild jaundice
      e) Murphy's sign (sudden involuntary arrest of inspiration when the right upper quadrant is palpated during inspiration) more often observed after several days
   2. Laboratory tests
      a) Granulocytosis common
      b) Serum amylase, serum aminotransferases often increased
      c) Mild hyperbilirubinemia in 20%
      d) Biliary scintigraphy the test of choice (e.g., TcHIDA scan): if isotope excreted, sensitivity 100%, specificity 95%
   3. Treatment
      a) Hospitalize: if signs and symptoms intensify, emergency cholecystectomy; otherwise, elective cholecystectomy within a few days
      b) Parenteral narcotic prior to admission may be necessary if pain is intolerable

B. Chronic
   1. Signs and symptoms
      a) Character and location of pain identical with that of acute cholecystitis
      b) Variably associated with nausea, occasionally vomiting
      c) Tenderness to deep palpation in right upper quadrant of abdomen but no muscle guarding
      d) No Murphy's sign (see above)
      e) Gallbladder not palpable
      f) No jaundice
      g) Fever unusual
   2. Laboratory tests
      a) White blood count, serum amylase, serum aminotransferases, serum bilirubin normal
      b) Ultrasound test of choice for diagnosis of gallstones
      c) Oral cholecystogram if ultrasound equivocal
   3. Treatment
      a) Elective cholecystectomy (almost always by use of laparoscope)
      b) Gallstone dissolution and gallstone lithotripsy no longer used

SYMPTOMATIC PATIENTS WHO HAVE NO DETECTABLE GALLSTONES

A. Adenomyomatosis of the gallbladder
   1. Thickening of the gallbladder wall due to hyperplasia of the epithelium with the formation of glands and of diverticula through the muscular wall
   2. Often asymptomatic but may have symptoms indistinguishable from chronic cholecystitis
   3. Diagnosis often suspected by ultrasound or cholecystography but can be made definitively only by pathologist

B. Biliary dyskinesia
   1. Abnormally decreased emptying of the gallbladder, associated with pain suggestive of gallbladder disease
   2. Normal ultrasound
   3. Best diagnosed by cholecystokinin-stimulated TcHIDA scan

4. If associated with severe symptoms, cholecystectomy warranted
C. Biliary sludge
   1. Symptoms suggestive of gallbladder disease and ultrasound characteristic of sludge
   2. Diagnosis can be confirmed by duodenal drainage with microscopic identification of cholesterol crystals or bilirubinate granules
   3. Unpredictable course; severely symptomatic patients should have cholecystectomy

CHOLEDOCHOLITHIASIS
A. Epidemiology
   1. Occurs in approximately 15% of patients with chronic cholelithiasis
   2. May originate either in gallbladder or in intrahepatic or common bile ducts
   3. May occur before or after cholecystectomy
B. Signs and symptoms
   1. Typically, severe colicky right upper quadrant abdominal pain often associated with jaundice, mild fever, nausea, vomiting
   2. Rarely, painless jaundice will be the presenting symptom
   3. If no intervention, repeated attacks ultimately lead to cholangitis (see below)
   4. If patient asymptomatic, no physical signs; if patient symptomatic, same signs as in acute cholecystitis
C. Laboratory tests
   1. Tests in an ambulatory setting not appropriate
   2. If studies are done, granulocytosis, increases in serum alkaline phosphatase activity, serum bilirubin, serum aminotransferase activity, serum amylase activity are likely
D. Treatment
   1. Hospitalization
   2. If ultrasound shows dilated biliary tree with probable distal obstruction, removal of stone(s) by endoscopic retrograde cholangiopancreatography (ERCP) indicated
E. Cholangitis
   1. Bacterial infection of biliary tree
      a) Usually associated with obstructing stone, tumor, or stricture
      b) Symptoms are fever, chills, abdominal pain, often jaundice
      c) Abdominal tenderness, often rebound tenderness
      d) Granulocytosis, elevated serum alkaline phosphatase activity, sometimes elevated serum aminotransferase activity
      e) Blood cultures often positive
      f) Hospitalization mandatory for antibiotics, relief of obstruction
   2. Primary sclerosing cholangitis
      a) Chronic inflammation of unknown cause
      b) Leads to fibrosis and to cholestatic liver disease
      c) Mostly in men
      d) Very high correlation with chronic inflammatory bowel disease; most commonly, ulcerative colitis
      e) Diagnosis by ERCP
      f) No effective treatment

Table 73.2   Frequency and Etiology of Postcholecystectomy Syndrome (PCS)

	Bodvall and Oevergaard (1967)	Stefanini et al (1974)	Hess (1977)	Brandstatter et al (1976)
Number of patients with cholecystectomy	1930	800	919	
PCS total	764 (40%)	249 (31%)	142 (26%)	
Severe PCS	104 (5%)	32 (4%)		
Etiology				
Organic total			58%	66%
Organic biliary	9%	14%	4.5%	43%
Organic extrabiliary			53.5%	23%
Nonorganic total			42%	34%

After Tondelli P, Gyr K. Stalder GA, Allgower M: The biliary tract. Part I. Cholecystectomy. *Clin Gastroenterol* 8:486, 1979.

g) Unpredictable course, but death from hepatic failure in patients with advanced disease

POSTCHOLECYSTECTOMY SYNDROME
A. Incidence and cause (Table 73.2)
  1. Organic biliary: e.g., retained stones, papillary stenosis, bile duct stricture, cystic duct remnant, bile duct tumor
  2. Organic extrabiliary: e.g., esophagitis, peptic ulcer disease, pancreatitis, adhesions
  3. Nonorganic: e.g., irritable bowel syndrome, psychiatric disease
B. Symptoms
  1. Mild: dyspepsia, constipation, diarrhea, and intolerance to some foods
  2. Severe: severe upper abdominal pain, symptoms of cholangitis or biliary fistula

74/ ABDOMINAL HERNIAS

DEFINITIONS
A. Hernia: protrusion of a viscus or part of a viscus from its normal location
B. Reducible: contents can be pushed back to its original location
C. Irreducible or incarcerated: contents cannot be pushed back
D. Strangulated: blood supply to herniated viscus is compromised

HERNIAS OF THE GROIN (FIGURE 74.1)
A. Inguinal
   1. Classification
      a) Direct: bowel or omentum protrudes directly through the floor of the inguinal canal, emerges through the external inguinal ring above the inguinal ligament
      b) Indirect: bowel or omentum enters the inguinal canal through its internal ring, traverses the canal, emerges through the external inguinal ring
   2. Epidemiology and etiology
      a) Eighty-five percent occur in men
      b) Commonest groin hernia even in women
      c) All indirect due to a congenital defect in combination with a predisposing condition that increases abdominal pressure (e.g., straining, obesity)

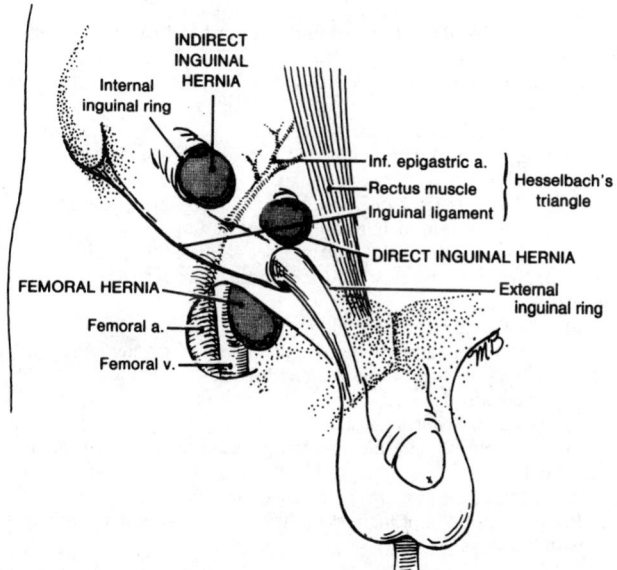

Figure 74.1. Artist's rendition of groin region, illustrating femoral hernia and indirect and direct inguinal hernias. (Modified from Dunphy JE, Botsford TW: *Physical Examination of the Surgical Patient,* 3rd ed. Philadelphia, WB Saunders, 1964, p 118.)

      d) Direct due to increased abdominal pressure associated with deterioration of supporting structures with age

      e) Direct and indirect hernias much more common after age 50

3. History

    a) Dull ache in groin

    b) Bulge in the groin, sometimes extending into scrotum (labia in women), often before pain has been experienced

    c) Incarcerated hernias may or may not be more painful

    d) Strangulated hernias always very painful and tender; nausea, vomiting, abdominal distention, fever are common

4. Physical examination

    a) First, with patient standing

    b) Indirect hernia, an elliptical swelling descending toward or into the scrotum

    c) Direct hernia, an isolated oval swelling near the pubis

    d) An attempt should be made to reduce hernia, first with patient standing

    e) If hernia not visible, the finger should be placed at base of scrotum, then cephalad and laterally into the inguinal canal: when the patient coughs or strains, hernia will protrude into canal

5. Differential diagnosis

    a) Strain of the adductor muscles: pain but no bulge

    b) Hydrocele: identified by transillumination

    c) Varicocele: feels soft and worm-like, usually collapses when patient lies down (if it does not, neoplastic obstruction of left spermatic vein should be suspected)

    d) Spermatocele: vaguely circumscribed, persists when patient lies down

    e) In testicle and environs

      1) Epididymal cyst: in any part of epididymis, smooth or lobulated

      2) Epididymitis: tender swollen epididymis, often relieved by elevation, immobilization of the scrotum

      3) Torsion of testicle: sudden onset of unremitting pain

      4) Testicular tumors: indurated, usually not tender

6. Management

    a) All inguinal hernias should be repaired

    b) Risk of incarceration or strangulation much greater with indirect hernias: repair of direct hernias can be more confidently deferred

    c) Trusses are contraindicated

    d) Acute, but not chronic, incarceration warrants hospitalization and repair

    e) Strangulation requires emergency surgery

7. Recurrence: 1–7% of indirect, 4–10% of direct — 50% of both within 5 years

B. Femoral

1. Epidemiology and etiology

    a) Second most common type of groin hernia

    b) Ten times more common in women

    c) Probably a combination of a congenitally large femoral ring and deterioration of tissue with aging; increased pressure (e.g., straining, pregnancy) often contributes

2. History
    a) Bulge in groin primary symptom
    b) Dull pain less common than with inguinal hernias
    c) Symptoms of incarceration or strangulation same as with inguinal hernias

3. Physical examination
    a) Mass often palpable medial to femoral vessels, inferior to inguinal ligament usually reducible
    b) Often difficult to detect; therefore, if signs and symptoms of unexplained intestinal obstruction, suspect strangulated femoral hernia

4. Differential diagnosis
    a) Enlarged lymph node, lipoma, saphenous varix: not reducible
    b) Direct inguinal hernia

5. Management
    a) All should be repaired
    b) Postoperative complications same as with inguinal hernias; 5–35% recur

INCISIONAL HERNIAS

A. Definition: protrusion of omentum and/or bowel through a surgical incision
B. Risk factors: poor surgical technique, wound infection, obesity, peritoneal dialysis
C. Presentation: bulge through the incision
D. Management: should be repaired
    1. Obese patients should lose weight first
    2. Abdominal binders may help if operation is delayed

UMBILICAL HERNIAS

A. Definition: protrusion of omentum and/or bowel through the umbilical ring
B. Etiology: probably due to congenital defects; occur mostly in middle-aged multiparous women, cirrhotics, frail elderly
C. Presentation: bulge usually obvious
    1. Occasionally, vague pain without bulge until patient lies supine and coughs
    2. Most common complication is incarceration with or without strangulation
D. Management: all should be repaired

EPIGASTRIC HERNIAS

A. Definition: protrusion of fat or omentum through the linea alba between the umbilicus and the xiphoid
B. Etiology: probably due to a congenital defect; occur mostly between ages 20 and 50; 3 times more common in men
C. Presentation: small painless subcutaneous mass just to the left of the midline
    1. Small hernias more likely to incarcerate
    2. Local pain and tenderness; less often, deep pain, abdominal distention, nausea and vomiting
D. Management: all should be repaired (10% recurrence rate)

75/ BENIGN CONDITIONS OF THE ANUS AND RECTUM

PRURITUS ANI
A. Definition: perianal itch, particularly in men, usually worse at night, often intermittent
B. Etiology: often unknown but may be symptom of an anorectal disorder (Table 75.1)
C. Diagnosis
   1. History
      a) Occasionally, an excess intake of milk, coffee, tea, alcohol, cola, or spices may be associated
      b) Medications (Table 75.1) may be involved
   2. Physical examination
      a) General
         1) Look for dermatological problems (Table 75.1)
         2) Pelvic examination in women to exclude associated vaginal infection
         3) Inspection of perianal region, including asking the patient to strain to demonstrate prolapse or fecal incontinence or by flatulence

Table 75.1. Common Problems Associated With Pruritus Ani

Drugs
    Oral antibiotics (tetracycline)
    Colchicine
    Laxatives
Dermatological disorders
    Psoriasis
    Atopic dermatitis
    Contact dermatitis
    Lichen planus
    Condylomata
    Venereal warts
    Herpes simplex
    Tumors
Diarrhea
Fissures
Fistulas
Infection
    Fungi and yeast (especially in diabetic patients) (see Chapter 83, Common Problems of the Skin)
    Erythrasma
    Scabies (see Chapter 83, Common Problems of the Skin)
    Pinworm (*Enterobius vermicularis*) infestation — more common in children
    Vaginal infections (see Chapter 77, Nonmalignant Vulvovaginal Disorders)
Obesity and excessive sweating
Poor anal hygiene
Rectal prolapse
Prolapsed hemorrhoids (most often hemorrhoids are not associated with pruritus, and other causes should be sought)

      b) Rectal
         1) Should be done routinely
         2) Excessive tenderness in one area should raise the suspicion of an anal fissure
         3) All structures within reach of the finger should be assessed

  3. Anoscopy
      a) Side and oblique views are important
      b) Instrument must be inserted and withdrawn 3 or 4 times for adequate inspection

  4. Cellophane tape examination for pinworms
      a) Fold clear cellophane tape, sticky side out, over a tongue blade
      b) Have patient place blade at the anal verge on awakening in morning, before bowel movement or cleaning of area
      c) Mount tape on a microscope slide and examine under $10 \times$ objective within a day or two

D. Treatment

  1. Tepid sitz baths
      a) Excellent temporary relief (e.g., at bedtime)
      b) Often prove to be impractical

  2. Ensure anal cleanliness
      a) Use of soft, white, unperfumed toilet tissue after a bowel movement
      b) If paper irritating, use of moistened cotton swabs, or glycerin or cleansing tissues (e.g., Preparation H cleansing tissue)
      c) Clean the area once or twice a day with plain soap; between times apply dry talc (or zinc oxide paste at night, removed each morning)

  3. Patient should wear cotton underwear

  4. Patient should avoid prolonged sitting

  5. Treat specific problems (Table 75.1)

  6. Severe nocturnal pruritus may respond to hydrocortisone cream, 0.5% or 1%

  7. Modify diet (see above) as necessary; response may not be observed for 1 or 2 weeks

  8. Control diarrhea or constipation (Chapter 25)

  9. If simple measures do not work, consider acidification of stool
      a) Stool pH can be measured with litmus paper or urine dipstick after mixing some stool with water
      b) If stool pH above 8 or 9 (normally 6 or 7), acidify with *Lactobacillus acidophilus* (e.g., *L. acidophilus* 1 or 2 capsules 3 times/day) or with malt soup extract (Maltsupex)

 10. Antipruritic sedatives (e.g., Benadryl 25–50 mg before bedtime) may be of help

 11. Pinworms
      a) Once identified, all members of family should be tested
      b) Drug of choice is pyrantel pamoate (e.g., Pin-X), single oral dose 11 mg/kg (not more than 1 g); alternative drug is mebendazole (Vermox), one 100-mg chewable tablet
      c) Clothing and bed linen should be laundered with hot water and detergent on same day medication has been taken

ANAL FISSURE

A. Definition: a painful elliptical tear, usually in the posterior portion of the anal canal
B. Etiology
    1. Primary: due to trauma (e.g., passage of a large hard stool)
    2. Secondary: due to inflammatory bowel disease, infection, or an anatomical defect (e.g., postoperative scar)
C. Diagnosis
    1. History
        a) Sudden onset of sharp rectal pain that occurs during and immediately after defecation, followed by a dull ache that may last for hours
        b) Sometimes, spotty bleeding
        c) Occasionally, pruritus ani (see above), almost always with mucus discharge
    2. Physical examination
        a) Buttocks gently retracted; patient asked to strain: many times fissures can be seen
        b) If a rectal examination is to be done (not necessary if fissure seen unless another problem is suspected), cotton saturated with lidocaine gel may be placed over fissure beforehand
        c) Chronic fissure recognizable by indurated edges and redundant tissue at outer lip (sentinel pile)
D. Treatment
    1. Conservative
        a) Stool softeners, continued after fissure heals, plus high fiber diet and water (8 glasses/day) (Chapter 25)
        b) Sitz baths, 15–20 minutes 1–3 times/day, followed by 0.5–1% hydrocortisone cream or by topical anesthetics (e.g., Nupercainal cream) for no more than 2–3 weeks
    2. Surgery
        a) If no improvement in 3–4 weeks or if fissure appears chronic (see above)
        b) High (97%) success rate

HEMORRHOIDAL DISEASE

A. Definition
    1. Simplistically, a varicosity of the rectal venous plexus (Fig. 75.1)
    2. Classification: Table 75.2
B. History
    1. External hemorrhoids: perianal pain exacerbated by defecation; patient may feel a tender perianal lump
    2. Internal hemorrhoids
        a) Bleeding: intermittent, bright red, usually spots toilet tissue or towel, occasionally more sustained
        b) Prolapse: sensation of anal fullness, especially after defecation; if irreducible, may be associated with fecal soilage, mucus, pruritus ani
        c) Pain: suggests thrombosis or strangulation
C. Physical examination
    1. External hemorrhoids: a soft and painless mass just outside the anal verge, but if thrombosed, firm, nontender, blue
    2. Internal hemorrhoids sometimes can be seen if buttocks retracted

Table 75.2 Classification of Hemorrhoids

External skin tags: Small discrete skin tags arising from the anal verge.

External hemorrhoids: Hemorrhoids arising from the inferior hemorrhoidal plexus exterior to the anal verge, covered by pain-sensitive skin. Thrombosis may cause acute and sometimes severe discomfort.

Internal hemorrhoids: Hemorrhoids arising from the vascular cushions, normal structures lying above the anal verge, covered by pain-insensitive mucosa. Internal hemorrhoids may be classified further:

  First degree: Hemorrhoids bulging into the lumen of the anal canal that produce bleeding

  Second degree: Hemorrhoids that prolapse during defecation but that reduce spontaneously

  Third degree: Prolapsed hemorrhoids that require manual reduction

  Fourth degree: Hemorrhoids that are irreducibly prolapsed

Thrombosed internal hemorrhoids: An internal hemorrhoid may prolapse and strangulate, which leads to thrombosis, an excruciating painful condition. If swelling progresses, gangrene of the hemorrhoids with ulceration, local infection, or pylephlebitis (septic phlebitis of the portal venous system) may result.

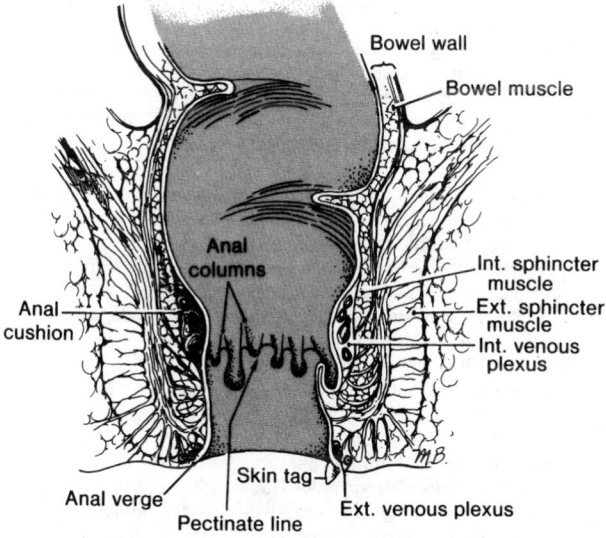

Figure 75.1. Important structures of the anal area.

and patient strains, but are diagnosed definitively by anoscopy (flexible sigmoidoscopy indicated if symptomatic hemorrhoids are of recent onset)

D. Differential diagnosis
  1. Hypertrophied anal papilla
    a) Along pectinate line (Fig. 75.1) in association with anal fissure, Crohn's disease, or no known cause
    b) Usually asymptomatic: occasionally erode, become infected, or bleed

2. Anal skin tags
   a) Small projections of redundant skin external to the anal verge
   b) May be associated with hemorrhoids or with Crohn's disease
   c) Asymptomatic: occasionally bleed, erode, or become infected
3. Prolapse of rectal mucosa
   a) More common in the elderly
   b) Identified by downward displacement of rectal mucosa without venous swelling
4. Protruding tumors: polyps, cancer, endometriosis — refer if in doubt

E. Course: symptoms usually resolve spontaneously but tend to recur

F. Treatment
1. Conservative (most patients respond)
   a) Avoidance of direct pressure (e.g., inflatable ring)
   b) Sitz baths 2–3 times/day for 15–20 minutes
   c) Stool softeners (Chapter 25), especially if stools are hard; increased bulk in diet; bulk laxative (Chapter 25); increased fluid consumption
   d) Topical hydrocortisone cream (e.g., 0.5–1% 3–4 times/day) may relieve pain or itching
   e) Analgesic rectal preparations (e.g., Nupercainal) 3–4 times/day
   f) Systemic analgesics (e.g., Tylox) occasionally necessary for pain of thrombosed hemorrhoid
2. Surgery
   a) Indications: doubt about diagnosis, no response in a week or two to conservative treatment, severe pain, evidence of strangulation, ulceration, or perianal infection
   b) Injection of sclerosing agents for first- or second-degree hemorrhoids (Table 75.2): office procedure
   c) Rubber band ligation for first-, second-, or third-degree hemorrhoids (Table 75.2): office procedure
   d) Manual dilation: unacceptable complications
   e) Partial internal sphincterotomy: ineffective
   f) Cryotherapy: no advantage over rubber band ligation and causes more discomfort
   g) Laser therapy and infrared photocoagulation for first-, second-, and third-degree hemorrhoids (Table 75.2): laser therapy has no special advantage and is expensive; photocoagulation efficacious in control of bleeding from stage 1 and 2 hemorrhoids
   h) Hemorrhoidectomy
      1) Only treatment for large internal and fourth-degree hemorrhoids
      2) Best chance of long-term control
3. Special considerations
   a) Conservative treatment, if possible, if patient has severe heart failure, debilitating disease, portal hypertension
   b) Hemorrhoids in pregnancy are common, best managed conservatively (unless strangulated)
   c) If coexistent with inflammatory bowel disease, should be managed with a gastroenterologist

ANORECTAL ABSCESSES AND ANORECTAL FISTULAS

A. Definitions
1. Anorectal abscesses involve the perineum and perianal structures and are classified by their location (Fig. 75.2)
2. Anorectal fistulas are tracts lined by granulation tissue and have an internal opening in the anal canal and an external opening in the perianal skin

B. History
1. Associated conditions: Table 75.3
2. More common in men
3. Abscess
   a) Abrupt onset of perianal pain intensified by sitting, walking, coughing, or defecating
   b) Malaise, chills, fever common
   c) Mucopurulent discharge or scant bleeding when draining
4. Fistula
   a) Most commonly, painful perianal swelling, frequently intermittent
   b) Often a purulent discharge

C. Rectal examination
1. Abscess
   a) Perianal (Fig. 75.2): warm, tender, subcutaneous swelling next to the anus
   b) Ischiorectal: fluctuation on digital examination; sometimes, only tenderness
   c) Higher anorectal: no findings, but patients often have severe pain, fever, and a high, very tender posterior rectal mass
2. Fistula
   a) External opening can often be seen in the perianal area
   b) Anoscopy may be of help

D. Treatment: referral to a surgeon for drainage of abscess, excision of fistula

PROCTALGIA FUGAX

A. History: sudden onset of severe, intermittent rectal pain lasting less than 30 minutes to 1 hour, often nocturnal, sometimes after intercourse
1. No associated organic illness
2. Often associated with psychiatric illness

B. Treatment
1. Sitz baths
2. Locally applied pressure
3. When severe, sublingual or cutaneous nitrates may be of help

RECTAL PROLAPSE

A. Definition: prolapse of the rectum through the anus
B. Epidemiology
1. More prevalent in women; peak incidence between ages 60 and 80 (in men, about age 40)
2. May be associated with chronic constipation or diarrhea
C. History
1. Initially, protrusion only with defecation; often a feeling of incomplete evacuation

   2. Eventually, prolapse, invariably with incontinence, occurs simply
      with walking or even standing
   3. Patients may complain of tenesmus, develop a mucous discharge
   4. Prolapse may become excoriated, bleed
   5. In advanced stage, there may be urinary incontinence; in females,
      uterine prolapse
D. Physical examination
   1. Inspect the anus when the patient strains (anticipate
      incontinence)
   2. Digital examination will reveal a patulous, relaxed anal sphincter
   3. Flexible sigmoidoscopy should be done routinely to exclude tumor
E. Treatment
   1. If prolapse is small, stool softeners and an irritant rectal
      suppository may prevent straining
   2. Otherwise, refer to a surgeon for ligation or sclerosis (mucosal
      prolapse) or operation (full-thickness prolapse)

VENEREAL DISEASE

A. Causes: Table 75.4
B. Diagnosis
   1. Perianal lesions
      a) Syphilis may be suspected by chancre, condyloma latum (wart-
         like excrescence) confirmed by dark-field examination
      b) Condyloma acuminatum: collection of warts extending into the
         canal
      c) Herpes simplex infection — first as vesicles, later as coalesced
         ulceration — requires fluorescent monoclonal antibody test or
         culture
      d) Proctitis
         1) Rectal discharge, pruritus, tenesmus, hematochezia,
            constipation common, no matter the cause
         2) Pain suggests herpetic infection (or syphilis) usually
            associated with constitutional symptoms (urinary retention,
            impotence, dysesthesias of perineum, buttocks, thighs)
         3) Inguinal adenopathy with syphilis, herpes,
            lymphogranuloma venereum (LGV)
         4) Anoscopy and flexible sigmoidoscopy required
            (a) Gonorrhea causes a nonspecific inflammation, diagnosed
                by culture
            (b) Syphilis requires dark-field examination
            (c) LGV causes linear and aphthous ulceration, requires
                culture or serial serological studies
            (d) Amebiasis causes punched-out ulcers with a yellow base
                and diffuse inflammation
C. Treatment
   1. Most conditions warrant referral to a gastroenterologist
   2. Patients with gonorrheal proctitis need not be referred: treatment
      is usually successful (Chapters 13 and 77)
   3. Luetic proctitis also easily treated (Chapters 16 and 77)
   4. Chlamydial (e.g., LGV) infections respond to tetracycline,
      erythromycin, or sulfa (Chapter 13)
   5. Condyloma acuminatum may respond to podophyllin (Chapter 82);
      large lesions may require excision or fulguration

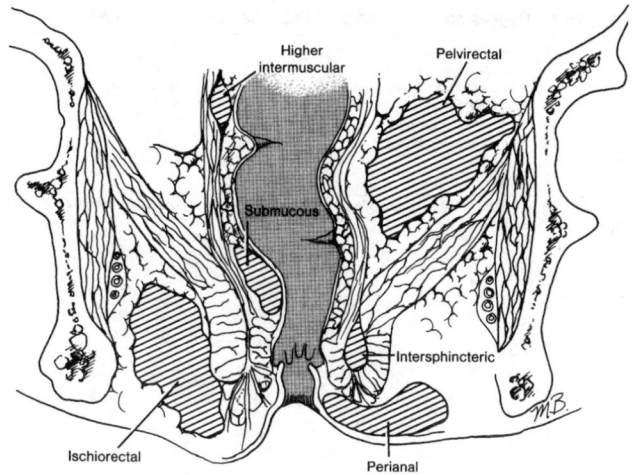

Figure 75.2. Anatomical classification of common anorectal abscesses.

Table 75.3 Conditions That May Be Complicated by Anorectal Abscess and Fistula in Ano

INFLAMMATORY BOWEL DISEASE
CHRONIC INFECTIONS (uncommon)
  Actinomycosis
  Tuberculosis
  Lymphogranuloma venereum
  Schistosomiasis (rare)
  Amebiasis (rare)
INFECTION ANATOMICALLY ADJACENT TO THE RECTAL AREA AND PRESENTING AS
  ANORECTAL ABSCESS OR FISTULA IN ANO
  In women
    Pelvic inflammatory disease
    Bartholin gland abscess
  In men
    Infections of a Cowper gland (small periurethral glands)
    Pilonidal sinus (occasionally occurs in females)
FOREIGN BODY (e.g., an ingested bone or a penetrating wooden splinter)
TRAUMA
  Surgery (e.g., hemorrhoidectomy or prostatectomy)
  Radiation
  Laceration (e.g., from an enema)
ABNORMALITIES OF HOST DEFENSE (e.g., bone marrow aplasia, leukemia or lymphoma, diabetes
  mellitus)
CARCINOMA OF ANUS OR RECTUM

6. Amebiasis is treated with metronidazole and, usually, with diiodohydroxyquin (Chapter 12)
7. Herpetic infection may be associated with HIV infection (Chapter 20), may respond to sitz baths and to topical analgesic cream, if mild; to topical or oral acyclovir, if severe

Table 75.4 Causes and Prevalence of Proctitis in Homosexual Men

Gonorrhea	13–45%
Syphilis	5–10%
Lymphogranuloma venereum (LGV)	Uncommon
Non-LGV *Chlamydia trachomatis*	8–15%
Condyloma acuminatum	50%
Herpes simplex virus[a]	6–30%
Amebiasis	20–30%
Cryptococcosis[a]	Rare

From Peppercorn MA: Enteric infections in homosexual men with and without AIDS. *Contemp Gastroenterol* 2:23, 1989.
[a] Especially associated with AIDS.

Section XII
Gynecological Problems

CONTRACEPTIVE DEVICES AND METHODS

A. General considerations
1. Methods of contraception, including mechanism, failure rate, adverse effects: Table 76.1
2. Before deciding about methods of contraception, elicit the medical history (to identify risks of becoming pregnant) and perform physical and pelvic examination [including cancer detection smear and, in a patient with multiple sexual partners, gonococcal culture and chlamydia smear (see Chapter 77)]
3. Protection is necessary until menopause

B. Oral contraceptives
1. Modes: Table 76.1
2. Some currently available preparations: Table 76.2
3. Contraindications: Table 76.3
4. Recommended dosages
   a) Start with a preparation containing 30–35 μg of estrogen and ≤1 mg of progestin
   b) If there is breakthrough bleeding, >35 μg of estrogen may be needed but should not be used for more than 2 or 3 cycles
   c) If there is persistent breakthrough bleeding or no withdrawal bleeding, refer to a gynecologist
   d) Combination tablet taken daily for 3 weeks, starting the fifth day of cycle or first Sunday after onset of the menstrual period
5. Noncontraceptive benefits: Table 76.4
6. Risks (Table 76.1)
   a) Thromboembolic disease (arterial and venous)
      1) Risk much higher if estrogen dose exceeds 35 μg/day
      2) Increased age (over 35 years) and smoking compound risk
   b) Hypertension: not a risk with estrogen doses of 35 μg/day or lower
   c) Neoplasia: Table 76.5
   d) Gallbladder disease: 2-fold increase within 1–2 years of taking oral contraceptives
   e) Headaches: migraine may be intensified and cause a change to another method of contraception
   f) Birth defects: no evidence to support an association
   g) Other side effects
      1) Alopecia: rare, usually transient
      2) Nausea: uncommon; can be eliminated by taking the contraceptive at bedtime
      3) Fatigue: occasionally reported but transient
      4) Change in menstrual flow: typically a reduction in amount and duration of flow
      5) Breakthrough bleeding: most common in first few cycles after starting regimen
      6) Weight gain: in about 5% of patients
      7) Chloasma (yellowish-brown discoloration of skin): relatively uncommon but will not abate if regimen is continued

Table 76.1. Summary of Methods of Contraception, Their Mechanism of Action, Failure Rate, and Major Adverse Effects

Method	Mechanism of Action	Failure Rate %[a] Low	Failure Rate %[a] High	Some Adverse Effects
No method		85	85	
Spermicide alone	Inactivation of sperm	21.6	25.6	Irritation can occur
Sponge with spermicide	Mechanical barrier to sperm; inactivation of sperm	16	51.9	Increased risk of vaginal infection
Withdrawal	Avoidance of coitus during presumed fertile days	14.7	27.8	
Periodic abstinence		13.8	19.2	
Diaphragm or cervical cap with spermicide	Mechanical barrier to sperm; inactivation of sperm	12	38.9	Increased risk of urinary tract or vaginal infection
Condom	Mechanical barrier to sperm	9.8	18.5	Allergic reactions
Oral contraceptives		3.8	8.7	
Combined	Suppression of ovulation, changes in cervical mucus and endometrium			Estrogen-related risk of thromboembolism, stroke; myocardial infarction in older smokers; hypertension
Progestin only	Changes in cervical mucus and endometrium, possibly suppression of ovulation			Irregular, unpredictable bleeding in some
Intrauterine device Progesterone T Copper T 380A	Inhibition of sperm migration, fertilization, or ovum transport	2.5	4.5	Pelvic inflammatory disease; uterine perforation; increase in menstrual blood loss with copper
Medroxyprogesterone (Depo-Provera)	Changes in cervical mucus and endometrium, suppression of ovulation	<1	<1	Menstrual irregularities; headache; weight gain
Levonorgestrel subdermal implants (Norplant)	Same as medroxyprogesterone acetate	<1	<1	Menstrual irregularities; headache; weight gain

Adapted from: Choice of contraceptives. *Med Lett Drugs Ther* 34:111, 1992.

[a] Percent accidental pregnancy during first year of use among women in the United States more likely (low failure rate) and less likely (high failure rate) than average to use the method correctly and consistently (Harlap S, et al: *Preventing Pregnancy, Protecting Health.* New York, Alan Guttmacher Inst, 1991, p 33).

Table 76.2.　Some Current Oral Contraceptives Available in the United States

Drug	Estrogen (μg)	μg per Month	Progestin (mg)[a]	mg per Month	Cost ($)[b]
COMBINATION					
Loestrin 1/20 21, 28 (Parke-Davis)	Ethinyl estradiol (20)	420	Norethindrone acetate (1)	21	22.33
Loestrin 1.5/30 21, 28 (Parke-Davis)	Ethinyl estradiol (30)	630	Norethindrone acetate (1.5)	31.5	22.33
Levlen 21, 28 (Berlex)	Ethinyl estradiol (30)	630	Levonorgestrel (0.15)	3.15	19.43
Nordette 21 (Wyeth Ayerst)	Ethinyl estradiol (30)	630	Levonorgestrel (0.15)	3.15	21.99
Lo/Ovral 21 (Wyeth-Ayerst)[c]	Ethinyl estradiol (30)	630	Norgestrel (0.3)	6.3	22.02
Tri-Levlen 21, 28 (Berlex)	Ethinyl estradiol (30, 40)	680	Levonorgestrel (0.05, 0.075, 0.125)	1.925	17.28
Triphasil 21 (Wyeth-Ayerst)[c]	Ethinyl estradiol (30, 40)	680	Levonorgestrel (0.05, 0.075, 0.125)	1.925	19.27
Ortho Tri-Cyclene (Ortho)	Ethinyl estradiol (35, 35, 35)	735	Norgestimate (0.18, 0.215, 0.25)	4.515	21.16
Ovcon 35 21, 28 (Mead Johnson)	Ethinyl estradiol (35)	735	Norethindrone (0.4)	8.4	21.02
Brevicon 21, 28 (Syntex)	Ethinyl estradiol (35)	735	Norethindrone (0.5)	10.5	20.32
Genora 0.5/35, 28 (Rugby)	Ethinyl estradiol (35)	735	Norethindrone (0.5)	10.5	8.23
Modicon 21 (Ortho)[c]	Ethinyl estradiol (35)	735	Norethindrone (0.5)	10.5	22.10
N.E.E. 0.5/35, 21, 28 (Lexis)	Ethinyl estradiol (35)	735	Norethindrone (0.5)	10.5	10.25
Nelova 0.5/35, 21, 28 (Warner-Chilcott)[c]	Ethinyl estradiol (35)	735	Norethindrone (0.5)	10.5	13.90
Generic (Spencer-Mead)	Ethinyl estradiol (35)	735	Norethindrone (0.5)	10.5	5.95
Tri-Norinyl 21, 28 (Syntex)	Ethinyl estradiol (35, 35)	735	Norethindrone (0.5, 1.0)	15	19.53
Ortho-Novum 7/7/7 21 (Ortho)[c]	Ethinyl estradiol (35, 35, 35)	735	Norethindrone (0.5, 0.75, 1.0)	15.75	20.10
N.E.E. 10/11 21, 28 (Lexis)	Ethinyl estradiol (35)	735	Norethindrone (0.5, 1.0)	16	10.25
Nelova 10/11 21 (Warner-Chilcott)[c]	Ethinyl estradiol (35)	735	Norethindrone (0.5, 1.0)	16	13.90
Ortho-Novum 10/11 21 (Ortho)[c]	Ethinyl estradiol (35, 35)	735	Norethindrone (0.5, 1.0)	16	22.10
Janest-28 (Organon)	Ethinyl estradiol (35)	735	Norethindrone (1)	21	16.40
Genora 1/35 21, 28 (Rugby)	Ethinyl estradiol (35)	735	Norethindrone (1)	21	11.00
N.E.E. 1/35 21, 28 (Lexis)	Ethinyl estradiol (35)	735	Norethindrone (1)	21	10.25
Nelova 1/35 21 (Warner-Chilcott)	Ethinyl estradiol (35)	735	Norethindrone (1)	21	12.38
Generic (Dixon-Shane)	Ethinyl estradiol (35)	735	Norethindrone (1)	21	11.90
Generic (Spencer-Meade)	Ethinyl estradiol (35)	735	Norethindrone (1)	21	6.25
Norcept-E 1/35 21, 28 (GynoPharma)	Ethinyl estradiol (35)	735	Norethindrone (1)	21	5.72

Norethin 1/35E 21, 28 (Schiapparelli Searle)	Ethinyl estradiol (35)	735	Norethindrone (1)	21	11.00
Norinyl 1+35 21, 28 (Syntex)	Ethinyl estradiol (35)	735	Norethindrone (1)	21	20.32
Ortho-Novum 1/35 21 (Ortho)c	Ethinyl estradiol (35)	735	Norethindrone (1)	21	20.05
Ortho-Cyclen (Ortho)	Ethinyl estradiol (35)	735	Norgestimate (0.25)	5.25	21.16
Demulen 1/35 21 (Searle)c	Ethinyl estradiol (35)	735	Ethynodiol diacetate (1)	21	21.27
Ovral (Wyeth-Ayerst)c	Ethinyl estradiol (50)	1050	Norgestrel (0.5)	10.5	34.35
Norlestrin 1/50 21, 28 (Parke-Davis)	Ethinyl estradiol (50)	1050	Norethindrone acetate (1)	21	21.27
Ovcon 50 21, 28 (Mead Johnson)	Ethinyl estradiol (50)	1050	Norethindrone (1)	21	23.20
Demulen 1/50 21 (Searle)c	Ethinyl estradiol (50)	1050	Ethynodiol diacetate (1)	21	23.72
Norlestrin 2.5/50 21, 28 (Parke-Davis)	Ethinyl estradiol (50)	1050	Norethindrone acetate (2.5)	52.5	22.01
N.E.E. 1/50 M 21, 28 (Lexis)	Mestranol (50)	1050	Norethindrone (1)	21	10.25
Genora 1/50 21, 28 (Rugby)	Mestranol (50)	1050	Norethinedrone (1)	21	11.00
Nelova 1/50 21 (Warner-Chilcott)	Mestranol (50)	1050	Norethindrone (1)	21	12.38
Norethin 1/50-M 21, 28 (Schiapparelli Searle)	Mestranol (50)	1050	Norethindrone (1)	21	11.00
Norinyl 1+50 21, 28 (Syntex)	Mestranol (50)	1050	Norethindrone (1)	21	20.32
Ortho-Novum 1/50 21 (Ortho)c	Mestranol (50)	1050	Norethindrone (1)	21	20.05
Generic (Spencer-Mead)	Mestranol (50)	1050	Norethindrone (1)	21	6.25
PROGESTIN ONLY					
Ovrette (Wyeth-Ayerst)	None		Norgestrel (0.075)	2.1	21.89
Nor-QD (Syntex)	None		Norethindrone (0.35)	7.35	23.63
Micronor (Ortho)	None		Norethindrone (0.35)	9.8	25.45

Adapted from: Choice of contraceptives. Med Lett Drugs Ther 34:111, 1992.

a Different progestins cannot be compared on a milligram basis.
b Cost to pharmacist for 1 month's use, based on manufacturer's listings in Drug Topics Red Book, 1992.
c Also available in 28-day regimens at slightly higher cost.

Table 76.3.   Absolute Contraindications to Oral Contraceptives

Thrombophlebitis or thromboembolic disorders (current or remote)
Cerebral vascular or coronary artery disease (current or remote)
Known or suspected carcinoma of the breast
Known or suspected estrogen-dependent neoplasia
Undiagnosed, abnormal genital bleeding
Known or suspected pregnancy

Table 76.4.   Noncontraceptive Health Benefits of Oral Contraceptives[a]

Disease	Rate of Hospitalizations Prevented per 100,000 Pill Users	Number of Hospitalizations Prevented	Number of Deaths Averted
Benign breast disease	235	20,000	
Ovarian retention cysts	35	3,000	
Iron deficiency anemia[b]	320	27,000	
Pelvic inflammatory disease (first episodes)			
Total episodes[b]	600	51,000	100
Hospitalizations	156	13,300	
Ectopic pregnancy	117	9,900	10
Endometrial cancer[c]	5	2,000	100
Ovarian cancer[c]	4	1,700	1,000

Adapted from Ory HW: The noncontraceptive health benefits from oral contraceptive use. *Fam Plann Perspect* 14:182, 1982.

[a] Rate of hospitalizations prevented and deaths averted annually by use of oral contraceptives, per 100,000 pill users, and estimated number of hospitalizations and deaths prevented annually, by specific disease in the United States. Except where noted, figures refer to hospitalizations prevented among the estimated 8.5 million current users of oral contraceptives in the United States.

[b] Episodes prevented regardless of whether hospitalization occurred.

[c] Based on an estimated 39 million United States women who have ever used oral contraceptives.

Table 76.5.   Oral Contraceptives and Neoplasia Risk

	Increased	No Effect	Decreased	Inconclusive Information
Hepatocellular adenoma	X			
Cervical neoplasia				X
Endometrial cancer			X	
Ovarian cancer			X	
Breast cancer		X		
Pituitary adenoma		X		
Malignant melanoma				X

8) Depression: occasional problem warranting discontinuation of medication
9) Effects on laboratory tests: Table 76.6
10) Drug interactions: Table 76.7

7. Follow-up
   a) Pelvic examination, cervical cytology yearly
   b) Oral contraceptives can be stopped abruptly if pregnancy is desired or another form of contraception is planned

C. Subdermal contraceptive (Norplant) (Table 76.1)
   1. The most effective method [with Depo-Provera (see below)] of reversible contraception

Table 76.6. Effects of Oral Contraceptives on Selected Laboratory Tests

Laboratory Test	Effects	Probable Mechanism
SERUM, PLASMA, BLOOD		
Albumin	Slightly decreased	Decreased hepatic synthesis
Aldosterone	Increased	Activates renin-angiotensin system
Amylase	Slightly increased (common)	Pancreatitis
	Markedly increased (rare)	
Antinuclear antibodies	Become detectable	Not established
Bilirubin	Increased (rare)	Reduced secretion into bile
Coagulation factors	Increased II, VII, IX, X	Increased synthesis
Cortisol	Increased	Increased cortisol-binding globulin
		Urinary free cortisol unchanged
Folate	Decreased or no change	Decreased folate absorption
Haptoglobin	Decreased	Decreased hepatic synthesis
High-density lipoprotein cholesterol	Increased with estrogens and decreased with progestins	Not established
Iron-binding capacity	Increased	Increased transferrin levels
Magnesium	Decreased or no change	Decreased bone resorption
Phosphatase, alkaline	Increased (rare)	Altered secretion bile
Platelets	Slightly increased	Not established
Prolactin	Increased	Not established
Renin activity	Increased	Increased synthesis of renin substrate
Thyroxine (total)	Increased	Increased thyroxine-binding globulin
Transaminases	Slightly increased	Not established
Triiodothyronine	Decreased	Increased thyroxine-binding globulin
Vitamin B_{12}	Decreased	Not established
URINE		
δ-Aminolevulinic acid	Increased	Increased hepatic synthesis
Calcium	Decreased	Decreased bone resorption
Prophyrins	Increased (may precipitate porphyria in susceptible patients)	Increased δ-aminolevulinic acid synthetase
17-Hydroxycorticosteroids	Slightly decreased or no change	Increased binding proteins
17-Ketosteroids	Slightly decreased or no change	Increased binding proteins

Adapted from: Effect of oral contraceptive on laboratory test results. *Med Lett Drugs Ther* 21:54, 1979.

Table 76.7. Selected Drugs That May Interact With Oral Contraceptive Preparations (OCPs)

Drugs that may decrease the effectiveness of OCPs, resulting in breakthrough bleeding, pregnancy, or both

A. Well-established, relatively commonly occurring drug reactions
1. Anticonvulsants: barbiturates, phenytoin (Dilantin), or primidone (Mysoline)
2. Antimicrobials: rifampicin
B. Reported instances of possible drug interactions
1. Antimicrobials
a. Breakthrough bleeding only: neomycin, nitrofurantoin, phenoxymethylpenicillin (penicillin V)
b. Breakthrough bleeding and pregnancy: ampicillin, chloramphenicol, sulfamethoxypridaxine (Kynex, Midicel)
2. Others: chlordiazepoxide (Librium), meprobamate, phenacetin, and phenylbutazone (Butazolidin)

Drugs whose effectiveness may be altered by OCPs

A. Anticoagulants: The effect of anticoagulants may be reduced by the simultaneous administration of OCPs.
B. Clofibrate (Atromid-S): Control of cholesterol and triglyceride levels may be lost when OCPs are simultaneously administered with clofibrate.
C. Thyroid hormone in patients without functioning thyroid gland: Mostly a theoretical concern; however, there may be a need for an increased dose of thyroid hormone in patients without a functioning thyroid gland.
D. Tricyclic antidepressants: Higher doses of estrogen may inhibit the effect of antidepressants, and tricyclic toxicity may be increased.
E. Caffeine: There may be decreased metabolism of caffeine induced by OCPs. Patients who take large amounts of caffeine (e.g., 4–8 cups of coffee/day) should be cautioned regarding symptoms of caffeinism.

2. Provides protection for at least 5 years; insertion and removal under local anesthesia in an office setting
3. Contraindications: pregnancy, thromboembolic events, undiagnosed genital bleeding, active liver disease, breast cancer
4. Side effects: Table 76.1
5. Rapid return of fertility when removed
D. Intramuscular injectable contraceptive (Depo-Provera) (Table 76.1)
1. Injection of 150 mg provides contraception for at least 14 weeks
2. Side effects: Table 76.1
3. Possible delay in return of fertility for 4–9 months after injection
E. Intrauterine device (Table 76.1)
1. Recommended only for women who desire no further pregnancies and who are in a mutually faithful monogamous relationship (multiple partners increase risk of pelvic inflammatory disease)
2. Types
a) Progestasert: a plastic device with a progesterone reservoir that is depleted in 12 months
b) ParaGard: contains copper but no hormone, can be used continuously for 8 years
3. Best inserted at the time of the menstrual period, often associated with transient cramping
4. Risks
a) Contraindications: Table 76.8
b) Adverse effects: Table 76.1
5. Follow-up

Table 76.8   Contraindications to Insertion of an Intrauterine Device (IUD)

1. Pregnancy or suspicion of pregnancy
2. Abnormalities of the uterus, resulting in distortion of the uterine cavity
3. Acute, or history of, pelvic inflammatory disease
4. Postpartum endometritis or infected abortion in the past 3 months
5. Known or suspected uterine or cervical malignancy, including unresolved abnormal Papanicolaou smear
6. Genital bleeding of unknown etiology
7. Untreated acute cervicitis until infection is controlled
8. Wilson's disease (copper-containing IUDs)
9. Known allergy to copper
10. History of ectopic pregnancy
11. Patient or her partner has multiple sexual partners
12. Conditions associated with increased susceptibility to infections with microorganisms, including leukemia, diabetes, AIDS, and those requiring chronic corticosteroid therapy
13. Genital actinomycosis
14. A previously inserted IUD that has not been removed

      a) Annual visit for interval history, pelvic examination including a cervical cancer smear, gonorrhea or chlamydia culture (if indicated)
      b) Device easily removed by gentle traction on the string at the time of a menstrual period
F. Contraceptive sponge (Table 76.1)
    1. Should remain in vagina no longer than 24 hours, should not be removed until 6 hours after intercourse
    2. Discarded after removal
    3. For women who have intercourse infrequently and for postpartum patients
    4. Associated rarely with toxic shock syndrome (Chapter 77)
G. Contraceptive diaphragm (Table 76.1)
    1. Prescribed by a physician or an assistant, and the first placement is checked by the prescriber
    2. May be inserted for as long as 4 hours before intercourse, should be checked for position and left in place at least 6–8 hours after intercourse (if intercourse repeated during that time more spermicidal jelly should be applied)
    3. Lasts 2 years, but new fitting needed after significant change in weight, pregnancy, or pelvic surgery
    4. Cervical cap, an alternative to the diaphragm, fits snugly over cervix; first placement must be done by a trained professional
    5. Risks: Table 76.1; contraindicated if there is a sensitivity to rubber or to the spermicidal jelly or if the woman will not or cannot (e.g., because of obesity) touch her vagina
H. Condom (Table 76.1)
    1. Effectiveness enhanced if combined with application of spermicidal jelly or foam in the vagina
    2. Also protects against sexually transmitted disease
I. Vaginal suppositories, foam, or jelly
    1. Inserted at least 10–15 minutes before intercourse in the vagina and (foam or jelly) over the cervix
    2. Useful to increase effectiveness of condom at midcycle or of diaphragm if repeated intercourse occurs

J. Rhythm method (Table 76.1)
  1. Calendar method: patient keeps a record of the duration of each menstrual cycle, subtracts 18 days from shortest cycle, 11 days from longest cycle, establishing time of fertile period
  2. Basal body temperature method: patient takes her temperature each morning from day 3 of the cycle until it has been elevated (usually 1°) above baseline for 72 hours, at which point she is postovulatory and intercourse may be resumed
  3. Cervical mucus method: requires patient to learn changes in mucus (becomes clearer) and to recognize abdominal discomfort associated with ovulation
K. Sterilization
  1. Vasectomy
    a) Under local anesthesia in a urologist's office; vigorous physical activity and sexual intercourse restricted for 5–7 days; patient not sterile for 4–6 weeks (established by sperm counts)
    b) Reanastomosis successful in 60% of patients, but vasectomy should only be done if intent is permanent sterilization
    c) Risks
      1) Short term: infection, hematoma, epididymitis, granuloma formation
      2) Long term: possibly increased risk of prostate cancer — data inconclusive
  2. Tubal ligation
    a) Under general anesthesia in an ambulatory surgery unit; normal activity may be resumed in 2–3 days; sexual intercourse permitted as soon as wound no longer hurts
    b) Reanastomosis often successful, but tubal ligation should only be done if intent is permanent sterilization
    c) Risks: bleeding, infection, operative trauma to bowel, bladder, or uterus

DIAGNOSING PREGNANCY

A. Tests for detection of β-subunit of human chorionic gonadotropin are highly sensitive and specific
B. Types
  1. Radioimmunoassay (serum): Chorio Quant, Beta Tec, HCG Beta III
    a) Nearly 100% accurate when used at least 7 days after conception
    b) No luteinizing hormone (LH) cross-reaction
    c) Used also for assessing abnormal pregnancy (e.g., ectopic, threatened abortion)
    d) Specimen must be sent to a laboratory; turnaround time is 1 day
  2. Enzyme-linked immunoassay (urine or serum): Icon, Confidot, Quest
    a) Accurate when used at least 12 days after conception
    b) No LH cross-reaction
    c) Results available in minutes
  3. Radioreceptor assay (serum): Biocept-G
    a) Accurate when used at least 14 days after conception
    b) LH cross-reaction possible

c) Specimen sent to the laboratory; turnaround time is 1 day
4. Immunoassay (urine or serum): Neocept, Pregnosis
    a) Accurate when used at least 28 days after conception
    b) LH cross-reaction possible
    c) Serum must be sent to a laboratory, but urine can be tested in the office

VULVOVAGINITIS

A. Candidiasis (Table 77.1)

1. Accounts for 40% of cases of vulvovaginitis
2. *Candida* a normal inhabitant of the vagina in 16% of nonpregnant women in their reproductive age
3. Predisposing factors: pregnancy, diabetes mellitus, immunosuppression, antibiotic or corticosteroid therapy, iron deficiency, vaginal surgery, oral contraceptives, use of tight-fitting synthetic underclothes or pants
4. Signs: inflammation of vulva and vagina; vaginal mucosa may show adherent white patches; there may be vulvar erosions and pustules
5. Diagnosis: confirmed by placing a few drops of 20% KOH on a slide over a few drops of vaginal secretions and finding budding filaments, pseudohyphae, and spores
6. Treatment topical: given first [before oral (see below)]
    a) Terconazole (Terazol): one 80-mg suppository or 0.4% cream intravaginally at bedtime for 3 days *or*
    b) Butoconazole nitrate (Femstat): one applicator full of 2% cream intravaginally at bedtime for 3 days *or*
    c) Miconazole nitrate (Monistat): one 200-mg suppository intravaginally at bedtime for 7 days *or*
    d) Clotrimazole (Gyne-Lotrimin or Mycelex): two 100-mg tablets intravaginally for 3 days, or one 100-mg tablet intravaginally at bedtime for 7 days, or one applicator full of 2% cream intravaginally for 7 days
7. Resistant/recurrent infection
    a) If a second infection occurs relatively soon, patient should be re-examined and have a KOH preparation (see above) within 1–2 weeks of treatment of second infection to see if organism has been eradicated
    b) Persistent infection warrants a 7-day course of an antifungal agent
    c) Recurrent infection warrants consideration of a different antifungal agent
    d) Reinfection dictates that the male partner be treated with antifungal cream placed on the scrotum, penile glans, and shaft for each of 7 nights; if there has been cunnilingus, the partner should be treated with oral nystatin
    e) Patients with recurrent infection should be instructed to wipe from front to back when bathing and after urination or defecation
    f) Eight ounces of *Lactobacillus acidophilus* yogurt eaten daily for 6–12 months may decrease recurrences
    g) Ketoconazole (200-mg tablets), 400 mg twice a day for 2 weeks followed by 100 mg (1/2 tablet)/day for 6–12 months, or fluconazole (50-, 100-, 200-mg tablets), 150 mg once a month (expensive, reserved for ketoconazole failures), may suppress reinfection

Table 77.1. Vaginal Discharge

	Symptoms	Malodor	Increased Mucosal Erythema	Consistency	pH	Wet Smear	KOH	Treatment of Choice (See Text for Doses)
Physiological	None	None	None	Floccular	3.5–4.1	Rare WBCs, large Gram-positive rods, squamous epithelial cells		None
Candida	Pruritus, burning	Yeast smell	Yes	Thick, curd-like	3.5–4.5	Budding filaments, spores, pseudohyphae	Budding filaments, spores, pseudohyphae	Imidazole or traizole derivative
Bacterial vaginosis	±Pruritus, burning	Fishy or musty	±	Thin, creamy	5.0–6.0	Clue cells	Fishy odor, musty odor	Metronidazole or clindamycin
Trichomonas	±Pruritus	Variable	Yes	Copious, frothy	6.0–7.0	Copious WBCs, trichomonads		Metronidazole
Atrophic	±Vulvar, vaginal dryness	Variable	±	Mucoid, blood tinged	As high as 7.0	Copious WBCs, parabasal and intermediate cells, paucity of superficial cells		Estrogen cream

WBC, white blood cell.

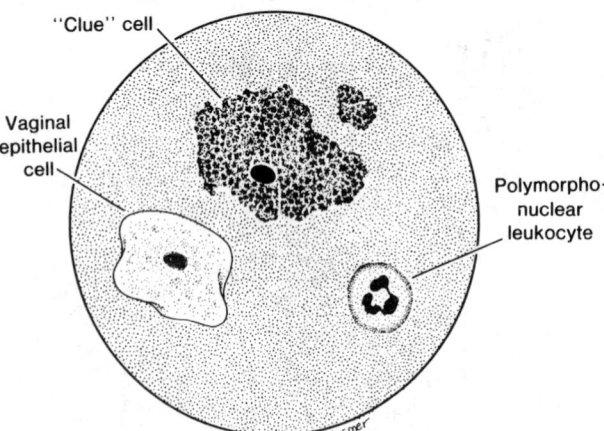

Figure 77.1. "Clue" cells.

    h) Recurrences related to specific events (e.g., menses) may be prevented by use of clotrimazole suppositories for each of 3 days before event

    i) If above measures fail, diabetes mellitus (Chapter 56) and HIV infection (Chapter 20) should be excluded, and if ruled out, referral to a gynecologist is indicated

B. Bacterial vaginosis vulvovaginitis (Table 77.1)
   1. *Gardnerella vaginalis* and various anaerobic bacteria found in vagina in increased concentrations
   2. Vagina and vulva may be mildly inflamed
   3. Fishy odor especially prominent after intercourse
   4. Clue cells seen on saline wet smear are vaginal squamous cells covered with bacteria (Fig. 77.1)
   5. Treatment
     a) Metronidazole (Flagyl) 500-mg tablets 2 times/day for 7 days, or 0.75% gel (Metrogel) intravaginally 2 times/day for 5 days, or 2% clindamycin phosphate cream (Cleocin vaginal cream) intravaginally for 7 nights
     b) Metronidazole contraindicated during first trimester of pregnancy or in alcoholics; in such cases use clindamycin 300 mg 2 times/day for 7 days or 2% clindamycin cream, as above
     c) Partner should use a condom during intercourse during treatment period

C. *Trichomonas* infection (Table 77.1)
   1. Symptoms, besides pruritus, may include vaginal burning, spotting, dysuria, increased frequency of urination, urgency
   2. Vaginal mucosa may show a typical reddish color with punctuation ("strawberry" appearance)
   3. Saline wet smear usually shows multiple white cells and trichomonads (Fig. 77.2) with moving flagella (if prepared at room temperature)

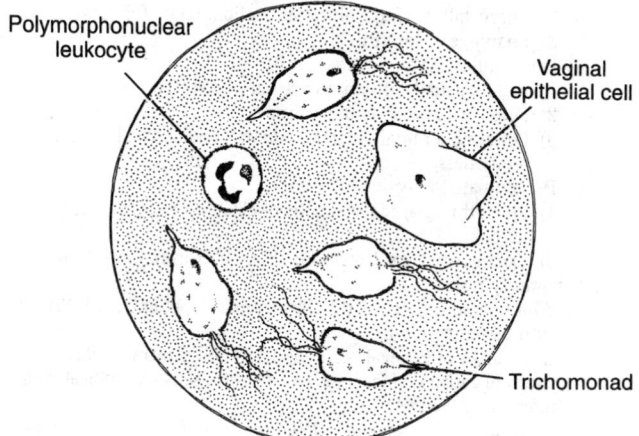

Polymorphonuclear leukocyte

Vaginal epithelial cell

Trichomonad

Figure 77.2.   Saline preparation showing trichomonads.

4. Treatment
   a) Single 2-g dose of metronidazole (Flagyl); if ineffective, 500 mg 2 times/day for 7 days or 2 g/day for 3–5 days
   b) Unresponsive patients should be referred to a gynecologist
   c) If metronidazole contraindicated, clindamycin should be prescribed (see bacterial vaginosis, above)
   d) Sexual partners should be treated also and should wear a condom during intercourse during period of treatment

D. Atrophic vaginitis (Table 77.1)
   1. Due to estrogen deficiency
   2. Treatment
      a) Estrogen cream, one-half to one applicator of estrogen cream every night for 1–2 weeks, then every other night for 2 weeks, then for 1 or 2 days if symptoms recur
      b) Patients should also be followed by a gynecologist
      c) If patient unwilling to use cream, Premarin 0.625 mg/day for 1 month can be prescribed
      d) Asymptomatic women with atrophic vaginas need not be treated

GONOCOCCAL AND CHLAMYDIAL INFECTIONS

A. Gonococcal infection
   1. Risk of transmission: 90% from infected men to uninfected women; 20% from infected women to uninfected men
   2. Symptoms and signs
      a) Initially none: routine screening important in women with multiple sexual partners or with other sexually transmitted diseases
      b) Uncomplicated infection
         1) Vaginal: purulent discharge, itching, dyspareunia, dysuria, vague lower abdominal pain

        2) Anorectal: itching, painful defecation, rectal fullness
        3) Pharyngeal: sore throat
   c) Pelvic inflammatory disease (PID)
        1) Begins usually after a menstrual period
        2) Fever, nausea, abdominal pain
        3) Lower abdominal, bilateral adnexal, and cervical motion tenderness
   d) Disseminated infection
        1) Polyarthralgia; tenosynovitis of elbows, wrists, or knees; skin lesions
        2) Usually develops 1 or more weeks after initial infection
  3. Laboratory tests
   a) White blood cell count usually elevated in patients with PID or with disseminated infection
   b) Gram stain of cervical material diagnostic if intracellular Gram-negative diplococci are seen; not a sensitive indicator of infection, however
   c) Cultures (chocolate agar), DNA probe test, fluorescent antibody test, or enzyme immunoassay is confirmatory
  4. Management: Table 77.2
B. *Chlamydia trachomatis* infection
  1. Symptoms and signs
   a) Lower tract infection and PID — similar to those of gonorrhea (see above)
   b) Cervical discharge less profuse than in gonorrhea, onset more indolent
  2. Laboratory tests
   a) Cultures are definitive but expensive, and growth is slow
   b) Diagnosis usually made by fluorescent antibody staining, enzyme immunoassay, or DNA probe test
  3. Management: Table 77.2

VULVAR ULCERATIONS
A. Herpes simplex (Table 77.3)
  1. Sexually transmitted, characterized by remissions and exacerbations independent of repeated exposure
  2. Factors influencing recurrence not well understood
  3. Systemic and local symptoms (Table 77.3) often appear before vaginal vesicles are seen; vesicles may at first be asymptomatic but eventually enlarge, rupture to form shallow painful ulcerations
  4. Confirmation of diagnosis made by culture through local health department or by Papanicolaou smear or Tzanck preparation (Chapter 83) from fluid from unroofed vesicle or from base of an ulcer; confirmation most likely during first 3 days of infection
  5. Ulcers crust over and heal in 1–3 weeks
  6. Treatment
   a) No means to eradicate virus
   b) Oral analgesics, topical anesthetics (e.g., compresses of Domeboro solution), witch hazel pads, warm tea bag compresses, sitz baths may alleviate discomfort
   c) Betadine solution applied twice a day for several days inhibits secondary bacterial infection, promotes drying of lesions
   d) Acyclovir decreases symptoms

Table 77.2. Management of Gonococcal and Chlamydial Infections

UNCOMPLICATED GONOCOCCAL INFECTION (asymptomatic, cervicovaginal, or anorectal symptoms; pharyngitis)

1. a. Ceftriaxone, 125 mg i.m. once (or equivalent cephalosporin)
      or
   b. Spectinomycin, 2.0 g i.m. (once)
      or
   c. Ciprofloxacin, 500 mg p.o. once, or ofloxacin, 400 mg p.o. once (contraindicated in pregnancy and in those age 16 and younger)
      or
   d. Norfloxacin, 800 mg p.o. once (contraindicated in pregnancy and in those age 16 or younger)
      or
   e. Amoxicillin, 3 g p.o. with 1 g probenecid if infection is known to have been acquired from a source proven not to have penicillin-resistant gonorrhea
2. Treat for chlamydia with doxycycline, tetracycline, erythromycin, or azithromycin (see below).
3. Treat partner(s).
4. Follow-up assay or culture 1 week after completing treatment.
5. Report to local health department.

CHLAMYDIA CERVICITIS; POSSIBLE GONORRHEA/CHLAMYDIA INFECTION (a common situation with manifestations of infection present but without culture confirmation)

1. a. Azithromycin, 1 g p.o. once for treatment of uncomplicated chlamydial infection, and ofloxacin, 400 mg p.o. once for treatment of uncomplicated gonorrhea
      or
   b. Doxycycline, 100 mg twice a day for 7 days
      or
   c. Ofloxacin, 300 mg p.o. 2 times/day for 7 days
      or
   d. Erythromycin base, 500 mg 4 times/day for 7 days
2. Treat partner(s).
3. Follow-up assay or culture for gonorrhea and/or assay for chlamydial infection 1 week after completing treatment.

PELVIC INFLAMMATORY DISEASE (gonorrhea, *Chlamydia*, or both may be the cause)

1. Ambulatory treatment[a]
   a. Ceftriaxone, 250 mg i.m., one dose
      or
      Cefoxitin (Mefoxin), 2 g i.m., one dose with probenecid, 1 g p.o.
      plus
      Doxyclycine, 100 mg p.o. 2 times/day for 14 days
      or
   b. Ofloxacin, 400 mg p.o. 2 times/day for 14 days
      plus
      Clindamycin, 450 mg p.o. 4 times/day for 14 days, or metronidazole, 500 mg. p.o. 2 times/day for 14 days
   c. Contact or observation every 24–48 hours to ensure improvement.
2. Indications for hospitalization
   a. Diagnosis uncertain (to exclude appendicitis, ectopic pregnancy, nongonococcal PID, pelvic abscess).
   b. When a pelvic abscess is present.
   c. Diagnosis is certain, but patient is toxic or unable to follow ambulatory treatment reliably.
   d. Patient does not respond promptly to ambulatory treatment.
3. Inpatient treatment
   a. Cefoxitin, 2 g i.v. every 6 hours, or cefotetan, 2 g i.v. every 12 hours
      and
      Doxycycline, 100 mg i.v. every 12 hours
      or

Table 77.2.   Continued

   b. Gentamicin, 2.0 mg/kg as an initial dose followed by 1.5 mg/kg every 8 hours
      and
      Clindamycin, 900 mg i.v. every 8 hours

GONOCOCCAL/ARTHRITIS-DERMATITIS SYNDROME (hospitalization is recommended)

1. a. Ceftriaxone, 1.0 g i.m. or i.v. daily for at least 48 hours
      or
      Ceftizoxime, 1 g i.v. every 8 hours for at least 48 hours
      or
      Cefotaxime, 1 g i.v. every 8 hours for at least 48 hours
   b. For patients allergic to β-lactam drugs, spectinomycin 2 g i.m. every 12 hours should be given.
   c. Patients may be discharged 48 hours after clinical improvement, with close follow-up (*see 4 below*).
2. When the infecting organism is proven to be penicillin sensitive, parenteral treatment may be switched to ampicillin 1 g every 6 hours.
3. Treat for potential coexistent chlamydial infection (see above)
4. The patient should complete 7 days of antibiotic therapy with either Cefixime, 400 mg p.o. 2 times/day,
   or
   Ciprofloxacin, 500 mg p.o. 2 times/day (contraindicated in pregnancy and in those age 16 or younger).

Adapted from: *MMWR* 42(RR–14):1–108, 1993 (see General References) and Specific References 3, 13, 28.
Note: Of the antibiotics listed above use erythromycin, azithromycin, amoxicillin, gentamicin, clindamycin, spectinomycin, or cefalosporins in pregnant women. Ceftriaxone is effective against penicillinase-producing *Neisseria gonorrhoeae* (as well as many other organisms).

     1) For initial attack, 200 mg p.o. every 4 hours 5 times/day for 10 days and, using a glove, acyclovir ointment on same schedule
     2) If severe systemic symptoms with initial attack or if patient immunocompromised, hospitalize for intravenous acyclovir
     3) Not effective during recurrence, not recommended
     4) If frequent severe recurrences, suppressive therapy of 200 mg p.o. 3–5 times/day for up to 12 months

B. Syphilis: see Chapter 16 and Table 77.3
C. Other causes: Table 77.3

MISCELLANEOUS LESIONS

A. Bartholin's cyst/abscess (Table 77.4)
   1. See Figure 77.3
   2. Small (1–2 cm) asymptomatic cysts require no treatment
   3. Abscess formation or a rapidly enlarging, painful, hemorrhagic cyst requires drainage, usually by a gynecologist
B. Condylomata acuminata (venereal warts, anogenital warts, genital warts) (Table 77.4)
   1. Sexually transmitted
   2. May be a risk factor for cervical and vulvar dysplasia (Chapter 78)
   3. Most often seen in association with vulvovaginitis
   4. More prevalent, more aggressive in pregnant women
C. Sebaceous cysts: Table 77.4 and Chapter 83
D. Vulvar papules: Table 77.5
E. Hypopigmented and hyperpigmented lesions of the vulva: refer to a gynecologist or dermatologist (Chapter 78) for biopsy

Table 77.3. Causes of Vulvar Ulcerations

Disease Entity	Etiology	Appearance	Transmission	Symptoms; Other Manifestations	Diagnosis	Treatment
Herpes simplex (see text)	Herpes simplex II Rarely herpes simplex I	Vulvar vesicle(s)	Sexual	Fever, malaise, lymphadenopathy, burning, paresthesia, dysuria, urinary retention, painful ulcer	Viral culture or Pap smear or Tzanck preparation	Oral acyclovir Topical acyclovir Palliative treatment of lesions
Herpes zoster	Varicella zoster	Ulceration following the distribution of dermatome	Previous varicella, zoster infection	Fever, malaise, lymphadenopathy, painful ulcer	Distribution of lesions Viral culture Pap smear or Tzanck preparation	Oral acyclovir Topical acyclovir Palliative treatment of symptoms
Syphilis (see text and Chapter 16)	Treponema pallidum	*Primary:* chancre — hard, painless lesions with central ulceration, lymphadenopathy *Secondary:* condyloma latum — multiple flat plaques, often confluent; rash — especially palms and soles, lymphadenopathy *Tertiary:* gummatous tumors or ulceration	Sexual	*Secondary:* Malaise, flu-like syndrome, arthralgias, lymphadenopathy *Tertiary:* CNS signs and symptoms	Positive FTA Rising VDRL titers	Benzathine penicillin G or Tetracycline or Erythromycin
Granuloma inguinale	Calymmatobacterium granulomatis	Painless, erythematous nodule that ulcerates; ulcers have irregular borders with a granulation ricine base; lymphadenopathy latter	Sexual	Nonhealing ulcer that becomes painful after secondary bacterial infection	Donovan bodies (macrophages containing intracytoplasmic pleomorphic rods)	Tetracycline Gentamicin Chloramphenicol Trimethoprim/ sulfamethoxazole (Bactrim Septra)

Table 77.3. Continued

Disease Entity	Etiology	Appearance	Transmission	Symptoms; Other Manifestations	Diagnosis	Treatment
Lymphogranuloma venereum	Chlamydia trachomatis Serotype L	Vulvar papule that ulcerates in 4–6 weeks; hallmark inguinal adenitis — nodes are unilateral and edematous; later, bubo formation (enlarged matted nodes held together by inflammatory reaction); fistula formation, vulvar fenestration stages — scarring and lymphedema	Sexual	Fever, malaise, initially painless	Titer of at least 1:64 on LGV complement fixation test	Aspiraton of fluctuant buboes Tetracycline Erythromycin Sulfamethoxazole Surgical reconstruction
Chancroid	Haemophilus ducreyi	Soft, painful, chancre-like ulcer	Sexual	Painful ulcer Inguinal adenopathy	Culturing the organism is difficult Diagnosis of exclusion	Ceftriaxone Erythromycin Trimethoprim-sulfamethoxazole
Hidradenitis suppurativa (see Chapters 11 and 63)	Inflammation/infection of apocrine sweat glands	Vulvar abscess formation with draining sinuses, scarring, and induration; fistula formation	Nontransmittable	Pruritus, burning	Appearance Biopsy	Surgical excision Occasionally, systemic antibiotics Rarely, systemic or intralesional corticosteroids
Behçet's disease	? Autoimmune	Vulvar ulcerations with associated oral ulcerations and ocular inflammation		Arthritis, erythema nodosum, pyoderma, thrombophlebitis, acne, ulcerative colitis, neurological symptoms	Diagnosis of exclusion	No definitive treatment High-dose oral contraceptives Intralesional corticosteroids Chlorambucil

Crohn's disease	Unknown	Linear ulcerations similar to a knife cut Draining sinuses Fistulous tracts	Oral ulcerations GI symptoms	Biopsy	Corticosteroids Sulfones Metronidazole Surgical reconstruction
Tuberculosis (see Chapter 15)	Mycobacterium tuberculosis	Painless ulceration Airborne Primary inoculation		Biopsy, acid-fast cultures	Antituberculous therapy

CNS, central nervous system; FTA, fluorescent titer antibody; GI, gastrointestinal; LGV, lymphogranuloma venereum; Pap smear, Papanicolaou smear.

Table 77.4. Common Nonmalignant Vulvar Lesions

Disease Entity	Cause	Appearance	Symptoms	Complications	Diagnosis	Treatment	Other
Bartholin's cyst	Obstruction of duct of gland	Discrete swelling of inferior aspect of labium majus	None or vulvar irritation due to enlargement	Infection, hemorrhage into the cyst Carcinoma, if age ≥ 40	Visual inspection	None unless symptomatic, infected, or hemorrhagic Marsupialization	
Bartholin's abscess	Infection and obstruction of duct of gland	Discrete swelling of inferior aspect of labium majus	Pain	Hemorrhage	Visual inspection	Incision and drainage Rarely, excision	Culture for gonorrhea
Condylomata acuminata	Human papillomavirus	Single or multiple 2–3-mm-diameter and 10–15-mm-high, fine, finger-like projections or flat-topped lesions; lesions may become confluent	Itching, vaginal discharge	Secondary ulceration and infection	Visual inspection, biopsy	Podophyllum 20–25% Trichloroacetic acid Liquid nitrogen or Nitrous oxide or interferon injection	5-Fluorouracil for intravaginal lesions Laser surgery, excision, or electrodesiccation Treat partner
Sebaceous cyst	Unknown	Discrete swelling often 1 cm in diameter; firm, solid with a yellow color	Vulvar irritation, due to enlargement Pain, if infected	Infection	Visual appearance, biopsy	None Excision, if infected or bothersome	

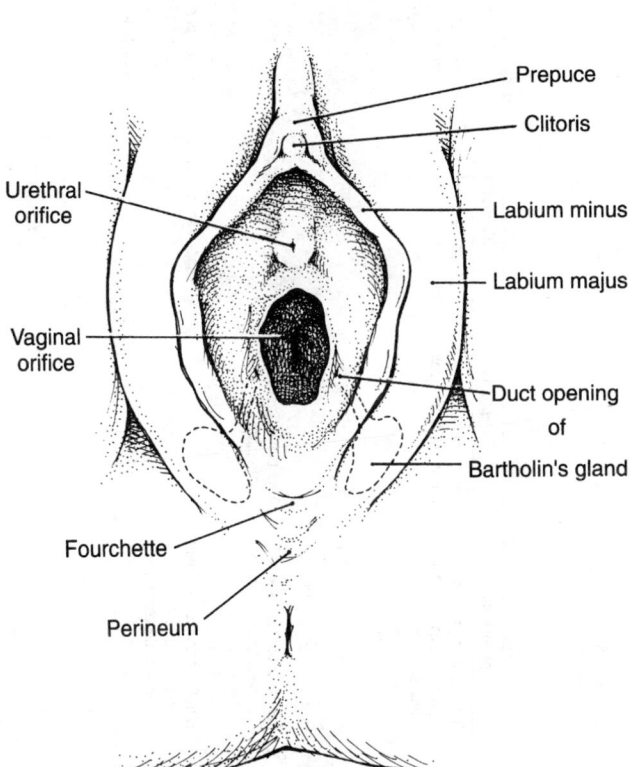

Figure 77.3.   Anatomy of the vulva.

F. Vestibular adenitis/vestibular adenoma
1. Adenitis is inflammation or infection of the minor vestibular gland (located lateral to the hymen)
   a) Causes chronic vulvar pain and dyspareunia
   b) Lesions may not be easily seen, but careful inspection, if necessary with a magnifying glass, will reveal them: tiny red macules or papules
   c) Usually exquisitely tender
   d) Patients should be referred to a gynecologist; treatment of choice is a plastic repair of the perineum
2. Adenomas are generally 1–2 cm in size, associated with dyspareunia, burning; patients should be referred to a gynecologist

Table 77.5. Common Vulvar Papules

Disease Entity	Cause	Appearance	Symptoms	Diagnosis	Treatment
Folliculitis (see Chapter 11)	Staphylococcus and/or streptococcus	Erythematous papules or pustules with a central hair shaft	Asymptomatic Vulvar irritation or pain	Appearance	Germicidal soap, e.g., pHisoHex Sitz baths or warm compresses Rarely, gentamicin or Neosporin ointment Rarely, systemic dicloxacillin or erythromycin
Acrochordon		Soft, skin-colored, sessile or pedunculated tags of skin	Asymptomatic unless infarcted	Appearance, biopsy	No treatment or Excision, electrocautery, laser, or cryotherapy
Molluscum contagiosum	Pox virus Possibly, sexually transmitted	Wart-like papules 1–10 mm in size with a central umbilical depression		Appearance, biopsy	Scraping open the papule, evacuating the contents, and cauterizing or curetting the base

G. Tampon-related ulceration/toxic shock syndrome
  1. Ulcers due to repeated tampon use during periods of diminished or absent menstrual flow
    a) Associated with intermenstrual bleeding and/or abnormal vaginal discharge
    b) Superficial, red, 1–2 mm in diameter, located usually in one of the vaginal fornices
    c) Heal spontaneously in a few days if use of tampons is stopped
  2. Toxic shock syndrome is due to coagulase-positive *Staphylococcus aureus*
    a) Symptoms: fever of >102°F, severe headache, sore throat, vomiting, diarrhea, rash, myalgias
    b) Signs: hypotension and shock may develop within 48 hours; palmar erythema; sunburn-like rash with desquamation; conjunctivitis; purulent vaginal discharge; inflamed, sometimes ulcerated vagina
    c) If tampon is in place, it should be removed and cultured
    d) Gonorrhea culture and chlamydial test (see above) should be done, as well as routine bacterial culture
    e) Vagina should be cleaned with Betadine; patient should be hospitalized for life support and for intravenous antibiotics

DETECTION OF VULVAR LESIONS

A. Preinvasive lesions called *vulvar intraepithelial neoplasia* (VIN)
   1. Average age of women with lesions is 40–50
   2. Pathognomonic lesion is a macule or maculopapule with a roughened surface, but appearance may be varied in pigmentation, size, shape
   3. Apparent condyloma acuminatum (Chapter 77) may be treated without biopsy but biopsied if no decrease in size in 2–4 weeks
   4. Patients with lesions other than condyloma acuminatum must be referred to a gynecologist for biopsy

B. Vulvar cancer
   1. Average age of women with lesions is 60–70
   2. Increased risk associated with condyloma acuminatum, increasing number of lifetime sexual partners, immunosuppression, smoking
   3. Most common symptom is itching; other symptoms include ulceration, bleeding, pain, or appearance of a mass
   4. Diagnosis requires biopsy
   5. Prevention of advanced disease requires that patient be taught to examine her vulva periodically by use of a mirror and to report any changes promptly

DETECTION OF CERVICAL LESIONS

A. Papanicolaou smear
   1. Technique
      a) Visualize the cervix
      b) Place the spatula firmly against the cervix and rotate at least 360°, preferably 720° in a continuous sweep
      c) Then sample the endocervical canal with a plastic brush (Cytobrush, Milex)
      d) Smear both specimens onto a clean slide and spray with or immerse in a fixative
      e) Send slides to a reputable laboratory
      f) Smear must be repeated if no endocervical cells are present
   2. Interpretation of report
      a) If atypical cells and inflammatory cells are present, treat for chlamydial infection (Chapter 77) and repeat smear in a few weeks
      b) If atypia or inflammation persists or if dysplastic cells are seen, patient should be referred to a gynecologist for colposcopy (to illuminate and magnify the cervix, vagina, and vulva)
   3. Frequency
      a) Every 2–3 years once sexual activity has begun or after age 18 if patient is virginal
      b) Not necessary to do routinely if, after patient is 60, three smears taken at least a year apart are negative

DETECTION OF ENDOMETRIAL CARCINOMA
A. Risks
  1. Polycystic ovarian disease, diabetes mellitus, extreme obesity
  2. Use of unopposed (i.e., without progestin) exogenous estrogen in postmenopausal women
B. Screening
  1. Various curettes and aspirators are effective, safe devices in experienced hands to sample endometrial tissue
  2. Any woman with unexplained postmenopausal bleeding should have endometrial biopsy

DETECTION OF OVARIAN CANCER
A. Risk increases with increasing age
B. Symptoms: abdominal fullness, bloating, pelvic pressure; pain and/or constipation occur relatively late in course
C. Most common sign is an adnexal or abdominopelvic mass
D. Computed tomography or ultrasound can determine extent of tumor but cannot distinguish a benign from a malignant process
E. Tumor markers (α-fetoprotein, human chorionic gonadotropin, carcinoembryonic antigen) are more useful in following course of a diagnosed patient than in establishing a diagnosis
F. Premenarche
  1. Two-thirds of ovarian tumors are benign
  2. Most common symptom of a malignant tumor is pain
G. Reproductive period
  1. Most ovarian masses are functional cysts; usually resolve spontaneously in 2–4 weeks
    a) Detected by ultrasound
    b) Oral contraceptive medication taken for 2 months will cause most benign cysts to shrink within 2 months
  2. Persistent masses often neoplastic but seldom malignant; referral of patients to a gynecologist for definitive diagnosis is warranted
H. Perimenopausal and menopausal periods: periodic pelvic examination best way to screen for ovarian cancer

Section XIII
Problems of the Eyes and Ears

79/ HEARING LOSS AND ASSOCIATED PROBLEMS

DETERMINING SEVERITY AND MECHANISM OF HEARING LOSS

A. History
  1. Is one ear or are both ears involved?
  2. Was hearing loss abrupt or gradual? Has it progressed rapidly? Has hearing acuity fluctuated?
  3. Is there tinnitus, vertigo, otalgia, otorrhea, or facial weakness?
  4. Is there a family history of hearing loss?
  5. Is there a history of noise exposure?
  6. Are there related causes of hearing loss (e.g., syphilis, diabetes mellitus, hypothyroidism, head trauma, or exposure to ototoxic agents such as aminoglycosides, diuretics, aspirin)?
B. Physical findings from otoscopy
  1. Inspection of external canal and tympanic membrane
  2. Assessment of membrane mobility by air insufflation (absence of mobility suggests a pathological condition such as negative pressure, middle-ear fluid, or a mass)
C. Preliminary hearing testing
  1. Tuning fork test: test conductive and sensorineural hearing by use of a 512-Hz tuning fork
    a) Weber test (Table 79.1): hold the vibrating tuning fork against the middle of the forehead
    b) Rinne test (Table 79.1): hold the vibrating tuning fork against the mastoid bone until it is no longer audible; then hold it about an inch away from the external meatus
  2. Speech recognition testing
  3. Audiometry
    a) Establishes precise level of hearing loss

Table 79.1. Classification of Probable Mechanism of Hearing Loss, Using Tuning Fork Tests

Classification	Rinne Test	Weber Test
NORMAL HEARING		
Both ears	AC > BC	Midline
CONDUCTIVE LOSS[a]		
Right ear	Right ear: BC > AC Left ear: AC > BC	Lateralized to right ear
Left ear	Right ear: AC > BC Left ear: BC > AC	Lateralized to left ear
Both ears	Right ear: BC > AC Left ear: BC > AC	Lateralized to poorer ear
SENSORINEURAL LOSS		
Right ear	AC > BC bilaterally	Lateralized to left ear
Left ear	AC > BC bilaterally	Lateralized to right ear
Both ears	AC > BC bilaterally	Lateralized to better ear

AC, air conduction; BC, bone conduction.
[a] Because sound transmission by air is much more efficient than by bone, air conduction may remain greater than bone conduction in early or minimal conductive hearing loss.

  b) Performed by an audiologist, takes about 20–30 minutes
D. A practical method for approximating the severity of hearing loss:
   Table 79.2

CAUSES OF HEARING LOSS (TABLE 79.3)

A. Conditions of the external ear
  1. Cerumen impaction
     a) Intermittent fullness and hearing loss on affected side,
        increasing in severity after showering or swimming; often a
        history of prior episodes
     b) Diagnosed by otoscopy
     c) Treatment
        1) If cerumen soft, may be removed by irrigation with warm
           tap water through a rubber bulb syringe
        2) If cerumen impacted, a few drops of hydrogen peroxide (or
           of Cerumenex) should be instilled twice a day for 1 week
           before irrigation
        3) If impaction is refractory to treatment or if there is a
           history of tympanic membrane perforation or of
           mastoidectomy, cerumen should be removed by an
           otolaryngologist
  2. Foreign body
     a) If an insect (often the case), should be killed first by
        instillation of mineral oil
     b) If vegetable, avoid irrigation (may cause swelling of the foreign
        body)
     c) Remove with alligator forceps or a wax spoon
  3. Otitis externa
     a) Most common in summer
     b) May cause itching at first, then pain aggravated by movement
        of the ear or the jaw
     c) Hearing may be impaired
     d) Copious or greenish exudate suggests *Pseudomonas,* the most
        common bacterial cause
     e) Yellow crusting and a purulent exudate suggests
        Staphylococcus aureus
     f) A moldy material, white to black, suggests fungus

**Table 79.2.   A Practical Method for Approximating the Severity of
Hearing Loss in the Office**

Severity of Hearing Loss	Social Difficulty	Office Voice Test	Pure-Tone Audiogram
Normal hearing	None	18 ft or more using normal voice	No loss over 10 dB
Slight hearing loss	Long-distance speech	Not over 12 ft using normal voice	10–30-dB loss
Moderate hearing loss	Short-distance speech	Not over 3 ft using normal voice	≤60-dB loss
Severe hearing loss	All unamplified voices	Raised voice at meatus	>60-dB loss
Profound hearing loss	Voices never heard	All speech and sound	>90-dB loss

Adapted from Mawson SR: *Diseases of the Ear.* Baltimore, Williams & Wilkins, 1974.

Table 79.3.   Causes of Hearing Loss in Adults

Causes	Mechanism	Onset Rapid (Hours to Days) or Gradual (Months to Years)	Bilateral or Unilateral
EXTERNAL AUDITORY CANAL			
Cerumen impaction	C	Either	Usually unilateral
Foreign body	C	Rapid	Unilateral
Otitis externa	C	Rapid	Unilateral
New growth	C	Gradual	Unilateral
MIDDLE EAR			
Serous otitis media	C	Either	Either
Acute otitis media	C	Rapid	Unilateral
Barotrauma	C or SN	Rapid	Unilateral
Traumatic perforation of tympanic membrane	C	Rapid	Unilateral
Chronic otitis media	C	Gradual	Unilateral
Cholesteatoma	C or SN	Gradual	Either
Ossicular chain problem	C	Gradual	Unilateral
Adhesive otitis media	C	Gradual	Either
Tympanosclerosis	C	Gradual	Unilateral
Traumatic injury	C or SN	Rapid	Unilateral
Otosclerosis	C and/or SN	Gradual	Bilateral
New growths	C or SN	Gradual	Unilateral
INNER EAR			
Presbycusis	SN	Gradual	Bilateral
Acoustic trauma	SN	Gradual	Bilateral
Drug-induced	SN	Either	Bilateral
Ménière's syndrome	SN	Rapid	Usually unilateral
Central nervous system infection			
Meningitis	SN	Rapid	Either

Syphilis	SN	Either	Either
Tuberculosis	SN	Either	Either
Acoustic neuroma	SN	Gradual	Unilateral
Mumps	SN	Rapid	Unilateral
ATRAUMATIC SUDDEN SENSORINEURAL HEARING LOSS	SN	Rapid	Unilateral

C, conducive; SN, sensorineural.

g) Scaling, cracked, weeping canal skin indicates eczema

h) Cultures unnecessary unless topical treatment fails

i) Treatment

1) General: remove all debris (preferably with a suction cannula) and apply appropriate topical therapy

2) For bacterial infection: have the patient instill an antimicrobial-corticosteroid combination (e.g., Cortisporin Otic Suspension) 3 or 4 drops 3 or 4 times/day for 5–7 days

3) For fungal infection: dust canal (in office) with sulfanilamide powder (single application ordinarily sufficient); alternative is 3 drops of clotrimazole (Lotrimin) 1% solution twice a day for 14 days

4) For eczema: apply a topical steroid cream (e.g., triamcinolone 0.1% daily for 14 days); once control is achieved, chronic symptoms can be suppressed by first weekly, then monthly, application

5) If canal is too swollen to apply medication, a cotton wick should be inserted (e.g., Oto-Wick) until only the end is visible, and then liquid medication should be applied to the wick, which can usually be removed in 2–3 days

6) Stop treatment when problem has resolved, usually in 5–7 days

7) During treatment, keep ear dry by plugging it with cotton impregnated with petroleum jelly

8) Refer promptly to an otolaryngologist if mastoiditis is suspected (slow response to treatment and mastoid tenderness) or if otitis associated with fever, excruciating pain, presence of friable, red granulation tissue in canal (malignant otitis externa, more likely in diabetics or in immunologically compromised persons)

4. New growths — basal cell carcinomas and squamous cell carcinomas — occur commonly in this area, and any patient with a suspicious lesion should be promptly referred to an otolaryngologist

B. Conditions of the middle ear

1. Serous otitis media

a) Fullness, decreased hearing in one or both ears with minimal or no pain

b) Often a history of recent viral upper respiratory infection (URI), exacerbation of allergic or vasomotor rhinitis or prior acute otitis media

c) Rarely, due to nasopharyngeal carcinoma

d) Otoscopy findings: closure-retraction of tympanic membrane, membrane immobility (see above), visible air-fluid level

e) Conductive hearing loss (see above)

f) Management

1) Systemic antibiotics for 10 days (e.g., erythromycin, 250 mg 4 times/day, and sulfisoxazole, 500 mg 4 times/day)

2) Topical nasal decongestants (e.g., Neo-Synephrine 0.25% or 0.50% spray or drops, 2 puffs or drops to each nostril followed 5–10 minutes later by 2 more puffs or drops, 4 times/day) for no more than 3 days

 3) Refer to an otolaryngologist if effusion persists beyond 4–6 weeks — myringotomy may be necessary

2. Acute otitis media
   a) Marked pain in the ear, usually after a recent URI
   b) Purulent drainage indicates perforation of tympanic membrane or concomitant otitis externa
   c) Otoscopy findings: injection, loss of luster of entire membrane, eventually bulging of membrane and loss of landmarks
   d) Conductive hearing loss (see above) in some patients
   e) Most common causative agents: *Streptococcus pneumoniae, Haemophilus influenzae, S. aureus,* β-hemolytic streptococcus
   f) Management
      1) Systemic antimicrobials for 10 days: amoxicillin 500 mg 3 times/day for 10 days is the first choice, but a high prevalence of β-lactamase-producing bacteria may dictate another choice (e.g., Augmentin 250/125 or 500/125); for penicillin-allergic patients, erythromycin, 250 mg 4 times/day, or trimethoprim-sulfamethoxazole, 2 tablets 2 times/day
      2) Aspirin or acetaminophen for pain
      3) If perforation with discharge, Cortisporin Otic Suspension 4 times/day for 1 week
      4) Refer to an otolaryngologist
         (a) If membrane bulging with pus or patient has severe pain or vertigo
         (b) If inadequate response after 2 days of treatment
         (c) If there is facial nerve dysfunction, persistence of a membrane perforation, or hearing loss that persists beyond 4–6 weeks

3. Barotrauma
   a) Symptoms and signs produced by a sudden pressure differential between the middle ear and the surrounding atmosphere (e.g., during rapid descents while flying or scuba diving)
   b) Fullness, pain, or decreased hearing in one or both ears
   c) Otoscopy findings: vary from mild membrane retraction to hemotympanum, with or without perforation
   d) There may be conductive or sensorineural hearing loss; if so, referral to an otolaryngologist is warranted because of possible inner-ear involvement
   e) Mild symptoms may respond to nasal or oral decongestants

4. Traumatic perforation of tympanic membrane
   a) From an applicator or other object used to remove wax, foreign bodies, forcefully directed water, blast waves from detonations, etc.
   b) Symptoms: decreased hearing, tinnitus, pain, and bleeding
   c) Otoscopy findings: perforation, immobile membrane after air insufflation (of help if perforation not seen)
   d) Management
      1) Small perforations usually heal spontaneously in several weeks; large ones may require grafting by an otolaryngologist
      2) If there is a possibility of middle-ear contamination, oral

Table 79.4.   **Chronic Otitis Media: Features Distinguishing Inactive and Active (Cholesteatoma) Forms**

Feature	Inactive	Active (Cholesteatoma)
Discharge	Mucoid or mucopurulent	Purulent, foul
Location of pathology	Middle ear; eustachian tube	Middle ear, attic, antrum, any part of temporal bone
Tympanic membrane perforation	Pars tensa (central)	Pars flaccida or marginal
Middle-ear mucosa	Mucous membrane	Stratified squamous epithelium
X-rays	Normal; clouding of mastoid cells	Underdevelopment of sclerosis of mastoid cells; bone destruction
Cholesteatoma formation	No	Yes
Bone erosion	No	Yes
Treatment of infection	Medical/surgical (surgery if the perforation fails to heal spontaneously)	Surgical

antibiotics (e.g., ampicillin or erythromycin 250 mg 4 times/day for 1 week) are indicated
3) Plug the ear with cotton covered with petroleum jelly to prevent water from entering the ear
4) Signs of inner ear injury — tinnitus, vertigo, sensorineural hearing loss — warrant referral to an otolaryngologist (there may be a fistula, which requires repair)
5. Chronic otitis media
   a) Signs: persistent or recurrent otorrhea, perforated membrane, usually some degree of conductive hearing loss
   b) Inactive versus active ("cholesteatoma" in Table 79.4 refers to debris that accumulates at the site of invasion of squamous epithelium from the canal into the middle ear)
   c) Complications (mastoiditis, facial nerve paralysis, intracranial infection, etc.) dictate immediate referral and hospitalization
6. Ossicular chain problems
   a) General
      1) All patients have conductive hearing loss
      2) All patients should be referred to an otolaryngologist for accurate diagnosis, possible surgical correction
   b) Adhesive otitis media
      1) History of ear infection
      2) Tympanic membrane retracted, atrophic in areas of healed perforations
      3) Mild hearing loss
   c) Tympanosclerosis
      1) History of ear infection
      2) Usually, a tympanic membrane perforation; discrete plaques of dense collagen with calcified hyaline may be seen in middle ear
   d) Traumatic ossicular injury
      1) History of trauma (e.g., basal skull fracture, traumatic membrane perforation) followed by unilateral hearing loss

Table 79.5. Drugs That May Cause Sensorineural Hearing Loss

ANTIBIOTICS	DIURETICS
Streptomycin	Ethacrynic acid
Neomycin	Furosemide
Gentamycin	OTHER DRUGS
Tobramycin	Salicylates
Chloramphenicol	Quinidine
Vancomycin	Quinine
	Cisplatin

      2) Usually, blood can be seen behind the eardrum
   e) Otosclerosis
      1) Slowly progressive hearing loss, usually bilateral
      2) Usually affects people in their second or third decades, more common in women; process accelerated by pregnancy
      3) Membrane usually appears normal
   f) New growths
      1) Can be seen on otoscopy
      2) Malignant tumors most commonly present with chronic, occasionally bloody discharge
C. Chronic sensorineural hearing loss
  1. Presbycusis
   a) Universal among elderly, high frequency initially
   b) Routine screening of elderly not recommended
   c) If patient (or family) recognizes a problem, counseling is indicated (see below), as is audiometry (see above)
  2. Noise-induced hearing loss
   a) Most commonly affects individuals employed in high-noise industries (loud music may cause hearing loss but usually many years after repeated exposure)
   b) Initially, high-frequency loss irreversible (acute loss due to acoustic trauma is reversible)
  3. Drug-induced hearing loss (Table 79.5)
   a) Prognosis varies depending on the drug (e.g., salicylate- or quinine-induced hearing loss usually reversible; aminoglycoside-induced hearing loss often irreversible and may progress after drug is stopped)
   b) Effect is dose related
  4. Ménière's syndrome
   a) "Classic" syndrome consists of fluctuating hearing loss, roaring tinnitus, aural fullness, and spontaneous peripheral pattern vertigo (Chapter 64), but all symptoms may not be present
   b) Attack lasts minutes to an hour, often associated with nystagmus
   c) Between attacks, tinnitus and sensorineural hearing loss (low frequency initially) often persist
   d) Unilateral in 70–80% of cases
   e) Treatment
      1) Referral to an otolaryngologist to confirm diagnosis and to initiate treatment (usually diuretics, meclizine, prochlorperazine)
      2) After acute attack, diuretics (e.g., hydrochlorothiazide 25–50

mg/day) are continued for a year, and, if no recurrence at that point, they can be stopped
   3) Patients whose disease is severe and refractory to medical treatment may be candidates for surgery, often successful
5. Acoustic neuroma
   a) Patients present with unilateral hearing loss and chronic, usually mild, positional vertigo
   b) Audiometry usually confirms sensorineural hearing loss
   c) Examination reveals neurological dysfunction of (in decreasing order of frequency) nerves V, VII, VI and cerebellum (ataxia, falling to side of lesion)
   d) Computed tomography or magnetic resonance imaging demonstrates the lesion
   e) Referral to an otolaryngologist is indicated for any patient with unilateral sensorineural hearing loss
   f) Surgery usually successful, although hearing loss is permanent
6. Sudden sensorineural hearing loss
   a) Otological emergency dictating immediate referral to an otolaryngologist
   b) Causes include viral cochleitis, arterial occlusion, inner-ear fistula, sudden expansion of a tumor, temporal bone fracture, noise trauma
   c) Hearing loss usually permanent

TINNITUS

A. Subjective tinnitus
   1. Patient complains of noises that cannot be heard by the observer
   2. Tympanic
      a) Usually the result of conductive hearing loss
      b) Often described as pulsating
   3. Petrous
      a) Associated with sensorineural hearing loss
      b) May be intermittent or continuous
   4. Management
      a) Reassurance that no serious intracranial condition exists
      b) Playing an FM radio at bedtime (FM delivers a broader range of frequencies than AM) may be of help
      c) Masking treatment, an apparatus that generates "white noise," is available from an audiologist
B. Objective
   1. Noise audible to patient and examiner and originates from the patient's ear
   2. Causes: aneurysm of the internal carotid artery, benign vascular tumors of the middle ear, temporomandibular joint instability, myoclonus of palatal muscles
   3. Patients should be referred to an otolaryngologist

DEALING WITH THE PATIENT WITH PERMANENT HEARING LOSS

A. Communication
   1. Counseling of family to face patient when speaking, use gestures, speak at a moderate pace and audibly
   2. Ensure adequate lighting and minimize background noise

   3. Be patient, ask how communication can be improved
   4. Sign language (for totally deaf people) most easily learned in
      childhood
B. Hearing aids
   1. Can increase intensity of a sound by up to 70 dB
   2. Expensive ($300–$1000), but a 30-day trial period is usually
      allowed
   3. Adjustments should be made, when necessary, by an audiologist
C. Cochlear implants for selected patients who do not benefit from a
   hearing aid

80/ COMMON PROBLEMS ASSOCIATED WITH IMPAIRED VISION: CATARACTS AND AGE-RELATED MACULAR DEGENERATION

CATARACTS

A. Definition: opacification of the lens of the eye
B. Etiology (Table 80.1): the majority of cataracts are senescent
C. Evaluation
   1. Symptoms
      a) Impaired vision, usually a fog over the eyes
         1) Early on, distant vision often impaired more than near vision
         2) Central opacities cause visual loss more noticeably in bright light (and visual acuity may be improved by mydriatics)
         3) Peripheral opacities cause visual loss relatively late
      b) Rings or halos around lights or objects may be seen
      c) Objects appear more blue and yellow
   2. Ophthalmoscopy: lens appears cloudy, best appreciated through a moderately plus lens of the ophthalmoscope
   3. Visual acuity examination

Table 80.1. Etiology of Cataracts

CONGENITAL
   Autosomal dominant inheritance: 25% of congenital cataracts
   Maternal malnutrition
   Maternal infections: rubella, syphilis
   Maternal metabolic disease (e.g., diabetes mellitus)
   Maternal medication: corticosteroids
   Prematurity
TRAUMATIC
SENESCENT
SECONDARY
   Drug therapy: corticosteroids
   Degenerative eye disease: severe myopia
   Retinal dystrophy
   Essential iris atrophy
   Retinal detachment
   Glaucoma
   Intraocular neoplasia
   Ocular ischemia (e.g., Takayasu's disease)
ASSOCIATED WITH METABOLIC DISEASE
   Diabetes mellitus
   Wilson's disease
   Hypoparathyroidism

Table 80.2.   Temporary Restrictions After Cataract Surgery*a*

Wear eye shield during sleep and wear glasses at other times; shields are usually worn for 1 month and then discontinued.

Minimize bending or stooping for 3 or 4 weeks.

Do not sleep on side of operated eye for 3 or 4 weeks.

Do not wash hair for 2 weeks.

No showers for 2 weeks, although a bath is allowed (but with assistance to prevent a fall).

No strenuous or excessive physical activity for 4 weeks and then only after approval of the ophthalmologist.

---

a These are suggested to prevent inadvertent injury to the eye, diminish disruptive pressure on the wound, avoid sudden rise in ocular pressure, and diminish the chance of infection. These recommendations are conservative. The ophthalmologist may very well prefer a more liberal set.

      a) Best done by use of a Snellen Chart

      b) Refer to an ophthalmologist if acuity reduced

  D. Surgery

    1. Indications

      a) Visual needs of patient

      b) Absence of other ocular abnormalities that preclude a successful operation [e.g., macular disease (see below)]

    2. Procedure

      a) Removal of entire lens (intracapsular extraction) or removal of anterior part of lens, leaving posterior capsule (extracapsular extraction, currently by far the procedure of choice)

      b) Both eyes usually require operation, done a few months apart

      c) Bifocal intraocular lenses inserted in 90–95% of patients

      d) Operation normally performed on an outpatient basis

      e) Restrictions after operation: Table 80.2

      f) Complications: best managed by operating surgeon

        1) Inflammation common, usually controlled by topical corticosteroids, but infection must be recognized early to avoid serious sequelae

        2) Hemorrhage: heralded by a sudden reduction in visual acuity

        3) Retinal detachment: characterized by sudden loss of visual acuity, flashes of light, floaters in the visual field

        4) Glaucoma (see Chapter 81): characterized by redness, tenderness, pain in the eye, perhaps decreased vision

        5) Delayed opacification of the posterior capsule, with a gradual decrease in vision over 1 or 2 years, can be treated effectively with a laser

AGE-RELATED MACULAR DEGENERATION

A. Clinical features

    1. Atrophic form

      a) Characterized by retinal pigment epithelial changes and by drusen formation (drusen are excrescences between the retina and the choroid that appear as tiny discrete white or yellow deposits)

      b) Visual acuity not necessarily reduced

    2. Exudative

      a) Characterized by edema, hemorrhage, or lipid accumulation beneath or within the retina; neovascularization (best detected by fluorescein angiography) and scarring may occur

b) Accounts for majority of cases associated with visual loss
B. Treatment
1. No dietary manipulation has been shown to be effective (value of vitamin supplementation being evaluated)
2. Subsets of patients may benefit from laser photocoagulation; routine referral to an ophthalmologist is appropriate

HELP FOR THE VISUALLY IMPAIRED

A. Resources available
1. Large print books, journals, and newsprint
2. *Talking Books Program* of the Library of Congress
B. Sources of advice
1. Volunteers for the Visually Handicapped, 4405 East-West Hwy., Bethesda, MD 20814
2. Visual Foundation, 770 Center St., Newton, MA 02158

81/ GLAUCOMA

ANATOMY: FIGURE 81.1

TYPES (TABLE 81.1)

A. Primary open angle
   1. Anatomy: Figure 81.1
   2. Epidemiology
      a) Prevalence increases after age 40
      b) African Americans are affected at a higher frequency and at an earlier age than whites
      c) Familial, but pattern of inheritance is unknown
   3. Manifestations
      a) Asymptomatic early
      b) Occasionally a patient may notice halos around lights and blurring of vision if intraocular pressure rises suddenly (e.g., after ingestion of a large quantity of fluid)

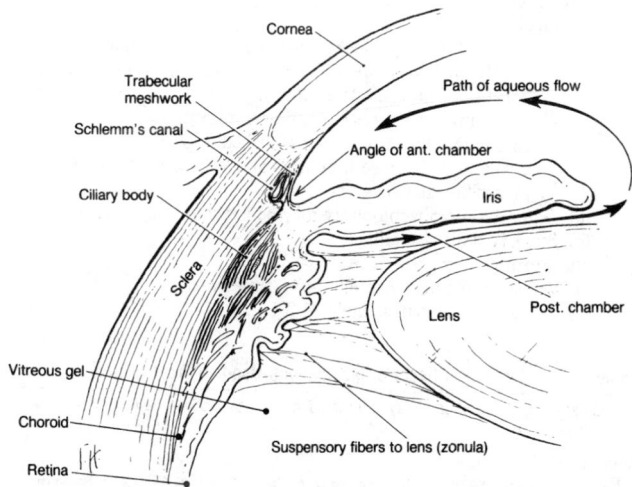

Figure 81.1. Anatomy of the eye — cross section at the cornea. (From Basmajian JV: *Grant's Method of Anatomy,* 8th ed. Baltimore, Williams & Wilkins, 1971, p 543.)

Table 81.1. Types of Glaucoma

PRIMARY
   Open-angle: 90% of patients
   Angle-closure: 5% of patients
   Congenital: infant and juvenile onset
SECONDARY
   Open-angle: results from topical or systemic steroids, ocular inflammation, or obstructed venous return from the eye (e.g., carotid cavernous sinus fistula)
   Angle-closure: results from trauma, neovascular change in the iris, ocular neoplasia, cataract surgery, and iris degeneration from various causes

      c) Central vision preserved until late in disease, so testing of visual acuity not reliable screening procedure

      d) Increased intraocular pressure causes increased cupping of disc; eventually disc pales

  4. Screening

      a) Techniques available to primary physician are insensitive; screening should be done by an ophthalmologist

      b) For African Americans, every year or two after age 40; for others after age 65

      c) Procedures: all should be done

         1) Tonometry: to measure intraocular pressure

         2) Funduscopic examination through the dilated pupil

         3) Visual field assessment

         4) Gonioscopy: to visualize the angle of the anterior chamber

      d) Findings: some patients will have only increased pressure without other abnormalities; about 1% a year of these people will develop glaucoma

  5. Treatment

      a) Medical

         1) First, a topical β-blocker (levobunolol hydrochloride ophthalmic solution — Betagan — is the preferable product because of minimal side effects)

         2) Sometimes, epinephrine and/or a mild miotic (e.g., carbachol, pilocarpine) is prescribed also

         3) Carbonic anhydrase inhibitors and stronger miotics are prescribed as necessary

      b) Argon laser trabeculoplasty may be effective if medical therapy fails

      c) Surgery if all else fails

  6. Monitoring

      a) Ophthalmological examination 3 times/year

      b) Side effects of drugs: Table 81.2

Table 81.2.   Systemic Effects of Medications Used to Treat Glaucoma

Considerable absorption of drug may occur through the nasal mucosa via flow through the lacrimal duct

β-Adrenergic blocking agents
  Pulmonary: bronchospasm — the incidence is markedly decreased with highly selective β_1-blockers
  Cardiovascular: bradycardia, hypotension, decreased cardiac contractility
  Central nervous system: fatigue, depression, memory loss

Miotics (e.g., pilocarpine)
  Refractive error, decreased night vision, especially in those with cataracts, ciliary muscle spasms, ocular burning; long-acting agents such as phospholine iodide, because of irreversible depletion of cholinesterase, may make general anesthesia dangerous

Sympathomimetics
  Increased respiratory rate, headache, tremor, tachycardia, arrhythmia

Carbonic anhydrase inhibitor
  Malaise, fatigue, anorexia, depression, decreased libido, systemic acidosis (especially a risk in those with severe respiratory disease or those taking large doses of salicylates), nausea, vomiting, diarrhea, alterations in taste of carbonated beverages

Developed from Everitt DE, Avorn J: Systemic effects of medication used to treat glaucoma. *Ann Intern Med* 112: 120, 1990.

B. Primary angle closure
  1. Diagnosis
    a) Early recognition important to prevent blindness
    b) Symptoms of an acute attack: pain (usually periocular or supraocular), blurred vision, halos around lights at night; symptoms may be relieved in lighted rooms or in daylight
    c) Examination during acute attacks reveals marked elevation of intraocular pressure and a red eye (see Chapter 82 for differential diagnosis)
    d) People predisposed to angle-closure glaucoma have shallow anterior chambers (Fig. 81.1) seen by shining a flashlight on the eye from the side and showing a shadow over the nasal part of the eye from the bowed iris
  2. Treatment
    a) Acute attack
      1) Refer immediately to an ophthalmologist (blindness will almost certainly occur within a few days if treatment is not initiated)
      2) If immediate referral not possible, give hyperosmotic glycerol 1 ml/kg mixed as a 50% solution with juice (highly effective), or Diamox 250 mg p.o., and a miotic (e.g., Pilocarpine 4%) every 15 minutes
    b) Asymptomatic patients with shallow anterior chambers
      1) Avoid mydriatics (e.g., anticholinergic drugs)
      2) Early peripheral iridectomy by laser, an office procedure

82/ THE RED EYE

ANATOMY: FIGURE 82.1 (SEE ALSO FIG. 81.1)

DIFFERENTIAL DIAGNOSIS (TABLES 82.1 AND 82.2)

A. Acute glaucoma: see Chapter 81
B. Iritis: rapid initiation of treatment (usually a dilating agent and local corticosteroids) important to prevent scarring
C. Corneal injury
   1. Pain is usually intense
   2. Abrasions can be patched for 24 hours; deeper injuries (revealed by fluorescein staining) require urgent referral
D. Scleritis
   1. Often part of a systemic disorder (e.g., rheumatoid arthritis)
   2. Often associated with iritis
E. Episcleritis

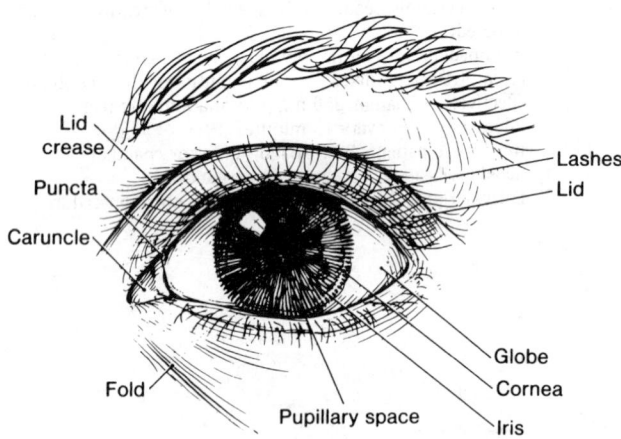

Figure 82.1. External landmarks of the eye.

Table 82.1. Major Causes of a Red Eye

CONDITIONS THAT REQUIRE REFERRAL
   Acute glaucoma
   Acute iritis
   Acute corneal tear or infection (keratitis)
   Acute scleritis and/or episcleritis
   Bacterial conjunctivitis (hyperacute)

CONDITIONS THAT USUALLY CAN BE MANAGED BY THE GENERAL PHYSICIAN
   Bacterial conjunctivitis (acute and chronic)
   Viral conjunctivitis
   Inclusion conjunctivitis
   Allergic conjunctivitis
   Chemical conjunctivitis
   Foreign body
   Subconjunctival hemorrhage

Table 82.2. Important Observations in the Evaluation of a Patient With a Red Eye

Condition	History of Previous Ocular Disorder or Condition Predisposing to an Ocular Disorder	Pain[a]	Visual Acuity	Appearance of Cornea	Discharge	Pupil	Redness	Selected Evaluations
Glaucoma	±	+	Diminished or blurred	May be hazy	None	Often dilated, middilated, or fixed	Around cornea	Ocular pressure[b] in eye is high (see Chapter 81)
Iritis	±	+	Blurred	Normal	None	Small and different from opposite side	Around cornea	Normal
Corneal injury	−	+	Usually diminished	May be streaky	Usually some	Normal	Localized or diffuse	Fluorescein stain[c] shows epithelial defect as brilliant green
Scleritis	+	+	Normal	Normal	None	Normal	Localized or diffuse	A drop of Neo-Synephrine 2½% or 5% in conjunctiva will constrict superficial but not deep vessels (see text)
Episcleritis	−	+	Normal	Normal	None	Normal	Localized	None
Bacterial conjunctivitis	−	Mild discomfort or burning	Normal	Normal	Present: thick or thin	Normal	Diffuse	None
Inclusion conjunctivitis	−	Mild discomfort or burning	Occasionally blurred, if chronic	Normal except if late when superior dots or streaking may be seen	None or mucopurulent	Normal	Diffuse (variable)	None
Viral conjunctivitis	−	Mild discomfort or burning	Normal	Normal	Watery	Normal	Segmental or diffuse	None

Table 82.2. Continued

Condition	History of Previous Ocular Disorder or Condition Predisposing to an Ocular Disorder	Pain[a]	Visual Acuity	Discharge	Appearance of Cornea	Pupil	Redness	Selected Evaluations
Keratitis	Often	+	Diminished	Usually some	Corneal opacity	Normal	Around cornea	A diagnostic scraping may be performed by an ophthalmologist
Allergic conjunctivitis	Previous history of allergies	−	Usually normal	Mild or none	Normal	Normal	Diffuse	None

[a]Photophobia in addition to pain may be seen in varying degrees with nearly any of these conditions, but its presence is neither universal nor diagnostic.
[b]Should not be measured if a discharge is present or if a corneal ulceration is seen.
[c]Use individually packaged sterile fluorescein strips.

Table 82.3.   Diagnosis Based on Cells in Material Scraped
From Conjunctiva

Cells	Significance
Polymorphonuclear leukocytes	Bacterial, fungal, chlamydial (inclusion conjunctivitis), trachoma, Sjögren-Larsson syndrome
Mononuclear cells	Viral
Eosinophils	Allergy, ocular pemphigoid
Epithelial metaplasia (atypical, large cells)	*Chlamydia*, herpes simplex

1. Etiology usually unknown, occasionally part of a systemic disease (e.g., rheumatoid arthritis) or due to an infection such as herpes zoster
2. Observation that the lining of the eyelid is not inflamed and that there is no discharge distinguishes it from conjunctivitis

F. Conjunctivitis, including hyperacute conjunctivitis, an urgent problem (see below)

CONJUNCTIVITIS
A. Presentation: see Table 82.2
B. Laboratory diagnosis
   1. Culture
      a) Usually unnecessary; diagnosis can be made from appearance of conjunctiva
      b) If done, material should be obtained, without anesthesia, by everting the eyelid, wiping with a sterile cotton swab
         1) Transfer immediately into transport medium or have delivered immediately to laboratory
         2) Both eyes should be cultured
   2. Scraping
      a) Apply a topical anesthetic (e.g., Ophthaine), use a sterile platinum spatula (from a medical supply house) or the dull side of a sterile scalpel blade
      b) Smear material on a slide, stain with Gram's or Giemsa stain (Table 82.3)
C. Specific types
   1. Hyperacute bacterial conjunctivitis
      a) Findings: thick copious discharge; both eyes involved within several days; aching pain; swollen lid; tender eye; often enlarged preauricular nodes; corneal ulcer may develop
      b) Usually caused by *Neisseria gonorrhoeae* or *meningitidis*
      c) Scrapings: numerous granulocytes, intracellular Gram-negative diplococci
      d) Culture: on Thayer-Martin medium or send to the laboratory on Transgrow medium
      e) Therapy: consult an ophthalmologist immediately; treatment will include topical and systemic antibiotics
   2. Acute bacterial conjunctivitis (Table 82.2)
      a) Most common cause is *Staphylococcus aureus,* but pneumococcal, *Haemophilus* and, rarely, other bacteria also cause conjunctivitis
      b) Often called "pink eye"; very often both eyes become involved

c) Therapy: topical antimicrobial (e.g., Sulamyd 10%, 2 drops every 3 hours while awake) for 5–6 days usually curative; symptoms abate in a day or two; cool compresses may provide some relief

3. Chronic bacterial conjunctivitis
   a) Most cases caused by *S. aureus*
   b) Patients complain of a sensation of a foreign body in the eye as well as redness, itching, eyelids sticking together after sleep
   c) Often a history of recurrent sties (see below) and of loss of eyelashes
   d) Examination shows erythema of lid margin; sometimes, a scant exudate; surrounding skin may show seborrheic dermatitis or may be excoriated; crusting at bases of eyelashes; conjunctiva may show papillary hyperplasia (mounds with a single central vessel); cornea may be ulcerated, clouded, or vascularized
   e) Scraping and culture may be of help in diagnosis
   f) Therapy: gentamycin solution or ointment every 4 hours for 2 weeks while awake, plus daily cleansing of the eyelids with a neutral soap

4. Viral conjunctivitis (Table 82.2)
   a) Both eyes often involved within a day or two
   b) Excessive tearing without purulent discharge
   c) Preauricular nodes may be enlarged and tender
   d) Scraping shows mononuclear cells
   e) Self-limited (a few days); cool compresses and vasoconstrictive drops (e.g., Albalon, Naphcon-A, Vasocon-A — all over-the-counter drugs), 2 drops 4 times/day, may give relief
   f) If there is corneal ulceration, immediate referral to an ophthalmologist is indicated

5. Inclusion conjunctivitis (Table 82.2)
   a) Caused by *Chlamydia* and seen frequently in sexually active young adults
   b) Untreated, becomes chronic, and in 2–3 weeks, a keratitis (Table 82.2) and, sometimes, an iritis may develop (see above and Table 82.2)
   c) Occasionally associated with genitourinary infection or with Reiter's syndrome (Chapter 55)
   d) Diagnosis can be confirmed, if necessary, by a commercially available slide test for detection of *Chlamydia* (Chapter 13) or by scraping (Giemsa stain shows large basophilic cytoplasmic inclusion bodies)
   e) Therapy: oral tetracycline 250 mg 4 times/day for 21 days (alternatively, erythromycin, 250 mg 4 times/day, or trimethoprim-sulfamethoxazole, 1 double-strength tablet twice a day for 21 days); sexual partner should be treated also, and male partner should wear a condom until treatment completed

6. Allergic conjunctivitis (Table 82.2)
   a) If diagnosis in doubt, scraping may be done to reveal confirmatory eosinophils
   b) Treatment: topical vasoconstrictor (Albalon, Naphcon-A, or Vasocon-A — over-the-counter drugs), 1–2 drops 4 times/day, and cool compresses; topical corticosteroids are highly effective, but because of possible side effects (corneal damage in

the presence of herpes infection, fungal infection, development of open-angle glaucoma, cataracts) should be used cautiously
7. Chemical conjunctivitis
   a) History of exposure to, e.g., smoke, sprays, chlorinated water, makes diagnosis obvious
   b) Patient should rinse eye with water promptly, apply cool compresses, apply vasoconstrictor drops (see above)
   c) Acid or alkali injury is an ophthalmological emergency — refer promptly after irrigation
8. Foreign body
   a) If not visualized, fluorescein staining is appropriate to detect corneal damage
   b) Irrigate with sterile normal saline or eyewash if object is not washed away; if object is embedded in cornea, remove with a sterile needle after applying local anesthetic (e.g., Ophthaine)
   c) After removal, apply a drop of an antimicrobial (e.g., Sulamyd 10%) and cover the eye with a patch for 24 hours
   d) If object cannot be removed or if symptoms persist for a day or more, refer to an ophthalmologist urgently

SUBCONJUNCTIVAL HEMORRHAGE
A. Sometimes occurs after straining or coughing but often appears apparently spontaneously
B. Occasionally a sign of viral conjunctivitis (see above)
C. No treatment required, resolves in a few days

EYELID CONDITIONS
A. Hordeolum
   1. Infection of the glands of the eyelid, caused by *S. aureus*
   2. Sudden onset of localized pain, swelling, redness, often a purulent discharge
   3. May point to conjunctival side of lid (internal hordeolum) or be associated with an eyelash follicle and point to the skin side, an external hordeolum or *sty*
   4. Treatment
      a) Hot compresses 15–20 minutes several times a day
      b) The lid should be scrubbed with neutral soap each morning
      c) A topical antimicrobial (e.g., Sulamyd 10%) should be applied every 3 or 4 hours for a few days
      d) If no response in 2 days, refer to an ophthalmologist for incision
B. Blepharitis
   1. Marginal (see Chapter 82)
   2. May be associated with chronic bacterial conjunctivitis (see above)
C. Chalazion
   1. Lipogranulomatous inflammation of a meibomian gland secondary to chronic inflammation, may follow a hordeolum
   2. Presents like an internal hordeolum (see above) but is chronic, is not acutely inflamed
   3. Usually requires excision

Section XIV
Miscellaneous Problems

NEVI AND MELANOMA

A. Atypical (dysplastic) nevi (moles)
   1. Typical nevi are round, tan to dark, sharply defined, present since early adulthood; average adult has 20 of these lesions
   2. Atypical nevi
      a) Asymmetrical, irregular, variably colored, often larger than 6 mm in diameter, but are not melanomas (see below)
      b) Patients should be referred to a dermatologist for biopsy or surveillance (examination every month by patient, every 6–12 months by physician)
      c) If no family history, risk of melanoma increased 2–8-fold
   3. Familial atypical mole and melanoma (FAMM) syndrome
      a) Criteria
         1) Family history of melanoma in at least one first- or second-degree relative
         2) Many nevi, some of which are atypical morphologically and histologically
      b) Risk of melanoma is 100%
      c) Patients should be examined every 4–6 months (and should examine themselves monthly)
      d) Should avoid sunburn, use sunblock (see below)
B. Melanoma
   1. Risk factors: atypical nevi, FAMM syndrome (see above), freckles, history of severe sunburns and easy burning, inability to tan, light hair, blue eyes
   2. Subtypes: Table 83.1
   3. Prognosis: dependent on thickness and on whether there are metastases; no effective medical treatment regimens have been developed; only chance for cure is surgical removal

ACTINIC KERATOSIS, KERATOACANTHOMA, NONMELANOMA SKIN CANCERS

A. Actinic keratosis (Table 83.2)
   1. Usually seen in fair-skinned persons in fourth or fifth decades
   2. Associated with an increased risk of skin cancer; precursors (although rarely) of squamous cell carcinomas
   3. Treatment: cryosurgery with liquid nitrogen; patients should be examined every 6 months thereafter to look for new lesions
B. Keratoacanthomas (Table 83.2)
   1. Develop on sun-exposed skin
   2. Should be biopsied or excised to exclude squamous cell carcinoma
C. Nonmelanoma skin cancers
   1. Risk factors
      a) Cumulative sun exposure (especially during childhood and adolescence); higher risk in fair-skinned people who do not tan
      b) Organ transplantation
   2. Basal cell carcinoma (BCC)
      a) Eighty percent develop on head and neck
      b) Subtypes: Table 83.2

Table 83.1. Features of the Subtypes of Melanoma

Melanoma Subtype[a]	Approximate Frequency (%)	Clinical Appearance	Location	Age Group Most Often Affected	Differential Diagnosis
Superficial spreading melanoma	70	Usually brown but may be variably colored brown-black-blue-red and white; flattish papule or plaque, or macular and papular lesions, usually over 6 mm in diameter	Anywhere; frequently on the back in men and on the legs in women	30–40 years	Nevus, seborrheic keratosis
Nodular melanoma	16	Colored as above or amelanotic, dime-shaped or polypoid papule or nodule; typically symmetric and uniform	Anywhere	40–50 years	Nevus Thrombosed Capillary Hemangioma Pyogenic Granuloma
Lentigo maligna melanoma[a]	5	Tan or brown, less often black, blue or red, irregular macule with focal surface elevation; later may develop distinct papules and nodules	Face most often; always on sun-exposed surface	50–70 years	Solar lentigo
Acral lentiginous melanoma	<5	Similar in appearance to lentigo maligna melanoma; when it occurs as a pigmented band in the nail fold, it is called Hutchinson sign (see text); seen most frequently in African Americans and Asians	Palms, soles, phalanges	All ages	Nevus, postinflammatory hyperpigmentation, fungal infection-induced nail dystrophy; pyogenic granuloma

[a]Other rare types combined make up less than 5% of melanoma.

Table 83.2. Nonmelanoma Skin Cancers, Keratoacanthomas, Actinic Keratoses

Clinical Type	Presentation	Key Features	Differential Diagnosis
I. ACTINIC KERATOSIS Actinic keratosis	Erythematous, scaly to hyperkeratotic macule; ill-defined border; usually multiple; always on sun-damaged skin	Scaly, ill-defined lesion on sun-damaged skin	Bowen's disease, superficial BCC, SCC, dermatitis, tinea
II. KERATOACANTHOMA Keratoacanthoma	Firm-to-hard, volcano-like crater with a central keratin plug	Keratin-filled "crater"	SCC, prurigo nodularis
III. BASAL CELL CARCINOMA (BCC) Noduloulcerative	Small, firm, waxy papule often with telangiectasias; may ulcerate; especially on the face	Waxy papule	Intradermal nevus, fibrous papule, folliculitis, seborrheic keratosis
Superficial	Erythematous, sharply circumscribed, scaly macule or thin plaque with a thin thready border; especially on the trunk	Thread-like	Actinic keratosis, Bowen's disease, nummular dermatitis, contact dermatitis, tinea
Morpheaform	Spontaneous scar-like lesion; whitish yellow, smooth shiny scar surface	"Spontaneous"	Scar, granuloma annulare, sarcoid, localized scleroderma
Pigmented	Blue, brown, or black waxy papule; mostly found in deeply pigmented Caucasian, Asian, or African American persons	Pigmented waxy papule	Seborrheic keratosis, nevus, melanoma
IV. SQUAMOUS CELL CARCINOMA (SCC) Common SCC	Firm-to-hard, erythematous, hyperkeratotic nodule, or ulcerated nodule; especially on the dorsal hands, forearms, and face	Firm-to-hard keratotic nodule	Keratoacanthoma, hypertrophic actinic keratosis, seborrheic keratosis, prurigo nodularis
Bowen's disease SCC in situ	Erythematous, sharply circumscribed, scaly macule or thin plaque	Circumscribed scaly erythema	Actinic keratosis, superficial BCC, dermatitis, tinea

BCC, basal cell carcinoma; SCC, squamous cell carcinoma.

3. Squamous cell carcinoma (SCC): Table 83.2
4. Prognosis
   a) BCCs rarely metastasize; SCCs metastasize 3–10% of time (especially if they develop in scars, in areas of chronic inflammation, or in an immunocompromised host)
   b) A person who has had one nonmelanoma skin cancer has a 50% chance of another within 5 years
5. Treatment
   a) All suspicious lesions should be biopsied
   b) Most tumors will be excised, often using Mohs micrographic surgery [a technique in which repeated (if necessary) histological examinations are done immediately to ensure a tumor-free margin]
   c) Electrodesiccation and curettage, cryosurgery, and radiation therapy are alternative modalities, depending on patient's preference, availability of procedure, and cost

ACNE AND RELATED DISORDERS

A. Acne vulgaris
   1. A chronic disorder of the sebaceous glands, particularly those on the face, chest, and back
   2. Begins in prepubescence with the formation of *comedones* (plugged sebaceous ducts, either closed — whiteheads — or open — blackheads), proceeding with inflammation and ending, in the worst cases, with cyst formation
   3. Evaluation
      a) History of medications: hormonal contraceptives; corticosteroids; lithium; iodides; phenytoin; anabolic steroids; high doses of riboflavin, cobalamin may cause or aggravate acne
      b) History of use of facial makeup, creams, moisturizers, hair products that may contain oil that occludes sebaceous glands
      c) History or physical examination that suggests a hyperandrogenic state (Chapter 61)
   4. Therapy
      a) Table 83.3
      b) Retinoic acid (Retin-A, topically, or Accutane, orally) is teratogenic, and sexually active women should use two methods of contraception when using these preparations, should be prepared for an abortion if contraception fails, or abstain from sexual activity during the treatment period (20 weeks for Accutane) if abortion is not acceptable to them
      c) Accutane will predictably cause dry skin and eyes and mild elevations of serum triglyceride and cholesterol levels and of liver enzyme activity

B. Acne rosacea
   1. A chronic inflammatory disorder of the central part of the face
   2. Most common in fair-skinned Caucasians with blue eyes
   3. Begins usually in the third or fourth decade with central facial erythema, telangiectasias, intermittent red follicular papules and pustules
   4. Rarely, rhinophyma develops; more often in men

Table 83.3. Acne Therapy

Type of Acne	Clinical Appearance	General Hygiene	Initial Therapy	Re-evaluate	Therapy if Not Responding[a]	Therapy Change if Responding Nicely
Comedonal acne	Open and closed comedones (blackheads and whiteheads)	Gently wash face with fingertips 2 times/day, using Lever 2000, Dial, or Almay antibacterial liquid soap; avoid lotions or cosmetics containing oil	Retin-A 0.01% gel or 0.05% cream, pea-sized amount at bedtime	8 weeks	Increase Retin-A to 2 times/ day if tolerated	No change
Inflammatory acne	Comedones and inflammatory papules ± pustules		Retin-A, as above; BPO gel 2.5% every A.M. *or* Erythromycin 2% or clindamycin 1% solution or gel 2 times/day[c]	8 weeks	Add oral antibiotics: tetracycline 500 mg 2 times/day or erythromycin 333 mg 3 times/day; change to erythromycin or tetracycline, whichever was not used previously; if still no response after 8 weeks, refer to a dermatologist	Decrease oral antibiotics by 1 tablet every 4–6 weeks; at dose when flare occurs, increase by 1 tablet and hold for several months; then re-evaluate
a) Cystic acne, or b) Scarring inflammatory acne[d]	a) As above plus cystic or nodular lesions b) Inflammatory acne with focal scarring		Retin-A and BPO or antibiotic solution as above, plus oral antibiotics as above	8 weeks	Discontinue all other treatments; begin Accutane[e] (see text); consider referral to a dermatologist	

BPO, benzoyl peroxide.

[a] If not responding, always review patient's regimen; he or she may be noncompliant or just incorrectly using medications.

[b] BPOs such as Desquam E or Benzac AC for dry or normal skin; Desquam X or Benzac W for oily skin. The advantage of BPO over topical antibiotic is that BPOs are bactericidal and antibiotics are bacteriostatic and, therefore, there is less chance for bacterial resistance; a theoretical disadvantage of BPO is that the Food and Drug Administration (FDA) is currently re-evaluating BPOs regarding carcinogenicity; this concern is felt by most experts not to be clinically relevant.

[c] Topical erythromycin such as A/T/S or EryMax; clindamycin such as Cleocin T solution or gel.

[d] Scarring inflammatory acne is not an FDA-approved indication for Accutane; recommend referral to a dermatologist who is willing to treat such patients with Accutane to prevent further permanent, disfiguring scarring.

    5. May involve the eyes (conjunctivitis, blepharitis, episcleritis, chalazion, hordeolum, keratitis — see Chapter 82)

    6. Treatment

      a) Tetracycline, 500 mg 2 times/day, or erythromycin, 333 mg 3 times/day, halved at 4-week intervals if response is good, increased to next higher dose if there is a flare

      b) Alternative to systemic therapy is topical metronidazole gel (Metrogel) twice a day after washing; response varies

C. Hidradenitis suppurativa

    1. Disorder characterized by inflammation and occlusion of apocrine glands (located in perineum, inguinal folds, pubic region, umbilicus, breasts, postauricular area, scalp, back)

    2. Multiple large comedones (see Acne, above), inflammatory papules, pustules, cysts (which rupture to form draining sinus tracts)

    3. Patients also have cystic acne (see above) and scarring scalp folliculitis (see below)

    4. Treatment

      a) During acute flares, short courses of antimicrobials based on culture of draining lesions

      b) Chronic antimicrobial therapy and topical benzoyl peroxide as for acne (Table 83.3)

      c) Surgery only for severe disease

D. Miliaria

    1. Disorder of sweat retention due to occlusion of ducts of eccrine glands (almost always on the trunk)

    2. Seen in persons exposed to high environmental temperatures or to high fever; also occlusive material on skin predisposes to the problem

    3. If occlusions are superficial, asymptomatic 1–2-mm vesicles are seen; if deep, pruritic red papules are seen

    4. Treatment: provide a cool environment, remove occlusive fabrics

DERMATITIS

A. Summary of diagnostic, therapeutic, and prognostic features: Table 83.4

B. Atopic dermatitis

    1. Typically associated with allergic rhinitis or asthma; 70% have a family history of atopy

    2. In adults, involves hands; face; flexural arms, legs, neck, wrists, ankles

    3. See Table 83.4

C. Nummular dermatitis: pruritic, sharply circumscribed, 1–2-mm, vesicular to lichenified red plaques on the extremities (for treatment, see Table 83.4)

D. Asteatotic eczema

    1. Dry scaly skin followed later by fissuring with erythema in the cracks

    2. Elderly most commonly affected

    3. Patients complain of stinging, tight skin with or without pruritus

    4. Treatment

      a) Dry skin treated with warm baths or showers with oilated soaps (e.g., Dove) used, followed by an oil-based emollient (see Topical Therapeutics below) and avoidance of harsh soaps and rough fabrics

Table 83.4. Summary of the Diagnostic, Therapeutic, and Prognostic Features of the Phases of Any Dermatitis

Phase	Typical Morphology	Primary Treatment of Dermatitis	Indicators of Colonization or Secondary Infection Requiring Therapy	Treatment of Infection	Second-Line Treatment for Unresponsive Dermatitis or First-Line Treatment for Very Severe Dermatitis	General Prognosis
Acute dermatitis	Papules, papulovesicles, erythema, serous discharge, and crusting	Saline compresses 4 times/day, switching when dry to corticosteroid creams[a] 2 times/day (high potency) and emollients ± antipruritics (menthol and camphor)	Moderate to severe crusting representing impetiginization or erythema representing erysipelas or cellulitis	Oral antistaphylococcal antibiotics (dicloxacillin or cephalexin) except in cases of erysipelas or cellulitis, which typically require i.v. antibiotics (see Chapter 11)	Prednisone 0.7–1 mg/kg/day tapered over approximately 2 weeks	Usually excellent
Subacute dermatitis	Erythema, edema, papules, and scale	Topical corticosteroid (high-potency) ointments[a] and emollients[b]	As above and/or numerous excoriations	As above	Phototherapy or photochemotherapy with UVB or PUVA, respectively	Usually good; however, recurrences are not uncommon
Chronic dermatitis	Lichenified or thickened papules and plaques	Topical corticosteroid ointments (high potency)[a]	As above and/or nonhealing fissures	As above	As above	Treatment is difficult, recurrences are very common

PUVA, psoralen-ultraviolet A light; *UVB*, ultraviolet B light

[a] Only low-potency corticosteroids should be used on the face; when using class supra-, high-, or mid-potency corticosteroids elsewhere, side effects such as atrophy, telangiectasia, striae, or systemic absorption are possible.

[b] Corticosteroids and ointments are discussed in detail in the section entitled, Topical Therapeutics.

       b) Erythema treated with low-potency to mid-potency topical corticosteroid ointment (not cream) twice a day; see Topical Therapeutics, below

E. Contact dermatitis
1. Irritant dermatitis
    a) Harsh chemicals, e.g., soaps and cleansers, cause a scalded appearance of the skin
    b) Mild irritants cause macular erythema, but chronic exposure causes scale and plaque formation
2. Allergic contact dermatitis
    a) Delayed hypersensitivity reaction after initial sensitization
    b) Most common cause is plant dermatitis (poison oak, ivy, or sumac)
    c) Typically, an acute vesiculobullous eruption that may continue to appear for up to 3 weeks
    d) If cause not obvious and lesions recur, patch testing by a dermatologist may be revealing
    e) Treatment (Table 83.4): topical treatment, but oral corticosteroids (prednisone 0.7 mg/kg, tapered over 2 weeks) if there are vesiculobullous lesions or if face, hands, or genitalia are involved

F. Contact urticaria
1. Most common cause is latex
2. Itching initially, then hives in area of contact
3. May cause anaphylaxis (Chapter 19) so allergic patients should wear a Medic-Alert bracelet and carry an epinephrine-containing autoinjector (Epi-Pen)

G. Hand dermatitis
1. Nummular (see above) and contact (see above)
2. Dyshidrotic hand dermatitis
    a) Tiny vesicles on the sides of the fingers and over the palms; intensely pruritic
    b) Tends to cycle over weeks to months
    c) Treatment: emollients and topical corticosteroid ointments (see Topical Therapeutics, below)

H. Perioral dermatitis
1. Minute papules and pustules on a background of erythema and slight scaling around the mouth alone or around the mouth, eyes, and nares; tends to burn rather than itch
2. Most common in young women
3. Treatment: as for acne rosacea, above

I. Intertrigo
1. Moist erythema and sometimes fissuring in skin folds or at angles of the mouth; tends to itch and burn
2. Treatment: talc, weight loss, cool environment; if unresponsive or if at angles of mouth, refer to a dermatologist to confirm diagnosis or for consideration of collagen injection to eliminate apposition of skin

J. Seborrheic dermatitis
1. Erythema and dry white to greasy yellow scale in affected areas (scalp, areas of facial hair, central face, ears, presternal chest, axillae, umbilicus, inguinal folds, gluteal cleft, perianal skin); *dandruff* is a nonerythematous scaling in same locations

2. Treatment
    a) For scalp
        1) First, selenium sulfide shampoo (e.g., Head & Shoulders Intensive Formula or Selsun Blue) every other night
        2) Then, if necessary, fluocinonide solution (e.g., Lidex 0.05%), 1 drop to each nickel-sized itchy, scaling area
    b) For face and body: hydrocortisone cream, 0.5% or 1% 2 times/day, or ketoconazole cream (e.g., Nizoral 2%), 2 times/day until clearing

PSORIASIS
A. General
    1. Psoriasis is a benign epidermal hyperproliferation of unknown cause
    2. One-third of patients develop disease before age 19; average age of onset is 27 years
    3. Lifelong disease with remissions and exacerbations
    4. Exacerbated by sunlight deprivation, infection, certain drugs (e.g., lithium and antimalarials), cutaneous trauma, psychological stress
B. Presentation
    1. Subtypes
        a) Chronic plaque psoriasis
            1) Most common type
            2) One to many deeply red, sharply demarcated oval plaques, several centimeters in diameter, with moderate to heavy silvery-white surface scale, commonly on scalp and over one or more extensor joints
            3) Intertriginous plaques may also be present, with little or no scale
        b) Guttate psoriasis
            1) Acute exanthem-like eruption of drop-like red, flat-topped scaly papules of 1 mm to 1 cm may be widespread over face, scalp, hands, feet
            2) Frequently triggered by an infection (e.g., Streptococcal pharyngitis or viral upper respiratory infection)
        c) Erythrodermic psoriasis and pustular psoriasis less common, more severe forms
    2. Nails: often show pitting, onycholysis (separation from the nail bed with a white color between the plate and the bed), or subungual hyperkeratosis
    3. Extracutaneous disease: psoriatic arthritis; may be debilitating, best referred to a rheumatologist
C. Treatment
    1. Avoid systemic corticosteroids
    2. Chronic plaque psoriasis
        a) Mild emollients (see Topical Therapeutics, below)
        b) Keratolytics (e.g., Lac-Hydrin)
        c) Low-potency to mid-potency topical corticosteroids (see Topical Therapeutics, below)
    3. Generalized plaque psoriasis: refer to a dermatologist for consideration for photochemotherapy (8-methoxypsoralen plus ultraviolet radiation in a light box 3 times/week) or, alternatively, methotrexate or etretinate (a synthetic retinoid)

4. Guttate psoriasis
    a) Usually responds to emollients, low-potency topical corticosteroids (see Topical Therapeutics, below)
    b) Treat promptly any triggering infection
5. Erythrodermic and pustular psoriasis: should be referred to a dermatologist urgently for systemic treatment with etretinate or methotrexate, followed by ultraviolet radiation

ACANTHOSIS NIGRICANS

A. Presentation
    1. Hyperpigmented velvety change in the skin of the base of the neck, extensor joints of the hands, flexor surfaces
    2. May be associated with endocrinopathies (insulin resistance, diabetes mellitus, obesity, polycystic ovaries, Addison's disease, acromegaly, hypothyroidism, pineal hyperplasia, or tumor)
    3. May be associated with certain drugs and peptides (e.g., nicotinic acid, glucocorticoids, adrenocorticotropic hormone)
    4. May be associated with malignancy, usually over age 40; in one-third of cases, tongue and lips are affected
B. Treatment: for cosmetic purposes, may be treated with topical retinoic acid (see Acne, above)

HAIR LOSS

A. Stages of hair growth
    1. Anagen: growing phase (years), 70–80% of scalp hair
    2. Catagen: transition phase (months), about 10% of scalp hair
    3. Telogen: resting phase before shedding (months), about 20% of scalp hair
B. Nonscarring alopecia
    1. Male or female pattern
        a) Common in both sexes
        b) In men: first frontal and vertex thinning, eventually confluent
        c) In women: diffuse thinning over the crown (male pattern hair loss in women may be a sign of virilization — see Chapter 61)
        d) Treatment
            1) Topical minoxidil: produces hair growth in only 20% of people but may reduce rate of hair loss in many more people; expensive (about $60/month)
            2) Hair transplants: expensive, some discomfort during procedure
            3) Hair prostheses: expensive, can be uncomfortable
    2. Telogen effluvium
        a) Shedding of telogen hairs (see above) diffusely over scalp, often noticed only because of excess hair on comb or brush
        b) May follow a stressful event or condition (e.g., surgery, childbirth, high fever, sudden weight loss, psychiatric stress) by 1 to several months
        c) Reversible
    3. Anagen effluvium
        a) Caused by chemotherapeutic agents
        b) Hair loss occurs over days; only sparse (telogen) hairs remain
        c) Reversible
    4. Other reversible drug-induced hair loss (commonly associated drugs are androgens, anticoagulants, cholesterol-lowering agents)

     5. Alopecia areata
       a) Typically, coin-shaped areas of hair loss over scalp but may be diffuse, may involve entire body
       b) Usually reversible within 1 year
       c) Increased incidence of autoimmune thyroid and adrenal disease and of pernicious anemia
       d) Often treated with topical corticosteroid solution (see below), 1 drop to each nickel-sized area

C. Scarring alopecia
  1. Associated with a variety of systemic disorders and of primary cutaneous disorders (e.g., discoid lupus)
  2. Scalp is scarred in areas of hair loss
  3. Irreversible

DERMATOPHYTE INFECTIONS

A. Common features
  1. Superficial fungal infection
  2. Symptoms of pruritus, burning, and stinging
  3. Transmissions may occur through direct contact but more often occur by indirect contact (e.g., shared linens and towels, baths, showers, and pools)
  4. Diagnosis confirmed by potassium hydroxide (KOH) preparation and/or a fungal culture
    a) Scale obtained by use of a #15 scalpel blade held perpendicular to the skin
    b) One drop of 20% KOH added to scale on a slide, and a coverslip is applied
    c) Preparation heated gently and examined through a microscope, using a 40 × objective
    d) Fungal hyphae look like refractile rod-shaped filaments of uniform width with characteristic branching (Fig. 83.1)
    e) *Candida* and *Pityrosporum* appear as pseudobranching or nonbranching hyphae and as clusters of budding cells (Fig. 83.1)

B. Tinea capitis
  1. Very unusual in adults
  2. Patchy hair loss with broken-off hairs
  3. Involved scalp is red, scaly
  4. Should be treated aggressively, preferably by a dermatologist, to prevent scarring
    a) Selenium sulfide shampoos (e.g., Selsun Blue, Head & Shoulders Intensive Formula) every day for 1 to several days
    b) Oral griseofulvin 375 mg once a day; be aware of teratogenicity

C. Tinea faciei
  1. Lesions vary from red, relatively ill-defined scaly plaques to sharply circumscribed plaques with central clearing
  2. KOH preparations often negative; culture may be necessary
  3. Treated with griseofulvin 375 mg once a day; be aware of teratogenicity

D. Tinea corporis
  1. Infection outside of head, groin, hands, and feet
  2. Annular plaques with a delicate scale at the advancing border
  3. KOH preparation positive

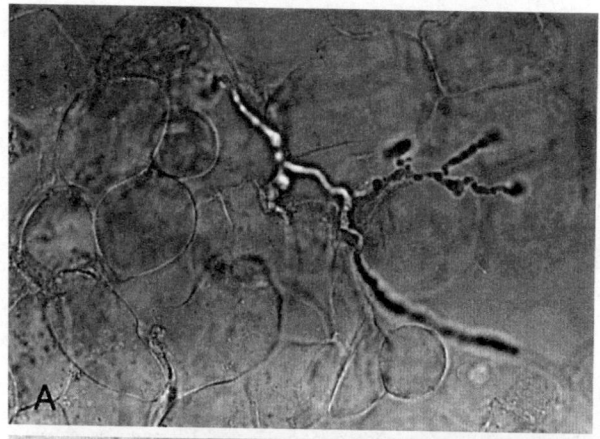

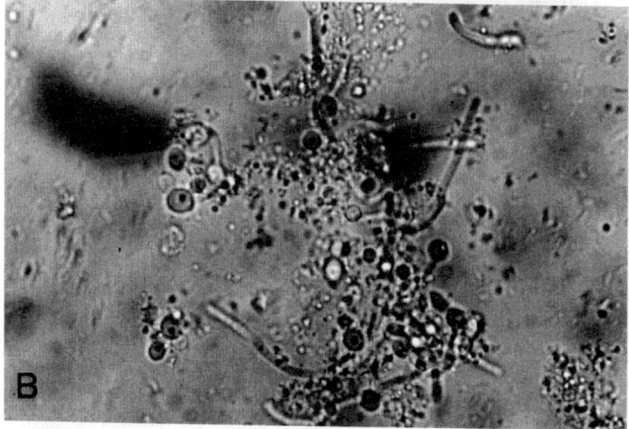

Figure 83.1.   A. Hyphae of tinea (KOH preparation, ×400). **B.** Pseudohyphae of *Candida.* (KOH preparation, ×400.) (**B** provided courtesy of William G. Merz, Ph.D.)

    4. Treated with topical imidazole antifungals (see Topical Therapeutics, below) twice a day for 4–6 weeks

E. Tinea cruris
1. Predominantly seen in men
2. Hemispherical, scaly plaques on the superiormost medial thighs extending onto the perineal and inguinal areas
3. KOH preparation positive
4. Treated with topical imidazoles (see Topical Therapeutics, below)

F. Tinea pedis
1. Interdigital and/or plantar involvement with variable erythema, diffuse scale, focal maceration; some patients form tense blisters
2. KOH preparation positive
3. Treated with topical imidazoles (see Topical Therapeutics, below), but refractory cases may require oral griseofulvin 375 mg/day

G. Tinea manus
1. Diffuse, usually noninflammatory scaling of the palms
2. KOH preparation positive
3. Treated with topical imidazoles (see Topical Therapeutics, below), but oral griseofulvin often required, ultimately 375 mg/day (be aware of teratogenicity)

H. Tinea unguium
1. Usually of the toenails, occasionally of the fingernails
2. Whitish-yellow discoloration, subungual debris, thickening of nails
3. Treatment usually ineffective

YEAST INFECTIONS

A. Candidiasis
1. Presentations
    a) Inflammatory summertime rash in women
    b) Vaginal infection in premenopausal women (Chapter 77)
    c) Oral infection in immunosuppressed patients or in diabetics (Chapter 84)
    d) Perineal and buttocks infection especially in incontinent or elderly people
2. Appearance on skin: red, slick, shiny patches with an irregular border of delicate scale and, often, satellite papules and pustules
3. KOH preparation (see above, Dermatophyte infections, and Fig. 83.1) confirmatory, usually unnecessary
4. Treated with nystatin cream or an imidazole cream (see Topical Therapeutics, below) twice a day until complete clearing (usually 2–3 weeks); topical drying powders (see below) may be of help in preventing recurrence; refractory cases may require oral ketoconazole 200 mg/day for 10–14 days; rare severe hepatotoxicity occurs, and liver function tests should be monitored before and after treatment

B. Tinea versicolor
1. Superficial infection caused by *Pityrosporum orbiculare* (also called *Malassezia furfur*)
2. Most patients are in their teens or early twenties
3. Especially common in warm months
4. Increased frequency in patients with exogenous or endogenous hypercorticoidism
5. Appearance: oval, scaly, hypopigmented, hyperpigmented or red

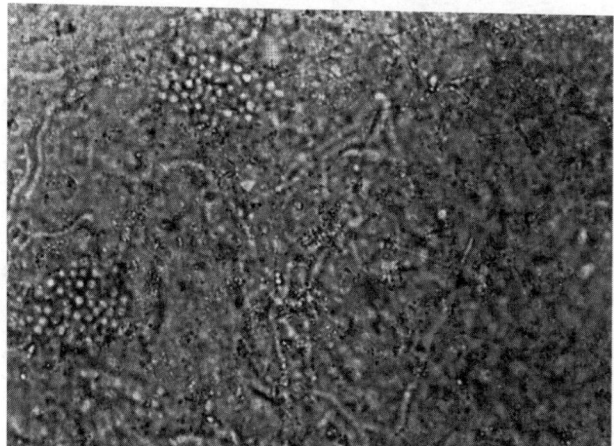

Figure 83.2. Short hyphae and spores of *Malassezia furfur* seen in tinea versi-color. (KOH preparation, ×400.)

patches that coalesce into larger lesions over upper trunk, less often on face, scalp, genitalia, proximal extremities
6. Usually asymptomatic but sometimes pruritic
7. KOH preparation (see above) shows pseudohyphae and spores (Fig. 83.2)
8. Treated with selenium sulfide 2.5% lotion, left on for 15 minutes, then washed off every night for 2 weeks, then once a month as prophylaxis (ketoconazole shampoo may be used, alternatively, on same schedule)

LOCALIZED VIRAL INFECTIONS OF THE SKIN
A. Warts
  1. Common features
     a) Caused by human papilloma virus
     b) Most common in children and young adults
     c) Disrupt normal skin lines
     d) Frequently have visible thrombosed capillaries on their surface that look like black dots
     e) Appear most often at sites of trauma
  2. Types
     a) Common warts (verruca vulgaris)
        1) Initially 1-mm, smooth, skin-colored papules that gradually enlarge to several millimeters with a rough hyperkeratotic surface; may coalesce to form large plaques
        2) Found most often on hands
     b) Flat warts
        1) Skin-colored to pink, flat-topped papules less than a few millimeters in diameter
        2) Occur most commonly on dorsal hands or on face
     c) Genital warts (condylomata acuminata)
        1) Begin as minute flat papules that become hyperkeratotic

2) Present on the external genitalia, perineal and pubic regions; may be in vagina or in rectum

3) Cervical warts in women and anal warts in homosexual men predispose to development of intraepithelial tumors

    d) Plantar warts

      1) Circumscribed, thickened, slightly elevated papules

      2) Distinguished from corns by paring with a #15 scalpel blade at a 45° angle: warts have minute black dots on surface; corns have a central core; corns are smooth, do not bleed when scraped; warts are rough, do bleed when scraped

    e) Treatment

      1) Common, flat and plantar warts

        (a) Soak in warm water for several minutes, then file smooth with a nail file or pumice stone, then apply 2–3 drops of 16% salicylic acid (Occlusal or Duofilm), letting each drop dry before applying the next

        (b) If no response after 6 weeks of daily therapy, cryosurgery with liquid nitrogen should be instituted (and continued every 1–2 weeks until resolution or 10 treatments)

        (c) Patients with refractory warts should be referred to a dermatologist, and those with plantar warts, to a podiatrist

      2) Genital warts

        (a) Podophyllin 25% in tincture of benzoin (Pod-Ben-25) applied (with a swab carefully) weekly by the physician; patient must not move until solution has dried; medication is washed off 2–4 hours after the first application, then left on for an additional 2–4 hours each week to 24 hours

        (b) Alternative is podofilox 0.5 (Condylox) applied by patient as instructed in package insert

        (c) Refractory lesions require cryosurgery

B. Molluscum contagiosum

  1. Common in young children and in HIV-positive people

  2. Caused by pox virus

  3. Lesions are umbilicated, skin-colored to whitish, 1–4-mm papules on neck, trunk, genitalia, eyelids

  4. KOH scrapings show eosinophilic intracytoplasmic inclusion bodies

  5. Treated initially with a salicylic acid solution (Occlusal or Duofilm, as for warts, above); if no response, topical retinoin (Retin-A 0.26% gel) twice a day and then cryosurgery or curettage

HERPES INFECTION

A. Herpes simplex infection

  1. Recurrent localized blistering often triggered by sun exposure, illness, menses, stress

  2. Most lesions are due to reactivation of latent virus, but virus may be transmitted by direct contact with an open lesion

  3. Oral infection

    a) As a primary infection, acute gingivostomatitis, with systemic symptoms (e.g., fever) (see Chapter 84)

      b) Recurrent infection manifested as herpes labialis with coalescing blisters on or about the lips; no systemic symptoms; lesions heal in about 1 week

4. Genital herpes: see Chapter 77
5. Herpes infection on body (other than oral or genital) through contact with a patient who has active lesions (a common site in health care workers is on the finger)
6. In immunocompromised patients, lesions are chronic, punched-out ulcers
7. Complications
      a) Cutaneous dissemination in a patient with generalized atopic dermatitis
      b) Erythema multiforme: a hypersensitivity response to herpes infection
      c) Herpetic keratitis (Chapter 82)
      d) Systemic infection in an immunocompromised patient
8. Treatment
      a) Primary infection: acyclovir 200 mg (200-mg tablet) 5 times/day for 10 days
      b) Recurrent infection: acyclovir 200 mg 5 times/day for 5 days
      c) In immunocompromised patients with chronic lesions, acyclovir 400–800 mg 5 times/day for 14 days; unresponsive patients should be hospitalized for parenteral therapy
      d) Prophylaxis
         1) More effective for genital than for oral herpes
         2) Acyclovir 400 mg twice a day for people who have had six or more recurrences or if lesions can be anticipated (increased sun exposure)

B. Herpes zoster (shingles)
1. Reactivation years after (two-thirds of patients are over age 50) an initial varicella (chickenpox) infection
2. Dermatomal distribution of coalescing vesicles (thoracic, 50%; cervical, 20%; trigeminal, 15%; lumbosacral, 10%)
      a) Accompanied (frequently preceded) by a sequential neuralgia
      b) Lesions develop crusts in 7–10 days, clear in 2–3 weeks; new lesions may appear for up to 7 days
3. Tzanck smear will confirm that the lesions are herpetic (i.e., either zoster or simplex)
      a) Unroof a vesicle; scrape the base and smear onto a glass slide
      b) Stain with commercially available Tzanck stain or with Giemsa stain (0.5 ml water and 0.5 ml Giemsa stain mixed and flooded over the specimen, rinsed with water after 30 seconds, and air dried)
      c) Search the slide for giant cells and for cells containing multiple nuclei that appear molded together
4. In patients with recurrent dermatomal lesions, culture is indicated (scraping is placed in a viral culture medium) to rule out simplex infection, a probable sign of immunocompromise
5. Treatment
      a) Acyclovir 800 mg (800-mg tablets) 5 times/day reduces development of new lesions only if it can be begun within 48 hours of eruption
      b) Topical wet to damp dressings

      c) Topical antibacterial agent (e.g., bacitracin ointment) to prevent secondary infection

      d) Analgesics as necessary

6. Postherpetic neuralgia

      a) Pain after healing of the cutaneous lesions is most commonly seen in people over age 80, usually abates within 6 months

      b) Treatment

         1) Capsaicin cream (Zostrix 0.025% or Zostrix HP 0.075%, available without prescription) 4 times/day; may be a delay of a few days or weeks before effect

         2) Amitriptyline 12.5–150 mg/day may give some relief

7. Other complications

      a) Ocular zoster requires emergent treatment by an ophthalmologist

      b) Ramsay-Hunt syndrome: facial and auditory involvement (facial palsy, tinnitus, vertigo, hearing loss)

      c) Paralysis of muscles corresponding to affected dermatome in 1–5% of people, usually with recovery

      d) Meningoencephalitis or disseminated skin or systemic infection in immunocompromised people

INFESTATIONS

A. Scabies

1. Caused by mite infestation

2. Pathognomonic lesions are thread-like ridges, ½–1 cm in length with a minute vesicle or papule at one end; also, ½–1 cm nodules containing mites, small red papules, eczematous plaques, and excoriations may develop

      a) Lesions itch intensely, worse at night

      b) Burrow most common on hands, wrists, penis, nipples, axillae, gluteal cleft; nodules most common on scrotum, penis, axillae

3. Diagnosis can be confirmed by scraping the vesicle or papule at the end of a burrow with a #15 scalpel blade, covering the scraping on a slide with a coverslip, applying mineral oil, and identifying the mite and/or eggs through the 10× objective of the microscope

4. Treatment

      a) Lindane (Kwell Cream, 60 g, enough for two people) or permethrin (Elimite 60 g) applied at bedtime, washed off the next morning; should not be used by pregnant or lactating women or by people with numerous excoriations

      b) After use of the scabicide, emollients or low-potency corticosteroids (see Topical Therapeutics, below) may be necessary to suppress skin hypersensitivity induced by the mites

      c) All bed linen and recently worn clothes should be washed in hot water and put through a hot dryer

B. Pediculosis

1. Lice infestation

2. Intense pruritus with excoriations that frequently become secondarily infected

3. Nits or eggs are >1 mm long, attached to hair shafts; lice are visible to the naked eye

4. Treatment
   a) Pyrethrin shampoo (RID — available without prescription) or lindane (e.g., Kwell lotion, cream or shampoo — requires prescription): shampoo left on for 5 minutes; lotion, overnight; lindane application must be repeated 1 week later
   b) Nits should be removed with a fine-toothed comb after an undiluted white vinegar compress is applied for 15 minutes
   c) Close contacts should be treated
   d) Linens, clothing should be washed in hot water, dried in a hot dryer

AUTOIMMUNE BLISTERING DISORDERS

A. Conditions characterized by flaccid to tense bullae, with or without erythema, localized or generalized
B. Serious and sometimes life-threatening
C. Diagnosis requires a biopsy with special staining
D. All patients should be referred to a dermatologist
E. Treatment includes high-dose prednisone, cytotoxic drugs or plasmapheresis

DRUG ERUPTIONS

A. Exanthems
   1. Appearance: usually macular and papular (morbilliform) but may be purely macular, often pruritic
   2. Common associated drugs: penicillins, cephalosporins, sulfonamides, quinidine, cimetidine, allopurinol, carbamazepine, phenytoin, isoniazid, nitrofurantoin
   3. Course: after 2–3 days (previous exposure) or 9–10 days
   4. Systemic involvement: usually none but occasionally kidneys or liver is involved
   5. Treatment
      a) If uncomplicated, stop offending drug, apply bland topical over-the-counter menthol or phenol containing preparations (e.g., Aveeno Anti-Itch Cream) many times a day
      b) If systemic involvement, consider referral to a dermatologist to confirm diagnosis and for consideration of more specific treatment
B. Erythema multiforme
   1. Erythema multiforme major
      a) Caused by drugs (e.g., sulfonamides, penicillins, phenytoin) or infections (see below)
      b) Usually a prodrome of malaise, myalgia, fever, sometimes upper respiratory infection
      c) Develops rapidly, involves skin and at least two mucosal surfaces (usually conjunctival or oral mucosa)
      d) Skin lesions progress from macules to bullae, often confluent; mucosa shows erythema, denudation, crusting, bullae
      e) Most frequent complication is secondary infection; most devastating remote complication is ocular scarring and impaired vision
      f) Immediate hospitalization warranted for corticosteroids, treatment of complications
   2. Erythema multiforme minor
      a) Caused less often by drugs, most often associated with a

preceding herpes simplex infection (see above), although a variety of other infections have also been implicated

b) Begins with red to violaceous macules that evolve into papules with an expanding border, leaving a nonblanchable, dusky, sunken center ("target lesions"); lesions may coalesce into plaques or become bullous

c) Lesions may be anywhere but favor hands, feet, knees, elbows; mucosal lesions may occur; occasionally, erythema multiforme may be limited to the mouth

d) Fever and malaise may occur

e) Treatment

1) Stop offending drug if one is identified

2) Treatment of causative infection would not alter course, so decision to treat depends on infection

3) For symptomatic relief

(a) Oral lesions may be treated, e.g., 4 times/day with a suspension containing equal parts Benadryl Elixir and Maalox; swish for 1 minute and expectorate

(b) Topical anesthetics, e.g., Xylocaine gel, may be applied to painful oral lesions before meals

4) Use of systemic corticosteroids is controversial; consult with a dermatologist

5) If herpes simplex was the trigger, prescribe acyclovir prophylactically (see Herpes simplex, above)

C. Toxic epidermal necrolysis

1. Caused by drugs (especially penicillin, sulfonamides, anticonvulsants, nonsteroidal anti-inflammatory agents, allopurinol, colchicine)

2. Begins with diffuse, painful erythema that spreads quickly over body; patchy, then coalescing areas of necrosis with sloughing develop rapidly

3. Patients are very sick; mortality rate is high (25–75%); hospitalization is mandatory

PHOTOSENSITIVITY

A. Phototoxic or sunburn reaction

1. Most often associated with phototoxic drugs (e.g., sulfonamides, tetracycline, doxycycline, phenothiazines, nonsteroidal anti-inflammatory agents, especially piroxicam (Feldene) and psoralens)

2. Will occur in anyone if drug level is high enough and if ultraviolet radiation is intense enough

B. Papular or papulovesicular erythema

1. Photoallergic eruption caused by a drug (e.g., thiazides, nonsteroidal anti-inflammatory agents, especially Feldene, sulfonamides, sulfonylureas, oral contraceptives, quinidine)

2. Polymorphous light eruption

a) Pruritic papular eruption on extensor arms, sometimes legs after first exposures to sun in spring and summer; eventually clear with tanning

b) Cause unknown

C. Treatment: soothing baths with additives such as Aveeno; analgesics if necessary

D. Sunscreens and sunblocks
  1. For photosensitive and normal people who will be out of doors a good deal in sunny seasons
  2. Most screens contain agents (benzophenones or cinnamates) that absorb ultraviolet B (cause of drug eruptions); newer screens contain parsol, which absorbs ultraviolet A (cause of polymorphous light eruption)
  3. Blocks contain zinc oxide and/or titanium dioxide, often less acceptable cosmetically
      a) Rated by sun protection factor (SPF); SPF of 15 is adequate
      b) Use 1 ounce of lotion, on average, for entire body surface to get adequate protection

TOPICAL THERAPEUTICS
A. Topical corticosteroids
  1. Preparations
      a) Low-potency: hydrocortisone 1% (e.g., Hytone)
      b) Mid-potency: triamcinolone 0.1% (e.g., Kenalog) or fluocinolone acetonide 0.025 (e.g., Synalar)
      c) High-potency: fluocinonide (e.g., Lidex)
      d) Super-potency: clobetrasol (e.g., Temovate)
  2. Dosages
      a) Generally only low-potency preparations should be used on face, in skin folds, on genitals
      b) One g covers 10×10-cm area; 2 g cover hands, head, face, or anogenital area; 3 g cover the anterior or posterior trunk or one arm; 4 g cover a single lower extremity; 30 g cover the entire skin
B. Emollients (moisturizers)
  1. Oil in water (mostly water), water in oil (mostly oil) or oil; the more oil, the more occlusive; oil in water (e.g., Moisturel, Keri Lotion), however, often a reasonable compromise
  2. Emollients with keratolytic or hydrophilic chemicals are useful in patients with dry skin (e.g., Lac-Hydrin lotion — requires a prescription)
C. Topical antifungal agents
  1. Polyene antibiotics such as nystatin (Mycostatin — requires a prescription) for *Candida* infection
  2. Imidazoles such as clotrimazole (Lotrimin AF — does not require a prescription) or ketoconazole (Nizoral 2% — by prescription) for dermatophyte and yeast infections
  3. Allylamines such as terbinafine (Lamisil — by prescription) for dermatophyte and yeast infections
D. Compresses and baths
  1. Compresses
      a) To dry and debride localized areas of acute dermatitis characterized by moist, red, edematous papules, plaques, vesicles, or bullae
      b) Solutions
          1) Saline
          2) Precipitating protein: e.g., Burows aluminum acetate, 1:20 solution; Domeboro's aluminum sulfate and calcium acetate solution, 2:30 solution; Aveeno-Colloidal Oatmeal packet

3) Germicidal: e.g., silver nitrate 0.1–0.5% solution, acetic acid 1–5% solution

2. Baths
   a) If more than one-third of body is covered by acute dermatitis, lukewarm baths (rather than compresses) are the treatment of choice
   b) Additives include Aveeno Oil packet, baking soda (3 cups), and hydrolyzed starch (Lint) 4 cups mixed with water and then added to the bath
   c) For dry, pruritic dermatoses, bath oil, ¼ cup, or Aveeno Oilated Oatmeal packet should be added to the bath water (be aware of slippery surfaces)

84/ COMMON PROBLEMS OF THE TEETH AND ORAL CAVITY

ACUTE PROBLEMS

A. Toothaches (pulpitis)
  1. Presentation
     a) Large carious lesion (see below), large restoration (filling), or both
     b) Pain in response to thermal stimuli, especially cold, may radiate to the face or the ear
     c) If pulp of tooth becomes necrotic, thermal sensitivity disappears, but there is exquisite sensitivity to percussion of the crown
     d) If toothache is left untreated, an abscess of the tooth or facial cellulitis may occur
  2. Treatment
     a) If patient is afebrile and there is no swelling of the face or the gums, analgesia (e.g., acetaminophen 650 mg every 4 hours) and referral to a dentist within 24 hours
     b) If there is low-grade fever (up to 101°F) and/or slight swelling of the face or gums, analgesia and antibiotics (e.g., penicillin, 250 mg, or erythromycin, 250 mg, every 6 hours) and referral to a dentist within 12–24 hours
     c) If there is fever above 101°F and more than slight swelling of the face or gums, immediate referral to a dentist is indicated
B. Pericoronitis (third molar or wisdom tooth pain)
  1. Presentation
     a) Patient usually between 15 and 25 years of age
     b) Pain that radiates to the ear, throat, floor of the mouth, and foul taste
     c) Swelling prevents proper closure of jaw (in severe cases, difficulty swallowing)
     d) Gingiva are markedly red, swollen, tender; occasionally, tender adenopathy and fever are present
     e) Possible complications: peritonsillar abscess, cellulitis, Ludwig's angina (cellulitis of the floor of the mouth)
  2. Treatment
     a) If patient afebrile, analgesics and referral to a dentist within 24 hours
     b) If patient febrile, add antibiotics as for toothache, above
C. Acute necrotizing ulcerative gingivitis (ANUG, Vincent's infection, trench mouth)
  1. Presentation
     a) Sudden onset, usually associated with debilitating illness, an acute respiratory infection, or acute psychological stress
     b) Fetid odor, foul taste, increased salivation, gingival bleeding, extremely sensitive gums, constant gnawing pain
     c) Punched-out ulcers, covering of the gums with a gray slough, at the edges of which is a linear erythema

d) Usually, submandibular adenopathy and slight fever; in severe cases, high fever and malaise
e) Potential for rare severe systemic infection and for local gangrene

2. Treatment
a) If severe, immediate hospitalization
b) If less severe, immediate consultation by a dentist for debridement, antibiotics

D. Recurrent aphthous stomatitis (RAS, canker sores)
1. Presentation
a) Superficial ulcerations on the mucous membranes of the lips, cheeks, tongue, floor of the mouth, palate, or gingiva
b) Begins with burning for 1–48 hours before painful vesicles (single or multiple) appear, rupture in 2 days to form ulcers with a red or gray-red center and an elevated red rim
c) Lesions heal in 7–10 days, although some people have constantly recurring lesions for years

2. Treatment
a) Mouthwash of equal parts Benadryl suspension (5 g/ml) and Kaopectate (prepared by a pharmacist), or
b) Viscous Xylocaine applied with a cotton-tipped applicator, or
c) Zilactin (available without prescription), a tannic acid suspension applied 4 times/day
d) In severe cases, tetracycline may be of help, i.e., a 250-mg capsule in 50 ml of water as a rinse, then swallowed 3 or 4 times/day for 5–7 days

E. Acute herpetic gingivostomatitis
1. Presentation
a) Relatively rare in adults except in immunocompromised patients
b) Diffuse, red shiny involvement of gingiva, oral mucosa with swelling and bleeding
c) Lesions are at first spherical gray vesicles that rupture in 24 hours to form small painful ulcers with a red, elevated margin and a depressed yellow or gray-white center
d) Regional adenopathy and fever are common, a distinguishing feature from RAS (above)
e) Lesions heal in 7–10 days

2. Treatment
a) As above for RAS
b) Immunosuppressed patients need to be seen by an expert in infectious disease

F. Sialadenitis
1. Presentation
a) Pain and enlargement of affected salivary gland
b) Bacterial infection may present as red, tense overlying skin and purulent discharge from a draining duct; relatively uncommon in adults
c) Obstructive sialadenitis associated with stone or mucous plug occurs most commonly in middle-aged men
1) Symptoms aggravated by eating
2) Submandibular glands most often affected
d) Mumps: usually bilateral, with systemic symptoms

   2. Treatment
      a) Bacterial: heat (moist packs for 15–20 minutes and intraoral
         warm rinses), analgesics (e.g., acetaminophen), antibiotics
         (e.g., penicillin V, 250 mg, or erythromycin, 250 mg, every
         6 hours for 10 days), and liquid diet for 2–3 days
      b) Obstructive: referral to a dentist or an otolaryngologist
G. Temporomandibular joint pain (TMJ)
   1. Epidemiology
      a) Most patients are women between ages 24 and 40
      b) There may be a history of grinding of teeth, jaw trauma,
         whiplash injury, or emotional stress
      c) Twenty percent of patients with rheumatoid arthritis have TMJ
         pain
   2. Presentation
      a) Pain and tenderness in muscles of mastication and in TMJ
      b) Crepitus when jaw is moved
      c) Decreased range of motion
      d) Incoordination on closing mouth sometimes
   3. Treatment
      a) Analgesics (e.g., acetaminophen 650 mg every 4–6 hours)
      b) Referral to a dentist for a variety of symptomatic maneuvers
         and exercises; conservative therapy almost always is effective
H. Local alveolar osteitis (dry socket)
   1. Most common complication of tooth extraction, especially of
      impacted third molar
   2. Intense localized pain 2–3 days after an extraction, often with
      accompanying foul odor
   3. Treatment
      a) Acetaminophen, 650 mg 3 or 4 times/day, plus codeine, 30 mg
         every 4 hours
      b) Prompt dental referral

CHRONIC DENTAL AND ORAL PROBLEMS
A. Periodontal disease (pyorrhea)
   1. Gingivitis
      a) Presentation
         1) Forms
            (a) Acute: painful; rapid onset; short duration
            (b) Subacute: less severe
            (c) Recurrent
            (d) Chronic: most common; slow onset; less painful than
                acute or subacute form
         2) Signs
            (a) Early: increased gingival fluid, bleeding of gums on
                gentle probing
            (b) Bright red color (normally coral pink)
            (c) Acute: diffusely edematous
            (d) Chronic: appears fibrous, pits on pressure
      b) Cause: unremoved plaque (bacterial and their by-products) that
         has formed calculus (tartar)
      c) Major complication is periodontitis (see below)
      d) Treatment: referral to a dentist for plaque and calculus removal
         and for instruction in plaque control (brushing with a soft

bristled toothbrush, flossing), visits to a dentist every 6–12 months, as necessary

2. Periodontitis
   a) Presentation
      1) Red, bleeding gums (painless unless there is infection superimposed), gingival inflammation, as above, and pus-filled pockets around the teeth
      2) Eventually, teeth loosen and spread apart, gums recede
   b) Treatment (to preserve teeth, restore function)
      1) As for gingivitis above
      2) Periodontal surgery to improve gingival architecture

B. Denture problems
   1. Presentation
      a) Looseness and discomfort are common problems
      b) Failure to remove dentures at night may be cause of problems in some cases (e.g., bony erosion, mucosal ulceration, candidiasis)
   2. Treatment: dental referral for denture remodeling, new dentures, remodeling of soft or hard tissue, or dental implants (expensive, still require dentures)

C. Dental caries
   1. Presentation
      a) Nonpainful, white, brown, or black spot on the enamel of a tooth, most often on biting surface
      b) Sometimes only identifiable by dentist's use of special equipment (e.g., x-rays, hand instruments)
   2. Treatment: removal of lesion, restoration (filling of lost portion of tooth)

D. Angular cheilosis
   1. Presentation
      a) Dryness and burning at corners of mouth
      b) Wrinkles appear at corners, eventually fissure
   2. Treatment
      a) Edentulous patients should be referred to a dentist for consideration of dentures or denture remodeling
      b) Patients with teeth should be treated with petrolatum-containing ointment (e.g., Chapstick); lesions usually heal spontaneously

E. Thrush (oral candidiasis)
   1. Presentation
      a) White, curd-like loosely attached plaque on an erythematous mucosa, begins as pinpoint spots
      b) Tongue often red, burning
      c) May occur in people with poor oral hygiene, in poorly nourished people, in people with debilitating illness, in people who are immunocompromised (e.g., HIV infection)
   2. Treatment
      a) Good oral hygiene (see Gingivitis, above)
      b) Nystatin oral suspension, 4–6 ml held in the mouth for several minutes before swallowing, 4 times/day; thrush usually resolves in 1–2 weeks
      c) For patients with HIV infection, see Chapter 20

F. Halitosis
   1. Causes: retention of odoriferous food particles, ANUG (see above),

caries, chronic periodontal disease, dentures, smoking, adjacent
infection (e.g., tonsillitis, sinusitis), pulmonary infection,
alcoholism, renal failure

2. Treatment
    a) Local: oral hygiene (see Gingivitis, above); dental treatment of
       specific problems, mouthwashes or breath fresheners every 2–4
       hours if necessary
    b) Extraoral: treat underlying cause

G. Xerostomia (dry mouth): inadequate saliva
    1. Presentation
        a) Cracking of the lips, difficulty swallowing, changes in tongue
           texture
        b) Infections, caries, denture problems often occur
        c) Often, a history of medication use (e.g., anticholinergics,
           decongestants, or antihistamines)
    2. Treatment
        a) Dental referral for evaluation and for caries prophylaxis
        b) Irrigation with methylcellulose, glycerin, or a saliva substitute
           (e.g., Glandosane, Oralube, Xerolube — without prescription)

H. Common tongue conditions
    1. Geographic tongue
        a) Asymptomatic inflammatory condition consisting of patchy
           areas of denudation outlined by a thin yellow-white line
        b) Heal quickly in one location, reappear in another
        c) Persists for weeks or months, may recur at a later date
        d) No effective treatment
    2. Hairy tongue
        a) Thick matted layer on the dorsum of the tongue of
           hypertrophied papillae, yellowish white to brown or black
        b) Majority of patients are heavy smokers
        c) Treatment: brush tongue with a tongue blade or toothbrush
    3. Median rhomboid glossitis
        a) Ovoid, rhomboid, or diamond-shaped reddish patch (that
           contains no papillae) on the dorsum of the tongue
        b) Present since birth; no clinical significance

I. Leukoplakia and erythroplakia
    1. Presentation
        a) Leukoplakia
            1) Varies from grayish-white, flattened scaly lesions to a thick,
               irregularly shaped plaque
            2) Associated with chronic irritation (tobacco, alcohol, poor
               dentures)
        b) Erythroplakia: velvety red lesion of ≤2 cm, with or without a
           hyperkeratotic component
    2. Significance: erythroplakia may be an important precursor of
       squamous cell cancer; malignant potential of leukoplakia is less
       but still exists
    3. Treatment
        a) Discontinuance of chronic irritants, followed by 14 days of
           observation
        b) Patients with persistent lesions should be referred to a dentist
           for biopsy and follow-up

J. Squamous cell carcinoma

1. Epidemiology: 4 times more common in men, most common after fourth decade
2. Presentation: persistent lesions
   a) On lip: 95% on lower lip, appear as an ulcer, wart, sore, or scale; more common in fair-skinned people
   b) In mouth: 50% on ventrolateral tongue, 16% on floor of mouth; appear as ulcer (60%), growths (30%), other lesions (10%)
3. Treatment: a cooperative effort between otolaryngologist, dentist, radiation oncologist

85/ COMMON PROBLEMS OF THE FEET

PREVENTIVE FOOT CARE FOR PATIENTS WITH DIABETES MELLITUS AND/OR ARTERIAL INSUFFICIENCY

A. Problems
1. Sensory neuropathy
   a) May cause burning, severe pain, especially at night
   b) Lessens ability to appreciate painful stimuli, e.g., corns, calluses, foreign bodies
2. Motor neuropathy
   a) Wasting of small muscles
   b) Increased tendency to hammertoe, calluses
3. Sympathetic neuropathy
   a) Excessively dry feet
   b) Increased risk of secondary infection
4. Vascular disease (see Chapters 70 and 71)
   a) Having the patient examine his or her feet every day for irritations, abrasions, calluses is important
   b) Proper shoe selection (comfortable, wide toes, low heels) is important
   c) Thick toenails, corns, calluses are best trimmed by a podiatrist
   d) Soft cotton should be worn between toes that tend to rub together
   e) Talcum powder should be used to prevent interdigital moisture and maceration
   f) Lanolin should be applied to dry, thickened skin to prevent fissuring

BUNIONS

A. Definition and pathogenesis
1. Deformity of the first metatarsophalangeal joint, including enlargement of the joint and lateral deviation of the great toe
2. Due to hypermobility of the first metatarsal and excessive pronation of the foot (flatfoot)
B. Symptoms: pain in the first metatarsophalangeal joint, intensified by wearing a shoe
C. Management
1. Acute symptoms
   a) Rest, not wearing shoe, soaks in warm water
   b) Nonsteroidal anti-inflammatory agent, e.g., Naprosyn, 500 mg every 12 hours, or Feldene, 20 mg every 24 hours
2. Long-term conservative management: molds (arch supports and protective shields, best made by a podiatrist), also worthwhile as preventives to deter symptoms
3. If conservative management fails, surgical correction (usually on an ambulatory basis) by a podiatrist or orthopedist

CALLUSES AND CORNS

A. Definition and pathogenesis
1. Callus: thickening of the epidermis, the result of repeated trauma
2. Corn: excessive or concentrated callus

3. Most common cause is excessive pronation of the foot (flatfoot), not shoes

B. Symptoms
1. Diffuse callus is asymptomatic
2. Concentrated calluses or corns produce pain on pressure (shoes or walking)
3. In a diabetic (see above), or in any patient with arterial peripheral vascular disease, may become ulcerated or infected

C. Management
1. Initial relief from debriding painful lesions with a #15 scalpel blade, kept nearly parallel to the skin
2. Conservative long-term management requires control of excessive pronation with orthotic devices (see Bunions, above)
3. If conservative management fails, surgical correction by a podiatrist or orthopedist of malaligned bones can be considered

OTHER HYPERKERATOTIC LESIONS

A. Verruca plantaris (plantar warts): see Chapter 83
B. Porokeratotic lesions
1. Circumscribed discrete very painful hyperkeratotic lesion on sole from occlusion of a sweat duct by keratin (looks like a large corn)
2. Made worse by debridement, needs curettage by a podiatrist or dermatologist
C. Foreign bodies, e.g., a hair, create a local hyperkeratotic inflammatory reaction; excision is curative

NAIL CONDITIONS

A. Onychomycosis (fungal infection): see Chapter 83
B. Ingrown toenails
1. Medial or lateral border of the toenail, almost always the great toe, penetrates the flesh
2. Treatment
   a) Refer to a dermatologist, podiatrist, or surgeon for excision of the offending border of nail
   b) Ten percent will recur; if so, the entire nail can be removed, and the matrix can be cauterized for permanent cure

HEEL PAIN

A. Presentation (see also Chapters 51 and 67)
1. Commonly localized to medial anterior aspect of heel
2. First step in morning is particularly painful; then pain eases after 5–10 minutes, becomes progressively worse during day
3. Tenderness approximately 4.5 cm from posterior margin of plantar surface, probably a plantar fasciitis (bone spurs, commonly seen on x-ray, do not cause pain)
4. Problem usually due to overuse (e.g., running), but gout (Chapter 53) and Reiter's syndrome (Chapter 55) should also be considered

B. Treatment
1. Nonsteroidal anti-inflammatory agent (Chapter 54), rest, soaking in warm water
2. If necessary, injection (by use of a 25-gauge 1-inch needle) of a corticosteroid-lidocaine solution (see Table 50.4) into the tender area
3. To prevent recurrence, the patient should insert a 1.4-inch felt

(not foam) pad into the heels of his or her shoes; if that does not work, refer patient to a podiatrist for an orthotic device

METATARSALGIA

A. Definition and pathogenesis
  1. Pain in the forefoot, mostly in women
  2. Most common cause is Morton's neuroma
     a) Two adjacent interdigital nerves become compressed and inflamed
     b) Pain enhanced by elevating the heel, compressing the forefoot (e.g., by wearing high-heeled shoes)
B. Symptoms and signs
  1. Shooting, burning, or cramping pain involving two adjacent toes
  2. Pain occurs during walking or running, relieved by rest, massage
  3. Palpation between affected toes reveals marked tenderness
C. Treatment
  1. Wearing of low, flat, wide, soft leather shoes
  2. Injection of corticosteroid-lidocaine solution (Table 50.4) into tender area may provide temporary relief
  3. Nonsteroidal anti-inflammatory drugs are not effective
  4. If symptoms persist, surgical excision is highly effective (4–6-week recovery period)

INDEX

Page numbers followed by *t* or *f* indicate tables or figures, respectively.